To Adri

Rome and America:
THE GREAT
REPUBLICS

Best of luck

Walter Signoriello

Rome and America:
THE GREAT
REPUBLICS

What the Fall of the Roman Republic Portends for the United States

WALTER SIGNORELLI

ARCHWAY
PUBLISHING

Archway Publishing books may be ordered through booksellers or by contacting:

Archway Publishing
1663 Liberty Drive
Bloomington, IN 47403
www.archwaypublishing.com
1 (888) 242-5904

Taken from the King James Version of the Bible.

ISBN: 978-1-4808-6340-8 (sc)
ISBN: 978-1-4808-6341-5 (hc)
ISBN: 978-1-4808-6342-2 (e)

Library of Congress Control Number: 2018907157

Print information available on the last page.

Archway Publishing rev. date: 08/13/2018

Contents

Introduction

The Roman Republic was at its height in the first century BC, and its armies dominated the Mediterranean world. When Pompey the Great was solidifying his conquests in the East, Julius Caesar was conquering Gaul in the West, and riches were pouring into the city, neither the leaders nor the people of Rome thought the structure of their society was about to fall apart. They did not know that decades of civil war were upon them; that their political system would be uprooted; and that their previously guaranteed civil liberties, property rights, and freedoms were about to be lost. But indeed they were lost, and history can repeat itself.

Might the people of the United States be similarly sightless about their future? In *Coming Apart*, Charles Murray wrote,

> But how much room does the American project have left? The historical precedent is Rome. In terms of wealth, military might, and territorial reach, Rome was at its peak under the emperors. But Rome's initial downward step, five centuries before the eventual fall of the Western Roman Empire, was its loss of the republic when Caesar became the first emperor. Was that loss important? Not in material terms. But for Romans who treasured their republic, it was a tragedy that no amount of imperial splendor could redeem.
>
> The United States faces a similar prospect: remaining as wealthy and powerful as ever, but leaving its heritage behind. The successor state need not be one ruled by emperors. We may continue to have a President and

a Congress and a Supreme Court. But the United States will be just one more in history's procession of dominant nations. Everything that makes American exceptional will have disappeared.[1]

Striking similarities between Rome and America have inspired many historians and commentators to make comparisons, and many have drawn pessimistic conclusions. However, our fate is not predetermined; our choices will determine our future. We have the advantage over the Romans of knowing how their history unfolded, and we have the opportunity to avoid their mistakes.

This book compares Rome and America, but its focus is confined to the republics. It's the Roman Republic that is relevant to the political and social problems of our times, not the Imperial Rome ruled by autocratic emperors. The republic was characterized by annual elections, legislation by popular assemblies, and equality before the law. It survived longer than the United States has so far survived, but it eventually disintegrated and mutated into an imperial autocracy. Although our republic has existed for more than two centuries, we cannot know whether it will continue to thrive or its constitutional structure will disintegrate. With that in mind, studying the Roman Republic can help us better understand ourselves; comparing Rome's strengths and weaknesses to those of our nation can provide helpful insights that will inform our policy decisions.

World history exhibits recurring patterns, and the core dynamics of human activity transcend the differences between epochs and cultures. Oswald Spengler, the German historian, noted, "[I]t might be accurate to conclude that each historical or cultural era traverses a series of stages in an ordered and obligatory sequence; each cultural era is a living entity with inner dynamics that may not be easily discernible; however, these dynamics may track those in other cultural eras. If so, recognizing the dynamics may assist us in understanding current circumstances and predicting future directions."[2] Thus, we can study the dynamics that led to

---

[1] Charles Murray, *Coming Apart* (New York: Crown, 2012), p.278-9.
[2] Oswald Spengler, *The Decline of the West* (New York: Alfred Knopf, 1926). I, 26.

Rome's growth and prosperity, and its subsequent demise; identify the signs of those same dynamics in our culture; recognize the persistent workings of time that either strengthen or erode social structures; and find ways to avoid dissolution and foster growth and prosperity.

Although the five centuries of the Roman Republic cannot be exactly matched with the history of the United States, many distinct periods and events in Rome and America present remarkable similarities. This book examines a wide array of subjects common to both nations, including the formation of the republic, the determined character of the people, military victories, slavery, class conflicts, political partisanship, exorbitant wealth, commitment to the rule of law, the responsibilities and dangers of world hegemony, and the leadership of extraordinary individuals who changed the course of history.

Both republics evolved from humble beginnings into the most powerful nations of their times, and they expanded commerce and prosperity in the broadest terms. They absorbed people from surrounding nations and cultures, gradually welcoming them as full citizens; they sanctified individual rights and liberties, protected nations and peoples beyond their own borders, and came to believe in their own exceptionalism and manifest destinies.

Beyond these simplified histories, countless political, economic, and social parallels exist between the republics. Some are superficial, but others are fundamental and significant. Both republics experienced similar events and evolutions although not necessarily in the same sequences. Illustrations depicting the timeline of historical events and evolutions cannot be superimposed one over the other to show the same linear pattern. An event from the later days of the Roman Republic may coincide with an event from the beginning of the American republic; conversely, a parallel event from the early days of Rome may coincide with an event from the later days of the United States. The ideological conflict between Alexander Hamilton and Thomas Jefferson that infused the early American republic, for example, parallels the ideological conflicts between Julius Caesar and Marcus Porcius Cato, which were so pivotal at the end of the Roman Republic. The Battle of the Orders, between plebeians and patricians during the early Roman Republic, parallels the fight for civil rights for women and African-Americans in the later

American republic. The military triumphs and conquests of the Romans over Carthage in the Punic Wars, leading to Roman hegemony over the Mediterranean world, occurred around the midpoint of its history. We hope America's Second World War triumph, which led to its superpower status, occurred early in its history, but that is uncertain; it may be that it occurred late in its history.

Although the Roman and American republics flourished in different times and places, and functioned on different technological platforms, they have been part of the same march of human evolution, and the same immutable laws of nature and human development have molded them in similar ways. We can discern their characteristics and how their histories coincide, and we can discern which characteristics and dynamics led to their successes, and which led to their failures. While it's easier to compare Rome to early America than it is to compare it to America after the industrial and technological revolutions, the fundamentals of human interactions have not changed, and the parallels remain and continue.

The American republic has reached a point in its evolution that is comparable to the time of the greatest Roman conquests. Notably, at their military and economic heights, both nations saw the strengths of their political and social institutions begin to decline. In Rome, political partisanship undermined respect for the Senate, the state religion, and the patron-client system. In America, the institutions of society—government, the church, the press, the police, education, Wall Street, and the banks—have all been the subject of intense criticism and systematic subversion.

In the political arena, recent presidential elections have become battlegrounds wherein ruthless and underhanded attacks against opponents have become the norm—and winning at all costs, the rule. Mischaracterizations, insults, and falsehoods have generated animosity and disrespect for the candidates and the system; and they continue long after campaigns.

Although every presidential election is called the most important election in the history of the nation, only an objective, historical assessment can determine whether an election was in fact the most important of its time. Nevertheless, we should always assume that the next presidential election may indeed be the most important one of our time. It may decide the future direction of our nation and, quite possibly, the survival of our republic. This statement may seem hyperbolic since the United States is the wealthiest nation on earth and is viewed as the dominant world power, possessing astounding technological capabilities and military bases around the world. However, other nations at the height of their success, including Rome, found themselves in serious and precipitous decline. It is not inconceivable that we in the United States could find ourselves in similar circumstances.

Extreme and inflexible partisanship has inhibited or prevented legislative compromise; in reaction, presidents have circumvented Congress by issuing executive orders to implement their programs and policies, leading many to characterize the office as the "imperial presidency." To draw a Roman analogy, this is akin to the consulship of Julius Caesar in 59 BC, when he circumvented the Senate; excluded and displaced his coconsul, Marcus Calpurnius Bibulus; and forced his programs through the tribal assembly without regard to constitutional checks and balances. Instead of naming 59 BC the consular year of Caesar and Bibulus, as consular years were normally named, it became known as the consular year of "Julius and Caesar."

Caesar's unlawful actions in 59 BC set in motion a chain of events that culminated in the crossing of the Rubicon in 48 BC, his assassination in 44 BC, and the emperorship of Augustus Caesar in 26 BC.

In the United States, the growing powers of the presidency and increasingly acrimonious partisan politics have brought the nation to a similar situation the Romans faced as they careened toward the civil war between the Caesarean and senatorial parties. Neither the Republican nor Democratic Party has demonstrated the capability to unify the nation; their primary missions seem to be to oppose and obstruct the other party. With legislation frequently stalemated, future presidents will increasingly resort to executive orders and other tactics to bypass Congress, further subverting our system of checks and balances. These and other troubling developments have raised questions about whether our republic will survive or fall apart as the Roman Republic did—or whether it will be transformed into a different form of government, perhaps something similar to Rome's imperial autocracy.

CHAPTER 1

Parallel Republics

IN INNUMERABLE WAYS, THE United States of America is the political and social descendant of the Roman Republic, and the influences of Rome reverberate throughout our world. Centuries have passed, and society has evolved, yet America reflects Roman structures, ideas, and principles. Despite the gulf of time, these parallels support drawing significant correlations between the two republics. Each nation, born out of unrelenting conflict with dangerous and threatening adversaries, developed military and civic structures that enabled them to surpass all other contemporaneous nations. Both societies idealized soldierly valor as well as civic and familial virtues; both were pragmatic, frugal, independent, and determined to fight to the ultimate extent rather than to submit to tyranny. Both imposed obligations on their leaders to act within the rule of law and invested their citizens with enforceable civil rights. Both incorporated foreigners, accommodated massive waves of new citizens, and assimilated diverse ethnic groups into their cultures. Not until the United States of America came forth did the world see a nation that has assimilated as many diverse peoples as Rome did.

The Romans emerged from the seven hills above the Tiber River to dominate the Mediterranean Basin and the world of classical antiquity. There is no parallel in antiquity to the success of Rome. At its zenith, Roman hegemony reached from England to the Black Sea, from Gibraltar to Egypt. Its system of government enabled millions of citizens to live together and work productively for centuries, and it created a melting pot in which its citizens and subjects enjoyed the opportunities of upward mobility, economic prosperity, and entry into the political class. Once the Roman Republic had established the benefits of citizenship, outsiders continually clamored for inclusion.

Tacitus summarized the Roman Republic, compacting five hundred years into one paragraph:

> In Rome's earliest years as a city, its rulers were kings. Then Lucius Junius Brutus created the consulate and free Republican institutions in general. Dictatorships were assumed in emergencies. The regimes of the Council of Ten did not last more than two years; and then there was a short-lived arrangement by which senior army officers— the commanders of tribal contingents—had consular authority. Subsequently Cinna and Sulla set up autocracies, but they too were brief. Soon Pompey and Crassus acquired predominant positions, but rapidly lost them to Caesar. Next, the military strength which Lepidus and Antony had built up was absorbed by Augustus. He found the whole state exhausted by internal dissensions, and established over it a personal regime known as the *principate.*[3]

We live in a time too early for us to summarize the American republic, but we can note that this republic also began by overthrowing a king and creating free republican institutions. Just as Rome empowered consuls to replace the kings, the founding fathers created a presidency with comparable executive powers. Rome instituted a dual legislature with its Senate and popular assembly, and we established a two-branch Congress comprising the Senate and House of Representatives. The Romans experimented with government institutions and made adjustments to match changing circumstances, and we adjusted the relationships between the

---

[3] Tacitus, The Annals of Imperial Rome (London: Folio Society, 1996) 3.

central and state governments, and between the federal branches. Despite early struggles and existential wars, both nations provided opportunities and upward mobility for millions of people.

REVOLUTION

Although historians have differed on determinations of the exact dates and sequence of events that constituted the founding of the Roman Republic, a consensus has held that in approximately 509 BC, the Romans expelled Tarquinius Superbus, the last Etruscan king, and established the republic.

Tarquinius abused his power, plundered the treasury for personal benefit, personally initiated and decided capital cases, and exiled citizens before confiscating their property.[4] His actions incited a revolution, which became a giant step in advancing constitutional and democratic government. The Romans replaced the monarchy with two consuls and other magistrates, whom an assembly of the people elected annually; and those magistrates became lifetime members of the Senate. Although the new government favored the aristocracy, it balanced the interests of competing factions and classes, and it eventually evolved into a more democratic, representative government.

After his expulsion, Tarquinius did not capitulate without a fight; he tried to regain his throne by enlisting the aid of his Etruscan allies, who still dominated the region. However, after several defeats, he gave up, and the Romans retained their independence.

Two millennia later, the American colonists overthrew King George III and won independence from Great Britain. With the Declaration of Independence, they renounced their allegiance to the king, formed a confederation of thirteen states, and declared war. They rebelled to redress grievances similar to those that had caused the Romans to rebel against Tarquinius. George III had obstructed the administration of justice, made judges dependent on his will alone, imposed taxes without representation, and deprived citizens of the benefits of trial by jury. The grievances listed in the Declaration of Independence justified the revolution, but

---

[4] Livy, *Histories* (Harvard University Press, Loeb Classic Library) bk 1. 49-60; bk. 2.1.

the essential justification was larger than any particular set of grievances. The declaration announced that humanity had taken another giant step toward democratic government, the greatest giant step since the Roman Republic.

When the American Revolution began, King George, like Tarquinius, did not give up his possessions without a fight. He sent fifty thousand soldiers and thirty thousand foreign mercenaries to suppress the rebellion; nevertheless, the Americans were victorious and forced the British to surrender. Again, however, like Tarquinius, King George also tried to regain control of his former possessions in the War of 1812. He was defeated, and America remained independent of the British as Rome had remained free of the Etruscans.

INHERITANCE

Both Roman and American revolutionaries benefitted from their positions as the successors of the nations they had overthrown. The Romans' Etruscan legacy gave them advantages over the other Italian tribes. Although historians and archaeologists still debate the origins of the Etruscans, most agree that they migrated from Asia Minor and settled in western Italy. They brought with them the skills of a more advanced civilization, and these proved to be more effective than those known in Italy at that time. They had a structured military organization, engaged in mining and manufacturing, and traded throughout the Mediterranean region. As they conquered or gained political dominance over Northern Italy, from the Po Valley to the Tiber and also the region along the west coast of Italy from Latium to Pompeii, they took control of Rome and established more than twenty cities; the most prominent were Tarquinia, Clusium, Caere, and Veii.

Etruscan cities enjoyed defenses superior to the settlements and villages scattered throughout Italy. When the Romans expelled the Etruscans, they inherited a well-constructed city with a water supply, drainage, pebbled streets, brick buildings, and a defensive rampart. As Livy recounted, Rome was well-situated geographically. "Not without cause did gods and men select this place for establishing our City—with its healthful hills; its convenient river, by which crops may be floated down from the midland regions and foreign commodities brought up; its sea, near enough for use, yet not exposing us, by too great propinquity, to peril from foreign fleets; a situation in the heart of Italy—a spot, in short, of a nature uniquely adapted for the expansion of a city."[5]

Rome, as a center for trade and commerce, offered advantages over competing tribes, and the prosperity of the city provided the resources to support a strong military. Like pupils who outshine their master, the Romans wrested supremacy in Italy from the Etruscans by building on the foundations the Etruscans had left behind.

Similarly, the Americans built on the institutions the British had planted in the New World. They inherited the British Empire's commercial institutions, trading arrangements, maritime enterprises, and legal system, which provided the rule of law necessary for investment and prosperity. When he advised the Parliament that he intended to send the British army and navy to suppress the rebellion, George III asserted, "The object is too important, the spirit of the British nation too high, the resources with which God hath blessed her too numerous, to give up so many colonies which she has planted with great industry, nursed with great tenderness, encouraged with many commercial advantages, and protected and defended at much expense of blood and treasure."[6]

After the Revolutionary War, Timothy Pickering, the secretary of state for presidents George Washington and John Adams, acknowledged this debt, proclaiming that Britain was "the country of our forefathers, and the country to which we are indebted for all the institutions held dear to freemen."[7]

THE FOUNDERS

Although the founders claimed British heritage and administered the colonies according to British customs and traditions, more than half of

---

[5] Livy, bk. 5, 54

[6] George III, "Address to Parliament," October 27, 1775.

[7] Henry Adams, ed., *Documents Relating to New England Federalism, 1800–1815* (Boston, Little, Brown, and Company, 1877) 389.

them wanted to break from the mother country. When it came time to adopt a new government, they didn't look to the British monarchy; instead they turned to the checks-and-balances system of the Roman Republic. They used the better parts of the Roman system as a model for the US Constitution, naming their most powerful legislative body the "Senate" after the Roman Senate rather than after the British Parliament. They adopted Roman symbols, such as the eagle for military standards and the goddess Liberty for coins. The Roman motto e pluribus unum (out of many, one) and Virgil's novus ordo seclorum (new world order) were inscribed on the great seal of the United States. Capitol Hill in Washington, DC, was named for the Capitoline Hill of Rome. In the chamber of the House of Representatives, behind the speaker's platform on either side of the flag, are two fasces. Each fasces comprises an axe surrounded by a bundle of rods. Such fasces were carried in procession before the Roman consuls as symbols of authority.

The founding fathers' attachment to Rome was embodied in the many obvious and direct imitations of Roman architecture. In 1784, Thomas Jefferson visited the Roman temple to Augustus's grandsons in Nimes, France; and he adopted its dignified design as the ideal for official American democratic government. The US Capitol, with its rotunda and classical facade, the Virginia Capitol Building in Richmond, and the Rotunda at the library of the University of Virginia were based on Roman models. Jefferson used the Doric designs of the Roman architect Vitruvius for his home at Monticello.

Subsequent generations copied Roman arch-construction engineering to build aqueducts, such as the forty-six mile Croton aqueduct (begun in 1840), which traversed from upstate New York across the Harlem River to the Central Park reservoir in New York City. In the Gilded Age, the Jay Gould Library in the Bronx, New York, replicated the Roman Pantheon. The original Penn Station in New York City, completed in 1910, was modeled after the Baths of Caracalla. The Lincoln Memorial, the Jefferson Memorial, and the National Gallery could have been Roman buildings. In 1935, the US Supreme Court building was constructed based on the design of the Temple of Jupiter Optimus Maximus on Rome's Capitoline Hill.

The most popular play of the revolutionary era, Joseph Addison's Cato, portrayed Marcus Portius Cato the Younger acting to save the Roman Republic and refusing to surrender to Caesar. Cato took his own life rather than submit to Caesar's pardon. If he had accepted the pardon, he would have been accepting Caesar's dictatorship, and the founders saw an analogy to any concession or accommodation to the British king. George Washington constantly quoted Addison's play, and many of his finest speeches were drawn from it. At his winter camp in 1778 at Valley Forge, General Washington staged the play as a motivational device for his officer corps as they prepared the famous surprise attack across the Delaware.

The founders used classical Roman pseudonyms for their essays, letters, and position papers. For *The Federalist Papers*, Alexander Hamilton used Publius after Publius Valerius Puplicola, one of the earliest consuls of the Roman Republic; for other essays and letters, he chose other names to suit the subject matter. Camillus, Cato, Cincinnatus, Fabius, Horatio, and Tully (Cicero) were some of the pseudonyms he and others adopted. During the Whiskey Rebellion in 1794, the secretary of state Edmund Randolph published thirteen essays denouncing the rebels in Western Pennsylvania. He used the pseudonym Germanicus, the Roman general who suppressed a tribal revolt on the border of the empire.

The postrevolutionary founders continued the attachment. Henry Clay published articles using the name Scavola after the Roman jurist. Daniel Webster often used Roman allusions in his speeches. Arguing before the Supreme Court in the Dartmouth College case against a government takeover of the college, Webster drew a Roman analogy. "Sir, I know not how others may feel, but, for myself, when I see my Alma Mater surrounded like Caesar in the senate-house, by those who are reiterating stab after stab, I would not, for his right hand, have her to turn to me, and say, *Et tu quoque mi fili! And thou too, my son.*"[8]

The attachment was further evident in the many statues and busts of leading statesmen clothed in togas: Washington, John Jay, Andrew Jackson, Sam Houston, and John Calhoun, among others.

To be clear, the founders admired the early Roman Republic but despised how it ended, and they despised the imperial emperorship even

---

[8] George Ticknor, "Webster's Speeches," *American Quarterly Review* 9 (1831): 434–5.

more. The most enduring legacies of Rome that influenced them came from periods well before the profligate luxuries, bathhouses, and decadence of the emperors. The founders admired the functional roads, bridges, and aqueducts built during the republic, and they adopted much of the early Roman political system, including its procedures, respect for private property, and adherence to constitutional principles. They admired Roman law, which, in addition to being the basis for European civil law systems, greatly influenced Anglo-American common law; and they admired the rights of Roman citizenship, which presaged American constitutional rights.

The founders felt a particular affinity to the self-sufficient Roman farmer. In both nations, the rugged individualism of the farming classes provided the core strength of their armies, since these free, land-holding farmers became citizen soldiers when necessary. Fighting to keep their land and their freedom, these citizen soldiers won most of their battles, and those they lost were quickly reversed. For the Romans, their struggle against neighboring tribes, marauders, and invaders from the North was the crucible that molded their character; for the Americans, it was their struggle against the natural elements, ferocious battles with Native American tribes, and wars with mercenary European armies. These struggles inspired otherwise-independent, individualistic actors to unite and fight for the survival of their communities—and later for their nation. As an outgrowth of their victories, both nations came to believe that nothing was impossible for them to achieve. This belief was the energizing force behind the passion for freedom and independence that inspired them to fight to the ultimate for their rights. The freedom for which they fought wasn't the freedom to disregard rules and obligations but the freedom to exercise the rights of independent communities. They fought against outside enemies to remain free of domination, and they fought against internal enemies to remain free of tyranny.

HEROIC MODELS

The heroes the Romans and the Americans looked to were the citizens who had sacrificed or fought bravely for their nations. Undoubtedly, the exploits of their heroes were embellished and mythologized; nonetheless, they provided exemplars for all citizens to emulate. The virtues of courage, endurance, piety, and honor were taught through the stories of the heroes; and at various points of comparison, the accomplishments of American heroes seemingly matched the accomplishments of the greatest Roman heroes.

George Washington is often referred to as the American Cincinnatus after the legendary Roman general Lucius Quinctius Cincinnatus (519–438 BC), who was appointed dictator when rival tribes threatened Rome. Cincinnatus defeated the tribes, then immediately resigned the dictatorship and retired to his small farm, declining to profit from his position. After his victory over the British, Washington also declined to seize the monarchical power that could have been his for the taking and returned to his farm. However, that comparison is limited because Cincinnatus won his war in sixteen days; Washington's war lasted eight years.

A better comparison can be drawn in the Roman general Marcus Furius Camillus (446–365 BC). Camillus and Washington were both military leaders who demonstrated unsurpassed leadership, courage, and discipline. Camillus has been honored as the second founder of the Roman Republic, and Washington has been called the father of his country.

Between 396 and 367 BC, Camillus was appointed dictator and given emergency powers five times, each because of imminent attacks. He fought and won great military victories that saved his nation and then retired to private life. In 396 BC, he was called on to take charge of the siege of the Etruscan city of Veii, which stood twelve miles from Rome on the north side of the Tiber River. The rival cities had fought several wars and dozens of battles over many decades without a decisive winner. Veii was a formidable rival for control of the Tiber and the nearby salt deposits. Situated on a steep plateau and surrounded on three sides by a deep moat, Veii held a strong defensive position. The siege had been ongoing for several years, and the Romans, on the verge of exhaustion, suffered a defeat outside the walls of the city as their soldiers fled. At that point, Camillus was appointed dictator and called on to save the faltering Roman campaign. He immediately set about motivating and instilling discipline in the soldiers.

Livy recounted, "The change in command at once made a change in all things else; there was a new hope and a new spirit, and even the fortune of the City seemed to be renewed. The dictator's first act was to visit military punishment upon those who had fled from Veii in panic, and to teach his men that the enemy was not the worst thing they had to fear."[9]

Camillus had new siege works constructed outside the walls of Veii, while he had a contingent of soldiers surreptitiously clear an agricultural drainage tunnel that passed under the city walls and into its citadel. On the day of the attack, as the Romans scaled the walls, they simultaneously emerged from the tunnel inside the city, surprising and overcoming the enemy. When it became clear the Romans were winning the battle, Camillus had the heralds proclaim that Etruscans who put down their weapons would be spared. Most put down their arms; those who refused to surrender were killed. Thus Camillus conquered Veii, taking great spoils that shored up Rome's depleted treasury.

As often occurs after a crisis passes, applause for a victorious leader turns to jealousy and accusations. Charges were brought against Camillus regarding the distribution of the spoils taken from Veii, and he retired into exile. However, he would be needed again, and in 390 BC, as the Gauls sacked Rome, he was called out of exile and appointed dictator for the second time. He expeditiously reorganized the army and rescued the city.

He was called on three more times, the last time in 367 BC, when the Gauls again were on the march, invading Central Italy and threatening Rome. In his fifth dictatorship, Camillus repulsed the Gauls at a battle near the River Anio, killing thousands and forcing the rest to flee.

After the battle, Camillus returned to Rome in triumph, but he immediately faced a political conflict between the plebeian and patrician classes. The plebeians demanded one of the consulships should go to a plebeian. When the patricians refused to give up their exclusive hold on the office, civil war loomed. Rather than precipitate war, Camillus reserved the use of his dictatorial powers and instead agreed to a compromise that resolved the crisis. Although a patrician himself, Camillus supported the demand that one of the two consuls must be a plebeian. As part of the bargain, a new magistrate position was created, a praetor to administer

---

[9] Livy, *Histories*, bk. 5, 19.

justice in the city, whom the patricians would elect from their ranks. The compromise changed the trajectory of the republic, and to commemorate the occasion, Camillus dedicated the Temple of Concord in the forum.

From this point on, the Romans were no longer so divided by continuous disputes between the classes, and the new nobility that developed, composed of both plebeian and patrician families, synergized the nation's strengths and launched its expansion. Livy summarized Camillus's accomplishments.

> He was truly a man of singular excellence whether in good or evil fortune; foremost in peace and in war before his banishment, and in exile even more distinguished, whether one thinks of the yearning of his countrymen who called on him in his absence to save their captured city, or of the success with which on being restored to his country he restored the country itself at the same time; after this for five and twenty years—for he survived so long—he maintained his glorious reputation, and was deemed worthy of being named next after Romulus, as Rome's second Founder.[10]

Washington's career bore many similarities to that of Camillus. In September 1775, he took charge of the makeshift Army of the Continental Congress after the Battle of Bunker Hill. The British army occupied Boston, and Washington put the city under siege to starve them out. The question was who would starve first. Through eight months and a bitter winter, Washington held his army together despite insufficient supplies, inadequate artillery, and a lack of funds to pay the troops. He was able to do so mostly by setting an inspiring example and by appealing to patriotism, but discipline was the real backbone of his leadership. In a general order to his army, he laid down the law.

---

[10] Livy, bk. 7, 1.

As the season is now fast approaching when every man must expect to be drawn into the field of action, it is highly necessary that he should prepare his mind, as well as everything necessary for it. It is a noble cause we are engaged in, it is the cause of virtue and mankind, every temporal advantage and comfort to us, and our posterity depends upon the vigor of our exertions. But it may not be amiss for the troops to know that if any man in action shall presume to skulk, hide himself, or retreat from the enemy, without the orders of his commanding officer, he will be *instantly shot down*, as an example of cowardice.[11]

As Camillus had done at Veii, Washington ended the siege at Boston by arduous preparation and a surprise attack. While the British were barricaded in the center of the city, they hadn't secured Dorchester Heights, a peninsula overlooking the city from a mile across the harbor. From the heights, cannon shots could reach the city, and no doubt, if the British saw the Americans moving onto the heights, they would have raced to secure that high ground.

To use the heights to their advantage, Washington needed artillery, and he sent General Henry Knox to Fort Ticonderoga, New York, to transport that fort's artillery to Boston. In an extraordinary effort, Knox transported one hundred twenty thousand pounds of cannon and mortars, first rowing it on barges forty miles down Lake George, then pulling it on sleds to Albany, and finally moving it three hundred miles east to Boston. It took three months to do so, but in February 1776, the artillery arrived.

On the night of March 4, 1776, to distract the British, Washington bombarded the city from Roxbury while he surreptitiously moved the Ticonderoga artillery and seven thousand troops onto the heights. In a night of tremendous effort, fortifications were built, and the cannons were placed. When dawn came, the British were stunned to see what had occurred in the darkness. The tactical advantage Washington had seized

---

[11] George Washington, "General Orders," 26 February 1776, (**http://founders/archives.gov/document/Washington/03-020275.**

forced the British to evacuate the city, providing a much-needed boost to what had been flagging American morale.

However, victory wouldn't be that easy. The initial boost of morale was short lived since the British were soon on the counterattack. After the Boston triumph, Washington suffered many losses and retreats, including the strategic and demoralizing loss of New York, yet he never contemplated surrender. He maintained strong discipline, sometimes by ordering the flogging or hanging of derelict soldiers.

Washington studied and admired Roman generals, evident by the bust of Julius Caesar in his Mount Vernon home and his collection of military treatises, including Caesar's *Commentary on the Gallic Wars*. His own military tactics followed those of both Camillus and Quintus Fabius Maximus—Camillus for his surprise tactics against overconfident and unprepared enemies and Fabius for his delaying and scorched-earth tactics used to combat Hannibal's army when it was ravaging Italy and threatening Rome. Using Fabian strategy against the British, Washington avoided major battles until conditions were favorable. He would trade ground for time to wear down the attention and patience of the enemy. Then, more like Camillus, Washington would employ stealth, speed, and surprise to attack at the least-expected moments, as on the icy morning of Christmas 1778, when he crossed the Delaware River to strike a momentum-changing victory at Trenton. His incredible steadfastness wore down the British until the final decisive battle at Yorktown forced their surrender.

After the decisive victory at Yorktown and the surrender of the British army in 1781, which resounded around the Western world, Washington was in a position to assume monarchical power. However, on December 23, 1783, two days after the British army evacuated their last troops, he entered the Maryland State House, where Congress was meeting, bowed to the delegates, and stated, "Having now finished the work assigned me, I retire from the great theatre of action, and bidding an affectionate farewell to the august body, I here offer my commission and take my leave."[12] His

---

[12] "Address to Congress on Resigning his Commission," *The Writings of George Washington*, Vol.27, ed. John Fitzpatrick (Wash.D.C.: US Government Printing Office, 1933-44), 284-285.

action spoke even louder than his words. His relinquishment of military power set the precedent for civilian control of the new republic.

When Washington's army disbanded in 1783, the officers formed the Society of the Cincinnati, a name honoring the Roman general Cincinnatus, and they elected Washington as their first president. More than two centuries later, the society still meets.

Washington retired to his Virginia farm, but six years later, in 1789, when the founders formed the new nation, he was persuaded to become the first president of the United States. During his eight years in office, he held the factionalized nation together. He was the bridge between the Jeffersonian Republicans and the Hamiltonian Federalists. His adamant refusal to involve the nation in foreign entanglements—namely, the war between Britain and France—enabled him to avoid an internal schism that would have torn the nation apart. After his two terms, he could have been easily reelected, but he voluntarily gave up his position and again retired to private life.

His retirement was interrupted in 1798. War with France seemed imminent, and President John Adams appointed Washington as commander in chief of the defense forces. Although Washington had been reluctant to reenter public life, he responded to the call of duty. Fortunately, the war was averted, and Washington returned to retirement for the last year of his life.

Camillus and Washington personified the values that lived in their citizenry and drove their young nations. They fought fiercely for independence from external enemies, but in domestic politics, they remained loyal to the principle that a leader shouldn't hold on to power beyond his term, believing that doing so would lead to despotism.

TYRANNICIDE

Roman opposition to autocracy was embodied in the lives of two famous members of the Junius Brutus family line. The first was Lucius Junius Brutus, who in 509 BC led the rebellion that drove out the Etruscan king. He became a coconsul of the new republic, and when he learned that his two sons had been plotting to restore the Etruscan king, he authorized their executions. He also demanded that all citizens swear an oath never to be ruled by a king, and throughout the history of the republic, antimonarchy was a rallying call that always aroused resistance to tyranny. Proof that someone aspired to be king was a death sentence.

The second was Marcus Junius Brutus, who traced his patrician ancestry to Lucius Junius Brutus. In 44 BC, 465 years after the expulsion of King Tarquinius, Marcus Brutus led the contingent of senators who assassinated Julius Caesar. The senators joined in the assassination because Caesar had assumed lifetime dictatorial powers and, so the senators believed, would soon declare himself king. Although it could be debated whether the assassination of Caesar was justified, the revolt against him exemplified the strength of the Roman commitment to liberty.

Marcus Brutus paid with his life for leading the assassination, and he became a hero to the American patriots as they contemplated rebellion against the British king. To the founders, despite the questionable legality of his act, Brutus personified freedom.

When rebellious sentiments become violent, the results are most often tragic. On April 14, 1865, the actor John Wilkes Booth shot and killed President Abraham Lincoln at Ford's Theater. As Booth made his escape, he jumped from the theater balcony onto the stage, shouting, "Sic semper tyrannis!" (Thus always to tyrants!), clearly identifying his act with Brutus's assassination of Caesar.

It's interesting to note how Booth's background led him to his murderous act. His father had been named Junius Brutus Booth after the Roman family so revered for their actions against tyrants; furthermore, Booth's English ancestors had been opponents of King George III. As an actor, Booth had played leading roles in John Howard Paynes's play *Brutus, or the Fall of Tarquin*, which dramatized the overthrow of the Etruscan king by the first Brutus, and he played in Shakespeare's *Julius Caesar*, which dramatized the assassination of Caesar by the second Brutus.

The notion of killing a supposed tyrant isn't confined to deranged minds; it has held an odd legitimacy. Even today, the Virginia state flag depicts Lady Liberty standing on the chest of a dead king and proclaiming the Virginia motto, Sic Semper Tyrannis.

Slavery

To the modern view, the proposition that Rome and early America advanced freedom and equality seems peculiar in view of the fact that both, in whole or in part, were slave societies that prospered by subjugation and exploitation. The proposition that the republics spread freedom and equality can stand only when limited to their core memberships. Slaves—whether people captured in battle, purchased in the slave trade, or born into slavery—were neither considered citizens nor included in the expansion of freedom and equality. In Rome, the putative justification for slavery was that Roman generals spared a defeated enemy's life rather than killing him or her.

Before the expansion of slavery, both Rome and America prospered through the efforts of citizen farmers who worked the land for themselves; the numbers of slaves and indentured servants were limited and didn't undermine the basic yeomen structure. However, in 326 BC, the Romans restricted debt bondage for citizens and increasingly turned to the acquisition of slaves through conquest as a means of obtaining cheap labor.

In the third century BC, the Romans captured and enslaved vast numbers of people. In 167 BC, the conquest of Epirus in Greece brought one hundred fifty thousand slaves. Julius Caesar's conquests reportedly brought as many as a million. Historians estimate that the slave population grew from a relatively small percentage to as much as 40 percent of the population, and by the first century BC, slaves formed the major component of the work force. While slavery made some property owners very rich, slavery displaced the citizen farmers, and as a result, landless and desperate citizens poured into Rome, altering the traditional structure of society.

Though the forms of slavery differed between Rome and America, parallels are evident in how the growth of slavery to overwhelming numbers engendered catastrophic consequences to each nation. A great evil to the individuals whom it subjugated, slavery proved to be an even greater evil to society.

In colonial America, a combination of slaves and indentured servants comprised nearly half the population, with almost as many bonded whites as enslaved blacks. Many viewed this circumstance as the natural order of things until the Declaration of Independence and the Revolutionary War. After the revolution, the recognition of individual rights led to the virtual disappearance of bonded white servitude. The notion that servitude was a condition that could affect either whites or blacks changed into the notion that servitude affected only blacks. In the South, black slavery continued to grow and infect that society. Despite all the speeches about liberty, the importation of slaves continued, and the overall slave population in the South grew to at least 40 percent. Slavery caused the Civil War, the deaths of more than six hundred thousand soldiers, and the destruction of the South's economy. Though the war officially ended slavery, it was replaced by a system of segregation and discrimination that persisted for another century.

To the contrary, the Roman Republic never contemplated ending slavery but allowed it to continually increase. As the number of slaves reached dangerous levels, sporadic insurrections threatened internal security; the most famous one, led by Spartacus in 73–71 BC, could have overthrown the state. The Romans responded to the insurrections with harsh measures, further coarsening their culture and leaving the corrosiveness of slavery to fester among their people.

Roman slavery was not always a permanent condition; many slaves found avenues out of bondage, especially the more fortunate household slaves who could save enough to buy their own freedom or were manumitted by their owners. The adage that what doesn't kill you makes you stronger applied to freed Roman slaves, many of whom went on to do great achievements and find financial success. Similarly, after America ended slavery, however imperfectly, and eventually ended the worst of its vestiges, the descendants of freed slaves strengthened the nation and made greater and greater contributions to society; many achieved spectacular successes.

Freedom, Equality, and Immigration

Violence in history is what makes news, but the burgeoning of rights, freedom, and equality was the more constant aspect of the Roman and

American stories, though with qualitative differences. Early Rome emphasized the freedom and independence of the group more so than those of the individual. It was a society based on the paterfamilias model, in which the patriarch of each extended family or clan controlled its members, and each family member lived by the rules of obedience and loyalty to the family. The paterfamilias pledged loyalty to the state, and in return the state respected the authority of the family to discipline its own members.

Over four centuries, within the framework of this family/clan society, the rights of Roman citizens increased, and the inequalities among classes decreased. Plebeians gained political equality with patricians, soldiers were granted land for their service, and landless citizens were given lands to colonize. Many slaves, perhaps nearly one million, were set free; and unlike other ancient states, freedmen received the vote and full political citizenship. Roman citizenship became a coveted and privileged status the Romans were willing to share. By the first century BC, citizenship had been extended to all the Italian allies and several other peoples within Roman territories without restrictions of ethnicity, religious belief, or social origins.

Immigration and assimilation reinvigorated and strengthened the Roman populace. Edward Gibbon compared the Roman policy to that of other ancient societies. "The narrow policy of preserving, without any foreign mixture, the pure blood of the ancient citizens, had checked the fortune, and hastened the ruin, of Athena and Sparta. The aspiring genius of Rome sacrificed vanity to ambition, and deemed it more prudent, as well as honorable, to adopt virtue and merit for her own where so ever they were found, among slaves or strangers, enemies or barbarians."[13]

As in Rome, American history was a story of inclusion, the expansion of rights, and furtherance of equality for common citizens. The commitment to individual liberty was more pronounced in America than in Rome, but irrespective of the qualitative differences, citizens of both nations would sacrifice their lives to protect their liberties. The famous statement of Patrick Henry before the Virginia legislature in 1775 as that

---

[13] Edward Gibbon, *The Decline and Fall of the Roman Empire,* vol. 1 (New York: Modern Library, 1931) 29.

body contemplated revolution epitomized the American sentiment. "Is life so dear, or peace so sweet, as to be purchased at the price of chains and slavery? Forbid it, Almighty God! I know not what course others may take; but as for me, give me liberty, or give me death!" In a 1777 letter to British General John Burgoyne, General George Washington explained that the Americans would win the Revolutionary War because "the associated armies in America act from the noblest motives, liberty. The same principles actuated the arms of Rome in the days of her glory; and the same object was the reward of Roman valor."[14]

Both societies saw landownership as the bedrock on which to build a strong society. American land was plentiful for anyone willing to risk settling on the ever-expanding frontiers and facing potential attacks by native tribes. Similar to the establishment of Roman colonies, the 1862 Homestead Act converted public lands to private farms and ranches, and as settlements expanded to the Mississippi River and beyond, the new landowners were elevated from disenfranchised persons to propertied members of the middle class. With property rights, they gained the right to vote and hold public office, and they wholeheartedly adopted the values of individual freedom and independence that would shape the nation. They valued the right to be free of arbitrary governmental action, to freely express their opinion, to come and go as they pleased, to associate with whomever they wanted, and to profess the religion of their choice.

RULE OF LAW

Romans idolized their laws and the concept of citizen equality before the law (excluding slaves). The Twelve Tables of Laws of 450–449 BC established that no laws could be enacted in favor of, or in detriment to, some citizens unless common to all citizens, and the tables reiterated that no citizen could be put to death except after trial. By and large, the Romans obeyed lawful decrees and verdicts, and powerful leaders, even with armies at their disposal, submitted to decrees of the people.

---

[14] John Shields, *The American Aeneas: Classical Origins of the American Self,* (Knoxville, Tenn.: University of Tennessee Press, 2001) xxix.

Americans, too, idolized their laws and the concept of equality before the law. Francis Grund, a German educator and immigrant to America, observed in 1837, "There exists in the United States a universal submission to the law, and a prompt obedience to the magistrates, which, with the exception of Great Britain, is not found in any other country."[15] Nevertheless, submitting to the law didn't mean they wouldn't resist officials who acted unlawfully or expropriated too much power. Time and again, citizens refused to submit to arbitrary and capricious rulings, and they held public officials to account at the polls and through indictments.

The American founders admired those Romans—Marcus Junius Brutus, Marcus Porcius Cato the Younger, and Marcus Tullius Cicero—who had resisted tyranny to the full measure. The founders especially idolized Cato for his loyalty to the law, defense of the republic, and principled stands against Julius Caesar. As for Cicero, although many of his actions in the rough-and-tumble of political life were criticized, his writings on the principles of law raised his status above mere politicians. The founders quoted Cicero and his memorable passage on natural law from *The Republic*.

> True Law is Reason, right and natural, commanding people to fulfill their obligations and prohibiting and deterring them from doing wrong. Its validity is universal; it is immutable and eternal. Its commands and prohibitions apply effectively to good men, and those uninfluenced by them are bad. Any attempt to supersede this law, to repeal any part of it, is sinful; to cancel it entirely is impossible. Neither the Senate nor the assembly can exempt us from its demands; we need no interpreter or expounder of it but ourselves. There will not be one law at Rome, one at Athens, or one now and one later, but all nations will be subject all the time to this one changeless and everlasting law.[16]

---

[15] Francis Grund, *The Americans, in Their Moral, Social, and Political Relations,* in Charles Murray, *Coming Apart,* 134.

[16] Cicero, *The Republic,* (Cambridge, MA: Harvard University Press) 3, xxii. 211.

The Romans applied natural law, emphasizing the civic and martial duties that were commensurate with citizenship. Their concept of equality was proportional equality. Citizens were ranked by the census according to status, and those in the higher ranks had more honors but proportionally more duties and obligations.

With qualitative difference, the Americans also applied natural law, emphasizing the freedoms and independence of citizenship, the notion of which was articulated so superlatively in the Declaration of Independence.

> We hold these truths to be self-evident: that all men are created equal, that they are endowed by their Creator with certain unalienable rights; that among these are life, liberty, and the pursuit of happiness. That to secure these rights, governments are instituted among men, deriving their just powers from the consent of the governed; that whenever any form of government becomes destructive of these ends, it is the right of the people to alter or abolish it, and to institute new government, laying its foundation on such principles and organizing its powers in such form, as to them shall seem most likely to effect their safety and happiness.[17]

Both societies recognized the benefits of government and collective action but also the dangers of autocratic power. They adopted the ultimate position that if government abrogated their natural rights, citizens could justifiably follow natural law by resisting the tyranny. Their commitment to freedom wasn't merely in the form of words but was backed up by a willingness to fight. At the end of their republic, Roman senators assassinated the tyrant Julius Caesar; and the Americans founders, at the beginning of theirs, declared war on King George III. The spirit to fight for freedom passed from the leaders to the citizen soldiers. As George Washington awaited the British invasion of New York City in August 1776, he issued a general order to his army, in which he defined fighting for freedom. "The

---

[17] Declaration of Independence, 1776.

hour is fast approaching on which the honor and success of this army and the safety of our bleeding country depend. Remember officers and soldiers that you are free men, fighting for the blessings of liberty—that slavery will be your portion, and that of your posterity, if you do not acquit yourselves like men."[18]

For the duration of the Revolutionary War, the American commitment to freedom was tested to the fullest. It not only passed the test but also set an example for subsequent generations to emulate.

A test of longer duration was to follow. The revolution preserved democratic liberty for the time being, but could it long endure? With so many commonalities between the two greatest republics, the obvious question was whether the American system of government would eventually disintegrate as had the Roman Republic. Abraham Lincoln said, "If this nation is ever destroyed, it will be from within, not from without." Lincoln based that statement on his knowledge of history. He knew that despite Rome's wealth and success on the world stage, Romans found issues on which to divide themselves, and he knew that "a house divided against itself cannot stand." When he uttered those words, he was thinking of slavery but knew other issues could also destroy the nation and that extreme partisanship and the demonization of adversaries assuredly destroyed the Roman Republic.

Despite Rome's great strengths, in the last century of the republic, the rule of law broke down, sending Rome hurtling from civil war to civil war. The antagonism between classes and factions led to poisonous hatred and the final dissolution of their republic. Lincoln understood that such poisonous hatred and extreme forms of partisanship could destroy the Union.

---

[18] George Washington, "General Order," August 1776, in David McCullough, *1776* (New York: Simon & Schuster, 2005) 159.

CHAPTER 2

Beginnings and Challenges

SOME MIGHT TAKE OFFENSE at comparisons between American civilization and ancient Rome. They would view the brutal history of Rome with all its wars, massacres, and political violence as alien to American history, and they would think Roman brutality disqualifies that civilization from being viewed in the same light as America. However, an honest and thorough assessment of both nations reveals striking correlations and a fundamental moral equivalency. While it is true that someone looking back will see that the Roman Republic compiled a terrible list of atrocities and slaughter, it is also true that someone looking back on American history will see a daunting list of wars and atrocities as well. For the most part, circumstances and the tide of history forced on them the participation of both nations in violent conflicts. Each faced brutal enemies and dire circumstances that compelled them to act in ruthless ways.

The Romans, situated on a navigable river near vital salt deposits, were surrounded by aggressive tribes who wanted what Rome had; the Americans, with a relatively small population, confronted a vast wilderness populated by warlike and alien tribes. Both the early Romans and early Americans had to fight ferocious battles to preserve themselves, toughening and preparing themselves for their later roles as conquerors and world leaders.

CONSTANT WAR

To judge the Romans fairly requires an understanding of the conditions people faced in the ancient world. Thomas Hobbes studied antiquity and reached the conclusion that in the state of nature, man's life is "solitary, poor, nasty, brutish, and short." Although his characterization ignores all the familial and joyful aspects of life people experience even in the most difficult circumstances, he correctly surmised that harsh realities and dangers affected every aspect of life. Groups of people—families, clans, or tribes—saw other groups not as kindred spirits but as natural enemies, competitors for scarce resources. In the times of the Roman kings and the early republic, life for most people was a Hobbesian struggle. Continuous war among tribes was the natural state of human affairs, and the Romans were in constant conflict, sometimes against their Latin relatives and sometimes while allied with Latin tribes against non-Latin tribes of Italy. They had to be prepared to fight annual wars. As Hobbes wrote, "War was not simply the act of fighting, but the period of time in which there existed both a propensity toward and a likelihood of fighting." No such thing as peace existed, only rest between battles.[19]

It would be tedious and depressing to describe in detail all the wars Rome fought. Suffice it to say, they lived in a dangerous and unstable world under the constant threat of violent death or enslavement. The tribes of the Apennine Mountains raided the Latin plains and tried to move into areas already settled. The Roman and Latin territories looked inviting, since life on the plains or in the coastal regions was less harsh than life in the mountains.

In mainland Italy, habitable land was well populated, and the migration of one tribe would precipitate the migration of another, often resulting in a domino effect and instigating new conflicts. Without a superior governing force to impose peace and order, tribes had to constantly defend their territories. The Romans, as just one of many tribes, were in a perpetual state of emergency, alternately fighting the Etruscans, Albans, Sabines, Oscans, Samnites, Aequians, or Volscians. If they weren't actively

---

[19] Thomas Hobbes, *Leviathan*, chap. 13.

engaged in fighting, they were preparing for imminent attack. Contrary to the prevailing view of the Romans as an overly aggressive people, Rome's initial campaigns were more often defensive than aggressive.

Adding to these dangers, tribes from Gaul, who had crossed into Italy and taken root in the northern regions, periodically overran the Italian regions. The controlling philosophy of the Gallic tribes was that rights were carried at the point of a sword and that everything belonged to the brave. [20] Defending against the incursions of the Gauls required an equally harsh stance. In addition, Roman citizens were under constant attack from the sea by Carthaginian and Greek raiders. Pirates attacked ships and took hostages to get ransom or to sell them into slavery. Living under such conditions affected the character of the people; if Romans were ruthless and brutal, they were so out of necessity for survival.

Although the Romans defeated most of their enemies, they lost their share of battles, and after defeats, many Romans were slaughtered or sold into slavery. Slaughter and slavery begat more of the same in what seemed like constant and unavoidable cycles of revenge. Tribes were forced to make choices: they could gamble and fight to win; they could retreat within the walls of a city and hope to fend off a siege; or they could submit to conquest and pay the consequences, giving up land, tribute, hostages, or freedom.

Rome's response to this constant state of war was to strengthen itself, develop a well-trained and disciplined army, conquer and suppress its enemies, and convince other potential enemies to accede to terms of peace. Their early successes reinforced the belief in conquest as the best security. However, conquest required more conquest, and as their territory expanded, new enemies appeared, and new battles had to be fought.

Unquestionably, winning battles was necessary for survival. The Romans knew the consequences of defeat, and all focused on military survival; thus, they valued courage, martial skill, and sacrifice for the nation. Their society was fully organized for war; being prepared to fight meant the difference between life and death, between freedom and slavery.

---

[20] Livy, *Histories*, bk. 5. 36.

Servian's Military System

Servius Tullius, the king who ruled from 580 to 530 BC, set the foundations of the Roman military state. He instituted the census and divided the population into classes and "centuries" according to criteria based on property ownership. The population was divided for both military and political purposes. Livy wrote, "The political reputation of Servius Tullius rests upon his organization of society according to a fixed scale of rank and wealth. He originated the census, a measure of the highest utility to a state destined, as Rome was, to future preeminence; for by means of it, public service, in peace as well as war, could thenceforward be regularly organized on the basis of property; every man's contribution could be in proportion to his means."[21]

Citizens were divided into six classes, from the richest in the first class to the poorest in the sixth. Citizen soldiers provided their own equipment. Those wealthy enough to provide the best armament and weapons, including warhorses for the cavalry, were the first class. The rest were assigned in steps to lower classes according to their wealth. The poorest were assigned to the lowest class and weren't incorporated into the fighting legions. According to Dionysius of Halicarnassus,

> Tullius made none of these regulations without reason, but from the conviction that all men look upon their possessions as the prizes at stake in war and that it is for the sake of retaining these that they all endure its hardships; he thought it right, therefore, that those who had greater prizes at stake should suffer greater hardships, both with their persons and with their possessions, that those who had less at stake should be less burdened in respect to both, and that those who had no loss to fear should endure no hardships, but be exempt from taxes by reason of their poverty and from military service because they paid no tax.[22]

---

[21] Livy, bk. 1, 42.

[22] Dionysius of Halicarnassus, *Roman Antiquites*, 4:19.3

Tullius revolutionized society and differentiated Rome from other social systems. Its civil and military structures coincided. No other society in history appears to have placed such a high value on military service and to have singled out its heroes with such regular and extravagant adulation. Victorious generals staged triumphant parades, and soldiers who participated in the victories were rewarded. Historian Leopold von Ranke noted, "The military and population institutions made Rome what it was. For the power of the Roman state had a military basis beyond that of any other state." Military organization and values permeated the Roman state; its ordered unity, social discipline, and civic responsibility were the secrets of its success.[23]

The early Romans employed a progressive tax system based on an ideology so "each would contribute according to his means." It didn't follow that "each would receive according to his need." The poor were relieved of the burden of contributing but didn't receive a dole from the state. When Servius Tullius established his system for contributions, he proclaimed, "In order to lighten for the future the burden also of the war taxes you pay to the public treasury, by which the poor are oppressed and obliged to borrow, I will order all the citizens to submit a valuation of their property and everyone to pay his share of the taxes according to that valuation ... for I regard it both just and advantageous to the public that those who possess much should pay much in taxes and those who have little should pay little."[24]

When funds were needed for war or disaster relief, the taxes on the wealthiest and most prominent citizens were increased. One might view this system as a reverse inequality, but the early Romans didn't see it that way. As Cicero put it, "Equality itself is inequitable, since it allows no distinctions in rank."[25] With the privileges of rank and status came responsibility to contribute to the state, and this value system was inculcated into the public mind. Romans believed it was an honor and a privilege to hold public office although the office was unpaid and the honoree often had to expend his own funds to carry out his duties.

---

[23] Leopold von Ranke, *World History: The Roman Republic and Its World Rule,* 1886.
[24] Livy, *Histories,* bk.1.42.
[25] Cicero, *The Republic,* 1. 43.

The quest for honor and glory became powerful motivators to engage in wars, but these wars weren't merely chivalrous skirmishes for knights to impress the populace. They were brutal contests for survival, dominance, and security. Winning a battle didn't prevent the adversary from returning at a later time to take revenge; therefore, in some circumstances, victorious tribes, rather than entering a peace treaty with a defeated enemy, would slaughter a defeated enemy or sell their citizens into slavery in distant lands. Camillus did just that when he conquered Veii in 396 BC. He killed the inhabitants who wouldn't surrender and sold the remainder into slavery, leaving the city empty and deserted.

Invasion of the Gauls

Six years after she subjugated Veii, it was Rome's turn to face slaughter and potential slavery when plundering Gallic tribes swept into the Italian Peninsula. Brennus, their formidable chief, led them. Plutarch provided an enlightening exposition of these events, illustrating the nature of battles for land, resources, and booty. While Brennus was besieging the Tuscan city of Clusium, the Clusiums asked the Romans to intercede and send ambassadors to Brennus. The Romans agreed and sent the ambassadors to ask what grievance Brennus had against the Clusium. In reply, Brennus laughed and said,

> The Clusiums wrong us in that, being able to till only a small parcel of earth, they yet are bent on holding a large one, and will not share it with us, who are strangers, many in number and poor. This is the wrong which ye too suffered, O Romans, formerly at the hands of the Albans, Fidenates, and Ardeates, and now largely at the hands of the Veientines, Capenates, and many of the Faliscans and Volscians. Ye march against these peoples, and if they will not share their goods with you, ye enslave them, despoil them, and raze their cities to the ground; not that in so doing ye are in any wise cruel or unjust, nay, ye are but obeying that most ancient of all laws which gives to the

stronger the goods of his weaker neighbors, the world over, beginning with God himself and ending with the beasts that perish. For these too are so endowed by nature that the stronger seeks to have more than the weaker. Cease ye, therefore, to pity the Clusiums when we besiege them, that ye may not teach the Gauls to be kind and full of pity towards those who are wronged by the Romans.[26]

Clearly, Brennus and the Gauls were confident in their strength, and they marched swiftly toward Rome. On July 18, 390 BC, a Roman army intercepted them near the confluence of the Allia and Tiber Rivers. The Romans were shocked at the sight of the Gauls with their long, streaming hair stiffened by wash of lime; their shaggy moustaches; their half-naked bodies painted with bright colors; their broad gold rings around their necks; and "the dreadful din of the fierce war songs and discordant shouts of a people whose very life is wild adventure."[27] In the battle, the Roman army was routed, and many of its fleeing soldiers were drowned as they tried to escape across the Allia River.

It was a catastrophic defeat for the Romans. A large contingent of soldiers fled to Veii, the nearby city they had recently conquered and which remained intact and defensible; others fled in disarray to Rome, where they ran into the city without stopping to shut the city gates and took refuge in the citadel on the Capitoline Hill.

Unopposed, the Gauls entered Rome. They occupied the major part of the city but couldn't scale the cliffs to the fortified citadel, where Marcus Manlius Capitolinus repulsed them. While the Gauls slaughtered the unprotected inhabitants and plundered and burned the rest of the city, the Roman leaders and soldiers remained in the citadel, resisting the siege. They held out for seven months until famine and disease overcame them. The Gauls also suffered from famine and disease, and an agreement was

---

[26] Plutarch, "Camillus" in *Lives*, trans. Perrin (Cambridge, MA: Harvard University Press, 1928).
[27] Livy, *Histories*, bk. 5, 129.

reached by which the Romans would pay Brennus a ransom of one thousand pounds of gold for him to depart the city.

In the meantime, the soldiers who had fled to Veii reassembled while other Romans from the countryside joined them, and they appointed Camillus dictator to rescue the city. He organized the army and marched to Rome, arriving as those on the citadel were weighing the gold they had collected to give to Brennus. Plutarch recounted,

> On learning what was going on, he [Camillus] ordered the rest of his army to follow in battle array … [H]e lifted the gold from the scales … and then ordered the Gauls to take their scales and weights and be off, saying that it was the custom with the Romans to deliver their city with iron, not with gold. When Brennus in wrath declared that he was wronged by this breaking of the agreement, Camillus answered that the compact was not legally made nor binding, since he himself had already been chosen dictator and there was no other legal ruler; the agreement of the Gauls had therefore been made with men who had no power in the case … At this, Brennus raised a clamor and began a skirmish, in which both sides got no further than drawing their swords and pushing one another confusedly about, since the action took place in the heart of the ruined city, where no battle array was possible. But Brennus soon came to his senses, and led his Gauls off to their camp, with the loss of a few only … During the ensuing night he broke camp and abandoned the city with his whole force, and after a march of about eight miles, encamped along the Gabinian way. At break of day Camillus was upon him, in glittering array, his Romans now full of confidence, and after a long and fierce battle, routed the enemy with great slaughter and took their camp.[28]

---

[28] Livy, bk. 5, 129.

The Sack of Rome was a near-death experience for the Roman people, a humiliation that steeled the Roman character ever harder. Immediately after the sacking, attacks from other enemies increased. In 389 BC, Etruscan, Volscian, and Aeduian tribes presumed that the Romans had been weakened, and they formed an alliance to wipe them out. They attacked on three fronts. The prospects for the Romans seemed so dire that their longtime allies, the Latins and Hernici, refused to send soldiers to fight alongside them, as had been their custom. To meet the threat, the Senate appointed Camillus dictator again, and he spent a year battling to stave off and defeat all three enemy armies.

Thereafter, almost every year a war was fought with one or another of the enemies that ringed Roman territory, and as soon as one threat was repulsed, another arose; the drumbeat was constant. Finally, in 353 BC, the Romans defeated the Etruscans from Tarquinia, the city from where the last Etruscan kings of Rome had come, and the other hostile tribes around Rome. Peace treaties were signed, and Rome's hegemony was acknowledged.

From 509 BC to 353 BC were Rome's formative years. Its character and government were strengthened and solidified for the next stages of its journey—the conquest of the Italian Peninsula, the defeat of Carthage, and the expansion throughout the Mediterranean region.

Tribal Wars in America

In America, the same forces that molded the Roman character molded the American character. Beginning with their first settlements in the early 1600s, the Americans confronted deadly perils, not only the perils of obtaining food and shelter in a wilderness environment but also the same kind of tribal warfare the early Romans faced. The settlers came to find land and economic opportunity, and to escape religious persecution in Europe. They settled in Roanoke, North Carolina, in 1587; Jamestown, Virginia, in 1607; Sagadahoc, Maine, in 1607; Plymouth, Massachusetts, in 1620; New Amsterdam, New York, in 1625; and Boston Bay, Massachusetts, in 1630. Native American tribes, some as fierce as any of the warlike tribes of ancient Italy, surrounded all of them.

Thousands of distinct Native American tribes lived throughout North America; most were in a perpetual state of war with one another. Continual raids, combat, and revenge murders were the norm for these warlike people, who valued courage and martial skills above all else. The first major tribe to substantially interact with the settlers was the Powhatan tribe, which controlled the area from Eastern Virginia to Maryland. The Powhatans were always ready for war and had fought many battles against enemy tribes to the north and west. In their culture, "war was the ultimate test for every male, a searching examination where only the strong, intelligent, or lucky would survive. Men were expected to display strength and courage in hand-to-hand combat, fortitude if captured and tortured (while they were slowly put to death in excruciating pain, they would throw insults at their enemies), and wisdom in council."[29]

SETTLEMENTS

The Roanoke settlement in Powhatan territory was short lived, and later expeditions found it abandoned. Although the British Parliament mounted an inquiry into the fate of the settlers, no definitive answer has ever been reached.

The Jamestown settlement by 1622 had expanded to more than forty plantations. Despite and series of raids and skirmishes with the Powhatans, the settlers reached a peace and trade agreement with Chief Opechancanough. However, the chief's word was no good. He used the peace to build up his forces while planning a surprise attack on the settlers. During the apparent peace "the warriors would wander, casually and unarmed, with provisions to sell, into the English settlements where they were well known, and then at a given time they would grab any object they could find—spade, ax, gun, knife, rock, log, tong—and murder every person they could reach, man, woman, or child, and they would burn all the buildings and crops."[30]

More than seven hundred settlers were killed. After the massacre, the

---

[29] James Horn, *A Land as God Made It* (New York: Basic Books, 2005) 19.
[30] Bernard Bailyn, *The Barbarous Years* (New York: Alfred Knopf, 2012) 101.

settlers consolidated, abandoned some of the plantations, fortified others, and began a ten-year war of revenge.

In Massachusetts, the Plymouth colony initially enjoyed peaceful relations with the local Wampanoag tribe; then, in 1630, eleven ships with seven hundred more settlers arrived, changing the demographic balance. The new congregation's leader, John Winthrop, the future governor of the Massachusetts Bay Colony, famously sermonized, "We shall be as a city upon a hill; the eyes of all people are upon us." He saw part of the Puritan mission as converting the Native Americans to Christianity. In accordance with this mission, Native Americans were admitted to Harvard College after it was founded in 1635, although only a few attended.

In 1636, the relative peace was interrupted when a war with another tribe, the Pequots, broke out. This was a war filled with vicious reprisals on both sides. The Puritans didn't have sufficient forces to defeat the Pequots, so they formed alliances with the Mohawk and Narragansett tribes. The Mohawks were part of the New York Iroquois alliance, traditional enemies of the Algonquin-speaking tribes of New England. The Narragansetts were on-again, off-again enemies of the Pequots; and now they saw an advantage in aligning with the Puritans.

With these allies, the Puritans waged war until the culminating battle of 1637, in which they destroyed a Pequot village at Mystic, Connecticut, and killed more than four hundred. The Pequot chieftain, Sassacus, fled; but the Mohawks later caught and beheaded him. The Mohawks sent his head to the Puritans as a show of good faith.

Modern historians have a penchant for placing the blame for the initial conflicts and massacres on the European settlers, but when civilizations clash, when the dynamics of the struggle for survival dominates human conduct, when the instincts for revenge are inflamed, reserve should be exercised before casting blame on groups that were caught up in the rush of history. Determining who insulted whom to incite a conflict, who resorted to violence first, and who retaliated is less helpful than understanding the dynamics of mass human migrations. History is an ongoing story of the migration and intermingling of formerly distinct peoples. One might observe that the circulation and integration of peoples is a necessary and natural process designed to sustain and improve the human race, as natural as the circulation of the atmosphere, the oceans, and the storms they produce. Invariably, human migrations involve violent conflicts. In light of the warlike character of the Native American tribes and the equally determined nature of the settlers, the only way by which conflict could have been avoided would have been for immigrants not to have crossed the Atlantic. But they did, and circumstances led to clashes between the tribes and the settlers. Making matters worse, the savagery and wanton slaughter in these clashes inflamed unquenchable hatred, and as a Hobbesian state of war took hold across the land, some settlers descended to the same level of barbarity as the most savage tribes.

For the Native American tribes, maintaining a sufficient population was critical to survival; otherwise stronger tribes would have overpowered them. Some tribes, to augment their numbers, regularly took captives and employed them as slaves, often intending to integrate them with their people. Sometimes they sold their captives into the slave market. The Occaneechi tribe controlled trading paths from North Carolina to Georgia, and ran a slave market on an island on the Roanoke River.[31]

The American settlers were made to order as slaves; they could be taken far from their settlements near the coast to areas inland, from where they couldn't escape or be rescued. The tribes took thousands of settlers as captives, most of whom died in captivity. Some adapted and became members of the tribes; a few escaped and found their way home to tell their stories.

Despite attacks, massacres, and kidnappings that inflamed hatred among the settlers, integration with the more peaceful tribes continued with regularity. It wasn't uncommon for whites to take Native American wives. The races mixed, and entire tribes assimilated into white society. However, the most recalcitrant tribes resisted assimilation and waged war to prevent the further spread of white settlements. The chiefs of these tribes justified their attacks on the settlers as necessary to protect their lands. Although the continent had abundant expanses of arable land and great forests, the chiefs faced a dilemma. Moving out of the way of the white settlers meant moving into the territory of other tribes, which would

---

[31] Lee Miller, *Roanoke* (New York: Arcade, 2000) 250-260.

lead to certain war. Native Americans weren't monolithic; they were fragmented. Each tribe claimed its own exclusive territory, and each viewed other tribes as enemies. An amalgamated Native American identity didn't arise until the twentieth century.

In Massachusetts after the first Pequot War, the Puritans enjoyed a period of peaceful coexistence with the nearby tribes. They established missions to convert the Native Americans to Christianity, and many "praying Indians" integrated into Puritan society. Some excelled in their relations with the English; John Sassamon, a student at Harvard College, was looked upon as one of the most enterprising converts. He acted as a go-between with the Algonquin-speaking Wampanoag and the English.

Compromises kept the peace for a time, but it didn't last because the Puritan population kept growing, and the settlements kept expanding into tribal hunting grounds. The settlers continued to arrive from Europe, and the settlers were prolific. They lived under the rule to "Go forth and multiply." They did, and their population doubled every generation.

KING PHILLIPS' WAR

The inevitable conflict broke out in 1675 when Metacom, whom the colonists called "King Phillip," became chief of the Wampanoag and immediately prepared for war. He sold land to certain non-Puritan colonists in exchange for gunpowder and flintlock muskets, which were superior to the matchlock muskets the Puritans used. Acting in the same fashion and for similar reasons as the Sabine, Aequian, and Volscian chiefs of Roman times, Metacom forged an alliance with other tribes, including the Narragansett, who had been aligned with the whites but switched sides. Metacom believed that if he defeated the English, he would become the most powerful chief in the region.

Sassamon, the translator, was related by marriage to Metacom. When he learned of Metacom's plans, he passed the information to the Puritans. Shortly thereafter, three of Metacom's Wampanoags murdered Sassamon. To exact justice on his behalf, the Puritans tried and hanged the murderers. Metacom retaliated by attacking and burning Puritan villages, thus precipitating King Phillip's War. From June 1675 to August 1676, with their superior weapons, Wampanoags wiped out twelve of New England's ninety towns and killed six hundred colonists, including women and children. The Puritans retaliated just as brutally. For two years, there was constant war until the tide turned in August 1676, when a Mohawk warrior, fighting with the Puritans, shot and killed Metacom; and a combined force of Puritans and Mohawks defeated the Wampanoag and their allies.

The war reduced the native population of New England by almost 40 percent, and many survivors fled north to join the Abenaki tribe. Consequently, southern New England was left without a substantial Native American population, and Metacom joined the long list of leaders throughout history who, for ill-conceived reasons, led their followers to disaster. His war deepened the Puritans' hostility toward the Native Americans and poisoned future relations.

ATROCITIES AND REVENGE

Metacom's demise didn't end the conflicts, and wars and atrocities with other tribes continued. In the French and Indian War (1756–1763), twenty Native American tribes fought with the French against the English army and the American colonists. These fierce warriors came from the territories of Pennsylvania, Ohio, and as far away as Wisconsin. They fought with fanatical zeal and measured the worth of a warrior by how many scalps he carried on his belt. Stories of atrocities these warriors had committed circulated like wildfire, and a nightmarish fear of them pervaded the consciousness of the colonists.

A notorious atrocity occurred at Fort William Henry, made famous by James Fenimore Cooper's novel *The Last of the Mohicans*. The British fort was situated at the base of Lake George, New York. In 1757, it was under siege by a French force of eight thousand, which included two thousand Native American warriors, mostly from the Huron tribes. The British and Americans defending the fort surrendered and were given safe passage to march out of the fort with their muskets but without ammunition. However, as the defenseless soldiers, with their wives and children, marched away, the tribal warriors attacked them. Most of the soldiers were killed and scalped or wounded, and many of the women and children were kidnapped. The Fort Henry massacre incited years of revenge attacks by soldiers and colonists against the Huron.

This massacre was strikingly similar to one the Gallic Eburones tribe inflicted on a Roman garrison of the XIV Legion in Belgic territory (modern Belgium) in 53 BC. The Gallic tribes were led by the formidable chieftain, Ambiorix, who negotiated a truce with the legion. But as the Romans marched away from their encampment, bands of tribal warriors ambushed them in the forest. The legion was virtually annihilated.

Julius Caesar took revenge. He wrote that the Eburones were "to be destroyed root and branch for their crime."[32] Within a few years, the Romans annihilated the Eburones, who disappeared from history.

During the American Revolutionary War, Native American tribes fought on the side of the British, and the atrocities attributed to the tribes deepened the colonists' animosity toward them. Justifying the revolution in the Declaration of Independence, Thomas Jefferson listed the British use of the tribes among the grievances against the king. "He [the king] has ... endeavored to bring on the inhabitants of our frontiers, the merciless Indian savages, whose known rule of warfare is an undistinguished destruction of all ages, sexes, and conditions."

The American victory in the Revolutionary War sent the British back to England and Canada, but the Native Americans remained, and for them the war wasn't over. For the Americans, victory inspired notions of a destiny to spread across the continent, but the tribes were seen as obstacles, and the consensus was that they would have to adjust or be driven away. Gordon Wood wrote,

> Although many whites admired the Indians for their freedom, the Anglo-American idea of liberty and independence was very different from theirs. Where ordinary white American men conceived of freedom in terms of owning their own plot of cultivated agricultural land, Indian males saw liberty in terms of their ability to roam and hunt at will. Like many American gentry, these

---

[32] Christian Meier, *Caesar*, (German: Basic Books, 1982) 197.

Indian warriors did not believe they should actually work tilling the fields. They thought, as one missionary to the Oneida reported in 1796, that "to labor in cultivating the Earth is degrading to the character of Man 'who (they say) was made for War & hunting & holding councils & that Squaws & hedge-hogs are made to scratch the ground.'"[33]

The warrior culture of Native American tribes the Americans confronted recalled the identical warrior culture of the Gallic and Germanic tribes the Romans had confronted. Tacitus described, "A German is not so easily prevailed upon to plough the land and wait patiently for harvest as to challenge a foe and earn wounds for his reward. He thinks it tame and spiritless to accumulate slowly by the sweat of the brow what can be got quickly by the loss of a little blood."[34]

Just as the Romans justified their aggression against the barbarians, Americans justified their aggression as they moved westward. They viewed the failure of the tribes to cultivate the land as a forfeiture of the right to hold it and as a justification for the Americans to take it. Although the Washington administration endeavored to establish peaceful relations with the tribes and to obtain tribal lands only through purchases and treaties, the administration failed to control the westward movement of the settlers and failed to prevent tribal war parties from raiding American settlements. The Shawnee, Wyandot, Ottawa, Miami, Potawatomi, and Kickapoo tribes residing west of the Allegheny Mountains and north of the Ohio River ignored peacekeeping efforts and conducted daring raids as far south as Kentucky. In autumn 1790, near the tribal town of Kekionga, tribal warriors led by Little Turtle, the Miami war chief, attacked a column of US cavalry and killed 183 soldiers.

President Washington and Congress sent additional troops to the area, and in November 1791, General Arthur St. Clair and his second-in-command, General Richard Butler, marched out of the fort

---

[33] Gordon Wood, *The Empire of Liberty* (London: Oxford University Press, 2009) 124.
[34] Tacitus, *Germania*, 14.

at Cincinnati with a regiment of about fourteen hundred soldiers. Only 427 were regular troops; the rest were untrained militia accompanied by about six hundred wives, children, and camp followers. On November 3, 1791, they camped near Kekionga. During the night, unbeknownst to them, the tribes, led by Little Tuttle, surrounded them. Before dawn on November 4, 1791, as the troops were preparing breakfast, a thousand painted warriors attacked "like a thunderstorm that came up quickly and rapidly." Surprised, many of the militiamen panicked, and death was everywhere. General St. Clair managed to gather his regulars, and they made a determined stand using their bayonets to push the warriors back. But the battle was lost, and at eight thirty, St. Clair led his troops in flight to a fort twenty-nine miles south. Of the original 1,400 troops, 657 were dead, and 271 were wounded; most of the civilians had been killed. General Butler was among the dead. His body had been desecrated, his heart cut into pieces and distributed to the tribes that had participated in the battle.[35]

Centuries earlier, in AD 9, when he learned that three of his legions had been ambushed and destroyed in the Teutoburg Forest, Augustus remonstrated in despair, shouting, "Varus, give me back my legions." Similarly, when he learned of St. Clair's defeat, Washington roared, "IT'S ALL OVER! St. Clair's defeated—ROUTED! The officers nearly all KILLED! I told him when I took leave of him—Beware of SURPRISE! He went off with that as MY LAST SOLEMN WARNING! Yet he let his army be cut to pieces—HACKED—BUTCHERED—TOMAHAWKED— by SURPRISE—the very thing I warned him against! The blood of the slain is upon him—the curse of widows and orphans—THE CURSE OF HEAVEN!"[36]

Congress conducted an inquiry into the causes of the defeat and found that inadequate equipment, untrained troops, and a lack of strategic planning had been the factors that were most responsible. The contrast between the disciplined and commendable conduct of the regular troops with the panic and flight of the militiamen pushed Congress to fund a professional, standing army. Henry Knox, Washington's secretary of war,

---

[35] Alan Taylor, *Divided Ground* (New York: Penguin Ransom House, 2007) 259.
[36] Thomas Fleming, *The Great Divide* (Boston: DaCapo Press, 2015) 115.

proposed that the army's strength should be 5,120 men, the same number as a Roman legion; that it should be organized into four cohorts of 1,280, each designed to coordinate the use of infantry, artillery, and cavalry; and that the units should train both separately and in unison, using signal systems essentially the same as those the Romans used.

By 1794, the legion was fully trained and ready to retaliate against the Little Turtle coalition. At Fallen Timbers, they won a decisive battle that forced the tribes to sign the Treaty of Greenville of 1795, ceding much of the land in the Ohio region to the United States.

The westward march continued, and as ever more American settlers moved across the Allegheny Mountains to the Mississippi River, atrocities both sides committed made peace a virtual impossibility. From the American point of view, if the tribes wouldn't make peace, give up their independence, and assimilate into the new society, as many had done in the East during the foregoing two centuries, they would have to be defeated. For the tribes, their choices were to submit, keep moving into less-bountiful lands, or make a final stand to preserve their independence.

Tecumseh

In the Indiana region, an extraordinary leader emerged who made a fateful decision. Tecumseh, chief of the Shawnee tribe, denounced the previous peace agreements and land concessions, and he assembled a confederation of tribes to resist any further white settlement. Tecumseh replicated the campaigns of Vercingetorix, the Gallic tribal chief, who in 52 BC assembled a confederation of Gallic tribes to resist Julius Caesar's conquest of Gaul. Supporting the notion that one man's terrorist is another man's freedom fighter, Vercingetorix and Tecumseh voiced the battle cry of freedom and led ruthless campaigns against the enemies overrunning their lands.

Tecumseh traveled across the country and recruited tribes, including the Creeks and Red Sticks. He instructed them to repudiate their treaties and increase their raids on white settlements. In October 1811, he reportedly told a gathering of warriors, "Let the white race perish! They seize your land. They corrupt your women. They trample on the bones of your dead! Back whence they came, upon a trail of blood, they must be driven!

Back—aye, back to the great water whose accursed waves brought them to our shores! Burn their dwellings—destroy their stock—slay their wives and children that the very breed may perish! War now! War always! War on the living! War on the dead!"[37]

When the War of 1812 began, Tecumseh aligned his confederation with the British, and in August 1812, he led six hundred Shawnee warriors, combined with a British force of 250 regulars, against Fort Detroit. The American general at the fort, William Hull, fearing that the Shawnee would massacre the women and children if the fort were taken by force, surrendered the fort without firing a shot. With the loss of Detroit and other forts in the territory, the Northwest was wide open to British-Indian raids. Hull was later court-martialed for cowardice.

In January 1813, an American regiment of about eight hundred was sent to Michigan to protect settlers. At the River Raisin, a combined total of twelve hundred British troops and Tecumseh's warriors attacked them. Outnumbered, the Americans surrendered. The British troops took prisoners and marched them toward Canada. About eighty wounded Americans who couldn't walk were left behind, and when the British left, the Indians massacred the wounded soldiers. "Remember the Raisin" became a rallying cry for retaliation against the tribes.

In September 1813, the Americans won a naval battle against the British on Lake Erie, which forced the British and Tecumseh's warriors to retreat into Canada. General William Henry Harrison, a future US president, led three thousand troops into Canada and defeated the British and Tecumseh's warriors at the Battle of the Thames. Tecumseh was killed, and his northern confederacy died with him; but other leaders emerged, and other tribes made a stand, fighting to near extinction.

In the South, the Creeks, whom Tecumseh had inspired, attacked and overran Fort Mims, which was about forty miles north of Mobile, Alabama. Within the fort were men, women, and children—about 250 whites, 150 blacks, and more than 100 friendly Indians. The Creeks slaughtered all but fifteen. A member of the American burial party described the

---

[37] R. David Edmunds, *Tecumseh and the Quest for Indian Leadership* (Boston: Little Brown & Company, 1994) 70-85.

remains. "Indians, Negroes, white men, women and children lay in one promiscuous ruin. All were scalped, and the females of every age were butchered in a manner which neither decency nor language will permit me to describe."[38]

ANDREW JACKSON

This occurrence, nearly two centuries after the Jamestown massacre, reinforced the belief that the Native Americans were incorrigible and eternal enemies. They had to be driven away or wiped out. Andrew Jackson was the man who embodied this belief of extermination. A fierce, charismatic leader with flaming red hair and blazing blue eyes, Major General Jackson led several thousand of his Tennessee militia into Creek territory in March 1814. At Horseshoe Bend, on the Tallapoosa River, they killed over eight hundred Creek warriors. Jackson then forced the Creeks to sign the Treaty of Fort Jackson, by which they surrendered half of their territory or twenty-two million acres, stretching from Georgia to Alabama.

Jackson's success against the Creeks led to his assignment to defend the city of New Orleans against the pending British invasion. He defeated the British spectacularly in the Battle of New Orleans, which made him the hero of the war, put him on a path to the presidency, and established him as a leader. He would come to be called "Old Hickory" by his troops and a Caesar by others, the latter not in a complimentary way.

Jackson would become the personification of the formative years of America, years that have many parallels to those of the early Roman Republic. Each nation was toughened for the difficult tests they would face when they dominated greater territories and took on the challenges of maintaining peace and order throughout their worlds. But it wasn't toughness alone that elevated them above other nations; their political systems provided the strength, flexibility, and resilience necessary for them to become the dominant powers of their times.

---

[38] Borneman, *1812* (New York: Harper Collins, 2004) 151.

CHAPTER 3

Political Systems

ON JULY 4, 1788, during an Independence Day celebration in Philadelphia, Pennsylvania, James Wilson, a delegate to the Constitutional Convention, spoke of the ratification of the Constitution. He declared to the assembled celebrants,

> You have heard of Sparta, of Athens, and of Rome; you have heard of their admired constitutions, and of their high-prized freedom ... But did they, in all their pomp and pride of liberty, ever furnish, to the astonished world, an exhibition similar to that which we now contemplate? Were their constitutions framed by those, who were appointed for that purpose, by the people? After they were framed, were they submitted to the consideration of the people? Had the people an opportunity of expressing their sentiments concerning them? Were they to stand or fall by the people's approving or rejecting vote?[39]

For Rome, the answer to each of Wilson's questions was yes. In the decades after the expulsion of the kings, the Roman people developed

---

[39] Robert Green McCloskey, ed., *The Works of James Wilson* (University Park, Illinois: Liberty Fund, 1967) 1304.

a set of governing rules and a set of basic individual rights. They established the powers of the magistrates, the Senate, the assemblies, and the tribunes of the plebs; the latter were given the power to act in defense of citizens against unlawful or unjust acts of the magistrates. In 451–450 BC, a committee of ten magistrates, the decemvirs, were tasked with writing the laws for all to know; and in 449 BC, the people approved the written laws, known as the "Twelve Tables," which included guaranteed rights and protections for all citizens. Most pertinent was this provision: "No privileges, or statutes, shall be enacted in favor of private persons, to the injury of others contrary to the law common to all citizens, and which individuals, no matter of what rank, have a right to make use of"[40]

This provision of the tables anticipated the Fourteenth Amendment of the United States Constitution. "No State shall make or enforce any law which shall abridge the privileges and immunities of citizens of the United States; nor shall any State deprive any person of life, liberty, or property, without due process of law; nor deny to any person within its jurisdiction the equal protection of the laws."

Rome's Constitution encompassed more than the Twelve Tables. It wasn't created at a particular moment; nor did it remain unchanged. It evolved and developed as the city and empire expanded. Subsequent to the promulgation of the Twelve Tables, the people of Rome, in their popular assemblies, passed additional structural laws to amend their constitution. At important turning points, they created new offices, altered the legislative process, or adjusted the relationships between the Senate and the assemblies. By direct popular voting, the Romans established their political order through a progression of laws, each building on or modifying prior ones. In effect, the Roman people amended their constitution as the American people amended theirs. In an environment of unusual transparency, the Roman Republic functioned within explicit parameters on which the assemblies of the free citizens agreed.

---

[40] *The Law of the Twelve Tables*, IX, 1 (Harvard University Press, Loeb Classical Library, 1938), 481.

Checks and Balances

The essential elements of the Roman and American constitutional systems were remarkably similar. Motivated by their hatred of monarchy, the founders of each republic built their political systems on the doctrines of separation of powers and checks and balances. They were wary not only of autocratic rule but also of unchecked popular democracy, since they knew that without restraints, an assembly of people could become just as tyrannical as a king. John Adams explained, "The Roman constitution formed the noblest people, and the greatest power, that has ever existed. But if all the powers of the consuls, senate, and people, had been centered in a single assembly of the people collectively or representatively, will any man pretend to believe that they would have been long free, or ever great?"[41]

Both nations designed their governments to adapt to changing circumstances and meet the demands of new interest groups without destroying the traditional order. To accommodate new groups, a republic adjusts the weightings of its checks and balances. It allows the new groups to participate, thus profiting the nation.

Through trial and error, the Romans developed a practicable form of republican government. As Cicero wrote, it was "based upon the genius, not of one man, but of many; it was founded, not in one generation, but in a long period of several centuries and many ages of men." At the republic's high points, the Romans enjoyed a governing system that was new in the history of mankind. They developed the first democratically based government that successfully administered an area far larger than a city-state. Most previous states, except for a few short-lived Greek city-states, had been controlled by force and ruled by either monarchs or oligarchies, with the majority of people living in servitude without individual rights. In contrast, the early Roman Republic invested its citizens with broad rights and equality under the law. It created a sense of belonging to a special community and inspired its citizens to accept and fulfill their civic duties.

Though the Roman constitution was unwritten in the sense that it

---

[41] John Adams, *Defense of the Constitutions of the Governments of the United States of America*, 1776, 30.

wasn't contained in a single cohesive document, its principles were contained within a continuum of traditions, laws, and decrees pronounced over the centuries. Rome's constitution mixed the elements of democracy, oligarchy, and executive authority into three branches of government: first, the executive magistracy, led by two annually elected coconsuls; second, the Senate, with its members drawn initially from the patrician aristocracy but later from all classes; third, the assemblies of the people.

The balance of power between the three branches of government fluctuated, but a workable balance was maintained between them for almost five hundred years, a remarkable accomplishment because Rome had the same class divisions that had destroyed other nations. The patrician class jealously guarded its hereditary privileges over the plebeians, while the plebeians vigorously demanded equality. At several points, class warfare almost tore the republic apart, but mutual interests overcame the divisions and held it together. Preventing one side from dominating the other was the key to a continuing state. John Stuart Mill wrote about republican government, "A party of order or stability, and a party of progress or reform, are both necessary elements of a healthy state of political life. Each of these modes of thinking derives its utility from the deficiencies of the other; but it is in a great measure the opposition of the others that keeps each within the limits of reason and sanity."[42]

Roman Senate

The Roman Senate had been an advisory body to the kings, comprising one hundred fathers of patrician families. At the founding of the republic, it was increased to three hundred members and by the end of the republic to nine hundred. Election as a magistrate made one eligible for admission to the Senate. When called into session, the Senate met from dawn until sunset within the city or within a one-mile radius of the city gates. A magistrate with imperium (supreme power), either a consul or a praetor, could summon it. The magistrate presented a subject for discussion, and each senator in his turn could voice his opinion with absolute freedom of speech.

---

[42] J. S. Mill, *On Liberty* (New Haven: Yale University Press, 2003) 113.

Although the Senate couldn't pass laws, it customarily passed resolutions approving proposed bills before they were submitted to an assembly. It didn't elect the magistrates, but in emergencies, it could appoint a temporary dictator. It determined foreign policy, ratified treaties, and received embassies. With the agreement of the assembly, the Senate authorized the consuls to raise armies and undertake wars, and it assigned proconsuls and propraetors to governorships and provinces. It held the power of the purse and oversaw the treasury, public lands, mines, quarries, salt works, and the sale and distribution of war booty.

The strength of the Senate was the popular consensus that it was the heart of the nation, composed of worthy individuals who had been elected as magistrates. The Senate balanced the competing interests of political and economic factions and, when necessary, checked the destructive impulses of the populace.

Senators served at their own expense since it was deemed an honor to serve. They fought in military campaigns, and the valor they displayed in war and their diplomatic abilities could affect their influence with the people. Life tenure for senators provided stability and a counterweight to the one-year tenure of the consuls, and the overall experience and maturity of the senators counteracted some of the more impulsive or radical acts of the popular assemblies. Through its influence over the magistrates and the tribunes, the Senate largely controlled the legislative agenda. Wolfgang Kunkel, writing of the third and second centuries BC, stated,

> All the power and experience of the politically dominant stratum of Rome was concentrated in the Senate, which amid the yearly change of magistrates was the one point of stability in Roman political life; and this is the reason for the immense power that this body enjoyed for centuries. Without possessing any legislative or executive power of its own, the Senate, as a standing source of advice for the magistrates, held the real leadership of the state firmly in its own hands.[43]

---

[43] Wolfgang Kunkel, *An Introduction to Roman Legal and Constitutional History*, trans. J. M. Kelly (Oxford: Clarendon Press, 1973) 20.

Until the late republic, the authority of the Senate was accepted as superior to the magistrates and the army. Without Senate approval, a magistrate was not to move his forces into another province. When it became necessary to send more legions into the field than the two consuls could manage, the Senate assigned proconsuls, or propraetors, to lead the additional legions. The army commanders sent their reports to the Senate, and that body could reprimand the commander or praise him by the grant of a public triumph (a parade through the city with his troops).

Senators performed quasi-public functions, such as arbitrating disputes and representing the interests of provincials. They often represented parties in lawsuits, and they sat as jurors in trials for public crimes such as treason, conspiracy, and corruption. Conversely, senators were not immune from prosecution, and they could be expelled from the Senate for crimes, immorality, or bankruptcy.

Over time, the power of the Senate alternately expanded and contracted. Events, emergencies, and personalities influenced the deference shown to its decrees. Open debate and full examination of proposals by conscientious senators contributed greatly to Rome's survival and success, as during the wars against Carthage and Macedon when the Senate demonstrated its greatest power and effectiveness, coordinating strategies in several military campaigns simultaneously over far-flung territories. The wars provided the ultimate stress tests, and the Senate was instrumental in guiding Rome to its triumphs. Coincidentally, the Senate provided the stage for scores of the most ambitious, self-confident, and charismatic leaders ever known to play their parts in steering the course of history.

ROMAN ASSEMBLIES

In Rome, popular assemblies voted on laws and elections. The most important assemblies were the *comitia centuriata* (assembly of the centuries), the *comitia tributa* (tribal assembly), and the *concilium plebis* (council of the plebs). Each assembly was organized differently and voted for different offices and measures. Voting was by groups, not by individuals, with the votes of some groups more heavily weighted than others.

Initially, the *comitia centuriata* was the dominant assembly. Convened by a consul, it met on the Field of Mars outside the city gates, and its members passed laws; elected the consuls, praetors, and censors; declared war or peace; and voted on capital cases.

The *comitia tributa* wasn't structured militarily but organized by geographic districts. Its eligible citizens voted on proposed laws and actions, and elected the lower magistrates, including quaestors and aediles. Quaestors were treasury officials, responsible for receiving taxes from the tax collectors, making payments, and keeping accounts. Aediles were responsible for the upkeep of temples, buildings, streets, markets, and public events.

By the second century BC, the *concilium plebis* became the dominant and most active assembly. It was organized like the tribal assembly, except that patricians were excluded. Tribunes of the plebs presided over it, although they weren't magistrates. They didn't have imperium; nor could they command armies, execute the laws, act as judges, or mete out punishment, but they could intercede on behalf of plebeians to protect them against unlawful or unjust acts of the magistrates. Their persons were inviolate, but their power applied only in Rome or to a mile from the city gates; and they couldn't intercede against the actions of a temporary dictator.

At first, resolutions of the *concilium plebis*, called "plebiscites," pertained only to plebeian affairs unless the Senate ratified them. However, in 287 BC, the passage of the *Lex Hortensia* removed the need for Senate ratification, and plebiscites became laws applicable to all citizens, including patricians. Thus, it became the dominant assembly of the late republic. Historians have agreed, "Though the legislative competence of all the assemblies was equal, the *concilium plebis* became the usual organ for the passing of laws in the later Republic as its presidents, the tribunes, had more time for, and interest in, legislation than the consuls, who were frequently engaged in military duties."[44]

In 457 BC, the number of tribunes was increased from two to ten, and with their veto power over Senate proposals, they gained substantial control of the legislative process. A consul who wished to submit a bill

---

[44] H.F. Jolowicz and Barry Nicholas, *Historical Introduction to Roman Law* (New York: Cambridge University Press, 1972) 26.

to the assembly had to deal with the tribunes because one tribune alone could veto the submission.

It might seem that such power put the tribunes in complete control of the state; nevertheless, the magistrates and senators weren't without means of influencing affairs, and they could enlist a tribune to intercede a veto on their behalf. More significantly, the people respected the nobility for its history and leadership, and often sided with the magistrates over the tribunes.

While the uncertainties of antiquity have veiled the exact procedures followed in each assembly, before votes were taken, preliminary meetings, or *contiones* were held, advocates on either side of an issue gave speeches. Consuls and senators often spoke and proposed laws in the interests of the nobility, and tribunes of the plebs, who generally represented the interests of the commoners, often opposed them. However, it wasn't uncommon for consuls to propose progressive and democratic reforms. On the whole, the adversarial nature of the process proved beneficial; arguments were tested and honed, and the process led to better policy and operational decisions.

Roman Consuls

To prevent the return of autocracy, the Romans replaced the king with two consuls, giving them equal but divided authority. Each could veto the actions of the other. The purpose of this divided authority was to prevent any one person from obtaining kingly power. The consuls were elected for only one year, which was a unique development in government. Ideally, it not only limited the power of the consuls but also reduced internal conflicts. Those opposed to the policies, actions, or personality of a particular consul needed to wait only one year for change. With no hereditary successions or lifetime appointments, there was no compelling need for the revolts, assassinations, or poisonings that later became the bane of the emperors.

Consuls were given the imperium, supreme authority to command both civil and military affairs. Their principal duty was to command the armies. Outside Rome, when dealing with external threats, their powers were greatest, almost absolute. In their provinces, they could install or depose foreign magistrates, demand troops from Rome's allies, destroy cities, enslave conquered peoples, and punish or execute soldiers for disobedience or desertion. Still, they needed senatorial support since the Senate held the power of the purse. Polybius related, "Without a decree of the Senate, they can be supplied neither with corn nor clothes nor pay, so that all the plans of a Commander must be futile, if the Senate is resolved either to shrink from danger or hamper his plans."

Inside the city, the consuls executed the laws, carried out the Senate's decrees, and summoned the popular assemblies for votes. Although they had great power, they acted within strict parameters. They could exercise their authority only in person, meaning that they had to be present to issue commands, and their commands were subject to the veto of the coconsul. Unlike the president of the United States, who appoints a cabinet to administer the executive branch, consuls didn't appoint the other magistrates and couldn't unilaterally dismiss them.

Unlike kings and temporary dictators, the consuls weren't immune from prosecution. When their terms expired, they lost their immunity, and they could be charged with crimes or offenses and be tried before the Senate or an assembly of the people. This was a powerful incentive for them to act within the law. Knowing they were subject to prosecution when their year of immunity expired, the consuls, for the most part, didn't engage in tyrannical practices to preserve their positions. They expected that as long as they performed their duties in accordance with accepted standards, they would gain the gratitude and respect of the citizens; nonetheless, charges against ex-consuls weren't uncommon.

For example, the tribune Gaius Sempronius Blaesus brought charges of treason and cowardice against the ex-consul Cneius Fulvius for loss of an army to Hannibal during the Second Punic War. According to Livy's account, the tribune spoke before the assembly.

> Many generals had by indiscretion and ignorance brought their armies into the most perilous situations, but none, save Cneius Fulvius, had corrupted his legions by every species of excess before he betrayed them to the enemy; it might therefore with truth be said, that they were lost

before they saw the enemy, and that they were defeated, not by Hannibal, but by their own general. No man, when he gave his vote, took sufficient pains in ascertaining who it was to whom he was entrusting an army. What a difference was there between this man and Tiberius Sempronius! The latter having been entrusted with an army of slaves, had in a short time brought it to pass, by discipline and authority that not one of them in the field of battle remembered his conditions and birth, but they became a protection to our allies and a terror to our enemies. They had snatched, as it were, from the very jaws of Hannibal, and restored to the Roman people, Cumae, Beneventurm, and other towns. But Cneius Fulvius had infected with the vices peculiar to slaves, an army of Roman citizens, of honorable parentage and liberal education; and had thus made them insolent and turbulent among their allies, inefficient and dastardly among their enemies, unable to sustain, not only the charge, but the shout of the Carthaginians. But, by Hercules, it was no wonder that the troops did not stand their ground in the battle, when their general was the first to fly; with him, the greater wonder was that any had fallen at their posts, and that they were not all the companions of Cneius Fulvius in his consternation and his flight. Caius Flaminius, Lucius Paullus, Lucius Posthumius, Cneius and Publius Scipio, had preferred falling in the battle to abandoning their armies when in the power of the enemy. But Cneius Fulvius was almost the only man who returned to Rome to report the annihilation of his army.[45]

After the tribune's speech, Fulvius, rather than waiting for the verdict of the assembly, fled into exile.

The most direct and important check on the power of the consuls

---

[45] Livy, *Histories*, bk. 26, 2.

was the law that forbade them from entering Rome with their armies. This unequivocally set the limits of their power. Montesquieu noted the following of the northern border of Rome at the Rubicon River: "But to secure the city of Rome against these troops, the famous *senatus consultum* which can still be seen engraved on the road from Rimini to Cesena was issued. It consigned to the infernal gods, and declared guilty of sacrilege and parricide, anyone who passed the Rubicon with a legion, an army or a cohort."[46]

For four centuries, the barrier wasn't breached; however, in the last century of the republic, several military commanders crossed the barrier and entered Rome with their armies. In 49 BC, when Julius Caesar crossed it, the final act of the republic opened.

TEMPORARY DICTATORS

In emergencies, the Senate could appoint a dictator for a maximum of six months. The dictator had absolute control over all matters and wasn't subject to vetoes by consuls or tribunes of the plebs. He was permanently immune from prosecution for any acts committed during his term. A dictator was first appointed in 458 BC, when Aequian tribes from the east had surrounded a Roman army in the field and Rome was in peril. The Senate called on retired general Lucius Quinctus Cincinnatus to take over the fight against the Aequians. To provide Cincinnatus with the necessary power he needed to deal with the crisis, he was given absolute powers and authority over all the other magistrates. In sixteen days of battle, Cincinnatus expeditiously defeated the Aequians and saved the city. Grateful, the Romans asked him to stay as dictator for the full six months of the term, but he declined the offer and returned to his farm.

---

[46] Montesquieu, *Considerations on the Causes of the Greatness of the Romans and their Decline*, trans. David Lowenthal (New York: The Free Press, 1965). II, 57

American Checks and Balances

The founders were steeped in the history of Rome, and they were obsessed with its mutation from a republic into an imperial dictatorship. They were avid readers of Edward Gibbon's *Decline and Fall of the Roman Empire*, the first volume of which was published in 1776, the year of independence; the sixth and last volume was published in 1789, the year the Constitution was ratified. The founders knew that when one political faction gained preeminence over the others, that faction inevitably imposed oppressive measures to maintain its preeminence. To avoid that result, the framers wrote into the Constitution a system of separation of powers and checks and balances similar to that of Rome's, but they adjusted and perfected them. Their goal was to prevent the disintegration of the republic or the establishment of a centralized autocracy. James Madison, the leading drafter of the Constitution and the fourth president, wrote, "In all political societies, different interests and parties arise out of the nature of things, and the great art of the politician lies in making them checks and balances to each other."[47]

What Madison and the other drafters established wasn't exactly the same system as that of Rome, but it was based on the same principles. Rufus Fears wrote of the framers, "They crafted our Constitution to reflect the balanced constitution of the Roman Republic, with the sovereignty of the people guided by the wisdom of the Senate, with a powerful executive in the form of the commander in chief, the consul." To preserve American liberty, power was divided vertically between the national government and the state governments, and horizontally among three separate federal branches: a Congress to make the laws, an executive branch to enforce the laws, and a judiciary to interpret the laws. John Adams, the nation's second president, explained, "By the authorities and examples already recited, you will be convinced that three branches of power have an unalterable foundation in nature; that they exist in every society natural and artificial; and that if all of them are not acknowledged in any constitution

---

[47] Robert Rutland, "For the National Gazette," *Papers of James Madison*, January 23, 1792, (Charlottesville, VA., University of Virginia Press) 198.

of government, it would be found to be imperfect, unstable, and soon enslaved; that the legislative and executive authorities are naturally distinct;
and that liberty and the laws depend entirely on a separation of them in
the frame of government."[48]

The founders knew that when the Roman *populare* factions began
bypassing the Senate and sending bills directly to the assembly, where
they were passed without the imprimatur of the Senate and where force
of numbers overwhelmed rational compromise, the republic was doomed.
To avoid such circumstances, the founders required the approval of both
branches of Congress to enact a law, thus maintaining equilibrium between the main factions. They gave the president the power to veto bills
passed by the Congress, which provided an additional check; but to check
the president, the Congress could override the veto by a two-thirds vote.

US Congress: House and Senate

The founders divided Congress into two branches: the House of
Representatives (its members elected for two-year terms) and the Senate
(its members elected for six-year terms). They made seats in the House
proportional to the population, with the more-populated states having
more representatives than the less-populated states. For the Senate, they
gave each state two senators regardless of population to prevent the states
with greater populations from dominating the less-populated agrarian
states. This served a similar purpose as Rome's one vote per tribe, which
favored the rural areas and landowning classes over the urban populace.

To mitigate the divisions between the propertied and the landless
classes, which had been so detrimental to the Roman Republic, the
American founders eliminated property requirements for either the
Senate or the House of Representatives, such as those required for the
English Parliament. In addition, members of Congress were given guaranteed salaries, making it financially feasible for individuals from all segments of society to serve in either branch.

For a bill to become law, it had to be passed in both branches of

---

[48] John Adams, *Works*, bk. 4, 579.

Congress. Special provision was made for the all-important taxing power, which must originate in the House, since that body is the closest and most accountable to the people.

The Senate was given powers the House of Representatives was not given. It shared executive power through its authority to ratify treaties the president entered into and to confirm presidential appointments to the cabinet, ambassadorships, top military positions, and all federal judgeships, including Supreme Court justices. If the House impeached a president or a federal judge, the Senate would hold a trial and render judgment. A conviction required a two-thirds vote.

Taking a lesson from Rome, American congressmen and senators were given absolute immunity for speeches on the floor of Congress, meaning that no action for defamation or otherwise may be brought against them for such speech. Unfettered debates came at a high price, but the benefits far outweighed the costs.

After establishing the system of checks and balances in the legislative process, clearly expressed in article 1 of the Constitution, the founders turned their attention to the executive and judicial branches in articles 2 and 3.

THE AMERICAN PRESIDENT

The founders debated having two presidents in the manner of the Roman coconsuls to avoid concentrating too much power in the hands of one person. Contributors such as Alexander Hamilton advocated a strong executive, but many others were fearful of reconstituting a kingly power. Responding to Hamilton, Governor George Clinton of New York, writing under the pseudonym "Cato," retorted, "You do not believe that an American can be a tyrant? [Y]our posterity will find that great power connected with ambition, luxury, and flattery, will ... readily produce a Caesar, Caligula, Nero, and Domitian in America."[49]

After much debate, the founders vested the executive powers in one

---

[49] Letter V of November 22, 1787, in Ralph Ketcham, ed., *The Anti-Federalist Papers and the Constitutional Convention Debates* (New York: Mentor, 1986) 317.

president. They didn't consider a provision for the appointment of a temporary dictator as the Romans had done but gave the president greater powers than the Roman consuls. The president is the commander and chief of the army and navy, while the consuls were in command of only that part of the Roman army the Senate designated. Neither the president nor the consuls could declare war, but both could take defensive military action. The president's power allowed for emergency action to respond to unanticipated circumstances, as was the case when President Lincoln exercised de facto dictatorial powers at the outset of the American Civil War.

The Constitution commands the president "to take care that the laws be faithfully executed," and the president is subject to checks and balances. If he or she violates or fails to enforce the laws, Congress could impeach and remove him from office. Whether a president could be prosecuted in a criminal court during his term hasn't been tested. If that were the case, the president's ability to function would be severely hampered. The Romans gave immunity to their consuls until the expiration of their terms, but a consul's term was only for one year. The president's term is for four years.

Though the United States has never tried to prosecute a president, either in or out of office, two presidents have been impeached, Andrew Johnson in 1868 and Bill Clinton in 1998; neither was convicted. Prosecution of Richard Nixon was contemplated after his resignation, but President Gerald Ford pardoned him, making a possible prosecution moot.

THE COURTS

The third branch of the federal government is the judiciary. Article 3 of the Constitution briefly defines the judiciary's structure and powers, leaving expansion to future developments. "The judicial Power of the United States, shall be vested in one Supreme Court, and in such inferior Courts as the Congress may from time to time ordain and establish."

The president appoints all federal judges with the advice and consent of the Senate. The judges have life tenure during good behavior, and their compensation cannot be diminished.

A major difference between the American and Roman systems was that the Roman judiciary wasn't an independent branch of government. The praetors, aediles, and quaestors, who presided over trials, were elected for one year at a time as opposed to lifetime appointments. Most had aspirations for higher office, and politics could have had a strong influence on them. Their rulings could be appealed to an assembly; thus Rome's justice system, for good or ill, was far more subject to democratic influence than ours.

In both nations, as time progressed, judicial powers expanded. In *Marbury v. Madison*, Supreme Court Chief Justice John Marshall established the power of judicial review, ruling that it was the purpose of the courts to determine the constitutionality of statutes and government actions. This power has provided a strong check on the other branches of government and has afforded the means for resolution of partisan arguments and conflicts.

FEDERALISM

The American system of federalism provides for a separation of powers between the federal and state governments in a system similar to separation of powers between the Rome's central government and its associated Italian territories and outside provinces. The Tenth Amendment of our Constitution certifies that the powers not specifically granted to Congress are retained by the states, and states continue to wield important powers. They enact and enforce their own laws and execute all governmental functions except in matters subject to a superior federal authority. The state governors exercise executive power, and independent state courts exercise judicial power.

Similarly, in Italy the towns and cities kept their powers in domestic matters, and they elected local magistrates, who enforced local laws. Central authority over the free local governments was limited to taxation, military levies, and diplomacy; in all other matters the locals could act as they saw fit. Italian allies eventually held dual citizenship as citizens of their locality and of Rome, just as Americans are citizens of their state and the United States. For the provinces outside Italy, the Senate appointed governors who imposed Rome's will to a greater or lesser degree, but the provincials retained authority over matters of no concern to Rome. Provincials didn't have direct representation in the assembly or Senate, but when conflicts arose, they could petition those bodies, usually by employing senators or tribunes as lobbyists.

Over time, both nations increased centralization and instituted programs that overpowered the principles of federalism, proving true the theory that bureaucracies only expand and never contract. In Rome, Julius Caesar and Augustus Caesar centralized authority and created powerful bureaucracies to impose their will; in similar fashion, in the United States, Franklin Roosevelt and his successors centralizing powers in the federal government that previously had been within the purview of the states. As the trend continues, future presidents will have the leverage and authority, such as the Caesars used to transform the Roman Republic into an autocracy. Unconstrained, a future president or series of presidents could readily impose despotic measures that abrogate our checks-and-balances systems, our individual rights, and the long-cherished ideals of American freedom and liberty.

CHAPTER 4

Class Struggles

FROM THE BEGINNING OF the Roman Republic, inequalities between the classes generated political and social conflict, but over a period
of four centuries, Rome achieved a greater degree of equality among the
classes than in any other ancient society. The poor and debtor classes gradually achieved greater representation in the assemblies and the Senate.
Slavery was never eliminated, but large numbers of slaves were set free,
and former slaves attained the right to vote and work equally with freeborn
citizens. Women, though they never obtained the vote, gradually gained
equal standing in the laws of marriage, divorce, property, and inheritance.

Romans were divided into the patrician or plebeian classes, with the
early republic dominated by the patricians. The word *patrician* stems from
the Latin word for "fathers." How the differentiation between patrician
and plebeian families came about is uncertain; Livy merely says King
Romulus appointed one hundred senators from among the fathers, and
"their descendants were called patricians."[50] These "fathers," as in most
archaic societies, were the heads of families who had gained possession of
the land and thus became the nobility.

Plebeians were non-patrician, freeborn citizens. On the whole, they
were small farmers who provided most of the labor for the economy
and most of the soldiering for the legions, but the patricians politically

---

[50] Livy, *Histories*, bk.1, 8

marginalized them. It was generally believed that the plebeians and patricians were of different blood; whether this was by tribal or ethnic differences is unclear. Family surnames distinguished patricians from plebeians, and social divisions persisted to varying degrees into the imperial period.

In the early republic, hereditary rights preserved the patrician hierarchy, and leaders selected from elite families took turns serving as consuls and praetors. This was justified by the contention that the qualities of leadership—intelligence, physical strength, courage, and composure during crisis—were attributes that ran within families and were likely to pass from father to son to grandson. Keeping leadership within the aristocracy was thought to be more prudent than exposing the state to the uncertain impulses of the plebeian multitude. An obvious disadvantage of this patrician hierarchy was the failure to fully utilize the talents of accomplished plebeians.

The plebeians complained that despite being subject to the military levies, they were neither represented in the highest state offices nor given access to economic opportunities. However, as Rome expanded and the duration of wars and levies increased, the plebeians, in return for their military service, gradually obtained political power and equality before the law.

Historians refer to these early-class struggles as the battle of the orders, meaning the process whereby the plebeians strove to achieve political equality while the patricians tried to preserve their favored position. The battle took many forms—political intrigues, trials, strikes, riots, and personal violence. Leading participants on both sides faced the prospects of prosecution, ruinous fines, exile, and death. Nevertheless, as potentially catastrophic as each conflict may have been, and as powerful as were the forces pulling the republic apart, countervailing forces and compromises kept it bound together. The marvel of Rome's political structure was that the continual tug-of-war between factions was balanced enough to prevent one side from pulling the other into the moat. As long as the patricians exercised their authority within the confines of the law and as long as the plebeian populace continued to accept and abide by the acknowledged rules, the nation remained united.

Step by step, the Romans developed a clearly defined set of governing rules and a set of basic individual rights. In 509 BC, the first year of the republic, the consul Publius Valerius Poplicola established a rule that whenever a magistrate (who at that time could be only a patrician) put the life or rights of a Roman citizen at stake, the citizen had a right of appeal to the tribal assembly. Somewhat akin to the Anglo-American right of habeas corpus, this right of appeal to the people fostered a rule of law based on democratic principles that rejected the absolute power of monarchies and dictatorships.

Implementing the rules and protecting citizen rights wasn't easily accomplished in that period of hard and brutal realities. Serious conflicts arose between the plebeians and the patricians over the laws of debt and military service. Rome had the same debt laws as other ancient societies. If a man couldn't pay his debts, his creditor could demand his involuntary labor under conditions not far removed from slavery. Although the rules were elaborate, in some cases the debtor could be sold into bondage. If he resisted, state officials were called on to enforce the laws, and they often did so in unjust and arbitrary ways that infuriated the debtor class. Livy described a conflict that arose in 495 B.C. "Internal dissensions between the Fathers and the plebs had burst into a blaze of hatred, chiefly on account of those who had been bound over to service for their debts. These men complained loudly that while they were abroad fighting for liberty and dominion they had been enslaved and oppressed at home by fellow-citizens, and that the freedom of plebeians was more secure in war than in peace, amongst enemies than amongst citizens."[51]

TRIBUNES OF THE PEOPLE

In 494 BC, the plebeians protested their second-class status by stopping all work and abandoning Rome. Their secession was more drastic than the modern labor strike—the plebeians moved out of the city with their families and threatened to set up a separate state. One of their demands was for the appointment of representatives who could protect their interests.

---

[51] Livy, bk. 2, 23.

To prevent the disintegration of the state, the Senate conceded to this demand and agreed that the plebeians could elect two tribunes from their own class. These tribunes of the plebs would be elected annually, and within the city boundaries they would have the power of intercession to protect plebs from unjust arrest, execution, or bondage. A citizen could appeal to a tribune, who could present the appeal to the assembly. Tribunes were also given the power to veto the submission of proposed laws to the assembly. To protect their persons, it was agreed that the tribunes were to be inviolate—meaning, immune from arrest or violence while in office—to the same extent as the consuls. To further protect the plebeians, no patrician could be a tribune of the plebs.

Once the tribunes obtained power, they readily exercised it against the patricians. Time and again they vetoed the submission of Senate-sponsored bills. In 473, 470, and 454 BC, they brought charges against ex-consuls, and for a time, the consulship seemed crippled by the might of the tribunes. Most importantly, the tribunes resisted levies of troops. In 457 BC, when the Volsci and Aedui tribes threatened Rome, the Senate directed the consuls to conduct a levy and lead an army into the field; however, the tribunes, with the support of the people, refused to allow the levy unless the number of tribunes was increased from two to ten. After a standoff, the patricians were compelled to agree. Consequently, two tribunes from each of five classes would be elected—the lowest class, because it paid no tax, wouldn't be represented.

APPOINTMENT OF THE DECEMVIRS

The conflict didn't abate, and in 451 BC, the animosity between the orders again reached a point that threatened the survival of the state. The plebeians abandoned the city to protest the arbitrary and unequal legal practices that favored patricians. To resolve the conflict, an extraordinary compromise was reached. The Senate was disbanded, elections for magistrates were canceled, and the consuls and tribunes were temporarily replaced by ten commissioners, the *decemviri legibus scribendis*, magistrates who were appointed jointly from both the plebs and the patricians to propose measures that should be advantageous to both sides, and secure equal liberty. To accomplish their task, they would investigate the reasons for the dysfunction within the state, and they would exercise whatever powers were necessary to resolve the problems.

The plebeians demanded a written code of law so that the laws would be known to all and couldn't be enforced in an arbitrary manner. It was agreed that the new laws written by the decemvirs would be codified and available for all to read and that they would have to be ratified by popular vote.

In the first year of the decemvir regime, they accomplished their task, crafting Ten Tables of Laws, which were posted for the people to read, make comments on, and offer amendments. The tables reaffirmed the traditional laws regarding heredity, burials, contracts, and property; and they outlined the rules for the initiation of trials, lawsuits, and the enforcement of judgments. Although written as procedural laws, the tables confirmed the underlying substantive law and the rights of citizens. Of great import, they reinforced the traditional social bonds of the paterfamilias—in other words, maintaining the rights of the head of a family to control his wife, children, and his sons' wives and children. They also reinforced the obligations of patrons and clients. The tables included a new provision limiting the number of times a debtor could sell his son into servitude to satisfy debts.

The tables provided notice, warning, and instruction to the people regarding the laws and their rights and obligations. No longer would the law be a matter of oral tradition known only to the ruling class. The written laws provided an objective basis on which citizens could argue against unlawful and arbitrary decisions. They included important provisions that only the *comitia centuriata* (assembly of the centuries) could pass laws authorizing capital punishment and also that a citizen accused of a capital crime had the right to a trial and the right of appeal to the assembly.

In the following year, another board of decemvirs was appointed, and they produced two additional tables; and in 449 BC, a vote in the *comitia centuriata* adopted the Twelve Tables of Laws. The laws were then inscribed on bronze tablets and posted in the forum. These laws became the fountainhead of all public and private Roman law, and their adoption may have marked the first time in history that the people of a nation, including the common people, ratified the foundational laws by which they would be governed.[52]

Unfortunately, one of the tables that the second board of decemvirs promulgated included the ill-conceived clause that banned marriages between patricians and plebeians. This didn't bode well for national comity, and egregious abuses of power marred the term of the second board. Foolishly, the citizens had given the second board combined consular and tribunal powers to rule the state; unchecked, several decemvirs blatantly abused their authority. Dionysius of Halicarnassus described the abuses. "Another was their treatment of the most reputable Romans who were dissatisfied with their actions, some of whom, on the strength of false and heinous accusations, they were expelling from the city and others they were putting to death, suborning some of their own faction to accuse them and themselves trying these cases. But more than anything else was the license they gave to the most audacious of the young men by whom each of them was always attended, to plunder and pillage the goods of those who opposed their administrations."

At the end of their term, the decemvirs refused to relinquish their magistracy, claiming it was necessary for them to remain in power because of ongoing attacks from neighboring tribes in Roman territory. Patricians who opposed this tyranny left the city, and in this unusual situation, they were joined by plebeians, who seceded from the city en masse, refused to work, and demanded a restoration of the constitutional order and the reinstatement of their tribunes. Faced with united opposition from both patricians and plebeians, also an insurrection in the legions, the decemvirs were forced to resign in disgrace. The Senate and assemblies reconvened, and new consuls and tribunes were elected. Promptly thereafter, the newly elected tribunes brought charges against the decemvirs; two were sentenced to death, and the others were forced into exile.

---

[52] *The Law of the Twelve Tables*, 8.10, vol. 329 (Harvard University Press, Loeb Classical Library, 1938), 481.

THE BATTLE OF THE ORDERS

In the following decades, the plebeian tribunes, through their influence in the tribal assembly, gained more than equality with the patrician consuls and Senate; at times, they had a de facto dominance. Nonetheless, the patricians still exercised great power, since much of their influence came from patron-client relationships, their control of religious rites, and the people's respect for the prominent families and their illustrious ancestors. Leading citizens could influence and persuade the people and often did so through powerful speeches to the assemblies. In his history, Livy reconstructed the speeches of the consuls and tribunes. Just how accurately he did so is uncertain, but like a great artist, he captured the essential elements. Through the perfection of his language, he illustrated the beliefs and passions that drove these extraordinary actors as they debated matters of life and death, loyalty and treachery.

Livy recounted that in 446 BC, the tribunes refused to allow a levy of soldiers when the Volsci and the Aedui were again plundering and burning Roman fields and villages outside the city. Titus Quinctius Capitolinus, the patrician consul, addressed the tribal assembly, many of whom owned property and farms outside the city. Quinctius challenged the motives of the tribunes and argued the necessity of meeting the enemy in the field.

> It is with great shame that I have come to this assembly to confront you … It was not cowardice in you that they [the Volsci and Aedui] despised … It was the discord betwixt the classes, and the quarrels—poison of this City—between the patricians and the plebs that aroused their hopes, as they behold our greed for power and yours for liberty; your disgust at the patrician magistrates and ours at the plebeian … Every man of you will presently be getting from the country a report of his personal losses …
>
> Shall the tribunes restore and make good to you your losses? Resounding words they will pour forth to your hearts' content, and accusations against prominent men, and laws one after another, and assemblies; but from

those assemblies there was never one of you returned
home the better off in circumstances or fortune ... Now
you suffer the foe to load himself with your riches and
depart. Hold fast to your assemblies and live your lives in
the Forum; you shall still be pursued by the necessity of
that service which you seek to evade ... the public flatterers—I mean your courtiers of the plebs, who still suffer
you neither to be at war nor to keep the peace—are exciting you and urging you on. Once thoroughly aroused
you are a source of advancement or of profit to them; and
because they see that so long as the orders harmonious
they themselves count for nothing anywhere, they had
rather lead an evil cause than none.[53]

Quinctius was persuasive, and the people voted for the levy to proceed. The next day the entire body of eligible young men appeared at the
Field of Mars to serve in the legions. The enemy tribes were repulsed.

Nevertheless, the acrimony between the classes continued. The tribunes proposed two laws: first, to rescind the law in the Twelve Tables
that forbade intermarriage between plebeians and patricians; second, to
allow one of the two consuls to be a plebeian. The patricians opposed both
proposals, and vehement debates ensued.

The plebeian tribune Gaius Canuleius called an assembly and spoke
for the proposals.

In the one bill we seek the right of intermarriage, which
is customarily granted to neighbors and foreigners—indeed we have granted citizenship, which is more than
intermarriage, even to defeated enemies; in the other we
propose no innovation but reclaim and seek to exercise a
popular right, to wit that the Roman People shall confer
office upon whom it will ... When we raise the question
of making a plebeian consul, is it the same as if we were

---

[53] Livy, *Histories,* bk. 3. 27.

to say a slave or freedman should attain that office? Have you any conception of the contempt in which you are held? That you breathe, that you speak, that you have the shape of men, fills them with resentment. Nay, they assert, if you please, that it is sinning against Heaven to elect a plebeian consul ... Do we not believe it possible that a bold and strenuous man, serviceable both in peace and in war, should come from the plebs ... Or shall we refuse, even if such a one appear, to let him approach the helm of state? Must we rather look forward to consuls like the *decemvirs*, the vilest of mortals, who nevertheless were all of patrician birth, than to such as shall resemble the best of kings, new men though they were?

But let me tell you that in the statutory prohibition and annulment of intermarriage between patricians and plebeians we have indeed at last an insult to the plebs. Why, pray, do you not bring in a law that there shall be no intermarrying of rich and poor? That which has always and everywhere been a matter of private policy, that a woman might marry into whatever family it had been arranged, that a man might take a wife from that house where he had engaged himself, you would subject to the restraint of a most arrogant law, that thereby you might break up our civil society and make two states out of one ... There is nothing we are seeking to gain from marriage with you, except that we should be accounted men and citizens. Neither have you any reason to oppose us, unless you delight in vying with each other how you may outrage and humiliate us.[54]

The battle of words between Titus Quinctius, expressing patrician sentiment, and Gaius Canuleius, expressing plebeian sentiment, exemplified the nature of the conflict between the classes. Though the immediate

---

[54] Livy, bk. 4, 4.

issues they raised were not the same—Quinctius challenging the loyalty of the plebs for denying the levy; Canuleius challenging the arrogance of the patricians for denying the right of intermarriage—the hostility both men expressed on behalf of their factions showed how deeply the nation was divided. Group association, as a basic psychological need, is the driving force behind most societal conflicts. Even in homogeneous societies, distinct groups and opposing factions have always formed and have always found issues to contest. During the republic, the initial patrician-plebeian dichotomy took various iterations—those born Romans versus freedmen; full citizens versus half citizens; the senatorial class versus the equestrians; *optimates* versus *populares*; and the citizens of urban Rome versus the citizens from the Italian Peninsula.

The early prohibition on intermarriage was a deeply divisive issue, and the plebeians persisted in their refusal to allow a levy until a vote was taken on the intermarriage issue. Consequently, the patricians were forced to allow a vote in the assembly, and the ban was rescinded.

After that victory, the tribunes continued pressing for a plebeian consulship, and the patricians continued to resist. Finally, in 444 B.C, a compromise was reached that created a substitute position—a military tribune with consular authority who could be chosen from either the patricians or the plebs. The new position was geared primarily to military matters, and it didn't carry the status and prestige of the consulship. At first, three such positions were filled; later, the number was increased to six.

This compromise was assumed to be a great victory for the plebeian tribunes who expected that they would be among those elected as military tribunes with consular powers. Ironically, when elections were held for the new positions, the people chose all three tribunes from among the patricians. Apparently, the people were satisfied enough with the concession that plebeians were allowed to stand for the office, but they weren't ready to abandon the traditional hierarchical system and the prominent and powerful patrician families. For more than four decades, from 444 BC until 400 BC, the plebeian citizens elected only patricians to the office of military tribune with consular powers. No plebeian was elected to that office, even though it had been created to accommodate plebeian interests and even after the number of positions was increased from three to six.

The plebeian tribunes complained of being held in contempt by their own constituents. It seems that patrician public relations efforts successfully painted plebeian leaders as opportunists who interfered with the military levies to obtain personal benefits and enhance their own importance.

The tribunes of the plebs nevertheless continued their efforts in the interests of the plebeian class. They pushed for land reform, proposing a law that the land that had been captured from enemies should be divided up among the citizens. If passed, it would have resulted in the confiscations of public land from the nobles who had accumulated large estates. The tribunes also pushed for debt relief, limits on the length of military service, and open eligibility for public offices.

Almost every other year, the same dance took place. The plebeian tribunes proposed reforms and tried to force a vote in the assembly, and the Senate responded by calling for a levy of troops to fight enemy tribes marauding throughout Roman territory. The Senate knew that with the citizen soldiers away from the city, fighting the enemy, a lawfully constituted assembly wouldn't be possible. The tribunes responded with threats to prevent the levy unless the Senate agreed to a vote on the reforms. These stalemates required negotiations that sometimes resulted in reforms but more often postponements because of more pressing needs to send the legions into battle. On occasion, when compromise couldn't be reached, the Senate resorted to the appointment of a temporary dictator. In any case, the patricians were unable to permanently obstruct the relentless efforts of the plebeians for reform.

Inexorably, the plebeian tribunes achieved their goals. In 409 BC, a plebeian was elected quaestor. In 406 BC, the Senate decreed that the soldiers should be paid a salary from the public treasury rather than serving at their own expense. This was an enormous boon to the citizen soldiers, since it broke the cycle of having to go into debt while serving in the legions during the summer and then having to pay off the debt after the fall harvest.

In 403 BC, the quid pro quo for the soldiers' salary came due during the siege of the city of Veii when the soldiers were required to maintain the siege throughout the winter. In protest, the plebeian tribunes prevented a new levy and proposed ending the siege, but the patrician tribune with consular powers, Appius Claudius Crassus, accused the tribunes of the plebs of abandoning the soldiers in the field for purposes of self-aggrandizement. In a diatribe to the assembly, and in the presence of the plebeian tribunes, he spoke as follows: "If it has ever been a question, Quirites [People of Rome], whether it was for your sake or their own that the tribunes of the commons have always encouraged sedition, I am certain that the doubt has this year been resolved ... Indeed they are like quack-salvers seeking employment, since they desire that there should always be some disease in the body politic, that there may be something which you may call them in to cure."[55]

Appius explained the need to continue the siege of Veii throughout the winter.

> Either we ought not to have undertaken the war, or we ought to conduct it as befits the Roman People, and end it as quickly as possible. And we shall end it, if we press our beleaguered foes, and quit them not till we have fulfilled our hopes and captured Veii ... Seven times they have renewed the war; never have they kept faith in peace; our fields they have pillaged a thousand times; they forced the Fidenates to forsake us; our settlers they have put to death; it was they who instigated, in violation of the law of nations, the impious murder of our envoys ...
>
> With such enemies ought we to wage a faint-hearted and dilatory war? ... [I]f we bring our army back, who can doubt that not only a desire for revenge, but also necessity, constraining them to plunder others since they have lost their own possessions, will cause them to invade our territory? So we are not postponing the war, if we act on your advice, but are receiving it within our own borders ... See how many undesirable consequences attend that line of policy: the loss of works constructed with such effort; the imminent devastation of our fields;

---

[55] Livy, *Histories*, bk. 5, 3

the Etruscans, instead of the Veientes only, aroused to war with us. It is thus, tribunes, that you would manage matters, much as though in dealing with a sick man, who if he would undergo a strict regimen might begin at once to recover, you should protract his illness and perhaps render it incurable, by indulging his immediate desire for meat and drink …

For perseverance, needful in every kind of warfare, is especially so in besieging cities, since fortifications and natural advantages make most of them impregnable, and time itself subdues them, with hunger and thirst, and captures them, as it shall capture Veii, unless the plebeian tribunes help our enemies, and the Veientes find in Rome those succours which they are seeking to no purpose in Etruria … Could anything happen which would so please the Veientes as that factions should spring up, first in the City of Rome, and then, as though by contagion, in the camp.[56]

Appius then returned to his attack on the tribunes. In a speech that anticipated Abraham Lincoln's castigation of the Northern politicians who undermined the Union's Civil War efforts, Appius accused disloyal tribunes of treasonous activities, which undermined the morale of the army and the nation.

Death by cudgeling is the wage of him who forsakes the standards or quits his post; but those who advise the men to abandon their standards and desert the camp gain a hearing, not with one or two soldiers, but with whole armies, openly, in public meetings; so accustomed are you to hear with complacency whatever a tribune says, even if it tends to betray the City and to undo the state; and captivated by the charm of that authority, you suffer

---

[56] Livy, bk. 5, 4

any wickedness whatsoever to lurk beneath it. It only remains for them to utter in camp and in the presence of the soldiers the view which they noisily publish here, and to corrupt the armies and not to suffer them to obey their leaders. For in the upshot liberty has come to mean at Rome, that a man respect neither senate nor magistrates, nor laws, nor ancestral customs, nor institutions of the fathers, nor military discipline.[57]

The speech of Appius in 403 BC had its desired effect, and the plebeians soon enlisted and rushed to the aid of the soldiers already conducting the siege. Not knowing the future, they surely thought the siege would last one year; however, it lasted seven more years until the capture of Veii in 396 BC. During this period, the strength of the plebeian bargaining position grew, and they continued their advancement.

In 400 BC, Publius Licinius Calvus became the first plebeian elected as a military tribune with consular powers. He served his term moderately and admirably, and in the following year, 399 BC, the people elected plebeians to five of the six positions. Then, in 398 BC, the patrician party, concerned about the loss of their authority, ran their most respected members for office, and the people elected patricians to all six positions. This ongoing political competition benefitted the common people because better candidates, more responsive to the people, ran for office.

CAMILLUS

In 395 BC, a new controversy between the orders arose after the conquest of Veii and the dispersal of its entire population. The plebeian tribunes proposed that half of the Roman citizens should leave Rome and occupy Veii and its lands. The patricians vehemently opposed the plan, offering that there was enough dissention in a single city, and there would be more in two. Of most importance, the patricians argued that no good would come to a people who abandoned their gods, the gods of their ancestors,

---

[57] Livy, bk. 5, 6.

and the gods of a victorious city. In another example of the cohesiveness of Roman society overpowering the dissensions within it, the patricians won the debate, and the proposal was defeated.

In 390 BC, the Veii issue reignited with the Sack of Rome by the Gauls. After the invaders departed, the Senate called on all the citizens to rebuild the ruins of the devastated city. The tribunes of the plebs, to the contrary, argued that to do so would be a task too overwhelming, and they urged the people to quit their ruined city and immigrate to the still-uninhabited city of Veii. To avoid the abandonment of Rome, Marcus Furius Camillus, the most prominent and respected patrician, spoke before the assembly.

> Even now I would gladly stop and hold my peace, were not this too the quarrel of my country; whom to fail while life endures is in other men disgraceful, but in Camillus impious. For why did we seek to win her back, why rescue her, when besieged, from the hands of the enemy, if, now that she is recovered, we voluntarily abandon her? And, although while the Gauls were victorious and in possession of the entire City, the Capitol nevertheless and the Citadel were held by the gods and men of Rome, shall we now, when the Romans are victorious and the City is regained, desert even Citadel and Capitol? ...
>
> We have a City founded with due observance of auspice and augury; no corner of it is not permeated by ideas of religion and the gods; for our annual sacrifices, the days are no more fixed than are the places where they may be performed. Do you intend, Quirites, to abandon all these gods, both of state and of family? ...
>
> For you remember how, before the coming of the Gauls, when our roof-trees, public and private, were unharmed and our City stood uninjured, that this same proposal was urged of migrating to Veii. And consider, tribunes, how wide is the difference between my view and yours. You think that even if then it ought not to have been done, yet now at any rate it ought; I on the

contrary ... even if it had been right to migrate then, with the City all intact, should not think it right to abandon these ruins now. For then our victory would have been a reason for migrating to a captured city—a reason glorious to ourselves and our posterity; but now such a removal is for us a wretched and humiliating course, and a glory to the Gauls. For we shall not seem to have left our country as victors, but to have lost it as men vanquished ... Have Gauls then been able to cast Rome down; and must Romans appear unable to have raised her up? What remains, if they should presently come with fresh forces—for all agree that their numbers are scarce to be believed—and should wish to dwell in this City which they have captured and you have abandoned ... What if not the Gauls but your ancient foes the Volsci and Aequi should migrate to Rome? Should you like them to be Romans, and yourselves Veientes? Or should you not prefer this to be your wilderness, rather than the city of your enemies? For my part I do not see what could be more abominable. Are you ready to stomach these outrages, these infamies, because it irks you to build?[58]

The speech of Camillus, particularly those aspects appealing to religion, won the day, and the people began rebuilding Rome. However, as soon as one crisis passed, another arose. Debt and the procedures for enforcing debt obligations continued to pit the plebeians against the patricians. Debtors could be forced into indentured servitude for a term agreed on to pay off the debt. If no agreement was reached or fulfilled, the creditor could commence a legal action, and debtors who failed to pay within thirty days of a judgment could be seized by the creditor and brought before a magistrate. The magistrate could authorize the creditor to keep the debtor in bondage for sixty days. Table 3 mandated, "If the judgment is not satisfied, and no one offers as surety on the debtor's behalf, the creditor may

---

[58] Livy, bk. 5, 51.

take his debtor and bind his hands or feet with fetters not exceeding fifteen pounds in weight, or less if the creditor so desires."[59]

During that time, the creditor had to publicly display the debtor on three consecutive market days or until someone paid the debt. If no one came forward, the debtor could be sold into slavery. Needless to say, within such a system injustices abounded. Soldiers came back from wars to face crushing debts, and they had to sell their farms for less than a fair price. It was a time when the economy was in a postwar depression, and destitute fathers, faced with dire consequences, sent their sons into bondage to pay off debts. Under such conditions, plebeian leaders and some patricians led movements for reform, even revolution.

MANLIUS ADVOCATES FOR DEBTORS

In 385 BC, the conflict over debt boiled over when a patrician, Marcus Manlius Capitolinus, took up the cause of the debtors. Manlius was a great hero for defending the citadel against the Gauls during the Sack of Rome. Now he came to the rescue of a soldier who had been condemned for debt. Manlius paid the debt for the soldier and began a campaign against the moneylenders. In his speeches, he accused the Senate of hoarding public gold, and he argued that the gold should be used to pay off the debts of the citizens. As could be expected, his proposal excited the populace, and an upheaval seemed imminent. Skeptics in the Senate claimed that Manlius acted more out of self-interest to advance himself than out of concern for the poor.

The Senate called back the dictator Aulus Cornelius Cossus from a military campaign to deal with Manlius. The dictator "insisted that he [Manlius] should either make his indictment good or confess to the crime of having accused the Senate falsely and exposed it to the unmerited odium of a charge of theft."[60]

When Manlius didn't respond to a summons from the dictator, he was arrested and jailed. However, the citizens protested so loudly that the

---

[59] *The Law of the Twelve Tables*
[60] Livy, bk. 6, 16.

dictator resigned, and the Senate released Manlius, thereby emboldening him more. He continued his protest with an absolutely seditious speech to the plebs.

> How long, pray, will you remain ignorant of your own strength, which nature has willed that even brutes shall know? ... Make but a show of war, and you shall have peace. Let them see you ready to resist, and they will give you your rights of their own accord. We must all unite in some bold stroke, or else, divided, submit to every evil ... Is there so little spirit in this great people that you are always satisfied with the help your tribunes lend you against your adversaries, and never quarrel with the senators, save as to the length you will suffer them to go in ruling you? And this is no native trait in you, but you are slaves by use ... Dictatorships and consulships must be leveled with the ground, that the Roman plebs may be enabled to lift its head. Stand by me, then; prevent all court-proceedings regarding moneys; I avow myself the patron of the commons—a title with which my zeal and loyalty have invested me: if you choose to give your leader a more striking title of authority or honor, you will find him the more able to make good your wishes.[61]

This speech went too far. It made clear to the plebeian tribunes that Manlius wanted to become a king, which would curtail their power or eliminate their positions entirely. The tribunes charged him with treason, and after a spectacular trial, he was convicted. In an irony of fate, Manlius was executed by being thrown from the Tarpeian Rock, on the same citadel where he had achieved his greatest fame in fighting off the Gauls. His execution reiterated the Roman hatred of monarchy, even when the proposed monarch was a military hero running on a platform to improve the lot of the ordinary citizens. This rabid anti-monarchy sentiment was

---

[61] Livy, bk. 6, 18.

uncommonly strong for ancient times, and the Romans suspected anyone who would aim for more power than their constitution allowed.

The end of Manlius didn't help the debtors; their plight persisted. In the next decades, the plebeian tribunes Gaius Licinius and Lucius Sextius continually and forcefully advocated for debt relief. The problem for the debtors was accumulated interest on the initial loan. As debtors fell behind in their interest payments, the total debt ballooned. Licinius and Sextius proposed the forgiveness of outstanding debts upon payment of the initial principle without the necessity of paying the accumulated interest. They also revived the proposal that plebeians could become consuls and indeed added that one of the consuls must be a plebeian, since that would allow the commoners the opportunity to gain honor and the rewards of authority.

Licinian-Sextian Compromise

The tribunes backed up their proposals with threats of strikes and violence. The patricians resisted and appointed Camillus as dictator with the idea of crushing the power of the plebeian tribunes. For more than a year, the sides threatened one another until Camillus in 367 BC, in a moment of great political sagacity, declined to exercise his dictatorial powers. Instead, he offered to compromise with Licinius and Sextius and conceded to most of the plebeian demands.

The Licinian-Sextian laws were passed, restoring the consulship and allowing the election of plebeians to that office. In 366 BC, Lucius Sextius became the first plebeian elected as consul. With the plebeian ascendancy to the consulship, the position of military tribune with consular powers was abolished. However, the plebeian consulship was permissive, not mandatory; that would come later.

To compensate the patricians for the loss of the exclusive right to the consulship, the position of urban praetor was established to assist the consuls with legal and civilian functions, and the position was to be filled from the patrician class. As events developed, the urban praetor provided a great benefit for the relationship between the classes because the praetors issued written edicts that improved the regularity and transparency of the law.

The Licinian-Sextian laws gave the plebeian *concilium plebis*, the power to elect plebeian aediles and quaestors—the former in charge of administrative matters, the latter in charge of financial affairs. The laws also gave the tribunes veto power—not only over proposed legislation but also over administrative decrees of the Senate that were considered counter to the interests of the plebs. This was an extremely important change to constitutional procedure, extending the power of the plebeian tribunes into areas that heretofore had been prerogatives of the Senate.

Of great importance, a limit of 500 *iugeras* (310 acres) was placed on the amount of public land one person could obtain. This concession was a setback for the patrician class, but it strengthened the republic. With more land available, it gave the plebeians a better opportunity to obtain parcels of public land and provided opportunities for upward mobility. Inevitably, a substantial number of plebeians amassed great wealth and became nobles in their own right.

Also of great importance, the plebeians became eligible for the college of priests—a significant development because the commencement of assemblies and other governmental functions often turned on the priestly interpretation of the oracles and quite often the manipulation of the oracles. Religious rites and auguries were intertwined with political events, and were used in political gamesmanship. When omens weren't favorable, assemblies, trials, and military levies could be delayed. To a modern view, auguries based on what section of the sky birds appeared or on interpretations of animal entrails seem primitive and nonsensical; nonetheless, they provided a set of rules for the conduct of public affairs that could be used as a means to force compromises between adversarial factions. As long as these rules were accepted as legitimate and authoritative, they provided common ground on which to settle issues. With a bad omen preventing a vote on an issue, the factions would often negotiate over the substance of the issue. When a compromise was reached, a new date and new auguries were scheduled.

Two years after the Licinian-Sextian compromise, Camillus died during an epidemic. He was lauded as the savior of the city and the preserver of the republic. His life had been exemplary, and even after his death his influence led to the compromise of 352 BC, in which the coconsuls—the patrician Publius Valerius Publicola (not to be confused with the founding consul of the republic) and the plebeian Gaius Marcius Rutulus—working together, appointed a commission of bankers to discharge or alleviate debts. It was fairly done, and much of the indebtedness was cleared away, which freed many plebeians from unending and crushing burdens.

A direct correlation existed between the plebeian gains and Rome's increasing prosperity. The recognition and gradual amelioration of plebeian complaints created the internal unity that was necessary to defeat external enemies. As the Romans established dominion over the Italian Peninsula, they distributed tracts of conquered land to their land-hungry citizens and military veterans. Plebeians were sent to establish colonies, where many became substantial landowners. Successful plebeians contributed greatly to Rome's military and economic strength, and many entered the class of equestrians, a term derived from the archaic equestrian order made up of those wealthy enough to equip themselves with horses and armor when serving in the legions. Equestrians became plebeian leaders while at the same time they integrated with the nobles to form an expanded propertied class. Thus the plebeians overcame their second-class status and became an integral part of the nation's leadership, making Rome strong enough to dominate its adversaries and expand beyond the Italian mainland.

The elevation of plebeian elites to the highest offices created a new class of nobility, based on wealth and achievement rather than on inherited status. Leading citizens of the plebeian class, those honored because of military or other public achievements, moved into the upper stratum of society. Nobility was no longer obtained by birth alone but could be won by merit, and intermarriages between patricians and successful plebeians generated a new and vibrant class of leaders and entrepreneurs. Plebeians elected to magistracies became senators, and with this new blood, the Senate became an institution of the able and energetic. New men grew in influence and power, and they helped embark Rome on more than two centuries of growing strength and prosperity.

In 342 BC, the plebeians took a major step forward when their right to seek the office of consul became a mandate that one of the two consuls must be from the plebeian ranks.

Rome's increasing prosperity brought further measures in favor of the plebeians. In 326 BC, the consul Gaius Poetelius passed the *Lex Poetelia*, which alleviated the harshest consequences of the debt laws. This legislation radically altered the rules for debtors by taking away the creditors' right to summarily sell an unexonerated debtor into slavery. The *Lex Poetelia* required a new court order, in addition to the initial sixty-day order, to sell the debtor. Livy called this change "a new birth of freedom." It established a Roman citizen's inalienable right to liberty. Undoubtedly, disputes over assessing the time and value of the debtor's labor were common, but the requirement of court intervention was a major step in the furtherance of due process of law. The law allowed property to be used as payment for a loan rather than the debtor's labor. This development brought an unexpected boost to Rome's economy, because it advanced the concept that credit could be extended on the security of landed property or personal possessions. This, in turn, generated the growth of professional banking, which led to Rome's decision to issue its own coined money rather than to rely on foreign coins.

In 287 BC, a confrontation between the orders resulted in another major advance for the plebeians. To protest the requirement of obtaining prior approval from the Senate before submitting a proposed bill to an assembly, they seceded from the city. The Senate appointed Quintus Hortensius as dictator to meet the emergency, and following the example of Camillus, Hortensius compromised with the plebeians. He passed the *Lex Hortensia*, which made plebiscites legally binding—not just on plebs but on all Romans—thus bringing triumph and equality to the plebeians after two centuries of conflict with the patricians.

The *Lex Hortensia* was an extraordinary law, in that the patrician *comitia centuriata* (assembly of the centuries) conceded its role as the dominant lawmaking body to the plebeian-controlled assemblies. It seemed that the plebs had gained political domination. Nevertheless, the *comitia centuriata* remained important since it still elected the consuls, praetors, and censors; and acted as a court of appeal in cases where citizens had been sentenced to death. Furthermore, deference to the Senate and patrician families prevented the plebeian tribunes from overstepping their bounds. Although the Senate didn't have formal de jure law-making powers, it continued debating and drafting laws before sending them to the tribal assembly. The tribunes could veto a proposed law, but through the legislative process, compromises were generally achieved. The equilibrium between the Senate and the assemblies fostered a period of prosperity and expansion lasting well into the second century.

CHAPTER 5

Roman Conflicts in America

AMERICAN HISTORY ALSO INCLUDES a story of competing classes, factions, and parties. At the outset of the republic, sectional conflicts between the agrarian interests on one side and the commercial/manufacturing interests on the other affected all aspects of political activity. Although the American revolutionaries tried "to form a more perfect Union," partisan politics immediately began the work of disunion. The founders established a checks-and-balances system based on the Roman model, but when they put their system into practice, the same discordant dynamics of partisanship the Romans had experienced confounded them.

Thomas Jefferson recognized the similarities between Roman and American partisanship. He wrote to John Adams, "Men have differed in opinion, and been divided into parties by these opinions, from the first origin of societies; and in all governments where they have been permitted freely to think and to speak. The same political parties which now agitate the U.S. have existed thro' all time. Whether the power of the people or that of 'the aristoi' should prevail were questions which kept the states of Greece and Rome in eternal convulsions, as they now schismatize every people whose minds and mouths are not shut up by the gag of a despot."[62]

The founders knew that throughout history when factions coalesced

---

[62] Jefferson to Adams, June 27, 1813, in Cappon, *Adams-Jefferson Letters*, vol. 2, 335.

around an ambitious, demagogic political leader, they tended to place extraordinary faith in that leader beyond what was prudent. Alexander Hamilton recognized the dangers such individuals posed to democratic institutions. He wrote the following in *Federalist*, no. 6, "Are not popular assemblies frequently subject to the impulses of rage, resentment, jealousy, avarice, and of other irregular and violent propensities? Is it not well known that their determinations are often governed by a few individuals in whom they place confidence, and are, of course, liable to be tinctured by the passions and views of those individuals?"[63]

Ambitious leaders have often gained the loyalty of faction members and then marched them into conflicts that were more important to the leaders than to the faction. As was seen in Rome, leaders endowed with the proverbial lust for power led their followers into ruinous conflicts, such as those between Marius and Sulla, Catiline and Cicero, Caesar and Pompey, and Antony and Octavian.

The founders saw the correlation between the partisan forces prevalent in the Roman Republic and the partisan forces in the fledgling American republic. James Madison emphatically made the point that good government must be designed to accommodate competing interests and protect against the evils of excessive partisanship. In *Federalist*, no. 10, he wrote,

> The latent causes of faction are thus sown in the nature of man; and we see them everywhere brought into different degrees of activity, according to the different circumstances of civil society. A zeal for different opinions concerning religion, concerning government, and many other points, as well of speculation as of practice; an attachment to different leaders ambitiously contending for preeminence and power; or to persons of other descriptions whose fortunes have been interesting to the human passions, have, in turn, divided mankind into parties, inflamed them with mutual animosity, and rendered them much more disposed to vex and oppress each other than

---

[63] *The Federalist Papers*, No. 6.

to co-operate for their common good. So strong is this propensity of mankind to fall into mutual animosities, that where no substantial occasion presents itself, the most frivolous and fanciful distinctions have been sufficient to kindle their unfriendly passions and excite their most violent conflicts.[64]

Madison saw that factions initially formed out of economic interests often evolved into factions driven by political ideologies and animosities. Such animosities were evident in colonial New York, where two factions—the DeLanceys and the Livingstons—represented respectively the merchant class and the landed Hudson River patroons. The DeLanceys, akin to the Roman equestrian class, advocated raising revenues by taxing land; the Livingstons, akin to the Roman landed senatorial class, believed trade should be taxed. Compounding the differences between them, the DeLanceys were members of the Anglican church, which enhanced their connections to the British government and London merchants; the Livingstons were Presbyterian and vehemently opposed the Anglican domination of public offices. On almost every public issue leading up to the revolution, the Anglicans and Presbyterians disagreed, as did the DeLanceys and Livingstons. Generally, Anglicans were Tories; Presbyterians were Whigs. After the revolution, Anglicans supported the Federalist Party; Presbyterians supported the Republicans.[65]

More divisive than the animosity between the landowning and merchant classes was the animosity between the creditor and debtor classes, and from the nation's inception, these conflicts threatened to divide it. Madison wrote, "But the most common and durable source of factions has been the various and unequal distribution of property. Those who hold and those who are without property have ever formed distinct interests in society. Those who are creditors, and those who are debtors, fall under a like discrimination."

During the years of the Articles of Confederation, many Revolutionary

---

[64] *The Federalist Papers*, No. 10.

[65] Richard Ketchum, *Divided Loyalties* (New York: Henry Holt, 2002), 56.

War veterans were unable to pay their mortgages or the crushing property taxes state governments imposed on them to pay war debts. Like the Roman citizen soldiers who had lost their farms to the latifundia (large conglomerate farms), American veterans lost their farms to foreclosures and government seizures; and, like the Roman citizen soldiers who rebelled, Americans rebelled in several states, resisting court orders and sheriffs. The most notable rebellion, Shays' Rebellion, occurred in Massachusetts in 1787, two years before the ratification of the Constitution. Daniel Shays, a Revolutionary War veteran, organized an army of farmers and marched them to the state capitol in Springfield to close down the courts. Shots were fired, and several government officials were killed or injured. The rebels asserted control of Western Massachusetts for several months before a national army suppressed the rebellion. However, the debtor-creditor conflict didn't subside. While some reforms were made, debtors remained subject to imprisonment or indentured servitude for another century. In some states the laws were extremely harsh, and injustices against debtors inflamed partisanship passions. Just as in Rome, in 385 BC, when Marcus Manlius Capitolinus used the plight of a soldier shackled for indebtedness to incite a rebellion against creditors and the oligarchy, American political leaders used the plight of debtors and small farmers to create populist movements in opposition to the creditor and landowning classes.

To accommodate opposing interests and ameliorate potential conflicts, Madison designed the Constitution's checks-and-balances system, a system that worked remarkably well to address economic conflicts, but it couldn't always contain cultural or ideological conflicts. Madison underestimated the reach of partisanship. Pragmatic compromises can be reached over issues relating to property ownership, income distribution, debt, taxation, or whether the highest tax rate should be 35 or 40 percent; however, compromises are far more difficult when people separate themselves on the basis of social, cultural, and religious differences. When people attach themselves to a particular group or party for emotional fulfillment for a sense of belonging or because of racial, ethnic, or religious affiliations, the attachment arouses ancient tribal instincts. Labels automatically pit one against the other, and the hostility exhibited by opposing parties can take the most noxious forms. As political debate moves from disagreement about economic and financial issues to social and moral issues, acrimony between parties intensifies.

Jefferson initially voiced approval of parties. In 1798, when his Republican Party was in opposition, he wrote, "In every free and deliberating society, there must from the nature of man be opposite parties, and violent dissensions and discords; and one of these for the most part must prevail over the other for a longer or shorter time. Perhaps this party division is necessary to induce each to watch and debate to the people the proceedings of the other.[66]

In later years, when his party was in power, Jefferson was less tolerant of political opposition, and he practiced partisan politics with as much vigor as anyone.

On paper, Jefferson, Hamilton, and Madison wrote about the evils of partisanship, and they knew intellectually that governing required reasoned compromise. But in practice they couldn't resist engaging in the most virulent forms of excessive partisanship, and they fully participated in the conflicts among political factions and sectional interests.

Near the end of Washington's presidency, political leaders split into two main parties—the Federalists and the Republicans. The Federalists supported Washington's policies and a strong central government. They were heavily supported in the Northeast, where they represented the combined interests of large-scale landowners and the wealthy merchants of the port cities, who controlled trade with Great Britain. The Republicans had two main blocs of support: a southern branch of plantation/slave owners and small farmers; and a northeastern branch, often described as Democratic Republicans, consisting of independent businessmen, working-class tradesmen, and artisans.

Hamilton, Adams, John Jay, and John Marshall were the leading Federalists; Jefferson, Madison, and Aaron Burr were the leading Republicans. Remarkably, at the beginning of the nineteenth century, the alignment of the American parties in many ways mirrored the alignment of the Roman parties of the late republic. Although the specific interests

---

[66] "Letter from Thomas Jefferson to John Taylor," 1798, *The Works of Thomas Jefferson* (New York: G.P Putnam's Sons, 1904) 430-433.

of the parties weren't exactly the same, the Federalists could be matched with the *optimates,* while the Republicans, especially the Democratic Republicans, could be matched with the *populares.* The Federalists, like the *optimates,* supported the status quo and resisted populist change; the Republicans, like the *populares,* wanted to lessen the nobility's domination of political power.

The terms *populare* and *optimate* didn't represent political parties in the modern sense, because Roman politics was primarily a competition for high offices and power between independent nobles. Some advocated populist reforms, some endeavored to protect the position of the oligarchy, and others switched their positions depending on expediency. Nevertheless, the independent actions of these nobles, in one direction or the other, had the same effect as a political party agenda.

Like the *populares* and *optimates,* the American parties held diametrically opposed views on the role of government. Federalists, with Hamilton as the prototype, believed in active central government, mercantilist economic policies, debt financing, and a strong standing army that would support nationalist policies and enforce domestic order. According to Madison, the Federalists "[a]re more partial to the opulent than to the other classes of society; and having debauched themselves into a persuasion that mankind are incapable of governing themselves, it follows with them, of course, that government can be carried on only by the pageantry of rank, the influence of money and emoluments and the terror of military force." He could have been describing the *optimates.*

As for the Republicans, Madison wrote that they believed "that mankind are capable of governing themselves." They believed in limited government, decentralized laissez-faire economics, and the supremacy of the states to govern their own affairs. They were against standing federal armies and control of the economy by politically connected elites. Madison described a party with many similarities to the *populares,* especially the latter's opposition to monopolistic power in the hands of an entrenched oligarchy.

President Jefferson was a proponent of limited government. In his first inaugural address, he declared, "A wise and frugal government, which shall restrain men from injuring one another, shall leave them otherwise free to regulate their own pursuits of industry and improvement, and shall not take from the mouth of labor the bread it has earned. This is the sum of good government." Jefferson held an idealistic belief in the people and belief that limited government would bring prosperity. "We must dream of an aristocracy of achievement arising out of a democracy of opportunity."

Jeffersonian Republicans believed the backbone of the nation was its self-sufficient, small-farm, agrarian-based economy, which they contended was the most meritorious form of society. Thus, they played a role similar to the Roman *populares*, who advocated on behalf of the small farmer against the *optimates*, who controlled the large estates—the *latifundia*.

To be sure, the conduct of the Jeffersonian Republicans didn't always comport with their professed ideals. Southern slavery contaminated their ideology, but the party was nonetheless able to represent the interests of the free farming class. Although some southern Republicans owned large slave plantations, the majority of farmers had relatively small farms and didn't own slaves, and Republican leaders claimed that slavery would be ended as soon as practicable.

With politics making strange bedfellows, the southern Republicans formed an alliance with northern Republicans, who, under the leadership of Aaron Burr and others, had organized fraternal societies and clubs that became a growing voting bloc. The northerners focused on business and taxation issues that differed from the issues that concerned the southern agrarian interests. They also took up the cause of immigrants, just as a faction of *populares* had taken up the cause of the non-Latin Italians, who had been vying for full Roman citizenship and equal voting rights.

Despite the differences between the northern and southern Republicans, their party was bonded together by a vehement opposition to the Federalists and a common hatred of British monarchy and mercantilist power. They had fought the Revolutionary War to rid themselves of the British hegemony, but they now saw the Federalists as simply replacing it with a pro-British oligarchy that would reverse the economic freedom and civil liberties the revolution gained.

The Federalists feared both elements of the Republican Party. They feared that the southern Republicans would turn the country back into a loose confederation of independent states and that the northern

Republicans would lead a populist uprising that would topple the hierarchy of the social and political order.

During the following decades, the parties would change names and revise their agendas several times, but their essential positions would remain the same, and they would maintain the same adversarial relationships to one another that the Roman *populares* and *optimates* had maintained for centuries.

CHAPTER 6

Caesars in America

WHAT REPUBLICANS AND FEDERALISTS agreed on was that ambitious men of the opposing party would try to seize unbridled political power. They carefully monitored the activities of their adversaries, sometimes even of their own associates. Obsessed with spotting American "Caesars," they constantly watched for potential tyrants, and the same accusations of tyranny the *populares* made against *optimates*, such as those against Sulla and Cato, were those the Republicans made against Hamilton and Adams. Conversely, the accusations of demagoguery the *optimates* made against *populares*, such as those against Caesar and Catiline, the revolutionary conspirator, were those the Federalists made against Jefferson and Burr. Public discourse routinely carried poisonous insults, and the greatest insult was to call someone a Caesar or Catiline. Both sides used these epithets against the other.

In a letter to George Washington, Hamilton referred to the Republican leaders as Whigs like Caesar. He wrote, "It has aptly been observed that Cato was the Tory—Caesar the Whig of his day. The former frequently resisted— the latter always flattered the follies of the people. Yet the former perished with the Republic, [while] the latter destroyed it. No popular Government was ever without its Catilines & its Caesars. These are the true enemies."[67]

---

[67] Alexander Hamilton to George Washington, August 18, 1792, in Harold Syrett, *Papers of Alexander Hamilton*, vol. 12, 252.

Hamilton wrote in the *Philadelphia Gazette* that "the Catilines and Caesars of the community who, leading the dance to the tune of liberty without law, endeavor to intoxicate the people with delicious, but poisonous draughts, to render them the easier victims of their rapacious ambition."[68]

Hamilton opposed Republicans on principle, but he was particularly antagonistic toward Burr, whom he saw as a potential tyrant. Hamilton declared, "In a word, if we have an embryo-Caesar in the United States, 'tis Burr … He is a man whose only political principle is, to mount at all events to the highest legal honors of the Nation and as much further as circumstances will carry him."[69]

Others thought it was Hamilton who was the reincarnation of Caesar, although they didn't mean it in the sense that he would use populist causes to gain support; they meant that if he gained power, he would wield it as a dictator on behalf of the oligarchy. Hamilton had told Adams and Jefferson that "the greatest man that ever lived was Julius Caesar"[70] Jefferson saw Hamilton as endeavoring to aggregate Caesar-like powers to the executive branch. In August 1792, Secretary of State Jefferson wrote to President Washington that Hamilton's conduct as secretary of the treasury "flowed from principles adverse to liberty, and was calculated to undermine and demolish the republic, by creating an influence of his department over the members of the legislature."[71] Jefferson's complaints to Washington were couched in relatively mild language, but he harbored much harsher thoughts. On the issue of the United States Bank versus state banks, he wrote, "For any Virginian to recognize a foreign legislature [meaning the US Congress] is an act of *treason* against the state, and whoever shall do any act under the colour of the authority of a foreign legislature—whether by signing notes, issuing or passing them, acting as director, cashier or any other office relating to it shall be adjudged guilty of high treason & suffer death accordingly."[72]

---

[68] Harold Syrett, "Catulus No.III," September 29, 1792, 500.

[69] Gordon Wood, *Empire of Liberty* (Oxford: Oxford University Press, 2009), 158.

[70] Carl Richard, *The Founders and the Classics* (Cambridge, Ma,, Harvard University Press, 1994) 267.

[71] Harold Syrett, *Papers of Thomas Jefferson*, vol. 23, 353.

[72] Thomas Jefferson, in Thomas Fleming, *The Great Divide* (Boston: DaCapo Press, 2015), 134.

Jefferson's harshness seemed in keeping with the malevolent conduct of the French Revolution. Although it's less than certain that Jefferson envisioned Hamilton being executed for treason, he truly saw him as a potential Caesar. Undoubtedly, Hamilton had that potential. As a young officer during the Revolutionary War, he demonstrated courage and competence, rising to become a lieutenant colonel and General Washington's chief of staff at twenty-two years of age. At the Battle of Yorktown, he led three battalions in a bayonet charge against the British. As a writer, he was prolific, and like a Caesar, he wrote superlatively, even while fully engaged in the real world of politics and administration. In politics, he was a brilliant strategist with immense energy and ambition. Driven by a desire for a historical legacy, he was obsessed with preserving his reputation. His eleven duels attested to the audaciousness of his Caesar-like character.

As secretary of the treasury, Hamilton steered the new nation toward becoming a centralized European-style government and economy. Overcoming resistance by the Jeffersonian Republicans, he established the First Bank of the United States and convinced Congress and President Washington to assume the war debts of the states. By doing so, he enlisted the loyalty of the creditor class to the new federal government. He saw that when the moneyed interests of the nation invested their assets in central government bonds, they would become supporters of a strong unified government rather than a loose federation of independent states. In addition, he dispensed patronage positions that tied prominent citizens to the government.

Consistent with the political structure of Hamilton's ideal government was his support of a classical hierarchical social structure in which people were held together by vertical ties similar to the Roman patron/clientele system. Hamilton believed that members of the general populace would elect their "betters" to office, and he wrote in *Federalist*, no. 35, "[M]echanics and manufacturers [tradesmen] will always be inclined, with few exceptions, to give their votes to merchants, in preference to persons of their own professions or trades ... They know that the merchant is their natural patron and friend."

Hamilton believed, like the Roman nobility, that the government should be run by persons of independent wealth, who would accept the responsibilities of office for the good of the general welfare, not for personal pecuniary benefit. However, Hamilton's aim to maintain a class-structured society ran against the tide of the spreading populism of the postrevolutionary period. It seemed that French Revolutionary ideas and slogans were gaining influence with the American working classes and the poor.

The French Revolution widened the split between the American parties. The Jeffersonian Republicans saw France's revolution as a welcomed extension of the American Revolution, while the Hamiltonian Federalists were pro-British and saw the French upheaval as the unleashing of chaos and mob anarchy. By inference, the Republicans would have favored the Roman *populares*, and the Federalists would have favored the *optimates*.

The Whiskey Rebellion (1792–1794) had the flavor of the French Revolution and of the plebian secessions from Rome and the Gracchi revolts. The rebellion began when Secretary of the Treasury Hamilton imposed excise taxes on whiskey. Farmers in Western Pennsylvania saw this tax as discriminatory because the tobacco and cotton crops of the South weren't subject to similar taxes. The excise tax would undermine their livelihoods, so they mounted an armed protest. Others soon joined them with other grievances. On August 1, 1794, more than seven thousand protesters gathered on a field outside Pittsburgh. David Bradford, the primary speaker, appeared in the uniform of a major general and urged the mob to secede from the Union and form an independent state; other speakers urged looting and burning Pittsburgh. The protesters imitated the rhetoric of the Jacobins. They flew their own flag, celebrated the 1793 executions of Louis XVI and Marie Antoinette, set up mock courts and mock guillotines, and talked of marching on Philadelphia and deposing their new "rulers."

Hamilton convinced Washington to suppress the rebels, and he and Washington marched an army of thirteen thousand troops into Pennsylvania. This army was larger than Washington's Revolutionary War army, and in the face of this show of strength, the rebellion collapsed.

Jefferson was more sympathetic to rebel causes and decried the use of military force to suppress the rebels. Conversely, he didn't decry popular violence against those in power; his ideology of liberty for the people had a dark side. He had been the minister to France, and it was said that he had a love affair with the French Revolution. He saw revolutionary violence as unavoidable, and when asked about the fate of Louis XVI, he merely stated that the king should be punished like other criminals. This comment was in keeping with his famous comment "The tree of liberty had to be watered from time to time with the blood of patriots and tyrants."[73] He wrote that he hoped the revolutionaries would "bring at length kings, nobles and priests to the scaffolds which they have been so long deluging with human blood."[74] He equated the American and French Revolutions with a worldwide movement for liberty, writing, "The liberty of the whole earth was depending on the issue. Rather than it should have failed, I would have seen half the earth desolated."[75]

In contrast, Hamilton distinguished the two revolutions, writing that their "difference is no less great than that between Liberty and Licentiousness." He thought that if the atheism of the Jacobins came to America, it would destroy the country.

In the war between England and France, Hamilton and the Federalists advocated alliances with England, which the Republicans vehemently protested. When it was made public in 1795 that the Federalist John Jay had negotiated a neutrality treaty with England, the outrage that followed threatened the Union. Political debate became violent, Republican protesters in the streets hanged both Jay and Washington in effigy, and angry rhetoric turned political adversaries into enemies for life.

As events unfolded, France defeated most of the continental European armies and seemed on the verge of invading England. The French viewed the American neutrality as an affront, and they began to seize American ships that carried British goods. To counter this effort, President Adams and Congress authorized the conscription of troops and other military expenditures. Many Federalists called for a declaration of war against France and for an alliance with Britain. The Republicans, led by Vice President

---

[73] Thomas Jefferson to James Madison, January 20, 1787, in *Papers of Thomas Jefferson*, vol.1, 438.

[74] Thomas Jefferson to Tench Coxe, May 1, 1794, in *Papers of Thomas Jefferson*, vol. 28, 67.

[75] Thomas Jefferson to William Short, January 3, 1793, in *Thomas Jefferson Writings* (New York: Library of Congress, 1984), 1003–1006.

Jefferson, were adamantly against war with France and urged delay. They expected that Napoleon would soon invade Britain and that the dilemma of which nation to side with would be resolved.

In an attempt to head off the crisis, President Adams sent a diplomatic mission to Paris. It included John Marshall, a moderate Federalist from Virginia, who was seen as a person whom the Virginia Republicans would respect. In Paris, however, the French demanded payments, a loan, and even a bribe before they would negotiate with the mission. This incident became known as the XYZ Affair. Marshall refused to make any payments, and after months of discussions, the mission ended in failure. When Marshall returned to the United States, the public applauded his resolute integrity and refusal to be intimidated. The nation prepared for war, and newspapers took up the rallying cry "Millions for defense but not one cent for tribute!"

The pendulum of public opinion swung toward the pro-British Federalists and against the Republicans, and some Federalists claimed that the Jeffersonian Republicans were in league with the French to spread democratic radicalism to America. President Adams, riding a wave of unexpected popularity, announced a "half-war" or quasi war against France. The United States abrogated prior treaties, embargoed trade, and authorized American naval vessels to attack French warships that were seizing American merchant ships.

Rumors of a French invasion spread, and Hamilton exploited the crisis. Although he had resigned from the government in 1795, he remained the recognized leader of the Federalist Party. In 1798, he convinced President Adams and Congress to authorize seven new regiments as a defense force. Ex-president George Washington was appointed as commander in chief of the armies, and Hamilton was appointed major general and second-in-command. Washington would be the figurehead; Hamilton would run the operations.

No doubt, Hamilton envisioned himself achieving great military triumphs, but events halfway around the world brought his grand enterprise to a close. In October 1798, British admiral Horatio Nelson won a decisive naval victory over the French fleet at the Battle of the Nile, thus ending the threat of a French invasion of either England or America. The crisis passed, and Hamilton's army was disbanded. Nonetheless, his conduct had made it abundantly clear that he was intent on achieving personal glory. In the public discourse of that time, he was often castigated and called an aspiring Caesar. Had war not been averted, Hamilton surely would have built on his authority of command to aggregate more power for himself. In any event, Hamilton wouldn't be the last celebrated American to be seen as a potential Caesar.

CHAPTER 7

Aaron Burr, the American Catiline

THE AMERICAN FOUNDERS HATED the dictator Julius Caesar, and calling someone a Caesar was a pernicious insult. What was worse than calling someone a Caesar was calling someone a Catiline. Aaron Burr was the object of this insult more than anyone else.

Lucius Sergius Catalina (Catiline), a charismatic aristocrat from an ancient and renowned family, fought courageously on the side of Sulla in the civil war and was instrumental to Sulla's victory at the Battle of the Colline Gate. During Sulla's reign, Catiline participated in the proscriptions of Sulla's adversaries and the confiscation of their properties, but he may not have benefitted as well financially as others, such as Marcus Licinius Crassus, who became the richest man in Rome. After Sulla's reign, Catiline fell deeply into debt, and he began to resent those in power who had become rich through cronyism and exploitation. Although born an aristocrat, Catiline became a populist demagogue, and since many of his class and generation had also fallen into debt, he became a spokesman for them, gaining a following as an advocate for broad debt relief.

In 68 BC, he was elected a praetor and in 67 BC was assigned as the governor of the North Africa province. When his term expired in 66 BC, he announced that he was running for consul, but he was promptly charged with committing extortion during his governorship. This was likely a ploy by his political opponents, because it was illegal to run for office while such criminal charges were pending. Although no substantial evidence was produced, Catiline had to end his campaign until his trial was over. He was acquitted, but the trial damaged his reputation, and he continued to be the subject of slanderous accusations of immoral and indecent conduct.

CATILINE AS POPULARE/DEMOCRAT

Despite the accusations, he had the support of *populares*, including Crassus and Caesar. He had the support of those whose land had been confiscated by Sulla, from expelled senators, those who had been denied patronage, to the struggling farmers who welcomed him as a new populare champion. According to the historian Sallust, they were "debauchees, adulterers and gamblers, who have squandered their inheritances in gaming dens, pot houses and brothels."[76]

In 64 BC, Catiline again announced his candidacy for consul. His platform was aimed at leading and strengthening the common people and weakening the entrenched oligarchy. He claimed that the latter had amassed their wealth and power by theft and abuse. He repeated the same theme over and over. "In the Roman Republic, there are two bodies. One is frail and sickly with an empty head; the other is strong and healthy, but has no head. I intend to be that head, if I can show I deserve to be, as long as I live." Such talk made him appear to be another budding dictator. The oligarchy mobilized a campaign against him, and the smears against him and his followers intensified.

Catiline's primary opponent for consul was Cicero, who mounted an aggressive campaign. Cicero brought up the old rumors and allegations of Catiline's immorality as if they were facts and claimed, "No one has ever had such a talent for seducing young men." Whether Cicero was implying scurrilous relations or merely an overly enthusiastic youthful following wasn't clear.

Cicero also repeated unsubstantiated claims that during the dictatorship of Lucius Cornelius Sulla (83-81 BC), Catiline had tortured and

---

[76] Sallust, *The Jugurthine War and the Conspiracy of Catiline* (New York: Penguin Books, 1963) 184.

murdered his own brother-in-law, Marcus Marius Gratidianus. Cicero's charge was dubious because Sallust, a contemporary and enemy of Catiline at the time of dictatorship, didn't list the murder of Gratidianus in his list of Catiline's misdeeds. It stands to reason that he wouldn't have left that out had there been merit to the charge; indeed, Sallust described Catiline as having "an evil and depraved nature. Civil war, murder, rapine, and civil discord were gratifying to the young man from a very early age."

As an accomplished lawyer, Cicero most likely didn't believe all the slanderous accusations he made against Catiline. Years later, he described him more thoughtfully.

> Never, I think, has the world seen such a strange being, such a mixture of disparate, divergent and mutually contradictory needs and passions. Who would have been more pleasing—for a while—to the most respected men? Who was more closely associated with the lowest characters? Who showed himself baser in his wiles, more steadfast in his endeavors? Who was greedier in taking, more generous in giving? And what was most amazing about this man was that he was able to win many friends and bind them by his loyalty; whatever he possessed he shared with them all, and he stood by his own in all adversities, with his money, his influence, his personal commitment, and if need be with crimes and reckless stratagems; he varied his behavior, adapting to the circumstances, twisting and turning it to all sides; among older men he was sedate, among younger men sociable, among the unscrupulous daring, among libertines licentious.[77]

But during the election campaign, Cicero spoke only of the scurrilous aspects of Catiline's character. On election day, Cicero and Gaius Antonius Hybrida won the coconsulship, coming in first and second respectively. Catiline, a close third, lost.

---

[77] Cicero, *Pro Caelio.*

After the election, Catiline was tried for the Gratidianus murder that had occurred twenty years earlier. He was quickly acquitted.

Undeterred by the continuing allegations against him, in 63 BC, Catiline ran for consul a third time, hoping to be elected for the upcoming year, 62 BC. However, when he proclaimed himself the champion of the oppressed and adopted an extreme radical platform, dubbed "Clean Slates," proposing to cancel all outstanding debts, Caesar and Crassus withdrew their support.

Catiline's strongest constituency, rural debtor farmers, came into the city to vote for him, but the consul Cicero tactically delayed the election, causing most of the farmers to return to their homes without voting. In the delayed election with fewer rural farmers in the city, Catiline lost again.

Catiline Conspiracy

Feeling cheated and betrayed, Catiline began planning to seize power for himself. Historians disagree on the interpretation of the facts and motivations of the actors, and we cannot know for sure whether Catiline initially plotted violence or events led him there. He organized a substantial group of rebels, including Publius Cornelius Lentulus Sura, an ex-consul who had been expelled from the Senate for immorality. Allegedly, the plot included a plan to assassinate Cicero and other leading senators. According to Sallust, Catiline held a conspiratorial meeting at his house where he told his supporters,

> As for my designs which I have formed, they have already
> been explained to you all individually. But my resolution
> is fired more and more every day, when I consider under
> what conditions we shall live if we do not take steps to
> emancipate ourselves. For ever since the state fell under
> the jurisdiction and sway of a few powerful men, it is al-
> ways to them that kings and potentates are tributary and
> peoples and nations pay taxes. All the rest of us, energetic,
> able, nobles and commons, have made up the mob, with-
> out influence, without weight, and subservient to those

to whom in a free state we should be an object of fear. Because of this, all influence, power, rank, and wealth are in their hands, or wherever they wish them to be; to use they have left danger, defeat, prosecutions, and poverty. How long, pray, will you endure this, brave hearts? Is it not better to die valiantly, than ignominiously to lose our wretched and dishonored lives after being the sort of others' insolence? Assuredly (I swear it by the faith of gods and men!) victory is within our grasp. We are in the prime of life, we are stout of heart; to them, on the contrary, years and riches have brought utter dotage. We need only to strike; the rest will take care of itself.[78]

Subsequent events would show that Catiline meant what he said.

The alleged Catiline conspiracy to seize power came to light when Cicero, as the consul of 63 BC, learned of it from a scorned woman. Her information was only hearsay, and Cicero lacked corroborating evidence sufficient to warrant action. Subsequently, he received a midnight visit by Crassus, who turned over a packet of unsigned letters addressed to him and a group of other prominent senators, warning them to leave the city because Catiline was planning to seize power by force. Armed with this evidence, Cicero convened the Senate and presented the letters. The senators were alarmed, but the letters weren't traceable to Catiline, so no immediate action was taken against him.

In the following weeks, Cicero continued investigating and obtained additional information about the conspiratorial meeting that had taken place at Catiline's house. He reconvened the Senate, and when Catiline appeared, Cicero confronted him directly and castigated him in a devastating speech.

When will you stop testing our patience? How long will you mock us? How long must we endure that famous audacity of yours? The people are alarmed—doesn't that

---

[78] Sallust, *Bellum Catilina*, 20, 1–9.

mean anything to you? Even the Senate feels the need to defend itself against you. Don't the worried faces in the august assembly worry you? Don't you know that your plans already have been found out? Everyone here knows what you are up to. We know where you were last night, and the night before that, where you met, whom you met with, the schemes you hatched. Didn't you think we'd find out?[79]

Attempting to defend himself, Catiline pointed out the irony that, while he came from a long line of patrician ancestors, Cicero, an alien without any Roman lineage, was accusing him. Catiline walked out of the Senate and fled the city, but five of his coconspirators, including the ex-consul Lentulus, were arrested before they could flee.

The fate of these alleged conspirators greatly affected the course of history. An urgent debate in the Senate ensued in which Cicero and Marcus Porcius Cato the Younger argued for summary execution of the five conspirators as a necessary measure to ensure the security of the state. They argued that Catiline had an army outside the city and would enter Rome to rescue the prisoners and seize power. To the contrary, Caesar, as *pontifex maximus* (the highest office of the priesthood) and praetor-elect, spoke against summary execution and argued that the conspirators should be afforded trials. He conceded that "any torture would be less than these men's crimes deserve," but, he argued, they were citizens and possessed the constitutional right to trial by jury. He proposed that the conspirators be held until Rome was secured, at which time a trial could be conducted.

Despite Caesar's eloquent speech, Cato and Cicero won the argument, and the five conspirators were executed without trial. When Catiline heard of the Senate's vote for execution, he didn't slink away but took command of his waiting army. As a military standard for his rebel army, he used the silver eagle standard that had belonged to Marius, a hero to soldiers and commoners. For years, Catiline had kept Marius's standard in a shrine in

---

[79] Cicero, *In Catilinam.*

his home and had often shown it to trusted visitors. Now he displayed it openly as a rallying symbol for his followers.

The true motivations of political figures are always open to question. Were Catiline's actions undertaken to achieve economic and social reform. Were they undertaken to redress his personal grievances or a combination of both? A letter he wrote from his military camp to Quintus Catulus (the leading senator) reveals as much egoism as altruism.

> Lucius Catiline to Quintus Catulus: Your eminent loyalty, known by experience and grateful to me in my extreme peril, lends confidence to my plea. I have therefore resolved to make no defense of my unusual conduct, that I offer an explanation is due to no feeling of guilt, and I am confident that you will be able to admit its justice. Maddened by wrongs and slights, since I had been robbed of the fruits of my toil and energy and was unable to attain to a position of honor, I followed my usual custom and took up the general cause of the unfortunate; not that I could not pay my personal debts from my own estate ... but because I saw the unworthy elevated to honors, and realized that I was an outcast because of baseless suspicion. It is for this reason that, in order to preserve what prestige I have left, I have adopted measures which are honorable enough considering my situation.

In January 62 BC, two consular armies trapped Catiline's forces in the hills of Tuscany. Though they were severely outnumbered, Catiline exhorted his followers to fight.

> Two armies of the enemy, one on the side of Rome, and the other on that of Gaul, oppose our progress; while the want of corn, and of other necessaries, prevent us from remaining, however strongly we may desire to remain, in our present position. Whithersoever we would go, we must open a passage with our swords.

I conjure you, therefore, to maintain a brave and resolute spirit and to remember, when you advance to battle,
that on your own right hands depend riches, honor, and
glory, with the enjoyment of your liberty and of your
country ... Besides, soldiers, the same exigency does not
press upon our adversaries as presses upon us; we fight
for our country, for our liberty, for our life; they contend
for what but little concerns them, the power of a small
party. Attack them, therefore, with so much the greater
confidence, and call to mind your achievements of old ...

You must exert all your resolution, for none but conquerors have exchanged war for peace. To hope for safety
in flight, when you have turned away from the enemy the
arms by which the body is defended, is indeed madness.
In battle, those who are most afraid are in most danger;
but courage is equivalent to a rampart ...

But should fortune be unjust to your valor, take care
not to lose your lives un-avenged; take care not to be
taken and butchered like cattle, rather than fighting like
men, to leave to your enemies a bloody and mournful
victory.

During the furious battle that ensued, Catiline realized that only a few
of his men remained alive; and true to his word, he charged into the midst
of the enemy to meet his death.

The judgment of historians has been that he was a crass demagogue
who cynically tried to use the cause of democratic reform to gain personal
power. And like so many before and after him, he used the poor and disenfranchised as pawns in the service of his political ambitions. But history
is written only by the winners. Catiline may have genuinely believed in
the need for reform. If he hadn't been genuine, he had ample opportunity
to alter his course of action. Absent of the slanders against him, his career
might have taken a different course; and it is conceivable, though admittedly speculative, that the unsigned letters Crassus delivered to Cicero
were fraudulent. How incompetent would the conspirators have to have

been to send forewarnings well before the time of the attack? Catiline might have recognized a plot against him and called the strategy meetings at his home to plan his defense. When the meetings were revealed, he had no choice but to take the military option.

Comparable Lives

Among the early American founders, comparisons of Burr to Catiline were initially based on reports of Burr's immoral behavior and licentiousness. In hindsight, these comparisons were exaggerated, grossly unfair, and obviously politically motivated. It was only at the end of Burr's career that more salient grounds for comparisons to Catiline arose.

Pride was the nemesis of both men. Catiline, with his long aristocratic lineage, was offended by his electoral defeat to Cicero, the "new man" from Arpinium, who had schooled him in political tactics and castigated him in public speeches called the Catiline Orations. Similarly, Burr, from a highly respected and accomplished family, was affronted by Alexander Hamilton, the immigrant from the island of Nevis in the West Indies, who had impugned his character and honor in public speeches and in planted newspaper stories.

In truth, Burr's early career was a model of patriotism and honorable conduct. Born in 1756, he demonstrated the same quality of intellect, talent, courage, and ambition as the more favored founders. He was a dashing Beau Brummel type with a sterling academic background. John Adams wrote that he had "never known, in any country, the prejudice in favor of birth, parentage, and descent more conspicuous than in the instance of Colonel Burr."[80]

Burr's grandfather and father were both presidents of Princeton University, where Burr was a brilliant student himself. However, he left his studies early to serve in the Revolutionary Army and served superbly as a lieutenant colonel, enduring hardships and displaying decisive leadership. In November 1775, he marched from Boston to Quebec, a brutal

---

[80] Gordon Wood, "The Real Treason of Aaron Burr," *Proceedings of the American Philosophical Society* 143, no. 2 (June 1999).

350 miles across the rugged Maine territory, to reinforce General Richard Montgomery at the Battle of Quebec. Although the Americans were defeated and Montgomery was killed, Burr fought bravely and risked his life while trying to retrieve Montgomery's body, an act that earned him great acclaim.

In August 1776, the British invaded New York with a fleet of more than four hundred ships that landed an army of more than twenty thousand. General Washington's smaller army was forced to retreat, escaping at night across the East River from Brooklyn to Manhattan. The British followed quickly and almost surrounded Washington in Harlem Heights, but Burr, seeing the encirclement developing, led an attack against the British flank, which forced the British to pull back and allowed Washington's army to escape across the Hudson River to New Jersey. Without Burr's courageous and decisive action, the war likely would have been lost then and there, and the course of American history would have been vastly different.

Burr later fought alongside Washington at the Battles of Trenton and Monmouth. His battlefield actions brought him great fame and admiration, but in 1779 he resigned his commission, claiming physical exhaustion.

In 1783, when the British evacuated New York, he moved into the city and opened a law office on Wall Street. Coincidentally, Alexander Hamilton, who resigned from the army in 1782, also opened a law office on the same street. Both were highly successful in their legal practices and in New York politics.

As was common at that time, both Burr and Hamilton gained financially from their political influence, and each gained advantages from representing clients on either side of the anti-loyalist laws. These laws, similar to the Roman proscriptions, though not as draconian, allowed the revolutionary victors to confiscate the property of English citizens who had remained loyal to the Crown. The 1779 Confiscation Act allowed the state to take possession of the estates of known Tories. In 1782, the Citation Act permitted debtors to repay loyalists in depreciated or worthless Continental Congress dollars. In 1783, the Trespass Act gave New Yorkers the right to sue loyalists who had taken over or damaged their properties during the 1776–1783 British occupation.

Burr as Democratic/Republican

The political views of Burr and Hamilton affected the manner in which they conducted their law practices. Burr tended to represent small businessmen and tradesmen, while Hamilton favored the propertied class and represented former loyalists. Hamilton criticized the confiscatory laws as an attack on property rights and a threat to the social order; he viewed Tory citizens as valuable members of the upper class and their flight to England, Canada, and Nova Scotia as financially and culturally detrimental to the nation. To the contrary, Burr viewed the confiscation laws as a tool to finance disaster relief and provide compensation for the patriotic Americans whom the onerous British occupation had damaged. Burr's position was more popular.

The political divide between Burr and Hamilton became personal in 1791 when Burr defeated Hamilton's father-in-law, Phillip Schuyler, in the election for US Senator. The Schuylers were an American version of aristocracy. During the colonial period, they had been granted large tracts of land, including the Saratoga Land Patent of 1684. Hamilton did well to marry into the family.

Burr, as the primary leader of the New York Democrat Republicans, built his political support from the middle and working classes, debtors, and even slaves. He used the New York branch of the Tammany Society as a political club, and he was the first of his generation to personally engage in get-out-the-vote-type campaigning, a break from the more staid tradition of only allowing others to offer recommendations on a candidate's behalf. Personal campaigning had been viewed as overly ambitious and demeaning.

The rivalry between Hamilton and Burr personified the conflict between the parties and the ongoing class warfare that divided the nation. Hamilton and his Federalist Party acted to protect the interests of the moneyed classes; Burr and his Democrat Republicans advocated positions that were radical for the time, including debt relief, women's rights, and the abolition of slavery. In his campaign for governor, Burr supported reforms to democratize government, reforms that would have reduced property requirements for voting, eliminated greater weight to the votes of the wealthy, and changed the New York City mayoralty from an appointive office to an elective office. Critics claimed that Burr's program was an American version of Catiline's "Clean Slate" debt relief and his voting reforms.

The Federalist Party had been in power since the nation's beginning. Its popularity had been intertwined with the public's trust of George Washington. However, when John Adams succeeded Washington as president, two major issues gave the Democratic-Republicans an opportunity to oust the Federalists from power—an anticipated war with France and the Alien and Sedition Acts.

Vice President Jefferson, the leader of the Virginian Republicans, enlisted Burr to his camp, aligning the Virginia Republicans with the New York Democrat Republicans in a potent coalition. The plan was expected to produce a Jefferson presidency, with Burr as vice president. As fortune would have it, however, Jefferson and Burr tied with seventy-three electoral college votes each. Without a clear winner, the election was thrown into the House of Representatives, creating an awkward situation, since Burr was as much entitled to the presidency as Jefferson. To demonstrate his loyalty, Burr proclaimed that he wouldn't compete against Jefferson and claimed he had declined Federalist offers of support for his candidacy. Nevertheless, his critics contended that he had solicited Federalist support and had tried to steal the election.

Whatever the actual case, Jefferson won the vote in Congress. Ironically, his victory was due in large part to Hamilton, who worked in favor of Jefferson despite their opposing political philosophies. "If there is any man in the world I should hate," Hamilton said, "it is Jefferson." He supported Jefferson because he hated Burr more and felt strongly about Burr's proclivities for self-interest and self-dealing. Hamilton considered Jefferson's temporizing character less dangerous than Burr's boldness.

To counter members of his own party, who advocated voting for Burr, Hamilton undertook a letter-writing campaign. He wrote, "For heaven's sake, let not the Federal party be responsible for the elevation of this man ... Burr is sanguine enough to hope everything—daring enough to attempt everything—wicked enough to scruple nothing."[81] Hamilton's

---

[81] Alexander Hamilton to Theodore Sedgwick, December 22, 1800, in *Papers of Hamilton*, 25:270–272.

efforts had their effect; Jefferson was elected president, and Burr became vice president.

Despite finishing second, Burr, as vice president, triumphantly returned to New York and seemed to be on the brink of even greater achievements. However, to paraphrase Euripides, do not call a man fortunate while he still lives. Within a year, fortune turned against Burr.

To Jefferson, the tie vote had marked Burr not only as his rival but also as a rival of his chosen successor, the secretary of state James Madison, a fellow Virginian. To undercut Burr, Jefferson denied the vice president's recommendations for patronage appointments, thus weakening Burr in the eyes of his New York constituents. Burr's rivals, particularly Hamilton and DeWitt Clinton, took advantage of this situation and continued their campaign to discredit him. Using newspaperman James Cheetham as their vehicle, they accused Burr of trying to steal the election from Jefferson and attacked his personal conduct in the most scurrilous manner. They were responsible for the distribution of pamphlets, handbills, and newspaper articles that called Burr a Catiline, implying that he possessed the Roman's immoral and indecent character traits. At this time, the Catiline allusions didn't refer to allegations of treason; those would come later. Cheetham accused Burr of "abandoned profligacy" and of seducing and discarding women. Also, reminiscent of Cicero's remark about Catiline that "no one has ever had such talent for seducing young men," Cheetham claimed Burr attracted young men around him, insinuating a sexual connotation. He wrote that Burr was another Catiline, whose "malignant, secret, and duplicitous force … corrupts whatever it touches."

The Duels

Burr tried to remain aloof from the attacks, but his closest supporters were infuriated. His friend John Swartwout accused DeWitt Clinton of instigating Cheetham's attacks to destroy Burr. Swartwout challenged Clinton to a duel. While many duels, like lawsuits, were often settled before the event, on July 31, 1802, this one went forward on the dueling field in Weehawken, New Jersey. Five shots were fired, and Swartwout suffered two leg wounds. Clinton proclaimed that he would rather have shot Burr.

The libel and slander campaigns against Burr were effective. As the 1804 presidential election approached, Jefferson withdrew his support for Burr's second term as vice president, and on February 25, 1804, the Republican Party caucus failed to nominate him. Not ready to leave the political arena, Burr ran for governor of New York. On May 1, 1804, he suffered a decisive defeat, after which he learned that Hamilton had slandered him during the election campaign. A newspaper reported that Hamilton had given a speech to a group of influential businessmen, in which he proclaimed that Burr was a dangerous man who was not to be trusted with the reins of government. This was the usual political invective; however, Hamilton crossed a line when he referred to Burr as "despicable," a word that at the time carried a connotation of sordid sexual conduct.[82]

Burr demanded a retraction and an apology. In earlier years, these men had drawn back from the precipice of duels, but now the bitterness between them prevented a retrenchment. Burr blamed Hamilton for his dismissal as Jefferson's running mate and his loss in the election for governor. For his part, Hamilton was bitter over the Federalists' defeat and his party's declining power. His plans to control the nation's course were essentially dead, and he focused his blame on Burr. Letters and negotiations to resolve the dispute were unproductive. Besides the personal animosity, there was ideological animosity as well. On the night before the fatal duel, Hamilton said there was "no relief to our real disease, which is democracy."

On July 11, 1804, Burr and Hamilton met on the Weehawken dueling field high above the Hudson River. The vice president faced the former secretary of the treasury, and although the exact sequence is unclear, each fired one round. Burr was unhurt; Hamilton was hit and died the following day.

Undoubtedly, Hamilton's death affected the course of history. The Federalists had no one of his ability to replace him. John Adams wrote, "When Burr shot Hamilton, it was not Brutus killing Caesar in the Senate-House, but it was killing him before he passed the Rubicon."[83]

It wasn't safe for Burr to remain in either New York or New Jersey.

---

[82] Milton Lomask, *Aaron Burr* (New York, Farrar Straus Giroux, 1982), 1: 347.

[83] John Adams, *Boston Patriot*, 10 June 1809; Adams, *Works,* 9: 305—6.

Many Federalists wanted to take physical revenge rather than wait for the outcome of criminal charges, so he fled to the South where he was safer. There dueling was prized, and many viewed him as a hero. Instead of being ostracized, he was welcomed, and he even dined with President Jefferson.

New York indicted Burr for murder, as did New Jersey. The New York indictment was later dismissed for lack of jurisdiction, and the New Jersey indictment was dismissed because of insufficient evidence of criminal conduct.

Burr returned to the capital and completed his term as vice president. As president of the Senate, he presided over the impeachment trial of Federalist Supreme Court Justice Samuel Chase, accused of being unfit for office because of his political bias. Federalist critics pointed out the irony of Burr, an indicted murderer, presiding over the trial. Nevertheless, he was undeterred and effectively handled the trial in a manner that brought him high praise.

At the end of his term, Burr delivered a renowned speech in praise of the Senate. He called it "[a] sanctuary; a citadel of law, of order, and of liberty; and it is here—it is here, in this exalted refuge; here, if anywhere, will resistance be made to the storms of popular frenzy and the silent arts of corruption; and if the Constitution be destined ever to perish by the sacrilegious hands of a demagogue or the usurper, which God avert, its expiring agonies will be witnessed on this floor."[84]

The Burr Conspiracy

Burr's handling of the Chase trial and his respectful farewell speech to the Senate belied the later speculation about a Burr conspiracy to seize power by armed force and separate the western states from the Union.

Just as Catiline had a loyal following, Burr also had many devoted supporters, the Burrites. Burr's charisma, courage, and eloquence attracted friends and admirers, and he drew on their support for his next project—a plan to buy cheap land in western territories, lead settlers west, and resell or lease the land to them. On barges with about eighty supporters, he

---

[84] Nancy Isenberg, *Fallen Founder* (New York: Viking, 2007), 279–282.

traveled to Nashville, Tennessee, to Fort Massac on the Ohio River, and down the Mississippi to New Orleans. In each locale, he was greeted with honors as a war hero and former vice president. At Fort Massac, he met with General James Wilkinson, the commander of the army and governor of the Northern Louisiana territory. Unknown to Burr, Wilkinson was a spy in the pay of the Spanish government since 1787 and had previously made a secret agreement, known as the "Spanish conspiracy," to lead Kentucky's secession and incorporation into what was then Spain's Louisiana territory. This meeting marked the beginning of Burr's worst difficulties.

Just as Catiline was the subject of trials and conspiracy theories on the basis of unreliable evidence and uncertain accusations and speculations, Burr was accused of conspiracy against the interests of the United States on the basis of speculation and hearsay. Rumors began circulating that part of Burr's plan was to assemble a private army and lead a filibuster—a military expedition without government sanction—into the territories of Florida and Mexico. Allegedly, his goal was to free them from Spanish rule and establish a democratic government that would either be attached to the United States or become an independent nation. Without a declaration of war, such an expedition would be unlawful but not necessarily treasonous. As for the other part of his alleged plan, rumor had it that Burr intended to detach the western territories of the United States and combine them with his newly formed nation. That would have clearly amounted to treason.

Although nobody ever definitively proved that Burr had such a treasonous intent, when news of his preparations and speculations about a conspiracy began to circulate, his longtime enemies again compared him to Catiline. An article in Cheetham's *American Citizen* concluded, "To raise a rebellion in this quarter against the government would complete Mr. Burr's Catalinian character"[85]

Even President Jefferson adopted the epithet. On October 22, 1806, at a cabinet meeting called to discuss the allegations that Burr planned to separate the western territories from the Atlantic states, Jefferson ordered

---

[85] James Cheetham, *American Citizen*, September 17, 1804.

an investigation with the highest priority. He commented that Burr had raised "suspicions, as every motion does of such a Catalinian character."[86]

In 1806, the newspapers raised the specter of a conspiracy against the government. Rumors and incomplete information were built into a case against Burr and his collaborators. Jefferson read the reports, and in October 1806 he received a confidential letter from General Wilkinson, in which Wilkinson claimed that an association of ten thousand men had been assembled for the purpose of toppling New Orleans and invading Mexico. Wilkinson didn't name the leader of this conspiracy; however, he followed up by sending Jefferson a coded cipher letter, purportedly written by Burr, which outlined the conspiracy.

The circumstances surrounding the appearance of this letter bore a striking similarity to the unsigned letters Cicero received from Crassus about the alleged Catiline conspiracy. Just as Cicero used the unsigned letters to condemn Catiline, Jefferson used the letter from Wilkinson to label Burr a conspirator. Not until it was too late was it revealed that Wilkinson had doctored this cipher letter, but once the ink was out of the bottle, the stain couldn't be erased

Jefferson met with Wilkinson, and in one of the greatest misjudgments of character in American history, he believed Wilkinson's accusations. He did this despite continuing reports that it was Wilkinson who had been colluding with the Spanish government to detach the western territories from the United States. Most likely, Wilkinson accused Burr of treason to deflect suspicion from himself. Jefferson apparently couldn't see what his fellow Virginian Congressman John Randolph saw. Randolph described Wilkinson as "the most finished scoundrel that ever lived."

The Trials

For Burr, a series of legal actions followed. He was arrested and brought before several different state grand juries. All those charges were dismissed; then in January 1807, he was arrested in the US territory of Mississippi.

---

[86] Jefferson's "Anas," in Lipscomb and Bergh, eds., *The Writings of Thomas Jefferson*, Vol. 1: 458–60.

The grand jury there failed to indict him for any crime, but the judge refused to dismiss the charges. Burr fled the district, and the governor of Mississippi issued a fugitive warrant for his arrest. In February 1807, soldiers arrested and transported him to Richmond, Virginia, where he was arraigned before Chief Justice John Marshall and released on $10,000 bail.

In May, proceedings were held, and the prosecution charged Burr with treason for the assembly of a military force with the intention of levying war against the United States and with a misdemeanor involving the alleged plan to wage war with Spain. Although the prosecution claimed that Burr's grand army had marched through the states toward Mexico, they produced no witnesses who could say they had seen an actual army. Despite pressure from Jefferson, Chief Justice Marshall ruled that treason hadn't been proved. Marshall said that "an invisible army is not an instrument of war," and he asked, "What could veil his troops from human sight?" He dismissed the felony treason charge but ruled that probable cause for a misdemeanor had been established in that Burr had organized a conspiracy against the Spanish territories. With only the lesser misdemeanor charge viable, Marshall released Burr on bail.

President Jefferson wasn't pleased and sent agents across the country to find evidence of treason. He sent blank pardons to several prosecutors, which they could use to give immunity to any collaborators who would testify against Burr. As a result, the government produced fifty witnesses, including Wilkinson. The grand jury indicted Burr for treason, and Chief Justice Marshall remanded him to prison to await trial.

On August 3, 1807, the former vice president's trial began. The issues were clear. As Chief Justice Marshall explained, if Burr had attempted to wage war against a country at peace with the United States (Spain), he could be guilty of a misdemeanor; if he had attempted to wage war against the United States, he could be guilty of treason. Burr's defense asserted,

> Our ground of defense is that Mr. Burr's expedition was in concurrence with General Wilkinson, against the dominions of the king of Spain, *in case of war* [emphasis added] … If we prove that, at the time Wilkinson was pretending to favor Burr's expedition … he was receiving

a Spanish pension, this will explain his conduct. He defeated the enterprise of Burr by hatching a charge of treason against the United States, on purpose to serve the king whose money he was receiving! ... What we charge General Wilkinson with is having united with Colonel Burr, and deserting him; turning traitor, and representing the case quite different from the truth.[87]

On August 31, 1807, Justice Marshall for the second time dismissed the treason charge, ruling that the government had failed to prove an overt act of war against the United States. Consequently, no treason could be attached. In September, the remaining misdemeanor charges went to a jury, and after a half hour of deliberation, the jury found Burr not guilty.

After his ordeal, most people thought Burr would retire from public life; instead, to the great astonishment of many, he traveled west in an attempt to rekindle his plan for a military filibuster into Mexico. He was unsuccessful. Three years of fighting the treason charges had taken their toll. His reputation and stature had been irreparably harmed, and he couldn't garner sufficient support or resources. Undeterred, he traveled to Europe in an attempt to interest nations there in his idea to liberate South America from Spain, but his scheme evaporated. In 1812, he returned to New York, reopened his law practice, and conducted himself as a respected attorney until his death in 1836 at the age of seventy-nine.

Months after Burr's trial, evidence came to light that between 1792 and 1796, General Wilkinson had received payments totaling more than $35,000 from the Spanish governor of Louisiana. In 1808, a military board of inquiry was convened to investigate the charges. Wilkinson acted as his own lawyer and, using fraudulent documents, convinced the board that the monies he had received were merely payments for tobacco he had sold to the Spanish government. He was exonerated and remained a military commander until 1815.

In 1904, the truth came out when Dr. W. R. Shepherd, an American

---

[87] T. Carpenter, *The Trial of Aaron Burr on an Indictment of Treason* (Washington, DC: Westcott, 1808) 391.

scholar doing research in the archives at Seville, Spain, found government records that proved Wilkinson had been an agent in the pay of Spain. He had been known to his Spanish handlers as Agent 13 and had received annual payments from Madrid. Shepherd also uncovered a memorandum from Wilkinson outlining his plan to detach the western territories from the United States and join them with Mexico. Even more astonishing, Shepherd found a document showing that in 1787 Wilkinson had renounced his American allegiance and submitted a Declaration of Allegiance to the Spanish Crown. In the declaration, Wilkinson explained his actions as follows:

> Self-interest regulates the passions of nations as well as of individuals, and he who imputes a different motive to human conduct either deceives himself or endeavors to deceive others. Still, while I maintain this truth, I will not deny that every man owes something to the land in which he was born and educated …
>
> When a person of distinction intends to expatriate himself, he ought to proceed with caution and circumspection. He has to ponder well the obligations which subsist between him and his country, ascertaining dispassionately whether he is bound to its service by any tie of confidence, public, positive, or implicit. He ought to bear in mind that this resolution will wound the self-love of those whom he abandons, and consequently will expose his whole life and actions to the severest scrutiny, and his reputation and character to the shafts and flings of slander and calumny. Profoundly impressed with these important truths, laying aside every passion or prejudice, I call upon the reflection with which the goodness of God has endowed me and matured my decision in accordance with reason, honor, and conscience.
>
> Having these principles, and holding to this opinion, I hope that no one can say of me with justice that I break any law of nature or of nations, of conscience or of honor,

in transferring my allegiance, from the United States to his Catholic Majesty.[88]

Wilkinson's self-justification rings hollow, especially in consideration of the fact that in 1791 he accepted the commission as commander in chief of the US Army from President Washington without deigning to inform the president that he was actually working for the Spanish Crown. A treasonous and dishonorable con artist of the worst sort, Wilkinson remained in command of armies throughout the presidencies of Washington, Adams, Jefferson, and Madison. To the contrary, Burr, a recognized war hero and proponent of many admirable causes, was castigated and driven from public service on the basis of rumor, speculation, and the testimony of a deceitful traitor. With marked similarities to Catiline's career, Burr's political career was ruined because of falsehoods spread about him that set in motion a chain of increasingly drastic actions and reactions. Both men held themselves in the highest regard, and they couldn't tolerate accusations upon their character or motives. Responding to personal attacks and their declining circumstances, they each embarked on unsound and self-destructive courses of action. Catiline's became manifestly treasonous; Burr's rode a line of uncertainty and illegality that for more than a century cast him in ill repute.

---

[88] William Shepherd, "Papers Bearing on James Wilkinson's Relations with Spain," *American Historical Review* 9 (April 1904).

CHAPTER 8

Rome's Manifest Destiny

THE CENTURIES AFTER THE Licinian-Sextian compromise, from 367 to 133 BC, might be considered Rome's best. As the plebeians achieved political equality and economic opportunity, Roman society flourished, and its military strength, trade, and influence grew. Military victories led to diplomatic victories, and through voluntary alliances or imposed treaties, Rome methodically spread it hegemony across Italy. With its victory in the Latin War of 340–338 BC, some Latin cities, such as Tusculum and Aricia, were incorporated into the Roman state and given full citizenship while keeping control of their independent local governments. The aristocrats of these cities could become Roman senators and even consuls. Others cities, such as Tivoli and Praeneste, were given half citizenship (*civitas sine suffragio*). They weren't given the right to vote in Roman elections, but they gained access to the courts and the protections of Roman commercial, matrimonial, and estate law. In exchange, they were subject to Rome's foreign policy and liable for military service when called on to supply troops.

After the Latin War, Rome turned her attention to the non-Latin tribes of Italy, beginning with the Samnites, a longtime enemy. The Samnites controlled a large mountainous area in southwestern Italia. Organized like Native American tribes, they didn't live in towns but were spread across the mountainous country from where they conducted raids and then retreated to safety. Independent Samnite tribes formed a federation—the

Samnite League—that had the power of declaring peace and war. They had a fierce warrior spirit and survived against Rome for more than two centuries, but after many years of on-again, off-again warfare, Rome defeated them in 311 BC, though not decisively enough. In 298 BC, the Samnites attacked again, this time as part of a coalition with Etruscans, Umbrians, and Gauls (the latter in the pay of the Etruscans). War raged each year until 295 BC when at Sentinum, on the eastern slopes of the Apennines, a major battle was fought in which Rome was victorious. The Roman army suffered eighty-seven hundred casualties; the Samnite coalition suffered twenty-five thousand killed and eight thousand taken captive. Nonetheless, the Samnites continued fighting skirmishes until 280 BC, when they finally succumbed and agreed to a peace treaty.

For the Roman legions, fighting the Samnites required adjustments. The Romans had used the standard phalanx formation, which grouped the troops in a single block of heavy infantry drawn up in unbroken lines many ranks deep and operated best on flat, unbroken ground. In mountainous terrain, however, the phalanx was at a disadvantage; it lacked the mobility to deal with fast-moving skirmishers. Thus, the Romans changed their formations from the phalanx to more maneuverable maniples or smaller formations consisting of soldiers spaced in three lines. The first line of soldiers could fall back through the openings in the second line while the second line could advance to engage the enemy. The maniples were arranged in a checkerboard pattern, each distinct maniple separated from the next by a space equivalent to its own size, allowing for greater flexibility and tactical deployment. This tactical system made great demands on the individual line soldier who had to respond to orders and signals and move in unison with his comrades. Rigorous discipline and training were required, and the Romans quickly learned the new system, making their legions the most proficient military machines in the world.

Proud of what they had accomplished, the Romans assumed it was their destiny to impose order on conquered territories and spread their culture and values. To accomplish this, they built roads and bridges to connect their growing empire. In 312 BC, the Censor Appius Claudius Crassus began the construction of the Appian Way, which would run 132 miles from Rome to Capua. The road was fifteen feet wide, paved with close-fitting basalt stones so precisely set that cement wasn't needed. By 300 BC, the road reached its destination; afterward it was extended to Brindisi on the heel of Italy, for a total of 366 miles. Other roads branched off and crisscrossed Italy—the Via Campania traversed fifty miles from Capua to Naples; the Via Flaminia, begun in 264 BC, exited Rome northeast to Arminium on the Adriatic coast; and the Via Aemilius, begun in 187 BC, continued from the end of the Via Flaminia 180 miles northwest to the foothills of the Alps. The Via Aurelia ran northwest from Rome, along the coast into Gaul. By the end of the republic, eighteen roads exited Rome like the spokes of a wheel.

In the provinces the Romans built roads to solidify their military conquests. In Gaul, near Arles, the Via Aurelia met the Via Domitia, begun about 118 BC by the proconsul Domitius Ahenobarbus, the grandfather of a consul of the same name who would be a bitter enemy of Julius Caesar. The Via Domitia connected Spain to the western Alps. The Via Agrippa, built by Augustus's great legate, ran north from Arles to Lyon, the primary city of Gaul. In the Balkans, the Via Egnatia ran through rough terrain from the Adriatic to the Aegean Sea, connecting Macedon and Greece to Rome. Wherever Roman legions went, roads were built, eventually totaling fifty-three thousand miles.

The roads connected the mother city with what would become its colonies, and these colonies provided the framework for the empire. Instead of posting full-time military garrisons in the conquered territories, Rome sent contingents of between three hundred and seven hundred families to establish colonies, some in combination with other tribes, some purely Roman. The colonists received part of the conquered land. Appian explained, "As the Romans gradually conquered Italy, they took portions of the conquered territories and built cities on them, or sent their own citizens to colonize previously existing cities. These settlements served to garrison the conquered countries. They took the cultivated land which they had won, and immediately divided it up among their settlers, either gratis or for purchase-money, or for rent."[89]

The colonists were free from taxation and usually free of military

---

[89] Appian, *Civil War*, 1, 7.

levies because manning of the colonial outposts was deemed equivalent to military service. They elected their own Senate and magistrates, but they were subjects and citizens of Rome.

Along with military prowess and engineering skills, the Romans exhibited a genius for diplomatic negotiations that advanced their relationships with cities and tribes from the Alps to the southern end of the Italian Peninsula. After their victory over the Samnites at Sentinum, the Romans made treaties with seven Etruscan cities and several other non-Latin tribes, making them all allies of Rome. Like the half-citizenship cities, the allied cities had to provide troops when requested. Although the allies weren't equals, Rome protected their elite families and allowed them to rule their own people under their own laws. Many of these elite families were as influential in their own regions as the senatorial families were at Rome, and their leading citizens typically demonstrated their wealth and status by providing public services and amenities to their communities and clientele. Thus, with their status intact, they weren't alienated from Rome; and, of great importance, they didn't have to pay taxes to Rome, which reduced the incentive to rebel. Rome's relatively lenient treatment of those they conquered furthered the acceptance of its hegemony throughout Italy, and Rome established alliances with 120 Italian communities, plus a dozen Greek cities in Southern Italy.

An exception was the Greek city of Tarentum, a seaport city on the Bay of Tarentinus and originally a colony of Sparta. It refused to accept subordination. In 280 BC, it called on the Greek mercenary commander Pyrrhus of Epirus to wage a military campaign on its behalf. Pyrrhus invaded Italy and won several battles, but he lost so many soldiers in these battles that the expression "Pyrrhic victory" was coined. While still in a position of strength, he offered Rome peace terms. The Senate debated the terms, and as it was about to accept them, Appius Claudius, the censor who had built the Appian Way, now old and blind, rose to speak. He began by saying that he wished he was deaf as well as blind so he couldn't hear Romans accept such humiliating terms. The Senate promptly rejected the terms, and war continued. In 278 BC, Pyrrhus was defeated and returned to Greece. Tarentum then conceded to a treaty with Rome, and at that point, it could be said that Rome controlled the entire Italian Peninsula;

and her statecraft, as much as her military victories, was responsible for the first unification of Italy. Rome's success bred loyalty, which proved crucial in her next existential challenge.

WAR WITH CARTHAGE

The city of Carthage, located within modern-day Tunisia, had established a great maritime trading empire that dominated the western Mediterranean with ports on the North African coast, Spain, Corsica, Sardinia, and Sicily. A clash with Rome was inevitable, and the first of three Punic Wars began in 264 BC.

The First Punic War began when Rome's *centuriata comitia* voted to invade Sicily, sending an army overseas for the first time. Confronting the Carthaginian superior naval resources and maritime experience, Rome was overmatched at first but wasn't to be denied. In 261 BC, she built a fleet of one hundred quinqueremes (five decks of rowers), each carrying three to four hundred sailors and marines, and twenty triremes (three decks of rowers). This was the beginning of a navy that would conquer the entire Mediterranean.

Although three fleets of warships were lost in battles or storms, Rome quickly rebuilt them, making improvements each time. The warships were equipped with metal rams, grappling hooks, and a *corvus* (a boarding bridge). The *corvus* consisted of a walkway that had iron spikes on the bottom side. One end was hoisted to a mast, and when an enemy ship was close, the *corvus* was dropped. The spikes impaled the planks of the enemy's deck, pinning the ships together, and the Roman soldiers raced across the walkway on the attack.

The *corvus* allowed the Roman legionaries to use their close-combat skills, and they won several battles, including the decisive battle at Ecnomus on the southern coast of Sicily, the modern Bay of Gela. Defeated, Carthage was forced to sign a crushing treaty, giving up Sicily, eliminating most of its navy, and paying an enormous indemnity. Subsequently, with the Carthaginians weakened and unable to resist, Rome also took control of Sardinia and Corsica.

Deciding factors in the war were the unity and spirit of the Romans.

At this time, the common people and the governing class were united in their aims. Declarations of war were voted in the *centuriata comitia* by the people who had to do the fighting. In contrast, the Carthaginian people did as their rulers decided, and Carthage relied mostly on mercenary troops hailing from diverse countries and cultures who were no more committed to the Carthaginian cause than they would be to any other paymaster.

What occurred after the war exacerbated Carthage's defeat. The mercenaries turned on their employers, initiating a savage three-year conflict marked by some of the worst atrocities known to history. Deserters who knew that if they were captured they would be spared no mercy led the mercenaries; thus, they had no incentive to treat prisoners lawfully, but they tortured and mutilated them. The atrocities these mercenaries committed inspired Polybius's profound and damning observation about human nature.

> Similarly such malignant lividities and putrid ulcers often grow in the human soul, that no beast becomes at the end more wicked or cruel than man. In the case of men in such a state, if we treat the disease by pardon and kindness, they think we are scheming to betray them or deceive them, and become more mistrustful and hostile to their would-be benefactors, but if, on the contrary, we attempt to cure the evil by retaliation they work up their passions to outrival ours, until there is nothing so abominable or so atrocious that they will not consent to do it, imagining all the while that they are displaying a fine courage. Thus at the end they are utterly brutalized and no longer can be called human beings.[90]

Rome came to the aid of Carthage; and together, they defeated the mercenaries, executing all they captured.

In 237 BC, the Carthaginians, to compensate for their losses of Sicily,

---

[90] Polybius, *Histories*, bk. 1, 81.1–9.

Sardinia, and Corsica, established new colonies in Spain/Iberia, including the city of New Carthage as their Iberian capital for their territories below the Ebro River. Clearly, Carthage hadn't renounced its imperialistic policies, and another clash with Rome was forthcoming.

The Second Punic War began in 218 BC, when the Carthaginian general Hannibal Barca attacked the Iberian city of Saguntum, a Roman ally. Hannibal had inherited a lifelong hatred of Rome from his father, Hamilcar Barca, who had lost Sicily to the Romans in the First Punic War. A fierce thirst for revenge inspired Hannibal's attack.

In response to the attack on Saguntum, Rome sent an army to Spain, but Hannibal deliberately avoided it and surprised the Romans by invading Italy. He embarked from New Carthage with ninety thousand infantry, twelve thousand cavalry, thirty-seven elephants, and a train of pack animals. His army was composed of Iberians, Carthaginians, Greeks, and North Africans, including Numidian cavalry. The column of soldiers and animals stretched seven miles long as it began its march of fifteen hundred miles to Italy. During five months of travel, Hannibal encountered ambushes by local tribes; difficulties crossing the Pyrenees, Gaul, and the Rhone River; and then a disaster-filled passage over the Alps. When he descended into the Po Valley of Italy, he had only about twenty-three thousand men remaining. Nevertheless, he convinced the Gauls of that region that he was their liberator against the Roman oppressor and that they should join his crusade. The Gauls joined, as did several other tribes, including putative Roman allies. To encourage cooperation, Hannibal slaughtered those who resisted him.

In the late autumn of 218 BC at the Ticinus River in the Po Valley, Hannibal, reinforced by the Gauls and skillfully using his Numidian cavalry, caught the Romans by surprise and forced them to flee. In the battle, the consul Publius Cornelius Scipio was severely wounded. A month later, Hannibal defeated four more Roman legions at the Trebia River, a tributary of the Po River.

The winter passed without another major battle, but in June 217 BC, about sixty miles north of Rome at Lake Trasimene in the Umbrian region, Hannibal lured two more Roman armies into a trap as it marched in a column along a narrow road between the lake on one side and steep hills on the other. Pinned against the lakeshore and unable to maneuver, the Romans had no chance, and fifteen thousand soldiers perished, including the consul Gaius Flaminius Nepos.

With each of these battles, matters grew progressively worse for the Romans. To deal with the crisis, the Senate appointed Quintus Fabius Maximus as temporary dictator. He was from the prominent Fabii family. At a relatively old age to lead an army in the field, his strategy was not to confront Hannibal but to methodically wear him down, shadowing his army, staying on high ground, avoiding a major battle, and only engaging in small skirmishes.

In the autumn of 217 B.C., Fabius found himself in a favorable battle position. Hannibal had moved into the region of Campania to resupply his army with grain and livestock. He camped in the *Ager Falernus* area of the Volturnus River Valley and planned to move east to Apulia for the winter. But his choice of routes was limited. The wide, meandering Volturnus River, with steep banks in places, hemmed him in, as it was difficult to ford with an army.

Fabius occupied the high ground around the valley and stationed troops to block the exits out of the valley. He blocked the Appian Way south and the Casilinum Pass north. Sure that he had Hannibal trapped, he retired for the night believing that the next day would close the trap. However, during the night, Hannibal concocted his most famous ruse. At three o'clock on a dark night, he had his troops tie thick bundles of branches between the horns of his two thousand cattle and light the branches on fire. Cattle drivers then drove the flaming animals up a ridge away from the Casilinum Pass. To the suddenly awaked Romans, it appeared that Hannibal's army was escaping over the ridge using torches for light. The Romans charged after this phantom army. As they did, the pass was left unguarded and the bulk of Hannibal's army hurried through the pass to escape.

For the Romans, this lost opportunity had enormous repercussions. Fabius was widely criticized, and his term as dictator expired in December 2017. New consuls, Lucius Aemilius Paullus and Caius Terentius Varro, were elected. They were determined to confront Hannibal, and on 2 August, 216 BC, on the plain of Cannae in Apulia in southeastern Italy,

Hannibal inflicted on Rome the most devastating defeat in its history and the worst loss ever suffered by a western army on a single day. Hannibal had about forty thousand soldiers, and he faced two Roman consuls with sixteen legions, including allies, which totaled about eighty-six thousand. The armies lined up about a mile apart from each other, each line stretching several miles across the plain.

When the trumpets sounded and the battle was joined, Hannibal outgeneraled the Romans by employing a double-envelopment military tactic that has been imitated in wars ever since. The fighting lasted a few hours until the Carthaginians turned it into an out-and-out slaughter. As many as fifty thousand Romans and their allies were killed. One of the new consuls, Lucius Aemilius Paulus, had a chance to escape on horseback but chose to fight to the death with his troops. The other consul, Terentius Varro, saved himself and escaped. In all, one consul, two proconsuls, eighty senators, two quaestors, and twenty-nine military tribunes were killed—mounds of dead and dying lay across a square mile of ground.

The Romans lost not because their soldiers didn't fight as well as the Carthaginian forces but because of Hannibal's superior generalship. In the Roman infantry, a soldier fought shoulder to shoulder with his comrades in arms. He followed signals and commands from his centurion and attacked or defended against the enemy immediately before him. He couldn't see beyond his immediate surroundings and didn't know what was happening on the full battlefield; thus, he might find himself suddenly hemmed in so he couldn't use his weapons freely, or he might be attacked from two sides at once.

Roman soldiers fled to their camps, and of those who couldn't flee, ten thousand surrendered their arms and themselves. Hannibal had reached the apex of his glory. The march to Italy, especially the treacherous trek through the snow-covered Alps, and his four tremendous victories over Rome proved he was a great leader but a leader overzealous in his cruelty. Throughout his sixteen-years of war in Italy, Hannibal repeatedly inflicted unnecessary cruelty, ordering the execution of town leaders who refused to surrender and, for good measure, having their wives and children executed before their eyes.

Hannibal's cruelty and evil conduct might be judged as the equivalent of Rome's cruelty and evil conduct, but evil is a relative term. Portraying history as a battle between good and evil is overly simplistic; most often, it's a battle between the lesser evil and the greater evil. In this case, Hannibal was the greater evil. He came from a people who often sacrificed infants rather animals to their gods—Baal, Hammon, and Tanit. Motivated by personal revenge and self-glorification, Hannibal callously disregarded his own troops and manipulated them to follow him no matter the danger while knowing that, according to his strategic plan, most of them would die. His soldiers were merely pawns in his megalomaniacal scheme.

To finance his scheme, he would make deals, and for the prisoners who surrendered to him at Cannae, he offered to free them in return for a ransom of five hundred denarii for a horseman and three hundred for a foot soldier. The captives were certainly willing, and they sent a delegation of ten to the Roman Senate to plead for the ransom. Many senators urged payment, but a severe, elder senator, Titus Manilius Torquatus, spoke against it, chastising the delegates. "What would you do if you had to die for your country? Fifty thousand of your countrymen and allies on that very day lay around you slain. If so great carnage did not move you, nothing ever will … Too late you now endeavor to evince your regard of her when degraded, and become the slaves of the Carthaginians."[91]

The speech convinced the Senate not to pay the ransom. Had they paid, it would have shown they were beaten, and the rest of Italy would have abandoned them. Their refusal to pay epitomized the stern morality at the heart of Rome's invincibility. Surely, Hannibal must have been amazed and disappointed. He sold the captives into slavery, and the war continued.

The Romans had lost most of their soldiers along with their weapons and armor. Their treasury was depleted, and they suffered betrayal by longtime allies and attacks from foreign nations who sensed their plight. The Carthaginian victories convinced much of Southern Italy, including the cities of Capua and Tarentum, to defect from alliances with Rome and join Hannibal. Another Carthaginian army landed on Sicily, and

---

[91] Livy, *Histories*, bk. 22, 60.

the largest city on the island, Syracuse, defected to them. Meanwhile, Hannibal made a mutual aid treaty with King Phillip V of Macedon.

Prospects for the Romans could not have been bleaker, yet they refused to surrender or sue for peace. No other nation in history had withstood such a series of assaults and catastrophic defeats. Indomitable, they changed strategy and elected Quintus Fabius Maximus dictator. Fabius held the distinction of being the only dictator elected by the assembly, and he became known as the Great Delayer for his tactic of avoiding a major battle and methodically wearing down the enemy. To replace the fallen Roman soldiers, Fabius resorted temporarily to levying landless citizens and slaves—groups normally exempt from military service. Weapons and armor that had been taken in former wars as trophies were collected and furnished to the new recruits. Landowners voluntarily paid heavy property taxes to finance the war. Nobles serving in the legions declined to accept pay, and the centurions followed their example. These temporary measures bought time, and Rome survived, partly because Hannibal did not immediately attack the city itself, though he continued plundering and devastating the surrounding towns and countryside. Fortunately for the Romans, in a testament to the alliances they had built, most of their closest allies remained loyal. This dedication was crucial, because in this long war of attrition, time and again these allies supplied new waves of troops to replace those who had fallen to the onslaught of Hannibal's army.

In a strategic move, the Romans entered a mutual defense treaty with several cities in Greece. Under the treaty, these cities agreed to fight Phillip V in Greece to keep him from invading Italy and joining up with Hannibal. In addition, the Romans besieged the defecting city of Syracuse and convinced it to switch back to their side.

Another part of Rome's strategy was to bolster its attack in the Carthaginian territory of Spain. Under the dual command of Publius Cornelius Scipio, who had been wounded at Ticinus, and his brother, Gnaeus Cornelius Scipio, new legions were raised and sent by sea to the Spanish coast. The strategy to fight in Spain was effective for a time since it prevented Carthage from sending additional troops to Italy; however, in 211 BC, another catastrophe occurred when Hannibal's brother, Hasdrubal, an accomplished general, defeated the Roman legions. Both Scipios fell in battle.

The loss of these accomplished generals was devastating; neverthe-less, Rome was still resilient, and the following year, the Senate sent an-other army to Spain. In command, they placed Publius Cornelius Scipio Africanus, the son and nephew of the two slain consuls. Although he was only twenty-five, he was given proconsular imperium; his youth was overlooked because of his merit and the extraordinary circumstances. He came from an aristocratic lineage that had already produced thirty-five consuls. Publius was his given name; Cornelius was for his branch of the Scipio clan; Africanus was the name later given to him in honor of his conquest of Africa. The Scipios, like other great patrician families—the Fabians, Claudians, Aemilians, and Valerians—revered the achievements of their ancestors. The quest to protect the family reputation and add to its fame drove the aristocratic military commanders as fervently as any religious faith. Their concept of the afterlife depended on how their descendants remembered them. Saint Augustine wrote in 422 AD that the Romans demonstrated "what heights civic virtues could reach even without true religion … Out of love for honor and glory, [they] did not hesitate to place the safety of the fatherland ahead of their own, to subor-dinate greed for money and many other vices to one single weakness—the desire for praise."[92]

For Scipio Africanus, devotion to his family honor and his quest for fame inspired his life of heroism. He was bred to be a military commander. As a boy he had been brought on campaigns and had learned generalship firsthand from his father and uncle. He had been seventeen at the Battle of Ticinus when Hannibal surprised his father's legion and his father was wounded. Reportedly, he saved his wounded father from death. When his father and uncle were sent to Spain to fight the Carthaginians, he remained in Rome, devoting himself to the study of Hannibal's military tactics. He planned reforms for the army and devised new maneuvers to counteract Hannibal.

When his father and uncle were killed in Spain and the Senate sent him to replace them, he immediately began implementing the plans and reforms he had developed, adjusting the Roman battle formations and

---

[92] Saint Augustine, *Epistolae*, 138,17; *DeCivitate Dei*, 5, 13.

tactics, and placing his best legionaries on the flanks rather than the auxiliary troops his allies supplied. He improved the army's training and instituted a more effective signal system for issuing commands. In uneven terrain, he gave the maniple commanders more flexibility to act on their own initiative. To offset too much flexibility, he combined three maniples into a cohort. Legions—which consisted of thirty maniples, too many to allow independent action—were reconfigured into ten cohorts that could act independently without overly disrupting the cohesion of the legion. This balance proved successful.

As a result of these simple but significant adjustments, Scipio Africanus won several battles in Spain. Of major significance, he captured New Carthage with its fully stocked warehouses of supplies. More important, he freed hostages from the Iberian tribes, whom the Carthaginians had held to prevent their tribes from rebelling, and these tribes then transferred their allegiance to Scipio. In 208 BC, with their support he defeated Hasdrubal at the Battle of Baecula. This wasn't a complete victory because Hasdrubal escaped with his army around the western side of the Pyrenees and marched across Gaul into Italy to join up with Hannibal. This posed a deadly threat, but in 207 BC, the Romans snatched victory from the jaws of what could have been their ultimate defeat. As Hasdrubal marched south to meet Hannibal, he sent messengers with a letter to Hannibal, outlining his direction and the location where they should meet. However, the messengers and the letter were intercepted, giving the Romans vital intelligence. The Roman commander, Gaius Claudius Nero, rapidly marched his legions for six days and cut off Hasdrubal at the Metaurus River, where they surprised Hasdrubal and destroyed his entire army. After the battle, Nero sent Hasdrubal's severed head to Hannibal in his camp, where he had been waiting for his brother.

The Battle of Metaurus diminished Hannibal's chances of conquering Rome. By that time, his army had lost most of the experienced warriors who had come with him over the Alps. Without badly needed reinforcements, Hannibal reduced his operations, and throughout the next four years, no major battles were fought, though he remained an ever-present threat in Southern Italy.

In 205 BC, Scipio Africanus returned from Spain, and the assembly elected him to the consulship. Scipio immediately proposed a bold strategy to draw Hannibal out of Italy by attacking the Carthaginians in North Africa and threatening Carthage itself. After much debate, the Senate agreed and assigned him to the province of Sicily with permission to cross into North Africa. In the spring of 204 BC, Scipio raised an army, built a fleet, and crossed the Mediterranean.

In addition to his military skills, Scipio was a master diplomat, and he convinced Masinissa, a Numidian prince who had fought against him in Spain, to switch sides and fight with him. Now the Numidian horsemen, who had fought for both Hasdrubal and Hannibal, would be fighting for Scipio. With Numidian help, the Romans defeated a larger Carthaginian army at the Battle of the Great Plains, leaving the city of Carthage vulnerable. The Carthaginians negotiated for peace but were really playing for time while they recalled Hannibal from Italy to defend the city.

In 202 BC, Hannibal returned to North Africa, and two of the greatest generals of history confronted one another at the Battle of Zama. Before the battle, as if to dramatize the culmination of the titanic struggle that had been waged for sixteen years, Scipio and Hannibal came face-to-face in an extraordinary meeting. Their lives had been intertwined. To fulfill a promise to his father to destroy Rome, Hannibal ravaged Italy. Scipio Africanus was determined to avenge his father and uncle.

From the opposing camps, Scipio and Hannibal, each accompanied by a guard of horseman, rode out with banners of truce. Then they left the guards and met to discuss peace or war. An interpreter, from whom Polybius learned what had transpired, was present. After some preliminary remarks, Hannibal spoke first.

> I myself am ready to do so as I learnt by actual experience how fickle Fortune is, and how by a slight turn of the scale either way she brings about changes of the greatest moment, as if she were sporting with little children. But I fear that you, Publius, both because you are very young, and because success has constantly attended you both in Spain and in Africa, and you have never up to now at least fallen into the counter-current of Fortune, will

not be convinced by my words, however worth of credit they may be. Consider things by the light of one example, an example not drawn from ancient times, but from our own. I, then, am that Hannibal who after the battle of Cannae became master of almost the whole of Italy, who not long afterwards advanced even up to Rome, and encamping at forty stades [five miles] from the walls deliberated with myself how I should treat you and your native soil. And now here am I in Africa on the point of negotiating with you, a Roman, for the safety of myself and my country. Consider this, I beg you, and be not over-proud, but take such counsel at this present juncture as a mere man can take, and that is ever to choose the most good and the least evil. What man of sense, I ask, would rush into such danger as that which confronts you now? If you conquer you will add but little to the fame of your country and your own, but if you suffer defeat you will utterly efface the memory of all that was grand and glorious in your past.[93]

Hannibal then proposed new modified peace terms. Scipio was neither overawed by Hannibal's presence nor taken in by this master manipulator. Confident in the knowledge that Masinissa's cavalry had grown to four thousand horsemen, Scipio insisted that the parties stick to the more onerous peace terms that had been negotiated before Hannibal's return. He told Hannibal, "Of what further use is our interview? Either put yourselves and your country at our mercy or fight and conquer us."

The next day the battle was joined. Scipio had thirty-six thousand troops; Hannibal had fifty-five thousand plus eighty war elephants in front of his army. He intended to use them as he had in the past to break up the Roman infantry ranks. To counteract the elephants, Scipio adjusted the formation of his maniples, leaving open lanes for the elephants to run through rather than collide with the infantry; and as the elephants

---

[93] Polybius, *Histories*, bk. 15, 6.3.

pounded toward his lines, Scipio ordered hundreds of war trumpets to blast simultaneously with roaring shouts from his troops. The tremendous, jarring noise frightened many of the elephants, causing them to turn and stampede their own lines. Those that kept running forward were steered down the open lanes and then attacked from behind with javelins.

As the battle continued, Hannibal's old guard veterans of the Italian campaign moved toward a flanking position. Scipio sounded a recall and a reformation, and his thoroughly trained troops rapidly altered the battle formation to negate Hannibal's intended flanking move. As the lines clashed, Masinissa's Numidian cavalry made a timely charge into Hannibal's flanks. Effectively, the battle was over, and it turned into a massacre with twenty thousand Carthaginians killed and twenty thousand captured. Hannibal didn't stay to fight to the death with his troops.

Thus, with meticulous planning and execution, Scipio forced Hannibal to flee and Carthage to surrender. The terms of the peace treaty were now harsher, limiting Carthage to ten ships and forbidding it from engaging in war without the consent of Rome.

The torturous war against Carthage demonstrated the strength of Rome's political system, the staunch allegiance of its closest allies, the fortitude of its people, and its absolute determination to prevail at all costs, whatever the price in treasure and lives. The legions manned by citizen-soldier farmers who fought for their homes and hearth proved indomitable. As quickly as soldiers were killed or injured, they were replaced with new recruits. The people suffered enormous hardships, but they remained steadfast, and the leaders of the nation remained dedicated to their duties, fighting alongside their troops, evident by the deaths of twelve consuls who fell in combat. Although the war had all but exhausted Rome's finances and manpower, she would never surrender, and in the end she would triumph. Other nations recognized her as the world's ascendant power.

In the aftermath of the war, the republic was at its strongest, and its political system functioned at its best. The Senate enjoyed the deference of the people and the respect of its neighbors. It directed the actions of the magistrates, guided the assemblies, and exercised absolute control over the public treasury. Consuls, magistrates, and senators acted out of honor and duty not only for themselves but also for the honor of their ancestors and families. Believing it had a special destiny, the nation marched across the world with the intent to spread Roman law, justice, and order. Rome's foreign policy shifted from acting in response to the urgencies of the moment to a more purposeful and strategic program of conquest. Notwithstanding the terror and destruction they had spread, they hoped for peaceful resolutions by offering reasonable terms of surrender and convincing nations that it was simply in their best interests to accept Roman hegemony rather than resist the march of history.

According to Livy, the Carthaginian general (another Hasdrubal) who negotiated the peace treaty compared Roman diplomacy to other nations that had been victorious but less prudent.

> That it rarely happened that good fortune and a sound judgment were bestowed upon men at the same time. That the Roman people were therefore invincible, because when successful they forgot not the maxims of wisdom and prudence; and indeed it would have been a matter of astonishment did they act otherwise. That persons to whom success was a new and uncommon thing, proceeded to a pitch of madness in their ungoverned transports in consequence of their not being accustomed to it.
>
> That to the Roman people the joy arising from victory was a matter of common occurrence, and was now almost old-fashioned. That they had extended their empire more by sparing the vanquished than by conquering.[94]

GREECE

After defeating Carthage, Rome turned its attention to the East, where Macedon had overrun much of Greece and was threatening the rest. The Macedonian ruler Phillip V was from the same lineage as Alexander the Great, and he seemed determined to replicate Alexander's conquests and

---

[94] Livy, *Histories*, bk. 29. 42.

glory. The Roman Senate wanted to settle the score with Phillip V for his alliance with Carthage during the Second Punic War and proposed sending legions across the Adriatic to fulfill treaty obligations to the Greek cities that had requested aid. The assembly rejected the Senate's proposal. The people were tired of war, but the Senate persisted. The proconsul, Publius Sulpicius Galba, delivered a rousing speech in the assembly. He argued that Phillip V was as dangerous as either Pyrrhus or Hannibal had been and that if they didn't fight Phillip in Greece, they would have to fight him in Italy. Galba was persuasive, and in 200 BC, the assembly ratified the senatus consultum, a decree declaring war on Macedon. This was a critical decision since it set Rome's course for the next century.

The Senate directed Titus Quintius Flamininus to drive Phillip out of Greece. Flamininus had become consul at the young age of twenty-nine because of his outstanding performance as a praetor and then as governor of the city of Tarentum, a former Greek colony on the southern shore of the Italian boot. In Greece, he assembled his troops and fought several indeterminate skirmishes with the Macedonians. Finally, in 197 BC, Flamininus maneuvered Phillip into a battle at Thessaly on broken and hilly ground, the least favorable to the Macedonian phalanx formations. The more flexible and mobile Roman legions routed the Macedonians, and Phillip was forced to give up the territories he had conquered in Greece. The borders of Macedon returned to those before the time of Alexander the Great.

Many Greeks complained that they were merely exchanging one master for another, but Flamininus was an ardent admirer of Greece nd set about to protect its liberty. At the 196 BC Isthmian Games at Corinth, he issued a Proclamation of Liberty that astounded the Greek world; he granted liberty and independence to the Greek cities. He announced that Rome would neither demand tribute nor require conscripts or install garrisons. The Greeks were so astounded that they asked for the proclamation to be read a second time. In return for this liberty, Flamininus proclaimed that he only wanted the world to know that "there does exist in the world a nation which, at its own expense, risk, and travail is willing to wage war in order to bring the gift of liberty to other peoples." The Greeks expressed their gratitude by issuing their own proclamation.

> There was a nation in the world, which, at its own ex-
> pense, with its own labor, and at its own risk, waged wars
> for the liberty of others. And this was performed, not
> merely for contiguous states, or near neighbors, or for
> countries that made parts of the same continent; but they
> even crossed the seas for the purpose, that no unlawful
> power should subsist on the face of the whole earth; but
> that justice, right, land law should everywhere have sov-
> ereign sway. By one sentence, pronounced by a herald all
> the cities of Greece and Asia had been set at liberty. To
> have conceived hopes of this, argued a daring spirit; to
> have carried it into effect, was a proof of the most con-
> summate bravery and good fortune.[95]

Of course, shortly after the proclamation, its high-minded ideals crashed on the rocky terrain of Greece. By claiming the role of arbiter, the Romans took sides in boundary disputes and long-held rivalries, embittering whomever they ruled against and inciting grievances for ambitious politicians to exploit. Disorders and rebellions invariably erupted.

In 194 BC, to extricate themselves, the Roman army departed Greece and returned to Italy, but the relationship of arbiter to petitioner remained. Rome tried to maintain its hegemony from afar, and Greek advocates traveled to the Roman Senate, seeking arbitrations. Soon Rome's liberality toward foreign nations under its sway began drifting to a more imperious relationship of conqueror to conquered. Events forced this. The Seleucid King Antiochus III saw the vacuum the Macedonian defeat had created and joined with rebellious Greeks in a campaign against Rome. In 191 BC, the Romans returned to Greece, and in 188 BC, they defeated Antiochus and suppressed the rebellious states.

These wars changed the Eastern world's view of Rome. The idealistic notion of Rome as the guarantor of liberty lost its luster, and the more prosaic notions of stability, order, and control dominated the political environment. Deference to Rome became the norm; it was seen as the

---

[95] Livy, bk. 33. 33.

policeman of the world, and conflicts of any magnitude were brought to the Senate for resolution. In 171 BC, these entanglements caused Rome to send an army back to Greece again when King Perseus of Macedon aligned himself with the Achaean League and attacked rival Greek cities. Rome sent legions under consul Lucius Paulus Aemelius Macedonus, the son of Lucius Paulus Aemelius, the consul who had been killed at Cannae. The son proved more fortunate than the father—and more ruthless. In 168 BC, Paulus destroyed the Macedonian army and its Achaean allies at the Battle of Pydna in Thessaly. This time there was no Proclamation of Liberty; Rome plundered the possessions of her defeated foes and imposed severe restrictions on Macedon and its Achaean League allies. The Senate abolished the Macedonian monarchy, shut down the gold and silver mines, and redirected half of the taxes previously paid to the monarchy to the Roman treasury. The destruction of Macedon marked the end of Flamininus's policy of Greek freedom and the beginning of Greek subjugation. Paulus annihilated any nation that had fought on the side of Perseus, and he punished any nation that hadn't aided Rome. He destroyed the city of Epirus and enslaved one hundred fifty thousand of its citizens in the most ruthless way, sending a severe message to all Greece.

To discourage further rebellion, Rome took a thousand hostages from the Achaean ruling class for internment in Italy, including Polybius, a young man who would later write the greatest history of the period. Because of his social and intellectual status, Polybius was a guest of the Scipio family, and he became tutor, companion, and adviser to Publius Cornelius Scipio Aemilianus, the adopted grandson of Publius Cornelius Scipio Africanus. From his position, Polybius observed Roman politics and society firsthand. He wrote his history to explain "how and under what form of government almost all the inhabited world came under the single rule of the Romans in less than fifty-three years."[96]

Polybius contrasted Rome with its vanquished enemies—Carthage, Macedon, and Greece. He attributed much of Rome's success to its mixed form of government, in which the consuls, the Senate, and the tribunes coexisted to represent the interests of the competing elements of society

---

[96] Polybius, *Histories,* bk. 1, 1.

in a balanced manner. He also believed the Romans lived the virtues of discipline, courage, and sacrifice to a greater degree than any other people, allowing them to conquer less-worthy nations.

A well-known anecdote illustrates the power of Rome's spreading hegemony. In 168 BC, the king of Syria, Antiochus IV, had invaded Egypt and was marching with his army toward Alexandria when he met a Roman ambassador, Gaius Popillius Laenas, who was accompanied by only a small contingent. Antiochus held out his hand to Popillius, but Popillius declined and instructed Antiochus to read a decree from the Roman Senate that forbade him to wage war against Egypt and ordered him to evacuate the country. Antiochus read the decree and said he would confer with his council to decide what to do. He said he would inform Rome of his decision later. Popillius used a stick and drew a circle in the sand around the king, saying, "Before you step out of that circle give me a reply to lay before the Senate." Astounded, Antiochus hesitated for a moment, then said, "I will do what the Senate thinks right." He returned with his army to Syria.

Antiochus exercised more prudence than the rulers of the Greek city of Corinth. In 146 BC, they insulted and roughed up a Roman delegation. Four Roman legions responded to Corinth. They captured and razed the city, plundered all its riches, including four centuries of bronze and marble statues, and sold all its surviving inhabitants into slavery. Ironically, Corinth was where the Proclamation of Liberty had been announced fifty years earlier.

That same year, Rome ended its third war with Carthage. Peace with Carthage had lasted until 149 BC when Rome, blaming Carthage for a breach of their treaty, demanded that the Carthaginians abandon their city and move ten miles inland from the seacoast. Carthage refused, and the Third Punic War began. The war didn't go well at first, and the people wanted a new leader. They elected Publius Cornelius Scipio Aemilianus as consul despite his being under the legal age for the office. This was history repeating itself. Although Aemilianus was the natural son of the great general Lucius Paulus Aemelius Macedonus, through adoption, he had become the grandson of Scipio Africanus, who also had been elected consul while underage. Aemilianus would prove to be a worthy descendant of both his natural and adoptive ancestors.

Aemilianus led the assault against Carthage. He blockaded the harbor and built extensive siege works around the city. Polybius accompanied him as a trusted adviser and observed the events.

The war lasted three years, and in 146 BC, the final battle took place. The Carthaginians knew the Romans were intent on total destruction, and they fought to the death. After a week of terrible house-to-house fighting, the Romans overwhelmed them. Thousands were killed, fifty thousand survivors were sold into slavery, and the remainder were forced to settle inland.

The Romans set the city ablaze. Aemilianus cried as he watched the city burn. When Polybius asked him why, he replied, "A glorious moment, Polybius, but I have a dread foreboding that someday the same doom will be pronounced on my own country."[97]

The destructions of both Corinth and Carthage announced the hardening of Roman foreign policy. Treaties and alliances as a means of indirect rule had proved effective only on a temporary basis, so Rome instituted a system of direct rule over its provinces. In the next decades, governors were appointed and garrisons stationed in the provinces of Macedon, Greece, North Africa, Sicily, Sardinia, Near Gaul, Farther Gaul, Illyria, Spain, Asia Minor, and Syria.

---

[97] Appian, *Punic Wars*, 16.

CHAPTER 9

American Manifest Destiny

THE 1803 LOUISIANA PURCHASE from France by President Thomas Jefferson initiated a period of geographic expansion, economic prosperity, and social mobility. It was a major step toward America's manifest destiny. Adding eight hundred sixty-eight thousand square miles of land to the nation, it provided the opportunity for willing citizens to cultivate the land and build new communities. Thus, during the twenty-four years of the Jefferson, Madison, and Monroe administrations, the population doubled; settlers moved west across the Allegheny Mountains and beyond the Mississippi River. Agricultural production increased tenfold with the invention of the cast-iron plow and automatic planters and reapers. Thousands of enterprises were formed to initiate business ventures; the steamboat revolutionized river traffic; public and private corporations built bridges, canals, roads, and schools; and citizens organized a broad range of fraternal, charitable, and educational organizations.

Jefferson espoused states' rights, limitation of the federal government, and expansion westward. As soon as he and the Republican-controlled Congress took office, they began dismantling the mercantilist programs of the Adams-Hamilton Federalists. They reduced taxes, government debt, and the size of the bureaucracy. The military budget was cut in half, and the majority of Federalist military officers retired. In 1811, Jefferson's successor, President James Madison, ended the charter of the First Bank of the United States Hamilton had established. However, the Jefferson and

Madison presidencies suffered serious setbacks and were marred by several strategic blunders, including the self-imposed trade embargo against Britain and the declaration of war in 1812.

As would happen so often to future American presidents, war overwhelmed their ideology; although Madison had ended Hamilton's First Bank of the United States, he was forced to charter the Second Bank of the United States to fund the war against Britain.

The War of 1812

The War of 1812 had its roots in the ongoing war between Britain and France. The United States had tried to remain neutral, but British and French naval forces repeatedly boarded American merchant ships in search of cargo destined for their enemy. When they discovered banned cargo, they seized the ships and held them for forfeiture. Between 1803 and 1812, more than a thousand American ships were seized, mostly by the British, who searched the ships for deserters. Thousands of British sailors had signed onto American ships to avoid the harsh conditions and severe discipline of the British navy and the constant dangers of war. The United States didn't contest Britain's right to impress its sailors when they were found on American ships in British ports, but they protested the boarding of their ships on the high seas. Britain, of course, viewed the high seas as their province and their sailors as subjects who weren't free to sell their labor elsewhere.

When the Royal Navy discovered British sailors on American vessels, they impressed them onto their ships, a problematic endeavor because Americans were easily mistaken for British, and hundreds of American sailors were unjustly impressed. Such errors could take years to correct, if ever. A major incident occurred on June 22, 1807, when officers on a British ship off the coast of Virginia tried to board the USS *Chesapeake* to search for deserters. The American captain refused the boarding, and the British fired cannon shots, striking the *Chesapeake* twenty-two times. Three Americans were killed and seventeen wounded. In response, Jefferson ordered a trade embargo and a buildup of military stores. Congress ratified his order.

The trade embargo was costly to American commerce, but both Jefferson and Madison continued the embargo, believing it was the only feasible way to command respect for American shipping without resorting to war. The embargo caused substantial losses for American businesses and a reduction in federal revenues. South Carolina Congressman Langdon Cheves said of the embargo, "[I]t puts out one eye of your enemy, it is true, but it puts out both your own. It exhausts the purse; it exhausts the spirit, and paralyses the sword of the nation."[98] By the end of Jefferson's tenure, clearly the embargo had failed. On June 18, 1812, without other viable options to protect the nation's commerce, President Madison signed a declaration of war against Britain.

It would have been just as logical to declare war against the French, who had been engaging in the same conduct as the British, but the Jeffersonian Republicans hadn't lost their affinity for the French, even in the face of Napoleon's usurpation of power. Republicans justified their uneven policy on the grounds that French intrusions into American sovereignty weren't as severe as those of the British, and the French had aided the colonists during the Revolutionary War. Moreover, it was important and a matter of honor to demonstrate that America wasn't slipping back into British colonial status.

Although Congress declared war, the nation was ill prepared for it. Other than a few limited victories, the American armed forces didn't acquit themselves well. The army was a mixture of enlisted federal troops and state militias, and this divided structure proved unworkable. During three campaigns on the Canadian border, the state militias refused to cross the border, claiming they were only a defensive force and couldn't lawfully fight outside the United States. As a result, the British Canadians, with their Native American allies, won several major battles and captured several American forts.

The Americans surprisingly had more success at sea than on land. They shocked the British in August 1812 when, 750 miles east of Boston, the USS *Constitution* defeated a British thirty-eight-gun frigate. In the battle, British cannonballs bounced off the sides of the *Constitution*, earning

---

[98] Annals of Cong., 12th Cong., 2d Sess., 25:249 (Dec. 1812).

her the nickname "Old Ironsides." In October 1812, six hundred miles west of the Canary Islands, the USS *United States* captured the HMS *Macedonian* and sailed it to Newport, Rhode Island, making it America's first prize of war. In December 1812, the USS *Constitution* won another battle, defeating the HMS *Java* off the coast of Brazil. All totaled, in 1812, the Americans' navy captured seven British warships and fifty merchant vessels while losing only three small warships. In addition, American privateers captured hundreds of British merchant vessels.

In 1813, the tide turned when the Royal Navy asserted its superiority. By the end of the year, most of the US warships had either been destroyed or were blockaded in port. American merchant ships couldn't sail, and the government lost revenue from tariffs and excise taxes.

Trouble for America increased in 1814, when the British defeated the French at Waterloo and Napoleon abdicated, freeing the British to concentrate on the war with the United States and to reassign soldiers and warships to the fight. In June 1814, the British launched an invasion from Canada into New York. The Americans turned them back in a naval battle on Lake Champlain, but the British kept coming from another direction. In August 1814, two dozen British warships and four thousand soldiers entered Chesapeake Bay, overran Washington, DC, and burned down the White House and the Capitol building.

On September 13, 1814, the British attacked Fort McHenry in Baltimore, bombarding it constantly for twenty-four hours. A witness to the spectacular event, Francis Scott Key, was inspired to write "The Star-Spangled Banner," which became the national anthem. The fort withstood the bombardment, but the Americans were clearly on the defensive. President Madison, running out of money and with no means of borrowing more, sent a delegation to Britain to negotiate a peace treaty. The British were willing, and on Christmas Eve 1814, the Treaty of Ghent was signed. The slow speed of communications at the time meant that news of the peace didn't reach America before the Battle of New Orleans on January 8, 1815, the battle in which British troops commanded by General Edward Pakenham, the brother-in-law of the Duke of Wellington, attacked the city with five thousand regulars, expecting an easy victory. Waiting for them was Andrew Jackson, a backwoodsman from Tennessee, now a general, who had assembled a makeshift army of regulars, militiamen, volunteers, and even pirates to defend the city. Jackson had the strength of character to hold his troops together against what seemed overwhelming odds. From the advantage of his barricaded defensive positions, he won a decisive victory—two thousand British casualties to seventy American. General Pakenham was among the dead.

Because the news of the peace treaty didn't reach America until after news of the New Orleans victory spread, many believed the United States had won the war and dictated the terms of the treaty. This view increased support for a strong military force and inspired patriotic fervor and national optimism, which contributed greatly to another surge in economic activity.

The war and the embargo that had cut off English-manufactured goods sparked an American manufacturing revolution. Instead of exporting cotton, leather, and lumber to Europe and then importing the finished products, Americans kept the manufacturing at home. Investors redirected their capital from overseas trading ventures to domestic manufacturing. Cotton mills and factories sprang up everywhere, and merchants subcontracted piecework to farming families who supplemented their incomes by spinning yarn, weaving fabric, and making products, ranging from hats to boots. The engagement of the population in the manufacture of every kind of product led to a burst of inventiveness and more efficiency. With the growth of manufacturing, America would no longer be primarily an agricultural society dependent on foreign sales to raise capital. It became a self-sufficient economy, and its free enterprise system created new industries.

The war brought about other explosive consequences. In politics, the Federalist Party lost public support and dissolved, its reputation irretrievably tarnished by its opposition to the war. This occurred because in the years before and during the war, the Federalists, as the out-of-power party, had complained about every anti-British position the government took. They saw the embargoes and nonimportation acts as most detrimental to the New England merchant constituents. Many Federalists still had deep attachments to their English heritage. They resisted the nationalization of the state militias and voted against appropriations for the war. Some talked of secession; others discouraged lending to the government for the war effort and hoped for military defeat. Furthermore, some Federalists engaged in conduct that bordered on treason, urging people to withhold their federal taxes, giving speeches and writing articles that were libelous of the government. The Federalist governor of Massachusetts conducted an unauthorized and secret negotiation with the British for the New England states to end their participation in the war.

The victory at New Orleans destroyed the Federalists. It vindicated the Republican war and turned the nation against the Federalists for their disloyalty. As it was said, those Tories could never be trusted again.

The Tories, indeed, were finished; and James Monroe, a Republican, was elected president in 1816 against only token opposition. He had served as an officer under Washington at the Battle of Trenton, negotiated Jefferson's Louisiana Purchase, and served as Madison's secretary of war and of state. His presidency was characterized as the Era of Good Feelings, and during his terms in office, he obtained territories in the Pacific Northwest from Britain, Florida from Spain; and lands from Native American tribes. His Monroe Doctrine warned European imperialist powers to desist from colonizing territories in either North or South America—in effect, claiming hegemony over the Americas. In 1820, Monroe's reelection was virtually unopposed.

Nevertheless, the Republicans wouldn't remain perpetually in power. Ironically, their ultimate victory over the Federalists led to the demise of their own party. An anti-Tory, anti-Federalist, anti-elite sentiment spread across the country and throughout the broader population. Democratic ideas more radical than those the Republicans offered took hold. All that was needed to oust the Republicans was a strong politician who could truly represent the common people. Andrew Jackson, the hero of New Orleans, answered the call.

ANDREW JACKSON

Jackson was an extraordinary individual whose life experiences had scarred and toughened him. He had lived through a hard childhood. At twelve years old, he joined the militia to fight against the British in the

Revolutionary War. His older brother was killed in battle, and Jackson was wounded and captured. During his capture, a British officer struck him with a sword because Jackson had refused to shine the officer's boots. Ever since, Jackson harbored a deep-seeded grudge against the British; he was also hostile to people on a spectrum from eastern elites to Native Americans.

He lived in accordance with the advice his mother had given as she was dying. "[A]void quarrels as long as you can without yielding to imposition. But sustain your manhood always. Never bring a suit in law for assault and battery or defamation. The law affords no remedy for such outrages that can satisfy the feelings of a true man. If you ever have to vindicate your feelings or defend your honor [by dueling], do it calmly." In 1806, Jackson engaged in a duel over a wager on a horse race. He killed his adversary but not before he took a bullet that remained embedded in his chest for the rest of his life.

As a general, he was just as staunch during the military occupation of New Orleans. After the victory over the British but before news of the peace treaty arrived, Jackson imposed martial law. When a newspaperman criticized him for this decision, he had him arrested and imprisoned. When a judge issued a writ of habeas corpus on behalf of the newspaperman, Jackson had the judge arrested.[99]

After news of the treaty arrived, Jackson remained in command of his army and became the unofficial proconsul of the South, with the responsibility of addressing the continual raids by the Creek and Red Stick tribes. Those tribes had moved from the Georgia territory into the Spanish territory of Florida and joined forces with the Seminoles. Together they made cross-border raids on American settlements in Georgia. In 1817, they ambushed a boat transporting soldiers and their families traveling upriver to Fort Scott. The Seminoles killed or captured forty-five of the fifty-one passengers. In response, the War Department directed General Jackson to campaign against the Seminoles and take all necessary measures to terminate the threat, even if it meant attacking them in Spanish territory.

---

[99] Mark Neely Jr., *Lincoln and the Triumph of the Nation* (Chapel Hill, NC: University of North Carolina Press, 2011) 96.

Jackson was a man suited for the job; to his mind, the tribes needed to be destroyed. He declared that "[t]reaties answer no other purpose than opening an Easy door for the Indians to pass through to Butcher our citizens"[100] Interpreting his orders as a mandate to invade and annex Florida, he assembled eight hundred regular troops from Fort Scott, a thousand militiamen from Georgia, and two regiments of Tennessee volunteers who had fought with him at New Orleans (without the governor of Tennessee's permission).

In March 1818, with his forces augmented by friendly Native American warriors, he invaded Florida. In one village, his men found over fifty scalps, some readily identified as belonging to the soldiers and family members killed near Fort Scott. As could be expected, Jackson destroyed the village. He pursued the Seminoles across Florida, captured two of their chiefs, and ordered them hanged at once. Then, without a declaration of war from Congress or official authorization from President Monroe, he routed the Spanish from Fort St. Marks and captured Pensacola, the seat of the Spanish provincial government. He shipped the Spanish troops, the governor, and his officials to Cuba. Then he took control of the territory, setting up an American provisional government.

While campaigning against the Seminoles, he captured two British citizens, Alexander Arbuthnot and Robert Ambrister, and charged them with inciting the Seminoles to wage war against the United States. The two men were court-martialed, convicted, and sentenced to death. Arbuthnot was immediately hanged, but Ambrister was sentenced to the firing squad. While awaiting his execution, Ambrister filed a plea of mercy. The court showed mercy and reduced his sentence to fifty lashes and a year of hard labor. But Jackson wouldn't have it; he overruled the court's decision and ordered Ambrister's execution to go forward.

News of Jackson's exploits spread across the country, and despite the uncertain legality of his actions, his popularity soared. People likened his decimation of the tribes and his annexation of Florida to Caesar's conquest of Gaul. On the whole, the nation applauded Jackson's forcefulness, though some saw his ruthlessness in his treatment of the tribes as an attribute to be feared.

---

[100] Gordon Wood, *Empire of Liberty* (Oxford: Oxford University Press, 2009), 133.

Not surprisingly, his actions brought diplomatic protests: from Spain for the seizure of Florida and from Britain for the execution of the two British citizens. In 1819, Henry Clay, the Speaker of the House, brought a censure motion against Jackson for his alleged unconstitutional acts. On the floor of Congress, Clay spoke for two hours with his usual eloquence. "[R]emember that Greece had her Alexander, Rome had her Caesar, England her Cromwell, France her Bonaparte, and that, if we are to escape the rock on which they split, we must avoid their errors." He warned, "[I]n the provinces were laid the abuses and the seeds of the ambitious projects which overturned the liberties of Rome."[101]

The Senate committee recommended censuring Jackson for his unlawful recruitment of the Tennessee troops, for the capture of Fort St. Marks and Pensacola, and for the executions of Arbuthnot and Ambrister. The recruitment of the Tennessee troops, who were personally loyal to Jackson, particularly incensed many senators as it seemed a replay of the subversive actions of the Roman generals who had recruited armies more loyal to them than to the state. However, the committee's report wasn't finalized until the end of the congressional session, and the full Senate never voted on the matter. No doubt most senators weren't keen to censure the nation's most popular hero.

By 1821, all was forgiven or forgotten: Spain conveyed the territory of Florida to the United States, and Jackson was appointed governor. Other than the Louisiana Purchase, Jackson's appropriations of land in Florida, Georgia, and Mississippi were the largest extensions of US territory up to that time. He became more popular than ever. In 1824, Jackson ran for president, presenting himself as a reformer aiming to deal with the corruption of the elite ruling class. He campaigned on the slogan "Turn the rascals out." Although he won the most votes, he won only a plurality, not a majority, and the election was thrown into the House of Representatives. A backroom-brokered deal denied Jackson victory when the Speaker of the House, Henry Clay, gave the presidency to John Quincy Adams. Jackson was angry, and he wasn't a man to make angry.

He ran again for president in 1828, forming an alliance with Martin

---

[101] Annals of Cong., 15th Cong., 2d Sess., 645–55.

Van Buren of New York, who had built a campaign machine on the foundation of Aaron Burr's Republican Democratic clubs. As the combination of Jefferson and Burr had "dethroned" John Adams, the combination of Jackson and Van Buren "dethroned" John Quincy Adams.

The election signified not only a political change but also geographic and cultural shifts. The backwoodsman from Tennessee defeated Adams, a polished statesman from Massachusetts and the son of the second president. During Jackson's administration, commoners filled government jobs, and the nation's attention shifted to westward expansion.

Jackson was a genuine Democrat who believed in elevating the voice of the common man, and he transformed the Jeffersonian Republican Party into the Democratic Party. He not only demolished the Federalist notion of rule by the elites for the elites but also ridiculed the Republican version of rule, wherein a virtuous and enlightened agrarian aristocracy would impartially govern for the collective good. On the contrary, Jackson believed the common people should rule themselves. He believed in the wisdom of the populace over what he believed was the entrenched and corrupt ruling elite. Viewing the Senate as patrician oppressors of the common people, he identified with the plebeian struggle for democratic equality. He pushed for the elimination of property requirements to vote. In a letter to James Buchanan, he wrote, "[T]he great constitutional corrective in the hands of the people against usurpation of power, or corruption of their agents, is the right of suffrage; and this when used with calmness and deliberation will prove strong enough—it will perpetuate their liberties and rights."[102]

The public saw Jackson as a man of the people fighting for the liberties of the people. But one man's liberties are another man's oppression, and Jackson's critics saw him as a demagogue who used populism to overturn the natural aristocratic hierarchy and install himself as a Caesar, supported by the mob. Albert Gallatin, former secretary of treasury under Jefferson and Madison, spoke against Jackson, stating, "General Jackson

---

[102] Andrew Jackson to James Buchanan, June 25, 1825, in Robert Remini, *Jackson*, (New York: Harper Pereennial, 1966) 2, 30–1.

has expressed a greater and bolder disregard for the first principles of liberty than I have ever known to be entertained by any American."[103]

When thirty thousand of Jackson's followers came to Washington for his inauguration, Senator Daniel Webster wrote of it, "I never saw such a crowd here before. Persons have come five hundred miles to see General Jackson and they really seem to think the country has been rescued from some general disaster."[104]

Jackson consistently acted in accordance with the motto used by Brennus, the Gallic chieftain who sacked Rome: "to the victor belong the spoils." In his first term, Jackson removed sitting officials and replaced them with his cronies, qualified or not. After his reelection in 1832, he ordered the withdrawal of all federal funds from the Second National Bank and the transfer of the funds to state and private banks. When the secretary of the treasury refused to transfer the funds, Jackson fired him. Speaker Henry Clay compared Jackson's actions to Caesar's seizure of the Roman treasury during his war with Pompey. Newspapers and cartoons portrayed the Democratic president as an aspiring king or emperor. One article commented, "I cannot but recollect that Caesar was the greatest democrat Rome ever produced … and that his first steps were to cypherize the Senate and judicial tribunals; to take into his own hands the whole power of appointment to office, and to distribute the spoils of victory among his adherents. It was these measures … that enabled him to lay deep the foundations of the imperial throne … it is time to look about us, and anxiously consider, whether the days of the constitution and the republic are already numbered."[105]

Articles and cartoons implied that Jackson was a Caesar who ought to have a Brutus, and in January 1835, at the Capitol Rotunda, an assassin unsuccessfully tried to shoot Jackson. The assassin missed, and Jackson beat him with a stick.

Often compared to Julius Caesar, Jackson certainly possessed the courage, fortitude, and ruthlessness of Caesar. His accomplishments were

---

[103] Paul Johnson, *History of the American People* (Harper Perennial,1997), 330.
[104] Johnson, 339.
[105] "On Presidential Usurpation," *Farmer's Cabinet*, September 28, 1832, 2.

as momentous but not of the same magnitude. During his military career, Jackson commanded hundreds, sometimes thousands, of soldiers; Caesar commanded as many as a hundred thousand. Jackson won the Battle of New Orleans against the British and defeated several Native American tribes; Caesar won scores of major battles, defeated large tribal nations, and defeated other well-trained and well-organized Roman armies. While Jackson annexed Florida, Caesar subjugated Gaul, Near Spain, and Illyria. Caesar also invaded Britain and Germany.

Jackson differed most from Caesar in his treatment of the native tribes. Caesar established alliances with many Gallic tribes. Those who abided by peace terms, he incorporated into the Roman state and even admitted their chiefs into the Senate. Jackson drove the Native Americans into exile. He signed the Indian Removal Act of 1830, which provided for their resettlement to lands west of the Mississippi River, and he allowed no exceptions, even for the Cherokee Nation, a relatively advanced society that was not a nomadic, hunter-gatherer tribe but a stable, agricultural society. The Cherokees used slaves prior to European contact, and when cotton came into demand, they established plantations on which they used African-American slaves in the same way Southerners did. The Cherokees established schools, courts, and a republican constitution, but Jackson decided that independent nations couldn't exist within the confines of the United States; the Cherokees would have to move west with the other tribes. When the Cherokees were forced to move west to Oklahoma, they took their slaves with them. The census of 1835 counted 1,592 slaves, and more than 7 percent of Cherokee families owned slaves.

Jackson's Democratic successors, Presidents William Tyler and James Polk, continued his aggression. In 1845, the United States annexed part of Texas, and with the Mexican-American War of 1846–1848, it acquired the remainder of Texas and the territories that would later comprise New Mexico, Arizona, Nevada, Colorado, Utah, and California.

CHAPTER 10

Religion, Gods, and Oaths

IT HAS BEEN SAID that the strength of the early Romans came from their disciplined adherence to the religious and civic practices of their ancestors. Romans prized fidelity, fortitude, courage, and devotion to the People and Senate of Rome. They taught these values to their children through anecdotes and legends that often included the intercession of the gods. Thus, with religious foundations supporting the civic virtues, they built the steadfast national character necessary to survive in a challenging and turbulent world.

Historian F.R. Cowell wrote, "The creators of the Republic showed well enough in their speech what manner of men they were. The indications that language affords need confirmation from other quarters. It is forthcoming in many anecdotes and in the more substantial evidence provided by the known achievements of the early Romans. A general picture emerges of a stolid, matter-of-fact and puritanical people, intensely loyal to their family, their State and their gods, willingly accepting such authority with perfect discipline."[106]

The founders of the Roman Republic understood the advantages of religion as the basis for civic morality. When they renounced their monarchy and deposed Tarquinius, they didn't eliminate religion as an element of government. They replaced the king with two secular consuls and

---

[106] F.R. Cowell, *Cicero and the Roman Republic* (London: Pittman, 1948) 16.

transferred many of the king's religious functions to the *pontifex maximus* and the college of priests. This transfer of religious authority didn't diminish the state's critical religious and ritualistic functions; it wasn't a separation of church and state but a transfer of powers within the state. The priests weren't distinct from the state, and often they were secular magistrates. Rituals and sacrifices remained part of secular functions, and before conducting assemblies or embarking on war, magistrates invoked the gods and watched for signs of divine approval. The Romans also believed that the proper performance of rituals and sacrifices demonstrated their piety and morality. Failure to appease the gods would invite catastrophe because the gods couldn't be asked to preserve the health and prosperity of an impious or immoral people.

In discussing their polytheistic religion, the Romans favored practical questions and answers rather than metaphysical concepts. Their religion didn't concern the broader questions of man's inhumanity to man; kindness to their defeated enemies wasn't the focus of their thought. They wanted the gods on their side and prayed and sacrificed to gain protection from their enemies. Believing that the entire community would suffer for affronts to the gods, they endeavored to avoid the collective retribution that might be meted out by an angry deity, and they made extraordinary efforts to appease the gods through sacrifices and vows.

Believing the gods favored them because of their piety translated into a belief in a positive Roman destiny. Believing they were in the right enhanced their strength. Fighting only "just wars," only in self-defense, or fighting to revenge an unwarranted attack assured them that the gods would be on their side. In open debate in the Senate and the assembly, they argued the case for or against war. The people's vote for approval was the equivalent of divine approval.

But approval incorrectly obtained through mistaken arguments, imperfectly performed rituals, misread auspices, or disregarded omens would cause disastrous consequences for the state. When a disaster occurred, the arguments that had been made and the rituals that had been performed would be second-guessed, and blame would be cast on those responsible.

At times of great crisis, they intensified their propitiations. After the disaster at Lake Trasimene in 217 BC, when Hannibal annihilated two legions, the Romans appointed Quintus Fabius Maximus as dictator to save the nation. His first act wasn't military but religious. Plutarch related, "The first solemn action of his dictatorship was very fitly a religious one: an admonition to the people, that their late overthrow had not befallen them through want of courage in their soldiers, but through the neglect of divine ceremonies in the general. He therefore exhorted them not to fear the enemy, but by extraordinary honor to propitiate the gods. This he did, not to fill their minds with superstition, but by religious feeling to raise their courage, and lessen their fear of the enemy by inspiring the belief that Heaven was on their side."[107]

Religious oaths and contracts made with the invocation of the gods underpinned Roman affairs; the gods would punish breaches of such oaths or contracts.

At the pinnacle of importance were military oaths, the *sacramentum dicere*. When a soldier took the oath, he was obligated to obey his commander, adhere to military discipline, and never desert his comrades. The oath also legitimized his right to commit acts of war, which otherwise would be crimes. Violations of the oath had the added sanction of secular authority and could be treated as treason. Dionysius of Halicarnassus described, "For not only does the military oath, which the Romans observe most strictly of all oaths, bid the soldiers follow their generals wherever they may lead, but also the law has given the commanders authority to put to death without a trial all who are disobedient or desert their standards"[108]

Astute military commanders emphasized the religious authority of their imperium (supreme power). In 371 BC, Quintus Fabius, an ancestor of Fabius Maximus, became consul and took charge of a legion that had retreated in battle without authorization. Though the soldiers wanted to redeem themselves, Fabius refused to order them into battle until he could be sure of their full commitment, stating, "Unless they swear that they will return victorious from this engagement. Once, in a battle, the soldiers betrayed a famous consul, they will never betray the gods."

---

[107] Plutarch, "Fabius Maximus" in *Lives.*

[108] Dionysius of Halicarnassus, *Roman Antiquities,* bk. 11, 43, 1–5

In the tumult of the Roman world, oaths were often tested. Punishment reinforced the duty to abide by an oath. Livy recounted a speech of Scipio Africanus to a cohort of mutinous soldiers in Spain. When a rumor had spread that Scipio had died, these soldiers threw off all discipline, ejected their military tribunes, and plundered the native inhabitants. Scipio, using other troops, captured the mutineers. He identified thirty-one ringleaders and, in front of the assembled soldiers, had the ringleaders chained. He then spoke to the soldiers, giving them an accounting of the duties they had betrayed.

> [E]ven in my own camp, so much was I deceived in my opinion, the report of my death was not only readily believed, but anxiously waited for. Not that I wish to implicate you all in this enormity; for, be assured, if I supposed that the whole of my army desired my death, I would here immediately expire before your eyes; nor could I take any pleasure in life which was odious to my countrymen and my soldiers. But every multitude is in its nature like the ocean; which, though in itself incapable of motion, is excited by storms and winds. So, also, in yourselves there is calm and there are storms; but the cause and origin of your fury is entirely attributable to those who led you on; you have caught your madness by contagion. Nay, even this day you do not appear to me to be aware to what a pitch of frenzy you have proceeded; what a heinous crime you have dared to commit against myself, your country, your parents, your children; against the gods, the witnesses of your oath; against the auspices under which you serve; against the laws of war, the discipline of your ancestors, and the majesty of the highest authority.[109]

To emphasize the importance of the duties that had been forsaken, Scipio had the thirty-one ringleaders scourged and beheaded in front of

---

[109] Livy, *Histories*, bk. 38. 27.

the soldiers. He then showed leniency to the remaining soldiers, allowing them to take another military oath.

Oaths to the gods touched all aspects of life, and the Romans attributed difficulties and disasters of all kinds to violations of oaths and vows. In the Roman mind, religion and daily life were intertwined; oaths underscored business transactions, and temples were regularly used for business and political agreements. Contracts signed before a deity in his or her temple gave the contract legal force and also carried the threat of supernatural punishment for violations.

Polybius, a Greek nonbeliever, observed that religion was a necessity. He thought superstition was "what holds the Roman republic together." It underpinned business and the growing Roman economy. He wrote,

> If you lend a Greek the sum of one talent only, even if you had ten securities and as many promises and twice the number of witnesses, it is out of the question that he should keep his word, nor can you make him do it. Whereas among the Romans, however large are the sums to be disposed of, whether in the magistracies or the provinces, they keep faith to the letter, on account of the oath they have taken. In other peoples it is rare indeed to find a man who refrains from laying his hands on the public funds; among the Romans on the contrary it is very seldom that anyone is accused of peculation.

This superstition also underpinned their legal system. Testimony in court was overseen by the gods, and perjury was a public crime punished by the god in whose name the oath was sworn. Even assuming that a perjurer went without detection, it was believed that he or she would be punished by the avenging gods either in this life or the next; sometimes, instead of punishing the perjurer, the gods would punish the person's family or his or her unborn descendants. Lord Gibbon wrote, "The pontiffs managed the arts of divination, as a convenient instrument of policy; and they respected as the firmest bond of society, the useful persuasion that, either in this life or in a future life, the crime of perjury is most assuredly punished by the avenging gods."[110]

During the census, citizens had to declare under oath what property they owned. The censors used the declarations for tax assessments and to assign citizens to classes.

Treaties were sanctified by oaths, and the Romans punished their own citizens who broke oaths to other nations. The sociologist Jonathan Haidt described how an oath was made before Jupiter to sanctify a treaty with Carthage. "The man who is swearing to the treaty takes in his hand a stone, he says, 'If I abide by this my oath may all good be mine, but if I do otherwise in thought or act, let all other men dwell safe in their own countries under their own laws and in possession of their own substance, temples, and tombs, and may I alone be cast forth, even as this stone,' and so saying he throws the stone from his hand."[111]

The sanctity of the treaties with other nations required the recognition of the gods of those nations, and the Romans took no chances with the gods. They readily recognized and appeased the gods of other peoples. To maintain allegiances from conquered tribes, they respected their gods and allowed the people to continue their traditional religious practices. Whatever the Romans did, they did it wholeheartedly, and they appropriated to themselves the gods of the people they conquered, for they assumed that by doing so, they would gain the favor of those gods. The most-renowned example occurred when Camillus, after conquering the city of Veii, took the statue of their goddess Juno to Rome and had a temple built for her. The worship of Juno grew, and she joined Jupiter and Minerva in the triad of the greatest gods. Gibbon observed, addressing a later period but equally applicable to the republic, "The various modes of worship which prevailed in the Roman world were all considered by the people as equally true; by the philosopher as equally false; and by the magistrate as equally useful. And thus toleration produced not only mutual indulgence, but even religious concord."

---

[110] Edward Gibbon, *The Decline and Fall of the Roman Empire*, (London, Penguin Random House, 1776, 2010). Chap. II.

[111] Jonathan Haidt, *The Righteous Mind* (New York, Vintage Books, 2013) 59-61.

Religion controlled personal conduct. The people believed their actions would be judged by a higher authority and would have consequences, either in this life or the next. Clans and families worshipped and feared a variety of private gods. These gods scrutinized their daily conduct and would avenge an individual's failure to abide by an oath or obligation. The people also had to fear the greater gods, who might administer collective punishment on the nation for national sacrileges.

Thus, Rome's dedication to the sanctity of oaths underpinned her rule of law, making her a strong and stable society, a society that believed it was its destiny to impose order and security throughout ever-widening regions. Self-confident that spreading Roman ways would be best for the world, they justified their aggressions.

Not unlike the Romans calling on Jupiter or other gods to approve their undertakings, whether wars or building projects, early American congregations asked God to approve of their major public projects. In 1747, Benjamin Franklin organized the building of a fort on the Delaware River to defend Philadelphia from attacks by Spanish and French privateers. At the dedication of the fort, Franklin drew up a public proclamation, declaring, "It is the duty of mankind on all suitable occasions to acknowledge their dependence on the Divine Being," and he expressed in a prayer "that [God] would take this province under His protection, confound the designs and defeat the attempts of the enemies, and unite our hearts and strengthen our hands in every undertaking that may be for the public good, and for our defense and security in this time of danger."[112]

In concord with the Romans, the American founders knew that in a free republic, both individual and collective virtues were essential elements. Patrick Henry said, "No free government, or the blessings of liberty, can be preserved to any people but by a firm adherence to justice, moderation, temperance, frugality, and virtue." James Madison agreed. "To suppose that any form of government will secure liberty or happiness without any virtue in the people is a chimerical idea."[113]

---

[112] Van Doren, *Benjamin Franklin*, 188.
[113] Kurland, Phillip, eds., *The Founders' Constitution* (Chicago: University of Chicago Press, 1986). Madison, Papers, 11:163.

As a foundation for a cohesive civic society, the leaders of the first American colonies and congregations knew the importance of religious belief, and while the framers of the Constitution declined to endorse any particular religion (some were clearly agnostics), most pragmatically saw the necessity to advance religious belief. They subscribed to John Locke's adage that "promises, covenants, and oaths, which are the bonds of human society, can have no hold upon an atheist."

Like the Roman equestrian class, the American Protestant middle class was instilled with a spirit of capitalism underpinned by religious and moral obligations. The Romans sealed their contracts with oaths to the gods and developed commercial laws that supported the reliability of contracts. The American Protestant ethic made honesty in business an important aspect of a religious life. Thrift, frugality, and industry were not only practical values but also moral values. Benjamin Franklin's aphorisms—time is money; credit is money—reflected America's early adoption of a business-centered society. Although Franklin was a secular deist, his advice had a religious component, which was the cornerstone of good business. "Remember this saying, *The good paymaster is lord of another man's purse*. He that is known to pay punctually and exactly to the time he promises, may at any time, and on any occasion raise all the money his friend can spare. This is sometimes of great use. After industry and frugality, nothing contributes more to the raising of a young man in the world than punctuality and justice in all his dealings; therefore never keep borrowed money an hour beyond the time promised, lest a disappointment shut up your friend's purse for ever."[114]

George Washington's personal religious beliefs were masked, but he saw religion as a pragmatic virtue. In his Farewell Address, he explained, "Of all the dispositions and habits which lead to political prosperity, religion and morality are indispensable ... Whatever may be conceded to the influence of refined education ... reason and experience both forbid us to expect that national morality can prevail in exclusion of the religious principle." Washington and other founders, through encouragement and example, ensured that the practice of religion remained a conspicuous

---

[114] Benjamin Franklin, "Advice to a Young Tradesman," 1748.

element of the American value system, and they were wise enough not to impose a state-established religion. While Christianity was accepted as a cornerstone of the nation, the founders advocated separation of church and state, and state governments disestablished their relationship with their predominant churches, whether Anglican, Presbyterian, or Puritan.

All methods of Christian practice were accepted, and President Washington set the example by attending services at more than twenty different denominations during his presidency. The number of American denominations rivaled the number of gods the Romans worshipped, and the tolerance and acceptance of all religions engendered national strength rather than divisiveness. Non-Christian religions were also accepted. Although the number of Jewish people in American was small, on August 18, 1790, Washington wrote a letter to the Touro Synagogue of Newport, Rhode Island, assuring them that "happily the Government of the United States, which gives to bigotry no sanction, to persecution no assistance, requires only that they who live under its protection should demean themselves as good citizens … May the Children of the Stock of Abraham, who dwell in this land, continue to merit and enjoy the good will of the other Inhabitants; while everyone shall sit in safety under his own vine and fig tree, and there shall be none to make him afraid."[115]

In the first half of the nineteenth century, Christian religion flourished in the Second Great Awakening, which greatly affected the spirit and politics of the nation. In 1840, Alexis de Tocqueville made this appraisal:

> Religion in America takes no direct part in the government of society, but it must be regarded as the first of their political institutions; for if it does not impart a taste for freedom, it facilitates the use of it. Indeed, it is in this same point of view that the inhabitants of the United States themselves look upon religious belief. I do not know whether all Americans have a sincere faith in their religion—for who can search the human heart?—but I am certain that they hold it to be indispensable to the

---

[115] Gordon Wood, *Empire of Liberty* (New York: Oxford University Press, 2009) 584.

maintenance of republican institutions. This opinion is not peculiar to a class of citizens or to a party, but it belongs to the whole nation and to every rank of society.[116]

American religion wasn't static; as the nation changed, religions adjusted. Churches that had controlled distinct communities lost followers, while newer denominations gained followers. The notion of a person's religious affiliation being a matter of birth was replaced by the notion of individual choice or conversion, and Baptist and Methodist churches became the largest denominations in America. Religiosity based on individual choice fit well with notions of freedom and individual liberty.

The nation's ideals and realities didn't always coincide. Religion could provide the impetus for war. Leading up to the Civil War, the Northern Presbyterian minister and abolitionist Henry Ward Beecher preached that Southern leaders would be "whirled aloft and plunged downward for ever and ever in an endless retribution."

Although Lincoln tried to discourage such sentiments, he evidently believed God's retribution could be rendered not only in the afterlife but also in this life, and not only to individuals but also to nations. In his Second Inaugural, he noted the Almighty in the struggle over slavery between the North and South.

Both read the same Bible, and pray to the same God; and each invokes His aid against the other. It may seem strange that any men should dare to ask a just God's assistance in wringing their bread from the sweat of other men's faces; but let us judge not that we be not judged. The prayers of both could not be answered; that of neither has been answered fully. The Almighty has His own purposes: "Woe unto the world because of offenses! For it needs be that offenses come, but woe unto that man by whom the offenses cometh!" … Fondly do we hope—fervently do we pray—that this mighty scourge of war may

---

[116] Alexis de Tocqueville, *Democracy in America*, 1830.

speedily pass away. Yet if God wills that it continue, until all the wealth piled by the bond-man's two-hundred-and-fifty years of unrequited toil shall be sunk, and until every drop of blood drawn by the lash shall be paid with another drawn by the sword, as was said three thousand years ago, so still it must be said "the judgments of the Lord are true and righteous altogether."[117]

Lincoln invoked the Roman categorical imperative of fighting only a "just war" and also the Roman idea that the gods would punish a nation for its immorality. The Union victory confirmed the righteousness and divine approval of its cause, and the nation felt redeemed, self-confident, and ready to accomplish great things. The victory reinforced the idea that divine approval wasn't based on rituals and sacrifices but on righteous and just conduct. How people conducted their personal and public lives would determine their destiny.

In the post-Civil War era, religion became an increasingly more powerful influence on American life. Strains of Calvinism and Puritanism informed business practices, and almost without exception, business leaders imbued their commercial endeavors with religious overtones. Organizations opened their meetings with prayers; religious imperatives drove charities; and businessmen and clergy combined to spread capitalism, democracy, and Christianity. Beyond the borders of the United States, Americans began preaching their political and moral values to the world.

America was a Christian nation with a crusading spirit. Its leaders invariably conflated Christianity and patriotism, and military leaders appealed to the Christian cause to inspire their troops to fight. Between the First and Second World Wars, General Douglas MacArthur wrote, "I can think of no principles more high and holy than those for which our national sacrifices have been made in the past. History teaches us that religion and patriotism have always gone hand in hand, while atheism had invariably been accompanied by radicalism, communism, bolshevism,

---

[117]   Abraham Lincoln, Second Inaugural Address, March 5, 1865.

and other enemies of free government … I confidently believe that a red-blooded and virile humanity which loves peace devotedly, but is willing to die in defense of the right, is Christian from center to circumference, and will continue to be dominant in the future as in the past."[118]

---

[118] Douglas MacArthur, *World Tomorrow*, June 2, 1931.

CHAPTER 11

Wealth, Populism, and Civil War

AFTER ROME'S VICTORY IN the Second Punic War in 202 BC, it turned its military attention to Greece, and its successes there brought gold and silver, tracts of land, and valuable objects of all kinds into its possession. Plunder was the norm for the winners of a battle, and at the end of a campaign, the victors distributed slaves, livestock, and property to the legionaries. Soldiers could expect land or a cash bonus, enough to buy a small plot. Generals received a larger share, and after taking their share, they were expected to fill the state treasury with the remaining profits. Their conquests provided opportunities for Roman traders and entrepreneurs beyond Italy, and their successes transformed the overall economy from a Spartan-like subsistence to a vibrant market economy that generated profits and wealth.

As trade and commerce expanded into ever-wider areas, Rome's talent for organization, engineering, and investment moved it ahead of its more static neighbors. In 187 BC, the Roman silver denarius coin became the preferred medium of exchange throughout the Mediterranean world, which further enhanced Rome's economic advantages.

Rome's wealth increased even more so after her victory over King Perseus of Macedon at the Battle of Pydna in 167 BC. There was so much plunder taken that the Senate repaid the special taxes that had been levied on Roman citizens during the Second Punic War. It also abolished direct income taxes, which weren't permanently reinstated for more than a century. Abundant capital ignited trade and business, generating wealth for families and individuals, many of whom invested in large farms—latifundia.

The growing revenues were used for public purposes. Examples included a new drainage system and the Pons Aemilius, the first stone bridge across the Tiber River. Private individuals used their wealth to fund public projects, and consuls donated revenues obtained during military campaigns to stage festivals and build temples. In 146 BC, Quintus Caecilius Metellus, a conqueror of Macedon, used the spoils of war to fund the first marble building in Rome—the Temple of Jupiter on the Campus Martius.

The equestrians, a wealthy non-office-holding class, one formal rank below the senatorial class, profited from inflowing revenues and the public projects. Originally the equestrians formed a prestigious cavalry division of knights, composed of men wealthy enough to outfit a warhorse, but over time they evolved into a class of businessmen that included industrialists, financiers, tax collectors, builders, and merchants. By the late republic, they no longer had a military function.

In comparison to the military and political activities of the senatorial class, the activities of the equestrians were only superficially mentioned in the histories, but it was their activities in business, trade, and shipping that fueled the growth of the empire. They engaged in overseas trading, bid for public works contracts, and set up companies in which any citizen could buy a share.

The best record of equestrian commercial activity is at the site of Ostia Antica, a port city at the mouth of the Tiber River. Ostia was one of the first Roman colonies; its ruins attest to its role as Rome's commercial connection to the sea, though the remnants of the city are no longer in direct contact with the sea due to the accretion of mud and sand at the river delta. Ostia housed the headquarters of some sixty equestrian trading companies, and for a thousand years, ships from around the Mediterranean docked there to unload their cargoes onto barges for transport upriver to Rome. The port handled imports and exports to and from countries as far away as India.

Ostia's equestrians built luxurious homes in the city with fine atriums, gardens, statues, mosaics, and frescoes; they also funded numerous temples, a forum, and a large amphitheater. Equestrians also benefitted from state contracts for public works and from the management of state-owned mines, forests, and fisheries, which provided substantial profits. Although equestrians couldn't become senators without giving up the ability to engage in commerce, they could provide the funds for campaigning politicians, and thus they gained substantial political influence. Equestrian money, energy, and interests encouraged the constant expansion of commercial activity and societal changes.

After the Third Punic War, the Romans became the masters of the Mediterranean. Their most dangerous rivals had been subjugated. Carthage was no more, Macedon was a province, and the other Hellenic states were under their control. The nobility enlisted talented and ambitious new men into its ranks, and the people were proud of their special status as Roman citizens. New bridges, roads, aqueducts, public buildings, and temples proliferated; and engineering achievements reached historic levels.

Changes accelerated in all aspects of society, but not all the changes from conquests and expansion were positive, and several trends moved in crosscurrents. The immense profits pouring into Rome widened the income gap between classes, and although the general population benefitted to some degree, seeing the exorbitant wealth of those on the top evoked resentment and calls for reforms. For small farmers, the increasing wealth worked to their detriment. The growing number of latifundia that employed slaves imported to Rome with each foreign conquest overwhelmed them. Cheap labor pushed aside the free farmers, making it nearly impossible for them to compete. As a result, displaced farmers in great numbers gravitated to the city, where many joined the ranks of the unemployed, ripe for demagoguery.

Military expansion exacerbated the problems in the agriculture system. The Roman legions had been built on the obligation of the yeomen farmers to answer the military levies and to serve honorably, but as campaigns stretched farther afield and the fighting seasons were prolonged, soldier farmers returned from the legions injured, sick, or too late for the harvest. Many small farms fell into ruin by a thousand small cuts. Many of the soldiers died without sons to carry on; their plots passed to the state and were then leased to large-scale landowners.

Historian Robert Shaffern summarized, "The lands of the men who died without heirs reverted to the state, and often passed into the control of the politically well-connected. Senators, who had displayed such great leadership and patriotism during the dangerous era of the Punic Wars, now shamefully despoiled men who had served the republic with honor and courage. The Italian allies, too, wondered what benefits they enjoyed for fighting alongside Romans."[119]

Depending on one's perspective, the world could have been described as either progressing or decaying. Sallust (Gaius Sallustius Crispus), the defrocked politician turned historian, chose the latter. He painted a bleak picture of that period, which was surely colored by the events of his own tumultuous career. It would seem that he projected his personal difficulties into his account of the prior era, reconstructing facts in ways in accord with his viewpoint.

> Now the institution of parties and factions, with all their attendant evils, originated at Rome a few years before this as the result of peace and of an abundance of everything thing mortals prize most highly. For before the destruction of Carthage the people and senate of Rome together governed the republic peacefully and with moderation. There was no strife among the citizens either for glory or for power; fear of the enemy preserved the good morals of the state. But when the minds of the people were relieved of that dread, wantonness and arrogance naturally arose, vices which are fostered by prosperity. Thus the peace for which they had longed for in time of adversity, after they had gained it proved to be more cruel and bitter than adversity itself. For the nobles began to abuse their position and the people their liberty, and every man for himself robbed, pillaged, and plundered. Thus the community was split in two parties, and between these the state was torn to pieces.

---

[119] Robert Shaffern, *Law and Justice from Antiquity to the Enlightenment,* (New York: Rowland and Littlefield, 2009) 55.

But the nobles had the more powerful organization, while the strength of the commons was less effective because it was incompact and divided among many. Affairs at home and in the field were managed according to the will of a few men, in whose hands were the treasury, the provinces, public offices, glory and triumphs. The people were burdened with military service and poverty. The generals divided the spoils of war with a few friends.[120]

Despite Sallust's less-than-impartial evaluation, to a significant degree his cynical portrayal of the state of affairs was true, and reforms were necessary. The commoners found champions, sometimes from among their own, sometimes from nobles who took their side. These reformers inspired a movement labeled *populares,* a loose term for those advocating a redistribution of land, debt relief, and a lessening of the nobility's political and economic domination. As would be expected, most of the nobility opposed reforms, and those who actively resisted populist change were labeled *optimates.* However, not all nobles opposed reforms, and there was no reliable way of predicting to which side individuals might align themselves; several became prominent leaders of *populare* causes. *Populares* could be persons from the most noble of families who identified with the middle and working classes, and conversely *optimates* could be small farmers or businessmen who sided with the nobility.

Tiberius Gracchus

The most prominent reformers were the Gracchi brothers, Tiberius Sempronius Gracchus, and Gaius Sempronius Gracchus. They were from an elite family. Tiberius married Claudia, whose father, Appius Claudius Pulcher, was the pater of one of Rome's most prestigious families and also the *princeps senatus* or leading senator. Although born an aristocrat, Tiberius sympathized with the free citizen farmers and took on the role of spokesman for the landless. He didn't become a consul,

---

[120] Sallust, *Histories* (Penguin Classics, 2007), ch. 41.

as might be expected for members of his class, but instead he became a tribune.

Plutarch and others described Tiberius as a man gifted by nature, temperate and modest yet fearless in the face of adversity. He had been among the first to scale the walls of Carthage in that city's final defeat. Reputedly incorruptible, he took up the cause of land reform. Plutarch recounted that Tiberius traveled through the countryside, observing that now slaves rather than free citizen farmers tilled the land.

> Then the poor, who had been ejected from their land, no longer showed themselves eager for military service, and neglected the bringing up of children, so that soon all Italy was conscious of a dearth of freemen, and was filled with gangs of foreign slaves, by whose aid the rich cultivated their estates, from which they had driven away the free citizens.
>
> Tiberius was passing through Tuscany and observed the dearth of inhabitants in the country, and that those who tilled its soil or tended its flocks there were imported barbarian slaves, he then first conceived the public policy which was the cause of countless ills to the two brothers.
>
> Tiberius sought to win the favor of the multitude by fresh laws, reducing the time of military service, granting appeal to the people from the verdicts of the judges, adding to the judges, who at that time were composed of senators only, an equal number from the equestrian order, and in every way at length trying to maim the power of the senate.[121]

Some have judged Tiberius as an idealist committed to alleviating the plight of the lower classes and restoring the number of citizen farmers who would be eligible for military service. Others have judged him as an opportunist, who turned against his own class because the Senate had severely

---

[121] Plutarch, "Life of Tiberius Gracchus" in *Lives.*

criticized him for a treaty he had negotiated in Spain to surrender several legions in exchange for their safe passage out of that country.

Tiberius was determined to restore his standing, and in 133 BC, he campaigned for tribune, proposing land reform measures. He was elected and immediately proposed a 500-*iugera* limit (about 310 acres) on public land possession, which threatened the large holdings of the upper classes. This law, the *Lex Agraria*, was a renewal of the Licinian land laws of 367 BC, which had been increasingly neglected by the authorities and circumvented by the large landowners, who directly or indirectly controlled far more than the five-hundred-*iugera* limit. They would have to divest any excessive land holdings, making the land available to small farmers and landless citizens.

Tiberius's proposal had the support of several prominent and wealthy citizens, but it was blocked by a senatorial faction of landowners, who accused him of introducing the redistribution of land to bribe the rabble of the cities and incite revolution so he could seize dictatorial powers. The landowners complained that they had tilled and improved the land and spent decades growing vineyards and erecting buildings. They had paid their neighbors for parcels of land, sometimes using borrowed money, sometimes using their wives' dowries. Were they to lose their investments?

Tiberius proceeded nonetheless. To circumvent the customary legal procedure of submitting proposals to the Senate for its imprimatur, he broke with tradition and submitted his bill directly to the assembly, where he spoke in the most forceful manner on behalf of the landless. "The wild beasts have their own lairs, they have places of rest and refuge; but the men who bear arms, the men who risk their lives for the safety of their country, all they can enjoy is air and light; they have no houses or dwelling of their own, and are compelled to wander from place to place with their wives and children."[122]

His speech overwhelmed any opposition, and his law would have been easily enacted, but a fellow tribune, Marcus Octavius, exercised a veto. At this point, the bill should have stalled, and further debate and adjustments should have followed as the legislative system was designed.

---

[122] Plutarch, "Life of Tiberius Gracchus" in *Lives*.

Instead, Tiberius embarked on a revolutionary course, resorting to illegal methods in the assembly and using the power of the mob to intimidate his adversaries.

He introduced and passed an unprecedented bill that any tribune who defied the will of the people could be deposed. He then convinced the assembly to vote to depose Octavius, who, with his imperium stripped, was dragged off the rostrum. Expelling an elected tribune from the assembly by popular will was an illegal act that abrogated the safeguards at the heart of the Roman constitution and inevitably produced dire consequences.

With Octavius out of the way, the land redistribution bill overwhelmingly passed, and a permanent commission was set up to bring about its implementation. This might have been good public policy; however, instead of appointing impartial commissioners, Tiberius appointed himself; his younger brother, Gaius Gracchus; and his father-in-law, Appius Claudius Pulcher, to the commission. Keeping it all within his family further antagonized his enemies.

Coincidentally, it happened that the king of Pergamum had died and left his kingdom in Asia Minor to the people of Rome. Tiberius seized this opportunity and, bypassing the Senate again, proposed a bill in the assembly to accept the inheritance and use the revenues from this windfall to pay for the land distribution. To compensate the people of Pergamum, he granted them immunity from taxation.

The assembly passed the bill. This act struck another blow at the heart of the constitution, undermining the Senate's control of foreign and financial affairs, so it could only have been expected that the senators would take drastic action to protect their prerogatives.

In 132 BC, despite the illegality of serving two consecutive terms, Tiberius proposed to run for reelection as tribune, another abrogation of the traditional rules. His claim of the right to permanent reelection convinced many citizens, including fellow tribunes, that his aim was to seize dictatorial control of the state. The Roman hatred of monarchs was aroused, and conflict between the factions escalated. In the assembly, supporters of Tiberius clashed with opponents, and when reports reached the Senate that Tiberius had been offered a crown in the assembly, Publius Cornelius Scipio Nasica (183–132 BC), the *pontifex maximus*, demanded that the consul Publius Mucius Scaevola take forceful action against the treason. Scaevola, a learned jurist, refused, stating that he was uncomfortable with using force or killing a citizen without a trial. Scipio Nasica then donned his formal *pontifex maximus* attire and led two hundred senators to the forum to confront Tiberius. Violence erupted and quickly raced out of control, with Tiberius's supporters battling the senators and their supporters. Tiberius was clubbed to death, and many of his followers were killed.

Modern commentators usually frame the event in terms of the oligarchs suppressing a democratic movement. But from the viewpoint of the senators, they were dealing with an insurrection, led by a demagogue who had abrogated the constitution in the most flagrant way and surrounded himself with a mob that attacked the lawful representatives of the republic.

After the slaying of Tiberius, the Senate ex post facto (after the fact) issued a senatus consultum ultimum, a decree directing the magistrates to protect the republic, in effect ratifying the suppression of Tiberius. Trials and convictions of Tiberius's supporters followed. To the senators, proving their guilt proved the guilt of Tiberius and thereby justified his "execution." Though ratified ex post facto, Tiberius's slaying would inevitably boomerang on the Senate. It was a watershed event that set the republic on a roller-coaster course to its destruction. Tribunes had been inviolate since the first decades of the republic, and legend had it that their inviolability was so strictly upheld that a man had been put to death for failing to make way for a tribune passing through the forum. Once political violence superseded this inviolability, it was only a matter of time before the rule of law disintegrated.

Notably the slaying of Tiberius wasn't followed by a repeal of his land reform or his land commission. Opposition to Tiberius was political, not economic. Even the *optimates* recognized and acknowledged the necessity of reform; the distribution of land furthered conservative principles and provided a safety valve for the growing urban population.

GAIUS GRACCHUS

The death of Tiberius didn't dissuade his brother, Gaius Gracchus, from public life. He was also gifted by nature, particularly as an orator, and he used his brother's martyrdom to elevate his own stature. As a member of the land distribution commission, he wielded great power, and for several years he contemplated seeking election as a tribune but held back at the behest of his mother, Cornelia. A letter from Cornelia, written in 131 BC, supported that inference. She wrote,

> I would take a solemn oath, that apart from those who killed Tiberius Gracchus, no one has given me so much pain as you in this matter, who ought to undertake the part of all the children I have ever had, and to make sure that I should have as little worry as possible in my old age, and that, whatever your schemes might be, you should wish them to be agreeable to me, and that you should count it a sin to take any major step against my wishes, especially considering that I have only a little part of life left.
>
> Is it quite impossible to cooperate for even that short space of time without your opposing me and ruining our country? Where will it all end? Will our family ever cease from madness? Can a bound ever be put to it? Shall we ever cease to dwell on affronts, both causing and suffering them? Shall we ever begin to feel true shame for confounding and destroying the constitution? But if that is quite impossible, when I am dead, then see the Tribunate.[123]

Cornelia apparently disapproved of the challenge to the constitutional order her first son had undertaken, but in 123 BC, Gaius Gracchus sought and became tribune. Learning from his brother's mistaken reliance on a single constituency, Gaius appealed to a variety of interest groups. With their support and by exploiting a loophole in the law, he won a second consecutive term for 122 BC

---

[123] Cornelius Nepos, fragment, in Mary Lefkowitz and Maureen Fant, *Women's Life in Greece and Rome* (Baltimore: John Hopkins University Press, 2005) 191.

Gaius followed his older brother's policies and proposed expanding the land distribution and establishing more colonies. He even proposed a colony at Carthage, which would have been the first Roman colony overseas. In addition, recognizing that not all the urban poor were equipped or amenable to becoming colonist farmers, he provided subsidized grain at half the market price as an alternative. It was seemingly a reasonable measure at the time; in hindsight, it initiated a rudimentary welfare system that drew hordes of people into the city, people who could be manipulated by ambitious politicians vying for power. The *optimates* opposed this, and when the dole began, a senior senator and ex-consul, L. Piso Frugi, theatrically demonstrated his opposition by lining up with the people to receive his dole. Gaius wasn't amused and, with his fiercest invective, mocked Piso's grandstanding.

Gaius proposed road construction projects to provide employment, bringing him into favor of the equestrian contractors. The land distribution, construction projects, and grain subsidies were expensive. To defray the costs, he increased tax collections from the provinces, offering contracts to businessmen, called *publicani*, to collect the taxes and keep a percentage for themselves. The tax contracts were publicly auctioned, and the winning bidder had to pay the stipulated tribute in advance. Anything collected above that, they kept for themselves. The sums were enormous, so to raise the necessary capital, shares were offered and could be traded; the value of the shares fluctuated on projections of profit or loss and on the risk of world events.

As tax collectors with almost unlimited discretion, the *publicani* garnered enormous wealth from these enterprises and became a powerful part of the equestrian commercial class. They regularly exploited the provinces for high profits, and they continually challenged the authority and interests of the old senatorial order. Gaius further ingratiated himself with the *publicani* by rescinding the immunity from taxation his brother, Tiberius, had granted to the people of Pergamum. Adding insult to injury to these formerly independent people, he auctioned the lucrative tax contracts, which meant that the higher the winning bid, the greater the taxes extracted from the Pergamites.

Most important, Gaius gave the *publicani* immunity for their activities so they couldn't be prosecuted for tax collection abuses. As expected, the *publicani* joined Gaius's *populare* supporters, giving him a stronger coalition than that of his older brother.

This arrangement was a clear example of the inherent problem in democracies wherein a demagogue gains power by promising benefits to the common people, then uses that power for his own benefit and the benefit of his connected associates and other moneyed interests.

In addition, Gaius passed legislation allowing equestrians to sit on the jury courts that oversaw charges of corruption against retiring provincial governors. Thus, the equestrian class became nearly as powerful as the senatorial class.

In his two terms in office, Gaius changed the Roman constitution, effectively making himself the uncrowned king of Rome. Plutarch described, "All persons, even those who hated or feared him, stood amazed to see what a capacity he had for effecting and completing all he undertook. As for the people themselves, they were transported at the very sight, when they saw him surrounded with a crowd of contractors, artificers, public deputies, military officers, soldiers and scholars. All these he treated with an easy familiarity."

Gaius seemed invincible as he campaigned for his third consecutive term as tribune; however, when he put forward proposals to grant citizenship and distribute land to all the Latin tribes, he learned how fickle the populace could be. His proposals backfired because the urban plebs saw them as a dilution of their rights, and the *optimates*—led by Marcus Livius Drusus the Elder, a candidate for tribune; and Lucius Opimius, a consul—outmaneuvered him by proposing a more ambitious land distribution program for the urban plebs. This political triangulation undermined Gaius's support, and he lost his bid for a third term.

After Gaius's defeat, his supporters demonstrated in the streets, and Gaius, suspecting that he might suffer the same fate as his brother, employed armed bodyguards. He organized a massive demonstration on the Aventine, and when the consul, Lucius Opimius, sent a messenger with an offer to negotiate, Gaius's bodyguards killed him. The Senate responded by declaring a public emergency, suspending the constitution, and issuing another senatus consultum ultimum. Faced with the decree, most of Gaius's supporters defected, and Lucius Opimius led an attack on those who remained. Gaius was surrounded, and rather than surrender, he committed suicide by ordering his slave to kill him with a sword.

Apart from their indiscreet fomenting of violence, commentators have posited that the Gracchi failed because their movement was launched prematurely. Organized political parties as we know them today didn't exist then, and the Gracchi acted in their individual capacities without organizational support. They lacked the legitimacy of an established political party platform and were subject to charges of self-promotion and treason. Gaius was accused of being a tool of the *publicani* tax collectors, an accusation that would resurface time and again against later *populare* demagogues. Despite Gaius's downfall, the tax contracts remained in force after his death, and the *publicani* grew stronger and increasingly exploitative until the end of the republic.

Undeniably, the Gracchi brothers were charismatic leaders who exploited their noble status and natural gifts to gain personal power, but they also may have been genuinely motivated to act in the interest of the public good. Had they been less extreme and more patient, accepted political defeats as temporary, and eschewed violence, they may have been more successful. Although their careers were brief, the Gracchi brothers left an indelible mark on Roman politics. They spawned a line of successors, inspiring some to push for additional democratic reforms and others to imitate their grabs for power. Two millenniums later, they became heroes to modern populists and Marxists.

CHAPTER 12

Hellenism

DURING THE REPUBLIC'S LAST century, despite recurring periods of civil tumult and temporary military setbacks, Rome continued to expand its reach and power, and wealth and riches continued to pour into its coffers. However, though it appeared an invincible nation of granite, its foundations were showing cracks, and insidious changes affected its people.

While Rome's armies were overseas subjugating other nations, the homeland population was freed from the fear of attack, and affluent Romans began to abandon the discipline and military virtues of their ancestors. Enormous wealth at the upper strata of society afforded the leisure to engage in intellectual, artistic, and hedonistic pursuits; and contact with the East naturally raised interest in the profligacy and peculiarities of those cultures.

Many Roman elites saw Greek culture as superior to their own outdated rustic values, and they sent their children to study in Greek schools. Their children became fascinated not only with Greek arts and theater but also with Greek sophistry, atheism, and skepticism—notions that would have been intolerable to their ancestors.

A growing spiritual divide separated members of the elite classes, with traditionalists on one side and those more amenable to new ideas on the other. This spiritual and intellectual divide provided the Romans reasons to fight among themselves and exacerbated the ever-present competition between the great noble families. The Scipiones, Claudii, and Metelli competed for power, honor, glory, and wealth; and they treated each other as adversaries. Thus, they fulfilled Hannibal's prediction that the Romans, once threats from foreign enemies were subdued, would turn their aggressions against one another. According to Livy, Hannibal said, "No great state can remain at rest long together. If it has no enemy abroad it finds one at home in the same manner as over-robust bodies seem secure from external causes, but as encumbered with their own strength."[124]

Scipio Africanus, Scipio Aemilianus, and their families were enamored of Greek culture. Though they were members of a class rooted in tradition, they actively sought out new ideas and viewpoints. Velleius Paterculus wrote, "The elder Scipio prepared the way for Rome's power, the younger for Rome's luxury. When the fear of Carthage was removed and Rome's rival cleared from her path, the passage from virtue to vice was not a gradual process but a headlong rush. The old moral code was abandoned and a new one supplanted it. Rome gave herself up to sleep instead of watching, to pleasure instead of the use of weapons, to leisure instead of business."[125]

Fiercely opposing the adoption of Greek culture were traditionalists, led by Marcus Porcius Cato the Elder, the ultraconservative consul and censor. Cato was a powerful orator who spoke of the ancient republican virtues and railed against the changes he saw overtaking Roman society. Determined to suppress Hellenization and the libertine influences he thought would destroy the fabric of the Roman state, he played the role of a puritanical policeman.

Cato showed the extent of his ultraconservative view when he opposed a motion to lift outdated restrictions on women. In 195 BC, women demonstrated in the forum for the repeal of the Oppian Law, which had been imposed during the Second Punic War and required women not to wear gold jewelry or expensive clothes in public and to deposit their valuable possessions in the treasury. With victory over Carthage won and peace restored, the women demanded the repeal of the law. However,

---

[124] Livy, *Histories*, bk. 30.
[125] Velleius Patervuus, *Compendium of Roman History*.

Cato argued that the Oppian Law should remain in force to prevent the corruption of women by luxuries and the subversion of Rome's traditional values and religion. He complained,

> The community suffers from two opposite vices—avarice and luxury—pestilential diseases that have proved the ruin of all great empires. The brighter and better the fortunes of the Republic become day by day, and the greater the growth of its dominion ... so much the more do I dread the prospect of these things taking us captive rather than we them ... I hear far too many people praising and admiring those statues that adorn Athens and Corinth and laughing at the clay images of our gods standing in front of their temples. I for my part prefer these gods who bless us.[126]

Cato would lose this fight, since Roman women weren't so easily repressed, and the justice of their demands won out. The tribune Lucius Valerius spoke in the assembly for the repeal of the law.

> What, may I ask, are the women doing that is new, having gathered and come forth publicly in a case which concerns them directly? Have they never appeared in public before? Allow me to unroll your own Origins before you. Listen to how often they have done so—always for the public good ... Indeed, as no one is amazed that they acted in situations affecting men and women alike, why should we wonder that they have taken action in a case which concerns themselves? What, after all, have they done? We have proud ears indeed, if, while masters do not scorn the appeals of slaves, we are angry when honorable women ask something of us ...

---

[126] Cato the Elder, *Pro Lege Oppis,* in *Oratorum Romanorum Fragments XI–IXX,* quoted in Goodman and Soni, *Rome's Last Citizen* (New York: St. Martin's Press, 2012).

Who then does not know that this is a recent law, passed twenty years ago? Since our matrons lived for so long by the highest standards of behavior without any law, what risk is there that, once it is repealed, they will yield to luxury? For if the law were an old one, or if it had been passed to restrain feminine license, there might be reason to fear that repeal would incite them. The times themselves will show you why the law was passed. Hannibal was in Italy, victorious at Cannae. Already he held Tarentum, Arpi and Capua. He seemed on the verge of moving against Rome. Our allies had gone over to him. We had no reserve troops, no allies at sea to protect the fleet, no funds in the treasury. Slaves were being bought and armed, on condition that the price was to be paid their owners when the war was over. The contractors had declared that they would provide, on the same day of payment (after the war), the grain and other supplies the needs of war demanded. We were giving our slaves as rowers at our own expense, in proportion to our property rating. We were giving all our gold and silver for public use, as the senators had done first. Widows and children were donating their funds to the treasury. We were ordered to keep at home no more than a certain amount of wrought and stamped gold and silver. At a time like that were the matrons so taken up with luxury and fancy trappings that the Oppian law was needed ... To whom is it not clear that poverty and misfortune were the authors of that law of yours, since all private wealth had to be turned over to public use, and that it was to remain in effect only as long as the reason for its writing did?[127]

When the speeches for and against the motion for repeal had been made, vetoes were imposed to block the motion, but a vociferous crowd

---

[127] Livy, *Histories*, bk. 34

of women besieged the forum until the vetoes were rescinded and the Oppian Law was repealed.

Cato lost that battle, but he persevered in his war against any liberalization of traditional values. He was assuredly motivated by his fanatical hatred for those he believed undermined the old Roman morality, and he would use any means necessary. The Cornelius Scipio clan was his main target, and he would bring corruption charges against them.

In 190 BC, at the Battle of Magnesia, Publius Cornelius Scipio Africanus and his brother, Lucius Cornelius Scipio, defeated King Antiochus III of Syria. The king had invaded and seized the Roman province of Asia Minor. The brothers forced the king out of the province and made him pay an annual indemnity to Rome. However, years later, Cato brought charges against the brothers for misappropriations from the war booty and the indemnity. Cato couldn't have picked a more difficult prosecution. At his trial, Scipio Africanus spoke in his defense with a single sentence. "Romans, this is the date on which I conquered Hannibal." The conqueror of Hannibal was immediately acquitted.

Cato didn't quit. Three years later, he again charged Lucius Scipio with the misappropriation. Lucius was found guilty and imprisoned until his property was sold to pay the fine. Seeing the conviction, Scipio Africanus didn't wait around to be charged again, but he left Rome and retired from public life, bitter toward his countrymen. He died in 184 BC at age fifty-two. Cato outlived him by thirty-five years.

What happened to the Scipios forecast the bitter partisanship that would later fully infect the republic when cultural differences exacerbated partisan political differences.

Despite his efforts, Cato's faction failed to stem the returning tide from the East, and Greek ideas and practices continued to flood into Rome. Adaptations of Greek plays, art, and poetry began to dominate the culture of the educated classes, and by the second century BC, most Roman elites prided themselves on speaking Greek. Aristocrats staged the plays of Plautus and Terence, largely adaptations from Greek originals, which were popular with the commoners. Elites widely read Greek verse that provided models for the poetry of Catullus, Virgil, Ovid, and Horace.

In addition to intellectual ideas from the classic Greek academies,

Romans absorbed Greek social mores. Polybius observed, "The Romans maintained their integrity until they crossed the seas to do battle, until they forgot the laws and customs of their ancestors ... Some abandoned themselves to shameful love affairs, others to harlots, by now almost everyone went wild for the music, the banquets, and the luxury they learned to enjoy from Greece."[128]

Rome also absorbed some of the East's more nefarious and licentious cults. Rome's polytheism gave individuals or groups the opportunity to practice new cults, and the cult of Bacchus spread in Etruria and parts of Southern Italy. Apparently, it originated in the Greek cities as an offshoot of the cult of Dionysius, the god of wine. Its priests conducted secret rituals at night that involved frenzied dances and promiscuous sexual practices. When the bacchanalia spread to Rome, panic broke out over the reports and rumors of orgies and ritualistic murders.

Livy told us that when the consul Postumius learned of the rituals, he addressed the assembly.

> A great number of the adherents are women, which is the origin of the whole trouble. But there are also men like women who have joined in each other's defilement, fanatics maddened by night-watching, by wine, by nightly shrieking and uproar ... What then do you think of these assemblies which take place late at night, which are attended by men and women indiscriminately? If you knew the age at which the men are initiated, you would be filled not only with pity for them, but with shame. Do you think citizens, that young men who have taken this oath can be made soldiers? Are they to be trusted with arms when they leave this obscene sanctuary? Are they defiled by their own and others' sins to fight in defense of the honor of your wives and children? ... The evil grows every day ... It affects the whole commonwealth of Rome ... If any man has been drawn into that gulf by lust

---

[128] Polybius, *Histories*, 18.35; 35.11.

or madness, judge him to belong not to you but to those with whom he has conspired to commit every shameful and criminal act … Our fathers and grandfathers often gave the magistrates the duty of forbidding foreign rites, banning fakirs and prophets from the marketplace, the circus and the city, of collecting and burning prophetic books, and of forbidding all sacrificial ritual which was not Roman. For they were skilled in human law and divine law alike: they judged that true religion was never destroyed so quickly as when the old rites were abandoned and foreign ones introduced. I have thought it necessary to give you this warning so that you may not be disturbed by superstitious scruples when you see us, the magistrates, destroying the Bacchanalia and breaking up their unlawful assemblies.[129]

In 186 BC, the Senate banned the rites of bacchanalia and persecuted those worshippers who didn't flee. This episode bolstered the perception that Greek culture and ideas were harmful to the nation's morality and would weaken the state; it caused a conservative backlash with demands for a return to Roman austerity and rectitude. Notwithstanding this, with each Roman conquest in the East, the influence of Hellenization grew.

In 167 BC, the consul Lucius Aemilius Paullus completed the conquest of Macedon. At his spectacular three-day triumph at Rome, Paulus displayed the mounds of treasures and arms his troops had plundered. He also displayed Perseus, the captive Macedonian king, who in chains was made to walk behind Paullus's chariot. Paullus also confiscated the king's extensive library and brought it to Rome. This was a monumental event that stimulated great interest in Greek ideas.

Paullus's teenage son, Publius Scipio Aemilianus, accompanied him on the Macedon campaign to learn how Romans conducted war. The teenager learned well, and later he would use his learning to destroy Carthage.

As part of the peace treaty with Macedon, Paullus took a thousand

---

[129] Livy, *Histories*, 34.1.

Greek nobles as hostages to secure the good conduct of their families. Many of them were incorporated into Roman society and families, and one of the hostages, Polybius, became the tutor of Aemelianus. Polybius taught him Greek history, literature, and philosophy; and Aemelianus became an avid admirer of Greece culture. When he later became the most prominent man in Rome, his interests encouraged others to think and feel the same.

Also at this time, Cornelia, the daughter of Scipio Africanus, led a salon of elite Romans who were eager for Greek literature, art, and philosophy. Thus, Greek ideas of popular democracy influenced Cornelia's sons, Tiberius Gracchus and Gaius Gracchus. They became leading actors in the newest round of class warfare.

To be sure, many conservatives still reviled Greek culture and philosophy. In 155 BC, Cato the Elder heard the Greek sophist Carneades take one side of an argument one day and then take the other side on the next. Carneades did this to demonstrate that justice didn't exist and that there was no such thing as truth, except the proposition that there was no such thing as truth. So Cato expelled Carneades and other Greek philosophers from Rome. Expelling them, however, didn't stop the infiltration of their ideas.

Later censors, magistrates, and priests also tried to curtail the growing Greek influence. In 92 BC, the censors issued an edict, banning certain schools that taught Greek rhetoric. They were concerned that the young who attended these schools spent whole days in idleness, instead of being taught and attending to the uses and customs of their ancestors.

Appian wrote of the period. "About this time the consul Scipio [Nasica] demolished the theatre begun by Lucius Cassius, and now nearly finished, because he thought it far from desirable that the Romans should become accustomed to Grecian pleasures."[130]

Despite the efforts to resist Greek influences, inexorably Rome was overcome. Horace penned, "Captive Greece conquered the fierce victor, and brought the arts to rustic Latium."[131]

---

[130] Appian, *Civil Wars*, bk. 1, 28, 55.
[131] Horace, *Epistles*, 2, 1.

Over the course of a century, many in the upper classes increasingly discounted the old traditions and religious beliefs, though they observed state religious rituals for the sake of outward appearances. For them, philosophy gradually supplanted traditional religion. By the end of the republic, what had begun as curiosity and the dabbling in novel ideas grew to full acceptance. Many adopted Epicureanism or Stoicism. The Roman writer Lucretius (94–55 BC) expounded Greek Epicurean philosophy in *The Nature of Things*. He proposed an atom-based materialism that left no room for the gods; and most significantly, he denied the existence of an afterlife. He endeavored to teach that the gods were unconcerned with either piety or sin. He ridiculed the folly of clinging to life for love of material pleasure or fear of torment after death.

Lucretius was in step with the changing culture of the late republic. While deference to the gods persisted, the denial of an afterlife wasn't uncommon. Death was a relief from pain and affliction. Epicureanism claimed many followers, apparently including Julius Caesar, who in his speech against the execution of the Catiline conspirators argued that death was the end of everything; and since criminals wouldn't suffer in the underworld, the death penalty was an inadequate punishment.

Stoicism was another Greek philosophy Roman elites adopted. Cicero leaned toward Stoicism, and while he often alluded to the gods, he also discounted an afterlife. In his oration in defense of Aulus Cluentius Habitus, a man charged with murder, Cicero was surprisingly candid and somewhat comic. He argued that the victim of the murder, Oppianicus, had been so miserable that he should be glad to be dead. Cicero stated,

> He is dead now, and what harm can his death be said to have brought him? Unless we believe the stupid tales which would have us suppose that he is enduring the tortures of the damned in the underworld; that he had encountered even more of his enemies down there that he left behind him on earth; that the avenging furies of his mother-in-law, his wives, his brother and his children have driven him headlong into the regions reserved for the habitation of the damned. But if these stories are

untrue (as everyone knows they are), then it is clear enough that death has deprived him of nothing whatever—except the capacity to feel pain and to suffer.[132]

Apparently, Cicero believed his client, the defendant, should be rewarded for the murder instead of punished.

Epicureanism and Stoicism are often portrayed as opposites, but they had much in common, and each discounted an afterlife. They proposed that the gods, if they existed, weren't concerned about human affairs. Both philosophies espoused that living a virtuous life was the sole end for man. Epicureanism emphasized the enjoyment of the simple pleasures of life; Stoicism emphasized that a virtuous man calmly accepted the vicissitudes of life and was neither lifted nor diminished by extraneous events. In their purest forms, Epicureanism and Stoicism aimed to encourage rationalism, the simple virtues, and intellectual pursuit. In any case the practices, viewpoints, and attitudes that arose from deviant interpretations of these philosophies undermined the simple assumptions of Roman religion, customs, and values that had been so important to early Rome's character and strength. The culture of Roman elites evolved from one obsessed with appeasing the gods to one that adopted materialistic explanations for the universe, bringing about deep and far-reaching consequences for their society.

---

[132] Cicero, "Cluentius," in *Murder Trials*, trans. Michael Grant (New York: Dorset Press, 1975).

CHAPTER 13

The Jugurthine War

WITH THE DEFEAT OF the Gracchi brothers, the *optimates* coalesced, and for a time domestic stability was restored. However, the conflict was far from over. New *populare* leaders emerged to revive the Gracchan revolution, and they would be opposed by a new cadre of *optimate* leaders. As was usual in Roman politics, the new leaders came from the military ranks, and the military campaigns produced a new generation of capable and prominent men from both sides of the political spectrum.

North Africa presented the Romans with both military and political challenges. The Romans directly controlled their province of North Africa, an area in and around modern Tunisia, and they indirectly controlled the adjacent kingdom of Numidia as a protectorate situated in modern Algeria. The Numidian people were descendants of Persians who centuries earlier had migrated to North Africa. As Sallust related, "The Persians' state soon developed, and later, now with the name Numidians, they left their parents on account of their large numbers and took possession of the area closest to Carthage, which is called Numidia." The Numidian king Micipsa was the son of Masinissa, the great ally of Scipio Africanus in the war against Hannibal.

Micipsa bequeathed that upon his death his kingdom should be divided equally between his two natural sons, Hiempsal and Adherbal, and his adopted son, Jugurtha. The latter was an incomparable horseman and soldier known as the "lion of the desert." Jugurtha had served brilliantly as an ally of Rome in Spain and had developed relationships with many senators and generals. When the king died in 118 BC, the princes agreed to divide the kingdom in three parts, but Jugurtha arranged the assassination of Hiempsal and instigated a war with Adherbal. After Jugurtha defeated Adherbal in a decisive battle, the latter fled to Rome and petitioned the Senate to intercede. A senatorial commission sent to Numidia brokered a compromise, partitioning the nation between Jugurtha and Adherbal. At first, Jugurtha agreed but then invaded his brother's territory and surrounded Adherbal in the capital city of Cirta (modern Constantine), placing the city under siege. Residents of Cirta, including Roman and Italian businessmen who defended the city, convinced Adherbal to surrender himself alone. They expected that their association with Rome would protect them from Jugurtha; however, when Adherbal surrendered, Jugurtha tortured and executed him, and he ordered the executions of Roman and Italian businessmen in the city.

Jugurtha assumed the throne of Numidia for himself, and Rome faced a dilemma—although many senators supported Jugurtha, he had violated an agreement Rome guaranteed. The Senate, after debating the issue and considering the massacre of the merchants, decided against Jugurtha and sent the legions under the command of L. Bestia Calpurnius to Numidia. As the legions assembled a campaign, Jugurtha began bargaining for a peace treaty, and he allegedly bribed Calpurnius and other generals to delay the military action and accept his surrender on extremely lenient terms. He handed over silver, elephants, horses, and cattle. With that, peace was restored, and Jugurtha remained in power.

In Rome, the alleged bribery became known. Gaius Memmius, a fierce *populare* tribune of the people, denounced the pseudo-surrender and the bribe takers, whom he associated with the oligarchs who had killed the Gracchi.

Memmius's brilliant and powerful speeches inflamed the populace. One of his speeches was especially vitriolic.

> But who are they who have seized upon our country?
> Men stained with crime, with gory hands, of monstrous
> greed, guilty, yet at the same time full of pride, who have

made honor, reputation, loyalty, in short everything honorable and dishonorable, a source of gain. Some of them are safeguarded by having slain tribunes of the commons, others by unjust prosecutions, many by having shed your blood. Thus the more atrocious the conduct, the greater the safety ... But if your love of freedom were as great as the thirst for tyranny which spurs them on, surely our country would not be torn asunder as it now is, and your favors would be bestowed on the most virtuous, not on the most reckless ...

Let those who have betrayed their country to the enemy be punished, not by arms or violence ... but by the courts and Jugurtha's own testimony ...

For my own part, although I consider it most shameful for a true man to suffer wrong without taking vengeance, yet I could willingly allow you to pardon those most criminal of men, since they are your fellow citizens, were it not that mercy would end in destruction. For such is their insolence they are not satisfied to have done evil with impunity ...

I warn and implore you not to let such wickedness go unscathed. It is not a matter of plundering the treasury or of extorting money from our allies—serious crimes, it is true, but so common nowadays as to be disregarded. Nay, the senate's dignity has been prostituted to a ruthless enemy, your sovereignty has been betrayed, your country has been offered for sale at home and abroad. Unless cognizance is taken of these outrages, unless the guilty are punished, what will remain except to pass our lives in submission to those who are guilty of these acts? For to do with impunity whatever one fancies is to be a king. I am not urging you, Romans, to rejoice rather in the guilt than in the innocence of your fellow citizens; but you should not insist upon ruining the good by pardoning the wicked. Moreover, in a republic it is far better to forget a kindness than an injury. The good man merely becomes less active in well doing when you neglect him, but the bad man grows more wicked.[133]

Memmius summoned Jugurtha to Rome under safe conduct to testify at a hearing in the Senate to investigate the alleged bribery and the mismanagement of the war. At the hearing Memmius tried to get Jugurtha to identify any Romans he had bribed, but another tribune, who may himself have been bribed, ordered Jugurtha to remain silent, and the hearing adjourned without a resolution. When Jugurtha returned to Africa, he renewed his aggressions against Roman interests and reportedly remarked about Rome, "It was a city for sale and soon to be doomed—if only it found a buyer."

In 109 BC, the Senate sent the consul Spurius Albinus to Africa. He mounted a military campaign, but when he returned to Rome to conduct elections, he left his son Aulus Albinus, a propraetor, in charge. Aulus foolishly attacked the city of Suthul, a stronghold of Jugurtha. The Romans were surrounded, starved, and defeated. Jugurtha offered terms for surrender: If Aulus agreed to a peace treaty, Jugurtha would leave the Roman troops unscathed. However, they would have to walk in humiliation under the symbolic yoke of spears, and they would also have to withdraw from Numidia within ten days. Aulus accepted.

Hearing this crushing news was the last straw for the Roman people. The tribunes empaneled the Mamilian commission to investigate the bribery allegations and the conduct of the generals, and the Senate sent the new consul, Quintus Caecilius Metellus, to take charge of the army in North Africa.

Metellus was of the Metelli, the familia fast replacing the Scipiones as Rome's most powerful faction. Like his grandfather of the same name who had conquered Macedon, Metellus proved to be a highly competent and incorruptible general. He instituted a strict regimen of discipline, restored morale, won several difficult battles, captured Cirta, and implemented a

---

[133] Sallust, *The War with Jugurtha* (Cambridge, Ma.: Harvard University Press) 31, 22-29.

steady course to victory. Based on his progress, the Senate renewed his command for another year. When Metellus defeated Jugurtha's army in a major battle at the Muthul River, Jugurtha fled but continued to engage in guerilla warfare. He set numerous ambushes, but the Romans avoided or overcame them. At points when Jugurtha's fortunes were low, he offered terms of surrender, most likely as a stalling tactic. Sallust described, "During these activities Jugurtha was simply more unstinting, sending legates in supplication, begging for peace, surrendering everything to Metellus apart from the lives of himself and his children." But when the time came to surrender, he changed his mind and resorted to guerilla warfare again. Meanwhile, Metellus, by sure and steady management of his campaign, had gained control of Numidia, and it was inevitable that he would capture Jugurtha. In Rome his accomplishments were applauded.

Glory invites envy, and Metellus was envied. His legate, Gaius Marius, a new man of Volscian ancestry, born at Arpinum in the Apennine Mountains, was a soldier's soldier whose bravery and exploits earned him the respect of the troops. He was wounded several times, and on one occasion, while a doctor treated him for a battlefield wound, he famously remarked, "I see the cure is worse than the pain."

Ironically, Marius had received the appointment as Metellus's legate despite having betrayed the Metelli ten years earlier. In 119 BC, with Metelli support he had been elected as a tribune of the plebs but promptly turned on his patrons by advocating for a bill they opposed. Moreover, he threatened to arrest the consuls who blocked the measure. But times had changed, and since that conflict, he had married into the patrician Julian family, marrying Julia, the aunt of Julius Caesar. The Metelli, apparently thinking Marius had renewed his allegiance to the patricians, supported him again. Now, serving as second-in-command to Metellus and riding a wave of popularity among the troops, Marius decided to run for consul. He asked for permission to leave camp and return to Rome to do so, but Metellus, surprised by the request, denied it. This act affronted Marius, who began spreading word that Metellus was purposely protracting the war. He claimed that were he appointed to replace him, he could end the war sooner. Metellus realized that a discontented legate, at odds with his commander, was of little value to the army, so he agreed to the furlough.

Although Metellus may have been surprised by Marius's ambition, others wouldn't have been. Sallust wrote, "Even before this Marius had been possessed with a mighty longing for the consulship, for which he had in abundance every qualification except an ancient lineage; namely, diligence, honesty, great military skill, and a spirit that was mighty in war, unambitious in peace, which arose superior to passion and the lure of riches, and was greedy only for glory."[134]

Marius presented himself as an avenger for the common soldier, soliciting approval from the larger body of citizens by disparaging the nobles. As Plutarch described, he made

> boldly insolent and arrogant speeches with which he vexed the nobles, crying out that he had carried off the consulship as spoil from the effeminacy of the rich and well-born, and that he had wounds upon his own person with which to vaunt himself before the people, not monuments of the dead nor likenesses of other men ... Such talk was not mere empty boasting, nor was his desire to make himself hated by the nobility without purpose; indeed the people, who were delighted to have the Senate insulted and always measured the greatness of a man's spirit by the boastfulness of his speech, encouraged him, and incited him not to spare men of high repute if he wished to please the multitude.[135]

The Senate didn't condone Marius's candidacy, but his supporters mounted an aggressive election campaign, attacking Metellus and praising Marius. Sallust wrote, "The general's noble rank, which before had been an honor to him, became a source of unpopularity, while to Marius his humble origin lent increased favor; but in the case of both men their own good or bad qualities had less influence than party spirit. More than this, seditious magistrates were working upon the feelings of the populace,

---

[134] Sallust, 31, 22–29, tr. Rolfe.
[135] Plutarch, "Life of Marius," in *Lives*.

in every assembly charging Metellus with treason and exaggerating the merits of Marius."[136]

Marius gained public support, and the assembly elected him consul in 107 BC. Overriding the Senate, the assembly sent him to replace Metellus in North Africa.

Metellus refused to meet Marius. He believed he was on the verge of winning the war and that Marius would snatch victory from his grasp. Beyond the personal insult, Marius's election and assignment by the assembly was an affront to the *optimates* and an abrogation of senatorial power, which further exacerbated the internecine conflicts within the state.

As the new commander in North Africa, Marius was unable to effectively defeat Jugurtha and the Numidians. Fortunately for Marius, he had under his command an extraordinarily capable and shrewd quaestor, Lucius Cornelius Sulla, a patrician from the Cornelian clan. Sulla was an unusually tall Roman with red hair who quite correctly believed he was destined for great achievements.

Sometimes chance and treachery will accomplish what force cannot. While Marius was away from his main camp to conduct a siege and Sulla was left in charge, envoys from Jugurtha's ally, King Bocchus of Mauretania, appeared at the camp to invite Sulla to visit the king. This might have been a trap, but Sulla, seeing an opportunity, went nevertheless. With only a small escort, he traveled to the king's residence where he convinced the king to set a trap for Jugurtha. The king agreed and lured Jugurtha to a meeting, captured him, and turned him over to Sulla. This move effectively ended the war.

Sulla took his prisoner to Marius, who, as consul in 104 BC, brought Jugurtha to Rome in chains, displayed him in a triumphal parade, and had him executed. Although Sulla had engineered the capture, Marius reaped the bulk of the credit, planting a seed of resentment that began a lifelong feud between them. It was one of many feuds for Marius, who had already made an enemy of his former superior, Metellus, and now an enemy of his subordinate, Sulla.

---

[136] Sallust, *War with Jugurtha*, 73.

The war with Jugurtha was over, but its consequences would be far reaching. It would generate prosecutions for bribery and incompetence, exacerbating the growing partisan divide between *populares* and *optimates*, which would eventually undermine the cohesiveness of the republic. Sallust pointed to the war as an important turning point in Roman politics. He wrote, "I will write of the war the people of Rome fought with Jugurtha, king of the Numidians: first, because it was great, fierce, and with varying fortunes; but also then for the first time there was resistance to the arrogance of the *nobilitus*—a contest which confused everything, human and divine, and reached such senselessness that political divisions resulted in war and the devastation of Italy."[137]

During and after the war, various factions accused each other of corruption, incompetence, and disloyalty. Investigations and prosecutions poisoned the political atmosphere, protests and riots erupted, and the cultural divide expanded, which wasn't unlike that of the United States two millenniums later during the Vietnam War era.

Infighting within factions bred more uncertainty and distrust. The people's tribune, Gaius Memmius, who had exposed the wartime bribery, was assassinated—not by the oligarchy but by his own side. Other assassinations followed, and internal conflicts escalated, each bringing Rome closer to civil war.

---

[137] Sallust, 3.

CHAPTER 14

Marius and Sulla

GAIUS MARIUS SERVED SEVEN terms as consul, the first in 107 BC, then five consecutive terms from 104 to 100 BC, then the last in 86 BC, which he illegitimately seized by force. During his consecutive consulships, he led armies against the fearsome Cimbri and Teutonic warrior tribes, which were migrating to Northern Italy with their wives, children, and livestock. Although outnumbered by these enormous tribes, he defeated both in separate battles. His victories were largely due to his reorganization of the army in several practical ways. First, he improved its mobility and effectiveness by doing away with long baggage trains and by having the troops carry their own equipment and rations; thus, his troops became known as "Marius' Mules." Second, he modified the throwing spear by replacing the metal rivets holding the spearhead to the shaft with wooden pins so the pin broke on impact if it struck a shield, making the spear useless for throwing back. Third, young, inexperienced aristocrats were no longer made regimental officers but were relegated to assistant positions. Regiments would be led only by battle-tested officers from whatever class.

The most significant part of his reorganization later proved costly. Marius broke the customary rules for military service, ignored property requirements, and replaced the volunteer citizen soldiers with mercenary soldiers from the poorest classes. Thus, the army transitioned from a citizen's militia to a mercenary force. Although seemingly expedient, his reforms led to an army infiltrated by self-interested soldiers whose loyalty to their generals took precedence over loyalty to either the Senate or the nation. His soldiers, without land or assets, had every reason to stay in the legions where they saw the potential for plunder and reward. Upon completion of their service, they demanded land allotments and weren't reticent to threaten disruption or violence to get them.

Marius's reforms affected not only the complement of the army but also the political balance. From then on, the character of the legions changed, making them malleable for the political ambitions of their generals. As a consequence, daring, unscrupulous, and ambitious commanders, not tradition-minded nobles, wielded the most power within the republic. In alliance with aggressive tribunes, they cast aside the customary parameters of the republic and abandoned its checks-and-balances system.

While the military victories of Marius were crucial to Rome, his consecutive terms as consul abrogated customary law, and they further diminished the Senate's authority. Marius strengthened his political position by an alliance with Lucius Appuleius Saturninus, an aggressive and radical tribune, who held office from 103 to 100 BC and frequently resorted to mob violence to intimidate his adversaries. He championed populist causes and asserted the preeminent powers of the assembly over the Senate. For Marius, although the alliance politically strengthened him, it eventually dishonored his military record, undermined his popularity, and brought him new enemies.

Saturninus, for his own reasons, sponsored the *Lex Appuleia* (100 BC), which redefined treason as any act "damaging the greatness of the Roman People" or *maiestas laesa*. This overbroad and vague statute, with its inadequate definition of what would constitute damaging the *maiestas* of the Roman people, opened the door to arbitrary and politically motivated prosecutions. Originally sold as a means to hold incompetent generals accountable (such as those in the early war against Jugurtha), the statute was quickly applied to political disputes and accusations. One example was the prosecution of Quintus Caecilius Metellus, the enemy of Marius from the Jugurthine War. Saturninus charged Metellus with failing to swear to uphold a measure to distribute land in Gaul to Marius's veterans and thus forced him into exile.[138]

---

[138] Appian, *Civil Wars*, bk. 1.4.29–31.

In return, Marius supported the tribune's populist programs, including the renewal of Gaius Gracchus's overseas colonization plan and his grain distribution program for the urban population. Saturninus enacted these programs, as he had done to Metellus, by threatening senators with exile if they didn't swear to uphold his law and by using street thugs to intimidate his adversaries.

In a short time, however, the people turned against Saturninus when his thugs killed Gaius Memmius, the popular tribune who had famously railed against corruption during the Jugurthine War. The Senate responded by declaring a senatus consultum ultimum, which ordered Marius to protect the state. This was a pivotal moment in Roman history. Marius had benefited greatly from his alliance with Saturninus, but now the nobility was calling on him to act. Memmius's friends wanted revenge, and the equestrians wanted an end to the turmoil. Marius decided against Saturninus. He raised an army from among his veterans and surrounded Saturninus and his supporters inside the city. Saturninus evidently believed his prior relationship with Marius would hold him in good stead, and he surrendered on Marius's promise of fair treatment. To his surprise, he and his aides were quickly thrown into prison and executed without trials.

Marius's betrayal of his former ally cast him as a man whose word couldn't be trusted. *Populares* turned against him, and *optimates* still distrusted him; consequently, he chose not to run for consul again and left Rome. So with Marius discredited and Saturninus dead, *optimate* consuls were elected. Metellus was recalled from exile, senatorial power was restored, and the potential for civil war was abated. However, the Senate's failure to assent to reforms augured ill for the future.

ITALIAN SOCIAL WAR

Ten years later, the republic faced another existential threat when a coalition of Italian allies demanded changes in their status. Some, notably the Samnites, wanted complete freedom from their obligations to Rome; others wanted full Roman citizenship. Both groups protested that the Gracchan agrarian reforms unfairly dispossessed Italians from lands they had lived on for generations, and they protested the constant levies for military service. Italian veterans who had fought side by side with Romans wanted land grants equal to those of the Roman veterans. Italian businessmen, who had extended their interests throughout the provinces, wanted citizenship to protect their interests in the courts and influence foreign policy. Italian aristocrats and landowners had seen Marius rise from merely a second-generation Roman family to consecutive consulships; with citizenship, their families could also rise to become Roman elites.

In 91 BC, Marcus Livius Drusus the Younger, a Roman tribune, became the champion of the Italian coalition as well as an advocate for land and judicial reforms. He had been well schooled in political infighting since he was the son of Marcus Livius Drusus, tribune of 122 BC, who had helped to defeat Gaius Gracchus. He enjoyed being in the midst of controversy and was quite sure of himself. Reputedly, he asked, "When will Rome ever see my like again?"[139]

As for his political astuteness, he was exactly right. He knew the Italians had reached the boiling point and that their landless veterans had to be accommodated. He argued in the Senate and the assembly that the Italian allies had supplied the troops to fight with Rome against Jugurtha, the Teutons, and the Cimbri; they therefore deserved full citizenship.

Public debate on the issue was intense. Rumors circulated that the Italians had pledged themselves to be clients of Drusus. In response, an odd coalition of the most conservative *optimates* together with the urban lower classes opposed his call for Italian enfranchisement. Both groups saw the prospect of large numbers of new citizens eligible to vote in the assemblies as diluting their power. Drusus won over the *optimates* by pledging to assign the Italians to only five of the thirty-five tribes, and only those in the urban area, so their voting power would be limited.

While the Italian coalition of allies waited for the outcome of the citizenship vote, they made preparations for war in the event that their demands weren't met. The catalyst occurred in 90 BC when unidentified assailants assassinated Drusus. His death ignited a full-scale Italian rebellion. The Italians formed a federation, established a capital at Corfinum, and assembled a formidable military force, equal in fighting capacity to

---

[139] Velleius Paterculus, *Compendium of Roman History*, 2.14.2.

the Romans, since their soldiers had previously trained and fought with the legions. Three years of war followed, spreading throughout Central and Southern Italy. It became immediately apparent that the Italians were more than a match for the Romans; they won several hard-fought battles. Then, when Marius took command in the north and Sulla in the south, the Romans began to win battles. In 89 BC, Sulla led a lightning campaign against the Samnites, drove them out of Campania, and stormed their city of Bovianum, defeating them decisively.

On the basis of his victories, Sulla was elected consul in 88 BC, but the war continued, depleting the treasuries of both sides and leaving both Italy and Rome desolate. Prudently, the Romans made concessions, agreeing to confer Roman citizenship on all Italians who had remained loyal and on any of the rebels who put down their arms. This concession surfeited most of the Italians and weakened the impetus of the rebellion, which gradually came to an end. Italians south of the River Po gained full citizenship with constitutional protections against arbitrary Roman army officers or magistrates, the right to vote in the assemblies, the right to hold office, and access to the courts.

With this widespread grant of citizenship, Rome was transformed from a city-state into an Italian nation but a nation difficult to administer because its soldiers had become accustomed to fighting against one another, and full citizenship didn't preclude new partisan disputes. Though the Italians could vote, their voting power was limited to the five urban tribes. They protested, and a *populare* tribune, Publius Sulpicius Rufus, a friend of the deceased Drusus, championed their cause. He saw an opportunity to oust the *optimates* and nullify senatorial power. A persuasive orator, Sulpicius was an aggressive and ambitious demagogue who used social unrest to his advantage. Combining his support from the Italians with his support from equestrians and urban street gangs, he organized an anti-senatorial coalition and introduced laws that would strengthen the voting power of the newly enfranchised Italians. Rather than assigning them to the five urban tribes, where their votes would be minimized, he proposed distributing them to all thirty-five tribes, where their votes would overwhelm the senatorial powerbase outside the city and create a conflict between the new voters and preexisting ones.

The *optimates* adamantly opposed Sulpicius, and the consuls Quintius Pompeius and Sulla delayed the vote. Escalating violence soon followed. To protect himself and avoid the fate of the Gracchi, Saturninus, Drusus, and others, Sulpicius surrounded himself with a bodyguard of six hundred young men he called his anti-senate. Needing additional support and protection, Sulpicius enlisted the aid of Marius, the former consul and war hero, older now but still seeking power and glory. Marius agreed to support Sulpicius in exchange for command of the war against Mithridates, the king of Pontus, a country situated on the Black Sea in the northeast of Anatolia (modern Turkey).

MITHRIDATES

Mithridates claimed to be a descendant of Darius I, the Persian king, and Alexander the Great. He presented himself as the restorer of the combined greatness of the Greek and Persian empires, and the savior who would free the East from Roman oppression. He was incredibly ruthless; during his life, he killed his mother, brother, sister-wife, and children. Unusually tall with a massive, robust physique; he was a great horseman and chariot racer and also a master of botany, poisons, and antidotes. A. E. Housman immortalized him this way:

> There was a king reigned in the East:
> There, when kings will sit to feast,
> They get their fill before they think
> With poisoned meat and poisoned drink.
> He gathered all that springs to birth
> From the many-venomed earth;
> First a little, thence to more,
> He sampled all her killing store;
> And easy, smiling, seasoned sound,
> Sate the king when healths went round.
> They put arsenic in his meat
> And stared aghast to watch him eat;
> They poured strychnine in his cup

And shook to see him drink it up:
They shook, they stared as white's their shirt:
Them it was their poison hurt—
I tell the tale that I heard told.
Mithridates he died old.[140]

Mithridates died old but not before he spread death and destruction. Influential in the territories around the Black Sea, with close allies in Armenia and Scythia, he systematically began taking control of Anatolia and the Aegean Islands from potentates Rome supported.

Through political intrigue, poisonings, and military threats, he tried to annex Cappadocia, Bithynia, Paphlagonia, and Galatia but retreated when Rome ordered him to do so. He bided his time until 89 BC when, in the First Mithridatic War, he defeated a Roman army in Bithynian and openly proclaimed his intention to drive Rome out of Anatolia and Greece.

In those regions, large numbers of Roman and Italian merchants, moneylenders, slave dealers, tax collectors, and shopkeepers had settled and mingled with the native populations to conduct trade and business. They were the object of enmity because the local populations resented Roman dominance and the exorbitant taxes paid to Rome. Mithridates encouraged hatred of them with a widespread propaganda campaign, in which he repeated the motto "Romans, the common enemy of mankind," counteracting Rome's portrayal of itself as "the common benefactor of mankind."

In 88 BC, as the Social War, or war of the allies, divided Rome, Mithridates launched the greatest surprise attack against a civilian population in history. Determined to drive Rome out of the East, he concocted an elaborate terrorist plot to execute all the Latin-speaking people in the region in a single day. When he gave the word, the local populations rounded up the Romans and Italians and killed them all by whatever means was convenient. Cities, such as Pergamon, the capital of Rome's Asia province, and Ephesus, where many Latins had settled, saw massive

---

[140] A. E. Housman, "Terence, This Stupid Stuff," *Shropshire Lad.*

slaughter. Reportedly, in one day eighty thousand people were massacred, including women and children.

Mithridates followed up by sending armies into Greece to take control of Athens and the Aegean; in addition, his army slaughtered all the Romans and Italians on the Island of Delos in the Aegean Sea, about twenty thousand persons.

POLITICS IN THE FORUM

For Rome, not only did justice call for vengeance, but if its growing empire was to stay intact, retaliation was imperative. Marius wanted to lead the legions to the East, but he would have been a poor choice; at seventy years old, he wasn't in the physical condition for what certainly would be an arduous campaign against the formidable king. The Senate chose Sulla, the consul in 88 BC, as the best commander for the war. At fifty years of age, he was in the prime of his career, one that had followed the traditional path of honor. After serving admirably during the Jugurthine War and capturing Jugurtha, he commanded superlatively in Gaul against the Germans, in Spain against recalcitrant tribes, and against the Samnites in the Social War. An adversary described him as "cunning as a fox and brave as a lion."

The assignment of Sulla to fight Mithridates was a straightforward military decision, but Sulpicius needed a way to replace Sulla with Marius, so he demanded that Sulla and the other consul, Quintus Pompeius Rufus, proceed with a vote to redistribute the new Italian citizens to all thirty-five voting tribes. When the consuls refused, Sulpicius's thugs threatened them and their supporters with daggers. Pompeius Rufus went into hiding in the city while his son, also Sulla's son-in-law, was stabbed to death. Then Sulpicius had the assembly depose Pompeius Rufus from the consulship. Tribunes had deposed other tribunes before but never a sitting consul.

Sulla evaded the assassins, then under threat, agreed to support the pro-Italian legislation in exchange for continuing as consul. No mention was made of his command against Mithridates. He immediately went to Capua to take command of the five legions waiting to embark to the East. These legions included many of his loyal veterans from the Social War. At the same time, Sulpicius used Sulla's absence to uphold his bargain with Marius. He passed a law in the assembly, rescinding the Senate's assignment of Sulla to the eastern command and giving the command to Marius. It was another act in violation of Rome's constitutional system, comparable to the US House of Representatives firing and replacing a four-star general whom the president had commissioned and the Senate had confirmed. With mobs in the streets threatening anyone who opposed Sulpicius, Rome was in chaos.

A messenger was sent to Sulla with an order relieving him of his command. Sulla did not take it lightly. Not only did he see his dismissal as a violation of traditional order and the constitution, but he also saw the eastern command as his right and his chance for the fame and glory that drove Roman nobles. For years, he had been in the shadow of Marius; he was the unrecognized hero of the victory over Jugurtha, and he resented Marius for taking all the credit; he had been the most effective commander in the Social War, but Marius proclaimed himself the victor. Sulla wouldn't stand by while the aged Marius took over his command. He refused to accept his dismissal, and, joined by the deposed Pompeius Rufus, he marched on Rome with his legions. For the first time, a Roman army marched to Rome, not to protect it from external enemies but to free it from internal tyrants.

Waiting in Rome for the attack, Sulpicius had the assembly declare Sulla an enemy of the people while Marius put to death many of Sulla's supporters. Marius called for recruits and proclaimed freedom to slaves who would fight on his side, but his calls were largely ignored. With limited troops, Marius couldn't stop Sulla's army from taking the center of the city. Marius fled, and with the tables turned, Sulla had the Senate declare both Marius and Sulpicius enemies of the people. Sulpicius was captured and put to death; Marius escaped to North Africa. At this juncture, though he surely could have, Sulla chose not to seize absolute power for himself. He had never sought power by becoming a mob leader who bribed the masses with promises of free grain or land. He favored the traditional form of Roman government, led by established leaders from noble families who had proved themselves as military commanders and who took turns in the consulship and other magistracies. With temporary peace restored, Sulla modified the arbitrary and overbroad *maiestas* law of Saturninus, and he repealed the voting law of Sulpicius. Most significantly, he reduced the power of the tribunes and reinstituted the customary constitutional provision that bills required Senate approval before they could be submitted to the assembly.

Sulla held elections for new consuls. Lucius Cornelius Cinna, a *populare*, and Cornelius Octavius, an *optimate*, were elected as coconsuls in 87 BC. Although Sulla could have imposed his will and picked his successor, and even though Cinna was a political opponent, he accepted the results of the election. He did so upon extracting a solemn oath from Cinna in the Temple of Jupiter that his reforms would be left intact and because he expected that the coconsul, Cornelius Octavius, an *optimate*, would uphold his laws. Eager to confront Mithridates, Sulla led his legions across the Adriatic Sea. As soon as he did, Cinna betrayed his solemn oath, and civil war began again.

CHAPTER 15

Cinna Revolts: War between the Consuls

LUCIUS CORNELIUS CINNA WAS a patrician from an obscure branch of the Cornelian *gens*. Little is known about his early history other than that he fought as a legate in the Social War. It may be that he was an average person thrust by critical events into a leadership role, elected as consul because of his availability and because he vowed to maintain the status quo and Sulla's reforms. However, as soon as Sulla took his five legions across the Adriatic to invade Greece, Cinna revived the voting proposals of Sulpicius that Sulla had nullified, and he threatened to prosecute Sulla. His coconsul, Octavius, protested; and full-scale street battles erupted in the city. For the first time in the history of Roman civil conflicts, coconsuls warred against one another, with thousands of lives lost. Octavius gained the upper hand, forced Cinna to flee the city, and declared him an enemy of the people. Under this existential threat, Cinna invited Marius to return to Rome and share power with him, a pivotal decision that would cause events to spin out of control.

Marius returned from North Africa with an army that included mercenaries and slaves. He captured the port city of Ostia and cut off Rome's grain supply. His forces put Rome under siege, and with Rome facing starvation, the Senate arranged a peace treaty. Cinna and Marius were invited to enter the city, and Cinna resumed his consulship.

Once in control of the city, Cinna and Marius disregarded the peace treaty and sent their forces to hunt down opposition leaders. Marius, acting in a half-crazed manner, ordered his forces to systematically murder citizens who had supported Sulla. They killed Octavius as he sat in his consular chair, cut off his head, and delivered it to Cinna. Cinna declared Sulla an outlaw and enemy of the people, and he repealed his laws.

According to Appian, "All of Sulla's friends were put to death; his home was razed to the ground; his property confiscated; and himself made a public enemy. A search was made for his wife and children, but they had already escaped."[141]

The political murders of 87 BC foreshadowed the worst years of the French Revolution. Appian recounted,

> Now the victors sent out spies to search for their enemies in the senatorial and equestrians orders. When any knights were killed no further attention was paid to them, but all the heads of senators were exposed in front of the rostra. Neither reverence for the gods, nor the indignation of men, nor the fear of odium for their acts existed any longer among them. After committing savage deeds they turned to godless sights. They killed remorselessly and severed the necks of men already dead, and they paraded these horrors before the public eye, either to inspire fear and terror, or for a godless spectacle.[142]

Without holding an election, Cinna and Marius declared themselves consuls in 86 BC. No one opposed them, and the reign of terror continued. Marius took revenge on anyone who had opposed him over his career, especially on those whom he believed had caused him to flee in humiliation from the city he had saved with so many military victories. He exercised his hatred ruthlessly, butchering members of the most distinguished families of Rome, including former consuls and sitting senators. The Metelli faction was decimated as Marius and Cinna displayed no moderation. Sham charges were brought against the ex-consul Quintus Lutatius

---

[141] Appian, *Civil Wars*, bk. 1.73.
[142] Appian., bk. 1.71.

Catulus (149–87 BC). His relatives and friends appealed to Marius but to no avail, and Catulus committed suicide. Marius also had Lucius Crassus, the father of the future triumvir, murdered.

A tribune of the plebs, Sextius Lucilius, had opposed the actions of Marius and Cinna. He was unmolested in 87 BC, but when his inviolability expired in 86 BC, he was thrown to his death from the Tarpeian Rock in a revival of a long-abandoned practice.

How could a madman such as Marius have convinced his followers to commit such atrocities? It was a mix of envy and greed. By proscribing or outlawing wealthy victims on trumped-up charges, the murderers would share the victim's property. The bloodbath lasted until 86 BC, when Marius died—some sources say of a mental breakdown.

F. R. Cowell described the rule of Marius and Cinna.

> With a cold brutality new in Roman public life, they murdered the leading men of the Senate and of the governing class. From this appalling slaughter the Senate never recovered. The oldest, most eminent and most experienced of the traditional rulers of Rome disappeared in a blood-bath of revolting horror. Among them was Q. Mucius Scaevola, *Pontifex Maximus* and holder therefore of a most sacred office ... None but the lesser men, with some fortunate exceptions, remained. The weakness of the Senate as a political force in Cicero's lifetime must be attributed in part to the work of the butcher Marius and his accomplices.[143]

With Marius dead, Cinna remained as consul but ruled as a de facto military dictator. Some scholars point to the moderation of these post-Marian years, but he had already countenanced the executions of six *consulares*, the *pontifex maximus*, and other prominent nobles. Any Cinnan moderation or reconciliation was of necessity; he needed the cooperation of the remaining factions. To cement cooperation, he arranged marriages

---

[143] F.R.Cowell, *Cicero and the Roman Republic* (London: Pittman, 1948) 167.

to establish alliances; one of his daughters went to the up-and-coming Gaius Julius Caesar of the Julian clan. Regarding Italian citizenship, he was cautious. Although he had promised to extend the franchise, he didn't want to alienate the urban citizenry by overwhelming the assemblies with masses of new voters, so he had the censors only gradually add Italians to the citizenship rolls.

A major problem for Cinna was that the wars in the East and domestic turmoil in Italy had disrupted commerce and drained the treasury. As businessmen faced ruin, creditors called in loans. Cash was withdrawn from circulation; panic and hoarding followed. Cinna's response was to pass radical legislation that remitted three-quarters of all outstanding debt. This legislation helped debtors but destroyed many creditors and devastated the economy. Social unrest was rampant, and as Cinna's government teetered, *optimates* urged Sulla to return to Rome to restore order.

In the meantime, Sulla retook Athens from Mithridates after a long, arduous siege, and with his battle-hardened army of about forty thousand, he destroyed two much larger Mithridatic armies in ferocious battles at Chaeronea and Orchomenus on the plains of Attica. Sulla's army was smaller, but it was cohesive, while Mithridates's army was composed of soldiers from diverse nations and cultures, with different languages and dialects that were unintelligible to one another. They had different styles of fighting, and most had never fought together before; thus, they presented problems of discipline and coordination.

Sulla led his troops from the front. At the Battle of Orchomenus, at a point where the Romans were being overwhelmed by enemy cavalry and beginning to panic and flee, Sulla jumped from his horse, grabbed a standard, and ran to the forefront of his lines, shouting, "Romans, I'll win an honorable death here without you! When they ask where you betrayed your commander, you'll have to tell them about Orchomenus!" Of course, the Romans rallied and won the battle.

Mithridates, in the tradition of Persian kings, didn't engage in battle but left it to his generals. At his headquarters in the fortress at Pergamon, he heard the news of his losses and sent ambassadors to Sulla to seek peace.

Sulla had gained the momentum, but the campaign had lasted three years; and because of the problems back in Rome, he didn't have the time to completely finish the king. In 85 BC, Sulla met with Mithridates on the plain of Dardanus near the ruins of Troy to sign a peace treaty. According to Appian and Plutarch, Mithridates arrived with twenty thousand infantry and six thousand cavalry; Sulla had only one thousand infantry and two hundred cavalry. The two leaders met in front of their soldiers. Mithridates remained silent, but Sulla said, "Surely, it is the victor who has the right of silence, while a suppliant should ask forgiveness!" Mithridates began recounting the wrongs done to him, but Sulla cut him off and demanded to know whether he agreed to the peace terms that had been tentatively worked out. After some back-and-forth for the benefit of the audience, Mithridates agreed. Considering the carnage Mithridates had wrought, the terms were lenient—he had only to withdraw to his kingdom, dismantle part of his navy, and pay an indemnity.

Sulla Returns

In 83 BC, Sulla returned to Italy and for the second time marched toward Rome. He was joined by a host of nobles, who had raised troops from among their tenants and clients, including twenty-three-year-old Gnaeus Pompey, whose father had died while fighting the Marians; Marcus Licinius Crassus, whose father had been slain by the Marians; and Quintus Caecilius Metellus Pius, the son of Caecilius Metellus Numidicus, the longtime enemy of Marius from the Jugurthine War. As Sulla moved toward the city, he sent word that he wouldn't repeal the voting rights of the Italians; thus, he undercut opposition from that quarter.

Defections of several of their troop contingents to Sulla's side had weakened the Cinnan-Marian factions; in fact, Cinna had been stoned and stabbed to death in a mutiny by his own soldiers. His coconsul, Papirius Carbo, took sole command. Short on soldiers, he enlisted the support of a Samnite army to defend Rome. Ultimately, several battles were fought between a *populare* army augmented by the Samnites, totaling one hundred thousand, and Sulla's forty thousand well-seasoned and loyal troops. A year of fighting culminated at the Battle of the Colline Gate at Rome, where Sulla's troops destroyed the *populare* and Samnite coalition and slaughtered all the Samnite fighters, even the captives.

It seemed that the Cinnan-Marian *populare* faction was finally crushed, and Sulla, with a bodyguard of ten thousand known as "the Cornelii," took control of the city and government. In light of Cinna's betrayal of his oath, Sulla was distrustful of successors and had the *comitia centuriata* appoint him as dictator for an indefinite term. To his mind, the Senate had proved ineffective in containing the outrages of Marius and Cinna, and the state of affairs necessitated emergency measures. He would have to restore order and stability himself.

To purge the city of those he considered traitors; and to exact justice on behalf of the nobles who had been murdered or driven from their lands, he published proscription lists, announcing the names of those to be executed. To keep within the law, he had the assembly pass laws ratifying the death warrants. In this way, he was not acting outside the law; therefore, he wouldn't be subject to a subsequent prosecution for unlawfully executing citizens without trial.

The rationale for the proscriptions was that they ended the civil war by identifying and limiting the enemies of the republic. Anyone was authorized to kill a proscribed person and to receive a reward for doing so. The estates of the proscribed were sold at auction with the proceeds supposedly going to the treasury. Among those proscribed were forty senators, mostly Cinnan-Marians who had financially benefitted from the persecution of the nobility. Sulla called these persons "moneybags." He also proscribed Marius's son, who in the last days of the Cinnan regime had ordered the killing of the leading *optimate* senators remaining in Rome, including Quintus Mucius Scaevola, the renowned jurist and *pontifex maximus.*

Just as the agents of Marius and Cinna had benefitted from the murder of rich *optimates,* so also the agents of Sulla benefitted from the proscriptions and murders of rich *populares.* Although Sulla couched his actions with legal authority, he allowed his subordinates to engage in vengeful practices. Perhaps from Sulla's point of view and in the context of the time, such ruthless action was justified as necessary to prevent a resurgence of anarchy and violence. He had left Cinna in power, and Sulla's reprisals came only after Cinna and Marius had allowed slaves and street mobs to slaughter property owners and heads of families.

To diminish the memory of Marius, Sulla ordered the destruction of the memorials, plaques, and trophies that commemorated Marius's many victories. As could be expected, Marians removed and hid many of them.

In 81 BC, after six months, the addition of names to the proscription lists ended. Other than those proscribed, Sulla took into his government many of those who had cooperated with the Cinnan regime but hadn't directly participated in the atrocities. Nevertheless, some Cinnan holdouts remained in control of areas in the provinces outside Italy. The most formidable was Quintus Sertorius in Spain, and civil wars there would continue sporadically until 72 BC, when Sertorius was assassinated by his own associates.

To restore normalcy and order, Sulla enacted new laws. The *Lex Cornelia de Sicariis et Veneficiis* established standing criminal courts and proscribed a wide range of violent acts, including the use of violent street gangs. He also passed a law strengthening the law against *ambitus*, election bribery. This law imposed a prohibition on anyone convicted of election bribery from holding office for the next ten years.

To gain the support of the Italians, Sulla reversed himself and ratified the voting law of Sulpicius, which distributed Italian voters into all thirty-five tribes.

As for the tribunes, he reimposed the political reforms he had previously instituted, reduced the power of the tribunes to propose legislation, and revived the requirement of Senate approval before a bill could be submitted to the assemblies. In addition, he abolished the tribune's veto power in criminal cases. As for the extortion courts, he reversed the policy that only equestrians could sit as jurors and mandated that only senators could sit as jurors on this court. At the same time, he doubled the size of the Senate to six hundred members and allowed equestrians and Italian allies who supported him to be inducted. This was a practical necessity because so many senators had been killed, and replacements were needed to administer the growing empire.

Paradoxically, Sulla seized dictatorial power to restore the Senate's authority and the traditional balances of constitutional government. He restored the Senate's control of provincial governors and forbade the governors to make war outside their provinces or even leave their provinces without prior senatorial authorization. He passed a law reiterating the prohibition on consuls and proconsuls leading an army into Italy, something he had done himself. This law would later have a significant impact as a marker between the Senate and military commanders—Pompey would obey; Caesar would violate. Sulla reimposed the graduated age requirements for magistrates, the rule that only elected magistrates could become senators, and the prohibition against consuls running for consecutive terms or for reelection within ten years. The last would also become a pivotal factor in the subsequent dispute between Caesar and the Senate.

He established several colonies for his veterans, notably one in Pompeii. He sponsored the rebuilding of the Senate house, the construction of a great Tabularium (document office), and the Temple of Fortuna, among many other projects. In 81 BC, he resigned the dictatorship and was elected consul for the following year.

In 79 BC, when his projects and his restoration of order and the republic were completed, he voluntarily retired to private life, dying a year later. Although historians have castigated him as a tyrant, his actions weren't unusual in the maelstrom of the ancient world. He did not apologize for his actions and wrote the inscription for his monument. "No friend has ever done me a kindness and no enemy a wrong without being fully repaid."

CHAPTER 16

Competitors for Power

AFTER SULLA'S DEATH IN 78 BC, new actors filled the power vacuum left in his absence. These actors realized the path to power was to garner the support of the populace by promising benefits at the expense of the wealthy (although they were wealthy themselves) and, at the same time, enlisting the support of an army more loyal to them than to the state.

POMPEY AND CRASSUS

One such actor was Gnaeus Pompey Magnus (Pompey the Great). When Sulla marched on Rome, Pompey was only twenty-three years old, but he raised three legions to join Sulla from among his deceased father's tenants, clients, and veterans. Not authorized by the Senate, this was a private army. As a Sullan commander, he won several battles against Marian forces, and Sulla dubbed him "The Great." To further solidify his alliance, Pompey married the dictator's daughter.

After Sulla's death, the Senate authorized Pompey and Quintius Lucius Catulus to suppress the 77 BC revolt of Marcus Aemilius Lepidus, which they did and then disputed who deserved the most credit. Next, the Senate gave Pompey a five-year commission to take his army to Spain to root out the rebel army of Quintus Sertorius, the exiled Marian general who had conducted a guerilla war in Spain against the Roman Senate for eight years. In 72 BC, as Pompey neared victory, Sertorius's fellow rebels murdered him, and the war quickly ended.

Returning to Rome, Pompey requested a triumph. However, Sulla at first refused because Pompey wasn't even a senator yet. Pompey made a strong point. "More people worship the rising son than the setting sun." Sulla conceded and granted Pompey the first of his triumphs.[144]

The other major actor of the period was Marcus Licinius Crassus, who commanded a wing of Sulla's army when it defeated the Samnites at the Colline Gate. As a powerful figure during Sulla's reign, Crassus rebuilt his family's wealth, which had been degraded during the Marian-Cinnan regime. Crassus enriched himself by buying the properties of proscribed persons and amassed a fortune through opportunistic business enterprises. As he prospered, the slave rebellion of Spartacus (73–71 BC) was wreaking havoc in the Italian countryside. Spartacus, a Thracian gladiator, led a marauding army of escaped gladiators and slaves through Italy by looting, raping, and murdering. At first, the Senate didn't take Spartacus seriously enough and sent forces inadequate for the task to suppress the brigands. As the fame of Spartacus grew, thousands of slaves and criminals joined his ragtag army, turning an escape into a rebellion. Then, in 71 BC, Crassus took command of the army and raised an additional six legions with his own resources to crush the rebels. After fierce fighting, Crassus defeated Spartacus and infamously crucified six thousand rebels, spacing their crosses forty feet apart along the length of the Appian Way, from Capua to the gates of Rome. This act made Crassus one of Rome's most feared and respected men.

Pompey returned to Rome in 71 BC in time to assist in the suppression of the Spartacus rebellion and, to the annoyance of Crassus, to share in the credit. As natural competitors for preeminence in the state, neither Crassus nor Pompey completely disbanded their armies, which were camped not far from Rome. A clash between Crassus and Pompey seemed probable. However, they formed an alliance to become coconsuls in 70 BC, using the implied threat of their armies to pressure the Senate to assent to their elections in absentia, a violation of constitutional law.

---

[144] Plutarch, "Pompey," in *Lives*, 14.

Pompey's election as consul also violated the constitution since he had neither reached the qualifying age nor been a senator.

Although Pompey and Crassus had been aligned with Sulla and the *optimates*, they now reversed many of Sulla's conservative and prosenatorial measures, formed closer ties with the equestrian class, and courted the favor of the *populares*. They expelled sixty-four of Sulla's senators from the Senate and reduced the number of senators on jury panels to one-third, leaving two-thirds for the equestrians and others. Far more important, they restored the powers of the tribunes, thereby reviving the strength of the *populares*, which Sulla had so diminished. They removed Sulla's requirement of Senate approval before new laws were submitted to the public assembly, substantially reducing the Senate's ability to block controversial proposals. Although these measures were popular, they eventually led back to the chaotic state of affairs that existed before Sulla's restoration of the Senate's authority.

The laws passed during the coconsulship of Crassus and Pompey set the stage for the next act of the republic's deconstruction. Conflict between conservative elements in the Senate and populists in the assembly became inevitable. Although the tribunes had regained their power, the Senate was still formidable. It retained the power of the purse and could refuse to provide the funds to implement a law. It could issue a senatus consultum ultimum to declare a state of emergency and order the consuls to take whatever action was necessary to protect the republic.

Crassus, after his term as consul, continued on course to become the richest man in Rome, using his political power as a means to this end. As Rome's greatest lender, he benefitted from tax-farming contracts and building projects. Not a sentimentalist, he supported *populare* leaders despite the fact that his brother had died while fighting against the *populares* and his father had committed suicide when Cinna and Marius seized Rome. He most likely foresaw their growing power and hoped to protect his property from confiscation.

Pompey, more interested in military glory, sought an extraordinary commission to suppress the pirates who had been plundering Roman ships and taking hostages for ransom. The *optimates*, led by the leading *consulare* Quintus Lutatius Catulus, opposed giving him the commission. They resented Pompey for obtaining his consulship by threat and dismantling Sulla's reforms; they also suspected his ambition to secure overwhelming power for himself. Nonetheless, when pirates attacked Ostia, Rome's port at the mouth of the Tiber River, driving up the price of grain, the demand for action against the pirates overcame the senatorial opposition. In 67 BC, the assembly passed a bill, giving Pompey an extraordinary commission to eliminate the pirates. He was given supreme imperium over all the seas of the Mediterranean and for fifty miles inland from every coast. His imperium would be superior to the provincial governors in those areas. Under his command would be five hundred ships, one hundred and twenty thousand Roman troops, two quaestors, and twenty-four propraetor legates. In addition, he could levy troops and ships from the coastal regions and cities.

The grant of such authority by the assembly diminished the Senate, which again saw its authority to assign military commands circumvented. In any case, the results were good; from the moment of Pompey's commission, the price of grain fell, and confidence in the markets returned. Within a few months, Pompey obliterated the pirate menace and became the most renowned man of Rome.

Pompey's next opportunity for glory was the campaign to finally crush Mithridates, who had revived his fortunes after Sulla's departure from the East and had begun reconstituting his empire. In 74 BC, Mithridates marched into Roman-controlled Bithynia in Asia Minor— in effect, declaring war. Fearing a new Hannibal, Rome sent the consul Lucius Licinius Lucullus to destroy Mithridates. For eight years, Lucullus tried; he won several battles, but he couldn't capture him, and in 66 BC, Lucullus's legions mutinied. He was relieved of command and replaced by Pompey.

Pompey, fresh from his success against the pirates, lobbied to replace Lucullus. Again, Pompey overcame the resistance of the Senate, and the assembly passed a law replacing Lucullus and giving Pompey an extraordinary five-year commission to campaign in the East against Mithridates. This extended imperium abrogated the traditional principles of collective rule wherein elite families shared the magistracies and held them for limited terms, with limited powers, but Marcus Tullius Cicero, a fast-rising senator, persuasively argued that extraordinary circumstances required extraordinary measures. He argued that the stain of the unavenged atrocity of 88 BC, when Mithridates ordered "all the Roman citizens in all Asia, scattered as they were over so many cities, to be slaughtered and butchered," hadn't been cleansed. Mithridates, he said, "has never yet suffered any chastisement worthy of his wickedness ... Now, twenty-three years later, he is still a king."[145]

Pompey took three new legions to the East, adding to those of Lucullus. He tracked Mithridates to a stronghold near Dasteira in Pontus and launched a surprise nighttime attack that devastated the king's army. However, Mithridates escaped and fled to Armenia, seeking refuge with his longtime ally, King Tigranes.

When Pompey attacked Tigranes's stronghold in Artaxata, the king surrendered, accepted terms, and prostrated himself on the ground before Pompey. Tigranes transferred his rule over Mesopotamia, Syria, and Phoenicia to Rome.

Meanwhile, Mithridates with his remaining army fled over the Caucasus Mountains, around the Sea of Azov, to the Crimea, where he took control of the kingdom of Bosporus and established his headquarters in the fortress in Pantikapaion (modern Kerch). For three years he ruled, killing many he thought disloyal, including two of his sons.

Mithridates tried to negotiate peace with Pompey, who demanded that Mithridates appear before him and prostrate himself as Tigranes had done. Refusing to do so, Mithridates began planning to invade Rome. He heavily taxed the people to raise funds for his war, but all saw that his plan was madness; the Bosporan kingdom had been at peace for twenty-five years, and the people didn't want war. In 63 BC, Mithridates, facing rebellion by the people and betrayal by his allies, including his remaining son, Pharnaces, committed suicide rather than be turned over to the Romans. Reputedly, he tried to poison himself, but after a life of building up immunity to poisons, the poison didn't work, and he ordered his loyal bodyguard to finish him with a sword.

Pompey received all the credit though he didn't actually capture

---

[145] Cicero, *Pro Lege Manilia*, 121.

Mithridates. Nonetheless, during his five-year commission, he had achieved much. He had exercised his imperium to the fullest, displayed remarkable military and administrative abilities, conquered territories from the Black Sea to Egypt, and plundered many castles and kingdoms. He reorganized Rome's hegemony in the East, annexed Syria, and ended the kingdom of the Alexandrian Seleucids. He installed rulers loyal to Rome and founded thirty-nine cities, raised an extraordinary amount of revenue for the treasury, and, as expected, gained enormous personal wealth in the process, becoming as rich as Crassus. In a display of arrogance, when he captured Jerusalem, he entered the holy of the holies in the temple, ignoring its sanctity. He made Judea a client state; Herod the Great would become a Roman puppet king, who often acted in the interests of Rome rather than in the interests of his own subjects.

Pompey's prestige and wealth had grown far beyond the norm and made him superior to all others in a way that upset the balance of power. The leading senators resented Pompey for circumventing the Senate and securing the eastern command from the assembly, and they rejected the notion of one man, even a great hero, coming home to dominate the state. Consequently, they resolved to contain him. When Pompey sent requests to the Senate to provide land for his veterans and ratify the political and financial agreements he had made in the East, the senators denied his requests. Their denial was made with apprehension; many feared he would return with his army and march on Rome as Marius and Sulla had.

JULIUS CAESAR

While Rome awaited Pompey's return, Gaius Julius Caesar rose to prominence. He was from a patrician family and might have been expected to side with the *optimates*, but his aunt Julia had married the "new man" Gaius Marius, and Caesar favored the *populare* Marians, not the *optimates*. In 84 BC, when Marius and Cinna were aligned against Sulla, Caesar married Cinna's daughter, Cornelia, clearly announcing which side he supported. Fortunately for Caesar, he didn't fight in the battles against Sulla and thus escaped the proscription lists. However, Caesar's mettle was tested when Sulla insisted that he divorce Cornelia. Caesar refused, demonstrating his courage and independence. But he wasn't a fool, and fearful of Sulla's response, he left Rome and joined a legion in Asia Minor, keeping a low profile until Sulla's retirement.

Caesar's extraordinary character and self-esteem became evident when pirates captured him and demanded a ransom of twenty talents. Caesar told them they didn't know whom they had caught and that he was worth fifty talents. For the thirty-eight days of his captivity, he performed as though he were in command, joking with the pirates and ordering them about. When the ransom money arrived and he was released, he told them he would come back and crucify them all. His captors laughed.

Not long after, he came back with ships and captured the pirates. He delivered them to a prison at Pergamum, where he had them crucified as he had promised, though he exercised relative mercy. Suetonius related, "Even in avenging wrongs he was by nature most merciful, and when he got hold of the pirates who had captured him, he had them crucified, since he had sworn beforehand that he would do so, but ordered that their throats be cut first." Apparently, Caesar was concerned with his image. He wanted it known that he would exact revenge but wouldn't unnecessarily be cruel.

When Caesar returned to Rome, he entered the political arena, and in 69 BC, at the funeral of his aunt Julia, he displayed the images of her husband, Marius, which had been hidden since their disfavor in the reign of Sulla. This act sent another strong message of where he stood.

He was elected to the office of aedile, becoming responsible for the games and the upkeep of roads and public places. Again he displayed his attachment to the Marians, restoring for public display the plaques, statues, and trophies of Marius, which the Sullans had removed. The *optimates* led by Catulus accused Caesar of stirring up old hatreds, which is exactly what he did. He used the controversy to espouse the platform of the Gracchi—populism, land redistribution, and debt relief. Whether he was genuinely committed to radical causes or merely using them to obtain personal power was debatable. What wasn't debatable was Caesar's quest for power; it was fierce, calculated, and unrelenting. He tactically aligned himself with Crassus, and they resorted to buying votes and intimidating opponents to serve their ends.

In 63 BC, Caesar skipped the usual stepping-stones to become *pontifex maximus*. Borrowing heavily from Crassus to finance his election campaign, he defeated Catulus, the *princep senatus*, for that highly coveted office. Caesar's win contravened the tradition of giving that office to senior *consulares*. Although nominally a religious office, it carried secular political power; the *pontifex maximus* Scipio Nasica had led the assault against Tiberius Gracchus. Now it would be in the hands of a *populare* rather than an *optimate*, and the authority of the *pontifex maximus* would prove useful for Caesar's ambitions. The position also provided an illustrious dwelling, paid for by the state.

In 63 BC, Caesar was also elected to the office of urban praetor. With his meteoric rise to prominence, the leading actors—Caesar, Crassus, and Pompey—were assembled for an explosive drama. Three enormous egos were on the same field with room for only one—war, in one form or other, was inevitable but not yet.

Initially, Caesar and Crassus formed an alliance, and they supported the same proposals. Caesar introduced an empire-wide agrarian bill that would affect every province in the empire. The bill called for the last remaining public land in Italy to be distributed and for all leases on conquered lands in the provinces to be recalled at a fair price. A commission of ten members would administer the land reallocations. Of course, the entrenched, landowning class opposed the bill. Cicero, the consul of 63 BC, also opposed it, and he delivered a powerful speech against it, arguing that the bill would create not one king but ten. Rome's hatred of even the word *king* spelled the bill's defeat.

By defeating the bill, Cicero won a victory and ingratiated himself with the *optimates*, but Caesar and Crassus would later make him pay for his win. For the present, they threw their support behind Lucius Sergius Catilina (Catiline) for the next consulship. Their plan was to have an ally in position to advance their interests, but they got more than they bargained for; their protégé proved to be as ambitious, opportunistic, and formidable as they were, though not as clever.

When Catiline ran for consul but lost, he allegedly initiated a conspiracy to decimate the oligarchy and seize power for himself and his associates. The rebellion was suppressed, and five of the main conspirators were captured. Cicero argued for their immediate execution without trial.

To the contrary, Julius Caesar argued against their execution and said that the Senate should consider not only the immediate problem but also the broader implications of their decision. His words were prescient.

> But, you may say, who will complain of a decree which is passed against traitors to their country? Time, I answer, the lapse of years and Fortune, whose caprice rules the nations. Whatever befalls these prisoners will be well deserved; but you, Fathers of the Senate, are called upon to consider how your action will affect other criminals. All bad precedents have originated in cases which were good; but when the control of the government falls into the hands of men who are incompetent or bad, your new precedent is transferred from those who well deserve and merit such punishment to the undeserving and blameless.[146]

Despite Caesar's eloquent speech, Cicero won the argument, and the five conspirators were executed. For Cicero, in the fullness of time, his execution of the conspirators without affording them a trial plagued the remainder of his life. Conversely, Julius Caesar's speech against the executions proved the more judicious and won for him further popular support and influence, enhancing his stature to a level equal to Pompey and Crassus.

In 61 BC, at the end of Caesar's term as praetor, the Senate assigned him as the governor of Farther Spain with two legions, the Eighth and Ninth, under his command. Caesar wanted more, and he recruited a new legion from among the Spanish tribes, naming it the Tenth Legion. He personally selected the centurions, and by his extraordinary skill as a leader, he established a bond of loyalty with his legionaries that would endure for the sixteen years of their service. The Tenth would be with him throughout his military campaigns and throughout the civil war.

---

[146] Sallust, *War with Catiline*, 21–28.

CHAPTER 17

The First Triumvirate

FROM THE FIRST TRIUMVIRATE in 60 BC, the stability of the republic continuously deteriorated until its ultimate demise and the dictatorship of Caesar.

POMPEY'S TRIUMPH AND THE FIRST TRIUMVIRATE

When Pompey returned from the East, the Senate feared he would aggregate all powers into his hands; however, to the surprise and relief of many, he discharged his army in a demonstration of allegiance to the republic. In return, the Senate awarded him a triple triumph for his victories over Mithridates, the pirates, and the nations he'd conquered from Spain to the Black Sea. Some of his victories were later summarized in an inscription on the temple of Minerva he had built. "Consul Pompeius Imperator, having ended thirty years of war, defeated, killed or subjected 12,183,000 men, sunk or captured 846 ships, brought under Roman protection 1,538 towns and fortified settlements and subjected the lands from the Sea of Asov to the Red Sea, fulfilled his vow to Minerva in accordance with his merit."

This triple triumph was the pinnacle of Pompey's life. A triumph personalized the Roman quest for fame and glory, and it signified divine approbation of Roman conquest. No extravagance was spared. Pompey rode in a jeweled chariot while dressed in a purple toga decorated with golden stars; around his shoulders hung a cloak taken from Mithridates, which had belonged to Alexander the Great. Since the triumph was not only for the people but also for the Roman gods who had ordained the victory, Pompey's face was painted red to illustrate that Pompey represented Jupiter, king of the gods, and the true conqueror. To mitigate the effects of the extraordinary flattery on the man portraying the god, a slave rode in the chariot with Pompey and continually whispered in his ear, "Remember you are only human."

Pompey was only human. Although he had received his triumph, which was of overriding concern to him, he had failed to obtain land for his veterans or convince the Senate to ratify his eastern settlements. Foolishly, the Senate failed to accommodate him. Urged on by Lucius Licinius Lucullus, whom Pompey had replaced in the eastern command, the Senate refused to grant land to Pompey's veterans and insisted on a country-by-country examination of each of the eastern settlements rather than an approval in one comprehensive measure. Frustrated, in 60 BC, Pompey joined the alliance of Caesar and Crassus, and the three agreed to support one another's interests and divide control of the empire between them. To solidify their ties, Pompey married Caesar's daughter, Julia; and Caesar married, Calpurnia, the daughter of L. Calpurnius Piso, a close associate of Pompey. The three-way partnership was called the First Triumvirate, though it wasn't an official body. At the time, it strengthened their positions but eventually led to fatal consequences for each.

CAESAR'S FIRST CONSULSHIP

In 59 BC, with the support of his triumvirate partners, Caesar became consul. His first act as per the agreement of the triumvirate partners was a land-reform bill that favored Pompey and his veterans, and a bill to ratify Pompey's settlements in the East. For Crassus, Caesar passed legislation that improved existing tax-collection contracts controlled by Crassus's *publicani* supporters.

Caesar also proposed another land bill that was more moderate than the defeated empire-wide land bill he had proposed in his 63 BC praetorship. This one was well thought out and beneficial to the expanding nation. Thousands of veterans and citizens with three or more children would be given plots of public farmland in central Italy. To avoid specu-lation or transfer to larger combines, the plots couldn't be sold for twenty years. Any additional land needed would be purchased at a fair price from owners who agreed to sell, and the expenditure would come from the treasury filled by Pompey's eastern conquests. Nevertheless, *optimates* in the Senate opposed the land grants because this was their standard ideo-logical position, and they didn't want to give Caesar a victory that would increase his popularity.

In the Senate, Cato tried to filibuster the bill. Caesar lost patience and had him arrested and removed from the chamber, but most of the sena-tors rose and left with Cato. One of the Senators leaving with Cato said, "I would rather be in prison with Cato than in the Senate with Caesar." Caesar immediately relented and had Cato released. In the meantime, the session expired, and the bill failed.

Undeterred, Caesar presented the land bill to the assembly without the imprimatur of the Senate. Presenting a bill to the Senate for its advice was customary but no longer legally necessary. Nevertheless, in the as-sembly Caesar met further resistance. His coconsul, Marcus Calpurnius Bibulus (Cato's son-in-law), and three tribunes attempted to veto the bill, but Caesar's supporters physically prevented them from reaching the plat-form. This move evoked memories of Tiberius Gracchus presenting his land bill directly to the assembly and expelling the tribune Octavius from the assembly for trying to veto the bill.

Bibulus and others protested Caesar's strong-arm tactics by refusing to participate in governmental functions, and Bibulus announced that he was retiring to his house for the remainder of his consul year to watch the skies for omens. He claimed that until he observed a good omen and favor-able auspices, no public business could be lawfully conducted. According to the constitutional procedures in effect at that time, he was correct, but Caesar ignored him and proceeded with public activities irrespective of his coconsul's absence.

With Bibulus and the tribunes excluded, Caesar's bill passed in the assembly. It included an added provision that required all senators to swear that they wouldn't resist the bill, and any senator who opposed it would be subject to exile. This wasn't an original tactic; it was the same tactic Saturninus had used to exile Metellus for failing to swear to uphold the land grants for Marius's veterans. The Senate ratified the bill.

The land bill was a victory for Caesar. However, breeching the inviolability of the coconsul and the tribunes tainted the remainder of his career. With the threat of prosecution hanging over his head, he was pushed in directions he otherwise wouldn't have taken, directions that led to the culminating events of his life.

In the meantime, Caesar proved himself to be an outstanding administrator and political leader. He passed important laws to deter extortion in the provinces by rapacious officials. These laws were in keeping with Caesar's history of defending provincials and supporting the extension of citizenship to them. In summary, Caesar defeated the conservative Senate at every turn. As he pushed through his legislative program and had his allies elected as consuls for the upcoming year, it was said that the consulship of that year wasn't the consulship of Bibulus and Caesar but of Julius and Caesar.

Caesar anticipated that at the end of his consulship he would be appointed to a lucrative province, where he could raise money to pay the exorbitant debts he had accumulated during his election campaigns. The Cato-Bibulus faction of the Senate tried to obstruct his plans by assigning him to the lesser job of caring for the roads and forests of Italy, a job that wouldn't bring him money but would, in fact, cost him money. However, with the backing of Pompey and Crassus, a tribune passed a bill in the assembly, giving Caesar a five-year commission as proconsul and governor of three provinces at once—Cisalpine Gaul (Northern Italy), Illyricum (Dalmatia), and Transalpine Gaul (Southern France)—an extraordinary grant of power.

Caesar immediately assumed the commission. He didn't want a break in his imperium (authority) because if he reverted to the status of a private citizen, he could be prosecuted for the violent and illegal acts he'd committed during his consulship.

Clodius

To protect his interests and neutralize his enemies while he was away from Rome, Caesar formed an alliance with Publius Clodius Pulcher, an arrogant and unsavory character who could mobilize gangs, labor guilds, and trade organizations. He had been born a patrician, named Publius Claudius Pulcher, a member of the venerable aristocratic Claudii clan. But planning to become a tribune (patricians couldn't be tribunes), he changed his name to the plebeian Clodius, and he convinced Caesar, as *pontifex maximus,* to approve his adoption into a plebeian family, clearing the way for his election as a tribune.

Clodius had no loyalty to the patricians or anyone. Years earlier, in 66 BC, while campaigning against Mithridates under the command of his brother-in-law, the distinguished old-line general Lucius Licinius Lucullus, Clodius stirred up a mutiny, either because he didn't want to endure the hardships of a further campaign or because he was an agent of Pompey, who wanted the command. In either case, Lucullus was thoroughly undermined and replaced by Pompey.

As a tribune in 58 BC, allegedly acting as Caesar's agent, Clodius staged street demonstrations and employed his street gangs to threaten and intimidate his adversaries. He restored the legality of collegia (social clubs), which had previously been banned. These clubs maintained temples and crossroads but frequently acted as political gangs Clodius used as demonstrators and rioters. With them Clodius ruled the streets, and anyone could become a target. Ambitious to be the most powerful man in Rome, Clodius played ruthless politics to the extreme and blatantly fomented class warfare, at times targeting Pompey's faction—at other times, the conservative aristocratic circle. At one point, his demonstrators even blockaded and trapped Pompey in his house.

Clodius undercut traditional political procedures and passed a plebiscite that prohibited the magistrates from using unfavorable auspices to suspend meetings of the tribal assembly, thus eliminating a tactic the oligarchy often used to thwart populist measures or to de-escalate heated conflicts.

Despite Senate opposition, he passed the most far-reaching *populare* bills yet. The most significant bill provided for grain, previously subsidized, to be distributed entirely free to all freemen in Rome. As an unintended consequence, many slave owners released their slaves, making them freedmen and eligible for the free grain. Most of these freedmen still worked for their former masters as they had as slaves, but others swelled the population of the urban unemployed and joined Clodius's followers for the next half decade.

Apparently with Caesar's blessing, Clodius used his political power to settle personal scores. He took revenge on Cicero, who years before had testified against him during his trial for defiling a religious ceremony. Now, Clodius used his tribuneship to pass a bill that any public official who had executed a citizen without trial must be denied "fire and water," meaning exile. This bill was clearly aimed at Cicero for ordering the summary execution of the Catiline conspirators. Cicero knew charges would be forthcoming and reluctantly went into exile in Greece rather than stand trial. After Cicero left Rome, Clodius passed a second bill that specifically named Cicero, pronouncing that Cicero was to be denied fire and water and that his goods were to be confiscated. Clodius then had his gangs tear down Cicero's house on the Palatine Hill and burn his country villas to the ground.

Clodius's revenge against Cicero furthered the interests of the triumvirate; removing Cicero from Rome eliminated a potential obstacle to their plans. In 56 BC, the triumvirs met at Luca, in Cisalpine Gaul, Caesar's province, where they renewed their partnership, agreeing that Crassus and Pompey would be consuls again for the next year and that Caesar would guarantee their election by sending his soldiers to Rome to vote for them. They arranged five-year commands for themselves: Pompey would get Spain, Crassus would get Syria, and Caesar would get a five-year extension of his command in his three provinces. These extraordinary commands limited the Senate's authority to appoint magistrates to provinces on an annual basis and further weakened the checks-and-balances system.

In 57 BC, Clodius's term as tribune ended. He still had his gangs and continued his threats and demonstrations, but now he ran into opposition. The tribune, Titus Annius Milo, was a favorite of the *optimates*, and he twice prosecuted Clodius for violence under the Sullan law. However, Clodius's brother was the praetor for that year, and the charges were dismissed.

Clodius sent his gangs to Milo's house to intimidate him, but Milo had organized his own gang. He had hired ex-soldiers and gladiators who could more than match Clodius's strength. Street fighting continued throughout the year.

In 56 BC, when Milo's term ended, Clodius prosecuted him for violence, but at the trial, fighting broke out, and the trial had to be abandoned. Indeed, partisan violence had usurped the Roman law courts.

THE GALLIC WARS

While Clodius and Milo were creating chaos on the streets of Rome, Caesar was building a nation that would be far greater than the city of Rome. Caesar's extraordinary three-province, five-year command provided him a powerbase beyond the support of the capricious urban masses. Though he would maintain relations with Clodius and other popular leaders, his growing clientele would now include his troops, provincials, and even conquered tribes. As proconsul in his three provinces, he conducted perhaps the most astounding military and political campaign in history, and he publicized his achievements with regular dispatches back to Rome in a relentless propaganda campaign. In his memoir *The Gallic Wars*, Caesar described not only his military achievements in defeating several large and formidable Gallic and Germanic tribes but also his diplomatic achievements. As an example, he described his conferences with the Gallic tribal chiefs regarding the threatened invasion and immigration of Germanic tribes into Transalpine Gaul (Gaul west of the Alps).

> Then the Aeduan, Diviciacus, speaking on behalf of them all, told the following story. In the whole of Gaul there were two factions, one led by the Aedui, the other by the Arverni. For many years they struggled fiercely between themselves for supremacy until eventually the Arverni and the Sequani sent for German mercenaries; about 15,000 came across the Rhine in the first contingent. But after those uncivilized savages had developed a liking for the good land and high standard of living enjoyed by the Gauls, more came across, until by now there were some 120,000 of them in Gaul.

The Aedui and their dependent tribes had been involved in armed conflict against these Germans more than once, but they had suffered a disastrous defeat and had lost all their nobles, their entire council, and all their cavalry. They had previously been the most powerful people in Gaul because of their own valor and their ties of hospitality and friendship with the Roman people; but they were broken by these disastrous defeats. They were compelled to hand over to the Sequani as hostages their leading men and to bind their tribe by an oath that they would not try to get their hostages back or ask the Romans for help, but would submit forever to being under the power and control of the Sequani.[147]

Naturally, Caesar described how he favorably resolved the conflicts between tribes, either through force or through treaties. No doubt his memoir served the purposes of self-promotion, but real achievements supported its boasts. He proved himself to be an excellent diplomat, brilliant military tactician, and astute manager of people. With his great oratorical skills and the force of his personality, he won the loyalty of his troops, and his self-confidence made the difference between victory and defeat. His army's military and engineering feats were unmatched for nearly two thousand years.

The Gallic tribes defined themselves by their territories and viewed one another as adversaries; the largest tribes were the Helvetians, the Nervii, and the Belgae. By dividing and conquering them, Caesar established Rome's domination over Gaul. His achievements raised his popularity among the people to new heights, and in 55 BC, from a position of strength he met with Pompey and Crassus to renew the triumvirate and extend his command for another five years.

However, his success wasn't necessarily permanent. The Gauls had learned that divided they couldn't resist Rome, and Vercingetorix, the king of the Arverni tribe of southern Gaul, emerged to unite them. A highly

---

[147] Julius Caesar, *The Gallic Wars*.

gifted and imposing man, Vercingetorix traveled the country to convince all the Gallic tribes that they must be free. In a campaign remarkably similar to what Tecumseh, the Native American chieftain, conducted eighteen centuries later, Vercingetorix organized a coalition of more than twelve tribes to revolt against Roman rule. He had closely observed Roman tactics and had designed ways to defeat them. With a united tribal army, he invaded the Roman province of Narbonensis (modern Narbonne); cut off the Roman armies from one another by blocking roads; and set fire to farms, villages, and towns in a scorched-earth campaign to prevent them from obtaining supplies.

Vercingetorix won battles and came close to defeating Caesar, but in 52 BC, he retreated with eighty thousand men to Alesia, a fortified town that stood on the plateau of a hill and seemed impregnable. In one of the most astounding feats of military history, Caesar built an eleven-mile-long siege wall, twelve-feet high, topped with a walkway and turrets every eighty feet, surrounding the town. Without enough men to occupy the entire fortification, he devised additional means to contain the Gauls. He had deep trenches dug and filled with water diverted from a nearby river. Behind the trenches, he built palisades, augmented with pits, sharpened stakes, and traps. Behind his army, to protect it from the Gallic reinforcements that were sure to come to relieve Vercingetorix, he built additional walls and fortifications.

Meanwhile, inside the town, to preserve food for his fighting force, Vercingetorix expelled the women, children, and elderly who couldn't fight. These people approached the Roman lines and offered themselves as slaves in return for food. Caesar turned them away. Vercingetorix didn't allow them back into the town, so they camped outside the walls; many starved to death. When a Gallic army of tens of thousands arrived to relieve the siege and attacked the Romans from the rear, Vercingetorix sent his soldiers out to fill up the Roman trenches with branches and earth, preparing to attack the Romans from the front. Three days of ferocious fighting followed until the fortunes of war shifted in favor of the Romans. Unable to break the siege and facing starvation, the Gauls surrendered. Vercingetorix, wearing his best shining armor, rode out of town alone to the Roman camp and submitted himself. Caesar chastised him, chained him, and held him in prison for six years until he celebrated his triumph in 46 BC in Rome, where he displayed Vercingetorix as a trophy and then had him strangled.

Caesar achieved his victory with the aid of friendly tribes from Cisalpine Gauls (Gaul on the Italian side of the Alps). He gained their loyalty by granting them Roman half citizenship and making promises of full citizenship in the future. These tribes would later constitute a large part of his following.

After subjugating Gaul, Caesar built a bridge across the Rhine River and invaded Germany, supposedly to discourage the tribes there from invading Gaul. He then turned his attention west, built a fleet, and twice crossed the English Channel to invade England, planting the seeds of a Roman hegemony that would endure for three centuries. Despite his successes, his actions invited criticism. The Senate hadn't instructed him to conquer lands outside his provinces, but he justified his conquests as necessary to protect his provinces from neighboring threats. To be sure, his reasoning stretched the Roman principle that a just war could be one fought only to repulse or seek revenge through an attack. Cicero had Caesar in mind when he wrote, "Unjust wars are those that are undertaken for no reason, for a war can be deemed just only when it is a question of taking vengeance on enemies and repulsing them, not otherwise."[148]

As Caesar's term wound down, rebellions in Gaul and Germany repeatedly flared up, and he concluded that the tribes couldn't be trusted to abide by treaties, so he increasingly resorted to even more ruthless and cruel measures to suppress insurrections and intimidate potential rebels. On one occasion, after suppressing a revolt by the town of Uxellodenum in southwest Gaul, Caesar, as a warning to other towns, ordered the hands of every captured rebel cut off. He ordered similar atrocities in Germany, and Cato, his eternal enemy, suggested that Caesar should be turned over to the Germans for his crimes against them. Despite these merciless acts, reports of his victories made him a hero among the Roman populace. The Senate, on the contrary, distrusted him. They remembered his ruthless conduct during his consulship and feared his growing popularity and ascendancy as the leading member of the triumvirate.

---

[148] Cicero, *The Republic*, 3.35

THE TRIUMVIRATE DISINTEGRATES

The triumvirate collapsed when the third leg was removed. In June 53 BC, Crassus was the governor of the province of Syria and tried to prove himself the military equal of Caesar and Pompey. Despite domestic opposition, he proposed to invade the Parthian empire, a nation that originated from the northeastern area of modern-day Iran, which had conquered territory in Syria and Iraq. Cicero called it an unjust war, and a tribune, who tried to prevent it, conducted a ritual of execration, asking the gods to curse the war as the army departed. Crassus proceeded nonetheless.

Crassus's seven legions were ill prepared, and his strategy was flawed. He allowed his army to be lured into the desert near Carrhae without adequate food and water, and a Parthian army comprised of superior desert fighters encircled and attacked it. The Parthian cavalry rained a constant barrage of arrows on the Roman heavy infantry; it was constant because the Parthians had a thousand camels carrying bundles of arrows, with which to resupply their troops. Thus, Crassus suffered utter defeat, and more than thirty thousand Roman soldiers were killed or captured and sold into slavery. The standards of the seven legions were lost, a disgrace of paramount importance, and the Parthians would hold the standards for thirty-three years. Worse for Crassus, when he went to meet the Parthian generals to negotiate a surrender, they murdered him. The fabled story spread that the Parthians poured molten gold down his throat to ridicule him for his lifelong pursuit of wealth. While that might not be true, Crassus was indeed beheaded.

In August 53 BC, the alliance suffered another momentous stroke of ill fate—Julia died in childbirth. As Caesar's daughter and Pompey's wife, her death diminished the familial links between the two leaders. The child, who would have been Pompey's son and Caesar's grandson, died within a few days of his mother's death. Had this tragedy not occurred, history surely would have been altered.

After Julia's death, Caesar tried to reaffirm his bargain with Pompey, offering another member of his family to be Pompey's next wife. Pompey rejected the offer and instead married into the heart of the patrician nobility. He married the daughter of Quintus Metellus Scipio, a descendant of both Scipio Africanus and Quintus Caecilius Metellus; the latter was the bitter adversary of Marius. This marriage aligned Pompey more with the *optimate* faction and away from his *populare* triumvirate partner.

Coinciding with the end of the triumvirate alliance, street fighting between the gangs of Clodius and Milo reignited, and as the elections for 52 BC approached, Clodius campaigned for praetor while Milo campaigned for consul. The fighting and chaos were so severe that the elections had to be delayed, and no magistrates were in place for the next year.

POMPEY AS *OPTIMATE*

On January 18, 52 BC, Clodius was killed on the Appian Way in a brawl with the gladiators of Titus Annius Milo. When his body was brought to the forum, catastrophic riots erupted, and buildings were burned, including the Senate house. Disorders continued for months, and the uncertain facts surrounding Clodius's death ignited rumors and accusations that inflamed further conflicts between *populares* and *optimates*. The Senate was neither unified nor in a position to deal with the crisis, partly because the elections for new consuls had been delayed. With the chaotic situation threatening public order, the Senate was forced to turn to Pompey. Reluctant to make him a dictator, they devised a solution. They declared a state of emergency, made Pompey the sole consul, and empowered him to use military force to restore order. The sole consulship was a deviation from the traditional checks and balances of coconsuls but not a total capitulation to a one-man dictatorship.

The Senate ordered the mobilization of military-age youth throughout Italy, and Pompey, with his notable efficiency, restored order. He also brought many who had engaged in political violence to trial. He charged the supporters of Clodius and prosecuted Milo for Clodius's murder. Pompey prudently stationed troops at Milo's trial and banned alcohol in Rome, knowing an acquittal would likely spark more riots. Milo didn't wait for his conviction and fled into exile.

These events brought Pompey into a stronger alliance with the *optimates*, and the Senate extended Pompey's extraordinary commission for another five years, something it was unwilling to do for Caesar. Moreover, as a demonstration of the *optimate* revival, the Senate house was rebuilt and named the Curia Cornelia after Lucius Cornelius Sulla. The project was commissioned to Sulla's son, Faustus, who happened to be Pompey's son-in-law. Further solidifying the alliance between the *optimates* and Pompey, his new father-in-law, Quintus Metellus Scipio, was appointed as his coconsul.

CHAPTER 18

Caesar's Recall from Command

WHILE POMPEY'S STAR CONTINUED to rise with the *optimates*, the Senate's disaffection with Caesar deepened. A block of senators— led by Cato, Catulus, Bibulus, Lucius Domitius Ahenobarbus, and the two consuls Gaius Claudius Marcellus and Cornelius Lentulus Crus— was determined to thwart Caesar's ambitions and deny his demand that he be allowed to run for consul in absentia, which he needed to do to avoid a break in his imperium and immunity. The senators resisted not only out of personal animosity but because of their strong belief that Caesar had arbitrarily acted outside the law and blatantly violated the traditional rules that had enabled Rome to preserve and foster its special destiny. The consul Marcellus proposed rescinding the citizenship rights of Novum Conum, a colony Caesar established in Cisalpine Gaul, upon whose people he had conferred citizenship without the approval of the Senate. Marcellus alleged Caesar granted the citizenship in exchange for votes. Making his point, the consul ordered the whipping of one of these "citizens" to demonstrate that the man wasn't a Roman citizen and, more to the point, to humiliate Caesar.

Caesar believed the senators had insulted his *dignitus*—the esteem and status Romans so greatly valued. The Senate denied him a triumph despite his having conquered Gaul and having equaled Pompey in military victories. Of more concern, he well knew of the Senate's animosity toward him and the possibility that he could be prosecuted for crimes committed during his consulship a decade earlier. Cato had openly declared that he would prosecute him. Caesar's defense strategy was to avoid a lapse in his *imperium*, which would expire at the end of the year, thus ending his immunity from prosecution. He knew that even the greatest of Roman generals, Camillus and Scipio Africanus, had been prosecuted and forced into exile after their victorious consulships. The dilemma he faced was that his governorship was scheduled to end in January 49 BC, but he couldn't run for consul again until the end of that year. Furthermore, no one could run for consul from outside Rome, so he proposed that he should be able to run for consul in absentia while maintaining command of his armies. Negotiations and political intrigue followed for a year. Caesar sent promises that if his demands were met, he would disband his army. When Pompey was asked his opinion of Caesar's promises, he famously replied that "actions speak louder than words." As expected, the Senate rejected the proposal and didn't renew Caesar's command or allow him to run for consul in absentia.

The Senate proposed to assign the proconsuls for the upcoming years, which would include a proconsul to replace Caesar; however, tribunes loyal to Caesar, Marc Antony and Quintus Cassius Longinus, vetoed the proposal, thus preventing the assignment of Caesar's replacement. Then, on January 7, 49 BC, the Senate, with Pompey's backing, ignored or overrode the veto and passed a senatus consultum ultimatum, an emergency decree authorizing Pompey to take control of all the legions, including Caesar's legions, and to take whatever actions necessary to protect the republic. The Senate ordered Caesar to retire his command, disband his army, and return to Rome, decreeing that if he refused to comply, he would be judged an enemy of the republic.

THE RUBICON

On January 10, 49 BC, when Caesar learned of the senatus consultum ultimatum, clearly he was in personal jeopardy; and to him, his own interests were paramount to the interest of peace. He crossed the Rubicon into Italy proper with his most loyal troops. The crossing violated Sulla's law, which made it illegal for a general to lead troops into a province to which the Senate hadn't assigned him. This was a gamble for either supremacy or destruction, and as he gave the order to cross, according to various sources, he exclaimed, "Let the dice fly high" or "Let the die be cast" or "The die is cast."

Historians have debated whether Caesar's actions emanated from pure self-preservation or from a genuine belief that Rome's institutions, designed for a city-state, had become incapable of administering its growing world empire and that he was the man destined to restructure the nation. Surely a combination of these and other factors motivated his actions. Hegel saw Caesar as an instrument of a broader historical phenomenon, which moved of its own volition, using the will of great personalities to lead society to the next stage of its development. The time had come for change, and Caesar was the most eligible instrument of it. Hegel wrote of Caesar, "What he gained for himself by attaining his at first negative end—absolute power over Rome—was ... at the same time a necessary destiny in the history of Rome and the world, so that not only his personal advantage, but all his activity, proceeded from an instinct that brought about what was in itself timely." It would follow that if Caesar hadn't acted to transform Rome, some other leader would have.

Montesquieu had a similar view of historical events. To him, Caesar wasn't controlling the direction of the world, but the world was controlling his direction. When he rolled the dice, the stars were already aligned. Montesquieu wrote,

> It is not chance that rules the world. Ask the Romans, who had a continuous sequence of successes when they were guided by a certain plan, and an uninterrupted sequence of reverses when they followed another. There are general causes, moral and physical, which act in every monarchy, elevating it, maintaining it, or hurling it to the ground. All accidents are controlled by these causes. And if the chance of one battle—that is, a particular cause— has brought a state to ruin, some general cause made it necessary for that state to perish from a single battle.

In a word, the main trend draws with it all particular accidents.[149]

On the other hand, perhaps it was Caesar's will alone that changed the course of history; had it not been for him, Rome might have remained a republic. In any case, as events played out, the Senate didn't send an army to defeat Caesar's legions as they had sent an army to destroy Catiline; instead they evacuated the city.

Pompey had seven legions in Spain and two in Italy at his disposal, but his veterans, whose loyalty he could count on, hadn't fought in twelve years. Caesar had eleven legions that were fresh from their battles in Gaul, confident in both their superiority and invincibility. Facing this situation, Pompey retreated to Greece, where he could enlist reinforcements from among his allies. He intended to spread his military campaign over the East and West to take advantage of his superior naval power. Retreating to buy time might have seemed the most prudent strategy, but it came with the psychological price of being on the defensive and the political price of appearing disorganized.

With the forces he had on hand, Pompey moved down the peninsula to the port city of Brundisium, modern Brindisi; and from there, he embarked across the Adriatic. Caesar rushed to blockade the port, but he was too late; and Pompey, with twenty-five thousand troops, escaped to Greece.

Caesar's Dictatorships

After Pompey abandoned Rome, Caesar entered the city and set about solidifying his authority through the dual use of force and clemency. He declared martial law and had the twenty-two remaining senators appoint him dictator. Encountering resistance to his demands, he asserted his authority and forcibly seized fifteen thousand gold bars, thirty thousand silver bars, and thirty million sesterces from the treasury.[150] When a tribune

---

[149] Montesquieu, *Considerations on the Greatness of the Romans and Their Decline*, 169.
[150] Pliny, *Natural History*, 33, 56.

protested that the seizure was contrary to law, Caesar responded, "Laws and arms have each their own time. If you don't like what I am doing, get out: war doesn't permit of free speech. When I've finished the war, and made peace, come back and talk as much as you like." On the conciliatory side, he released senators and equestrians who had been captured in return for their oath not to take up arms against him. In 1588 Michel de Montaigne wrote of Caesar,

> The examples of his mildness and clemency toward those who had done him harm are infinite; I mean besides those he gave clemency during the time when the Civil War was still in progress, which, as he himself makes palpably enough in his writings, he used in order to cajole his enemies and make them less afraid of his future victory and domination … It often happened that he sent back to the enemy whole armies after having vanquished them, without even deigning to bind them by oath, if not to favor him, at least to hold back and not make war on him … Pompey used to declare all those his enemies who did not accompany him to war; Caesar had it proclaimed that he considered as his friends all those who did not stir and did not actually take arms against him … The cities he had taken by force he left at liberty to follow which side they pleased, assigning them no other garrison than the memory of his mildness and clemency.[151]

Liberally dispensing clemency helped Caesar win the public relations war, and many recruits joined his camp. Further strengthening his position, he had a law passed, conferring full citizenship on all the freemen of his Cisalpine Gaul province, something he had promised and spent years trying to achieve. Thus, he secured a large bloc of loyal support.

Of course, he knew public sentiment would swing to the one who

---

[151] Donald Frame, ed., *Complete Works of Montaigne* (Stanford, CA: Stanford University Press, 1948), 2:33.

proved his point by military victories, and in a surprise move, he led his troops to Spain to fight the Senate's legions and prevent them from joining Pompey in the East. Allegedly he declared, "I am off to meet an army without a leader; when I return, I shall meet a leader without an army." He fought several battles in Spain, maneuvered Pompey's generals into an unfavorable position, and sent word to Pompey's troops that, in exchange for surrender, they would receive clemency and a discharge from the legions. Pompey's troops demanded that their generals agree to the surrender terms, which they did.

In late 49 BC, with Spain secured, Caesar returned to Rome and had himself elected consul, thereby obtaining the lawful authority to command the legions for a year. In contrast, the Senate, away from Rome, couldn't convene an assembly to elect consuls. Ironically, Caesar now had lawful, constitutional authority to command the state and the legions, and Pompey was technically acting without lawful authority.

In January 48 BC, Caesar took the initiative rather than waiting for Pompey to invade Italy. He left half of his troops in Italy under the command of Marc Antony, his Master of the Horse; and he transported the other half, about fifteen thousand men, across the hazardous winter seas to Greece. Pompey was waiting with nine legions, cavalry, and a naval fleet. Caesar immediately sent the transport ships back to Italy to pick up the remainder of his troops. However, when Antony's troops embarked for Greece, Pompey's navy intercepted them under the command of Admiral Marcus Calpurnius Bibulus, the former consul whom Caesar had humiliated in 59 BC during their co-consulship. Bibulus forced Antony to turn back but not before capturing one of the transports and executing all on board.

In March 48 BC, Antony tried crossing again. He only evaded the navy and succeeded in landing because a storm drove Pompey's warships into the rocky shore.

Caesar and Antony reunited their troops into an army of twenty-six thousand, and they fought several inconclusive battles against Pompey's forces around the city of Durres. Had Caesar and Pompey called it a draw, made peace, and combined their armies, they could have imposed their will on the world; but Rome was irreconcilably divided, and the final battle had to be fought.

On August 9, the two armies clashed near Pharsalus in an enormous battle with eighty thousand soldiers engaged. Caesar's forces won a decisive victory. When Pompey realized the battle was lost, he fled to his tent, where he was found in a stupor. He had never lost a battle before and didn't know what to do. His aides whisked him away, and he fled to Egypt, where he believed he had allies. When he landed, the Egyptians assassinated him in the sight of his wife, Cornelia, and his younger son, Sextus.

Caesar didn't rest after Pharsalus; he had to address other issues in the East and couldn't return to Rome. He sent instructions to Marc Antony, who was in Rome, to have the Senate appoint him dictator for another year so he could continue campaigning in the East.

Unaware of Pompey's death, Caesar followed him to Egypt, intending to capture him. Pompey's death made the trip unnecessary, but while in Egypt, Caesar interceded in a power struggle for the Egyptian throne between Cleopatra and Ptolemy III, her thirteen-year-old brother. Caesar sided with Cleopatra, and her enemies attacked him. He had only a small force and was in dire straits for several months. At one point, he had to swim to save himself from capture, but he was able to fend off attacks until reinforcements from Syria and Jerusalem arrived. In a difficult tactical battle, Caesar defeated the enemy, then famously installed Cleopatra as the queen, made Egypt a client state, and for a month sailed up the Nile with the queen.

Caesar left Egypt and moved his legions to Asia Minor to secure areas Pompey had subjected but were now in revolt. He defeated King Pharnaces of Pontus, the son of Mithridates VI, at the Battle of Zela. Describing his victory, he wrote the famous phrase *"Veni, vedi, vici!"* (I came, I saw, I conquered!).

Upon his return to Italy in October 47 BC, Caesar continued his policy of clemency toward those who had fought against him, and this went far toward ending hostilities and reconstituting a functioning government. Many who had fought with Pompey accepted Caesar's clemency, notably Marcus Junius Brutus and Gaius Longinus Cassius, who each returned to Rome and became praetors. Cicero, who had sided with Pompey, was also forgiven. Other survivors of Pharsalus—including Caecilius Metellus Scipio (Pompey's father-in-law), Sextus Pompey, and Cato—refused the offer of clemency, reorganized their forces in North Africa and Spain, and recruited more than one hundred thousand soldiers.

Before dealing with them, Caesar set about restoring stability, and his actions are what stood him above so many other rulers in history. The civil war had worsened the debt problems and encouraged the hoarding of coined money. Without available legal tender, debtors were forced to pay their creditors with real assets, usually getting less than what the assets were worth. Loans were given only at high-interest rates, about 12 percent, exacerbating the economic difficulties. Caesar's more radical supporters expected him to adopt proposals for complete forgiveness of debt; the conservatives feared that he would. As a compromise, Caesar took a middle path and decreed practical and sensible measures. Creditors would have to accept land or other property in repayment of loans, which would be valued not at marked-to-market prices but at prewar prices. He appointed commissioners to value the property and set the level of rents for a full year, decreeing that the landlords had to carry the losses.

While this was necessarily acceptable to the creditor class, it failed to satisfy the most radical advocates for debt relief. At first, the advocates demanded a moratorium on interest payments, then a moratorium on principal payments; then they asked that all debts be completely wiped away. They threatened that if their demands weren't met, riots would follow, and the riots materialized. Caesar, who had benefitted from such tactics in the past, now opposed them. But, remembering how unpopular Marius had become for suppressing Saturninus and his mobs, Caesar was conveniently away from Rome when Marc Antony brutally suppressed the rioters. Between eight hundred and one thousand people were killed.

The riots were suppressed, but the urban mobs were still volatile and angry. To placate them and to distance himself from Antony, Caesar replaced him with Lepidus as his master of the horse. Then, going to the heart of the matter, Caesar took further measures to alleviate the debt problem. He canceled all interest due since the beginning of the current civil war. For interest previously paid, the equivalent would be deducted from future payments. Because of these measures, about one-quarter of all debts were absolved. Creditors were alarmed, but the settlement brought a degree of financial stability and confidence. Moreover, property rights hadn't been completely abrogated, and the distempering of the mobs brought many who had been fearful to Caesar's side.

In December 47 BC, with stability restored, Caesar embarked for North Africa to fight a brutal campaign against republican armies, which Caecilius Metellus Scipio and Cato led. After Caesar defeated their armies, both nobles committed suicide. Notably, Cato's death affected subsequent events more than the battle. He believed that accepting clemency would have been tantamount to granting Caesar the power of life and death, and as a Roman citizen, he couldn't submit to such tyranny. His suicide greatly affected those who clung to the hope of restoring the republic, and it became the accepted wisdom that Cato died for the republic's values. His act shamed those who had accepted Caesar's clemency, and eventually this shame would find a release.

In the summer of 46 BC, the Senate extended Caesar's dictatorship for ten years and added proconsular powers throughout the empire and command of all armies. He was given a new office, the prefect of morals, which usurped powers of the censors and allowed him to appoint or impeach senators. As dictator, he was immune from the veto of the tribunes, which meant the people lost the protection against the exercise of arbitrary power. Caesar controlled the treasury and was given the power to issue edicts, which meant he need not submit bills to the assembly for approval. He was in full control of the city, but forces loyal to Pompey were still in control of Spain, so he led his legions across the Pyrenees to crush this last opposition. In March 45 BC, at Munda, Caesar defeated the Pompeian forces of thirty thousand troops led by Pompey's son Gnaeus. It was Caesar's last and final military victory. The battle was fierce, and Caesar said, "Today, for the first time, I fought for my life." Gnaeus fought bravely but was killed as he fled. Pompey's other son, Sextus, escaped.

At this point, no doubt existed as to who would rule the empire. Vigorously exercising his extraordinary powers, Caesar rewarded those who had supported him. He increased the number of senators from six hundred to nine hundred and appointed bankers, businessmen, military officers, and provincials, completing the transformation of the Senate's character to a body of "new men," or men who had recently risen to attain success and status.

For his veterans, he established colonies in Italy and the provinces, the two most notable being at Corinth and Carthage. These are cities the Romans had destroyed but now would rebuild as great trading ports.

In complete control of the state and responsible for its survival, he moved in directions more compatible with those of the *optimates*. He reversed Clodius's free grain program and reinstituted the rule that some payment had to be made for the grain, excepting the very poorest. He culled noncitizens from the dole and sent eighty thousand citizens to colonies in the provinces, thus reducing the welfare rolls from three hundred twenty thousand to one hundred fifty thousand. These were astute measures; feeding the urban populace drained the treasury, and the discontented always posed a threat to riot. Caesar wouldn't neglect threats to his authority, and with some irony he banned collegia (social clubs) of the kind Clodius had used to stir up unrest in the streets and intimidate the Senate, often for Caesar's benefit.

To heal wounds, Caesar made conciliatory gestures to the *optimates*. He restored numerous statues of Sulla and the great statue of Pompey, which the people had destroyed in celebration of Caesar's victory. He allowed those adversaries whom he hadn't yet pardoned to return to Italy and even allowed them to hold magistracies and command armies. For the properties taken from the proscribed, he didn't allow his subordinates to abuse the process as Marius and Sulla's subordinates had. He knew that to rebuild the state he needed the cooperation of the governing class; otherwise the attempt to rebuild would be doomed to perish in another civil war.

His reforms were more practical than ideological. He reformed the Roman calendar, establishing the one still in use today; to curtail slave labor, he mandated that one-third of all shepherds and cattlemen in Italy had to be freemen. To encourage the birth rate, he gave special privileges to fathers of large families. To increase employment, he initiated major construction projects: the draining of marshes, a new road across the Apennines to the Adriatic, and a great Greek and Latin library. These weren't the drastic and radical reforms his enemies had predicted, but they were reasonable and pragmatic measures to address critical problems. As he had throughout his career, as quaestor in Spain, as proconsul during his ten-year commission over his three provinces, and as Rome's ruler, he liberally granted citizenship to certain allies and provincials, sometimes in Rome's interest and sometimes in his own. His inclusive policy set a beneficial course that contributed to the preservation of Rome for centuries to come, though not as a republic.

Cicero provided a succinct summary of Caesar's character and accomplishments.

> In him [Caesar] there was a great mind, a powerful brain, logical ability, a tenacious memory, literary talent, capacity for taking pains, power of reflection application; he had accomplished feats in war, however, disastrous to the constitution, that were still great; having planned for many years for absolute rule, he accomplished what he had in mind through great exertion and at great hazards; by public shows, by bonuses to veterans, by public feasts, he used to woo popularity with the unlettered populace; he had bound his followers to his side by gifts, his opponents by a show of forgiveness—in short, he had already brought to a free community the habits of slavery, partly out of fear, partly out of passivity.[152]

CAESAR TRIUMPHANT

The paradox and tragedy of Caesar were that while he implemented pragmatic policies aimed at strengthening and preserving the nation, he took on the trappings of autocracy and oriental emperorship. His image appeared everywhere on coins and statues. An ivory statue of him was placed in the Temple of Romulus, the first king of Rome, with the dedication "To the Invincible God." He built a temple to Venus, claiming that his family descended from Venus through Aeneas, the legendary Trojan founder of Rome. He brought his concubine, Queen Cleopatra, to Rome and placed a gilded bronze statue of her in the temple of Venus alongside the goddess.

---

[152] *Second Philippic, Horizon Book of Ancient Rome*, trans. Norman DeWitt (New York: American Heritage) 2:33.

He arranged four triumphs for himself, one more than Pompey had, and Caesar's lasted an unprecedented eleven days, one more than Pompey's. The triumphs celebrated his victories over non-Roman enemies—Gaul, Egypt, Pontus, and Numidia. Tactfully, in consideration of public sentiment, he didn't include his victories over Pompey and Cato.

The virtues Caesar exhibited were mixed with the most powerful of vices and with an unflagging self-glorification. Montaigne assessed him as follows:

> But all these fine tendencies were spoiled and stifled by the furious passion of ambition, by which he let himself be so forcibly carried away that one may easily maintain that it controlled the tiller by which all his actions were steered. Of a liberal man it made a public robber, to provide for his profusion and largesse, and it made him utter that ugly and very unjust saying, that if the most wicked and the lost souls in the world had been faithful to him in the service of his aggrandizement, he would cherish and advance them by his power as well as the most worthy men. It intoxicated him with a vanity so extreme that he dared to boast in the presence of his fellow citizens that he had made the great Roman Republic a name without form and without a body, and to say that his answers must henceforth serve as laws, and to remain seated while receiving the Senate when it came to call on him in a body, and to allow himself to be worshipped and have divine honors paid him in his presence.
>
> To sum up, this single vice, in my opinion, ruined in him the finest and richest nature that ever was, and has made his memory abominable to all good men, because he willed to seek his glory in the ruin of his country and the subversion of the most powerful and flourishing republic that the world will ever see.[153]

---

[153] *Second Philippic, Horizon Book of Ancient Rome,* 2:33.

In the few years in which he dominated Rome, Caesar's view of himself grew, and he increasingly exercised his extraordinary power in arbitrary ways, including unwarranted executions. Surely, Caesar's dictatorship was in Lord Acton's mind when he penned his great truism: "Power tends to corrupt, and absolute power corrupts absolutely. Great men are almost always bad men, even when they exercise influence and not authority, still more when you super-add the tendency or the certainty of corruption by authority."[154]

The Senate watched Caesar's every move, and in February 44 BC, when Caesar had himself declared dictator for life, the republic was all but dead. The will of one man had replaced almost five centuries of democratic republicanism. But, resistance was not dead, and a cabal of senators conspired to restore the republic. On March 15, 44 BC, the most famous assassination of history followed. In a scene more astounding than any fictional drama, Caesar walked without bodyguards to a Senate meeting in Pompey's theater, where men he had either promoted or pardoned stabbed him more than twenty-three times. In pure irony, Caesar bled to death as he lay at the pedestal of the statue of Pompey, which he had ordered restored.

The assassination may have been unnecessary. Caesar had been preparing to leave in the spring of 44 BC for a three-year campaign in the East, ultimately against the Parthians to erase the stain of Carrhae. For the period of his absence, he arranged for the upcoming magistracies and governorships to be filled by loyal and trustworthy officials, balanced between Caesarean and Pompeian associates; however, with the assassination, any hopes that the vestigial bonds that had held the *populares* and *optimates* together could be restored were finally and completely shredded.

Whether in time Caesar would have voluntarily given up the dictatorship, as Sulla had, or become a king as the conspirators suspected is unknowable. What is known, and is more important for history, is that the conflict between the populist movement that began with mostly noble intentions by the Gracchi brothers on one side and the aristocratic fear of a takeover by radicals and mobocracy on the other divided the nation into irreconcilable factions, and the division inexorably led to the ultimate destruction of the republic.

---

[154] Lord Acton to Mandell Creighton, a bishop in the Church of England, 1887.

CHAPTER 19

John Adams and Cicero

IN MANY WAYS, JOHN Adams (1735–1826), the second president of the United States, was the reincarnation of Marcus Tullius Cicero (106–43 BC), a consul of Rome. Both men were influential participants in the events of their times. They had similar talents, interests, and ambitions; and each rose to prominence—not by following military careers, as was the usual path for ambitious politicians of their times, but by their skills as advocates. These two historic figures are better known than most because each left a treasure trove of letters that revealed not only the history of their times but also their personal and intimate thoughts. They also published essays and other writings for the purpose of shaping their legacies.

While Cicero endeavored to preserve the Roman Republic as it stumbled toward its end, Adams endeavored to formulate the American republic at its beginning. Both held similar principles and values, were irresistibly drawn into the political fray, and were compelled to express their opinions. As lawyers, each risked their careers in the cause of justice and exhibited remarkable skills during politically charged trials.

They each began their political careers in alliance with factions for change: Cicero as a new man challenging the entrenched ruling class and Adams as a reluctant revolutionary who helped write and signed the Declaration of Independence. Eventually, both sided with conservative factions. Cicero aligned with the *optimate* Senate against *populare* revolutionaries as the best means of preserving the republic against mob-supported demagogues. Adams favored a pro-British oligarchy—even a possible monarchy—against the radical Jeffersonian Republicans.

Both enjoyed years of success, but at the height of their political careers, each made mistakes that undermined their accomplishments and reputations. Were it not for the divergent histories of their times, their lives may have exhibited even more similarities, but fateful decisions brought them to dissimilar ends. Cicero's life disintegrated into an unfortunate conclusion, including exile, proscription, and a violent death; while Adams reached a fulfilled old age without having to die for his convictions. Cicero divorced his wife of thirty years; Adams enjoyed a close and loving marriage with his wife, Abigail, until her death. Cicero, upon his death, left his family with a precarious future; his brother and nephew were also proscribed and killed. Adams's son, John Quincy Adams, became the sixth president of the United States.

CICERO AS LAWYER AND PROSECUTOR

Cicero came to prominence in 80 BC at twenty six years of age when he defended Roscius Amerinus, a man accused of murdering his father, a landowner from a town in Northern Italy. The case arose amid the turbulent aftermath of the Sullan-Marius civil war, when Roscius's father was murdered while visiting Rome. No one was arrested for the crime.

Chrysogonus, an official close to the dictator Sulla, seeing an opportunity, had the father's name retroactively added to the proscription lists and his property confiscated. This was part of a larger scheme by Chrysogonus and his cohorts to confiscate the properties of Sulla's enemies and buy them at far below-market prices. The Roscius property was valued at six million sesterces but was sold to Chrysogonus for two thousand sesterces. As a result, Roscius was left virtually penniless, and when he mounted a protest, Chrysogonus had him charged with patricide to silence him and conceal the illegal confiscation of the estate.

No prominent lawyer in Rome would take Roscius's case since they feared the power and ruthlessness of the Sullan administration, but Cicero took the case. He mounted a forceful defense and won an acquittal, and in doing so, he exposed the corrupt conspiracy including the involvement of Chrysogonus. For Cicero, implicating officials so high in the Sullan regime was a dangerous matter, as Sulla didn't hesitate to punish his enemies. Although Cicero suffered no immediate or direct retaliation, he decided it would be a convenient time to go to Greece for a few years of study.

After Sulla died, Cicero returned to Rome, reentered politics, and won the election to be a quaestor. He served his term in Sicily, where he established a reputation for integrity. Several years later, in 70 BC, a group of Sicilian provincials sought him out in Rome and complained of an egregious instance of official corruption and the filing of false charges against one of their colleagues. They complained that their provincial governor of Sicily, Gaius Verres, had extorted money and art treasures from them and from Sthenius, a prominent Sicilian businessman. When Verres attempted further extortion, Sthenius complained. To silence him, Verres used his offices to file a fraudulent capital charge against him, and Sthenius fled to Rome to avoid execution and find an advocate to argue his case. The Sicilians convinced Cicero to represent Sthenius and prosecute Verres. For Cicero to take the side of the Sicilians against Verres was a dangerous stance because Verres was well connected in the Senate, and the jury would be composed of senators. But what he had done for Roscius, he also did for the Sicilian provincials.

Cicero's prosecution of Verres was important not only for the parties to the case but also for the future political direction of the nation. In Rome, struggles for power were regularly fought in the courts, especially in the extortion court that handled cases against public officials charged with abuse of authority. The faction that controlled the jury pool often controlled the outcome of the trials. Traditionally, senators sat as jurors. However, when Marius came to power, he banned senators from the jury pool of the extortion court and replaced them with equestrian business-men. Conversely, when Sulla replaced Marius, he reinstated the senators and banned the equestrians. At the time Cicero charged Verres in the extortion court, the senatorial faction was in control, and the glaring question was whether a jury of senators would convict one of their own. Addressing them directly, Cicero challenged them to do justice despite political and financial considerations.

Today the eyes of the world are upon you. This man's case will establish whether a jury composed exclusively of Senators can possibly convict someone who is very guilty—and very rich. Let me add that because the defendant is the kind of man who is distinguished by nothing except his criminality and his wealth, the only imaginable explanation for an acquittal will be the one that brings the greatest discredit to you. No one will believe that anybody likes Verres, or that he is related to any of you, or that he has behaved well in other aspects of his life, no, nor even that he is moderate in his faults. No such excuses can extenuate the number and scale of his offenses.[155]

Cicero's adversary was Hortensius, the most prominent advocate in Rome. Cicero sarcastically pointed out the difficulties Hortensius would have defending a client such as Verres.

But look at the dilemma of Hortensius. Can he refute the indictment of avarice by praising his client's thrift? He has to defend a man who is thoroughly dissipated, thoroughly licentious, thoroughly vicious. Can he distract your attentions from his client's bad qualities by mentioning any of his virtues? There is no man weaker, more cowardly, [more] effeminate. And as for personality, there is no man more obstinate, more impertinent, more [arrogant]. But these are the comparatively harmless aspects of his character. No man more implacable, more cunning, and more [cruel] has ever lived! Not even a Crassus or an Antonious could have successfully defended him. They would have refused to take such a case, lest they lose their own good reputations by smearing themselves with another's vileness.[156]

---

[155] Cicero, *In Verrem*, 46-47.
[156] Cicero, *In Verrem*, 46–47.

As Cicero methodically presented the incriminating evidence, Verres decided prudence was better than taking his chances with the jury and fled into exile before the verdict of guilt was announced. The case established Cicero as the leading advocate in Rome and a champion of justice.

JOHN ADAMS DEFENDS BRITISH SOLDIERS

John Adams also gained prominence as an attorney in turbulent times. During the tensions leading up to the American Revolution, two regiments of British troops occupied Boston. On the night of March 5, 1770, a crowd of several hundred colonists surrounded the eight-man British contingent guarding the customs house. The crowd hadn't appeared by chance but had been sent as part of a plot by Samuel Adams (John Adams's cousin) to provoke an incident with the troops. The crowd taunted the troops and threw ice, lumber, and rocks at them. A member of the crowd ran forward and struck one of the soldiers with a club, knocking him down. The soldier got up, but another object hit him. He pointed his musket toward the crowd and fired. Other soldiers followed suit, shooting into the crowd, killing five, and wounding six. The shooting was dubbed the "Boston Massacre," and Samuel Adams spread news of the incident to incite revolutionary fervor. To calm the rising flames of protest, the authorities charged the soldiers who had fired on the crowd with murder.

When no other defense lawyer in Boston would take the case, John Adams stepped forward and offered to defend the soldiers. Although he was associated with those advocating independence from England, he saw that the soldiers had been doing their duty and had acted in self-defense. At the risk of alienating his cousin, Samuel Adams, and his fellow Bostonians, and ruining his law practice, Adams took the case to trial. In summation, he thoughtfully argued, "It is more important that innocence be protected than it is that guilt be punished, for guilt and crimes are so frequent in this world that they cannot all be punished. But if innocence itself is brought to the bar, and condemned, perhaps to die, then the citizen will say, 'Whether I do good or whether I do evil is immaterial, for innocence itself is no protection' and if such an idea as that were to take hold in the mind of the citizen that would be the end of security whatsoever."

Adams concluded his oration with an explanation of self-defense that was destined to become famous.

> Facts are stubborn things. And whatever may be our wishes, our inclinations, or the dictates of our passions, they cannot alter the state of facts and evidence. Nor is the law less stable than the fact. If an assault was made to endanger their lives, the law is clear—they had a right to kill in their own defense. If it was not so severe as to endanger their lives, yet if they were assaulted at all, struck and abused by blows of any sort, by snow balls, oyster shells, cinders, clubs, or sticks of any kind, this was a provocation, for which the law reduces the offense of killing down to manslaughter, in consideration of those passions in our nature which cannot be eradicated. To your candor and justice I submit the prisoners and their cause.[157]

Six of the soldiers were acquitted on the grounds of self-defense; two were convicted of manslaughter, and as punishment their thumbs were branded.

Adams's sound conduct and arguments during the trial earned respect from all sides, boosting his political career. As a politician, Adams held a middle-ground position between those who advocated revolution and those who remained loyal to the Crown. He played a role similar to that Cicero had played when negotiating between the *populares* and the *optimates*. Both Adams and Cicero tried to balance the interests of the working middle class on one side and the propertied ruling class on the other. Each at various junctures had to switch alliances, and each sometimes sided with those whom he had previously opposed. At first, Adams advocated remaining part of the empire while protesting excessive taxes and seeking representation in parliament. However, after the Battles of

---

[157] L. Kinvin Wroth, ed., *Legal Papers of John Adams* (Cambridge, MA: Bellnap Press, 1965).

Lexington and Concord between the colonists and the British, Adams advocated full-scale rebellion, and his speech in favor of the Declaration of Independence was one of the most persuasive. After America's victory in the Revolutionary War, he advocated reconciliation and renewed relations and trade with Britain.

CICERO IN THE POLITICAL TURMOIL

During Cicero's long career, he switched allegiances more times than could be counted. Recognizing that he could be criticized for acting out of expediency, he wrote in a letter, "Unchanging consistency of standpoint has never been considered a virtue in great statesmen. At sea it is good sailing to run before the gale, even if the ship cannot make harbor; but if she *can* make harbor by changing tack, only a fool would risk shipwreck by holding the original course rather than change it and still reach his destination"[158]

After Sulla's death, Cicero supported Pompey's proposal to restore the power of the tribunes. In a public speech delivered as though he were talking directly to the dead dictator, he stated, "As long as it could and as long as it had to, the Republic put up with that monarchical domination of yours in the courts, and in the whole of public life. But in case you don't yet realize it, all that was snatched from you and taken away on the day the tribunes were restored to the Roman people."[159]

At other times, Cicero opposed Pompey's proposals and embroiled himself in dangerous controversies. He presented himself as a person who could smooth over conflicts, arbitrate between the classes, and resolve differences for the common good, but this wasn't always easy to accomplish. When he was praetor and ambitious to run for consul, he needed to show the people that he was a *populare*, but he had to do so without alienating the *optimates*. In 66 BC, when the people demanded that Pompey be given the special commission to campaign against Mithridates in the East, the Senate opposed the appointment because they suspected Pompey of too

---

[158] Anthony Everitt, *Cicero* (New York:Random House, 2001) 163.
[159] Cicero, *In Verrem* 2, 5.

much ambition. Cicero equivocated but came out in support of Pompey. He did so in contemplation of the *populare* vote despite his own misgivings about Pompey's ambitions. On another issue, when Crassus proposed the annexation of Egypt and the Senate opposed him, Cicero joined the *optimate* side to show that he supported the preservation of the Senate's authority.

Cicero's political balancing act paid off. In 63 BC, he was elected consul, an extraordinary accomplishment for a "new man" from a provincial background and a family that had never produced a senator. He had to overcome opposition from conservative elements of the aristocracy who viewed him with disdain and suspicion. They hadn't forgotten the horrors perpetrated by Marius, the last "new man" who had become consul and also come from Arpinum, the same country town as Cicero. Nevertheless, Cicero's prodigious talents made him useful to the aristocracy. During the Catiline conspiracy, his decisive and resolute action to investigate and thwart the conspiracy saved Rome from what would have been a bloody coup. As he confronted the treachery at the height of the crisis, he demonstrated his resolute temper, saying to Catiline's face, "The Senate is aware of these things, the consul sees them, and yet this man lives!" From that point on, Cicero became more acceptable to the oligarchic branch of the Senate.

When five of the principal conspirators were captured, Cicero convinced the Senate to authorize their immediate execution, and the five conspirators were executed without trial. Cicero famously announced their deaths, saying, "They have lived."

Although the Senate had voted for the execution, Cicero, as consul, was deemed to be the most responsible; this would come back to haunt him in 58 BC when his bitter enemy, the vengeful Clodius, became a tribune. Paying Cicero back for his testimony against him when he was charged with sacrilege, Clodius passed a law that called for death or exile for anyone who had condemned a Roman citizen to death without trial. The law, though general, was aimed directly at Cicero, who didn't wait for arrest or trial but fled into exile in Greece.

Cicero's exile proved to be a great benefit for history. During this period, he turned his astounding energy to philosophical, political, and literary studies; and his prolific writings preserved the thoughts, beliefs, and accomplishments of classical antiquity for posterity. In a personal letter, he wrote, "Now that power has passed to three uncontrolled individuals, I am eager to devote all my attention to philosophy. I only wish I had done it from the outset."[160] Among many works, he produced *Of the Republic* and *Of the Laws*, which the American founders widely read and are still studied today.

In January 57 BC, Cicero's friends began a campaign to rescind his exile. Clodius was no longer a tribune but still wielded great power. When a motion was proposed to allow Cicero's return, Clodius and his cohorts prevented its introduction in the assembly. Violence erupted between the factions, and fighting in the streets continued for weeks.

To counteract Clodius's influence, Cicero's friends convinced both Pompey and Caesar to support a bill for Cicero's pardon and return. They agreed, but even that didn't assure success. In July, to outmaneuver Clodius, the Senate convened the *comitia centuriata* or military assembly, where it would be easier to pass the bill than in the tribal assembly. Citizens from outside the city were encouraged to attend the assembly to offset the city mobs Clodius controlled. In addition, Pompey sent his veterans to vote for Cicero. The bill was passed, and Cicero enjoyed a celebrated return to Rome.

After his return from exile, he resumed his advocacy and defended numerous associates of the triumvirs charged with political or financial crimes. On his own terms, he might not have defended many of them, but he was obligated to do so because Pompey and Caesar had cleared the way for his return, and he was compelled to patronize them and do their bidding. Except for a few attempts at independence, he complied with their wishes and even accepted a loan of eight hundred thousand sesterces from Caesar, putting himself further under Caesar's influence.

In 52 BC, Clodius was killed at the hands of Milo's troops. But the pleasure Cicero took in this news was tempered with foreboding. Instigated by Clodius's followers, the city raged with riots, and the Senate

---

[160] Cicero, *Selected Letters*, trans. P. G. Walsh (Oxford: Oxford University Press, 2008), 49–50.

house was burned. Pompey was made sole consul and brought troops into Rome to restore order.

To assuage the mob, Pompey charged Milo with Clodius's murder, and Cicero felt obligated to defend Milo. Winning an acquittal would have been fitting revenge against Clodius, but this wasn't Cicero's finest hour. He appeared intimidated by Pompey and the troops surrounding the trial. The cards were stacked against Milo, who fled into exile.

With Clodius and Milo removed, the immediate danger of political chaos subsided. Cicero was relieved, but although the cloud that had loomed over his head had lightened, it was never fully gone. As the prospect of war between Pompey and Caesar accelerated, Cicero had to tread carefully. He couldn't maintain a neutral stance indefinitely, and in 49 BC, when Caesar crossed the Rubicon, he asked Cicero to join and support him. Cicero had to make a critical choice. Although Caesar claimed that he intended to preserve the republic, Cicero believed he intended to seize absolute power. He declined the offer and instead aligned himself with Pompey, whom the Senate had authorized to levy an army.

When Pompey retreated with his army to Greece, Cicero joined him. Later, when Caesar defeated Pompey's army at Pharsalus, Cicero returned to Brundisium in Italy where he remained, waiting to discover his status and learn whether Caesar would grant him clemency. In October 47 BC, Caesar passed through Brundisium on his return from Egypt, and Cicero greeted him, surely with trepidation. They walked and talked for an hour, and Caesar forgave him for his alliance with Pompey, allowing him to return to Rome and the Senate. This was a prime example of Caesar's policy of clemency, which temporarily brought Cicero into his fold.

From the time of his unofficial pardon, Cicero outwardly supported Caesar's decrees, and as Caesar finished off Cato and the last of the republicans in North Africa, he refrained from expressing his inner convictions. But Cicero wasn't totally silent. When he wrote on the crucial topics of his time, his writing was sometimes courageous. He wrote about the death of Cato in exalting terms, calling him a republican martyr for whom "it seemed fit for him to die rather than to look upon the face of a tyrant."[161]

---

[161] Cicero, *De Officiis*, 1, 31.

Praising Cato risked the wrath of Caesar, which came not in the form of arrest but merely in a counter-polemic by Caesar himself.

Cicero enjoyed polemics and the academic life, and he might have retired to it. But Caesar's assassination thrust him back into the political maelstrom. In the turmoil that followed Caesar's death, Cicero tried to use his position as an elder statesman and his persuasive powers to avert civil war. Seeing the assassination as an opportunity to restore the republic, and believing that reconciliation was the best course, he took a pragmatic position and didn't denounce the assassins.

The Senate assigned three of the leaders—Marcus Junius Brutus, Gaius Cassius Longinus, and Decimus Junius Brutus (a relative of Marcus)—to governorships in Asia Minor, Syria, and Cisalpine Gaul respectively. With their governorships came armies, which became the forces of the senatorial block determined to restore the constitutional republic.

Marc Antony, consul for 44 BC, denounced the assassins but didn't immediately move to crush them. He went along with a temporary truce because as Caesar's lieutenant, he had come close to assassination himself and was susceptible to prosecution. However, as soon as he felt secure enough, he changed course and tried to assume Caesar's mantle. With *populare* support, he declared vengeance against the conspirator assassins, and a clash between Antony's legions and the republican forces was on course.

When Octavian, the eighteen-year-old grandnephew and adopted son of Julius Caesar, thrust himself into the midst of the power struggle, political intrigues began spinning one after another. At first, Octavian aligned himself with Cicero and the Senate's republican side rather than with Antony's Caesarean party. Cicero must have been confident that, aligned with Octavian, the republican side was stronger, so he gave a series of scathing speeches critical of Antony. These speeches, which have been titled the *Philippics*, later became nails in Cicero's coffin.

Cicero's confidence was misplaced. To his surprise and consternation, Octavian switched sides, left the republicans, and joined the Second Triumvirate with Antony and Lepidus.

After the triumvirs were victorious over the republicans and seized power, they instituted proscription lists. Although Cicero hadn't been a conspirator against Caesar and had supported the young Octavian, Antony insisted that he should be on the list and marked for death, no doubt because of the *Philippics*. Not only Cicero but his entire family was proscribed. Hearing the news, Cicero decided to flee to Greece and join Marcus Junius Brutus. However, in December 43 BC, while he was carried in a liter on his way to the coast, bounty hunters surrounded him. Trapped, he leaned his head out of the liter, and like a gladiator, he bared his throat for the sword. His decapitated head became a striking symbol of the end of the republic. It was taken to the forum and nailed to the rostrum, where he had often spoken so eloquently.

ALIEN AND SEDITION ACTS

The fall of John Adams from grace wasn't so drastic; he merely lost an election, though it was a bitter loss, leaving him to spend two decades defending the record of his presidency.

The major cause of Adams's unpopularity was a series of laws called the Alien and Sedition Acts. Adams passed these laws in response to the severe and vitriolic criticism directed at him and his administration by Republicans who opposed the president's pro-British policies. The laws were also aimed at aliens who were spreading French revolutionary ideas in America. The Alien Friends Act of June 25, 1798, authorized the president to expel any alien whom he judged dangerous to the peace and safety of the United States. This could be done without a hearing or even a reason. The Sedition Act of July 14, 1798, applied to all persons, not only aliens, and forbade anyone to "write, print, utter or publish ... any false, scandalous, and malicious writing or writings against the government of the United States, or either House of the Congress of the Unites States, with intent to defame ... or bring them ... into contempt or disrepute, or to excite against them, or either or any of them, the hatred of the good people of the United States."

A violation of the act could cause a fine of up to $2,000 and a penalty up to two years in prison. Adams might as well have reenacted the Roman law of *laesa maiestas*, passed by the tribune Saturninus in 100 BC, which made any affront to the majesty of Rome a capital crime.

The Sedition Act criminalized seditious libel of a federal official because such libels brought the government into disrepute and incited challenges to its authority. It was passed because the pro-French Republicans, angered by Adams's favoritism toward Britain, expressed themselves vociferously in newspapers, handbills, and other publications, castigating Adams and his government. To the Federalists, the Sedition Act was necessary to protect the country. They saw the libels and slanders radical Republicans propagated as evidence of collaboration with France and a coming Jacobin revolution. What had been written about Adams infuriated him, and he called it "the most envious malignity, the most base, vulgar, sordid, fish-woman scurrility, and the most palpable lies."[162]

Immediately upon passage of the act, the Adams administration arrested twenty-five Republican journalists and editors, obtained convictions against ten of them, and shut down numerous newspapers. Several newspaper editors were sent to prison. During the trial of one of the editors, Supreme Court Justice Samuel Chase charged the jury on the law of seditious libel. "If a man attempts to destroy the confidence of the people in their officers, their supreme magistrate, and their legislature, he effectively saps the foundation of government." On the conviction, Justice Chase sentenced the defendant to a fine of $400 (a substantial sum at the time) and six months in prison. He sentenced other convicted defendants to longer prison terms, one of them to eighteen months.

Congressman Matthew Lyon of Vermont was convicted of sedition, fined $1,000, and sentenced to four months in prison for condemning Adams's "continual grasp for power ... unbounded thirst for ridiculous pomp, foolish adulation, and selfish avarice." While incarcerated, Lyon ran for reelection and won.

Instead of quelling incivility and potential insurrection, the sedition prosecutions inflamed partisanship. More Republican newspapers opened than closed, and some Virginia Republicans advocated secession from the Union. Jefferson wrote to Madison that Virginia and Kentucky should "sever ourselves from that union we so much value, rather than

---

[162] Charles Warren, *Jacobin and Junto* (Cambridge, MA, Harvard University Press, 2014) 96.

give up the rights of self-government which we have reserved, and in which alone we see liberty."[163] Jefferson and Madison didn't act on their thoughts of secession but instead protested by drafting resolutions for the Virginia and Kentucky legislatures that declared the Alien and Sedition Acts unconstitutional. In support of the resolutions, they argued that states retained the right to judge the constitutionality of federal mandates and could decline to abide by those they deemed unconstitutional. This argument would later be revived in the debates over secession in the years leading up to the Civil War.

Adams alienated not only the Republicans but also his own party. As a Federalist, he became president with a pro-British stance in the war between Britain and France. However, in 1798 he secretly arranged a peace treaty with the French at a time when Federalist Party members had become consumed by conspiracy theories that the French would attack the United States and that the Jeffersonian Republicans would support them.

Without the knowledge of leading Federalists, Adams arranged the treaty to avoid war, but he gained no political benefit from this. The Republicans welcomed the treaty, but there was nothing that would convince them to vote for him, and the Hamilton-led Federalists abandoned him.

In the election year of 1800, the perceived threat of a French invasion had dissipated, and the defense forces were disbanded, but Adams's popularity had been badly damaged, and he lost a bitterly fought election to Thomas Jefferson. Interestingly, Adams placed more blame for his loss of the presidency on Hamilton than on Jefferson because Hamilton had publicly attacked him in a derogatory fifty-four-page open letter, titled "Letter from Alexander Hamilton, Concerning the Public Conduct and Character of John Adams, Esq., President of the United States." The letter destroyed Adams's chances for reelection.

In 1801, when President Jefferson took office and the Republicans took control of Congress, the Sedition Act lapsed, but the acrimony it had engendered persisted. In 1804, the Republican House of Representatives impeached Justice Chase for his biased role in the sedition prosecutions.

---

[163] Thomas Jefferson to James Madison, August 23, 1799, in *Republic of Letters*, 1119.

Adams was out of office, but the impeachment trial of Chase might as well have been a trial of Adams. After a close vote, the two-thirds majority required for conviction in the Senate wasn't reached, and Chase was acquitted. This thin margin represented another judgment unfavorable to Adams.

The Alien and Sedition Acts not only immediately diminished support for Adams but also came close to destroying his reputation in history. Adams believed the acts were necessary emergency measures because of the threat of war and insurrection, just as Cicero believed it had been necessary to execute the Catiline conspirators without trial because of the imminent dangers. For both Adams and Cicero, posterity has viewed these acts as unlawful violations of the most fundamental rights.

Adams knew his reputation was tarnished; coincidently, he drew solace from his identification with Cicero. He was a lifelong reader and admirer of Cicero; in a letter he wrote in 1809, he exposed his disappointments and consolations.

> Panegyrical romances will never be written, nor flattering orations spoken, to transmit me to posterity in brilliant colors ... Yet, I will not die wholly unlamented. Cicero was libeled, slandered, insulted by all parties—by Caesar's party, Catiline's crew, Clodius' myrmidions, aye, and by Pompey and the Senate too. He was persecuted and tormented by turns by all parties and all factions, and that for his most virtuous and glorious actions. In his anguish at times and in the consciousness of his own merit and integrity, he was driven to those assertions of his own actions which have been denominated vanity. Instead of reproaching his with vanity, I think them the most infallible demonstrations of his innocence and purity. He declares that all honors are indifferent to him because he knows that it is not in the power of his country to reward him in any proportion to his services. Pushed and injured and provoked as I am, I blush not to imitate the Roman.[164]

---

[164] John Adams to Benjamin Rush, March 23, 1809, in *Republic of Letters*.

Adams knew he would never receive accolades for his courageous decision to make peace with France and avoid an unnecessary war, a decision he'd made in contravention of his own party's position and at the price of his own popularity. On his tombstone, he had the following words inscribed: "Here lies John Adams, who took upon himself the responsibility of Peace with France in the year 1800."

Dying peacefully in his old age, Adam left a newly born republic. He had nurtured it through the dangers of its early years. Cicero, dying at the hands of murderers, left behind a republic in extremis. He had tried but failed to preserve it. These were two men with equal talents, interests, and determinations, whose fates were determined by the times in which they lived.

CHAPTER 20

Roman and American Law

A GREATER AND MORE lasting legacy than Rome's conquests was the body of law it gave to the world and America. Rudolph von Jhering, the German legal scholar, noted that Rome conquered the world three times: first through its armies, second through its religion, and third through its laws.[165] Henry Sumner Maine, the eminent legal historian, described Roman law as "the staple of the civil institutions by which modern society is even now controlled."[166] The system of law born in the Roman Republic resounds in our society today, and contributions of Roman advocates, jurists, praetors, and legislators have significantly affected American law and the nature of our society. The Romans established the fundamental legal principles and procedures that are evident in our legal thought and practices.

Like the Romans, the American founders chose committees to write the founding documents that set the parameters for their governments and citizens. The Romans decemvirs wrote the Twelve Tables, and the delegates to the Philadelphia Convention wrote the US Constitution. By adopting these founding documents, both nations committed to defined rights, equality before the law, and due process—the core principles that separate nations the rule of law governed from those governed by tyranny.

---

[165] Jhering, *The Struggle for Law.*
[166] Maine, *Ancient Law* 180.

The Twelve Tables were based on customary law or what the Romans called *mos maiorum*, the traditions of their ancestors. They codified the rights and duties of citizens in relationship to the state through a series of procedural and substantive laws, and they satisfied the need for laws to be expressed in clear and precise language, an important factor in the advancement and democratization of society. Once the tables were publicly available, the doors were opened to further development of the law.

The tables were prominent in the Roman consciousness. They emphasized the obligations of citizens and reflected the Roman character. Cicero reported that every schoolboy memorized them. Historian Thomas Duffy wrote, "The Laws of the Twelve Tables ... sank deep into the temperament of a Roman, and made him an obedient and cautious citizen, loyal to the state and to all superior society, reverential towards rules of conduct or ritual, innocent of questioning analysis, and chary of initiation." Duffy's assessment suggests differences between Romans and Americans. Contrary to the tables, the US Constitution brings to mind an independent populace not overawed by authority and conventions; constitutional liberties and rights are embedded in the American temperament. Such generalizations invite a thousand exceptions, but it is incontrovertible that the founding documents of each nation reflected the character of their people.

The tables addressed a broader range of subjects than the US Constitution. While the Constitution addressed the functions of the government and the relationship of the citizen to the state, the tables addressed all society and the legal relationships of citizens to one another. This was the case because early Romans viewed their society not as dominated by a state exercising power over its subjects but as a collection of extended families, or paterfamilias, with members having rights and obligations according to their status in relation to others. They didn't call themselves the State of Rome but the People of Rome, the *Populus Romanus*. Their political and social orders coincided. The people enforced the law, most often by the patriarch of a family exercising his patria potestas, or authority, over members of his familia or by citizens bringing charges against other citizens, even against government officials.

Although there were substantial differences between the nations, the Roman Republic created the great body of legal principles that underpin the Western world and thus American society. Roman law took many forms: statutes passed by an assembly, resolutions of the Senate, court decisions, jurist opinions, praetors' edicts, and enforceable customs. The Romans established substantive law in the areas of contracts, property, family, marriage, inheritance, wills, gifts, guardianships, debt, torts, crimes, remedies, and restitution. In procedural law, they instituted the basics of legal process—for example, the service of a summons, the formulae for claims, pretrial discovery, default judgments, and jury trials.

The Romans were proud of their legal system, believing it raised them above other nations, even the Greeks. Cicero pointed out how "incredibly muddled—almost verging on the ridiculous—other legal systems compared to their own"[167]

THE PATERFAMILIAS SYSTEM

Roman society was built on the foundations of its paterfamilias system, under which the pater, or father, exercised lawful authority over his natural and adopted children. The wives of his sons were also considered members of his familia if the marriages were performed by *convenire in manum*, or "in a handing over." If the wife remained independent, she stayed within the familia of her father.

The pater controlled the family's estate and was responsible for the preservation and proper distribution of the family property. He also controlled all the property his descendants under his authority acquired, irrespective of the descendant's age. Under appropriate circumstances, the property of a married son could still be under the control of the pater.

The pater decided family business, disputes, and disciplinary matters; and within legal constraints, he had the power of life and death over his family members. The Twelve Tables reiterated patriarchal authority, as ordained by Table IV. "A father has absolute power over his legitimate children throughout their life: he may imprison, flog, chain or sell them, or even take their life, however exalted their position and however meritorious their public services."

---

[167] Cicero, *On Oratory*, 197.

Legendary tales of fathers executing their own children instilled family discipline and obedience, but the record doesn't support proof that such events were anything but a rarity. Patriarchal authority was primarily exercised regarding marriages, inheritances, and finances. The state respected the independence of the paterfamilias as long as they functioned in ways that were compatible with the state's interests, and the state rarely needed to intervene because the paterfamilias system was accepted and obeyed. Family bonds and voluntary compliance with social norms were strengths of Roman society.

An informative case arose in 140 BC, when D. Junius Silanus, praetor of Macedon the previous year, was charged with extorting money from provincial citizens. Before judicial proceedings were initiated, Silanus's father, T. Manlius Torquatus, a well-respected former consul and pater of a prestigious noble family, intervened and begged leave of the Senate to conduct an inquiry within his paterfamilia. The Senate agreed to hold off putting Silanus on trial. Torquatus conducted his inquiry, pronounced his son guilty, and banished him. In disgrace, Silanus committed suicide.

The pater could discipline those under his power for punishable acts committed within the family. However, the supposed absolute power of the paterfamilias was not absolute; other laws constrained a father's conduct. A father had an obligation to act in good faith and treat his family members fairly. Table IV contained a specific restraint. "Three consecutive sales of a son by his father [to pay off debts], releases the son from the father's power." Furthermore, abuses within a paterfamilia could lead to judicial intervention; a family member or a citizen on his or her behalf could bring charges to a praetor, censor, or assembly.

Advocates

Although most disciplinary matters were decided within the family, some family disputes and other interfamily disputes required formal litigation and the assistance of advocates. Rome's adversarial system, with skillful advocates representing defendants and plaintiffs, distinguished Rome from other ancient societies. In Greek courts, a party to a case had to speak for himself; the common practice was to have someone else write a speech for the party to recite by heart. There were no summations and little room for oratory. In Rome, the parties rarely spoke for themselves; they had advocates. This practice stemmed from Rome's elaborately developed patron/client system, wherein patrons were obligated to represent their clients in court. To fulfill their obligations, patrons trained themselves in rhetoric and forensics—not only to win the contests for their clients but also to enhance their own status and prestige. Those patrons who declined to perform the duty themselves would call on another leading citizen to substitute for them, usually one well versed in the law. While enhancing their own prestige during the give-and-take of courtroom argument, the patron advocates developed precedents and practices that had the effect of protecting the liberties and rights of all Roman citizens. Honore wrote, "In Rome, in contrast with Greece, there was a legal profession, a body of initiates, conscious of its moral worth ... that conceived itself as the guardian of the rule of law, the living justification of Rome's claim to rule."[168]

PRAETORS

The praetors were second in authority to the consuls, and in 367 BC, the Lician-Sextian Laws transferred the consuls' supervision of the courts to the *praetor urbanus* or urban praetor. At the beginning of his term, a praetor published edicts outlining the legal actions that would be recognized, and the policies and procedures followed. An incoming praetor could follow the prior edicts, change some, or add new ones. In time, these edicts came to constitute an extensive body of practical and effective law that augmented and interpreted statutory law. The annual publication of the edicts provided an opportunity to add new remedies or modify what was antiquated. It was more practicable to develop the law in this way than by amending venerable statutes, for the conservative Roman mind wasn't amenable to repealing the time-honored codes of their forebears. For a private civil lawsuit to proceed, the plaintiff's allegations had to fit within the definition of a specifically recognized statute or edict, and the praetor could dismiss the lawsuit if he thought the claim was misconceived. This

---

[168] Honore, *Ulpian.*

was the same as the Anglo-American requirement for a plaintiff to allege a recognized cause of action and for a judge to decide on its sufficiency before allowing a case to proceed to trial. Praetors could issue preliminary interdictions ordering parties to do or not do something, just as our judges issue injunctions.

Praetors imposed equitable relief to avoid injustices that would result from a strict application of civil law in a particular case. For example, the law of succession did not recognize the claim to inherit by a widow whose husband died intestate, leaving no children or other blood relatives. Technically, she would no longer be in his paterfamilias and would return to her own. A praetor's ruling allowed her to claim her husband's property.

Expanded commercial activity required adjustments to archaic laws. For example, at the time of the Twelve Tables, theft was limited to the carrying away of another's goods. By the end of the republic, theft encompassed any deliberate conduct that deprived a person of his or her goods or their value. Buyers or sellers of fungible, or interchangeable, goods who rigged the measuring weights in their favor committed theft.

Newer laws were also modified. The *Lex Aquilia* was a statutory law from the third century BC that defined the *delict* (tort or crime) of damaging the property of another. The first section provided, "If anyone wrongfully slays a slave belonging to another person, or a four-footed herd animal, let him be condemned to pay to the owner as much money as the maximum the property was worth in the year previous to the slaying." This statute needed interpretation and expansion. A narrow reading would imply that the statute contemplated only direct causation, which was the early interpretation. However, a praetor later interpreted the statute more broadly as encompassing indirect slayings, such as wrongfully committing an act that set in motion a chain of events that caused a slaying. This concept parallels our modern concept of proximate cause for negligence liability.

Praetor Peregrinus

As Roman trade and commerce expanded, contact with foreigners (*peregrinus*) increased. In 242 BC, to address commercial disputes in which at least one of the parties was a foreigner, the position of *praetor peregrinus* was established, and standardized written pleadings, or formulae, were developed that contained both the action on which the claim was based and the defenses that could be raised against it. This simplification of process was an improvement on the prior practices. Rulings of the *praetor peregrinus* and the juristic opinions on which they relied were followed throughout the empire, thus contributing to the security and growth of foreign trade.

In *Rome the Law Giver*, Joseph Declareuil neatly summarized Rome's contribution to Western law.

> Hence the special service rendered by the edict; for the formulas devised by the praetor imposed their form and plastic character upon the Law to such an extent that, after the system had been abandoned and the molds broken up, it still retained their impression. Centuries afterwards, the language of the Law Courts still sometimes uses Latin titles that once belonged to the forms of procedure wherein this Law was framed. These institutions, coined in the Roman mint and preserving its stamp, were begotten of practical experience and have survived to outlive a whole series of abstractions of metaphysical Law and jurisprudence to which they remain the best antidote.[169]

Jurists

In early Rome, the powerful interplay between religion and law gave the college of pontiffs a profound influence over the interpretation of the laws. Then, in 253 BC, Titus Coruncanius, the first plebeian *pontifex maximus*, opened the study of law to secular students, thus cultivating a college of jurists. Since praetors and other judicial magistrates were elected for one year and wouldn't necessarily have extensive knowledge of the law, they

---

[169] Declareuil, *Rome, the Law Giver* (New York: Alfred Knopf, 1926) 377-378.

asked the best jurists to attend hearings to advise them on legal matters. Cicero stated, "For private lawsuits involving highly important matters depend, in my opinion, on the wisdom of the jurists. For they are often present at the trials and are invited to join the judge's advisers; and they provide weapons for careful advocates who look for help in their skill … It is they who have defined fraud, good faith, equity, what a partner owes a partner, what a person looking after another's affairs owes that person, or the reciprocal rights of principal and agent and of husband and wife."

The jurists weren't courtroom advocates; nor were they paid by the parties to a case. They were guardians and promoters of the law, and their impartiality earned them great respect. Over time, their opinions added layers on the edifice of the Twelve Tables, statutes, and praetorian edicts; and it came about that legal rules couldn't be laid down merely by the arbitrary act of the presiding magistrate, but a court's ruling had to conform to established precedents. Adherence to a consistent body of law advanced Rome beyond other nations of the period. Bruce Frier wrote,

> For the first time in history, a secular legal system was examined as a distinct and coherent body of knowledge: individual legal decisions, rules, and statutory enactments were considered objectively and were explained through reference to general principles and truths basic to the legal system as a whole. Law was finally sundered from the elaborate apparatus of case-oriented rhetorical argument and was made over into an abstract body of norms, on the basis of which legal claims could in principle be scrutinized without special reference to the persons of the claimant.[170]

The jurists issued written responsa prudentium (answers of the learned in the law). The form and content of these responsa varied at different periods since Roman jurisprudence wasn't static but constantly

---

[170] Bruce Frier, *The Rise of the Roman Jurists* (Princeton, NJ: Princeton University Press, 1985) 286.

evolving. At first, they interpreted the Twelve Tables and the statutes, but over time responsa relaxed the strictest statutory laws and updated the more archaic provisions of the Twelve Tables. For instance, the courts recognized new defenses that were equitable to the case at hand, and these become precedents for subsequent cases. Wolfgang Kunkel wrote,

> In this way the law was adapted, purely through the practice of magistrates' courts, and without the necessity of any great help from legislation, to meet the requirements of a developing economy and of a refined legal instinct orientated according to the principles of contractual good faith and equity. In form this huge advance was the work of a long series of annual magistrates ... We shall, however, see that behind the decisions of these men there stood opinions and advice which the leading jurists of the day used to give partly to the litigants and partly to the jurisdictional magistrates themselves.[171]

The jurists engaged in wide-ranging explorations of legal institutions and concepts. Their opinions drew on both factual and hypothetical situations to develop points of law, and their well-thought-out conclusions and definitions influenced the history of Western law. Alan Watson wrote,

> Each legal institution such as *emptio venditio* (buying and selling) and *furtum* (theft) would itself raise continuing questions of classification in juristic discussions on the essential nature and boundaries of each. Does sale require a price in coined money? Can there be a sale in which the vendor retains an interest in the thing to be sold? For theft to be committed must the thief intend to make a gain? Can land be stolen? And so on. The high achievement of the Republican jurists here is best seen

---

[171] Wolfgang Kunkel, *An Introduction to Roman Legal and Constitutional History*, trans. J. M. Kelly (Oxford: Clarendon Press, 1973) 52.

in the large extent to which the boundary lines which they set between one institution and another can still clearly be recognized in the laws of the modern Western world.[172]

The jurist Quintus Mucius Scaveola, who was *pontiff maximus* for almost a decade and consul in 95 BC, organized the civil law in a treatise of eighteen books that were the source of law for centuries. Unfortunately, they didn't survive intact, but they were referenced for centuries in later treatises, including the 530 AD *Digest of Justinian*. Mucius Scaevola was the most respected living jurist until 82 BC; unfortunately, that year Marius's son murdered him during the purge of the *optimates*. Nonetheless, his work and that of other praetors and jurists bolstered the rule of law for posterity.

CRIMINAL LAW

It's in criminal law that significant differences lie between the Roman and American systems. In Rome, the state didn't prosecute all crimes; private citizens brought charges in the same manner in which civil lawsuits were brought to obtain compensation for delicts (torts). For a crime, once a defendant's guilt was established, the victim of the crime had a right to enforce the penalty by prescribed methods. In America, private citizens don't prosecute or punish crimes.

Roman punishments could be harsh. The intentional arsonist was to be burned alive; the man who stole crops by night was to be hanged at the site of his crime. Parricide was treated with the utmost severity because it attacked the core structure of their society. "A parricide is flogged with blood-colored rods then sewn up in a sack with a dog, a dunghill cock, a viper, and a monkey; then the sack is thrown into the depths of the sea."[173]

The Twelve Tables prescribed that an offender who bore false witness

---

[172] Alan Watson, *Law Making in the Later Roman Republic* (London: Oxford University Press, 1974) 183.

[173] Justinian, *Digest*, 48.9.

was to be thrown from the Tarpeian Rock; for a judge taking a bribe, the punishment was death.

Roman laws for self-defense and protection of home and property weren't unlike modern law. If the victim of a theft caught the thief at night, or if the thief put up armed resistance, the victim was entitled to summarily kill the thief. However, the victim had to summon the neighbors with a loud cry for help so no doubt could exist as to the propriety of the killing. In the daytime, if the thief didn't resist but was caught red-handed, the victim had to bring him or her before a magistrate. If the magistrate ruled that the thief was guilty, the victim might execute the thief or sell him or her into slavery. If the thief hadn't been caught in the act, the Twelve Tables allowed the victim only to demand a monetary restitution from the thief and hold him or her in bondage until it was paid.[174]

Though Roman punishments were harsh, the law provided great protections for the accused, and the protections extended to citizens in provinces throughout the empire. In the New Testament, we learn that a Roman tribune arrested and bound Saint Paul of Tarsus in Jerusalem.

> When they had tied him with the thongs, Paul said to the centurion who was standing by, "Is it lawful for you to scourge a man who is a Roman and un-condemned?" When the centurion heard that, he went to the tribune and said to him, "What are you about to do? For this man is a Roman citizen." So the tribune came and said to him, "Tell me, are you a Roman citizen?" And he said, "Yes." The tribune answered, "I bought this citizenship for a large sum." Paul said, "But I was born a citizen." So those who were about to examine him withdrew from him instantly; and the tribune also was afraid, for he realized that Paul was a Roman citizen and that he had bound him.[175]

---

[174] *Law s of the Twelve Tables*, 8.12-13 (Loeb Classics, 329:483).
[175] *Acts* 22:25-29.

Over the centuries of the republic, the Romans developed important concepts and rights Americans have inherited. Citizens were entitled to jury trials. At times, as many as seventy-five citizens sat as jurors in criminal cases. To reduce possible intimidation, jurors weren't allowed to talk to each other, and from 137 BC, they voted by secret ballot. The accusing party had the burden of proof. Although the term "proof beyond a reasonable doubt" wasn't used, the proof to sustain a conviction had to be "as clear as the daylight."

The accused could put on a defense, something not done in most other ancient societies. An accused could employ as many as six defense advocates and had the power to compel witnesses to appear at trial. Affluent defendants, then as now, had better prospects than the poor, but the poor or others without sufficient means might find support in the patron or client system, in which a patron had an obligation to protect his clients from injustices. Moreover, a citizen could appeal a death sentence to the assembly, and a sentence of capital punishment couldn't be carried out without an order of the people.

In the early years, only an injured party or relative could prosecute a case. This system worked well enough when Rome was still mainly an agrarian society, but in the second century BC, the growing urban population and the influx of slaves produced higher crime rates. In response, the Romans adjusted and strengthened the capacity for criminal prosecutions, allowing any reputable citizen to prosecute a crime, even though the citizen wasn't the direct victim or a relative of the victim. Political figures often assumed the role of any citizen, thus increasing the number of prosecutions.

To address new problems that arose with the growth of Rome's expansion and complexity, several new standing courts of investigation, or *quaestiones perpetuae*, were set up to prosecute specified criminal offenses. The new courts were established by statutes, and their jurisdiction was limited to the subject matter of the statute. Separate courts handled prosecutions for violence, arson, poisoning, election bribery, extortion, and theft. The *Lex Calpurnia* in 149 BC established the *quaestrio de repetundae* to investigate and prosecute charges of extortion. In 122 BC, Gaius Gracchus amended the extortion law, clarifying who could bring charges and providing assistance for complainants.

In 81 BC, the dictator Sulla enacted the *Lex Cornelia de iniuriis* to prosecute personal assaults and public violence. Previously, most assault cases had been handled as civil delicts requiring restitution, but the escalating violence of the period required public punishments.

In each court, the procedures to initiate a prosecution had to be strictly followed. The first step was the postulation, a request to the praetor for permission to bring the charge. If more than one person wanted to prosecute, a preliminary hearing was held to decide who would be most suitable as the lead prosecutor. The praetor would then define the charge and the court in which it would be tried. A trial date was set with a minimum notice of nine days to the defendant.

At the trial, the accuser or his or her advocate would deliver an opening statement, outlining the facts of the case and the argument for conviction. The defendant or his or her advocate would deliver an opening statement in rebuttal. Then the evidence was heard through witnesses, who were subject to cross-examination. After completion of the evidence, there were no closing arguments, the judge didn't instruct the jurors, and the jurors didn't retire for deliberations—they simply cast ballots: *A* for acquittal, *C* for condemnation. Verdicts required only a majority; a tie meant acquittal.

Penalties, fixed by statute, were a fine, exile, or death. Long-term incarceration wasn't an option because there was no prison system. Upper-class defendants convicted of capital crimes seldom suffered execution. They could leave Rome before the pronouncement of a verdict and go into exile. The citizen's absence avoided his or her execution but meant the loss of whatever property the person had left behind. He or she was "interdicted from fire and water," meaning none could harbor him or her in Rome, and if the person returned, anyone could put him or her to death with impunity. Cicero went into exile in Greece to avoid prosecution by Clodius; Milo went into exile during his trial for murdering Clodius, avoiding a final judgment.

A defendant could avoid the confiscation of his or her property by committing suicide before the rendering of a verdict. In this way, the defendant's family wouldn't be deprived of their inheritance and sustenance. Tacitus told us regarding treason trials, "This kind of death was often put into people's minds by fear of the executioner, and also because, if con-victed, a man's property was confiscated and his burial forbidden, whereas those who settled their own fates had their bodies buried and their wills respected—a bonus for getting it over quickly."[176]

Social status affected all aspects of the justice system. In an action for defamation of character, a *humiliore* (a person of lower status or ill repute) would have difficulty prosecuting an *honestiore* (a reputable person of elite rank), while an *honestiore* could easily prosecute a *humiliore* for the same offense. Furthermore, those convicted of a crime or censored for disrepu-table conduct could be labeled *infamia* and banned from bringing charges in court or even testifying as a witness. This may seem strange from a modern perspective, but in America until the mid-nineteenth century, it wasn't so strange since criminal defendants, convicted felons, and atheists couldn't testify under oath.

Legacy to America

Perhaps the most consequential connection between the Roman and American legal systems is in their inheritance laws. Colonial America adopted a Roman-based inheritance system and rejected England's pri-mogeniture system. Primogeniture preserved large estates in a family by granting the major part of an inheritance to the eldest son. This was part of the feudal system that required landed estates to remain as large as possible to maintain the wealth and power of the noble families.

American colonists enacted statutes that provided a more equitable distribution of a decedent's property in accordance with Roman inher-itance law. In 1776, Thomas Jefferson introduced a bill in the Virginia House of Burgesses to abolish primogeniture, and in his *Autobiography* he lauded the end of primogeniture as one of the greatest achievements of republican government. To Jefferson, the more equitable distribution of inherited property prevented an "aristocracy of wealth" and substi-tuted "an opening for the aristocracy of virtue and talent." The new laws reinforced republican government and counteracted the stagnation of

---

[176] Tacitus, *Annals*, 6, 29, 1.

hereditary privilege. Abundant land made it feasible and advantageous to discard the remnants of feudalism.

Roman inheritance law made no distinction between the oldest or youngest, male or female. If a Roman citizen died without leaving a will, the estate was distributed equitably among the family members. If a will was left, an outside legatee couldn't take more than an heir. Consequently, Roman estates weren't concentrated in the hands of a single person, and the Roman nobility was thus fluid, not static. Noble sons were expected to build their own fortunes rather than relying on their inheritances. [177]

Likewise, American sons of the elite were expected to build their own careers. They engaged in business and commerce, acting more like Rome's equestrian class than England's aristocracy. Democratic republicanism was advanced, and European-style aristocracy was banished. The founders made inherited nobility unconstitutional. Article 1 of the Constitution forbade aristocratic titles: section 9, clause 8, stated, "No Title of Nobility shall be granted by the United States"; and section 10, clause 2, stated, "No State shall ... grant any Title of Nobility."

Other aspects of American property law are remarkably similar to Roman law. Both advanced the right to invest, own, and derive profits. The word *property* is derived from the Latin *proprius*, meaning "one's own." Property was not only land but also anything to which a monetary value could be assigned. With a high degree of sophistication, the Romans established several distinct property classifications. They distinguished between tangible and intangible, movable and immovable, unique and fungible, divisible and indivisible. These distinctions are still used today.

The jurists identified degrees of ownership and possessory interests in a property, and they recognized the superior claims of those who were in possession. Our maxim that "possession is nine tenths of the law," meaning that the possessor of property has greater rights than anyone but the true owner, conveys the same idea as the Roman saying "Happy are those who possess."

The jurists developed the equity action of unjust enrichment and

---

[177] Alan Watson, *Roman Law and Comparative Law* (Athens, GA. University of Georgia Press, 1991) 112.

developed the rules of easements, bailments, and transferring property (*mancipatio*). Our current laws of adverse possession of real property came from the Roman concept of *usucapio*, meaning "I seize by use."

Roman law recognized jus in re, which gave laborers and contractors the right not only to sue for the value of their work on a property but also to hold the property itself as security for the debt. Their right was comparable to the American mechanics' lien. Thomas Jefferson, well versed in Roman law, was a member of the committee that recommended the first mechanics' lien law in the United States. Contrary to the English common law, which generally favored landowners, the new law helped workmen.[178]

The Roman wills, trusts, and estates law had far more commonalities to our law than differences and wouldn't seem out of place today. Their law of transfer (*traditio*) developed the concepts pertaining to the intent of the transferor and the transferee, and they developed the concepts of gifts inter vivos (during life) and gifts causa mortis (at death), which still apply today.

Laws of contract were developed and refined. In early Rome, the requirements to establish an enforceable contract involved strict formulations involving vows, stipulations, and promises, but as commerce increased during the middle republic, the praetors recognized the creation of a contract by a simple consensual agreement of the parties. This ability to enter enforceable contractual relationships with diverse parties promoted freedom of action and economic prosperity.

Rome introduced bankruptcy law to ancient civilization. Under archaic law, an insolvent debtor could be forced into servitude for a period of years to satisfy the unpaid debt. This presented the problem that only one creditor could be satisfied at a time, so a legal process was instituted wherein the praetor could put the debtor's estate into receivership, assign a trustee to sell the property at public auction, and distribute the proceeds pro rata among all the creditors. American bankruptcy law is essentially the same.

The Romans developed the corporate form and the juristic corporate

---

[178] Henry Farnam, *Chapters in the History of Social Legislation in the United States to 1860* (Carnegie Institute of Washington, 1938).

person, distinct from the individuals who comprised it. Legal status was given to *sodalitates*, collegia, and societas—private groups such as American associations and partnerships—that combined resources to achieve a common purpose and had broad powers to govern themselves and their own property, and to sue or be sued.

Many other legal concepts were passed from Rome to America through English common law. In his *Commentaries on the Laws of England* (published between 1770 and 1783), England's leading jurist, Lord William Blackstone, referenced the *Corpus Juris Civilis* of the Emperor Justinian and perpetuated its legal principles. The *Commentaries* sold as many copies in America as in England and were the authority for much of American law. After the revolution and the rejection of English rule, Americans jurists felt they should develop their own jurisprudence by selecting the best principles and procedures from wherever they could be found. They drew further away from England, and between the revolution and about 1850, they incorporated additional segments of Roman law into our laws. Supreme Court Justice Joseph Story advocated teaching Roman law as a part of a complete legal education. "Where shall we find such ample general principles to guide us in new and difficult cases, as in that venerable deposit[e] of the learning and labors of jurists of the ancient world, the Institutes and Pandects of Justinian. The whole continental jurisprudence rests upon this broad foundation of Roman wisdom; and the English common law, churlish and harsh as was its feudal education, has condescended silently to borrow many of its best principles from this enlightened code."[179]

In 1832, Josiah Quincy, president of Harvard University, favored Roman law in his speech at the dedication of the Dane Law College. "It is an admitted fact, that a great proportion of the boasted wisdom of the English common law, was acquired by a silent transfer into it of the wisdom of Roman law, through the medium of the courts of justice, and that thereby the English law was raised from its original state of rudeness and imperfection."[180]

---

[179] Joseph Story, *Address to the Suffolk Bar*, 1829, American Jurist 1, 13–4.
[180] Josiah Quincy, *The Legal Mind in America*, ed. Miller (1962), 206–7.

The similarities between Roman and American law can be striking. American courts regularly reach the same results the Romans would have. For example, the Roman jurist Ulpian outlined the Roman principle of setting an equitable penalty proportionate to the seriousness of the injury. He described how compensatory damages were set in a case in which an object falls from a building and injures a citizen. "When in consequence of the fall of one of these projectiles from a house, the body of a free man shall have suffered injury, the judge shall award to the victim in addition to medical fees and other expenses incurred in his treatment and necessary to his recovery, the total of the wages of which he has been or shall in future be deprived by the inability to work which has ensued."[181]

While following most Roman legal concepts proved beneficial for America, following Roman slavery laws didn't. When questions arose about the treatment of slaves, some American courts looked to Roman precedents. In 1827, a Virginia court in *Commonwealth v. Turner*,[182] sounding like Cato the Elder, ruled that it wasn't a crime for a slave owner to beat his slave with "certain rods, whips and sticks" as long as the slave didn't die.

In 1854, during a critical period in the battle over slavery, Luther Cushing, the renowned Harvard Law professor, noted, "An example of the Roman law occurs with reference to the institution of domestic slavery in this country. Wherever that relation has been introduced, it has been followed and regulated, in the absence of other legislation, by the principles of the Roman law."[183]

In some legal matters, Americans learned from the mistakes of Rome. Our ex post facto (after-the-fact) laws corrected the defect in Roman law wherein conduct could be made unlawful retroactively; such laws made security and peace of mind impossible. In Rome, not only could the assembly pass a law making conduct unlawful that previously had been lawful, but individuals could be proscribed because of a military or political defeat.

The US Constitution prohibits ex post facto laws. Article I, section 9,

---

[181] Justinian, *Digest*, 10, 3, 5, 7.
[182] 26 Va (6 Rand.) 678.
[183] Luther Cushing, *An Introduction to the Study of Roman Law* (Boston, 1854), 129.

states "No Bill of Attainder or ex post facto Law shall be passed." Article I, section 10, stated, "No State shall … pass any … ex post facto Law."

The American founders recognized the same potential conflicts of interest the Romans recognized when they established the *praetor peregrinus* to adjudicate cases between citizens and foreigners. To deal with the inherent conflicts in lawsuits between parties from different states, article 3 of the Constitution created diversity jurisdiction, whereby such suits could be removed from state courts to federal courts.

For criminal trials, both societies recognized the value of citizen juries as a protection for the accused, and both systems provided strong protections for jury independence and integrity. Trial lawyers played prominent roles, and both systems countenanced creative lawyering. Cicero, in describing the trial lawyers' function, wrote, "The judges' business, in every trial, is to discover the truth. As for counsel, however, he may on occasion have to base his advocacy on points which *look like* the truth, even if they do not correspond with it exactly."[184] Cicero didn't exclude himself from such conduct, writing, "Anyone who supposes that in my forensic speeches he has got my personal views under seal is making a great mistake … We orators are brought in to say not what we personally think but what is required by the situation and the case in hand."[185]

In our courts, as in Cicero's day, lawyering skills can affect the outcome of a case as much as the evidence. American lawyers are expected to zealously represent their clients, and it is acceptable for them, like their Roman counterparts, to "manage the facts" either through meticulous witness preparation or by obfuscation of the truth.

As both nations matured, the number of lawsuits increased exponentially. Aggressive instincts were channeled from the battlefield into courtrooms where glory and wealth could be obtained with less physical risk. Lawyers became like military generals, using witnesses instead of soldiers to accomplish their goals. The better tactician had the advantage, and the more determined advocate often won the case irrespective of the

---

[184] Cicero, *On Duties*, in M. Grant, *Cicero on the Good Life* (New York: Penguin Classics, 1971), 147.
[185] Cicero, "Pro Cluentio," 139.

merits. As Walter Olson put it in *The Litigation Explosion*, "It was a playground for bullies, an uneven battlefield, where the trustful, scrupulous, and plainspoken were no match for the brassy, ruthless, and glib."

Despite the negatives associated with adversarial litigation, the Roman and American judicial systems helped to maintain the necessary balance between security and liberty. Although most cases dealt with localized or personal conflicts, many dealt with broader issues that encompassed important political considerations. The Roman tradition and practice of great speechmaking in debates in front of juries and assemblies—by such as Memmius, Appius, and Cicero—brought important issues before the people for their decision. Similarly, in early America, great orators—Patrick Henry, Henry Clay, and Daniel Webster, among others—were lawyers who followed in the footsteps of great Roman orators.

In both Rome and America, the give-and-take of argument by great legal advocates bolstered the respect for law, enriched civil discourse, and facilitated the advancement of society.

CHAPTER 21

Roman and American Senators

MOST WRITTEN HISTORIES HAVE emphasized the steps toward democratic progress, rightfully giving great attention to agents of change and leaders of democratic movements. Some have emphasized democratic expansion to such a degree that they have left the reader wondering why society hadn't yet reached a plateau of complete democracy and egalitarianism. One reason may be that these histories didn't present balanced approaches to either political or social dynamics. They neglected the forces opposed to change—the guardians of traditional values, customs, stability, and the status quo. When describing leaders of the establishment or leaders who blocked democratic or egalitarian measures, they described those leaders as reactionaries, as protectors of the wealthy or the landed aristocracy; and they rarely acclaimed them as great men. Guardians of the status quo were simply not as attractive or exciting as the up-and-coming activists fighting for change in the face of establishment opposition. The activists made good protagonists; the reactionaries made good antagonists, easily portrayed as villains.

In fact, both the protagonists and the antagonists played the roles necessary for the healthy development of society; they provided the needed political opposition to check extreme and questionable proposals. The Romans designed a dual system, in which advocates for change played a starring role in the people's assemblies while the guardians of the status quo played their roles in the Senate. The American founders designed a similar system in which congressmen in the House of Representatives, closer to the populace, advocated changes in accordance with popular opinion, while senators either prevented change or slowed it down.

Credit shouldn't be withheld from those Romans who worked to preserve the status quo and the balance of power between classes and factions, thus allowing society to persevere, develop, and advance. These guardians were often accused of resisting reforms out of greed and pride; however, greed and pride alone couldn't have prevented popular forces from taking control. The Roman guardians believed in the righteousness of their constitutional institutions, and these beliefs motivated them to resist the subversion of these institutions. They strongly believed in the traditional values of the early Republic and persuasively conveyed those values to all classes of society, counteracting the appeals and demands of demagogues and revolutionaries. They pointed to the time when the senatorial class enjoyed the deference and respect of the people; when the nobles acted out of honor and duty, not only for themselves but for the honor of ancestors, family, and country; when the elites governed the masses for the benefit of all; when honorable and courageous military service was a prerequisite for political office; when high office was earned by following the course of honor (from quaestor, aedile, praetor, and, for a selected few, consul). To them, the republic thrived when the senatorial class shared control among themselves and the leading nobles took turns filling high offices and governorships, when all those eligible were given a chance to prove their worth and earn glory.

The guardians demanded adherence to traditional religious practices and in times of crisis reverted to archaic rituals. They wholeheartedly believed in the connection between the proper performance of rituals and sacrifices to bountiful harvests and military victories. They believed in the fulfillment of duties and oaths as the prerequisite for military success. When Camillus took charge of the army after the Gauls sacked Rome, and when Fabius Maximus was appointed dictator after the defeat by Hannibal at Lake Trasimene, the first act of each man was to mandate extraordinary religious sacrifices and devotions to the gods.

In the late republic, secular approaches began to supplant religion, and *populares* proposed major political and social reforms. A line of senators resisted the proposed changes and resisted the transfer of power from the Senate to popular demagogues. These senators opposed the reforms of the Gracchi, the repeated consulships of Marius, the usurpation of power by Cinna, and the extraordinary commands of Pompey and Caesar. They supported Sullan reforms because these reforms revived senatorial power and the traditional constitution.

Debate between change agents and guardians of the status quo flourished in the Senate, assemblies, and courts; and an extraordinary group of leaders rose to prominence, each possessing great oratorical skills. On the *optimate* side, Cicero, Cato, and Catullus played the role of an informal triumvirate opposed in principle to the *populare* triumvirate of Caesar, Pompey, and Crassus.

CICERO

The best orator of the three, though not the most consistent, was Marcus Tullius Cicero. Although his political positions shifted over the years, on the whole he defended Rome's traditional institutions and its checks-and-balances system. Unfortunately, as a mediator between opposing political factions, he often alienated one side or the other.

The year of his consulship, 63 BC, was marked by his victory over the Catiline conspirators. To achieve his victory, he had to overcome a major obstacle: the prosecution Cato brought against the consul-elect for 62 BC, Lucius Licinius Murena. Allegedly, Murena had used bribery to win his election for consul, defeating Catiline and Servius Rufus. The defeated candidates took different courses; Catiline mounted his revolt against Rome; Rufus brought ambitus (election bribery) charges against Murena.

The establishment needed to rally together to face Catiline's revolt, and Murena was a reliable *optimate* who would help defend the state. While the unadaptable, unbending Cato saw it as his duty to prosecute Murena and did so in the role of lead prosecutor, Cicero made the opposite decision. He agreed to defend Murena because the conviction and exile of the consul-elect would have led to political chaos and strengthened Catiline's hand.

Ironically, Cicero had pushed to amend and strengthen the law of ambitus, increasing the penalty to exile for ten years. Now he had to defend against the enforcement of his own law.

Cicero was the better lawyer, and he applied the lawyer's adage—when you have a guilty client, change the subject. Despite the seriousness of the matter, he used humor to disarm the jury, switching the focus from Murena's guilt to the absurdities of Cato's Stoic beliefs. He told the jury that Stoics believed "that no one is merciful except a fool and a trifler … that wise men, no matter how deformed, are the only beautiful men; that even if they are beggars, they are the only rich men; that even in slavery, they are kings. And all of us who are not wise men, they call slaves, exiles, enemies, lunatics. They say that all offenses are equal, that every sin is an unpardonable crime, and that it is just as much of a crime to needlessly kill a rooster as to strangle one's own father."[186]

Murena was acquitted, and after he was installed as consul, he led an army to defeat Catiline's forces.

As successful as Cicero was in court and in the Senate, he was frequently the subject of criticism. He always felt personally offended by the criticism and responded with forceful justifications for his conduct. In 54 BC, he tried to justify his temporary support of the triumvirate in a letter to the *optimate* Publius Cornelius Lentulus Spinther, writing,

> I should like it to be clear to you that my attitude would have been just the same if I had had an open and completely untrammeled choice. I should not be in favor of fighting such formidable power, nor of abolishing the preeminence of our greatest citizens, even if that were possible. Nor should I be for sticking fast to one set of opinions, when circumstances have changed and the sentiments of honest men are no longer the same. I believe in moving with the times. Unchanging consistency of standpoint has never been considered a virtue in a great statesman. At sea it is good sailing to run before the gale, even if the ship cannot make harbor; but if she can make

---

[186] Cicero, *Pro Murena*, 61–62.

harbor by changing tack, only a fool would risk shipwreck
by holding to the original course rather than change and
still reach his destination.[187]

As a respected statesman, Cicero's opinion was valued, but in giving
his opinions, he made numerous enemies. After Caesar's assassination,
when the Senate turned against Antony, Cicero delivered several speeches,
describing the events and personages of the day. In one speech, he subtly
criticized the deceased Caesar, which didn't endear him to Caesar's adopted son, Augustus. "In [Caesar] there was genius, calculation, memory,
letters, industry, thought, diligence; he had done in war things, however,
calamitous to the State, yet at least great; having for many years aimed at a
throne, he had by great labor, great dangers, achieved his object; by shows,
buildings, largess, banquets he had conciliated the ignorant crowd; his
own followers he had bound to him by rewards, his adversaries by a show
of clemency: in brief, he had already brought to a free community—partly
by fear, partly by endurance—a habit of servitude."[188]

He followed his speech with twelve political pamphlets called the
Philippics. In the second, Cicero responded to Antony's accusation that he
had been involved in the assassination plot. Although filled with qualifi-
ers, the pamphlet ultimately praised the assassins—Brutus, Cassius, and
others—and implied that they should have also killed Antony.

> For heaven will bear witness that Rome—that any nation
> throughout the whole world—has never seen a greater
> act than theirs! There has never been an achievement
> more glorious—more greatly deserving of renown for all
> eternity. So if you pen me in a Trojan horse of complicity
> with the chief partners in the deed, I do not protest.
>
> Enroll me among such heroes, I beg you! I am afraid
> that one thing may not be to your liking. If I had been
> among their number I should have freed our country not

---

[187] Cicero, *Letters to Friends*, ed. D. R. Shackleton-Ailey, 3 vols. (London, 2001) 1.9.21.
[188] Cicero, *Philippics*, ed. W. Ker (London, 1926), 2.116.

> only from the autocrat but from the autocracy. For if, as
> you assert, I had been the author of the work, believe me,
> I should not have been satisfied to finish only one act: I
> should have completed the play!

He castigated and accused Antony.

> But suppose that someone prosecutes you; that he applies
> the test of the jurist Lucius Cassius Longinus: "who ben-
> efited thereby?" Then you will have to take care, for you
> might be implicated. ... Whom did its performance ben-
> efit most? Yourself! You, who far from being a slave, are
> an autocratic ruler: you, who employed the treasure in
> the Temple of Ops to wipe off your gigantic debts, who af-
> ter manipulating these same account-books squandered
> countless sums, who transferred enormous possessions
> from Caesar's house to your own ... Nothing short of
> Caesar's death could have rescued you from your debtor's
> ruin.[189]

Ultimately, Cicero's criticism of Caesar and his attack on Antony would cost him his life.

CATO

Marcus Portius Cato the Younger was an *optimate* in the extreme. He argued and fought to preserve Roman traditions of old, not only in the realm of political process but also in social values. Austerity in expenditures and conduct, he believed, would keep Rome strong. His model was his great-grandfather, Cato the Elder, who had fought to preserve Roman discipline and integrity.

It would be an understatement to say that Cato the Younger was an eccentric. His eventful life molded his unusual character. As an orphaned

---

[189] Cicero, *Selected Works*, trans. Michael Grant (Baltimore, MD: Penguin Books, 1960).

child, he lived in the household of his uncle, Marcus Livius Drusus, at the time Drusus was assassinated in the portico of his house. As a teenager, Cato excelled in the training exercises of young nobles, bringing him to the attention and favor of the dictator Sulla. He spent time in Sulla's orbit, but he detested dictatorship and, according to Plutarch, once asked for a sword to kill Sulla.

As a military tribune, he saw combat against Spartacus and Mithridates, demonstrated extraordinary bravery and leadership, and won the respect of his legionary comrades. He was elected quaestor and became a member of the Senate. However, because he had partial plebeian ancestry, he ran for and was elected as a tribune of the people, an office that allowed him to assert vetoes in the assembly against proposals that would have undermined the traditional constitution. Initially, his main concern was that Pompey would seize dictatorial powers when he returned from the East with his army, and he declared to all that Pompey's troops would enter Rome over his dead body. Later, he would become more concerned with Caesar's ambitions.

When necessary, Cato would conduct all-day filibusters in the Senate or the assembly to block proposals with which he disagreed. He wasn't a charming speaker but a combative one, who spoke the raw truth. In the Senate debate about whether to execute the Catiline conspirators, Caesar had argued that the ancients would have shown mercy. Cato challenged that contention and also the lack of fortitude and moral weakness of the senators.

> Do you support that our ancestors, from so small a be-ginning, raised the Republic to greatness merely by force of arms. If that been the case, we would be safe; because allies and citizens, arms and horse, we have in more abun-dance than they did. There were other things that made them great, which we lack: industry at home; equitable government abroad; minds impartial in council, uninflu-enced by any immoral or improper feeling.
>
> Instead of such virtues, we have luxury and avarice, public distress and private superfluity; we extol wealth

and yield to indolence; no distinction is made between good and bad men; and ambition usurps the honors due to virtue. Since each of you focuses on his individual interests and since at home you are slaves to pleasure, money, or favor, it happens that an attack is made on the defenseless state. ...

We are completely surrounded. Catiline and his army are ready to grip us by the throat ... The conspirators have planned massacres, fires, horrible and cruel outrages against their fellow-citizens and their country. Punish them in the spirit of our ancestors.[190]

Cato, along with Cicero, won that argument, and the conspirators were executed.

In 54 BC, Cato, as praetor, introduced an election reform law, one that would have curtailed the "generosity" of candidates running for office. It was a widespread practice for candidates to distribute gifts and favors, free meals and entertainments, even gifts of money to the urban populace. When the proposal became known, Cato was cursed and stoned. A tribune vetoed the proposal.

When Cato ran for consul in 52 BC, he refused to provide "generosity." Although his principled stand garnered substantial votes for him, they weren't enough to overcome the other candidates who spent liberally.

Cato's consistent adherence to his principles won him respect but not friends. When Cicero requested a triumph for his actions as the governor of Cilicia, Cato refused to support him, and he even refused to vote in favor of a thanksgiving (a lesser honor) that the Senate awarded him. In a letter to Cicero, he explained his position with a lecture.

That a thanksgiving was decreed I am glad, if you prefer our thanking the gods rather than giving you the credit for a success, which has been in no respect left to chance but has been secured for the Republic by your

---

[190] Sallust, *Bellum Catilinae* 52; Plutarch, *Cato Minor* 23. 3.

own eminent prudence and self-control. But if you think a thanksgiving to be a presumption in favor of a triumph, and therefore prefer fortune having the credit rather than yourself, let me remind you that a triumph does not always follow a thanksgiving; and that it is an honor much more brilliant than a triumph for the Senate to declare its opinion, that a province has been retained rather by the uprightness and mildness of its governor than by the strength of an army or the favor of heaven; And that is what I meant to express by my vote.[191]

In several instances, Cato's rigid adherence to his principles proved detrimental to the *optimate* cause and the preservation of the republic. Although he talked of sacrifice for the republic, he refused Pompey's request to marry one of his daughters. Marriages were how political alliances were cemented, and the marriage would have brought Pompey into the camp of the *optimates*. Instead, Pompey married Caesar's daughter as part of the deal to form the First Triumvirate, an alliance antithetical to republican principles.

Cato had bitten off his nose to spite his face, and his act would have far-reaching and severe consequences. A decade later, as his army lost to Caesar's army in North Africa, Cato committed suicide rather than surrender or appeal for clemency.

CATULUS

Quintus Lutatius Catulus Capitolinus (circa 120–61 BC), a leading *consulare*, represented the *optimate* cause throughout his career. He was called Capitolinus because he restored the Temple of Jupiter Optimus Maximus on the Capitoline Hill. Although a staunch supporter of the Senate against those he saw as radical demagogues, he took a far more pragmatic approach than Cato and was far more consistent than Cicero.

---

[191] Rob Godman and Jimmy Soni, quoted in *Rome's Last Citizen*, New York: St. Martin's Press, 2012) 214.

Understandably, he had a personal animosity toward the radicals, whom he saw as striving to undermine Rome's hierarchical structure. His father of the same name, Quintus Lutatius Catulus, the Elder (149–87 BC), had been coconsul in 102 BC with Gaius Marius. Despite their joint success in a major battle against the Cimbri, the coconsuls feuded, and after the war, each built a competing temple to commemorate his victory. Catulus, the Elder, dedicated the temple to the goddess Fortuna. The ruins of this temple can still be seen today at the Largo Argentina.

He was consul again in 87 BC, and in the conflict of that year between Sulpicius, Marius, and Cinna on one side and Sulla on the other, he sided with Sulla. Unfortunately for him, Marius and Cinna gained control of the city, and Marius's nephew prosecuted him. Rather than accept the inevitable guilty verdict, he committed suicide.

In 83 BC, when Sulla returned to Rome to dislodge the Cinnan-Marian faction, Catulus, the Younger, readily supported Sulla's annihilation of the usurpers. He applauded the restoration of the Senate's authority and the dislodging of the tribunes. After Sulla's death, Catulus shared the 78 BC consulship with Marcus Aemilius Lepidus (120–77 BC) in what was thought to be a balanced and stable power arrangement. However, at the end of their term, Lepidus illegally took control of the Po Valley with his private army, demanded that his consulate be extended, and proposed the overthrow of Sulla's constitution. The Senate issued a senatus consultum ultimatum against him, and Catulus, as proconsul with the aid of Pompey and Sullan veterans, defeated Lepidus at the Campus Martius. Lepidus fled to Sardinia, where he died.

That was the first test of the Sullan restoration, but there would be more. In the following years, Catulus endeavored to uphold the traditions of constitutional government while directing the operations of the Senate. This was a difficult challenge because the civil war had eliminated most of those who had been the leading *consulares*, and the Senate had increased to six hundred members, most of whom were new. Catulus took on the responsibility of directing Senate business, protecting its authority, and enforcing its code of conduct. For a decade he worked diligently to keep relative peace between warring factions by encouraging compromises and conciliations.

In 65 BC, the peace began to unravel. Catulus was cocensor with Crassus, and they disagreed over Crassus's plan to annex Egypt. Several other disagreements between them prevented them from conducting the census. Catulus also opposed the proposals to grant extraordinary powers to Pompey and Caesar. He consistently opposed Caesar and even attempted to implicate him in the Catiline conspiracy. In retaliation, Caesar attempted to prosecute Catulus for embezzlement of treasury funds earmarked for the restoration of the temple of Jupiter, but Caesar dropped the charges in the face of the high regard in which all sides held Catulus. The opinion of Catulus held great influence, and it was to him that Catiline wrote his letter of justification for his conspiratorial actions. It was to him that Caesar, Cicero, and Cato directed their arguments regarding the punishment of the captured Catiline conspirators.

Catulus voted with Cicero and Cato for the execution of the conspirators and for the declaration of Catiline as an enemy of the people. The defeat of the conspirators and Catiline's army was the last substantial victory of the *optimate* faction, and afterward Catulus faded in prominence as the *populare* faction strengthened. He lost the election for *pontifex maximus* to the younger Julius Caesar, an office that traditionally would have gone to the older man. From that point, Catullus gradually lost influence until his death in 61 BC.

Without Catulus, the weakened *optimate* faction lost control of the state to the First Triumvirate and then to the dictatorship of Caesar. Without him, Cicero was proscribed and murdered, and Cato committed suicide.

THE GREAT AMERICAN TRIUMVIRATE

From the beginning of the American republic, the Senate also endeavored to preserve traditional values, customs, and the status quo, particularly the constitutional system of the framers. This senatorial outlook helped to maintain the balance of power between classes, reducing conflicts and allowing society to develop and advance. As in Rome, the American Senate also produced groups of outstanding orators and debaters. With apologies to Patrick Henry and Abraham Lincoln, the most extraordinary group of American orators came of age in the postrevolutionary era. Senators Daniel Webster, John Calhoun, and Henry Clay equaled or surpassed the eloquence of the senatorial Romans—Cicero, Cato, and Catulus. Like the trio that opposed Julius Caesar, this American trio spent most of their careers opposing Andrew Jackson, the purported American Caesar.

WEBSTER

Daniel Webster (1782–1850) began his political life as a Federalist, but upon the demise of that party, he aligned with the National Republicans and later the Whigs. As a Whig, he served as secretary of state under Presidents Harrison, Tyler, and Fillmore. In addition to his service in the Senate and the government, Webster was the most outstanding lawyer of his era. In 1819, he successfully argued in the important case of *Dartmouth College v. Woodward* that the US Constitution protected private contracts from government interference. Dartmouth College had been incorporated by royal charter in 1769, and the case arose when the trustees of the college, who were Congregationalists and Federalists, removed John Wheelock, a Presbyterian and a Republican, from the presidency of the college.

The Republican-controlled New Hampshire legislature intervened to reinstate Wheelock. They did so by revoking the old charter of 1769 and creating a new corporation with a new set of Republican trustees. The new trustees reinstated Wheelock, and the deposed Federalist trustees sued. Webster represented the Federalist trustees before the Supreme Court, arguing that the original charter was a contract protected by article 1, section 10, of the US Constitution and that the government could not abrogate it. The court agreed with Webster, reinstating the old trustees, who removed Wheelock again. The decision established the freedom of privately funded universities from government interference; and more broadly, it had enormous implications for private property rights, giving private corporations constitutional protections. Corporations were no longer public institutions but private property belonging to individual shareholders, not the state.

Webster successfully argued more than one hundred cases before the Supreme Court. He was always persuasive, and his arguments were often used as models for the court's written opinions. In the Senate, where the parameters of legal argument didn't hinder him, his speeches often reached the heights of eloquence. Perhaps one of his greatest speeches was the reply he gave in 1830 to Senator Robert Haynes of South Carolina, who had supported the free distribution of public lands in the western states. Webster opposed the distribution of free land, making several pragmatic arguments and contending that the current policy of selling the land at market prices was the most sensible system because the proceeds were used to pay down the public debt. He augmented his pragmatic case with flights of eloquence. At one point, he spoke of the American settlers, discussing what they had achieved and the sacrifices they had made to obtain the land.

> These colonists, if we are to call them so; in passing the Alleghany, did not pass beyond the care and protection of their own government. Wherever they went, the public arm was still stretched over them. A parental government at home was still ever mindful of their condition, and their wants; and nothing was spared, which a just sense of their necessities required. Is it forgotten, that it was one of the most arduous duties of government, in its earliest years, to defend the frontiers against the north-western Indians ... Sir, it was not til General Wayne's victory, in 1794, that it could be said, we had conquered the savages. It was not til that period, that the government could have considered itself as having established an entire ability to protect those who should undertake the conquest of the wilderness. ...
>
> Over all that is now Ohio, where then stretched one vast wilderness, unbroken, except by two small spots of civilized culture, the one at Marietta, and the other at Cincinnati. At these little openings, hardly each a pin's point upon the map, the arm of the frontiersman had leveled the forest, and let in the sun. These little patches

of earth, and themselves almost shadowed by the hanging boughs of that wilderness, which had stood and
perpetuated itself, from century to century, ever since
the creation, were all that had then been rendered ver-
dant by the hand of man. In an extend of hundreds, and
thousands of square miles, no other surface of smiling
green attested the presence of civilization. The hunter's
path crossed mighty rivers, flowing in solitary grandeur,
whose sources lay in remote and unknown regions of the
wilderness. It struck upon the north, on a vast inland sea,
over which the tempests raged as on the ocean; all over
was bare creation. It was fresh, untouched, unbounded,
magnificent wilderness.

Webster then described how the government's policy of selling the
land at a fair price had contributed to the successful settlement of those
wilderness lands.

The debate on the issue wasn't over. Senator Haynes replied with an
equally admirable speech but one that suggested a possible dissolution of
the Union. Webster wasn't to be outdone, delivering his famous second
reply to Haynes, which many have called the greatest speech in Senate
history.

When my eyes shall be turned to behold for the last time
the sun in heaven, may I not see him shining on the broken and dishonored fragments of a once glorious Union;
on States dissevered, discordant, belligerent; on a land
rent with civil feuds, or drenched, it may be, in fraternal
blood! Let their last feeble and lingering glance rather
behold the gorgeous ensign of the republic ... not a stripe
erased or polluted, nor a single star obscured, bearing for
its motto, no such miserable interrogatory as "What is all
this worth?" nor those other words of delusion and folly,
"Liberty first and Union afterwards"; but everywhere,
spread all over in characters of living light, blazing on all

its ample folds, as they float over the sea and over the land, and in every wind under the whole heavens, that other sentiment, dear to every true American heart—Liberty *and* Union, now and forever, one and inseparable![192]

Words have consequences, and Webster's had favorable consequences, beating back those who cried "liberty" but actually meant "secession."

As an advocate, Webster was called the Cicero of his day. In fact, his record was far better than Cicero's. As a politician, he played a role more like that of Catulus—consistently defending property rights and opposing the distribution of free land but compromising to preserve the republic.[193]

CALHOUN

John C. Calhoun (1782–1850) also opposed free western land for settlers but for a different reason. He wanted to preserve slavery. From South Carolina, he served as a congressman, senator, secretary of war, and vice president. He was six foot two with a striking appearance; he was well spoken and learned. A slave owner, he had inherited his family mansion. A guest at the mansion said it was "like spending an evening in a gracious Tuscan villa with a Roman senator." He held some well-considered principles, but they were tainted by his support of slavery.

Throughout his career, Calhoun defended slavery with theoretical arguments, using exultant language that masked the inherent flaw in his thinking. Every issue was viewed through the eyes of slave owners. He opposed the land distribution bill for free land for settlers in the western territories because he believed the eventual addition of nonslave western states would upset the nation's political balance to the detriment of the slave states.

Calhoun's life was that of a brilliant man possessed by a fanatical ideology that could lead only to civil war. He advocated the theory of a

---

[192] Reg. Deb., 22nd Cong., 1st Sess.

[193] Paul Johnson, *History of the American People,* (New York: Harper Perennial, 1997) 316.

concurrent majority rather than a numerical majority. This meant that a popular majority couldn't impose its will on the minority; each cohesive political faction must approve a national law, because this was the only way to protect minority rights. Calhoun saw southern white slave owners as a minority, and his political theories, though couched in sophisticated language, seemed to be mere rationalization to preserve his comfortable lifestyle, obtained through the labor of others.

Calhoun's concurrent majority system would produce the same electoral outcomes as the Roman weighted-voting system in which the elite, a numerical minority, had to approve a law or candidate. Calhoun's system protected southern plantation owners; the Roman system protected latifundia owners.

As Andrew Jackson's vice president, Calhoun favored the annexation of Florida and Texas as slave-holding states, but he broke with Jackson over the Tariff Acts. In 1832, Calhoun resigned the vice presidency and was immediately elected to the Senate, where he delivered powerful speeches advocating states' rights. He argued that the United States wasn't a union but a compact from which states could secede or in which states could nullify laws that adversely affected their interests. At Calhoun's urging, South Carolina passed a Nullification Law and announced that it wouldn't abide by the tariffs.

Clay and Webster argued to the contrary and urged compromise. Calhoun and South Carolina stubbornly resisted any compromise, but the stakes were raised when President Jackson requested Congress pass a bill authorizing the use of force against South Carolina. Jackson called up the militia, ordered General Winfield Scott to move three artillery divisions into Charleston, South Carolina, and sent a battleship and seven cutters to Charleston Harbor. He also threatened to hang Calhoun and his compatriots for treason. Not willing to back down, the South Carolinians mobilized to fight, but as the crisis reached its peak, Henry Clay introduced the Compromise Tariff Bill of 1833, scaling down the tariff sufficiently for South Carolina to save face. The state rescinded Calhoun's Nullification Law, and a civil war was avoided for the time being.

To avoid Jackson's wrath, Calhoun reluctantly agreed to the 1833 compromise, but he didn't change his positions and became even more rigid in his beliefs until he died in 1850.

CLAY

Henry Clay (1777–1852) was the most prominent and influential of the triumvirs. In 1797, he moved from Virginia to Kentucky, where he established a lucrative law practice and became a leading statesman. Clay held positions as congressman, senator, Speaker of the House (five times), and secretary of state; he ran for president three times. His greatest attribute was his oratorical ability; he was known not only for his histrionics but also for his clear and thoughtful presentation of the issues in question. An astute political tactician, he became known as the Great Compromiser.

Clay was mostly self-taught. He knew the classics and wrote letters under the name Scavola, the Roman jurist. As a young man, he wrote a letter to the *Kentucky Gazette* on April 25, 1798, arguing for the emancipation of slaves, although he owned them. He wrote,

> Can any humane man be happy and contented when he sees near thirty thousand of his fellow beings around him, deprived of all the rights which make life desirable, transferred like cattle from the possession of one to another; when he sees the trembling slave, under the hammer, surrounded by a number of eager purchasers, and feeling all the emotions which arise when one is uncertain into whose tyrannic hands he must next fall; when he beholds the anguish and hears the piercing cries of husbands separated from wives and children from parents; when, in a word, all the tender and endearing ties of nature are broken asunder and disregarded; and when he reflects that no gradual mode of emancipation is adopted either for those slaves or their posterity, doubling the number every twenty-five years. To suppose the people of Kentucky, enthusiasts as they are in the cause of liberty,

could be contented and happy under circumstances like these, would be insulting their good sense.[194]

Clay might have been seen as a radical for his call for emancipation, but he was more talk than action. He owned slaves throughout his life, and political considerations always dictated his positions. At best, he advocated gradual emancipation; at worst, he advocated repatriation to Africa. In practical politics, he often played the role of mediator between Webster, the abolitionist, and Calhoun, the slaveholder. His main priorities were national security, national unity, and economic development.

He was the leading proponent of what he called the American System, which supported tariffs designed to allow America's fledgling manufacturing sector to compete with foreign goods. East Coast manufacturing would benefit most. To persuade western states to support the tariffs, he proposed that the revenue raised by the tariffs be used for infrastructure improvements—namely roads and canals that would connect eastern and western states. He also advocated for a national bank that would stabilize the currency and foster a vibrant financial system.

He differed from Calhoun and the states' rights proponents because he believed the Constitution contemplated greater capabilities for the federal government to protect national security and promote the prosperity of the people. Interpreting the Constitution expansively, he argued that Congress could establish post offices, build roads, and regulate interstate commerce. Although others might disagree, Clay believed tensions between states' rights advocates and those in favor of centralized power could be reduced through compromise. In his biography of Clay, Robert Rimini summarized,

> Perhaps better than anyone else of his generation, Clay also understood that differences of opinion among men would arise from time to time on a wide range of issues, not simply constitutional interpretation. Differences between the states and the national government, differences

---

[194] Clay, *Papers*, 1. 4–5.

between sections of the country, between competing economic interests, and between classes could be expected as the natural consequence of a people engaged in disparate occupations scattered across a huge country. It was therefore up to statesmen to find the means to resolve their differences in order to advance the material well-being of the American people and, most especially, to prevent the "convulsion and subversion of the government." That was the reason he placed such reliance on compromise over the next several decades. Men were bound to disagree on principles and issues, he said; if they were unwilling to work out their differences through a process of give-and-take, the result could be catastrophic. The result could produce savage civil conflict.[195]

Clay believed strongly in the checks-and-balances system, and his career was marked by his opposition to Andrew Jackson, whom he saw as the embodiment of Caesarism. His conflict with Jackson began in earnest on January 20, 1819, when Clay moved to censure General Jackson for his conduct surrounding the invasion and seizure of Florida. The motion to censure wasn't as drastic as Cato's proposal to prosecute Caesar for his expansive invasions in Gaul, but to Jackson it was just as threatening and insulting.

Before a packed House of Representatives, Clay spoke for two hours. He opened by claiming that he had nothing but the utmost respect for Jackson, but he decried the unauthorized seizure of Florida from Spain, the execution of two British subjects, and the Treaty of Fort Jackson, from which the Native American Creeks were forced to surrender their land. More potently, he decried that the Creeks were forced to deliver their religious leaders, their "prophets," to Jackson for execution. A people's religion should be respected. "When even did conquering and desolating Rome fail to respect the altars and the gods of those whom she subjugated?" Clay

---

[195] Robert Remini, *Henry Clay, Statesman for the Union* (New York: W. W. Norton, 1991) 142.

implored, "But, sir, spare them their prophets! Spare their delusions! Spare their prejudices and superstitions! Spare them even their religion, such as it is, from open and cruel violence!"

After suggesting that Jackson was a potential Alexander, Caesar, Cromwell, or Napoleon, Clay said that the republic would survive "by keeping a watchful and steady eye on the Executive; and above all, by holding to a strict accountability the military branch of the public force."[196]

The censure motion was shelved with the expiration of the congressional session. Jackson didn't immediately retaliate but began his lifelong crusade against Clay. A clash between these two men wouldn't have been a minor matter. They were both passionate and strong willed. Neither was reluctant to engage in a duel. Jackson had engaged in several, killing one man; Clay had engaged in two. In one he was shot in the leg; and in another against Virginia Senator John Randolph, shots were fired, but neither man was hit.

After the speech, Clay tried to assure Jackson that his argument wasn't a personal matter; thus, a duel didn't materialize. To be sure, the acrimony between them didn't disappear. Jackson wrote to a friend, "The hypocracy [sic] & baseness of Clay in pretending friendship to me, & endeavouring to crush the executive through me, make me despise the Villain."[197]

Clay was certainly a forceful adversary, but he was also an effective mediator. As a congressman in 1820–1821, he brokered the Missouri Compromise, which admitted Missouri, a slave state, and Maine, a free state, to the Union so the balance between slave and free states remained the same; thus, civil war was avoided and the Union preserved.

Abraham Lincoln took the same approach as Clay to the slavery problem, also hoping for its natural end without a war. Although Lincoln surely surpassed Clay as a statesman, it is debatable whether he surpassed him in lawyering. Robert Remini described Clay's mastery as follows:

---

[196] Annals of Cong., 15th Cong., 2d Sess., 631–655.
[197] Andrew Jackson to Major Lewis, January 25, 30, 1819 (New York Public Library: Jackson-Lewis Papers) in Remini, *Henry Clay*, 167.

He delighted juries. He even mesmerized them at times. In court he frequently regaled the juries with funny stories and anecdotes, told with gestures and grimaces and emotional outbursts. He quickly learned the arts that appealed to westerners, and he unashamedly employed them to his advantage. ...

In this setting he provided a thoughtful, lucid examination of the question, but couched in sharply focused, exciting, and sometimes dramatic language. His versatility, his extraordinary verbal range, his powers of argumentation were the reasons for Clay's meteoric rise to prominence in Kentucky. He could stampede audiences when sufficiently inspired and lift them out of themselves. He could reduce them to screaming, yelling, cheering mobs. Frequently, during the course of a long congressional career, he so ignited the galleries that the presiding officer was forced to clear them to restore order. ...

But it must be remembered that this success was not simply a triumph of style, theatrical wizardry, manner, or tone, although his consummate artistry constantly informed his public efforts. There was more. There was always enormous substance in what he said. With all stories and jokes and posturing, he made uncommon good sense when he spoke. He persuaded listeners; he did not bamboozle them.[198]

As a political manager, Clay was also a master. In 1823, as Speaker of the House, he cooperated with Webster to form the Nationalist-Republican Party to counteract the Jackson's Democratic-Republican Party. The Nationalist-Republicans would eventually become the Whig Party and then evolve into Lincoln's Republican Party.

The 1824 election for president exacerbated the acrimony between

---

[198] Remini, *Henry Clay*, 19.

Clay and Jackson. None of the four major candidates secured a majority in the electoral college. Jackson finished with the most votes, John Quincy Adams finished second, William Crawford third, and Clay fourth. At that time, the top three vote getters advanced to a runoff in the House of Representatives. Clay threw his support behind Adams, ensuring his win. When Adams assumed the presidency, he appointed Clay as secretary of state, and Jackson promptly accused Clay of making a "corrupt bargain" to secure the appointment. This accusation undermined the effectiveness of the Adams and Clay administration, and it was continually repeated for two decades, increasing in prominence with every vehement denial by Clay.

In 1828, Jackson ran for president as the standard bearer for the new Democratic Party. Clay campaigned for President Adams and repeatedly attacked Jackson. At a town meeting in Baltimore, he raised the fears of Caesarism and the worship of a military hero. He revived a theme from his 1819 censure motion, comparing Jackson to "the Phillips—the Caesars—the Cromwells—the Mariuses and the Scyllas [Sulla]." He excoriated "blind and heedless enthusiasm for mere military renown."[199]

Despite Clay's efforts, Jackson soundly defeated Adams for the presidency.

During Jackson's term, patronage abuses by his administration arose, and Clay reiterated his charge of Caesarism. He spoke at a dinner in Lexington, Kentucky. "Now persons are dismissed, not only without trial of any sort, but without charge ... by the will of one man ... But I must say that if an ambitious President sought the overthrow of our Government, and ultimately to establish a different form, he would ... proclaim, by his official act, that the greatest public virtue was ardent devotion to him ... Such an ambitious President would say, as monarchs have said, 'I am the State.'"

Clay described what Caesarism would mean for the presidency: "We should behold the victor distributing the prizes and applying his

---

[199] Clay, *Papers*, vol. 7, 272-273.

punishments, like a military commander, immediately after he had won a great victory."[200]

In 1832, Clay was nominated to run for president as the National-Republican Party candidate. From his seat in the Senate, he did everything he could to undermine the Jackson administration. At one point he aligned with Webster and Vice President John Calhoun in what was called the "Great Triumvirate."[201] Although they held different positions on many issues, the three men worked together against Jackson.

Vice President Calhoun suffered a falling out with Jackson when the latter belatedly learned that Calhoun had supported the censure motion against him in 1819. Now Calhoun joined with Clay and Webster to sabotage Jackson's nomination of Martin Van Buren as ambassador to Great Britain. As president of the Senate, Calhoun enjoyed casting the deciding vote to reject Van Buren and embarrass Jackson.

A greater issue was the re-charter of the Second Bank of the United States. In June 1832, Congress passed the re-charter bill, but President Jackson vetoed it, proclaiming that the bank was unconstitutional. He stated this despite a previous Supreme Court decision, *McCullough v. Maryland*, written by Chief Justice John Marshall that upheld the constitutionality of the bank.

The veto was vociferously attacked by Republicans who charged that Jackson had annulled two houses of Congress, the Supreme Court, and the Constitution of the United States. The *Washington National Intelligencer* proclaimed that the "Constitution is gone! It is a dead letter, and the will of a DICTATOR is the Supreme Law."[202]

The 1832 presidential election between Jackson and Clay was largely fought over the bank issue. Clay thought Jackson's assertion of preeminence over the Supreme Court would turn the nation against him. He thought that legal and economic arguments would persuade the people to vote against Jackson, but he underestimated the president's popularity. Jackson didn't emphasize the legal and economic aspects of the issue;

---

[200] Clay, *Papers*, 8, 41–54.

[201] Editorials, *Washington Globe*, January 28 and February 1, 1832.

[202] *National Intelligencer*, September 6, 1832.

he accompanied his veto with a message of populism and states' rights, writing,

> It is easy to conceive that great evils to our country and its institutions might flow from such a concentration of power in the hands of a few men irresponsible to the people ... It is to be regretted that the rich and powerful too often bend the acts of government to their selfish purposes. [When laws are enacted to] make the rich richer and the potent more powerful, the humble members of society—the farmers, mechanics, and laborers ... have a right to complain of the injustice of the Government. [The central government is best when it leaves] individuals and States as much as possible to themselves—in making itself felt, not in its power, but in its beneficence; not in its control, but in its protection; not in binding the States more closely to the center, but leaving each to move unobstructed in its proper orbit."[203]

Jackson's populist opposition to the bank and his states' rights positions were well received in the West and the South, and he soundly defeated Clay.

After recovering from the disappointment of his defeat, Clay returned to the Senate in 1833, where he enjoyed what was perhaps his finest hour. The triumvirate split temporarily because of differences over tariffs and protectionism. Former Vice President Calhoun led the South Carolina legislature to enact a nullification bill in protest against the federal tariffs that favored manufacturing but disfavored southern agriculture. The South Carolinians were adamantly opposed to the tariffs, announced they would refuse to honor them, and threatened secession rather than compliance.

Clay and Webster had championed the tariffs. President Jackson had not, but he now threatened to lead an army into South Carolina and,

---

[203] Richardson, *Messages and Papers*, 2, 1152–1154.

thinking of Calhoun, promised to hang any man who refused to obey the law. The serious possibility of civil war loomed.

Although Clay had been the primary proponent of tariffs and protectionism for his American system, he put aside his preferences, made necessary concessions, and supported the president, his nemesis. He brokered a deal in Congress in which the tariffs would remain at the same rate but would expire in seven years. This allowed the manufacturing sector time to adjust and gave the southern planters relief on a date certain. Clay was acclaimed for saving the Union, and with great satisfaction, he returned to Kentucky to contemplate retirement from politics. Of course, he returned to the Senate, where the bank issue reignited his battle with Jackson.

The bank issue was still a contentious problem. Jackson had vetoed the recharter, but the existing charter remained in effect four more years. Jackson wanted "the monster" killed immediately. During the summer, between congressional sessions and without authority from anyone but himself, Jackson fulfilled Clay's prophecy of Caesarism. Jackson ordered the secretary of the treasury to remove US funds from the bank and transfer them to state banks of Jackson's choosing. Secretary William Duane refused, so Jackson fired him and then nominated Roger Taney (subsequently the Supreme Court justice who wrote the infamous Dred Scott decision) to be the next secretary of the treasury. Before the Senate confirmed Taney, as required by the Constitution, Jackson ordered him to begin the "removal," which Taney did.

When Congress convened in December 1833, it was confronted by the bank fait accompli. Nicholas Biddle, the president of the bank, responded by curtailing loans and restricting bills of exchange. He stated, "This worthy President thinks that because he has scalped Indians and imprisoned Judges, he is to have his way with the Bank. He is mistaken."[204]

Biddle's actions caused a severe recession, led to numerous bankruptcies, and threatened a major economic collapse. Businessmen protested loudly, and the Senate became the site of daily diatribes, accusations,

---

[204] Biddle to Joseph Hopkinson, February 21, 1834, *Biddle Papers.*

and titanic speeches, with Clay, Webster, and Calhoun—the Great Triumvirate—taking the lead and heralding the Senate's Golden Age.

Clay moved to censure Jackson for the second time; this time, it was in the Senate, not in the House. Clay charged the president with exercising "[a] power over the treasury of the United States, not granted to him by the constitution and laws, and dangerous to the liberties of the people ... We are in the midst of a revolution, hitherto bloodless, but rapidly tending towards a total change of the pure republican character of the Government, and to the concentration of all power in the hands of one man."[205]

Clay outlined a case against Jackson, listing numerous threats to the people's liberty. Not holding anything back, he concluded his oration ominously. "The land is filled with spies and informers, and detraction and denunciation are the orders of the day. People, especially official incumbents in this place, no longer dare speak in the fearless tones of manly freemen, but in the cautious whispers of trembling slaves. The premonitory symptoms of despotism are upon us; and if Congress do not apply an instantaneous and effective remedy, the fatal collapse will soon come on, and we shall die—ignobly die—base, mean, and abject slaves; the scorn and contempt of mankind; unpitied, unwept, unmourned."[206]

Upon the conclusion of the speech, the Senate chamber exploded in applause and shouts of approval.

In the days following, Calhoun and Webster added their voices to the condemnation of the president. Calhoun compared the plundering of the Roman treasury by Julius Caesar to Jackson's plunder of the bank. He said Caesar had at least acted openly. "The actors in our case are of a different character—artful, cunning, and corrupt politicians, not a fearless warrior. They have entered the treasury, not sword in hand, as public plunderers, but, with the false keys of sophistry, as pilferers, under the silence of midnight."[207]

The speeches for and against Jackson continued until March 28, 1834, when the Senate voted, twenty-eight to eighteen, in favor of censure.

---

[205] Reg. Deb., 23d Cong., 1st Sess., 58–94.
[206] Reg. Deb., 23d Cong., 1st Sess., 58–94
[207] Reg. Deb., 23d Cong., 1st Sess., 220.

Despite the censure, Jackson had his way. He continued paying the government's bills from the US Bank but deposited incoming revenues into state banks of his choosing. By the time the bank's charter expired, its funds had been depleted, and it was out of business. Jackson had weathered all attacks, and his popularity continued to grow. Clay admitted as much. Speaking of the growing executive power, he said, "Its march has been steady, onward, and I lament to say, triumphant. It is now practically the supreme power in the State ... It is monarchy in disguise."[208]

In Jackson's last year in office, the Senate voted to expunge Clay's censure motion against him from the Senate record. Clay took this as a defeat and protested with another powerful speech but to no avail. In effect, Jackson won on almost every issue of disagreement with the Great Triumvirate. Although he had won, he never gave up a grudge. His last words as president were "My only regret as president is that I didn't shoot Henry Clay and hang John Calhoun."

More immediate for Clay, he lost the 1836 presidential election to Jackson's handpicked successor, Martin Van Buren.

Van Buren's first year was dominated by public debates on economic and financial matters and a proposal to establish an independent treasury, eliminating the state banks as primary deposit institutions. These issues caused a realignment of positions among the leading politicians and factions. The Great Triumvirate again fractured, creating great fodder for speechmaking. Robert Remini eloquently described the period.

> Never in the history of the Congress had there been such a debate, a debate of overwhelming dramatic and emotional power by three of the greatest statesmen and orators the nation had ever produced. The crowds that jammed the galleries, floor, and corridors enjoyed the unique experience of witnessing Clay's "glowing rhetoric," Calhoun's "nervous logic," and Webster's "overshadowing majesty." Here in full view of the entire country was the Great Triumvirate tearing their coalition apart

---

[208] Reg. Deb,, 24th Cong., 2d Sess., 360–376.

in oratory of unsurpassed eloquence. And they not only howled at each other's politics but over many months discussed and analyzed momentous national issues, such as slavery, abolition, expansion, depression, money and banking, public lands, and the nature of the Union. It was a stupendous moment in the parliamentary history of the United States. It set a level of debate never again equaled in this country.[209]

The debates of 1837 seemed like a culmination of two decades of presenting ideas with superlative rhetoric, two decades of testing, refuting, and refining them. Not since the Roman Senate when Cicero, Cato, Catulus, and Caesar debated the fate of their nation had rhetoric and logic so directly shaped events.

For the 1840 presidential election, the Whigs passed over Clay as their candidate, many saying they admired him greatly but didn't want to subject him to the humiliation of a third defeat. In 1844, he won the Whig nomination, but because of his stance against the annexation of Texas, he lost the presidency to James Polk, another Jackson protégé. Clay opposed the annexation of Texas because adding a slave state would have divided the Union and led to war with Mexico. He was right about the war, but his stance cost him the 1848 Whig Party nomination for president, which he lost to the war hero Zachary Taylor.

Clay's prediction about the war dividing the nation over slavery proved true. He took the lead in an effort to avoid civil war and, after six months of Senate debate, brokered the Compromise of 1850. The compromise admitted California into the Union as a free state and abolished the slave trade in the District of Columbia; for the south, it allowed several proslavery enactments, including the strengthening of the Fugitive Slave Act. Clay was lauded for avoiding civil war and was again called the Great Compromiser. Clay explained his views. "I go for honorable compromise whenever it can be made. Life itself is but a compromise between life and death, the struggle continuing throughout our whole existence, until

---

[209] Remini, *Henry Clay*, 517.

the Great Destroyer finally triumphs. All legislation, all government, all society, is formed upon the principle of mutual concession, politeness, comity, courtesy; upon these, everything is based ... Compromises have this recommendation, that if you concede anything, you have something conceded to you in return."[210]

At the end of his career, Clay felt defeated because he had never achieved the presidency, but on a grander scale, he hadn't been defeated. Assuming his goal was to preserve the Constitution, preserve the Union, protect liberty, and prevent tyranny, Clay had accomplished it all. He brokered a compromise over the Nullification Act and twice brokered compromises over slavery. Although he didn't fully stop Jackson, he slowed Jackson's onward march and clarified for future generations the principles of liberty that must always be defended. He accomplished all this by his words, logic, and prudence. The Kentucky *Commonwealth* wrote of him, "In five hundred years to come, it is not probable that an opportunity will occur to elevate his equal. Greece produced but one Demosthenes; Rome but one Cicero; and America, we fear, will never see another Clay."[211]

Clay died in 1852; and without him, the nation headed toward civil war.

---

[210] Clay, *Works*, 6, 410–418.
[211] *Commonwealth*, December 16, 1851.

CHAPTER 22

Slavery, Lincoln, and the Civil War

PARALLELS BETWEEN THE AMERICAN Civil War and the Roman civil wars are masked by time and circumstances, but they exist. Slavery was a major cause of the American war; less patently, slavery was also a major cause of Rome's internal conflicts. Rome's importation of great numbers of slaves from conquered foreign nations overwhelmed their society with enslaved people of different races and heritages. From the time of the Gracchi to that of Caesar, the enormous growth in the number of slaves drove small farmers and free workers into unemployment, poverty, and conflict.

Similarly, the American founders' failure to end slavery when they wrote the Constitution allowed the continued growth of the slave population, setting the nation on course to civil war. All indications were that the founders expected slavery to end gradually, but they were wrong. The Constitution provided for an 1808 end date for the importation of slaves. Article 1, section 9, states: "The Migration or Importation of such Persons as any of the States now existing shall think proper to admit, shall not be prohibited by the Congress prior to the Year one Thousand eight hundred and eight."

As 1808 approached, Thomas Jefferson, in his 1806 inaugural address, advocated for legislation to ban the trade. He said, "I congratulate you, fellow-citizens, on the approach of the period at which you may interpose your authority constitutionally, to withdraw the citizens of the

United States from further participation in those violations of human rights which have been so long continued on the unoffending inhabitants of Africa, and which the morality, the reputation, and the best interests of our country, have long been eager to proscribe."

In 1807, Congress passed an act to prohibit the importation of slaves into any port or place within the jurisdiction of the United States, beginning January 1, 1808, but it failed to ban already-existing slavery or impose further restraints on slavery. Congress limited the act to shipping and ports; it neglected the rest of the nation.

The reasons for the failure to ban slavery altogether weren't legal or moral, but economic. Industrial production of textiles increased the demand for cotton, and for the South to supply the demand, it needed slaves for cheap labor in its cotton fields. Fear was another reason to maintain slavery; fear that if the slaves were freed, a race war would follow. Those Southern leaders who otherwise would have preferred the end of slavery on moral grounds genuinely feared the consequences of an immediate abolition. The 1804 slave revolution in Haiti had deeply affected them; there the rebels, led by Jean-Jacques Dessalines, slaughtered all the whites on the island. The specter of the Haitian massacre haunted Thomas Jefferson and prevented him from taking substantive action against slavery. He claimed he would be personally willing to free all his slaves "if a scheme of emancipation and expatriation could be effected ... But as it is, we have the wolf by the ears, and we can neither hold him nor safely let him go." He predicted that were Congress to free the slaves, "all the whites south of the Potomac and the Ohio must evacuate their states, and most fortunate will be those who can do it first."[212]

Jefferson's concerns were reinforced by numerous local slave rebellions, particularly the 1831 Virginia rebellion led by the black preacher Nat Turner where fifty-seven whites, including women and children, were killed. The Southern response was to impose more stringent regulations on the conduct and movement of blacks to discourage them from meeting and organizing. As the percentage of slaves in the Southern population increased, the severity of punishments increased. Whipping was a standard punishment.

---

[212] Peterson, *Thomas Jefferson*, 995–998.

The Romans also feared their slaves, and after slave revolts, they too inflicted severe punishments but with a difference. The Romans did such things on a grander scale. They publicized their laws by visual display rather than by the printed word. The slave revolt led by Spartacus in 71–73 BC was punished by the crucifixion of six thousand rebellious slaves, with their crosses lined along the Appian Way for all to see. Smaller groups were executed at the public games by horrific methods. To discourage rebellious plots and incentivize slaves to carefully guard their masters from attack and report plots against them, the Romans instituted the draconian policy of executing all the slaves of a household wherein the master was murdered. In the fierce, harsh world of ancient Rome, such measures were accepted as necessary and justified. Ancient morality held that slaves lost their rights by surrendering in battle and by agreeing to be enslaved in return for preserving their lives. The spurious logic of this morality broke down when extended to those born into slavery. It was one thing for a captured soldier to accept enslavement instead of execution; it was another for him to relegate his descendants to slavery for time immemorial.

In America, punishments of slaves and rationalizations for slavery were irreconcilable to a people who purportedly believed in inalienable rights. Christian abolitionists tried to bring about an end to slavery through persuasion and appeals to religious principles, but they failed—not only because of Southern resistance but because their tactics made compromise virtually impossible. Instead of negotiating to solve the problem as Jefferson would have, the abolitionists vilified and alienated the slave-holding states. Although their stand was justified, it was counterproductive. William Lloyd Garrison and other abolitionists vilified not only slaveholders but also all Southerners. They characterized Southerners as the perpetrators of violence, drunkenness, sloth, and sexual depravity. In response, Southerners expressed hatred not only for the abolitionists but also for all Northerners, particularly New Englanders. They called the Yankees "money grubbers." Senator John C. Calhoun of South Carolina advocated secession, saying, "We have borne the wrongs and insults of the North long enough." Other slaveholders dug in, took a hard line, and resisted any attempt at compromise that might have led to the loss of their property.

Instead of slavery declining as the founders had hoped, by 1850 the United States became the world's largest slaveholding country with 3.5 million persons in bondage—and growing. The South provided two-thirds of the world's cotton supply, and with demand for cotton on the rise, the Southern planters pressed Congress to expand slavery into the western territories. This pressure led to the Kansas-Nebraska Act of 1854, which brought about the penultimate clash between abolitionists and slaveholders.

The Kansas-Nebraska Act allowed Kansas and other western territories to vote whether they were to be free or slave states. As the date for the Kansas election approached, supporters of slavery from Missouri, a slave state, infiltrated Kansas and mounted a campaign of violence, intimidation, and voter fraud, thus beginning several years of battles between proslavery and antislavery forces. In 1856, the slavers won the vote, and in response, the antislavery settlers drafted a new state constitution that banned slaves from Kansas. They elected an alternate governor and legislature, and applied for admission to the United States as a free state. Violence followed. Thomas Fleming related in *A Disease in the Public Mind*, "Anger mounted on both sides. The proslavery men struck first, after a proslavery sheriff was shot while sitting in his tent. About 750 Missourians, Alabamians, and South Carolinians stormed into Lawrence, Kansas's largest antislavery town, and wrecked the place. They burned and looted houses of antislavery leaders, blew up the Free State Hotels, and smashed up two antislavery newspaper offices."

John Brown, the vengeful abolitionist of later notoriety, lived nearby. The night following the Lawrence raid, Brown with his five sons and other followers invaded a proslavery district and dragged five men out of their cabins. Fleming wrote, "Brown ordered his sons to execute them before the horrified eyes of their wives and children, using two-edged cavalry swords that all but amputated arms and legs and heads."

Vitriol and Violence in the Senate

In the Senate, the violence in Kansas was the subject of rancorous debates nearly as heated as the violence. Senator Charles Sumner, a Puritan abolitionist from Massachusetts, in a speech called "the crime against Kansas," spoke for two days against the intimidation by the slavers. During his oration, he attacked the supporters of slavery in the most insulting and caustic terms, and he especially attacked the state of South Carolina. Sumner drew a parallel between the cause of liberty in Rome and the cause of liberty in Kansas. Some of his more memorable words follow:

> Against this Territory [Kansas] ... a crime has been committed, which is without example in the records of the past. Not in plundered provinces or in the cruelties of selfish governors will you find its parallel; and yet there is an ancient instance, which may show at least the path of justice. In the terrible impeachment by which the great Roman orator [Cicero] has blasted through all time the name of Verres, amidst charges of robbery and sacrilege, the enormity which most aroused the indignant voice of his accuser, and which still stands forth with strongest distinctness, arresting the sympathetic indignation of all who read the story, is that away in Sicily he had scourged a citizen of Rome—that cry, "I am a Roman citizen" had been interposed in vain against the lash of the tyrant governor ... It was in the presence of the Roman Senate that this arraignment proceeded, in a temple of the forum, amidst crowds—such as no orator had ever before drawn together—thronging the porticos and colonnades, even clinging to the house-tops and neighboring slopes, and under the anxious gaze of witnesses summoned from the scene of the crime. But an audience grander far, of higher dignity, of more various people and of wider intelligence, the countless multitude of succeeding generations in every land where eloquence has been studied, or where the Roman name has been recognized, has listened to the accusation, and throbbed with condemnation of the criminal. Sir, speaking in an age of light, and in a land of constitutional liberty, where the safeguards of elections

are justly placed among the highest triumphs of civilization, I fearlessly assert that the wrongs of much-abused Sicily, thus memorable in history were small by the side of the wrongs of Kansas, where the very shrines of popular institutions, more sacred than any heathen altar, have been desecrated; where the ballot-box, more precious than any work, in ivory or marble, from the cunning hand of art, has been plundered; and where the cry "I am an American citizen" has been interposed in vain against outrage of every kind, even upon life itself ...

But the wickedness which I now begin to expose is immeasurably aggravated by the motive which prompted it. Not in any common lust for power did this uncommon tragedy have its origin. It is the rape of a virgin Territory, compelling it to the hateful embrace of Slavery; and it may be clearly traced to a depraved longing for a new slave State, the hideous offspring of such a crime, in the hope of adding to the power of Slavery in the National Government.

Sumner turned his attention to Senator Andrew Pickens Butler of South Carolina, who had previously spoken in favor of slavery for Kansas.

With regret, I come again upon the Senator from South Carolina, who omnipresent in this debate, overflowed with rage at the simple suggestion that Kansas had applied for admission as a State; and, with incoherent phrases discharged the loosed expectoration of his speech, now upon her representative, and then upon her people. There was no extravagance of the ancient Parliamentary debate which he did not repeat; nor was there any possible deviation from truth which he did not make ... But the senator touches nothing which he does not disfigure with error, sometimes of principles, sometimes of fact. He shows an incapacity of accuracy, whether in stating the Constitution or in stating the law, whether in the details of statistics or the diversions of scholarship. He cannot open his mouth, but out there flies a blunder ...

Pray, sir, by what title does he indulge in this egotism? Has he read the history of "the State" which he represents? He cannot have forgotten its wretched persistence in the slave trade as the very apple of its eye, and the condition of its participation in the Union. He cannot have forgotten its constitution, which is republican only in name, confirming power in the hands of a few ... And yet the senator, to whom the "State" has in part committed the guardianship of its good name, instead of moving, with backward treading steps, to cover its nakedness, rushes forward, in the very ecstasy of madness, to expose it by provoking a comparison with Kansas ... In the one, is the long wail of slavery; in the other, the hymns of freedom. And if we glance at special achievements, it will be difficult to find anything in the history of South Carolina which presents so much of heroic spirit in an heroic cause as appears in that repulse of the Missouri invaders by the beleaguered town of Lawrence, where even the women gave their effective efforts to freedom. The matrons of Rome, who poured their jewels into the treasury for the public defense, did nothing of self-sacrifice truer than did these women on this occasion. Were the whole history of South Carolina blotted out of existence, from its very beginning down to the day of the last election of the senator to his present set on this floor, civilization might lose—I do not say how little, but surely less than it has already gained by the example of Kansas, in its valiant struggle against oppression.[213]

These were fighting words, and the next day, South Carolina Congressman Preston Brooks, a nephew of Senator Butler, approached

---

[213] Reg. Deb. 34th U.S. Congress, May 19, 1856.

Senator Sumner, who was seated at his desk in the Senate chamber. As Sumner began to rise, Brooks struck him repeatedly with a walking cane until Sumner fell senseless to the floor. He remained incapacitated and didn't return to the Senate for two years.

Congress censured Brooks, and he resigned his term. However, he was a hero in South Carolina, and the people of that state reelected him to Congress. He wasn't prosecuted.

The beating of Senator Sumner was just one example of the growing hatred between the opposing sides over slavery. Another incident raised hatred to a fever pitch when John Brown and twenty of his followers seized the arsenal at Harpers Ferry, Virginia, on October 16, 1959. Brown's goal was to incite a slave revolution by seizing and distributing the weapons. His plan didn't work. Within days, a Virginia militia unit under the command of Colonel Robert E. Lee recaptured the arsenal and imprisoned Brown. After a brief trial, in which Brown spoke against slavery, he was condemned and hanged. In the South, news of the raid increased the fear of slave insurrection; in the North, calls for abolition grew louder and more strident.

LINCOLN

Although Abraham Lincoln deplored Brown's violence, the shifting tide of public opinion swept him along. The Kansas-Nebraska Act had given birth to the new Republican Party, whose primary platform was to exclude slavery from the western territories, and Lincoln switched from Whig to Republican. Although he passionately hated slavery, he approached the problem in an analytical and noncaustic manner. He said, "I have no prejudice against the Southern people. They are just what we would be in their situation. If slavery did not now exist amongst them, they would not now introduce it ... I surely will not blame them for not doing what I should not know how to do myself. If all earthly power were given to me, I should not know what to do, as to the exiting institution ... But all this, to my judgment furnishes no more excuse for permitting slavery to go into our ... free territory than it would for reviving the African trade."[214]

---

[214] First Debate with Stephen Douglas at Ottawa, Illinois, August 21, 1858.

At six foot four inches tall, with a commanding presence, Lincoln came to national prominence—not as Caesar had, through bloody military battles, but largely due to his debates two years earlier against five-foot-tall Stephen Douglas. Lincoln and Douglas debated seven times during their race for the Illinois Senate. Lincoln lost that election, but the debates propelled him to the presidency. His exposition of the issues of the day secured his reputation as the most clear-thinking man in public life. His acceptance speech as the Republican candidate for the Senate clarified the nation's dilemma.

> A house divided against itself cannot stand. I believe this government cannot endure half *slave* and half *free*. I do not expect the Union to be *dissolved*. I do not expect the House to *fall*. But I *do* expect it will cease to be divided. It will become *all* one thing, or *all* the other. Either the *opponents* of slavery will arrest the further spread of it, and place it where the public mind shall rest in the belief that it is in course of ultimate extinction; or its *advocates* will push it forward, till it shall become alike lawful in all the states, *old* as well as *new*, *North* as well as *South*. (Emphasis Lincoln's)

Lincoln became president through his superior logic, understanding, and eloquence. Though he was self-educated, what distinguished him from most other politicians was his ability to correctly apply the lessons of history to the problems of his times. He knew how Caesar had conquered, and he knew the value of decisiveness, which enabled him to win victories against great odds. Unlike Caesar, Lincoln fought his war not for self-interest, power, or glory but to preserve the Union and achieve the ideals for which the Union was founded.

Secession and War

Weeks after Lincoln's inauguration, seven Southern states seceded, formed the Confederacy, and demanded the transfer of Fort Sumter in Charleston,

South Carolina, to the Confederacy. This demand was a precursor to war. Lincoln didn't want to be the initial aggressor, so he responded by notifying the Confederates that he was sending only provisions to the fort, not arms, a signal that he was not starting a war, but he would not surrender the fort. If attacked, he could respond by waging a just war, strengthening his moral position as the Romans always endeavored to do.

On April 12, 1861, Southern General Gerard P. T. Beauregard ordered cannon fire on the fort, and the Civil War began. For thirty-four hours, the Confederates bombarded the fort until flames engulfed it and the Union garrison surrendered. Beauregard allowed the Union troops to board a transport ship to New York. He also allowed them to take the fort's American flag, which at the time had sixteen stars for the sixteen states of the Union.

Fort Sumter was not only strategically significant as a bastion to protect Charleston Harbor but also symbolically significant as proof that the Confederates were in control of their territory. The Confederates repaired the fort and added ninety-five new cannons. On April 7, 1863, when the Union navy attacked the fort with nine newly built ironclad gunboats, the Confederate guns repulsed the attack. The battle bore striking similarities to sieges Roman armies conducted against ancient walled cities, when they used catapults to hurl boulders and fireballs at and over the city walls. If the walls couldn't be breached, the siege became a waiting game that depended on starving the inhabitants and preventing their resupply. At Fort Sumter, for two years the Union forces blockaded and bombarded the fort, shattering its redbrick walls, reducing it to rubble, and turning it into what looked like Roman ruins; but the Union forces were unable to force the Confederate troops to surrender because they were resupplied. Confederate volunteers ran the blockade on rainy or misty nights in low-to-the-water sloops, with sails painted gray or black, bringing food, water, and supplies.

The Confederates were never dislodged from the fort and abandoned it in February 1865 only as the war was coming to an end. On April 14, 1865, Union troops raised above the fort the very same US flag that had been lowered when the fort was surrendered in 1861. This occurred on the same day President Lincoln was assassinated.

War President

Lincoln as a war president, needless to say, faced great challenges. He hadn't had executive military experience, but he used his immense personal skills and political adroitness to manage the war and deal with each problem that arose. Exercising self-proclaimed presidential authority under his commander-in-chief powers, he acted without waiting for congressional authorization. Without a declaration of war by Congress, he assembled the state militias, enlarged the army and navy beyond their authorized strength, seized millions of dollars from the US Treasury without congressional authorization, spent non-budgeted funds, instituted a naval blockade of the Confederacy, and proclaimed martial law in parts of the North.

Lincoln ignored the letter of the law and acted as a Roman dictator would have acted when the nation was threatened and necessity required decisiveness. Like Caesar seizing the treasury and explaining to the protesting tribune that war takes priority over law, Lincoln explained that a law could be sacrificed to save the nation. As he so aptly put it, "Yet often a limb must be amputated to save a life; but a life is never wisely given to save a limb."[215] Not the least of the challenges he faced were threats of insurrection and sabotage in the North. When pro-Confederates burned railroad bridges and tore down telegraph wires, he suspended habeas corpus and imprisoned agitators and saboteurs without trial. Two of those he imprisoned for complicity in the destruction of the railroad bridges were the mayor and police chief of Baltimore. When the chief justice of the Supreme Court, Roger Taney, signed a writ for the release of the prisoners, Lincoln ignored it.

Lincoln arrested over fifteen thousand persons for acts of desertion or disloyalty. He didn't tolerate sedition and set aside First Amendment claims, jailing Northern political leaders who had subverted the Union cause by publicly speaking in favor of the South. He issued an order through his secretary of war that made illegal any "act, speech, or writing,

---

[215] James Bryce, *The American Commonwealth*, vol. 1 (New York: MacMillan, 1888), 100.

in discouraging volunteer enlistments, or in any way giving aid and comfort to the enemy, or in any other disloyal practice."

Political leaders in the North who spoke against the war were arrested and held without bail. Former Ohio Democratic congressman Clement Vallandigham was arrested for making anti-Lincoln speeches and urging soldiers to desert the Union army. He was ordered to be held for the duration of the war.

Free speech was a cherished right, and many critics argued that it needed to be protected even in time of war. This was a dilemma not without precedent. Lincoln knew the problems created by the Alien and Sedition Acts of President John Adams, but he also knew Roman history. No doubt he knew of the speech in 403 BC of Consul Appius Claudius Crassus to the Roman tribal assembly, in which he pointed out the dangers created by the tribunes who advocated sedition and desertion. (As noted in chapter four), the consul argued,

> Death by cudgeling is the wage of him who forsakes the standards or quits his post; but those who advise the men to abandon their standards and desert the camp gain a hearing, not with one or two soldiers, but with whole armies, openly, in public meetings; so accustomed are you to hear with complacency whatever a tribune says, even if it tends to betray the City and to undo the state; and captivated by the charm of that authority, you suffer any wickedness whatsoever to lurk beneath it. It only remains for them to utter in camp and in the presence of the soldiers the view which they noisily publish here, and to corrupt the armies and not to suffer them to obey their leaders. For in the upshot liberty has come to mean at Rome, that a man respect neither senate nor magistrates, nor laws, nor ancestral customs, nor institutions of the fathers, nor military discipline.[216]

---

[216] Livy, *Histories*, bk. 5, 6.

Appius Claudius Crassus persuaded the assembly to reject the rebellious actions of the tribunes by pointing out the treasonous nature of their arguments. Lincoln drew upon Appius's theme to persuade the public that the arrests of the agitators were justified. He published a letter in the newspapers, known as the Corning letter, in which he explained that politicians shouldn't be exempt from loyalty to their nation and that he held people like Vallandigham more culpable than any of the soldiers persuaded to desert from the army. He wrote, "Must I shoot a simple-minded soldier boy who deserts, while I must not touch a hair on a wily agitator who induces him to desert? This is none the less injurious when effected by getting a father, or brother, or friend, into a public meeting, and there working upon his feelings, till he is persuaded to write the soldier boy, that he is fighting in a bad cause, for a wicked administration of a contemptible government, too weak to arrest and punish him if he shall desert. I think that in such a case, to silence the agitator, and save the boy, is not only constitutional, but, withal, a great mercy."[217]

Newspapers that were critical of the war presented another problem. Articles and editorials by their nature generally presented reasoned arguments, as opposed to the virulent passion of inflamed speeches to agitated crowds, and freedom of the press was a fundamental right, but Lincoln decided that the press could be curtailed during times of war or rebellion.

A Lincoln supporter, Dr. Oliver Wendell Holmes Sr., addressed the issue in a 1863 Fourth of July speech. He had a personal interest because his son, Oliver Wendell Holmes Jr., who later became an associate justice of the Supreme Court, was serving in the Union army.

> At a time when every power a nation can summon is needed to ward off the blows aimed at its life, and turn their force upon its foes; when a false traitor at home may lose us a battle by a word, and a lying newspaper may demoralize an army by its daily or weekly *sillicidum* of poison, they insist with loud acclaim upon the liberty of

---

[217] Roy Basler, Ed.,*Collected Works of Abraham Lincoln* (Abraham Lincoln Association, 2006) 6:302–3.

speech and of the press; liberty, nay license, to deal with government, with leaders, with every measure, however urgent, in any terms they choose, to traduce the officer before his own soldiers, and assail the only men who have any claim at all to rule over the country, as the very ones who are least worthy to be obeyed.[218]

Lincoln subscribed to Holmes's argument. His administration closed over three hundred newspapers, seized the printing presses of some, and arrested editors. To Lincoln, the necessities of war obviated other considerations and shaped his political strategies.

He knew slavery had to be ended. But he had to walk a tightrope, and at the beginning of the war, he believed that he dare not free the slaves. If he had, the loyal border slave states—Kentucky, Maryland, Missouri, and Delaware—would likely have defected. His most immediate goal was to preserve the Union; to do so, he couldn't cut the baby in half. He wrote, "My paramount object in this struggle is to save the Union, and is not either to save or to destroy slavery. If I could save the Union without freeing any slave I would do it; and if I could save it by freeing all the slaves I would do it: and if I could save it by freeing some and leaving others alone I would also do that."[219]

The Emancipation Proclamation he issued on September 22, 1862—more to weaken the Confederacy than to proclaim freedom for all—applied only to the slaves in Southern states that were still in rebellion and where he could exercise his power as commander in chief. It was only a partial emancipation. He didn't free slaves in the four border slave states. Nonetheless, the proclamation had the not-inconsequential effect of drawing two hundred thousand African-American soldiers and sailors into the Union ranks. Lincoln considered this a major factor in the Union victory.

Although he hadn't been a military man, Lincoln studied military history and strategy, and his iron will made him a great military leader. He

[218] Oliver Wendell Holmes, $r., Speech, *New York Evening Post*, July 8, 1863.

[219] Abraham Lincoln to Horace Greeley, August 22, 1862, in the Collected Works of Abraham Lincoln.

also studied the political and economic strategies necessary to support a war effort; and just as Sulla, Caesar, and Augustus had done to their enemies in the past, so also Lincoln proscribed secessionist property owners. In areas conquered by Union forces, Lincoln's Confiscation Act permitted the government to seize and sell rebel property, with the proceeds going to the treasury. Persons connected to the Union government carried on rampant profiteering at the expense of Southern families, just as Roman officials had profiteered at the expense of those on the proscription lists.

To counterbalance this hardline approach, Lincoln followed Caesar's policy of clemency to lessen opposition and gather support. He issued orders that Confederate states could be restored to the Union if a percentage of its citizens took an oath of allegiance to the Union and assented to and supported the emancipation of the slaves. He released thousands of deserters and disloyal Northerners in exchange for their oath of loyalty to the Union. However, as the war dragged on, Lincoln saw only one way to conclude it. With the forcefulness and determination of Caesar when he crushed the forces of Pompey and Cato, Lincoln urged Generals Ulysses S. Grant and William Tecumseh Sherman to employ all the horrors of war to destroy the South.

Looking from afar, one might see Lincoln as a callous tyrant no different from the Roman purveyors of war. However, in Lincoln's case, what he said in his famous "Cooper Union" speech ("Let us have faith that Right makes Might") distinguished him from the might-makes-right ethos of the Roman Generals. Lincoln viewed the world from a higher plateau. Like the Romans who viewed their gods as dispensing retribution or favor, he also saw divine intervention as a judgment of a nation's conduct. In his Second Inaugural Address, he said, "If we shall suppose that American slavery is one of those offenses which, in the providence of God, must needs come, but which, having continued through His appointed time, He now wills to remove, and that He gives to both North and South this terrible war as the woe due to those by whom the offense came, shall we discern therein any departure from those divine attributes which the believers in a living God always ascribe to Him?"

From the vantage of history, many other analogies can be drawn between the Roman and American Civil Wars. Each began when no foreign power offered a serious threat. The Roman civil wars began after all her enemies had been defeated, and the American Civil War began after the British, French, and Spanish no longer posed imminent threats to American regions or sovereignty. It seems conflict abhors a vacuum, and when one conflict is resolved, another one surfaces. Peace with foreign nations and the lack of a foreign enemy provided the opportunity for rival factions within both Rome and America to turn upon each other.

Both civil wars exploded with a ferocity that might have seemed counterintuitive when countrymen were fighting countrymen. But Rome's determination never to accept defeat in its wars with foreign nations became a curse when the civil war pitted Roman against Roman. Similarly, just as the Romans turned their experience from foreign wars on themselves, so the Americans turned their experience from fighting the Native American tribes on their fellow countrymen. The atrocities of the American Civil War, so horrendous to any rational mind, had been rehearsed in the wars against the Native Americans. To the settlers and Indian fighters, surrendering to a warrior tribe would have been inconceivable. War was to annihilate or be annihilated, and it brought forth a steeled determination never to retreat. It engendered a callous brutality toward the enemy and a mind-numbing belief that it would be an irrevocable disgrace to surrender. The mind-set of the wars against the Native Americans carried over to the Civil War and could be seen in the madness of Confederate and Union soldiers repeatedly charging into fusillades of bullets as they tried to reach enemy lines.

Despite the difference in weapons Roman and American armies used, their battles had remarkable similarities. The Romans launched spears, then closed to fight with swords; the Americans, until supplied later with repeating rifles, fired mostly single-shot, muzzle-loading guns, then closed to fight with bayonets. The amount and kind of courage required of the soldiers was the same. Instances of panic and failure were the same. At the First Battle of Bull Run, when the Union army broke and fled back into Washington, DC, to the horror of its citizens, the scene surely resembled the Roman army's flight into Rome after its defeat at Lake Trasimeno by Hannibal's army.

In many of the battles, the size of the armies, the tactical maneuvers, and the casualties were comparable. At Gettysburg, the armies suffered fifty thousand casualties; at Philippi, the casualties were similar in size, though most were on the republican side. Each of these monstrous wars began with one man's decision—Caesar's choice to cross the Rubicon and Lincoln's choice to resupply Fort Sumter. Both could have taken alternative courses; both could have waited but didn't, though for far different motives. Caesar with his extraordinary abilities, popular support, and his loyal legions could have affected a peaceful compromise that would have been far better for the nation, but his self-interests took precedence. Lincoln unquestionably acted for the nation. By going to war, he had nothing to gain personally; he embarked on war because the Union had to be preserved for the democratic experiment to continue and the stain of slavery to be washed away. He saw himself as the man made for the moment.

Perhaps, the most astonishing parallel between Caesar and Lincoln, two of the most brilliant men of history, was that despite threats on their lives, each imprudently disregarded his personal safety, and each suffered assassination as he basked in the light of his triumph.

History has judged Lincoln as America's greatest president. Besides preserving the Union, he ended slavery, broke the stranglehold of the South's landed oligarchy, confirmed the strength of republican government, and distributed the largest tract of free land ever given to homesteaders. Moreover, had he lived after the Union victory, he surely would have been reelected thereafter. There were no term limits on the presidency at that time. Probably his proven leadership, courage, and competence would have brought him Augustan authority, which he would have used to change the course of history, undoubtedly for the better.

To be sure, Lincoln's greatness came at a high cost. In four years of the American Civil War, 2.2 million men fought for the Union, with eight hundred fifty thousand fighting for the Confederacy. The war brought death to six hundred twenty thousand soldiers and sailors, a figure comparable to all the Roman civil wars. While the civil wars of each nation wrought comparable misery, what differentiated them was that the Roman Republic was dying, while the American republic was striving to fulfill the promises of the Declaration of Independence and the Bill of Rights.

The American Civil War prevented the dissolution of the republic, altered the nation's character for the better, and cleared the way for America to reach a new plateau on the evolutionary journey of humanity. These were Lincoln's objectives, which he proclaimed in his Gettysburg Address. Borrowing a phrase Livy used to describe Rome's relief of debtor bondage, "a new birth of freedom," Lincoln set the nation on a new course. "It is rather for us to be here dedicated to the great task remaining before us—that from these honored dead we take increased devotion to that cause for which they gave the last full measure of devotion—that we here highly resolve that these dead shall not have died in vain—that this nation, under God, shall have a new birth of freedom—and that government of the people, by the people, for the people, shall not perish from the earth."

George Washington in toga

Cicero

Forum in Rome

Capital, Washington D.C.

Arch of Titus in Rome, celebrating victory in Jerusalem

Arch at Washington Square New York, celebrating Civil War victory

Arched bridge over the Tiber with Hadrian's memorial (Castel St. Angelo)

Arched bridge over the Potomac with Lincoln's memorial

Pantheon in Rome

U.S. Supreme Court, Washington, D.C.

Arched aqueduct at the Pont du Gard, France

Arched aqueduct at Monocacy Creek, Maryland

CHAPTER 23

New Beginnings in America

THE OUTCOME OF THE Civil War transformed America and set the stage for a surge of invention and industry that had been pent up for decades. First, the availability of abundant land for free and independent farmers strengthened the nation's core. Second, new technologies and industries brought about the greatest societal leap forward in human history. Third, the organized labor movement began its march to secure rights and benefits for workers. Fourth, the freedom and equality promised in the Declaration of Independence, the Constitution, and the Bill of Rights would come closer to fulfillment. Fifth, the ongoing conflicts with the Native American tribes would be addressed with more positive solutions. Finally, with the stain of slavery purportedly cleansed, America resumed its expansion, free to forthrightly spread the principles of free enterprise, liberty, and democracy beyond its borders.

LAND

In the midst of the Civil War, Lincoln demanded that Congress pass the Homestead Act of May 20, 1862. The act offered 160 acres of free public land in the West to settlers who agreed to build a home on it and farm it for at least five years. If they fulfilled the agreement, the land was theirs, and after twenty-five years, they could sell or bequeath it. In the preceding decade, the Southern Democrat slave interests had vehemently opposed proposals for distribution of federal land; they feared it would lead to the creation of free states in the West, prevent the expansion of slavery, and thus facilitate its end.

This was the same kind of land distribution bill the Gracchi and Caesar implemented to alleviate population pressures, allay unrest, and avoid civil war. Lincoln's Homestead Act was more effective. In the *New York Tribune*, Horace Greeley exclaimed that the act was "one of the most beneficent and vital reforms ever attempted in any age or clime—a reform calculated to diminish sensibly the number of paupers and idlers and increase the proportion of working, self-subsisting farmers in the land evermore." Pioneers, war veterans, freed slaves, and black freemen moved westward to make their claims. While there were winners and losers, over the subsequent decades, over two million people settled 270 million acres (10 percent of the land mass of the United States), and because of Lincoln, this was done without the stain of slavery.

INVENTIONS, INVESTMENTS, AND WEALTH

After the Civil War, the nation turned to building the most prosperous economy in the world. Inventors, manufacturers, and entrepreneurial geniuses of all kinds lifted the American standard of living to levels never seen before, and they spread benefits of industry to a larger percentage of the population than at any time in history. During the war, when the Deep South Democrats weren't represented in Congress, the Republican Party was able to pass its legislative agenda, including the Homestead Act, the National Currency Act, the Pacific Railroad Act, and the Land-Grant College Act. After the war, these government incentives spurred economic enterprises across the nation. William Seward, Lincoln's secretary of state, proclaimed a new era of economic expansion and prosperity that would be America's bulwark against domination by European powers. He stated, "Open up a new highway through your country from New York to San Francisco. Put your domain under cultivation and your ten thousand wheels of manufacture in motion. Multiply your ships, and send them forth to the East. The nation that draws most materials and provisions from the earth, and fabricates the most, and sells the most of production and fabrics to foreign nations, must be, and will be, the great Power of the earth."[220]

Thomas Edison, George Westinghouse, Alfred Nobel, George Eastman, Cyrus McCormack, Alexander Graham Bell, Nikola Tesla, Guglielmo Marconi, Elisha Otis, and Henry Ford were giants among the thousands of inventors and entrepreneurs who improved the quality of life in America and beyond. Electric lights, motors, cameras, radios, telegraphs, telephones, railcar air brakes, hydraulic motors, bicycles, barbed wire to contain cattle, automatic reapers, weaving looms, sewing machines, elevators, movie projectors, dishwashers, milking machines, condensed milk, canned goods, and refrigeration were among the thousands of inventions that improved living standards and the efficiency of industry. Inventions and new products reduced untold hours of tedious manual labor and improved the lives of millions, freeing people to expand their horizons and redirect their energies. Lincoln's secretary of war, Edwin Stanton, said of the McCormack reaper, "The reaper is to the North what slavery is to the South. By taking the place of regiments of young men in the Western harvest fields, it released them to do battle for the Union at the front and at the same time keeps up the supply of bread for the nation and its armies." After the war, the reaper freed workers for the industrial revolution and greatly contributed to ending hunger around the world.

On May 10, 1869, the transcontinental railroad was completed when the Pacific and Union tracks were joined at Promontory Point, Utah. This stupendous project required tunneling through the granite of the Sierra-Nevada Mountains. Laborers with pickaxes, sledgehammers, and shovels accomplished the task in a manner not much different from the way the Romans had built their aqueducts, roads, tunnels, and bridges. The railroad cut the time to cross the continent from three months to one week. More railroads were built and became the connecting rods of the nation, fostering the spread of commerce to all regions, much like the Roman roads that connected the regions of the empire and accelerated the spread of commerce.

---

[220] Cong. Globe, 32nd Cong., 2d Sess., App., 127.

Energized by new discoveries and inventions, America's industrial and commercial activity boomed. Great fortunes were built by the barons of industry and finance: John D. Rockefeller, Andrew Carnegie, Cornelius Vanderbilt, and J. P. Morgan, among others. Carnegie epitomized the Horatio Alger rags-to-riches stories that were so popular across America. Born in Scotland, Carnegie came to America, where he worked, saved, and invested. He led the expansion of the steel industry and built the world's largest and most efficient steel mill. Using the steel-manufacturing process a fellow Scotsman, Sir Henry Bessemer, had invented, he supplied the steel for rails and railcars, oil rigs, and bridges across America. As the rail-laying boom neared completion, he supplied steel girders for multistory buildings, which the Otis Elevator Company made practicable. In 1901, Carnegie sold his business to J. P. Morgan; the sale made him the richest man in the nation.

It was a period in which leading individuals and families assumed great civic responsibilities and supported great charities. Like the wealthy Romans who had built temples, rendered assistance to their clients, and sponsored public festivals and games, wealthy Americans sponsored public enterprises—colleges, hospitals, libraries, churches, parks, charitable organizations, and educational foundations. Carnegie again was the prototype. Before the end of his life in 1919, he gave his fortune away to charity and public projects. He was a benefactor of Booker T. Washington's Tuskegee Institute and the National Negro Business League. He financed the building of Carnegie Hall in New York City, Carnegie-Mellon College, numerous other college buildings and foundations, and more than twenty-eight hundred free public libraries. He set up and helped fund pension plans for teachers and his former employees. He also contributed to the building and establishment of The Hague Peace Palace in the Netherlands.

Not only the very wealthy but tens of thousands of prosperous citizens in towns and counties across the nation sponsored local projects, events, and organizations. They built churches and public buildings, organized civic clubs to advance beneficial social causes, and established the structures of a cohesive society.

Organized Labor

As the captains of industry were reinventing the American economy and building industrial conglomerates, workers found that their lives and work environments were also being reinvented. In the free-wheeling, laissez-faire capitalism of the times, employers sought to keep the costs of labor as low as possible. Besides keeping wages and benefits low, some employers inadequately ensured safe working conditions. With the pace of industry moving at faster and faster rates, accidents were frequent, and workers often suffered serious injuries, sometimes paying with their lives.

When unions began organizing to represent the interests of the workers, strikes soon followed. Between 1879 and 1885, there were more than three thousand strikes. Most were nonviolent, but it wasn't uncommon for violent conflicts to occur. In the Great Railroad Strike of 1877, both sides instigated violence. The unionists were given the blame for most of it; public opinion turned against them; and the strike failed.

On May 4, 1886, a union rally was held at Haymarket Square in Chicago. Anarchists infiltrated the crowd, and a bomb was thrown at the police. Panic, gunfire, and fighting erupted. Eight policemen and four workers were killed; many more were injured. Subsequently, seven anarchists were tried and convicted in connection with the bombing. Four were executed by hanging. As they marched to the gallows, they reportedly sang the "Marseillaise," the anthem of the international revolutionary movement of that period.

Most union leaders denounced the anarchists and communists who had infiltrated the trade union movement. In 1886, Samuel Gompers founded the American Federation of Labor (AFL), which represented the more highly skilled tradesmen. Gompers wasn't a revolutionary. He subscribed to the capitalistic system, kept the labor movement moderate, and prevented anarchists and communists from wresting control of his union. Negotiations between the AFL and management were generally productive, and the union succeeded because the high-skilled workers couldn't be easily replaced.

Although some unions clashed with management during strikes

that turned violent, such as the Homestead Steel Strike in 1892 and the Pullman Railroad Car Strike in 1894, most strikes or labor actions were relatively peaceful. Over the next century, organized labor played a significant role in building the American middle class, raising the standard of living for all, and strengthening the economy.

Rights and Equality

With the passage of the Civil War amendments, the nation renounced the initial Constitution's acknowledgment of slavery and set profound political and social changes in motion.

In 1865, the Thirteenth Amendment abolished slavery. The amendment proclaimed, "Neither slavery nor involuntary servitude ... shall exist within the United States, or any place subject to their jurisdiction." Nevertheless, Southern resistance to equal rights for the newly freed slaves was stubborn and violent. Federal armies were sent to occupy the South, and Northern administrators were sent to oversee reconstruction and the dismantling of slavery.

Charles Sumner, the senator who in the acrimony leading up to the war had been beaten senseless in the Senate house; and Thaddeus Stevens, a congressional chairman from Pennsylvania, demanded that the South be compelled to comply with the new, more inclusive Constitution. Some of those resisting the Thirteenth Amendment argued that the freed slaves weren't citizens. In response, Sumner, Stevens, and others pushed through the Fourteenth Amendment, which was ratified in 1868 and proclaimed that the freed slaves were citizens entitled to all the unqualified rights of citizenship. The first section of the amendment held profound consequences for American society. "Section 1. All persons born or naturalized in the United States and subject to the jurisdiction thereof, are citizens of the United States and of the State wherein they reside. No State shall make or enforce any law which shall abridge the privileges and immunities of citizens of the United States; nor shall any State deprive any person of life, liberty, or property, without due process of law; nor deny to any person within its jurisdiction the equal protection of the laws."

Despite the Fourteenth Amendment, resistance to bona fide equality for freedmen persisted, and they were prevented or discouraged from voting. In response, Congress proposed the Fifteenth Amendment, ensuring voting rights for all male citizens, including the freed slaves. It was ratified in 1870 and proclaimed, "The right of citizens of the United States to vote shall not be denied or abridged by the United States or by any State on account of race, color, or previous condition of servitude."

The amendments, however, didn't end Southern resistance, which escalated as segregationists and ex-Confederates used guerilla tactics, vigilantism, and intimidation to undermine the reconstruction program. President Andrew Johnson, who had become president upon Lincoln's assassination, was a former slave owner and a senator and governor from Tennessee. He equivocated about how to deal with the South, and his equivocation bolstered the resistance. Johnson pushed to restore the Southern states to their prewar status without exacting concessions, and he failed to act decisively to prevent reprisals against African-Americans who tried to exercise their newly won rights. Johnson's defiance of the will of the Republican-controlled Congress led to his impeachment and narrow acquittal in 1868.

In 1869, when Ulysses S. Grant became president, he acted decisively, establishing military zones in the South, imposing martial law, and sending additional federal troops to enforce the reconstruction laws. He suspended habeas corpus and jailed thousands of Ku Klux Klansmen. Despite all Grant's efforts, however, the segregationists would achieve their objectives. In the presidential election of 1876, neither Samuel Tilden nor Rutherford Hayes obtained a clear majority in the electoral college, so the election was thrown into the House of Representatives, where a deal was cut. Southern Democrats threw their support to the Republican Hayes in exchange for a guaranteed withdrawal of federal troops from the South. What followed was the dismantling of reconstruction, the disenfranchisement of the freedmen, and the imposition of Jim Crow laws. This was a devastating setback for the nation, and African-Americans continued to suffer abuses and injustices. Nevertheless, most African-Americans, freed from the constraints of slavery, continued working to overcome obstacles and improve their situations. Leaders such as Frederick Douglass, Harriet Tubman, Booker T. Washington, George Washington Carver, and W. E.

B. Du Bois led what might be called a nation within a nation to greater accomplishments and relative prosperity. Booker T. Washington preached self-reliance, sobriety, religion, and education as the means to overcome discrimination; and the values he instilled helped to sustain the core of the African-American community. Thousands of successful black-owned businesses were established, and many members of the black communities prospered, particularly in the North. Unfortunately, many other members were unable to overcome the obstacles to their full participation in the economy and society.

Social and political progress was sporadic and sometimes in retreat. The 1896 Supreme Court *Plessy v. Ferguson* decision upheld a Jim Crow law that required separate black and white railroad cars, holding that separate-but-equal public facilities were constitutional. The decision was eight to one, but the lone dissenter, Justice John Marshall Harlan, wrote a powerful dissenting opinion to which later courts would subscribe.

In 1901, President Theodore Roosevelt sent a positive signal of progress in race relations by inviting Booker T. Washington to dine at the White House. However, the invitation raised complaints from segregationists, and many in the country still harbored racist attitudes, even many in elite circles. In 1915, President Woodrow Wilson had the movie *The Birth of a Nation* shown in the White House, apparently endorsing its racist and anti-reconstruction message. The film became a recruiting tool for a revived Ku Klux Klan.

Setbacks aside, African-Americans joined Lincoln's "new birth of freedom," and they would eventually gain the fulfillment, or near fulfillment, of the promises of the Civil War amendments. Their centuries-long struggle for equality bore a striking resemblance to the struggles of the Roman plebeians for their equality, though the plebeians were better positioned to achieve their objectives, because they resided in contiguous areas and were cohesive enough to mount total strikes. The plebeians had official representatives, the tribunes, who possessed the power and leverage to exact concessions from the Senate. In 445 BC, by threatening a total strike and secession from the city, the plebeians forced the Senate to rescind the law barring intermarriages between patricians and plebeians. To the contrary, until the twentieth century, the African-American population was mostly scattered in rural areas and had limited political representation, making it difficult to take concerted action or achieve the repeal of discriminatory laws.

In 367 BC, the Roman law barring plebeians from the consulship was changed, and in 366 BC, Lucius Sextius became the first plebeian elected as consul 144 years after the founding of the republic. Then, in 342 BC, the law was strengthened to require that one of the two consuls must be a plebeian. With this political power, the plebeians gradually gained full legal and social equality.

Slavery produced different consequences for the republics because freed Roman slaves became citizens with the right to vote, regardless of their racial or ethnic origins. In the United States, although the Fourteenth and Fifteenth Amendments assured former slaves of citizenship and a right to vote, in actuality, their voting power was substantially suppressed until the mid-twentieth century.

Despite this suppression, African-Americans steadily gained greater political representation and more equality. In 1954, Thurgood Marshall, who would later become the first African-American Supreme Court justice, argued *Brown v. Board of Education,* the case in which the Supreme Court desegregated public schools by overturning the *Plessy v. Ferguson* separate-but-equal doctrine. The decision had profound social and economic consequences. As the new civil rights movement gained momentum, Rev. Martin Luther King Jr. emerged as an eloquent and powerful leader. His "I Have a Dream" speech, delivered on August 28, 1963, on the steps of the Lincoln Memorial, inspired the nation and led to the Civil Rights Act of 1964.

Subsequent decades brought much turmoil and many setbacks, but on the whole the nation continued to improve its race relations and equal employment opportunities. The election of Barack Obama in 2008 as the first African-American president, 146 years after the Emancipation Proclamation and 45 years after Reverend King's Lincoln Memorial speech, symbolized progress not only for African-Americans but also for America.

Native Americans

The Civil War interrupted the nation's expansion, but immediately upon its ending, the westward expansion recommenced at an even greater pace. As settlers moved into the Great Plains, clashes with Native Americans escalated because the settlers' farms and ranches were incompatible with the buffalo-hunting tribes. This led to the Great Sioux War of 1876–1877, a war noted for Custer's Last Stand, in which the celebrated General George Custer was killed and his troops annihilated at the Little Bighorn River in Montana. The slaughter of Custer and his troops, which included scalpings and other atrocities, led to calls for the brutal response that followed. The war with the Sioux was one of several in which the remaining tribes of the West were decimated.

In 1887, the United States tried a new policy. Seeking an alternative to these continuing wars, Congress passed the Dawes Act, which encouraged tribe members to switch to individualized land ownership rather than tribal ownership. The Dawes Act allotted 160 acres of land to each head of a Native American family, with additional acres for each dependent. Those who took advantage could obtain full citizenship, and many became successful members of the broader farming community. In 1924, efforts to encourage assimilation received a boost with the Indian Citizenship Act, signed into law by President Calvin Coolidge. The act granted full citizenship to all indigenous peoples.

Granting land and citizenship to Native Americans was the same solution the Romans reached to settle the Italian Social War. For four centuries the Romans had engaged in off-and-on-again wars with Italian tribes and nations. Ultimately, the Romans and Italians agreed that the only solution was complete assimilation, full citizenship, and an equitable sharing of land distributions. Most of the Italians fully embraced their citizenship, and the infusion of new blood revitalized Rome's population. In contrast, instead of accepting the land grants, a large number of Native Americans chose to live on reservations, where they did not prosper.

IMPERIALISM

The American consolidation of the continental United States paralleled Rome's consolidation of Italy and the Mediterranean Basin. Despite the constraints of their policy of initiating war only with a "just cause," the Romans, after long debate, decided to cross the seas to expand their empire. At the end of the nineteenth century, the Americans also debated whether to expand overseas. For a time, the anti-imperialists held the line against a growing imperialistic and jingoistic movement, but just as Rome annexed Mediterranean nations and established its hegemony, the United States asserted its influence outside its borders, often using a violent incident or confrontation to justify its actions, especially in South America. For example, in 1891, an incident in Chile nearly turned into a military confrontation when a crowd in Valparaiso, Chile, attacked a group of American sailors on shore leave from the USS *Baltimore*, killing two and injuring seventeen. President Benjamin Harrison threatened war if the Chilean government did not apologize for the violence and provide reparations for the families of the slain sailors. Chile complied with the American demand. Military action wasn't needed, but the incident sparked a wave of bellicose patriotism in the United States. Theodore Roosevelt criticized the administration, asserting that we should have declared war on Chile regardless of its compliance.

Roosevelt rode the jingoistic wave and became the leading advocate for American imperialism. In 1895, he advocated intervention in Venezuela, writing, "I rather hope the fight will come soon. The clamor of the peace faction has convinced me that this country needs a war."[221]

In 1898, Roosevelt got what he wished for with the Spanish-American War, when President McKinley declared war against Spain to support a revolution in Cuba. Roosevelt jumped at the chance to exhibit his military prowess. He formed a volunteer regiment, the "Rough Riders," which he led to victory in a battle against the Spanish at San Juan Hill in Cuba. It

---

[221] Theodore Roosevelt to Henry C. Lodge, December 27, 1895, in Elting Morison, Ed., *The Letters of Theodore Roosevelt*, vol. 1 (Cambridge, MA: Harvard University Press, 1958), 503–4.

is incontrovertible that Roosevelt sought glory and fame to advance his political ambitions just as so many Roman generals sought triumphs for their own advancement.

After defeating Spain, the United States established hegemony over Cuba and other Caribbean nations. It annexed the Philippines, Guam, Puerto Rico, and the Marianas, adding them to Alaska, Hawaii, and the Virgin Islands. As part of the deal to annex the Philippines, the United States paid Spain $20 million. American anti-imperialists lobbied against annexation, and Andrew Carnegie, a prominent member of the Anti-Imperialist Society, offered the Philippines $20 million from his own funds so the Filipinos could buy back their freedom, but nothing came of the offer.

As the Romans did, the United States granted a *civitas sine suffragio* status to the inhabitants of their territories: The inhabitants were citizens with civil rights, but they could not vote in national elections.

In 1901, Roosevelt became vice president and, in September of that year, succeeded to the presidency after the assassination of President McKinley. In 1904, Roosevelt was elected in his own right, and throughout his tenure, he advocated an aggressive foreign policy. He reinterpreted the Monroe Doctrine, changing it from an anti-colonist statement to one of American imperialism; and he strengthened the American hegemony around the Caribbean Sea and in Central America, not without threats of force. In one instance, when the Dominican Republic defaulted on its debts to European powers, Roosevelt seized the customs house of that nation to preclude a seizure by the Europeans. In doing so, he took on the hegemonic responsibility to see that the debts were paid.

His most lasting imperialistic achievement was securing the Panama Canal Zone with a ninety-nine-year lease. Allegedly this was accomplished by treaty, but the treaty was signed with Panamanian rebels who had taken over Panama, which at the time was a province of Colombia. When Colombia protested and threatened force to reclaim their territory, Roosevelt ordered a naval blockade to discourage any action; Panama became independent, and the Canal Zone became American.

Roosevelt's endeavors weren't confined to the Americas. In 1905, he helped negotiate the Portsmouth peace treaty between Russia and Japan;

and in 1906, to demonstrate America's role as a premier power, he sent the entire American navy around the world on a year-long cruise.

Roosevelt often acted without consulting Congress. In a letter to Henry Cabot Lodge, he bragged about his presidential accomplishments, writing, "The biggest matters, such as the Portsmouth peace, the acquisition of Panama, and sending the fleet around the world, I managed without consultation with anyone; for when a matter is of capital importance, it is well to have it handled by one man only."[222]

Indeed, one man had changed the nation's course. Roosevelt transformed the United States from a nation that had endeavored to avoid overseas entanglements to a nation that would project its power around the globe, a nation that would exercise hegemony over foreign territories in ways comparable to Rome's hegemony over her provinces and protectorates, and a nation that asserted itself as the democratic model for the world to emulate. Roosevelt made it clear that the United States was on its way to becoming the world's most powerful nation.

---

[222] Morison, *The Letters of Theodore Roosevelt*, vol. 6, 1497–8.

CHAPTER 24

Warrior Nations

"ONLY THE DEAD HAVE seen the end of war," a quote attributed to Plato, cannot be denied. War has been a constant from antiquity to modern times, and although the technology and weapons have changed, the same core strategies of war have been applied throughout history. Great nations have always prepared for war, and they have chosen their leaders from among those deemed most capable of conducting war. The Roman system was designed to elect consuls with military victories to their credit. In America, throughout the nineteenth century, victorious generals were held in such high regard that they almost held exclusive rights to the presidency or their party's nomination for president.

Rome fought enormous battles and large and small wars over several centuries, and they fought outside the Italian Peninsula for the first time in the First Punic War against Carthage. The United States also engaged in wars, large and small, first fighting overseas in the Spanish-American War in 1898.

The US fought its first war outside the American hemisphere in the First World War. On April 6, 1917, the United States declared war on Germany, immediately dispatching one division to France as a pledge of American involvement. Additional troops followed as soon as they could be trained. The Americans at first played a supporting role but quickly assumed a more prominent part, and in the autumn of 1918, they deployed more than 1.25 million soldiers to the Battle of the Argonne Forest, an astounding assemblage of men and equipment. After forty-seven days of savage warfare, the Americans and the Allies were victorious, and the Germans sued for peace.

On November 11, 1918, the armistice took effect. During negotiations to end the war, President Woodrow Wilson, hoping to make the world "safe for democracy," proposed his Fourteen Points. Among other items, they advocated "mutual guarantees of political independence and territorial integrity to great and small nations alike." Wilson's proposal was reminiscent of the 196 BC Proclamation of Liberty the Roman consul Flamininus announced to the Greek city-states after the Macedonian War. Though both the Fourteen Points and the Proclamation of Liberty were intended to promote peace, neither achieved its purpose. Wilson couldn't preserve peace because the Allies made the same mistake the Romans had made after defeating Carthage in the First Punic War—exacting onerous and unreasonable reparations. In the Versailles Treaty of 1919, they imposed harsh conditions on Germany, including disarmament, the loss of her colonies, the dismemberment of Austria-Hungary, the transfer of the mineral-rich region of Silesia to Poland, and exorbitant reparations. This "Carthaginian Peace" wouldn't last and planted the seeds of another war. Just as Hannibal had emerged in the Second Punic War to obtain revenge against the Romans, so would Hitler emerge as the avenger for Germany.

The United States officially entered the Second World War on December 7, 1941, after Japan attacked Pearl Harbor in Hawaii. Japan also attacked American naval bases in the Philippines, Guam, and Wake Island. Since Japan and Germany had a military alliance, Germany declared war on the United States.

During the war, 16.3 million Americans served in the armed forces, many in both the European and Pacific theaters; and after four years of all-out war, the American troops forced Germany and Japan to surrender. These victories weren't simply the result of greater material resources; they were also the product of America's collective will in the face of terrible casualties. Overall, the war claimed the lives of two hundred forty-five thousand American soldiers, sailors, airmen, and merchant marines.

The extraordinary courage and fortitude that propelled the American citizen soldiers to victory came from the same recesses of the human spirit, from the same cultural factors that had propelled the Roman citizen soldiers to victory over Hannibal two thousand years earlier. The Americans and the Romans faced different kinds of war, separated by millennia, but the soldiers displayed the same fidelity, discipline, and bravery. How and why their citizen soldiers possessed these attributes and values is an essential question. Many factors have been identified as shaping the strength of their character, but the complexity of the social, political, and economic factors precludes a definitive explanation. Quantitative accountings of natural resources or economic factors cannot satisfactorily explain the successes of these nations. As Einstein reputedly said, "Not everything that can be counted counts, and not everything that counts can be counted."[223] Any explanation of national success must include the intangible social and moral values ingrained in the people.

Neither nation could have achieved its military triumphs without the loyalty of the broader population and the willingness of its citizen soldiers to step forward and risk their lives for their country. In Rome, every spring for centuries, thousands of young men voluntarily reported for military duty. History focuses on unusual times when the tribunes resisted the levy as a political tactic, but those were exceptions. The levies were like the nation's biological necessity; at first they were compelled by external threats, but in time they were internalized as a moral obligation. Citizen armies were the backbone of the Roman social structure. Military service was a duty of all men from seventeen to forty-six, and soldiers were trained to function within the disciplined formations and signal systems of the legions. At times, 25 percent of the population served in the legions. The organization, discipline, and collective functioning of the legions allowed the Roman armies to defeat larger but less-organized armies.

The legions had loyal memberships with citizens volunteering each year to serve with the same centurions and comrades. Soldiers fighting alongside friends and companions inspired the courage men derive from union with their comrades in arms, and unity among soldiers discouraged flight and mitigated the sudden panic that normally overwhelms

---

[223] E. Calaprice, Ed., *The Ultimate Quotable Einstein* (Princeton, N.J.: Princeton University Press) 482.

individuals facing imminent death. They fought because those around them fought. A soldier's confidence that his comrades won't panic and flee strengthens his own resolve, and the combined resolve of the legionaries was the basis of Rome's military success.

Legions, cohorts, and centuries carried military standards, which originally were used in battle to communicate rallying points and signal tactics and formations. The standard bearer lowered, raised, waved, or pointed the standard to signal orders from the commander. Over time, the standards became symbols of pride soldiers would fight to the death to protect, and the significance of the standards became one of those factors Einstein referred to when he said, "Not everything that can be counted counts, and not everything that counts can be counted.".

Flavius Josephus, a Jewish aristocrat during the time of the rebellion in Jerusalem, described the Roman army.

> If you study carefully the organization of the Roman army, you will realize that they possess their great empire as a reward for valor, not as a gift of fortune. For the Romans, the wielding of arms does not begin with the outbreak of war, nor do they sit idly in peacetime and move their hands only during times of need. Quite the opposite! As if born for the sole purpose of wielding arms, they never take a break from training, never wait for a situation requiring arms. Their practice sessions are no less strenuous than real battles. Each soldier trains every day with all his energy as if at war. And therefore they bear the stress of battle with the greatest ease.[224]

At the pinnacle of the Roman military structure were the generals, legates, and military tribunes; beneath them were the centurions, career men who led centuries of between sixty and one hundred legionaries. The centurions conducted strenuous training drills and maintained the legion's traditions.

---

[224] Flavius Josephus, *Bellum Judaicum*. 310.

In many ways, the American military copied the Roman military structure and its methods of fostering unity, cohesion, and loyalty. The division, battalion, and company system was organized similarly to the Roman system, and the preservation of traditions through the use of flags, insignias, medals, and ceremonies instilled loyalty to one's military unit.

At the top of the American military structure were the commanding generals, supported by a corps of career officers—colonels, majors, and captains—who in turn were supported by career noncommissioned officers—sergeants, master sergeants, sergeant majors, and chief petty officers—who could be likened to Roman centurions. For both the Roman and American armies, the extraordinary competence of career soldiers was a crucial element of their military success. Inspired by honor, tradition, and duty, these soldiers with few exceptions overcame most obstacles and led their armies to victory.

The American officer corps, trained at West Point, Annapolis, and the Air Force Academy, studied the principles of leadership, most of which Roman examples could illustrate. American military leaders learned the importance of inspirational speeches, symbolism, faith in the cause, and appeal to honor and country. In some cases, the speeches were the difference between victory and defeat. With a little imagination and changes of names and place, the speeches of Roman consuls to their troops could be inserted in place of the speeches of American generals to their troops— and vice versa.

Caesar's speech to his mutinous Tenth Legion in 47 BC was well known to American generals. About to begin a new campaign in North Africa against the last-remaining republican forces, Caesar ordered the legion to prepare to embark. However, the legionaries had been fighting for eight hard years, and they demanded their discharges and bonuses. Violence broke out; two of Caesar's praetors were killed, and another praetor, Gaius Sallustius Crispus (the historian Sallust) was nearly killed. The soldiers then marched to Rome and assembled in the Campus Martius. Caesar faced them alone. He apologized for their long service but called them *quirites* (citizens) rather than *commilitones* (comrade soldiers), adding that they were no longer of any use. He agreed to their immediate discharge and told them he would reward them with land and bonuses for their past service when he came back from Africa to celebrate his next triumph with other soldiers, whom he would enlist. His reverse psychology worked; the legionaries dropped their demands and pleaded to go to Africa with him.

In a scene reminiscent of what Caesar faced, George Washington also had to deliver a speech to soldiers who were threatening mutiny in protest of the government's failure to pay them. On March 15, 1783, at Newburgh, New York, the soldiers met to plan their course of action. Washington unexpectedly showed up at the meeting and tried to persuade those present to remain loyal. His speech wasn't well received, but near its conclusion Washington took a letter from his pocket. The letter was from Congress. He squinted but still couldn't read it and fumbled to get his reading glasses, which few had seen him use. He apologized, "Gentlemen, you will permit me to put on my spectacles, for I have not only grown gray but almost blind in the service of my country." Whether staged or not, that poignant moment persuaded the troops to remain loyal.

Inspiring speeches, to be taken seriously, must be accompanied by real and tangible leadership. Like Caesar, who shared the same conditions as his legionaries in their camps, Washington for eight years shared camp life with his soldiers without affording himself the comfortable mansions available to him. Like Caesar, who wore a bloodred cloak when he rushed into battle so that all would know he was present, Washington made himself visible, traversing the battle lines on his white horse and placing himself in the same danger he asked his troops to face. At the Battle of Monmouth in 1778, Washington rode into the midst of the fray to rally his retreating troops. French Marquis de Lafayette, fighting for the Americans, declared, "General Washington was never greater in battle. His presence stopped the retreat; his strategy secured the victory. His stately appearance on horseback, his calm, dignified courage ... provoked a wave of enthusiasm among the troops."[225]

---

[225] Charlemagne Tower Jr., *The Marquis de Lafayette in the American Revolution* (Philadelphia: J.B. Lipincott, 1895), I:384.

PATTON

More than a century later, in the First World War, when the cavalry traded their horses for tanks, General George Patton led his tank divisions from the front, standing in the turret like a charioteer, wearing a white scarf so his troops would know he was with them.

Patton oversaw the mechanization of the US Cavalry. In 1917, as a major, he was appointed commander of the First Tank Brigade in France. Although the transition to mechanized warfare changed the tactics of warfare, tanks didn't change its basic nature. The essentials of military leadership stayed the same, and Patton displayed extraordinary leadership skills that would have been effective in any age. He was a student of military history, owned a copy of *Caesar's Commentaries*, and knew well the Roman campaigns in Gaul. When he visited the site of an ancient Roman military camp near Chamlieu, France, he said, "This place had once been home." He expressed his belief that he was a reincarnated Roman general and wrote a poem ending with these lines:

> And now again I am here for war
> Whereas Roman and knight I have been;
> Again I practice to fight the Hun
> And attack him by machine.[226]

Familiar with the memorable speeches given by Roman generals, Patton made his own speeches memorable, sometimes peppering them with barracks language for effect. In the Second World War, as a general in command of the US Army's Second Corp in North Africa as part of Operation Torch, he prepared for an assault against Erwin Rommel's German Panzer division. The battle would take place near the town of Thala in Tunisia, about twenty miles from Zama, where Scipio Africanus had defeated Hannibal. Patton delivered an address to his troops that Scipio Africanus, by substituting names, could have delivered to his

---

[226] Terry Brighton, *Patton, Montgomery, and Rommel* (New York; Three Rivers Press, 2008), 37.

legionaries. "Fortunately for our fame as soldiers, our enemy is worthy of us. The German is a war-trained veteran—confident, brave, and ruthless. We are brave. We are better equipped, better fed, and in the place of his blood-glutted Woten, we have with us the God of our Fathers, Known of Old ... If we die killing, well and good, but if we fight hard enough, viciously enough, we will kill and live. Live to return to our family and our girl as conquering heroes—men of Mars."[227]

After the Allied victory in Tunisia, they launched a massive invasion of Sicily with seven divisions in the first wave, two more than the later landing at Normandy. Patton was in command of the US Seventh Army, which landed on the southern side of the island. They landed at the Bay of Gela, where the Romans had defeated the Carthage navy to win the First Punic War. The plan was for Patton's army to support the left flank of the British army, commanded by General Bernard Montgomery, as the British moved north to capture the city of Messina. Patton didn't wait for Montgomery. He raced up the center of the island, turned west to take the city of Palermo, and then raced east to Messina, taking that city before Montgomery arrived.

It wasn't merely a competitive nature that drove Patton, but his race to beat the British to Messina was a means of motivating his troops; he was a master motivator but sometimes overcharged. He crossed the line when he visited a field hospital and slapped a shell-shocked soldier, whom he accused of cowardice and malingering. When this event was publicized, he was relieved of command and sidelined until the invasion of Normandy.

AMERICANS BATTLE TO CAPTURE ROME

Without Patton in September 1943, the Allies invaded the Italian mainland south of Naples on a forty-mile coastal stretch from Salerno to Paestum with Major General Mark Clark in command of the combined Allied Fifth Army. The British landed near Salerno. The American Thirty-Sixth Division landed at Paestum, an ancient city the Greeks had colonized in the sixth century BC, which boasted the most grand and well-preserved

---

[227] Blumenson, *Patton Papers*, 187–90.

Doric temples outside those at Athens. The temples were used as division headquarters and a hospital.

After weeks of fighting, the Germans began a controlled scorched-earth retreat northward. They evacuated Naples and destroyed much of the city as they left. The Fifth Army entered the city on October 1, 1943, then began a northward advance. However, the Germans had stopped retreating and set up the Gustav defensive lines across the mountain ranges that ran from the Tyrrhenian Sea to the Adriatic Sea.

Unable to fully pierce the Gustav line at the Rapido River and faced with formidable German defenses at Monte Cassino, the Allies adopted a plan to outflank the Germans, splitting off four of the thirteen divisions of the Fifth Army to make a surprise amphibious landing at the port city of Anzio, fifty-five miles behind the German lines and thirty miles south of Rome.

Anzio had a long history. It was where the Roman rebel Coriolanus had been defeated and killed in 490 BC, where Cicero had a villa, and where Nero supposedly fiddled while Rome burned.

On January 22, 1944, the four divisions successfully landed at Anzio without much opposition, but the Germans quickly sent reinforcements and contained them. Trapped on the beachhead, infantrymen dug trenches while planes, artillery, mortars, and machine guns took their toll. They suffered horrendous casualties, and it appeared for a time that they might be driven back into the sea; but after reinforcement by three more divisions and with the support of naval guns firing from destroyers off the coast, they moved forward meter by meter.

Meanwhile, the bulk of the Fifth Army was stalemated at the Gustav line at Cassino. In an effort to breach the line, Allied bombers and artillery obliterated the German positions, including the St. Benedictine Monastery at the top of the mountain; however, the rubble created by the bombing provided the Germans with impregnable cover that made it more difficult to root them out. Three attempts to break through the defensive line failed, and a stalemate settled over the battlefield. Then on May 11, 1944, the Allies launched a massive assault across a broad front. Under fierce fire, they crossed the Rapido River, captured Cassino and the monastery, broke through the defensive lines, and began heading north.

On May 22, 1944, with the breakthrough at Cassino, the Anzio divisions broke out of the beachhead where they had been held down for 125 days. According to plan, they began moving to assault the flank of the retreating German army, and they were to combine with the other Fifth Army divisions on Highway 6 at Valmontone. However, on May 23, 1944, General Clark, in a controversial move, changed plans and split his Anzio forces, sending half north toward Rome on Highway 7 and the other half to Valmontone.

Highway 7 tracked the path of the ancient Appian Way and was the most direct route to Rome; Highway 6 tracked the ancient Via Casilina, which also led to Rome but was farther east and would take longer. Over the centuries, many armies had used these roads. The Romans had fought the Samnites along the Via Casilina, and Hannibal had used it in his aborted attack on the city. Dan Kurzman neatly described it.

> On the other hand, Highway 7, the fabled Appian Way, was the ceremonious route to Roman heroes returning from battle in gilded chariots. It was too difficult a path for most invaders. Built more than two thousand years ago by slaves of the blind censor Appius Claudius Caecus, it was, in a sense, a road of peace. Ancient clans lined it with their tombs. St. Paul was greeted by his comrades at an Appian inn after surviving a shipwreck on the shores of Malta. And St. Peter, who had fled Rome to escape persecution of the Emperor Nero, turned back to suffer a martyr's fate after Christ appeared before him on this road; he had asked Christ: *"Domini, quo vadis?"* and Christ had replied: "To Rome, to be crucified again."[228]

As so many ancient armies had marched before, now an allied army was marching along the same routes, this time with tanks, trucks, cannons, and machine guns.

Military historians have criticized Clark for splitting his forces since

---

[228] Dan Kurzman, *The Race for Rome* (Garden City, NY: Doubleday, 1975).

this act diluted the strength of the army, slowed the advance, and cost lives. Critics alleged that he sent a division to Highway 6 to get in front of and stall the British army that was advancing on that highway. They surmised that his motivation was to reach and conquer Rome first. His soldiers thought he was obsessed with Rome and dubbed him "Marcus Aurelius Clarkus."

Fair or not, it seemed accurate that Clark enjoyed the fame of being named a conqueror of Rome; indeed, on June 4, 1944, two days before the D-Day landing at Normandy, the Americans entered Rome first. On the outskirts of Rome, Clark confiscated the city's entrance sign "ROMA" for his office, and he spent much of his time talking to the press and having his photograph taken in front of it. Then driving triumphantly through the streets in his jeep, he alighted at the ancient Theater of Marcellus and walked up the Capitoline Hill to city hall. He had arranged for the press to await him there for a supposed impromptu news conference. It wasn't quite an ancient triumphal parade, but it served the same purpose, since the press let the world know that Clark had conquered Rome.

Clearly, he experienced the same taste of glory, as had so many Roman generals. Although he was an invader, he did so as a liberator to free Rome from Mussolini's Fascists and Nazi occupiers. A comparison could be drawn to Sulla's return to Rome to free the city from the Cinnan-Marian tyranny. In any case, General Clark would have fit right in as a glory-seeking Roman consul.

Patton Returns

Meanwhile, as the June 1944 invasion of Normandy approached, Patton was given command of the Third Army. Most of his troops were inexperienced, and he gave several pre–D-Day speeches to inspire them to fight like hardened veterans. At six feet one inch tall, wearing his steel helmet, his medals, and his ivory-handled revolver, he cast an impressive figure as he spoke.

> Men, all this stuff you hear about America not wanting to fight, wanting to stay out of the war, is a lot of bullshit.

Americans love to fight! All real Americans love the sting and clash of battle. When you were kids you all admired the champion marble shooter, the fastest runner, the big-league ball players and the toughest boxers. Americans love a winner and will not tolerate a loser. Americans play to win all the time. That's why Americans have never lost and never will lose a war. The very thought of losing is hateful to Americans. Battle is the most significant competition in which a man can indulge. It brings out all that is best and it removes all that is base.

You are not all going to die. Only two percent of you right here today would be killed in a major battle. Every man is scared in his first action. If he says he's not, he's a Goddamn liar. But the real hero is the man who fights even though he's scared. Some men get over their fright in a minute under fire, some take an hour, and for some it takes days. But the real man never lets his fear of death overpower his honor, his sense of duty to his country, and his innate manhood …

An army is a team. It lives, eats, sleeps and fights as a team. This individual hero stuff is bullshit …

Each man must think not only of himself, but think of his buddy fighting alongside him. We don't want yellow cowards in the army. They should be killed off like flies. If not, they will go back home after the war, Goddamn cowards, and breed more cowards. The brave men will breed more brave men. Kill off the Goddamn cowards and we'll have a nation of brave men …

Sure, we all want to go home. We want to get this war over with. But you can't win a war lying down. The quickest way to get it over with is to get the bastards who started it … And when we get to Berlin, I am personally going to shoot that paper-hanging son-of-a-bitch Hitler …

Then there's one thing you men will be able to say when this war is over and you get back home. Thirty years from now when you're sitting by your fireside with your grandson on your knee and he asks, "What did you do in the great World War Two?" you won't have to cough and say, "Well, your granddaddy shoveled shit in Louisiana." No, sir, you can look him straight in the eye and say, "Son, your granddaddy rode with the great Third Army and a son-of-a-Goddamned-bitch named George Patton!"

All right you sons-of-bitches, you know how I feel. I'll be proud to lead you wonderful guys into battle anywhere, anytime. That's all.[229]

His speeches were effective, and his army battled eastward across France, outdistancing all other American and Allied armies. In 1944, the Germans mounted a surprise attack through the Ardennes Forest in an attempt to reach the port of Antwerp. The town of Bastogne blocked the path of the Germans, and it was crucial that it be defended. The 101st Army Airborne defended it, but they were quickly surrounded and placed under a withering siege of German firepower. Patton was ordered to detour northward to relieve the siege, but because of overcast weather, no air support for his tanks was available, and it was uncertain whether he would arrive in time. Acting as though he were a reincarnated Roman consul, he prayed to God as a consul would pray to Jupiter and Mars. "Grant us fair weather for Battle. Graciously harken to us as soldiers who call upon Thee that, armed with Thy power, we may advance from victory to victory, and crush the oppression and wickedness of our enemies."[230]

On December 23, 1944, the weather cleared, and American planes attacked the German forces. Three days later, Patton's army arrived, breaking the siege and blunting Hitler's last-gasp offensive.

After Bastogne, Patton crossed the Rhine into Germany, and he and his Third Army were acclaimed as the command most responsible for the

---

[229] Terry Brighton, *Patton, Montgomery, Rommel*, 261-265.

[230] Leo Barron, *The Christmas Battle for Bastogne* (New York: Penguin Group, 2012).

Allied victory in Western Europe. After the German surrender, Patton was appointed military governor of Bavaria with powers not unlike a Roman consul governing a conquered province. In a startling turn of history, as he was touring his province on his supposed last day in Europe, a truck accidently hit his jeep. He suffered a broken neck and was instantly paralyzed. At the hospital, he told the doctors, "If there's any doubt in any of your Goddamn minds that I'm going to be paralyzed the rest of my life, let's cut out all this horse-shit right now and let me die." Ten days later, he died.[231]

Patton's accidental death after major military victories in Germany echoed the death of Nero Claudius Drusus, stepson of Augustus, who between 14 and 9 BC commanded seven legions, crossed the Rhine, and conquered Germanic tribes and territories to the Elbe River. Drusus was a formidable warrior, winning the *spolia opima* award for a single-combat victory over a Germanic tribal king. Returning from a military success, he fell from his horse and died a month later from his injuries. Could Patton have thought he was the reincarnation of Drusus?

MacArthur Returns

Another American general who surely could have assumed the role of a Roman consul was General Douglas MacArthur. In October 1944, MacArthur fulfilled his "I will return" promise to the Philippines and achieved an enormous public relations victory. His genius for stagecraft provided an emotional lift for the war effort in the Pacific. A widely distributed photograph depicted him dramatically wading onto the beach at Leyte Gulf, with the surf splashing around his knees. He could have easily embarked from his landing craft onto a nearby dock without getting wet, but by staging the iconic photograph as he led his troops ashore to rescue the Philippines from Japanese occupation, he enriched the significance of his return. One might have half expected MacArthur to have plagiarized Caesar's "I came, I saw, I conquered."

MacArthur was a brilliant military administrator and strategist, but he knew his most important duty was to inspire the confidence of his

---

[231] Brighton, *Patton, Montgomery, and Rommel*, 385-6.

troops and his nation. He knew war was a test of willpower and that leadership and confidence from the top were categorical imperatives. Although the instruments of war had changed from Roman times, the same kinds of inspirational leadership that motivated the Roman legions were needed to instill confidence in American soldiers and sailors.

Since we know more about Caesar than any other Roman general, we can better see the parallels between him and MacArthur. William Manchester wrote in *American Caesar,* "Most of all MacArthur was like Julius Caesar: bold, aloof, austere, egotistical, willful. The two generals surrounded themselves with servile aides-de-camp; remained long abroad, one as proconsul and the other as shogun, leading captive peoples in unparalleled growth; loved history; were fiercely grandiose and spectacularly fearless; and reigned as benevolent autocrats."[232]

Caesar staged the elaborate surrender of Vercingetorix after defeating the Gauls at Alesia; MacArthur staged the elaborate ceremonies for the Japanese Second World War surrender on the battleship *Missouri* in Tokyo Bay.

Both men were natural-born military aristocrats, yet when they had full political authority, they implemented liberal democratic policies that favored the populace: Caesar as proconsul of Gaul and as consul and dictator of Rome; MacArthur as the de facto proconsul of the Philippines and then the de jure overlord and ultimate authority in Japan.

Both men believed that when war became necessary, it should be all-out war, and civilian authorities shouldn't interfere with military decisions. MacArthur testified to the joint session of Congress, "History teaches with unmistakable emphasis that appeasement but begets new and bloodier war. It points to no single instance where the end has justified the means—where appeasement had led to more than a sham peace. Like blackmail, it lays the basis for new and successive greater demands, until, as in blackmail, violence becomes the only other alternative." [233]

In the course of their careers, both men defied their civilian superiors. Caesar conquered northern Gaul and invaded Germany and Britain

---

[232] William Manchester, *American Caesar* (New York: Little Brown, 1978) 10.
[233] Manchester, 10.

without authorization. Eventually, the Senate recalled him. MacArthur forced the Roosevelt administration to approve his invasion of the Philippines rather than proceed on a straight path to Japan. During the Korean War, he fenced with the Truman administration over the possibility of bombing, even invading, China. Truman wanted to limit the war; MacArthur wanted all-out victory and went public with his criticism of Truman. The conflict escalated until Truman had no choice but to recall the general, who had won victory in the Pacific. The public reacted to the recall of MacArthur with as much furor as the Roman populace had reacted to Caesar's recall from Gaul. When MacArthur returned home, New York City gave him a ticker-tape parade that drew seven million people.

The conduct of both generals had historic significance. Caesar defied recall from his provinces by marching on Rome. To the contrary, MacArthur conceded to his recall without the slightest hint of military resistance. Different circumstances, different results. In Caesar's time, republican government was dying, and he thrust the civilian government aside and seized power for himself. In MacArthur's time, American democracy was strengthening, and all MacArthur could do was run for president. His campaign quickly faded.

It is an interesting what-if question whether in a different era or at a different age MacArthur would have acted in a more forceful manner than he did. Had MacArthur been in Caesar's situation, had he been younger, facing prosecution, he too may have crossed the Rubicon. Near the end of the Korean War, MacArthur was seventy; Caesar was fifty when he was recalled from Gaul. No doubt MacArthur, like Caesar, harbored resentment against politicians, whom he thought unjustifiably thwarted his plans. He testified at a Senate committee hearing, "I find in existence a new and heretofore unknown and dangerous concept that the members of our armed forces owe primary allegiance or loyalty to those who temporarily exercise the authority of the executive branch of government rather than to the country and its Constitution which they are sworn to defend."[234]

Notwithstanding his inclinations, out-and-out rebellion was unthinkable.

---

[234] Manchester, 631; Trumbull Higgins, *Korea and the Fall of MacArthur* (New York, 1960) 132.

The principles of civilian control were ingrained in the American military conscience. Conflicts between American generals and the civilian government had all been settled in favor of the government. Winfield Scott, George McClellan, William "Billy" Mitchell were just a few of those who lost contests of will with sitting presidents. Nonetheless, MacArthur saw himself in greater terms than any of his predecessors, no doubt likening himself to Caesar and other Roman generals, and not unjustifiably. He thoroughly studied the Roman conquerors and saw himself as a descendent of their line. He saw their greatness, the adoration they received, but also the criticisms and betrayals they encountered. He disdained critics and kept a quotation on his office wall from the Roman consul, Lucius Aemilius Paulus.

> In every circle, and truly, at every table, there are people who lead armies into Macedonia ... These are great impediments to those who have the management of affairs ... I am not one of those who think that commanders ought at no time to receive advice ... If, therefore, anyone thinks himself qualified to give advice respecting the war which I am to conduct, which may prove advantageous to the public ... he shall be furnished with a ship, a horse, a tent; even his traveling charges shall be defrayed. But if he thinks this is too much trouble, and prefers the repose of a city to the toils of war, let him not, on land, assume the office of a pilot.[235]

Throughout MacArthur's career, his peers and superiors deferred to him because of his invaluable talents, his remarkable speeches, and his ability to energize his forces. Long into his retirement, he continued to lead. On May 12, 1962, at West Point, he inspired the recruits and the nation with his powerful "Duty-Honor-Country" speech.

> Duty-Honor-Country: Those three hallowed words reverently dictate what you ought to be, what you can be,

---

[235] Manchester, 479.

what you will be. They are your rallying points; to build courage when courage seems to fail; to regain faith when there seems to be little cause for faith; to create hope when hope becomes forlorn. Unhappily, I possess neither that eloquence of diction, that poetry of imagination, nor the brilliance of metaphor to tell you all what they mean. The unbelievers will say they are but words, but a slogan, but a flamboyant phrase. Every pedant, every demagogue, every cynic, every hypocrite, every trouble-maker, and, I am sorry to say, some others of an entirely different character, will try to downgrade them even to the extent of mockery and ridicule.

But these are some of the things they do. They build your basic character; they mold you for your future roles as custodians of the nation's defense; they make you strong enough to know when you are weak, and brave enough to face yourself when you are afraid. They teach you to be proud and unbending in honest failure, but humble and gentle in success, not to substitute words for action, not to seek the path of comfort, but to face the stress and spur of difficulty and challenge; to learn to stand up in the storm but to have compassion on those who fail; to master your-self before you seek to master others; to have a heart that is clean, a goal that is high; to learn to laugh yet never forget how to weep; to reach into the future yet never neglect the past; to be serious yet never take yourself too seriously; to be modest so that you will remember the simplicity of true greatness, the open mind of true wisdom, the meekness of true strength ...

They teach you in this way to be an officer and a gentleman ...

You are the lever which binds together the entire fab-ric of our national system of defense. From your ranks come the great captains who hold the nation's destiny in their hands the moment the war tocsin sounds.

The long gray line has never failed us. Were you to do so, a million ghosts in olive drab, in brown khaki, in blue and gray, would rise from their white crosses, thundering those magic words: duty, honor, country ...

This does not mean that you are warmongers. On the contrary, the soldier above all other people prays for peace, for he must suffer and bear the deepest wounds and scars of war. But always in our ears ring the ominous words of Plato, that wisest of all philosophers: "Only the dead have seen the end of war."[236]

---

[236] Douglas MacArthur, *Reminiscences* (New York, 1964) 423–426.

CHAPTER 25

Partisan Divide

FROM THE BEGINNING OF the American nation, agricultural interests clashed with manufacturing interests, slaveholders clashed with abolitionists, Anglophiles clashed with Francophiles, and commoners clashed with the propertied classes. George Washington saw the poison of partisanship as he tried to keep Hamilton and Jefferson from tearing his cabinet apart. He wrote that political parties "kindle the animosity of one part [of the nation] against another, foment occasional riot and insurrection ... open the door to foreign influence and corruption [and] become potent engines by which cunning, ambitious, and unprincipled men ... subvert the power of the people and usurp for themselves the reins of government."[237]

Partisanship is innate and understandable. It has arisen everywhere and throughout history, but what Washington was referring to was excessive partisanship of the kind that can destroy a nation. Excessive partisanship is a form of mob psychology, a phenomenon that can be observed at sporting events, concerts, political rallies, and riots when participants adopt the mind-set of the crowd and lose their individual identities. This phenomenon has been observed in all ages and in all countries. Pliny the Younger, the Roman historian, pointed out that people tend to support a sporting team, regardless of the merit, content, or character of the team

---

[237] Fitzpatrick, *GW Writings*, vol. 25:214–215.

members. Of chariot-racing fans, Pliny wrote, "If they were attracted by the speed of the horses or the drivers' skill one could account for it, but in fact it is the racing-colors they really support and care about, and if the colors were to be exchanged in mid-course during a race, they would transfer their favor and enthusiasm and rapidly desert the famous drivers and horses whose names they shout as they recognize them from afar. Such is the popularity and importance of a worthless shirt."[238]

As did the sports fans of antiquity, modern sports fans exhibit the same irrational attachments to a name or team. They applaud players on their team who commit a hard foul in basketball, take out the second baseman in baseball, or unnecessarily slam an opponent in football. They call them good, hardnosed players; however, if the same players were on the opposing team, they would immediately condemn them as dirty players or cheap-shot artists.

Pliny's observation about sports fans and racing colors applies doubly to political fans. In politics, party members will view their own candidates who engage in misconduct, such as unscrupulously buying votes or making closed-door deals, as merely doing business as usual; however, they would see the same conduct by candidates of the opposing party as major corruption. Furthermore, party members view their candidates' personal immorality as irrelevant to the performance of their duties, while they would disqualify a member of the opposing party who engaged in the same conduct. It's not an overstatement to say that party members support whatever their candidates propose and oppose whatever the other party proposes.

Political partisanship has been a constant, although parties have shifted their focus and aims. The Democratic Party, which initially represented the slaveholding interests, eventually came to be seen as representing the working classes; while the Republican Party, which initially advocated the abolition of slavery and supported free labor, came to be seen as representing the propertied classes. As a further generalization, Democrats have looked to the presidency for strong centralized leadership, while Republicans have relied on Congress for moderate and diffused

---

[238] Pliny the Younger, "To Calvisius," *Letters*, (Harvard Classics, 1914).

leadership. Respectively, the modern political parties have traced the path of the Roman *populares* and *optimates*. The former sought charismatic and forceful leaders to challenge the hierarchy of the propertied classes, while the latter relied on the Senate to resist changes to the social and political order.

In the early American republic, the balance of political power favored the landowning classes, and governmental authority was decentralized among the states. Lincoln and Grant's presidencies were the exceptions, but after the Civil War and the reconstruction era, the states reasserted their preeminence, and in the laissez-faire economy, large industrial conglomerates gained widespread political influence. These conglomerates created great wealth for investors but also displaced and exploited workers. When the financial panic of 1893 struck, opposition to the conglomerates and complaints about the concentration of wealth in the hands of a few grew and became prevalent. Intellectuals and commoners alike believed the country was controlled by an oligarchy of monopolists who had state and federal officials in their pockets. Midwestern farmers, suffering from a recession, formed a populist movement, complaining that banks and the eastern mercantile elites were crushing them.

The conflict between big business monopolists, on one side, and democratic populist reformers, on the other, played out in the presidential election between William McKinley and William Jennings Bryan. McKinley was a Republican backed by the industrialists; he was committed to the gold standard and protecting the currency. Bryan was a populist leader running as a Democrat; he advocated a silver standard that would make more money available, aid debtors, and undercut bondholders.

At the 1896 Democratic Convention, Bryan delivered his powerful "Cross of Gold" speech, which won him the party's nomination for president. The speech was a rhetorical masterpiece that became a hallmark of the populist movement. The following are excerpts:

> I come to speak to you in defense of a cause as holy as the cause of liberty—the cause of humanity …
>
> Ah, my friends, we say not one word against those who live upon the Atlantic Coast, but the hardy pioneers

who have braved all the dangers of the wilderness, who have made the desert to blossom as a rose—the pioneers away out there who rear their children near to nature's heart … It is for these that we speak. We do not come as aggressors. Our war is not a war of conquest; we are fighting in the defense of our homes, our families, and posterity …

And now, my friends, let me come to the paramount issue. If they ask us why it is that we say more on the money question than we say upon the tariff question. I reply that, if protection has slain its thousands, the gold standard has slain its tens of thousands …

If they come to meet us on that issue we can present the history of our nation. More than that; we can tell them that they will search the pages of history in vain to find a single instance where the common people of any land have ever declared themselves in favor of the gold standard. They can find where the holders of fixed investments have declared for a gold standard, but not where the masses have.

Mr. Carlisle said in 1878 that this was a struggle between "the idle holders of idle capital" and "the struggling masses, who produce the wealth and pay the taxes of the country"; and, my friends, the question we are to decide is, Upon which side will the Democratic party fight—upon the side of the "idle holders of idle capital" or upon the side of "the struggling masses"?

You come to us and tell us that the great cities are in favor of the gold standard; we reply that the great cities rest upon our broad and fertile prairies. Burn down your cities and leave our farms, and your cities will spring up again as if by magic; but destroy our farms, and the grass will grow in the streets of every city in the country …

If they dare to come out in the open field and defend the gold standard as a good thing, we will fight them to the uttermost. Having behind us the producing masses of this nation and the world, supported by the commercial interests, the laboring interests, and the toilers everywhere, we will answer their demand for a gold standard by saying to them. You shall not press down upon the brow of labor this crown of thorns; you shall not crucify mankind upon a cross of gold.

Bryan's speech on behalf of the debtor farmers addressed the same issues between the Rome's small farmers and the latifundia interests that existed at the time of the Gracchi. It also aroused the same passions that drove Rome to political violence.

Although Bryan lost the election, the populist movement continued to grow, and in 1900, Bryan again challenged McKinley for the presidency. McKinley won, but the conflict between the factions didn't subside. The oratory of Bryan and others had inflamed passions, and a direct connection can be drawn to the assassination of President McKinley in 1901 by Leon Czolgosz, a radical anarchist. Czolgosz had attended a talk by the anarchist Emma Goldman and decided to kill the president. He confessed that he did it because he was against a government that was concerned only with making the rich richer.

Ironically, the powerbrokers of the Republican Party had picked Theodore Roosevelt to be McKinley's vice president. Their plan had been to quiet Roosevelt's outspoken criticism of monopolies by shifting him into the dead-end job of vice president. Their strategy backfired when McKinley was assassinated, and Roosevelt enthusiastically assumed the presidency, quickly becoming a thorn in the side of the industrialists. Roosevelt became known as a trustbuster for his litigation against monopolies and the corrupt politicians under their control. His most significant regulatory accomplishment was the breaking-up of John D. Rockefeller's Standard Oil Company. In retrospect, the transfer of power from McKinley to Roosevelt perfectly represented the shift from the nineteenth to the twentieth century and the trend away from admiration for big business and free enterprise, and toward an increasing distrust of unregulated capitalism and the super wealthy.

Roosevelt had promised not to run for another term, so in 1908 he supported William Howard Taft as his Republican Party successor. However, in 1912, dissatisfied with the Taft administration, Roosevelt formed a third party and ran for a third term. While he was giving a campaign speech, a mentally ill anarchist shot him. The anarchist stated that he did it because Roosevelt was a "third termer."

Roosevelt quickly recovered from his wound and resumed campaigning on a platform "to destroy this invisible Government, to dissolve this unholy alliance between corrupt business and corrupt politics is the first task of the statesmanship of the day." Among those in Roosevelt's camp, invective was rampart. Correlations were drawn between the American oligarchy and the Roman oligarchy of Augustus. In 1914, Louis Brandeis, a future Supreme Court justice, published *Other People's Money,* in which he explained how the system worked to the detriment of the general public. He saw a Roman parallel and the need for maintaining our system of checks and balances, writing, "The development of our financial oligarchy followed, in this respect, lines with which the history of political despotism has familiarized us: usurpation, proceeding by gradual encroachment rather than by violent acts; subtle and often long-concealed concentration of distinct functions, which are beneficent when separately administered, and dangerous only when combined in the same persons. It was by processes such as these that Caesar Augustus became master of Rome. The makers of our own Constitution had in mind like dangers to our political liberty when they provided so carefully for the separations of governmental powers."

Among the populace, the enormous wealth of a few was contrasted with the hard times for the many. Dissention grew as the young strove to push aside the old and the "have-nots" challenged the "haves." Criticism of the so-called robber barons spread among the population, and the growing union labor movement set the stage for combat between workers and management.

The dissention subsided for a time in the 1920s as economic prosperity mitigated class and factional conflicts, but the relative quiet ended with the 1929 stock market crash. The crash forecast or spurred the Depression, and the Depression reignited populist and revolutionary movements throughout the country. Existential challenges threatened the republic as labor strikes and armed combat punctuated the conflicts between the opposing sides. In 1932, workers marched on the Ford automobile plant in Dearborn, Michigan, to protest working conditions. The march was organized with the backing of William Z. Foster, the secretary of the Communist Party trade union federation, who in 1928 and 1932 ran for president on a platform to end capitalism and establish a workers' republic.

As the crowd assembled for the march, Foster gave a speech, demanding the restoration of the jobs and benefits that had been cut and the right to organize a union. The march began peacefully, but when it reached the plant, a pitched battle broke out between workers and security officers. The officers fired on the crowd, killing five people and wounding many others. This event became known as the River Rouge Massacre.

Another serious clash occurred in July 1932 when thousands of unemployed First World War veterans, known as the Bonus Army, camped in tents and shacks in Washington, DC, to demand their veterans' bonuses. The bonuses were due to be paid in 1945, but the veterans wanted immediate payment because of their economic plight. The sight of thousands of veterans camped outside the Capitol couldn't have differed greatly from the sight of Caesar's veterans camped in the Field of Mars in 47 BC to demand the bonuses that had been promised to them.

The American veterans, disappointed when the Senate refused to accelerate their payments, remained in Washington and continued their daily protests. On July 28, 1932, clashes occurred with police on Capitol Hill and around the Washington Monument, and President Herbert Hoover ordered General Douglas MacArthur, the army commander, to disperse the veterans. MacArthur, a conservative-minded traditionalist, believed the veterans were in the hands of communists; he dispersed them with tear gas, cavalry, and bayonets. Next, he bulldozed and burned their tents and shacks. Although MacArthur's actions were applauded by some, they were denounced by others, and there was significant debate about whether he had acted in defiance of President Hoover's order *not* to destroy the tent city. It wasn't the last time MacArthur would be accused of insubordination.

When President Franklin D. Roosevelt took office, the challenges from populists, socialists, and communists induced him to take positions that in another time he might not have taken. Although he was extremely wealthy and a patrician through and through, like the Gracchi, Roosevelt adopted a populist stance. For political advantage, he employed elements of class warfare and vilified the moneyed class. At his inauguration in 1933, he proclaimed, "The money changers have fled from their high seats in the temple of our civilization. We may now restore that temple to the ancient truths." He spoke of "the forgotten man" as his constituency, and he castigated "economic royalists" and the "privileged princes of new economic dynasties, thirsty for power."

In 1935, Roosevelt passed the Wealth Tax Act not only to fund his expanding government but also to mollify popular grievances. He introduced wealth redistribution programs. Some critics said he did so to mitigate the threat to his presidency posed by radicals such as Huey Long, the populist former governor and sitting senator from Louisiana. They said Roosevelt feared a challenge from Senator Long more than from any Republican. Roosevelt told his adviser, Rex Tugwell, that Long was "one of the two most dangerous men in the country." (General MacArthur was the other).

Senator Long, through the new medium of radio, appealed to the resentment of the poor and the unemployed against the superrich. He proposed a program he called "Share Our Wealth Society" with the motto "Every Man a King." He proposed a guaranteed $5,000 for each family; at the time that was enough for a home, an automobile, a radio, ordinary conveniences, and education for the children. To accomplish this, no one could own more than $10 or $15 million, which would be more than any one man and his children and grandchildren could spend in their lifetimes. He also proposed an old-age pension of thirty dollars per month for poor persons over sixty years old.

The essence of Senator Long's program mirrored the Roman *populare* programs—the Gracchan limitations on land ownership, Catiline's "Clean Slates" debt program, and Clodius's redistribution plans. Senator Long planned to run for president against Roosevelt in 1936, but like many of Rome's *populare* demagogues, he came to a violent end. In 1935, he was assassinated.

Senator Long's ideas didn't die with him. His populism bordered on communism, and this wasn't an aberration in the politics of the time. In 1941, Henry Wallace, a populist who had been accused of communist sympathies, was elected as Roosevelt's vice president. Had the Second World War not alleviated the Depression and had it not supplanted the economy as the major issue of the day, there's no telling what direction the country would have taken. The war changed the nation's mind-set; it fostered a deep antipathy to all forms of totalitarianism, including the Nationalist Socialist Party (Nazis), the Stalinist Communist Party, and Mussolini's Socialist Party.

Seeing the socialist-leaning Wallace as a detriment, Roosevelt dropped him from his upcoming ticket in favor of Harry Truman, a moderate Democrat. Truman, however, also harbored a deep-class consciousness, and in 1948, as president, he proclaimed that "Wall Street reactionaries are not satisfied with being rich. They want to increase their power and their privileges, regardless of what happens to the other fellow. They are gluttons of privilege."

After Truman's term, partisan attacks on the rich were less frequent for a time, and the communist/socialist movement diminished. However, by the 1960s, other less-overt antiestablishment movements, with similar anti-American and class struggle overtones, began gaining influence among the next generation and instigated partisan battles as serious as those of the earlier times.

CHAPTER 26

Marcus Livius Drusus and John J. Kennedy

THOUGH THEY TOOK PLACE two millennia apart, the assassinations of Marcus Livius Drusus the Younger in 90 BC and John Fitzgerald Kennedy in 1963 turned the course of their nations in remarkably similar ways. Both men were energetic, brilliant, appealing leaders; both inspired groundswells of positive and expansive feelings. Both were persuasive speakers who connected with their audiences. They followed a tradition of noblesse oblige, elites advocating on behalf of the common classes for the betterment of society. Both advocated civil rights and equality: Drusus for the Italians and Kennedy for American minorities. Both proposed major civil rights legislation but were killed before their legislation could be enacted.

Drusus was of mixed plebeian and patrician heritage. His father, Marcus Livius Drusus the Elder, of noble plebeian ancestry, had won a political victory for the Senate against Gaius Gracchus in 122 BC, and later became a censor. On his mother's side, Drusus was impeccably patrician, and it would have been expected for him to identify with the conservative faction. However, at the Battle of Arausio against Germanic tribes, he saw his Italian allies fight bravely before they were annihilated because of poor generalship. From that experience, he developed a strong affinity for the Italian allies and determined to become an advocate on their behalf. Like the Gracchi, he chose to become a tribune of the plebs rather than a praetor or consul. His aim was to enact reforms, and as a tribune with a respected military record and the support of the common people, he had a better chance to succeed. He was in a unique position since the oligarchic class was more likely to accept his proposals because of his background, his extensive clientele, and his outstanding reputation as a paterfamilias. Most important, his record as a dependable conservative who stayed within the traditional legal processes, rather than circumventing or violating the rules, distinguished him from the Gracchi. His objective was to persuade the oligarchy that his reforms, even at some sacrifice, would be better for them and the nation in the long run. At the same time, he tried to dissuade the Italians from outright rebellion, promising them that if they were patient, he would pass legislation for their full citizenship and equality.

Kennedy, an Irish-Catholic, could be compared to a "new man" of the Roman plebeian nobility. His father, Joseph Kennedy, was a self-made multimillionaire who had married Rose Fitzgerald, a woman from a prominent Boston family, the daughter of the city's mayor. The senior Kennedy served in the Franklin Roosevelt administration as the first chairman of the Securities and Exchange Commission. He had further political aspirations but was stymied. Thus, he passed his aspirations to his sons, Joseph Jr. and John Fitzgerald. The oldest, Joseph Jr., was expected to carry the political mantle, but he was killed in the Second World War when his plane was shot down over the Atlantic. With Joseph's death, the father concentrated on steering John to the presidency. John also served in the war and was injured when his torpedo boat was rammed and sank in the Pacific.

Although John Kennedy was the wealthy recipient of a $10 million trust fund, he became president as a Democrat and an advocate for the lower and middle classes. His advocacy was singularly attached not to specific reforms but rather to a broad call to arms for freedom and equality, support for American labor, civil rights for African-Americans, freedom for people enclosed by the iron curtain of the Soviet Union, and democracy for people not yet under the Soviet dome. In his inaugural speech, he said his generation had been given the responsibility to defend freedom everywhere. "I do not shrink from the responsibility. I welcome it." He made a commitment that America would "pay any price, bear any burden, meet any hardship, support any friend, oppose any foe, to ensure the survival and success of liberty." He inspired a generation with his famous call to arms, "Ask not what your country can do for you, but ask what you can do for your country."

Drusus and Kennedy each emerged as a perfect antidote for the factional conflicts that plagued his times. Both had the capacity to resolve issues, and if they had lived, they assuredly would have implemented positive solutions. Without them, the conflicts exploded: in Rome, the Italian Social War; in America, the social upheaval and civil violence of the 1960s and 70s.

Drusus proposed a comprehensive program for the unresolved problems that had continued unabated since the time of the Gracchi. His proposal accommodated all factions while demanding concessions from each. He proposed overseas colonies to provide land for the populace, winning support from the populace and also from a substantial segment of the oligarchy.

He next proposed reforms for the judicial system, which were badly needed because of the increasing number of politically motivated prosecutions. Even the most respected senators were dragged before the courts, and the outcomes of most of the trials were unsatisfactory. Verdicts weren't respected, and opposing factions accused the all-equestrian juries of bias, depending on "whose ox was being gored." Drusus proposed dividing the jury pools half-and-half between the equestrian and senatorial orders, hoping this combination would alleviate the political divide. To compensate the equestrians for losing total control of the jury pools, three hundred equestrians would be enrolled in the Senate. To compensate for the dilution of the Senate, it would regain its influence in the courts. The jury pool proposal passed with substantial support.

Drusus then turned to his most important and controversial proposal: full citizenship for the people of Italia. Reform was needed. The Italian population was angry because of their second-class status. Many Italians demanded full citizenship; others wanted complete independence. They complained about their treatment at the hands of Roman officials and the inequitable distribution of land and rewards for their soldiers who had fought alongside the Romans.

Rome's oligarchs had been divided over the issue for some time. Some were opposed to any upgrading of the Italians; they were satisfied with the status quo in which they received benefits from their Italian clientele. Others in the aristocracy saw the need for inclusion, and they saw disastrous consequences should the Italians be denied. Of the equestrians, most supported inclusion as they saw it as good for business. Others—particularly those *publicani* and equestrians with government contracts—opposed. Additionally, in what might seem counterintuitive, many *populare* leaders were against extending citizenship. Their base of support came from the urban masses and the rural plebeians; these groups saw that their own status would be diminished and their voting power diluted were the Italians to become their equals.

Unfortunately for Drusus, when it became known that the Italians were preparing for war, a backlash arose in the Senate, and his land and judiciary reforms were rescinded. Still determined, Drusus made a last-ditch effort to obtain citizenship for the Italians and avoid the pending war. He scheduled a vote in the assembly, but before the vote could be held, he was assassinated. His body was found in the atrium of his house. Several investigations were conducted, but the assassins were never identified, and it wasn't determined which faction, if any, was behind the assassination.

The consequences were monumental. The Italians declared war on Rome, and to Rome's surprise, the Italians were well prepared. The Italians won several battles before the Romans retaliated with decisive military victories. Although the Romans seemed to gain the upper hand, in 89 BC, they offered full citizenship to all Italians who had remained loyal and any of the rebels who put down their arms. The rebellion ended, and thousands of Italians traveled to Rome to register for citizenship. Nevertheless, it wasn't a happy ending: treasuries were depleted, and tens of thousands were killed. Mithridates took the opportunity to attack the Roman provinces in the East, infamously slaughtering all the Roman and Italian businessmen in Asia Minor and cutting off a major source of Rome's revenue.

Although *optimates* and *populares* had united to fight the Italians, when the war ended, the acrimony between factions resumed, with oligarchs prosecuting supporters of Drusus and members of the Drusus faction bringing reciprocal prosecutions against oligarchs. Worse still, civil war between the Marian and Sullan factions erupted over the command against Mithridates. Sulla retained the command, but while he was in the East, Marius tyrannized the oligarchs. When Sulla returned, he defeated the Marian faction and established his dictatorship. The dictatorship generated new problems and new factions. Consequences built on consequences until the end of the republic.

Had Drusus lived and enacted his citizenship law, the Social War would surely have been avoided, and the treasury wouldn't have been depleted. In all likelihood, Mithridates wouldn't have attacked, and Rome wouldn't have been compelled to go to war in the East. Business might have prospered at a greater rate; democratic progress might have developed and spread. Sulla wouldn't have marched on Rome and wouldn't have become dictator. Thus the stage wouldn't have been set for the later triumvirates and dictatorships. These are pure speculations, but peace instead of war incontrovertibly would have changed subsequent history.

The assassination of President Kennedy on November 22, 1963, in Dallas, Texas, also caused monumental consequences, though not as immediate as in Rome, but with similar far-reaching effects that changed the spirit and character of the American people. At the president's funeral procession, the image of his three-year-old son, John F. Kennedy Jr., saluting his father's casket as it rolled passed shattered the nation's heart.

Conspiracy theories regarding the assassination abounded. The assassin, Lee Harvey Oswald, was identified, but whether anyone was behind him has never been definitely established. One theory was that Kennedy's advancement of a civil rights agenda angered segregationists, who may have enlisted Oswald to kill the president.

During Kennedy's presidency, leaders of the African-American civil rights movement increased their demands for legislation to ensure desegregation and equal opportunities. The movement was committed to non-violent action, but resistance and violence by segregationists escalated and intensified. The southern segregationist resistance wasn't unlike the resistance of Rome's urban populace against the grant of citizenship to Italians. Freedom riders were attacked, churches were bombed, and demonstrations in Birmingham, Alabama, were broken up with dogs, water cannon, tear gas, and clubs. Expectations ran high that something had to be done to calm the waters and avoid an eruption of major racial violence. In June 1963, Kennedy proposed comprehensive civil rights legislation aimed at alleviating tensions and injustices. The bill would safeguard voting rights, desegregate public places and schools, prohibit federal funding of programs that practice discrimination, and guarantee equal employment opportunity. Southern Democrats, among others, opposed the bill, and political wrangling in the Congress held up its passage. The assassination may have been meant to prevent its passage; in fact, it had the opposite effect, making the nation more determined than ever to pass civil rights legislation.

Another theory was that the conspiracy emanated from communist Cuba. In the postwar world, communism had been on the march with takeovers in Eastern Europe, China, and North Korea. Fanatical communist adherents operated in America; a communist spy ring stole America's atomic bomb secrets and passed them to the Soviets. Oswald had aspirations as a communist. He had lived in the Soviet Union and had tried to visit Cuba. It is not inconceivable that he shot President Kennedy in revenge for the sponsorship of the ill-fated invasion of Cuba by Cuban exiles, the alleged CIA attempt to assassinate Castro, or Kennedy's naval blockade during the Cuban missile crisis, which had forced the Soviet Union to retire from the confrontation.

Another conspiracy theory involved organized crime. When Jack Ruby, the nightclub owner, shot Oswald at Dallas Police Department headquarters, some speculated that organized crime was involved and that Ruby shot Oswald to keep him from talking about who had aided or directed him. Support for the organized crime theory came from two fronts. The Chicago organized crime boss Sam Giancana had helped Kennedy win the election in Illinois in exchange for assistance regarding federal investigations; but Giancana felt betrayed because when Kennedy took office, he provided no help and ordered a crackdown on organized crime. Also, the Teamsters' Union had supported Kennedy in the election, and the president's brother, Robert Kennedy, as attorney general, set out to prosecute the leadership of the union. The ties between organized crime and the teamsters added fodder to the speculation.

The Warren Commission investigation concluded that Oswald had acted alone, not with or on behalf of others. In any case, as with the murder of Drusus, Kennedy's death had enormous consequences. While a shooting war didn't break out, the assassination changed American society. It smashed hopes of the youthful generation that the youthful president had inspired, depleted the nation's reserve of optimism, and diminished America's stature in the world. His loss raised the level of anguish among the disheartened, set the stage for waves of riots across American cities, and bolstered the claims of radicals calling for revolutionary action.

Kennedy's successor, President Lyndon Johnson, was presented with difficult problems he was unable to resolve. Although with his long experience as a legislator, he overcame the longest filibuster in Senate history and passed the civil rights bill in 1964; for other matters he didn't provide the kind of inspirational leadership Kennedy might have. Johnson's image as a wheeler-dealer politician added another layer of cynicism on top of the nation's troubled and distrustful state of mind. Some speculated that Johnson's escalation of the Vietnam War was partly to provide a distraction from the domestic unrest. While it's hard to believe a president would do such a thing, such things haven't been unknown to history. When Johnson found himself in the quagmire of the war, he sent more and more troops. The majority of the soldiers were draftees, not volunteers, and troop levels in the battle zone grew to five hundred thousand. Over the course of the war, 2.5 million soldiers were sent to Vietnam. Fifty-eight thousand were killed, many more were wounded, and many more suffered long-term psychological damage.

For a significant part of the population, demonstrating against the Vietnam War became a focal point for complaints about the inequalities of American society. Challenges to authority were applauded, and the social unrest and the antiwar atmosphere demoralized the troops, who knew politics had influenced military strategies. After the Tet Offensive in 1968, clearly the government was looking for a way out of the war rather than a way to win it. Army discipline deteriorated, and distrust between officers and soldiers placed everyone in jeopardy. As the war dragged on, drug addiction among the troops increased to levels that undermined the effectiveness of entire battalions. These problems, among others, eventually led to the United States' evacuating South Vietnam and leaving its allies at the mercy of the communists.

What-if questions can provoke a thousand speculations, but it's perfectly conceivable that had Kennedy lived, Vietnam might not have escalated as it did. Kennedy had demonstrated his mettle during the Berlin Wall standoff and the Cuban Missile Crisis. He had learned from the disaster of the Bay of Pigs invasion, and he wasn't one to be persuaded to act against his instincts by even the most forceful generals and advisers—as Johnson seems to have been. If Kennedy had committed the nation to the war, it might well have been fought with a different spirit. Kennedy's optimism was contagious; with Kennedy alive, the nation might have retained its optimism. The troops might have felt the nation's support instead of its disfavor and disavowal.

Had Kennedy lived, the nation may not have experienced the destructive drift of the 1960s and 1970s. In his absence, the Vietnam War precipitated a major cultural schism; trust in national institutions diminished, and the cultural polarization between left and right, young and old, widened. Had he lived, it's conceivable that the 1968 assassination of Martin Luther King Jr. would not have occurred.

As it happened, King's murder further damaged the national psyche. A wave of riots spread across the country, and alliances between some African-American groups striving for civil rights and extreme leftist groups seeking revolution led to a radical coalition and major instances of violence.

Parallels can be drawn to the time after the assassination of Drusus when the Social War raged with the Italians and the internal antagonisms among Romans almost dismantled the republic. In the wake of the violence following the assassinations in both nations, instability sought stability; Rome responded with Sulla, and America responded with Nixon.

CHAPTER 27

Prosecutions as War by Other Means

DURING PERIODS OF TURBULENT partisan conflicts, the Roman courts were used in place of battlefields to exact personal revenge or gain political advantage. Trials were public events, conducted on raised platforms in the forum, with crowds gathered to watch and make judgments of their own about the parties, witnesses, and advocates.

For the Romans, the personal and political were intertwined; their obsession with *virtus, dignitas,* and *auctoritus* drove leading Roman men to challenge and rechallenge one another. Trials conducted before the assembly, ad hoc special tribunals, or standing courts (perpetuae quaestio) provided a means to uphold individual or family honor without resorting to violence. In the late republic, trials were increasingly used to eliminate political foes by bringing prosecutions on any available grounds.

The immunity from prosecution Roman magistrates enjoyed lasted for only their one-year term; thereafter, magistrates were subject to prosecutions and lawsuits. Tribunes, senators, and private citizens initiating such legal actions were legion, and even the greatest of Roman magistrates were held to account for their alleged misdeeds.

In 149 BC, the *Lex Calpurnia* established the court of restitution (*quaestio de repetundis*) to prosecute extortion by public officials and recover ill-gotten property. It was a hybrid court that applied civil and criminal sanctions. About 139 BC, partisan factions increasingly began to use the restitution court as an instrument of political warfare and a venue for battles between *optimates* and *populares,* between equestrian businessmen and senatorial nobles, between provincials and governors, and between the Scipio circle and the Metelli circle. Political infighting that began in the assembly or the Senate wound up in the court, and as expected, trials led to retaliatory trials. As the court was initially constituted, the deck was stacked in favor of the senatorial class, with a jury pool that included only senators. But over time, as political conflicts escalated, the makeup of the jury pools became a major issue.

The watershed event that intensified partisan conflicts was the death of Tiberius Gracchus in 133 BC Appian related, "On the subject of the homicide of Gracchus, the city was divided between sorrow and joy. Some mourned for themselves and for him, and deplored the present condition of things, believing that the commonwealth no longer existed but had been supplanted by force and violence. Others considered that their dearest wishes were accomplished."[239]

After his death, the Senate passed a senatus consultum ultimum, which ratified the violence against Tiberius. Nonetheless, the adherents of Tiberius held firm and prosecuted Scipio Nasica, the *pontifex maximus,* for leading the march that had led to Tiberius's death. The trial was held before a *quaestio extra ordinem,* an ad hoc court convened by the Senate. The primary issue was the legality of the retroactive senatus consultum ultimum, but before a verdict could be rendered, the *optimates* who controlled the Senate sent Nasica on an assignment to Asia, giving him immunity for the term of his assignment. This tactic avoided the conviction of one of their own or an acquittal that might have unleashed another *populare* rebellion.

In 123 BC, the conflict reignited when Tiberius's brother, Gaius Gracchus, was elected as a tribune of the plebs with the support of commoners and the backing of equestrians. Suspecting that he would be the target of his adversaries and knowing that the outcome of political trials often depended on the makeup of the jury, Gaius passed a law mandating that equestrians would serve with senators on juries. This was a significant change because it shifted the balance of power away from the senatorial to the equestrian class.

---

[239] Appian, *Roman History,* 1.2.17

Gaius Gracchus also passed the *Lex Sempronia ne de capite civium* (Sempronia law— no new court without approval of the citizens), which restricted the Senate's authority to set up extraordinary ad hoc investigative courts by an ordinary senatus consultum decree. It also required the approval of the assembly to set up such courts. This law, Gaius thought, would protect him and his followers from Senate prosecution. Subsequent events, however, brought the opposite result. His law precluded the establishment of an extraordinary court without assembly approval, but by tying the Senate's hands, it forced the Senate to issue a more drastic senatus consultum ultimum, which authorized the consul Lucius Opimius to protect the republic by whatever means necessary. The consul and his forces promptly overwhelmed Gaius's supporters, and Gaius committed suicide.

Three years later, in 120 BC, Gaius's supporters regrouped and prosecuted Opimius for the death of Gaius. The prosecution was brought before the assembly, rather than a court. Cicero summarized the legal issues of the case. "Opimius killed Gracchus. What is the substance of the case? That he did this for the sake of the *res publica*, because he was called to arms by order of a *senatus consultum [ultimum]* ... Decius [the prosecutor], however, denies the legality of the decree itself, as being contrary to the laws. Therefore, the issue will be whether the senate's decree and the salvation of the *res publica* justified the act."[240]

Opimius was acquitted. In effect, the assembly ratified the legality of a senatus consultum ultimum, and thereafter the Senate employed it several more times during civil conflicts. But Opimius's acquittal didn't mean the Gracchan *populares* would forget. The martyrdom of the Gracchi hadn't destroyed their movement but invigorated it, and in 109 BC, when they had strengthened their political position, they prosecuted Opimius again, charging him with bribery. The transparent motive for the prosecution was pure revenge on behalf of Gaius Gracchus. Although the charges were surely trumped up, Opimius was convicted and exiled.

After the conviction of Opimius, *populare* tribunes increased the political prosecution of senators, and the Senate responded with several senatus consultum ultimums. In 100 BC, the Senate issued a senatus

---

[240] Cicero, *On Oratory*, 2. 132.

consultum ultimum aimed at Lucius Appuleius Saturninus, the tribune of the plebs who had driven Metellus into exile and had passed laws by strong-arm methods. The ultimum ordered the consul Gaius Marius to protect the republic. When Marius's troops surrounded Saturninus, the latter surrendered, but while he was in custody, a group of *optimates* including Gaius Rabirius killed him without a trial. At the time, no one was held to account for his death because it was apparently assumed that the ultimum had authorized his execution. This wouldn't be the end of the matter. Thirty-seven years later, in 63 BC, *populare* leaders prosecuted Gaius Rabirius for his participation in the killing of Saturninus, demonstrating the deep and long-lasting divide between the political factions.

From the death of Tiberius Gracchus in 133 BC to the prosecution of Rabirius in 63 BC, more than eighty significant political prosecutions were initiated. Though the charges varied, political partisanship was the motive for most of them. Often the outcome depended on the relative representation of senators and equestrians in the jury pools. Class representation on juries would be a matter of contention throughout the period. The faction that dominated the jury pools changed back and forth several times. When Gaius Marius came to power, senators were banned from extortion court (*quaestio de repetundis*) juries. As an unexpected consequence, the equestrians voted far more for acquittals than for convictions, primarily because the equestrian jurors were controlled not by political ideology but by what was good for business. They tended toward leniency. They declined to be a tool for politically motivated prosecutions, and they declined to convict defendants who had served Rome in war. Their verdicts shifted between the *populares* and the *optimates*.

For instance, they convicted Opimius for the death of the *populare* Gaius Gracchus, who had granted the *publicani* equestrians monopolistic contracts in Asia, but they sided with the *optimates* against the *populare* Saturninus when they saw the disorder and chaos he had instigated.

An aberration was the conviction of Publius Rutilius Rufus, who was tried in the *quaestio de repetundis* on a charge of extortion. Rutilius was a noble with a long and distinguished career. In the Jugurthine War, his exploits had included turning the course of a battle by capturing or incapacitating the enemy's war elephants. Elected consul in 105 BC, he instituted an improved system of military drill, and he passed a debtor reform law, the *bonorum venditio*, which established bankruptcy as an option. An accomplished advocate and jurist, Rutilius wrote treatises on the law that were quoted in Justinian's *Digests* five hundred years later.

His prosecution was an example of the aphorism "No good deed goes unpunished." In 94 BC, at an advanced age, he went to the province of Asia as a legate to the proconsul Quintus Mucius Scaevola. Their purpose was to deal with complaints of abusive tax farming by the *publicani* who had been plundering the province. This was a critically important assignment because Mithridates of Pontus coveted the Asia province, and the victimized provincials might welcome his invasion.

Scaevola and Rutilius reigned in the *publicani*, placated the provincials, and accomplished a wholesale reform of administrative practices. When Scaevola returned to Rome, Rutilius remained in Asia to complete the task of correcting the abuses and putting the reforms into operation. For these efforts, he was lauded, but in 92 BC, agents of the *publicani* prosecuted him for extortion in the Asia province—ironically, the offense he had attempted to curtail. His jury was chosen from the equestrian order, where the *publicani* exerted a strong influence. Rutilius was convicted, sending a message to discourage further senatorial interference with the practices of the tax farmers. Rutilius, a Stoic, accepted his exile and chose to spend it in the province in Asia where he allegedly committed his crime. He lived the rest of his life there and was treated with honors for the relief he had given the provincials.

In 91 BC, Rutilius's nephew, Marcus Livius Drusus, tribune of the people, affronted by the conviction of his uncle, proposed a law to return the jury pool to the Senate. In exchange, he proposed to enroll three hundred equestrians as senators. At the same time, he made other proposals, including the full enfranchisement of all Italians. His proposals met resistance from several sides at once, and in the midst of the debate, Drusus was assassinated. His proposals died with him, and the equestrians retained control of the jury pools.

The death of Drusus sparked the Italian Social War, which began badly for Rome. In the poisoned atmosphere of a war that wasn't going well, those associated with Drusus were prosecuted under the *Lex Varia*, a new law the tribune, Q. Varius Hybrida, enacted that broadened the *maiestas* law to encompass anyone who had sided with or even sympathized with the Italian demands for citizenship. Several members of the Metelli faction were put on trial. Even Lucius Cornelius Sulla was threatened with trumped-up charges, but they were dropped. The wheel turned quickly, and when the war turned in Rome's favor, Varius was prosecuted under his own law and convicted. He committed suicide—surely to the satisfaction of many.

The dictator Lucius Cornelius Sulla endeavored to ameliorate the poisonous atmosphere that had been created by the continual prosecutions. After returning from the East and ousting the *populare* faction, he reversed many of the *populare* laws, modified the arbitrary and overbroad *maiestas* laws, and enacted new criminal laws against violence. He restored the authority of the Senate and the integrity of the courts by adopting the jury pool proposals of Drusus, mandating that only senators could sit as jurors while adding three hundred equestrians to the Senate. As a practical matter, he needed the additional jurors to handle his newly enacted criminal laws. No doubt, Sulla enlisted the more conservative members of the equestrian class, and the new enrollees quickly accepted their senatorial privileges and adopted a senatorial outlook.

In 80 BC, the integrity of Sulla's senatorial restoration was tested when Cicero defended Roscius Amerinus on a charge of parricide. In defending his client, Cicero exposed the plot of Chrysogonus, an official in Sulla's regime, to steal the property of Roscius's father.

After learning of the death of Roscius's father, Chrysogonus retroactively added the father's name to the proscription lists and had his property confiscated and auctioned. Chrysogonus obtained the property for almost nothing, and to cover up his crime, he had the son, Roscius, charged with parricide.

For Cicero to successfully defend Roscius, he had to attack Chrysogonus. The attack could be taken as an attack on the Sulla, so Cicero proceeded carefully. He argued that Sulla's proscriptions were necessary and temporary measures but unintentionally had produced a breed of profiteers who used the umbrella of the proscriptions for their criminal schemes. Cicero offered that Sulla was unaware of the treachery going on beneath him. Roscius was acquitted, and Cicero gained prominence as the leading advocate of his time.

No reprisal was taken against Cicero, and Sulla's nonintervention spoke louder than words. The dictator stood by his institutions and the rule of law. However, the issue of senatorial bias and favoritism persisted, as shown in another test of the Sullan restoration. In 77 BC, Julius Caesar prosecuted Gnaeus Cornelius Dolabella, an ex-consul and Sullan loyalist, for extorting the inhabitants of Macedonia when he was governor of that province. Although Dolabella was clearly guilty, the senatorial jury acquitted him.

Caesar failed to convict Dolabella, but the case brought Caesar to prominence, and he became known as a brilliant orator and formidable advocate. The Roman quest for fame that drove so many nobles could be pursued in the courtroom as well as on the battlefield, and a curious overlap existed between courtroom success and military achievements. A nobleman who demonstrated outstanding oratorical skills in the courtroom would likely rise in the magistracy and be given military commands. By and large, this method of selection produced efficacious results, and many battles were won with the aid of inspirational speeches by military commanders who had honed their oratorical skills in the courtroom. Caesar employed his rhetorical skills throughout his military career.

The integrity of the Sullan system was tested again in 70 BC when Cicero, on behalf of Sicilian provincials, prosecuted Senator Verres, the ex-governor of Sicily, for extortion. Cicero argued to the senatorial jury, "Today the eyes of the world are upon you. This man's case will establish whether a jury composed exclusively of Senators can possibly convict someone who is very guilty—and very rich."[241] As the trial progressed, it appeared that the senators intended to convict Verres, and he fled into exile before the verdict.

The ability of citizens to hold ex-officials accountable helped to preserve the balance between citizens and government, and reined in corrupt and tyrannical officials. After Pompey, Crassus, and Caesar renewed the first triumvirate in their meeting at Luca, fears arose that the triumvirs

---

[241] Cicero, Verras I. 16, 46–47.

would dominate the state. Senators and other citizens used political prosecutions to resist their power. Although the triumvirs could not be prosecuted because they held imperium and immunity, their allies and associates were targeted by their enemies. Sources list at least fifty political prosecutions between the meeting at Luca and the outbreak of the civil war. Most resulted in acquittals, but they undermined the strength and unity of the triumvirs; thus, for a time they checked and held off the institution of tyranny.[242]

---

[242] Ercih Gruen, *The Last Generation of the Roman Republic* (Los Angeles: University of California Press, 1974) Ch. 7.

CHAPTER 28

Elections, Money, and Prosecutions

FREQUENT AND REGULARLY SCHEDULED elections strengthened the Roman Republic, but they also invited corruption. Roman elections for magistrates—consuls, praetors, aediles, and quaestors—were held every year, and candidates were required to convince voters of their abilities and good character. The word *candidate* comes from the Latin *candidatus*, the specially whitened toga Romans running for office wore to stand out as they walked through the forum, meeting potential voters. To win the favor of the people, candidates sponsored public games, gladiatorial contests, chariot races, and theatrical performances. They often borrowed heavily to fund the events, expecting to recoup their expenses later as proconsuls or pro-praetors, because in the Roman system magistrates became wealthy—not during their initial magistracies but later during their pro-magistracies when they were assigned as governors of provinces. Many governors stayed within the law, but many others crossed the line in a variety of creative ways, using their positions not for the public good but to pay back their creditors and accumulate fortunes. In any case, provincials gave donations, gifts, or bribes for favorable decisions and preferences.

Some governors borrowed much too heavily, and their debts pushed them to commit outlandish acts of extortion. Recognizing that such conduct damaged relations with the provinces, the Senate in 149 BC established the court of restitution (*quaestio de repetundae*) to prosecute governors who engaged in extortion and other misconduct. Nevertheless, complaints of extortion continued.

Recognizing that the extortion was connected to exorbitant election campaign spending, the Romans instituted several strict and complex procedures to regulate campaign spending, vote buying, and voter intimidation. An important measure was the secret ballot. The traditional voting practice had been for voters to assemble in their assigned tribes and announce their vote by moving to one side or the other in the voting arena where they could be seen, supervised, or intimidated by patrons, bribers, or others. In 139 BC, to discourage bribery and voter intimidation, the Romans mandated secret ballots in the *Lex Gabinia*. This may have helped but wasn't a complete solution to the problem of undue influence through bribery or intimidation.

In 116 BC, the Romans established the *quaestio de ambitu*, a permanent court to enforce previously enacted laws against election bribery in exchange for votes. This court investigated and punished not only outright electoral cash bribery but also gifts, such as free seats at games or gladiatorial contests. The penalty for a violation was forfeiture of the right to hold the office for which the candidate campaigned. Since retroactive enforcement would be ineffective, *ambitus* prosecutions were usually brought before winning candidates could assume office, and prosecutions under the law of *ambitus* became a regular part of political life.

In 80 BC, Sulla increased the penalty for *ambitus*: a candidate found guilty was prohibited from running for office again for ten years. Still, electoral corruption persisted as candidates used *divisors*, bribery agents, to get around the law.

In 67 BC, the *optimate* consul, C. Calpurnius Piso, proposed the *Lex Calpurnia de Ambitu*, which further enhanced penalties to include permanent exclusion from office, expulsion from the Senate, and a fine. The law extended liability not only to the candidate found guilty but also to his *divisors*. The *divisors* protested the bill and physically drove Piso from the forum. The Senate then provided a bodyguard for Piso, and he passed the bill at the next assembly.

In 63 BC, Cicero pushed through the *Lex Tullia de Ambitu*, which increased the penalty for *ambitus* to exile for ten years. Cicero's bill also clarified the rules by distinguishing lawful favors between patrons and clients from unlawful bribery for votes. Ironically, Cicero immediately had to defend an ally, Lucius Murena, who in 63 BC was prosecuted under his law.

Murena, an *optimate,* had won the election for the upcoming consulship, but Sulpicius Rufus, the losing *populare* candidate, prosecuted him for *ambitus,* claiming that Murena had bought votes. Sulpicius enlisted the tribune Marcus Porteus Cato as his advocate, an interesting choice since Cato strongly disagreed with the radical politics of Sulpicius and favored the more conservative Murena. But Cato had sworn to prosecute anyone who had used bribery in a consular election, and despite his political leanings, he agreed to prosecute the case against Murena.

In defense, Murena enlisted a stellar team, including Cicero, that year's consul; also Hortensius, Cicero's predecessor as the best orator in Rome; and Crassus, one of the richest and most powerful men in Rome. The trial resulted in acquittal, primarily due to the prestige of the defense advocates who highlighted Murena's good character and military accomplishments.

Cicero couldn't be pigeonholed as to what type of cases he would take or whom he would defend. The following year, in 62 BC, to great astonishment, he defended Publius Cornelius Sulla, the nephew of the dictator. The nephew was accused of participating in the Catiline conspiracy, the conspiracy that had targeted Cicero for death, the same conspiracy Murena was enlisted to fight against. Nevertheless, Cicero defended Sulla.

The background was that Publius Sulla had won the consulship for 65 BC but was prosecuted for *ambitus* (election bribery) and convicted. As a penalty, he was denied his consulship, fined, expelled from the Senate, and prohibited from ever again holding public office. Having been placed in such a ruinous position, he aligned himself with the disgruntled followers of Catiline. During the investigation into the conspiracy, Publius Sulla was charged with participation in the conspiracy on the basis of evidence given by an informant who had been involved. The informant named several individuals as participants, but when asked whether Publius Sulla had participated in the conspiracy, the informant said he didn't know for certain. The prosecution took this as an indictment, propounding that the informant had failed to exculpate the defendant. To the contrary, Cicero argued that the informant had affirmatively identified other conspirators, knew Publius Sulla wasn't one of them, but avoided saying so to make the conspiracy seem larger.

Cicero's argument succeeded, and Publius Sulla was acquitted. Cicero justified his defense of a possible member of the Catiline conspiracy as an exercise of justice and fairness. Others might have pointed to the loan from Publius Sulla to Cicero of two million sesterces, with which the latter bought a house on the Palatine Hill. It seems that the line between zealous advocacy for the public good on one hand and financial reward for the lawyer on the other was as blurred then as it is now.

The acquittals of Murena and Publius Sulla did little to help the cause of reform, and election corruption continued as Rome's expansion opened opportunities for vast profits in the provinces and raised the cost of election campaigns. Candidates for office were prone to optimism and continued to gamble by taking on large debts to fund their campaigns. In some cases, the candidate with the greatest potential amassed the greatest debt. Julius Caesar was the prime example. As an aedile, he spent extravagantly on public games, statues, and monuments; and he borrowed heavily from Crassus and Pompey to win elections for *pontiff maximus,* praetor, and consul. Caesar's campaign debt shaped the outcome of his career and was a major factor in the fate of the republic.

In 59 BC, Caesar was elected consul. During his term, his indebtedness to Crassus and Pompey surely influenced his conduct, and his actions on their behalf led to a constitutional crisis. He proposed a bill to provide land for Pompey's veterans at the expense of landowners in Italy and another bill to modify tax contracts for Crassus's *publicani* clients, giving them more favorable terms than the original contracts. He met strong resistance from several tribunes and from his coconsul, Marcus Calpurnius Bibulus. Twisting arms to get the bills passed, Caesar broke fundamental constitutional rules, breached the inviolability of the tribunes, arrested Cato in the Senate, and excluded Bibulus from the assembly.

Caesar passed the legislation, but he also made mortal enemies; and as his consulship neared its end, the Senate deprived him of his anticipated provincial governorship. Instead, they assigned him to the job of caring for the roads and forests, where he would lose money rather than gain it. But Crassus and Pompey came to his rescue, perhaps concerned about being paid back their loans. They persuaded the assembly to assign Caesar to the governorship of three provinces at the same time and for five years. This was an extraordinary grant of imperium, and in return Caesar supported five-year terms of imperium for Crassus and Pompey. Many historians mark the formation of this triumvirate as the event that precipitated the republic's end.

While the triumvirs dominated the republic, other candidates ran for magistrate offices. The costs of running for office were extremely high, and some candidates continued to engage in corrupt campaign practices in spite of the stringent penalties for *ambitus*. The frequency of prosecutions increased to a frenzy, escalating the animosity between rivals, sometimes culminating in violence. When the bitter enemies Milo and Clodius were campaigning for consul and praetor respectively, Clodius pointed to Milo's debt of six million sesterces. He maintained that one so deep in debt should be barred from standing for office because he would invariably abuse his office to recoup his debts, most often by preying on the provinces. Their elections never took place because the feud between them culminated in the murder of Clodius in 52 BC.

Major riots followed the murder, and to deal with them, Pompey was made sole consul. He had Milo tried for the murder, and Milo was convicted and exiled.

Pompey also tried to address the underlying causes of such bellicose campaign rivalries, not simply the symptoms. To break the connection between campaign debts and extortion by governors in the provinces, Pompey passed the *Lex Pompeii de Provinciis*. This law provided for a five-year period between serving as a consul or praetor and governing a province. Since the consuls and praetors ending their terms couldn't be assigned provinces for the next year, the assignments would be made to trustworthy ex-consuls and ex-praetors, whose magistracies had long since concluded and who presumably wouldn't be under the burden of crushing debts. Apparently, his law had effect since the number of prosecutions for *ambitus* and *repetundis* declined.

It would be difficult to definitively prove that the decline was a direct result of Pompey's law—correlation isn't necessarily causation—but the law was a well-constructed attempt to cure the problem of money in politics. Given more time, Pompey's law may indeed have proved to be the cure. However, the rise of Caesar and the advent of civil war changed Roman politics and eventually ended Democratic elections.

CHAPTER 29

US Political Prosecutions

IN THE UNITED STATES, as in Rome, the government's power to prosecute citizens and confiscate property has been frequently used for partisan political purposes rather than for appropriate and impartial governmental purposes. As political power shifted from one side to the other, the types of political prosecutions changed.

PROSCRIPTIONS AGAINST THE BRITISH LOYALISTS

During the Articles of Confederation, prosecutions similar to Roman proscriptions were used against Tories and loyalists who wanted the colonies to remain British. In New York, laws against Tories and loyalists allowed only the seizure of their property, but in other states, executions of those who had aided the British were possible. For example, in 1777, Pennsylvania passed a treason statute that included those who had "passively continued to adhere to the Crown," and bills of attainder (special acts of the legislature to impose penalties without a judicial conviction) were issued against 490 persons. Those attainted were ordered to surrender to judicial authorities for investigation and were subject to the death penalty and forfeiture of all property. Many of the attainted fled, but 113 surrendered. Of those, most settled their cases, but seventeen were tried, three were convicted, and two, John Roberts and Abraham Carlisle, were hanged.

In 1778, when the British army abandoned Philadelphia, Joseph Galloway, the president of the Pennsylvania Colonial Assembly, who had remained loyal to the British, fled to London. He owned Trevose, the finest estate in Bucks County, Pennsylvania; and he left his wife, Grace, behind to oversee the estate. However, the revolutionary government charged Galloway as a loyalist, confiscated the estate, and evicted Mrs. Galloway from the property.

In 1779, James Wilkinson, the future general and nemesis of Aaron Burr, acquired Trevose for one-third of its market value. Wilkinson apparently was given the inside track to get the property in return for making accusations of corruption against Benedict Arnold, who at the time was military governor of the area and had acted impartially, even sympathetically, toward the loyalists. One could draw a striking parallel between Wilkinson's conduct during this period to the notorious career of Chrysogonus, the Roman official who benefitted so conspicuously from the Sullan proscriptions.

In 1789, the framers of the Constitution prohibited such Tarquinian conduct and banned the federal and state governments from enacting bills of attainder. However, neither the constitutional ban nor the provisions of the Bill of Rights, ratified in 1791, could prevent subsequent politically motivated prosecutions.

FEDERALISTS VS. REPUBLICANS

In 1798, President John Adams signed the Alien and Sedition Acts into law, and his administration promptly arrested twenty-five journalists and politicians. Ten were convicted, among them Congressman Matthew Lyon, who successfully campaigned for reelection from prison.

In the most infamous case, the Adams administration prosecuted newspaperman James Callender for his seditious publications and libel of President Adams. The trial was presided over by Supreme Court Justice Samuel Chase, a staunch Federalist, who conducted the trial in a blatantly biased manner, forcing the defense counsels to quit the case. Callender was convicted, and Chase sentenced the journalist to nine months in prison. Understandably, the press wasn't kind to the judge. To Republicans, Chase was the most hated of all Federalists. *The Aurora* newspaper described him as "a character notorious for his enmity to Republican government, a man whose hostility to the cause of liberty will endure him never ending hatred."

In 1800, Justice Chase lived up to his reputation. He presided over the trial of John Fries, charged for what became known as Fries's Rebellion. The rebellion arose in Pennsylvania when a group of armed farmers, led by Fries, protested a federal property tax designed to finance the expansion of the army and navy for a possible war with France. The farmers threatened the tax assessors and intimidated a federal marshal into releasing some of their fellow farmers from jail. No shots or injuries resulted from the protests, and when the prisoners were released, the group dispersed.

The government charged Fries with treason, and Chase, doing what he had become known for, conducted the trial in such a biased manner that again the defense attorneys quit. The jury convicted Fries, and Chase sentenced him to death by hanging. President Adams, to his credit and against political advice, pardoned Fries, not because of the substance of the charge but because of Chase's outlandish conduct. Chase had contributed to the growing unpopularity of the Federalists.

The election of 1801 gave the Jeffersonian Republicans control of the presidency and Congress, but the Federalists still controlled the courts. Justice Chase continued to publicly assail Republicans, violating any semblance of judicial impartiality. In 1804, the Republican-controlled Congress, hoping to change the political makeup of the court, impeached Chase. The trial was held in the Senate, which acquitted Chase in a close vote. The senators decided that as obnoxious as his conduct had been, he hadn't committed high crimes or misdemeanors that would justify his conviction. Several Republicans voted with the Federalists to acquit because they were concerned that the independence of the judiciary would be diminished if judges were removable on less-than-constitutionally-defined grounds.

Politics motivated the prosecution of Aaron Burr for treason. President Jefferson saw Burr as a competitor for the leadership of the Republican Party and a possible threat to the unity of the nation. Jefferson encouraged the prosecution of Burr for his alleged schemes regarding Mexico and the western states. Few came to Burr's defense. The Republicans saw him as an overly ambitious usurper, and the Federalists hated him for the duel in which he shot and killed their leading light, Alexander Hamilton. As it turned out, after four years of battling the treason charges, Burr was acquitted. Most of the evidence against him proved bogus and insufficient to support a conviction.

Despite the cloudy aspects of the Burr prosecutions, the silver lining for American justice was the performance of Chief Justice John Marshall, who thwarted the efforts of Jefferson's agents to procure a conviction at any cost. In 1807, Marshall dismissed the felony indictment against Burr, leaving only a misdemeanor charge. Burr went to trial on the misdemeanor and was acquitted by the jury. Nonetheless, the damage was done; his political career was over.

Civil War Prosecutions

The Civil War generated numerous prosecutions of political figures. Lincoln prosecuted several Democrats because he believed their conduct and public statements undermined the Union cause. Other Republican officials, however, pursued prosecutions for what seemed purely partisan purposes. In Indiana, Governor Oliver Merton was a Republican; the legislature was controlled by the Democrats. The parties spent more time and energy on partisan disputes than on governing. Governor Merton insisted on the prosecution of several members of a supposedly secret Democratic group, the Sons of Liberty, for conspiracy and treason. A member of the group, Lambdin Milligan, had unsuccessfully run for governor with an acrimonious campaign. Frank Klement described him as follows: "He viewed himself as a Jeffersonian Democrat, devoted to states' rights, free trade, and agrarian principles. He hated New England and the 'isms'—protectionism, abolitionism, and Puritanism—emanating from that region and came to believe that Eastern industry and capital wanted to reduce the West 'to a state of pecuniary vassalage.' He convinced himself that Lincoln had trespassed beyond constitutional bounds, helping to transform a federal union into a centralized government."[243]

---

[243] Frank Klement, "The Indianapolis Treason Trials and Ex Parte Milligan," in *American Political Trials*, ed. Michael Belknap (Westport, CT: Greenport Press, 1981).

The trials were held before a military commission rather than a civilian court and would provide political fodder for Merton's reelection campaign. They also helped President Lincoln's campaign. Five defendants were prosecuted though the evidence sufficiently implicated only one, Harrison Dodd, who had formed a separate group, the Order of American Cincinnatus. As part of that group, he had engaged in overt conspiratorial activities. During the trial, Dodd escaped from custody and fled to Canada. He was found guilty in absentia.

The trial of the other four defendants was delayed until after the November election, and they were found guilty by association. Three were sentenced to be hanged. However, since Governor Merton and President Lincoln had won reelection, executing the men would have served little political purpose. Merton asked Lincoln to commute their sentences, which Lincoln intended to do, but he was assassinated before he could.

The defendants appealed their convictions on the grounds that as civilians they should have been tried before a civilian court rather than a military one. On April 3, 1866, the Supreme Court ruled in their favor, holding, "A citizen, not connected with the military service, and resident in a State where the courts are all open, and in the proper exercise of their jurisdiction, cannot, even when the privilege of habeas corpus is suspended, be tried, convicted or sentence otherwise than by the ordinary courts of law."[244]

The court's ruling set an important precedent and reprimanded Governor Merton for his politically motivated prosecution. The ruling also criticized the propriety of some of Lincoln's wartime policies.

Unions and Socialists

The half century between the Civil War and the First World War was a period of tremendous industrial development, and conflicts between management and labor precipitated a series of political trials. Prosecutions came from two sources: from the left, the 1890 Sherman Antitrust Act was used to target business monopolies; from the right, a host of new laws against anarchy, criminal syndicalism, and espionage were used to target radical revolutionaries.

---

[244] *Ex Parte Milligan*, 71 U.S. (4 Wall.) 2 (1866).

At the behest of management, the government prosecuted strike-related violence or the instigation of violence. Eugene Debs, the president of the American Railway Union, was prosecuted for contempt of court and conspiracy to commit violence in connection with the 1894 Pullman Railroad Strike. The available evidence exonerated Debs regarding the advocacy of violence; in fact, he had warned against violence. Nevertheless, the government proceeded against him. A jury acquitted Debs of conspiracy, but he was convicted of contempt of a court and was sentenced to six months in prison. After his prison experience, Debs became more radical, a study in the evolution of unionism to Marxism.

Debs ran for president five times as the Socialist Party candidate, advocating international socialism. In 1918, he was prosecuted and convicted under the Espionage Act for antiwar activities and sentenced to ten years in prison. At his sentencing, he was allowed to make a speech that revealed he had converted completely to international socialism. The following are excerpts:

> Your Honor, years ago I recognized my kinship with all living beings, and I made up my mind that I was not one bit better than the meanest on earth. I said then, and I say now, that while there is a lower class, I am in it; while there is a criminal element, I am of it; and while there is a soul in prison, I am not free …
>
> I believe, Your Honor, in common with all socialists, that this nation ought to own and control its own industries. I believe, as all socialists do, that all things that are jointly needed and used ought to be jointly owned—that industry, the basis of our social life, instead of being the private property of the few and operated for their enrichment, ought to be the common property of all, democratically administered in the interests of all …
>
> I am opposing a social order in which it is possible for one man who does absolutely nothing that is useful to amass a fortune of hundreds of millions of dollars, while

millions of men and women who work all the days of their lives secure barely enough for a wretched existence.

This order of things cannot always endure. I have registered my protest against it. I recognize the feebleness of my effort, but fortunately I am not alone. There are multiplied thousands of others who, like myself, have come to realize that before we may truly enjoy the blessings of civilized life, we must reorganize society upon a mutual and cooperative basis; and to this end we have organized a great economic and political movement that spreads over the face of all the earth.

There are today upwards of sixty millions of socialists, loyal, devoted adherents to their cause ... They are spreading with tireless energy the propaganda of the new social order ... They feel—they know, indeed—that the time is coming, in spite of all opposition, all persecution, when this emancipating gospel will spread among all the peoples, and when this minority will become the triumphant majority and, sweeping into power, inaugurate the greatest social and economic change in history.

In that day we shall have the universal commonwealth—the harmonious cooperative of every nation with every other nation on earth.[245]

Debs thought his impassioned speech advanced the cause of socialism, but, in fact, he was warning society of its dangers. He put a face on the "red scare." He also made clear the absurdity of the socialist/communist premises. His claim that the owners of industry "do absolutely nothing that is useful" seemed odd in an age in which the inventions of industry had relieved workmen of so much tedious, back-breaking toil; absurd in an age in which mass production had reduced the price of necessities to less than a tenth of their previous cost.

---

[245] American Voices, *Significant Speeches in American History*, Ed. J.Andrews and D. Zarefsky (New York, Longman, 1989).

With the 1917 Russian revolution raging and expanding into Europe, his talk of millions of socialists spreading propaganda in the United States raised the threat of a foreign-controlled government. He called for joint ownership of all property to be "democratically administered," but most citizens knew what Debs's ideas would mean—politicians in control of all property would become even more powerful than the wealthy industrialists. To spread the wealth, the new political administrators would confiscate the bank accounts of those believed to have accumulated millions by financial manipulations; they would confiscate the property of all the great American entrepreneurial inventors who had made their fortunes by creating products that improved life for all—Thomas Edison, George Westinghouse, and Alexander Graham Bell, among others. They would confiscate the businesses of those who had made consumer goods available and affordable for all—F. W. Woolworth, Richard Sears, Alvah Roebuck, Isaac Singer, R. H. Macy, Montgomery Ward, Levi Strauss, and so forth. The administrators would gain control of businesses without having built any of them, the kind of thing so often seen in third-world dictatorships, a sure formula for mismanagement and corruption. Entrepreneurship and invention would be stifled, and the standard of living for the masses would stagnate and decline.

During the war, antiwar activities were seen as a prelude to a communist revolution, and as the threat of communism grew, the federal and state governments instituted wide-ranging investigations and prosecuted hundreds of avowed communists and socialists. In 1919, using the Espionage Act, the government prosecuted and convicted Charles Schenck, the general secretary of the Socialist Party, for advocating resistance to the draft during the First World War. Schenck appealed his conviction to the Supreme Court on the grounds that it violated his First Amendment right of free speech. The court upheld the conviction ruling that his advocacy undermined the war effort. In dissent, Justice Oliver Wendell Holmes Jr. proposed the "clear and present danger" test for First Amendment cases. The majority rejected his proposal, but in later First Amendment cases, the Holmes test would be adopted by the court.[246]

---

[246] *Schenck v. United States*, 249 U.S. 47 (1919).

COMMUNISTS

New York State prosecuted Benjamin Gitlow, who set up the Communist Labor Party and published an article, "The Left Wing Manifesto," that criticized capitalism and advocated revolutionary Marxist principles. Because the article advocated the violent overthrow of the state government, he was prosecuted under the New York State Criminal Anarchy Act. He was convicted and sentenced to five to ten years in prison but appealed on the grounds that the statute violated the First Amendment.

While his appeals progressed through the courts, Gitlow unsuccessfully ran for mayor of New York City, governor of New York State, and vice president of the United States on the Socialist Party ticket with William Z. Foster. In 1925, Gitlow's appeal reached the Supreme Court. The Court upheld his conviction and the constitutionality of the statute.[247] Curiously, New York Democrat Governor Alfred Smith then pardoned Gitlow. Although Gitlow remained active, in 1929 he was forced out of the Communist Party because of a factional dispute in which Joseph Stalin interceded against him.

Of more importance, the Supreme Court's ruling in *Gitlow v. New York* set an important precedent for subsequent political prosecutions. At the beginning of the Second World War, when the Soviet Union was aligned with Germany, Congress passed the Smith Act, which was aimed at the Communist Party and made it a crime to "knowingly or willfully advocate, abet, advise, or teach the duty, necessity, desirability, or propriety of overthrowing or destroying any government in the United States by force or violence." When Germany broke its treaty and invaded Russia, thereby aligning Russia with the United States, President Roosevelt tactically declined to bring prosecutions under the Smith Act. However, when the war was over and the Cold War commenced, President Truman authorized prosecutions of communists. In 1948, using the Smith Act, a federal grand jury indicted twelve leading members of the Communist Party, including the party's national secretary, William Z. Foster; and the general secretary, Eugene Dennis. Because of a heart condition, Foster didn't stand trial. The

---

[247] *Gitlow v. New York*, 268 U.S. 652 (1925).

other eleven defendants were convicted, appealed on First Amendment constitutional grounds, and lost. In 1951, the Supreme Court upheld their convictions and constitutionality of the statute.[248]

Apart from any legal rationale, it was highly unlikely that the court would overturn the convictions of these communist activists while the Soviet spies Ethel and Julius Rosenberg were being prosecuted for stealing America's atomic secrets and passing them to the Soviet Union or while the United States was in a shooting war on the Korean Peninsula against communist China.

This was the McCarthy era when Senator Joseph McCarthy led what has been called a witch hunt for communists in the government and the media. This period paralleled the Roman period during the Italian Social War when the tribune Q. Varius Hybrida sought out for prosecution those suspected of inciting or supporting the Italian rebellion. As events turned, both Varius and McCarthy were discredited. Varius committed suicide; McCarthy was shunned and vilified until his death.

In the United States, after the Rosenbergs were executed and the Korean War ended, the Supreme Court liberalized its First Amendment jurisprudence, and courts began reversing convictions that had been based on the advocacy and promotion of communism or other radical causes.

The Vietnam War produced many political trials of antiwar activists. Although the defendants all claimed they were being prosecuted for their political beliefs, they were charged with common crimes such as arson, assault, riot, bombings, and murder. The riots at the 1968 Democratic Party Convention in Chicago spawned dozens of such prosecutions, but they, too, were for criminal acts designed to disrupt a public event.

A pure political prosecution was that of Daniel Ellsberg for leaking the Pentagon Papers to the press. The papers divulged government consultations and strategies about the Vietnam War, and because they were classified as secret, Ellsberg was charged with violating the Espionage Act. Eventually, the charges were dismissed when it was revealed that government operatives had burglarized Ellsberg's apartment to obtain evidence and that the FBI had recorded his phone conversations without a warrant.

---

[248] *Dennis v. United States,* 341 U.S. 494 (1951).

Watergate and Special Prosecutors

The Ellsberg burglary was a precursor to the burglary of the Democratic Party headquarters at the Watergate Hotel, in which operatives of the Republican Party were caught in the act. When it was learned that the operatives had an office in the basement of the White House, certain executive branch officials became suspects. Investigations led to the potential prosecution of President Nixon and the actual prosecution of several of his top staff members for conspiring to cover up the burglary.

Watergate was of enormous consequence for the nation. It was a major test of the checks-and-balances system; it exacerbated the acrimony between the political parties, and it brought to light the conflict of interests involved when the executive branch is the target of investigation.

Under federal law at that time, the US attorney general could appoint a special prosecutor to investigate cases that presented a conflict of interest within the executive branch; the appointee served at the discretion of the attorney general and, ultimately, the president. This arrangement proved problematic when President Nixon ordered Attorney General Eliot Richardson to fire Special Prosecutor Archibald Cox, who was investigating the Watergate burglary. Nixon wanted Cox fired because he refused to rescind a subpoena for presidential documents. Richardson resigned rather than carry out the order, but Solicitor General Robert Bork (of later notoriety for his failed nomination to the Supreme Court) fired Cox. Public criticism of this action forced Nixon to have Bork appoint a new special prosecutor, Leon Jaworski, to continue the investigation. Jaworski indicted seven Nixon aides but not Nixon. The grand jury characterized Nixon as only an unindicted coconspirator. Jaworski had dissuaded the grand jury from indicting the president by arguing that a sitting president could be indicted only after he left office. His argument followed the Roman precedent of consular immunity while in office. After Nixon resigned, his successor, President Gerald Ford, pardoned him. The pardon vitiated a potential indictment.

In 1978, to address the problems uncovered in the Watergate investigation, Congress passed the Ethics in Government Act. This law created the Office of Independent Counsel. The law established that the holder of that office, once appointed by a three-judge panel, could be removed only for "good cause" rather than at the discretion of the attorney general or the president, thus protecting the counsel's independence. As subsequent events unfolded, however, concerns about the dangers of such an independent counsel came to fruition. Politics could corrupt an independent counsel as it could any other official, and this became evident in 1992 when President George H. Bush was running for reelection.

President Bush had been vice president under President Reagan, and during that administration, the Iran-Contra arms-for-hostages deal came to light. Independent Counsel Lawrence Walsh was appointed to investigate the matter. One of the officials he targeted was Secretary of Defense Caspar Weinberger, who had served under President Reagan and was serving under Bush. Weinberger testified before a grand jury, but no action was taken against him for several years. Then, in June 1992, Walsh indicted Weinberger on charges related to the Iran-Contra deal. However, in what appeared suspiciously like a political hatchet job, four days before the November 1992 election, Walsh announced an additional indictment of Weinberger, and his office leaked a report that President Bush had lied when he said he was "out of the loop" in relation to the matter. This had a devastating effect, and Bush lost the election to Bill Clinton. A month later, a federal judge threw out the November indictment as unwarranted.

When Clinton became president, the Republicans retaliated for the Democrats' investigations of Nixon, Reagan, and Bush. Independent Counsel Kenneth Starr was appointed to investigate several land deals that had occurred when Clinton was governor of Arkansas, but Starr went far beyond that mandate. He investigated unrelated allegations involving Clinton's sexual conduct while president. Starr questioned Clinton before a grand jury, which was videotaped and shown to the public. Clinton was cited for lying to the grand jury, and he was later disbarred from practicing law.

The investigation led to Clinton's impeachment in the House of Representatives, but he was acquitted in the Senate. Undoubtedly, the cost of the investigation, impeachment, and trial was steep; more than the time and money expended, it was a major distraction for the entire government.

Because of these events, a consensus developed that the independent counsel had too much power. Congressional Democrats and Republicans agreed to let the independent counsel statute expire, returning to the prior system in which the attorney general had the discretion to appoint and terminate a special prosecutor for cases involving conflicts of interest.

Nevertheless, reinstating the limitations on the special prosecutor didn't solve the problem of prosecutorial overreach. During the presidency of George W. Bush, allegations surfaced that someone in the Bush administration had leaked the identity of a Central Intelligence Agency officer. Clearly motivated by partisanship, Democrats demanded a special prosecutor, and President Bush authorized the appointment of Patrick Fitzpatrick as the special prosecutor to investigate the allegation. Fitzpatrick was extremely thorough; some said overzealous. In 2007, he obtained a perjury indictment and conviction of Lewis "Scooter" Libby, an aide to Vice President Dick Cheney, even though Fitzpatrick knew Libby had nothing to do with the leak and that someone else had admitted to being the source of the leak.

As a convicted felon, Libby was forced to resign. Years later, Judith Miller, a *New York Times* reporter, a main witness against Libby in the grand jury and at the trial, alleged that Fitzpatrick had induced her to give false testimony. Fitzpatrick had jailed her for eighty-five days for refusing to testify. When she agreed to testify, she was released. During the preparation for her testimony, Miller alleged that Fitzpatrick had steered her to testify falsely by withholding exculpatory information from her that would have changed her testimony.[249]

Libby's prosecution made visible again the intractable problem of balancing the need for independent investigations of government officials against the tendency of prosecutors to become overzealous and engage in unscrupulous practices in the quest for convictions.

The prosecution of long-time Republican Senator Ted Stevens of Alaska illustrates the unscrupulous practices administration prosecutors sometimes engage in to obtain a conviction. In 2008, as Stevens campaigned for reelection, prosecutors in the Department of Justice Public

---

[249] Peter Berkowitz, "False Evidence against Scooter Libby," *Wall Street Journal*, April 7, 2015.

Integrity Section charged him with seven counts of making false statements on his Senate financial disclosure form and failing to properly report gifts and discounted renovation work performed on his home. The gifts included a puppy from a charity event, a massage chair, and a statue of a giant salmon. A federal grand jury in July 2008 issued the indictment, four months before election day. Assuming that he would be acquitted, Stevens pressed for a speedy trial so he could promptly clear his name as he campaigned for reelection. It was a mistake; he underestimated the deceitful tactics the prosecutors would use. The main issue of the trial was that Stevens had reported that a contractor had performed work on his house valued at $150,000, which Stevens paid, while the government contended that the work was actually valued at $250,000. The prosecutors contended Stevens had underreported the value by $100,000. The contractor who testified against Stevens was under threat of indictment in several matters and cooperated with the government in exchange for leniency.

During the trial, Stevens moved for a mistrial because the prosecutors had failed to turn exculpatory material over to the defense, as required by *Brady v. Maryland*[250]; but the judge, Emmet Sullivan, denied the request.

Just days before election-day, Stevens was convicted on all counts. He narrowly lost his reelection bid, undoubtedly because of his conviction.

After Stevens was replaced in the Senate by his Democratic opponent, the Democratic Party gained a sixty-seat filibuster-proof majority in the Senate. With the sixtieth vote, the Democrats passed the highly contested Affordable Care Act without any Republican votes, which intensified the deep partisan divide that so adversely affected the political climate for several years thereafter.

In February 2009, after Stevens's conviction and his election loss, an FBI agent who had worked on the case filed an affidavit, alleging that the prosecutors had conspired to withhold and conceal evidence that would have exonerated Stevens. Judge Sullivan ordered an investigation, which uncovered numerous *Brady* violations, including the concealment from the defense of an FBI interview with the contractor, who stated that the value of the work he provided was around $80,000, far less than the

---

[250] *Brady v. Maryland*, 373 U.S. 742 (1963).

$250,000 he had testified to at the trial and far less than what Stevens actually paid. The government also failed to disclose that the contractor had been under investigation for unrelated crimes, which might have shown his motivation for cooperating with the prosecutors.

Based on the *Brady* violations and other prosecutorial misconduct, Judge Sullivan vacated the conviction and dismissed the indictment. He also appointed a special counsel to conduct a criminal contempt investigation of six members of the prosecution team. The investigation wasn't completed until 2012. The special counsel didn't recommend criminal charges against the prosecutors but concluded, "The investigation and prosecution of U.S. Senator Ted Stevens were permeated by the systematic concealment of significant exculpatory evidence which would have independently corroborated Senator Stevens' defense and his testimony, and seriously damaged the credibility of the government's key witness."

Unscrupulous government prosecutions, on both the federal and state levels, pose a danger to our republic as great as the partisan political prosecutions the Romans encountered. In 2014, Democrat prosecutors indicted two prominent Republican governors, Rick Perry of Texas and Bob McDonald of Virginia. Both men were seen as potential presidential candidates, but the indictments destroyed their chances of running. In 2016, both cases were dismissed, too late for either man to mount an election campaign.

Balancing the risks of prosecutorial overzealousness against the need to hold public officials accountable was a problem that challenged both the Roman and American republics. Rome allowed its citizens, without government approval, to initiate charges against government officials, which they frequently did. Although these citizen-initiated prosecutions could be problematic, citizens could hold government officials accountable. In the United States, there is no comparable means for citizens to initiate a prosecution, and citizens cannot force the Justice Department or other enforcement agencies to initiate an investigation or prosecution of government conduct. In our system, federal, state, and local governments have exclusive authority to initiate criminal prosecutions. If the government refuses to prosecute its own officials and agents, the private citizen and the public are left without recourse. Moreover, even Congress in its oversight capacity is without recourse when the executive branch refuses to prosecute contempt of Congress or perjury before Congress. In short, the government cannot be forced to prosecute itself, and without an administration's voluntary compliance with the rule of law, the republic is at its mercy.

CHAPTER 30

Augustus Caesar Defeats All

GAIUS OCTAVIUS THURINUS (ANGLICIZED as Octavian), born in 63 BC, was the son of a wealthy plebeian senator and praetor. The father would have become a consul had he not died prematurely when Octavian was five years old. Octavian's mother, Atia, didn't remarry but dedicated herself to raising her son. She was a powerful influence on his life, but he had another powerful influence—Julius Caesar, his granduncle.

Atia taught Octavian well. At twelve, he delivered the funeral oration for his grandmother Julia, Caesar's sister, and this may have been when Caesar noticed the abilities of the precocious child. During the ensuing years, Caesar maintained an interest in him, took him on a campaign with him to Spain, and surely mentored him in military and political matters. When the young man was seventeen, Caesar sent him to Greece for his studies, then secretly adopted him as his son and made him heir to three-quarters of his estate. Evidently, Caesar had a discerning eye for talent, for he chose Octavian as his successor, and the youth would prove more than equal to the task.

Upon Caesar's assassination, Octavian took the formal name Gaius Julius Caesar Octavianus. The name and Caesar's imprimatur were important, for Octavian put himself forward as Caesar's heir apparent.

Octavian was either an eighteen-year-old political genius or a young man whose advisers steered him perfectly through a complex web of political intrigues. He patronized Cicero, seeking his acknowledgment, and obtained pledges of support from Caesar's devoted legions. He then openly challenged Marc Antony for the leadership of the Caesarean faction, accusing Antony of doing nothing to avenge Caesar's murder and questioning why Antony had failed to pay the citizens the stipend Caesar had promised them in his will. Octavian proclaimed that he would pay the money to the people from his own funds. This was a first step on his long road to power, which culminated in 27 BC when he was commemorated with the name Augustus, "the one who is to be venerated." To avoid confusion for the reader, the text from hereon will refer to him as Augustus, even though to be more accurate he wasn't formally given the name until later in the narrative.

In the contest between Augustus and Antony, Caesar's heir had built-in advantages. First, the urban plebs greatly admired Caesar; second, he had the familial right to avenge Caesar's murder; third, because of his inheritance, he had the money and the credit with which to recruit a large private army, promising to pay two thousand sesterces per soldier, which was far more than Antony's pay of four hundred sesterces. Two of Antony's legions promptly defected to him. Raising an army without Senate approval was unlawful and potentially treasonous, but the Senate barely protested, because they saw Augustus as a counterweight to Antony. All expected that a battle between them would erupt for the right to take Caesar's place as the leader of the *populare* party.

As for the leading assassination conspirators, the Senate had sent Marcus Brutus and Cassius to provinces in the East, where they took command of proconsular armies and levied troops from client-states, thus becoming potential counterweights to either Augustus or Antony.

Another conspirator, Decimus Brutus, had been assigned to Cisalpine Gaul and was in command of the legions in that province. Then, as Antony's consulship neared its end in 44 BC, the Senate assigned him as proconsul of Macedonia for the upcoming year; but Antony wanted Cisalpine Gaul, and, overruling the Senate, he had the assembly assign him to that province. When Decimus Brutus refused to surrender the province, Antony marched north with his legions to take it by force, besieging Decimus in the city of Mutina. This was treason, and the Senate, led by Cicero, declared Antony an outlaw and sent five legions under the command of the new consuls of 43 BC, Aulus Hirtius and Vibius Pansa, to relieve the siege.

To keep Augustus aligned with the Senate and opposed to Antony, Cicero convinced the Senate to make Augustus a propraetor and legitimize his private army. Augustus took the opportunity. He knew that on his own, he couldn't defeat the more experienced Antony, so to strengthen his hand, he joined the consuls, surprising many by going to the aid of Decimus Brutus, who had participated in the murder of Caesar.

The consular armies, led by Hirtius and Pansa, and supplemented by Augustus's army, relieved the siege and forced Antony to retreat. During the battle, both consuls fought bravely while leading their troops, but both were killed, leaving Augustus potentially in control of their legions.

At that point, the Senate with atrocious timing made the mistake of ordering Augustus to turn over the consular legions to Decimus Brutus for the remaining campaign against Antony. Realizing that he had been used and was being dismissed, Augustus defied the Senate and marched on Rome with his loyal troops. On August 19, 43 BC, with his army camped on the Campus Martius, Augustus sent armed centurions into the Senate to demand that he be allowed to run for consul. The Senate capitulated. Augustus was elected consul—the youngest in history at the age of nineteen years, ten months, and twenty-six days. He and his colleague, Quintus Pedius, Julius Caesar's nephew, ran unopposed. To preserve the formality of a lawful election, the people under military supervision filed through the voting pens and unanimously ratified the Senate's capitulation.

Augustus had outmaneuvered everyone, including Cicero. Once in power, he acted quickly, declaring the assassination of Julius Caesar a crime and appointing a tribunal to convict the conspirators in absentia. Then, as he proceeded north with his armies to confront Antony, Augustus made an astounding political reversal. He switched sides again, double-crossed the Senate, and, instead of continuing the fight against Antony, negotiated with him for an alliance.

Augustus, Antony, and Marcus Aemilius Lepidus Jr. formed the Second Triumvirate. Lepidus Jr. had been a close ally of Julius Caesar and was the son of the consul Lepidus Sr., who had led an unsuccessful rebellion against the *optimates* after Sulla's death. The new triumvirs met near Mutina on an island situated in the Lavernus River. This triumvirate wasn't arranged in secret like the First Triumvirate; it was titled "Three Men with Consular Powers for Confirming the Commonwealth" and was later ratified in the tribal assembly by the *Lex Tibia*. Each triumvir was given imperium in his province for five years; they were to be superior to all other magistrates, with the power to nominate governors, magistrates, and legates.

To their disrepute, they didn't follow Julius Caesar's example of clemency and protection for those who pledged their allegiance to the new regime. Rather, they replicated the atrocities of Marius and Sulla, treating any who had sided with their adversaries as enemies to be ruthlessly punished. In one of their first acts, they executed a tribune, an act that was ironic because Caesar had crossed the Rubicon supposedly to protect the inviolability of the tribunes. [251]

The triumvirs published proscription lists with hundreds of names. They also issued a decree to justify their actions.

> We shall not strike angrily at the crowd, nor take vengeance against all who have opposed us or conspired against us, or those who are merely rich, wealthy, or honored; nor as many as a previous dictator killed, a man who held supreme power before us. When he, too, was regulating the city in civil war, and whom you named Felix [Sulla] for his success though necessarily three have more enemies than one. But we shall seek revenge only on the worst and most deserving. This we shall do for you no less than for us: for it follows that while we are in conflict all will necessarily suffer terribly, and we must also appease the army, which has been insulted, provoked, and made an enemy by our common foe. Although we could summarily arrest whomsoever we had decided on, we choose to proscribe rather than seize them unaware; and this, also, we do for you, so that the enraged soldiers

---

[251] Appian, BC 4, 17, 65.

are prevented from surpassing their limits and exceeding their orders and acting against those not responsible,
but that they are limited to a certain number of known
names, and spare others by order.[252]

Although the triumvirs professed to be acting within restraints and on
behalf of the people, they acted in part for vengeance and in part to raise
the funds necessary to keep themselves in power. Funds had to be raised
from Italy, since there was no other ready source of revenue. The provinces
of the West had been depleted, and the provinces of the East were in the
hands of Marcus Brutus and Cassius. So, with Antony taking the lead,
the proscriptions increased because the collapse of property values necessitated more confiscations. In the end, more than two thousand names
were added to the lists. Many of the richest and most powerful senators
were executed immediately, with their properties confiscated. Cicero was
among them. In a heartless act, Augustus acceded to Antony's demand
for Cicero's death. Equestrians found themselves on the lists not for any
actions they had undertaken against the triumvirs but only because they
were wealthy. Most fled, abandoning their properties in exchange for their
lives. Those who weren't proscribed had to pay a tax up to 15 percent of the
notional value of their estates, even though the actual market value was
much lower. When the triumvirs needed more funds, the wealthy had to
advance loans to the government at minimal interest rates.

In addition, the triumvirs identified the territories of eighteen of the
wealthiest cities in Italy for total confiscation, the land to be used to reward the legions after they defeated the republican armies.

Fortified with funds and troops, the triumvirs turned their attention
to Caesar's assassins. In 42 BC, at Philippi, on the north shore of the
Aegean Sea, the armies of the Second Triumvirate, led by Antony and
Augustus, met the republican armies of Brutus and Cassius. The battle
was enormous, with perhaps two hundred thousand soldiers in the field.
They were evenly matched—nineteen versus seventeen legions—but the
triumvirs were quicker and more decisive. After a few hours, they were

---

[252] Appian, BC. 4.

victorious. Brutus and Cassius, defeated and knowing that the triumvirs wouldn't give them the clemency Caesar had, committed suicide. Thus, Antony, Caesar's legate; and Augustus, Caesar's adopted son, avenged the great man's murder.

In the aftermath of Philippi, the leadership of Rome seemed to have been resolved, but much sorting out remained. By agreement, the triumvirs divided the empire among themselves. Augustus took control of Italy and the West, including Cisalpine Gaul, which would no longer be a province but would be incorporated into Italy. Antony went to the East to reclaim the wealthiest provinces of the empire and to reopen their streams of revenue. Lepidus, the third member of the triumvirate, lost prominence and was given control of only North Africa, the least important province. Augustus and Antony divided de facto control of the empire. It was a replication of the situation after Crassus's death when only Caesar and Pompey remained of the first triumvirate. Inevitably, Augustus and Antony would vie for complete supremacy, but first an attempt was made to maintain peace through reciprocal marriages, like those to which Pompey and Caesar had agreed. Augustus married Antony's stepdaughter, Claudia; and Antony married Augustus's sister, Octavia.

For Augustus, his most urgent task was to pay his veterans and implement the resettlements. Twenty-eight legions had to be disbanded and settled on land, necessitating large-scale property confiscations and tax increases that provoked protests, intrigues, and revolts. Factions coalesced: middle-class factions against the urban proletariat, landowners against rapacious ex-soldiers, and Caesareans against Pompeians. For a decade, proxy battles were fought in courts, in assemblies, on streets, and on battlefields. Ronald Syme described the measures Augustus imposed.

> In desperate straits for money, he imposed new taxation of unprecedented severity—the fourth part of an individual's annual income was exacted. Riots broke out; and there was widespread incendiarism. Freedmen, recalcitrant under taxation, were especially blamed for the trouble and heavily punished. Disturbances among the civil population were suppressed by armed force—for the

soldiers had been paid. To public taxation was added private intimidation. Towns and wealthy individuals were persuaded to offer contributions for the army. The letters that circulated, guaranteed by the seal of the sphinx or by Maecenas' frog, [symbols of the Augustan administration] were imperative and terrifying.[253]

Throughout this chaotic period, Augustus gained recognition as a strong and effective leader. In control of Italy, he dispensed patronage and repaired damaged infrastructure. With the aid of his lifetime friends, Agrippa and Maecenas, he drew support from all factions; and as the son of Caesar, he held the loyalty of Caesar's veterans and *populare* followers. As Augustus gained strength, the surviving *optimate* landowners either joined his party or remained neutral. Their class had been thrice decimated by the confiscation of their property and the redistribution of their wealth to followers of the Augustan faction and the soldiers.

Meanwhile, Antony's conduct in the East alienated many of his followers. He initiated a campaign against Parthia to avenge the slaughter in 53 BC of Crassus's army. Eighteen battles were mostly successful, but the overall campaign was inconclusive. Antony had enlisted the Armenians as allies, but when Antony's advance stalled near the Caspian Sea, the Armenians deserted, and Antony had to retreat, pursued and harassed by the Parthians for twenty-five days until he reached safety in Syria. More than twenty thousand legionaries were lost during the campaign.

Further diminishing Antony's prestige, reports circulated that Cleopatra, the queen of Egypt, had distracted him and would use him to restore Egypt to its ancient extent and power. She, who had charmed Caesar, now captivated Antony. She was of pure Graeco-Macedonian descent, purportedly from the line of Alexander the Great. She possessed great intellect, spoke several languages, and dominated the court. Under her influence, Antony adopted the trappings and conduct of an oriental potentate.

In 33 BC, when the triumvirate expired, Augustus held the consulate.

---

[253] Ronald Syme, *The Roman Revolution* (Oxford: Oxford University Press, 1939) xix.

His partnership with Antony had dissolved, and he delivered a speech in the Senate in which he criticized Antony's conduct in the East, particularly his illicit alliance with Cleopatra. Antony lived openly with her, fathering two sons with her while still married to Augustus's sister, Octavia. This was an insult to the Julian clan, and the two leaders engaged in a virulent propaganda campaign, attacking each other's character. The final break occurred when Antony divorced Octavia. With Augustus keeping five legions under arms in Italy and Antony commanding six legions in the East, a clash was inevitable.

Although in January 32 BC, Augustus's term as consul and his official triumvirate imperium ended, he still controlled his loyal army. Surrounded by soldiers carrying concealed weapons, he entered the Senate as the leading citizen and sat in the chair between the two newly elected consuls to demonstrate he was still in charge of the state. He announced to the senators that he would provide evidence of treason against Antony and justification for war. In protest, the two consuls and many senators fled to Antony's side.

Undaunted, Augustus persisted. He obtained a copy of Antony's will and read it to the Senate. It showed that Antony had bequeathed legacies to Cleopatra's children and directed that when he died, he should be buried beside her in Alexandria. The will became the basis for wild rumors and a pretext for war. To further stir up war fever, rumors were spread that Antony and Cleopatra intended to conquer the West and transfer the capital to Alexandria.

Augustus won the propaganda war and succeeded in making all Italy swear an oath of allegiance to him, which initiated a patron-client relationship between him and all orders of Italian society. This relationship later became a foundation for his principate (supreme rule).

Augustus assembled an army of one hundred fifty thousand soldiers, and Antony assembled an equally large army. The only question remaining was who would attack first. Augustus, with astute political judgment, declared war—not on Antony but on Cleopatra. If Antony stood by the queen against Rome, he would be seen as a traitor.

Augustus invaded Greece, and as the sides skirmished and maneuvered for tactical position, Antony's side suffered serious defections; thus the outcome of the war was decided before the final battle was fought. In 31 BC at Actium, the forces of Augustus, under the generalship of Agrippa, defeated Antony's forces in a naval engagement. Antony fled to Egypt with Cleopatra; and in 30 BC, as his enemies closed in, he committed suicide. When Cleopatra heard of Antony's suicide, she did the same.

Augustus annexed the kingdom of Egypt as a Roman territory and seized Cleopatra's treasury, a treasury so enormous that it provided the means for him to pay his soldiers and settle his debts.

Many historians mark Augustus's triumph as the last episode of the battle for control of the burgeoning empire; more significantly, the ascent of Augustus marked the end of the republic. It wasn't until the birth of the United States of America that an authentic republican constitution again ruled a great nation.

CHAPTER 31

Augustus Reigns

AUGUSTUS CONTROLLED ROME FOR forty-five years from his victory in 31 BC at Actium until his death in AD 14 at seventy-six years of age. During his reign, he transformed the state and created an efficient and effective governmental structure, strengthening Rome's hold over its empire, and inaugurating the Pax Romana, an unprecedented two-hundred year period of relative peace, stability, and prosperity. His reign saw great building projects, capsulized by his remark "I found Rome a city of bricks and left it a city of marble." He established police and fire departments, the Praetorian Guard, and a body of civil servants to safeguard buildings, roads, and aqueducts.

In retrospect, what Augustus accomplished might have been exactly what was needed at the time. Speaking of Rome under Augustus and the American revolutionary period, Alfred North Whitehead said, "I know of only two occasions when the people in power did what needed to be done about as well as you can imagine its being possible." However, a closer look at Rome is more revealing and shows the appalling price that was paid— the end of republican liberty and the imposition of autocratic tyranny.

Undoubtedly, Augustus ranked among the most influential men of history, but he created with one hand and destroyed with the other. Always mindful of the fate of his adoptive father, he declined to openly make himself a dictator, but nevertheless, he incrementally transformed Rome from a republic to an imperial autocracy. Knowing it would be dangerous to affront the people's pride in their traditional rights and status, he used his talents for deception and manipulation to confound his competitors and seize authoritarian power. He was called the princeps or first citizen, and his new government was called the principate, after himself. By unique and ingenious artifices, he solved the problem of keeping the support of the people while leading them inexorably toward servitude, repeatedly speaking of the Senate's dignity and his respect for the republic, while his actions betrayed the opposite motives. He didn't destroy the republic by plunging it into a cauldron of boiling water. Instead, he gradually raised the temperature of the water so the citizens wouldn't realize their rights had been eliminated until it was too late. Scottish philosopher David Hume wrote, "It is seldom that liberty of any kind is lost all at once. Slavery has so frightful an aspect to men accustomed to freedom that it must steal in upon them by degrees and must disguise itself in a thousand shapes in order to be received."

Augustus preserved the ceremonial forms of the republic, keeping up the appearance that Rome was still a democratic body of free citizens while he absorbed all its real powers. The consuls, the Senate, and the assemblies continued to exist, but Augustus controlled them. They lost real independence and agreed to whatever Augustus decreed.

Step-by-step, he reorganized the legal foundations of his authority, taking for himself the offices of consul, tribune, proconsul of provinces, augur, and pontiff. With such executive, military, and religious authority, none could refuse his commands, and his word was law. Tacitus summarized, "Augustus seduced the soldiers with gifts, the people with grain, and all with the sweetness of leisure, and little by little grew greater. He amassed in himself and without opposition the functions of the senate, the magistrates, and the laws. For the most fierce had fallen in battle or by proscription, while the rest of the nobles, who were more ready for slavery, were raised up by honors and wealth and so elevated by the new order they preferred present safety to past dangers."[254]

In 27 BC and again in 23 BC, Augustus amended the constitution of his new order. In 27 BC, while declaring that he was restoring the republic,

---

[254] Tacitua, *Annals*, bk. 1.

he removed the proconsuls from the most important provinces and took control of them himself, directing the Senate to appoint him proconsul for ten years of Spain, Gaul, Cyprus, Cilicia, Syria, and Egypt. This gave him command of almost all the legions; and to solidify complete control, the proconsuls for the three remaining provinces were drawn from his party.

In 23 BC, he announced that he wouldn't hold the consulship year by year, but he took permanent proconsular imperium over the whole empire. His legates would run the provinces. To compensate in part for not holding the consulship, he took the power of a tribune for life, ensuring he could never be prosecuted since his term would never expire, and so twenty-one years after the demise of Julius Caesar's dictatorship, Augustus reestablished a dictatorship, which was far more comprehensive and absolute than Caesar had envisioned.

The legalization of his authority enhanced his power, but the support of the people was also necessary. All means of persuasion were employed to enhance his personal stature. Poets, historians, and pontiffs presented him as the savior of the nation who enjoyed the special favor of the gods. Festivals, ceremonies, and statues were all used to enhance his image. On his coinage, he was identified as "Caesar, the son of the deified." Eventually, throughout the empire, all gold and silver coins bore his image or a symbol associated with him. Idealized statues, depicting him as young, handsome, and robust, were erected in city centers and at main crossroads. The cult worship and deification of his adoptive father implied that he was the son of a god and would assume his own apotheosis.

Relying on his *auctoritas* or authority through personal prestige, Augustus simply exercised his will. He transferred the lawmaking powers of the assembly to the Senate, which he controlled. Although he left the election of magistrates in the assembly, he designated or preapproved who would run for office, allowing the assembly to hold a pro forma vote of ratification. So, from the outside, the government appeared to function according to constitutional procedures; in fact, it was a cloaked autocracy masquerading as a republic. It hardly needs saying, but the sovereignty of Augustus was above and beyond the forms and institutions of the outworn republic.

To secure his full control, Augustus appointed his personal loyalists to administer government functions. He appointed slaves and freedmen from the slave family of the emperor (*familia Caesaris*) as civil servants to run the bureaucracy. To control dissent, he banned the creation of new collegia (social clubs) without his approval and placed restrictions on the frequency of meetings and the number of collegia an individual could join.

Proclaiming that the taxes the triumvirs imposed were insufficient to run the government, Augustus began a step-by-step introduction of new taxes. Gibbon recounted in his *Decline and Fall of the Roman Empire,*

> The introduction of customs was followed by the establishment of an excise, and the scheme of taxation was completed by an artful assessment of the real and personal property of the Roman citizens, who had been exempted from any kind of contribution above a century and a half … In the reign of Augustus and his successors, duties were imposed on every kind of merchandise, which through a thousand channels flowed to the great center of opulence and luxury … The excise, introduced by Augustus after the civil wars, was extremely moderate, but it was general. It seldom exceeded one per cent; but it comprehended whatever was sold in the markets or by public auction, from the most considerable purchases of lands and houses to those minute objects which can only derive a value from their infinite multitude and daily consumption.[255]

Those taxes were just the beginning. As expenses mounted, Augustus introduced more taxes without seeming to do so unilaterally. He inveigled the Senate to join with him. Gibbon recounted,

> The ample revenue of the excise, though peculiarly appropriated to those uses, was found inadequate. To supply the deficiency, the emperor suggested a new tax of five per cent on all legacies and inheritances. But the nobles of

---

[255] Edward Gibbons, *Decline and Fall of the Roman Empire,*Vol. 1Chap. 6, III.

Rome were more tenacious of property than of freedom. Their indignant murmurs were received by Augustus with his usual temper. He disingenuously referred the whole business to the Senate, and exhorted them to provide for the public service by some other expedient of a less odious nature. They were divided and perplexed. He insinuated to them that their obstinacy to the inheritance taxes would oblige him to propose a general land tax and a capitation tax. They acquiesced in silence.

The nobles escaped the land and capitation taxes for the moment, but later emperors would impose them.

Those who still remained in possession of their land must have considered themselves fortunate. After Actium, Augustus initiated another wave of proscriptions, confiscating the properties of the senators who had fled to Antony and also the lands of Italian cities that had sided with Antony. The properties were taken initially for the benefit of the veterans, but over time Augustus and his partisans accumulated the wealth of the empire as they claimed the lands and the homes of the proscribed and the vanquished. They also reaped profits from the provinces, especially from Egypt after Augustus took control of its treasury. Well before the end of his life, Augustus was the richest man in the Western world. Any challenge to his authority was suppressed. In one instance in 20 BC, when an unapproved candidate, Marcus Egnatius Rufus, tried to run for consul, the Senate rejected him because he wasn't of the required age. Egnatius's supporters rioted but were suppressed, and Egnatius was executed, presumably with the approval of Augustus.

Augustus reformed the military, instituting a permanent army composed of career soldiers. Recruits now swore to serve the full sixteen years, which ended the recurring agitations of the troops for *en masse* discharges. Upon discharge, a veteran was given a stipend by the state, ending reliance on their generals for rewards. In addition, recruits included foreigners who were granted citizenship upon enlistment. To avoid collusion among ethnic groups, soldiers were separated and assigned to regions of the empire far from their origins.

In 20 BC, Augustus and Agrippa prepared to invade Parthian territory to complete unfinished business. They equipped a formidable army and arranged alliances in the area to further their objectives. The Parthians recognized the overwhelming threat and sued for peace. They returned the standards taken at Carrhae and recognized the Roman hegemony in Mesopotamia. This victory without a fight further enhanced the prestige of the principate.

Augustus used his army to execute the will of the state as it became more autocratic and its republican traditions deteriorated. He paid his army well and used them to control the people. He also took personal credit for their victories and downplayed the accomplishments of the officers actually in command. Triumphs for victorious generals gradually disappeared, and after 19 BC, no general unrelated to the Augustan family celebrated a triumph.

Of greater significance, he abrogated the traditional law that prohibited an army from entering the city of Rome and placed a permanent garrison in the city to maintain order. Throughout the empire, he initiated the use of soldiers for police duties, which lessened the tradition of civilian participation in criminal justice matters, reduced local control, and increased the central government's role in internal security.

In judicial matters, Augustus assumed the predominant role. Although the praetors still supervised the courts, their decrees could now be appealed to the princeps rather than to the assembly, and Augustus issued edicts and judicial decision without review. In criminal trials, the standing jury courts were replaced by delegates of the princeps, who could impose greater or lesser penalties than prescribed by the statute, and citizens lost their absolute right to appeal to the assembly to commute or nullify a death sentence. He also added the possible penalties of condemnation to hard labor in the mines or fighting in gladiatorial contests.

As for the jurists whose responses (legal opinions) had been so important in the development of Roman law, Augustus saw them as an unacceptable check on his power. Although he was careful not to subvert the jurists in a blatant way, he gradually reduced their independence by authorizing only certain of the jurists to issue responses with *ex auctoritate principis* (in the name of the princeps); and thus he seized control of the administration of justice. Henry Sumner Maine wrote, "The final blow to the Responses was dealt by Augustus, who limited to a few leading jurisconsults the right of giving binding opinions on cases submitted to them, a change which, though it brings us nearer the ideas of the modern world, must obviously have altered fundamentally the characteristics of the legal profession and the nature of its influence on Roman law."[256]

Only the opinions of the authorized jurists could be offered in court. If more than one opinion was submitted, the judge would choose which to follow, but he could decide cases only on the basis of an authorized opinion. Inevitably, the jurists were incorporated into the service of the government, acting as paid advisers to magistrates and princeps. As for the practice of advocacy and oratory under the Augustan system, the eloquence of free and independent advocates that had flourished in the republic degenerated into a formulaic model; speeches were carefully crafted not to offend the princeps or later the emperors.

Augustus tried to engineer Roman social life through legislation. In 18 BC, he enacted strict morality laws to redress the decadence that had spread as the republic expired. Despite the domestic unrest of the period, money had continued to pour into Rome, fostering extravagance and licentiousness. Among the wealthy, marriages were increasingly infrequent, and couples avoided having children, with adultery and divorce seeming more common than sound marriages. Augustus passed laws designed to counteract the breakdown of the old moralities by encouraging marriage and child-rearing. He imposed a duty to marry on men between ages twenty-five and sixty and on women between ages twenty and fifty. Those in breach of their duty lost certain privileges and rights. His law, known as the *Lex Julia et Papia*, made adultery a crime punishable by exile and the confiscation of property. A father who caught an adulterer with his daughter in his home or in the home of his son-in-law could kill the adulterer and his daughter without reprisal. Husbands couldn't kill their adulterous wives, but if they killed the adulterous partner, their punishment would be lenient. To discourage sexual immorality, cuckolded husbands had to

---

[256] Maine, *Ancient Law*. 605.

divorce their adulterous wives, which often entailed detrimental financial consequences for the wives and loss of parental privileges.

To insulate the nobility from libertine or degenerate influences, the law forbade any man eligible for the Senate to marry a freedwoman, actress, or daughter of an actor or actress. Also, any daughter of a man eligible for the Senate was forbidden to marry a freedman, actor, or son of an actor or actress; and no freeborn man could marry a prostitute, procuress, or woman convicted of a crime or adultery.

Augustus controlled the most important aspects of personal life. Cassius Dio reported that Augustus "assessed heavier taxes on unmarried men and women without husbands, and by contrast offered awards for marriage and childbearing."[257] Ironically, several years after enacting his morality laws, Augustus was forced to charge his own daughter, Julia, with adultery and send her into seclusion. He also banished the poet Ovid to the Black Sea coast near modern Romania either for immoral conduct or his sexually provocative writings.

In conjunction with his morality laws, Augustus conducted a census, the first in forty-one years. From the senatorial rolls he removed those he saw as immoral, corrupt, or disloyal to him.

In addition to micromanaging personal conduct, Augustus enacted broader social reforms. In 2 BC, fearing the impact of large numbers of slaves becoming freedmen, Augustus restricted manumissions by will to one-fourth of a decedent's slaves but never more than one hundred. To reduce the costs of the dole, he passed a measure that newly manumitted slaves could no longer receive free grain.

In AD 9, his Senate passed the senatus consultum silanianum, which revived the old law that authorized the execution of all the slaves of a household wherein the master was murdered. This was meant to discourage slaves awaiting manumission by will from prematurely bringing on the master's demise. It was also meant to ensure the aid of household slaves against rebellious slaves, poisoners, or invading criminals.

For his campaign against immorality, Augustus authorized the interrogation by torture of slaves to combat adultery. Using a first-person voice,

---

[257] Cassius Dio, *History of Rome*, 54. 16.1–3.

he issued an edict. "I do not think that interrogations under torture ought to be requested in every case; but when capital or more serious crimes cannot be explored and investigated in any other way than by the torturing of slaves, then I think that those [interrogations] are the most effective means of seeking out the truth and I hold that they should be conducted."[258]

With this edict he drastically changed the law of torture for cases against those suspected of disloyalty or conspiracy. Previously, a slave could testify for his master (though under torture by the adversary) but not against his master. Augustus changed this by allowing slaves to be transferred to the state so they could be tortured and so the evidence obtained could be used against their former masters. In effect, Augustus created an army of potential spies.

In 12 BC, Augustus became *pontifex maximus*. Of more import, all prayed to his household gods, Mars and Apollo, and prayers for the health and prosperity of the nation became prayers for the health and prosperity of Augustus. Throughout parts of the empire, especially in the East, he was seen as a living god.

Augustus's apotheosis diminished all others. Ronald Syme summarized the Augustan autocracy.

> A government had been established. The *principes viri* [leading men] were tamed, trained and harnessed to the service of the Roman People at home and abroad. Plebs and army, provinces and kings were no longer in the clientele of individual politicians. At Rome the Princeps seized control of all games and largesse. The descendants of great Republican houses still retained popularity with the plebs of Rome and troops of clients, arousing the distrust of the Princeps; not always without cause. But careful supervision at first and then the abolition of free elections soon diminished the personal influence of the *nobiles*. After the constructions of the *viri triumphales*, the friends of Augustus, there was scarcely ever a public

---

[258] Paul, *Adulterers*, bk. 2; D.48.18.8 pr.

building erected in Rome at private expense. Nor any more triumphs. At the most, a stray proconsul of Africa, fighting under his own auspices, might assume the title of imperator. Before long that honor too would be denied.

Military glory was jealously engrossed by the Princeps and his family. The soldiers were his own clients—it was treason to tamper with them. Hence constant alarm if generals by good arts or bad acquired popularity with the troops, and in time even an edict forbidding senators to admit soldiers to their morning receptions. For the senator no hope or monument of fame was left.[259]

The submission of the old republican institutions to the principate, and later the emperorship, not only diminished the independence and assertive spirit of the leading citizens; it also reduced the participation of the citizenry in the political process and lessened their sense of civic duty. The assembled people no longer actively participated in the selection and direction of their leaders; they became passive subjects. Juvenal captured the long-term effect. "Now that no one buys our votes, the public has long since cast off its cares; the people that once bestowed commands, consulships, legions, and all else, now meddles no more and longs eagerly for just two things—bread and circuses."[260]

In Juvenal's view, the people's acceptance of rule by emperorship traded not only liberty for security but also industriousness and dignity for sloth and degradation.

Historians have given great credit to Augustus for expanding government power, establishing an effective bureaucracy, and trying to revive public and private morality. Largely because of his longevity, his achievements were monumental. He has been given credit for selflessly seizing power and assuming the mantle of responsibility to transform the nation. However, from his own words, it is evident that he was mostly driven to

---

[259] Ronald Syme, *The Roman Revolution* (Oxford University Press, 1939) 404.
[260] Juvenal, *Satire*, 10.

seize and hold power by an ego-centered, Caesarian-sized ambition. In his last year of life, AD 14, he wrote a memoriam for himself titled *The Deeds of the Divine Augustus*, known as his "Res Gestae." He had it inscribed on two bronze tablets affixed to his mausoleum. Reproductions were affixed to monuments throughout the empire.

His *Deeds* comprised thirty-five paragraphs, all self-reverential. True, they reflected his unsurpassed accomplishments—the lands conquered; the temples, buildings, roads, and aqueducts constructed or repaired; and the great sums of money he "gave" to the plebs and soldiers. But many deeds were left out, and he downplayed the autocratic nature of his rule. The following paragraphs illustrate his evolution from a popular restorer of the republic to a near-godlike ruler.

> Twice I triumphed with an ovation, and three times I enjoyed a curule triumph and twenty-one times I was named emperor ... On account of the things successfully done by me and through my officers, under my auspices, in earth and sea, the Senate decreed fifty-five times that there be sacrifices to the immortal gods. Moreover, there were 890 days on which the senate decreed there would be sacrifices. In my triumphs, kings and nine children of kings were led before my chariot. I had been consul thirteen times, when I wrote this, and I was in the thirty-seventh year of tribunician power. (paragraph four)
>
> I was triumvir for the settling of the state for ten continuous years. I was first of the Senate up to that day on which I wrote this, for forty years. I was high priest, augur, one of the Fifteen for the performance of rites, one of the Seven of the sacred feats. (paragraph seven)
>
> The Senate decreed that vows be undertaken for my health by the consuls and priests every fifth year. In fulfillment of these vows they often celebrated games for my life; several times the four highest colleges of priests, several times the consuls. Also both privately and as a city

all the citizens unanimously and continuously prayed at all the shrines for my health. (paragraph nine)

By a Senate decree my name was included in the Saliar Hymn, and it was sanctified by a law, both that I would be sacrosanct forever, and that, as long as I would live, the tribunician power would be mine. (paragraph ten)

In my sixth and seventh consulates [28–27 BC], after putting out the civil war, having obtained all things by universal consent, I handed over the state from my power to the dominion of the Senate and the Roman people. And for this merit of mine, by a Senate decree, I was called Augustus and the doors of my temple were publicly clothed with laurel and a civic crown was fixed over my door and a gold shield placed in the Julian senate-house, and the inscription of that shield testified to the virtue, mercy, justice, and piety, for which the Senate and Roman people gave it to me. After that time, I exceeded in all influence, but I had no greater power than the others who were colleagues with me in each magistracy. (paragraph thirty-four)

When I administered my thirteenth consulate (2 B.C.), the Senate and Equestrian order and Roman people all called me father of the country, and voted that the same be inscribed in the vestibule of my temple, in the Julian senate-house, and in the forum of Augustus under the chariot which had been placed there for me by a decision of the Senate. When I wrote this I was seventy-six years old. (paragraph thirty-five)

The pretention that the republic still existed and that Augustus's authority was merely a matter of his *auctoritas*, the people's deference to him, was an early example of Orwellian double-speak. The Senate decreed that he would have the power of a tribune for life, though the people didn't elect him as a tribune each year, an essential characteristic of the traditional constitution. He claimed, "I had no greater power than the others who were colleagues with me in each magistracy." But they held one office; he held them all. He chose or approved most of the other magistrates, with the assembly only ratifying his choices.

Bold, timely, and skillful action was the key to his success. One of his first acts as a triumvir was to establish a formal state cult for Caesar, a deification that exalted Augustus's status and would eventually lead to his own veneration and deification while still living.

Inconsistency and irony didn't deter him. In his war against Antony, Augustus ridiculed Antony's submission to Queen Cleopatra and their adoption of the trappings of eastern-style divine monarchy. Yet Caesar, his "divine" father, had made Cleopatra a queen and brought her to Rome. Augustus didn't let logic or facts stand in his way; he became an eastern-styled emperor himself. Believing in his special inheritance from the deified Caesar, he transformed the republic into a hereditary monarchy. Tacitus, writing in his *Annals* a century after the principate, described Augustus's accomplishments.

> It was said, on the other hand, "that duty toward a father and the exigencies of state were merely put on as a mask: it was in fact from lust for domination that he had stirred up the veterans by bribery, had, while still a very young man, raised a private army, tampered with the Consul's legions ... wrested the consulate from a reluctant Senate and turned the arms that had been entrusted to him for a war with Antony against the republic itself. Citizens were proscribed and lands divided ... Undoubtedly there was peace after all this, but it was a peace that dripped blood.[261]

Any attempt to accurately and succinctly summarize Augustus's personality or identify the character traits that propelled him to such stupendous accomplishments would be riddled with contradictions. Still, he was a remarkable phenomenon—astonishingly confident and indomitably determined. He epitomized the Roman capacity to face down challenges

---

[261] Tacitus, *Annals*, bk. 1, 10.

and navigate through every kind of obstacle. At eighteen years of age, he demanded power in a treacherous city wherein his adoptive father had just been murdered; at seventy-six, he demanded that his wishes be followed after his death, designating Tiberius Claudius Nero, his son-in-law, whom he had adopted as his son, to succeed him as emperor.

Augustus surely thought he was establishing an enlightened monarchy, but there was no guarantee that the succeeding monarchs would even pretend to be enlightened. Tiberius, lacking the subtlety and diplomacy of Augustus, reigned through blatant tyranny, and the pretense that the republic still functioned lawfully soon died. Augustus had ended the lawmaking powers of the assemblies but left them the ceremonial power of electing the magistrates; Tiberius went further, removing even those ceremonial powers. Moreover, the election of magistrates in the Senate became hardly more than a rubber stamp for the candidates of the emperors. Wolfgang Kunkel wrote,

> As early as the time of Tiberius the election of magistrates was transferred from the people to the Senate, at any rate so far as any real choice between several contenders was concerned; it seems that even in later times a formal act of the people took place by which the Senate's suggestions of single candidates were approved, but his could be nothing more than an honorific ceremony. A little later popular legislation disappeared and its place was taken in practice by senatorial resolutions. After this the role of the people was limited to that of theatrical "extras" in the ceremonial acts of state whose dignity was thus intended to be augmented by the luster of old republican tradition.[262]

To discourage dissent, Tiberius expanded the *Lex Maiestas* (law of majesty) to criminalize any words, signs, or thoughts against the emperor.

---

[262] Wolfgang Kunkel, *An Introduction to Roman Legal and Constitutional History*, trans. J.M. Kelly (Oxford: Clarendon Press, 1973) 52.

He solicited senators to inform on their colleagues, and many did so. As a result, senators were reduced to pawns and flatterers who survived by infamy and intrigue.

This was nearly the end of meritocracy in the political realm. Without the people voting on the laws, electing the magistrates, or rendering judgments, prominent citizens increasingly retreated from public life and gave up seeking approval from their peers or the assemblies. For most, seeking fame in the service of one's nation became an anachronism.

Of the emperors who succeeded Tiberius, the only question was, Who was the worst? Citizens were treated as though they were conquered enemies. Many were put to death so emperors could confiscate their property, and the populace didn't intercede to protect the property of the wealthy. The urban poor continued to receive free grain, and in their idleness, they awaited the games and spectacles the emperors provided. To satisfy this mob's increasing bloodthirst, the promoters of the games and spectacles escalated the level of slaughter and inhumanity, further coarsening and debasing the populace.

The citizens were helpless against debauched emperors—Caligula, Nero, and Caracalla, to name a few—and continual intrigues at the top of the political world doomed the nation to its inevitable demise. With each new crisis that unfolded, the emperors assumed more autocratic powers, and the citizens lost more rights and protections. By the reign of Diocletian (circa AD 300), petitioners who entered the imperial presence, including senators, had to prostrate themselves before the throne and address his eminence as their "Lord" and "Emperor." Such citizens were ready for other nations to conquer them.

CHAPTER 32

The Imperial Presidency

AMERICA HAS NEVER HAD an Augustus, never one president who wholly transformed the foundational structure of its government. But America has had a succession of presidents who step-by-step moved the nation toward an Augustan transformation. Beginning with Theodore Roosevelt, they have transformed the nation from one dominated by Congress to one dominated by what has been called the "imperial presidency"—from a nation controlled by the private sector to one increasingly controlled by government, from a nation of independently acting states to one centrally controlled from Washington.

Theodore Roosevelt bragged about being a "one man only" leader. He believed presidents can take whatever action they deem necessary unless the Constitution or a statute expressly prohibits the action. Through executive powers, he implemented many transformative programs. Had he won a third term in 1912 under the banner of the progressive Bull-Moose Party, he would have expanded presidential powers further.

President Woodrow Wilson believed in an expansive executive branch, and he thought divided government was outdated. He also believed government should be deeply involved with matters of personal privacy. A progressive with an affinity for eugenics, in 1911, as governor of New Jersey, he signed the forcible sterilization law that targeted "the hopelessly defective and criminal classes." Many of Wilson's other planned big government projects were sidelined due to the First World War.

In 1932, when Franklin Delano Roosevelt won the presidency, he took up where Wilson and his cousin, Theodore Roosevelt, had left off. An outstanding and highly effective president, Roosevelt instituted domestic policy changes at a pace matching that of Augustus. He couldn't match Augustus only because he didn't enjoy the same longevity.

Demonstrating remarkable leadership during the Depression, Roosevelt instituted extensive public works projects, put the unemployed to work, and tried every means to stimulate the economy. His New Deal programs created multiple federal agencies to direct and control major aspects of the economy and society. Not an ideologue but a pragmatist, he would try one solution and then another to solve a problem. "The country demands bold, persistent experimentation," he said. "It is common sense to take a method and try it: if it fails, admit it frankly and try another."

He tackled the financial panic with bold measures, imposing a bank holiday and restricting the use of gold bullion as a means of payment. He implemented numerous programs to address the plight of people in dire circumstances. Many of his programs alleviated the worst conditions, but not every measure proved a success. He raised corporate and capital gains taxes to finance his programs; however, in 1938 when the Depression deepened, Congress rescinded the tax increases because they had proved destructive. Debate continues over whether Roosevelt's actions helped end the Depression or prolonged it. Nonetheless, no one can debate his extraordinary efforts and the patriarchal leadership he provided, calming and inspiring the nation during those difficult times. Justice Oliver Wendell Holmes said of him that "he did not have a first-class mind but had a first class temperament." Roosevelt surely had the perfect temperament to marshal the American nation and steer it through times of crisis.

For all the benefits of the New Deal projects and agencies, there were costs—most notably, cuts to the already-sparse defense budget and conflicts with the military. In 1935, Roosevelt's clashed with General Douglas MacArthur, the army chief of staff. While arguing over a 51 percent cut to the army budget, MacArthur reputedly told Roosevelt, "When we lose the next war, and an American boy with an enemy bayonet though his belly and an enemy foot on his dying throat spits out his last curse, I want the name not to be MacArthur, but Roosevelt."[263]

Despite that nasty encounter, Roosevelt assigned General MacArthur to command in the Pacific theater for the duration of the Second World War. MacArthur's prediction that the United States was ill prepared for the war proved accurate when the Japanese attacked the Philippines. The American and Filipino troops there fought bravely but were defeated because the United States couldn't provide reinforcements. Roosevelt ordered MacArthur to abandon his command on the islands, leaving his troops to be captured and imprisoned on Bataan.

Notwithstanding the disaster in the Philippines, Roosevelt proved to be a great wartime leader. He simultaneously oversaw the wars in Europe and the Pacific, and his extraordinary performance as commander in chief elevated the presidency. Conversely, Congress's lack of cohesiveness, isolationist positions, and neglect of the military diminished its stature. As late as August 1941, Congress was still equivocating over military preparedness; the House of Representatives renewed the Selective Service Act by only a single vote.

In an address to Congress on September 7, 1942, Roosevelt asserted his right to ignore an act of Congress if necessary to win the war. In 1943, he called the Senate "a bunch of incompetent obstructionists," and he indicated that the only way to get anything done was to bypass the Senate.[264]

Parallels to Augustus are clear. Just as Augustus emulated his predecessor, Julius Caesar, Roosevelt emulated his predecessor, Theodore Roosevelt. Just as Augustus had persuaded the Roman Senate to grant him unprecedented powers, Roosevelt persuaded Congress to delegate extensive powers to his newly created federal agencies. As Augustus passed legislation, empowering his government to regulate private conduct, Roosevelt's federal agencies vigorously regulated private-sector matters and social issues that hadn't previously come under federal jurisdiction. Just as Augustus replaced the independent republican jurists with those he selected, so also Roosevelt tried to pack the Supreme Court by adding

---

[263] MacArthur, *Reminiscences*, 99–100.

[264] Charles E. Bohlen, *Witness to History*, 1929–1969 (New York, 1973) 210.

six justices to the nine. But Roosevelt met resistance. The Senate balked, and Senator Henry Ashurst labeled the scheme "a prelude to tyranny." When Roosevelt's scheme failed, he converted the court to his side by encouraging retirements and pressuring other justices to render opinions more in accord with his policies.

Roosevelt's disregard of Congress raised concerns about a dictatorial presidency. During the Second World War, many saw his executive order to intern more than one hundred forty thousand Japanese-American citizens for the duration of the war as a violation of fundamental constitutional rights. Concerns about the internments and other issues were serious enough that the nation passed the Twenty-Second Amendment, which limited future presidents to two terms.

IMPERIALISM ABROAD

Despite the term limits, presidential power continued to expand, especially in foreign affairs and military matters. Presidents assumed the power to take military action without declarations of war by Congress: the Second World War was the last time Congress issued a declaration of war. Since then, all postwar presidents have asserted the right to unilaterally project American power, and they have led the nation into major wars in Korea, Vietnam, Iraq, Afghanistan, and Iraq again. Congress acted merely as a rubber stamp and regularly conceded foreign policy to the president because it was necessary to make strategic and diplomatic decisions expeditiously. Advanced technology necessitated the empowerment of the president. In an age of nuclear weapons and ballistic missiles, decisions might have to be made in an instant, and only the executive branch was suited to do so. With Congress acquiescing, the presidents assumed unbridled power to take immediate military action on their own initiative and then extended their emergency powers to longer-term military endeavors.

On the relatively few occasions when Congress acted to restrain presidential military action, the president either ignored it or marshaled public opinion to defeat its efforts. When President Harry S. Truman sent troops to Korea without congressional approval, a resolution was introduced in the Senate to limit his authority. One congressional critic argued against commitment of troops by executive decision, stating, "If the President alone is allowed to send anywhere abroad, at any time, hundreds of thousands of American troops without a declaration of war ... then, indeed, there is little left of the American constitutional government."[265] After spirited debates, the Senate passed a watered-down, equivocal resolution that had no effect on Korea and little effect on future presidents.

President Lyndon Johnson used the dubious Gulf of Tonkin Resolution to escalate the Vietnam War, sending more than five hundred thousand troops to Vietnam, and President Nixon bombed Cambodia and Laos to defend those troops. They justified their actions on the basis of the "domino theory," meaning that if even a small country thousands of miles from the United States fell to the communists, nations nearby would also fall like a row of dominoes.

The loss of Vietnam to the communists furthered a perception that America had weakened and lost its resolve. During President Carter's term, the nation was in a period he called a malaise, and the nation reached a low point in 1979 when the Iranians seized the US Embassy in Tehran and held fifty-two Americans hostage for 444 days.

President Reagan took a more confident and aggressive approach. On the day of his inauguration, January 20, 1981, the Iranians released the hostages.

Against communism, rather than merely preventing its expansion, he challenged the Soviet Union's core morality, political system, and economic viability. Calling the Soviet Union an evil empire, he reasserted America's special role in the world as a force for democracy. Counteracting the perception that the United States had lost its resolve and strength, he doubled the defense budget and projected American strength around the globe. He revived the B-1 bomber program the Carter administration had canceled and vastly expanded missile development programs as part of the arms race with the Soviet Union, thereby contributing to the Soviet collapse. He bombed the palace of the Libyan leader Muammar Ghaddafy in retaliation for the bombing by Libyan agents of a discotheque American soldiers frequented in West Berlin, Germany. In the Western Hemisphere,

---

[265] F. R. Coudert Jr. to the Editor, *New York Herald Tribune,* January 20, 1951.

he intervened in several Central American countries and, without congressional authorization, invaded the small Caribbean nation of Grenada to free it of a communist takeover.

President Clinton also took military action without congressional approval. In 1996, to support the independence of Kosovo from Serbia, he bombed Serbia, circumventing Congress by conducting the bombing under the auspices of NATO. President George W. Bush invaded Iraq on the basis of a congressional resolution but not a full-fledged declaration of war.

When and how presidents can unilaterally use military force without congressional authorization has been a matter of constant debate since the inception of the republic. Debates aside, American presidents have acted unilaterally, deploying troops and bombs as they saw fit, and Congress has never censured a president for doing so. The powers granted American presidents have far surpassed those of the Roman consuls, who didn't have the authority to initiate a war without authorization of the Senate or the assembly. When Hannibal was ravaging Italy during the Second Punic War, Scipio Africanus had to obtain the approval of the Senate to invade Carthage to draw Hannibal out of Italy. The tradition of senatorial control of the generals was sacrosanct.

Julius Caesar broke with tradition. He had been assigned as proconsul of Near Gaul, but he invaded Upper Gaul, Germany, and England, claiming that these invasions were necessary to protect his province. Caesar's unilateral aggression, without the deliberation and approval of the Senate or the assembly, precipitated a multiplicity of unintended consequences that contributed to the dissolution of the republic. Notably, Cato had threatened to prosecute Caesar for conducting the unauthorized wars, and when the Senate recalled Caesar, ending his immunity, the stakes were raised, and Caesar seized power to protect himself.

While it's incontrovertible that American presidents have the authority to act in response to imminent threats, questions arise when they commit forces on a long-term basis. Questions also arise about how presidents should respond to conflicts in the post-9/11 world of terrorism.

On September 11, 2001, the nation was shocked by the terrorist attack that killed almost three thousand Americans and destroyed the Twin Towers of the World Trade Center in New York, part of the Pentagon in Washington, DC, and four passenger airliners. Three days later, on September 14, 2001, Congress passed a joint resolution, authorizing President George W. Bush to use "all necessary and appropriate force against those nations, organizations, or persons he determines planned, authorized, committed, or aided the terrorist attacks that occurred on September 11, 2001, or harbored such organizations or persons, in order to prevent any future acts of international terrorism against the United States by such nations, organizations, or persons."

Short of a declaration of war on anyone, anywhere, anytime, the post-9/11 delegation of war powers to the president was the broadest possible. It compared to the extraordinary delegation of powers the Romans gave to Pompey to destroy pirates anywhere they could be found after pirates sacked the trading port of Ostia in 68 BC.

President Bush bombed and invaded Afghanistan to oust the Taliban tribes that had harbored the terrorists. The president then turned his attention to Iraq and Saddam Hussein, the dictator who had supported terrorism for three decades. President Bush argued that an invasion of Iraq was necessary to depose Hussein. He posed an argument similar to that of Publius Sulpicius Galba, who argued to the Roman assembly in 200 BC that if Rome didn't invade Macedonia to fight Phillip V there, Rome would have to fight him on her own soil in Italy. Bush argued that if we didn't fight terrorism and the sponsors of terrorism "over there," we would have to fight them "over here."

In response, Congress passed the war powers resolution of 2003. "The President is authorized to use the Armed Forces of the United States as he determines to be necessary and appropriate in order to defend the national security of the United States against the continuing threat posed by Iraq; and enforce all relevant UN Security Council resolutions regarding Iraq." The president then ordered the invasion and occupation of Iraq and subsequently initiated a drone missile program, targeting suspected terrorists in Iraq and Afghanistan.

President Obama continued the war on terrorism, though with a different set of priorities. He sent additional troops to Afghanistan while withdrawing troops from Iraq. He expanded the Bush drone missile program and authorized killing suspected terrorists in Iraq, Afghanistan,

Pakistan, Yemen, and Somalia. In addition, Obama went beyond the congressional authorizations of 2001 and 2003 by bombing Libya to oust Ghaddafy, the dictator of that country. The bombing continued until the Libyan rebels captured and killed Ghaddafy.

Presidents Bush and Obama justified their military commitments on the failed-state theory, meaning that if a government thousands of miles away lost control of its territories, jihadist terrorists would use them as a base to launch attacks against the United States. Under both the domino theory and the failed-state theory, the authority of the president to act unilaterally in defense of the homeland extended to any part of the world. Thus, the United States was in a position similar to that of the Romans when their empire reached its geographic zenith. J. A. Schumpeter described the Roman Empire this way:

> There was no corner of the known world where some interest was not alleged to be in danger or under actual attack. If the interests were not Roman, they were those of Rome's allies; and if Rome had no allies, then allies would be invented. When it was utterly impossible to contrive such an interest—why, then it was the national honor that had been insulted. Rome was always being attacked by evil-minded neighbors, always fighting for breathing-space. The whole world was pervaded by a host of enemies, and it was manifestly Rome's duty to guard against their indubitably aggressive designs. They were enemies who only waited to fall on the Roman people.[266]

Although Rome had seemed invincible for two centuries after its victory in the Second Punic War, it wasn't unchallenged. When its empire expanded to far-off regions, it encountered strong resistance from the Parthians, a people from northeastern Iran who conquered territories from Eastern Persia to Syria. Pompey could advance no farther than the Euphrates River, and in 55 BC, when Crassus invaded Parthian-controlled

---

[266] J. A. Schumpeter, *The Sociology of Imperialisms* (New York: World, 1955) 51.

territory, the Parthians wiped out his army at the Battle of Carrhae. Caesar had intended to erase the stain of Carrhae, but his assassination and the subsequent civil wars intervened. It was left to Antony to restore Rome's honor.

In 36 BC, Antony moved east with eighteen legions. His forward advance was slowed when he fell victim to treachery by his supposed Armenian allies. Becoming impatient, Antony impulsively rushed ahead, leaving his baggage train behind without adequate guard. The Parthian horsemen circled Antony's army and seized the baggage train, leaving Antony stranded in enemy territory without sufficient food or equipment. Antony had to retreat to avoid the fate of Crassus, and as he did so, the Parthians pursued and decimated his army.

At the completion of his civil war with Antony, Augustus had command of twenty-eight legions stationed in provinces outside of Italy. He continued Roman expansion and through forceful negotiations retrieved the standards of Crassus's army from the Parthians. However, in the north he wasn't as successful. In AD 9, Germanic tribes ambushed and annihilated three Roman legions in the Teutoburg Forest, and Augustus decided that Rome would expand no farther; he assumed a defensive posture. Still, defending the empire as it stood and maintaining order in the border nations were expensive drains on the treasury. Appian noted, "On some of these subject nations they spend more than they receive from them."[267]

After Augustus, the Romans conquered Britain; however, on the other end of the empire, the Parthians continued to battle them for control of the Middle East. In AD 116, the Emperor Trajan defeated the Parthians and established Roman hegemony beyond the Euphrates, but the conquest was short lived. Trajan's successor, Hadrian, pulled back Rome's reach to west of the Euphrates River.

The United States has more than seven hundred military installations in sixty countries around the globe and exercises various degrees of hegemony over numerous foreign nations and territories. This, too, is an expensive proposition. American hegemony differs from Rome's because we do not directly control these nations, but by providing military protection for

---

[267] Appian, preface to *Roman History*, 7.

them, these nations need not build large militaries to protect themselves; thus they become dependent on us.

Although seemingly invincible after its victory in the Second World War, the United States has encountered strong resistance in far-off places—for example, Korea and Vietnam. More recently, in the Middle East, it has faced hazards remarkably similar to those Rome faced. Military operations in Lebanon, Somalia, Iraq, and Afghanistan have suffered setbacks, and the outcome of the ongoing conflicts in the region cannot be accurately predicted. Remaining high is the potential for conflict with Iran, a country with a long history of warfare and incidentally with descendants of the Parthians among its population.

While the wisdom of presidents making unilateral decisions to engage in overseas military operations can be debated, it is incontrovertible that in foreign affairs Congress has deferred to the president. Just as the Roman Senate abdicated its responsibility for the direction of military affairs when it granted extraordinary imperium to Pompey, Caesar, and then Augustus, the American Congress largely abandoned its responsibility to control military operations.

IMPERIALISM AT HOME

Deference to the president in military and foreign policy has had domestic policy ramifications. Arthur Schlesinger wrote, "So the imperial presidency grew at the expense of the constitutional order ... And, as it overwhelmed traditional separation of powers in foreign affairs, it began to aspire toward an equivalent centralization of power in the domestic polity."[268]

During the Korean War, when a nationwide labor strike shut down the steel mills, President Truman seized the mills on the premise that the strike would hurt the war effort. He didn't consult Congress, and Congress's failure to react was tantamount to conceding that the president had the inherent authority to seize private property during an undeclared

---

[268] Arthur Schlesinger Jr., *The Imperial Presidency* (New York: Houghton Mifflin, 1973) 208.

war. However, the owners of the steel mills took the president to court, and the Supreme Court expeditiously declared Truman's action unconstitutional. Justice Robert Jackson wrote in his opinion, "No doctrine that the Court could promulgate would seem to me more sinister and alarming than that a President whose conduct in foreign affairs is so largely uncontrolled, and often even is unknown, can vastly enlarge his mastery over the internal affairs of the country by his own commitment of the Nation's armed forces to some foreign venture."[269]

Justice Jackson's point was similar to the point Rome's plebeian tribunes made about the Senate levying troops and sending them on campaign to avoid the constitution of a lawful assembly and votes on proposed legislation the Senate disfavored.

President Truman's steel-industry defeat aside, presidential command of foreign policy has translated into command of domestic policy. Just as Augustus's triumph in the Roman civil war empowered him and his bureaucracy to assume control of a broad range of domestic matters, so also the preeminence of modern American presidents in foreign affairs has empowered them to take control of aspects of domestic life of private concern or within the province of Congress or the states. Moreover, just as Augustus proscribed individuals and confiscated their property, so also the expanding powers of the executive branch have increasingly threatened or violated individual liberties and property rights.

Of all the modern presidents, Nixon was the most aggressive at converting his foreign-policy authority to domestic usages. With his background as a member of the congressional Committee on Un-American Activities, investigating communist infiltration of the government, he correlated domestic subversive activities with threats from foreign powers. This led him to believe in a need for strict executive branch secrecy, clandestine surveillance of American citizens in the name of national security, and suppression of criticism of the government. He used federal agencies, including the Internal Revenue Service, against his perceived political enemies. The climate he created within his administration led to the Watergate scandal, which drove him from office. Arthur Schlesinger said,

---

[269] Youngstown Sheet & Tube Co. v. Sawyer, 343 U.S. 579 (1952).

The belief of the Nixon administration in its own mandate and in its own virtue, compounded by its conviction that the republic was in mortal danger from internal enemies, had produced an unprecedented concentration of power in the White House and an unprecedented attempt to transform the Presidency of the Constitution into a plebiscitary Presidency. If this transformation were carried through, the President, instead of being accountable every day to Congress and public opinion, would be accountable every four years to the electorate. Between elections, the President would be accountable only through impeachment and would govern, as much as he could, by decree. The expansion and abuse of presidential power constituted the underlying issue, the issue that, as we have seen, Watergate raised to the surface, dramatized and made politically accessible.[270]

Nixon encapsulated his belief in presidential power when the interviewer David Frost asked him about the legality of his actions related to the Watergate scandal. Nixon said, "When the president does it—that means that it is not illegal." He later discovered that he wasn't quite correct when he had to resign from office.

In the wake of the Nixon scandals, Congress reasserted its authority by passing several laws that restricted executive branch powers. Within a few years, however, Congress reverted to its secondary position, passing broad and vague laws that delegated authority to regulatory agencies to make policy determinations and fill in specific details. In consequence, executive branch agencies have issued thousands of bureaucratic regulations and rulings that have grown to such an extent that the executive branch regulations outweigh congressional laws, unbalancing the separation of powers and erasing the difference between making the law and enforcing it.

Presidents in full control of federal agencies utilize regulatory

[270] Schlesinger, *The Imperial Presidency*, 377.

authority and discretionary powers to implement domestic policies that affect almost all aspects of the nation's life. Orders or even suggestions by imperial presidents ripple through the bureaucracy, affecting the life, liberty, and property of people among all walks of life.

Federal bureaucracies that are unchecked by Congress or courts often act in their own interests rather than for the general welfare of the people. Often political party zealots who are determined to implement their own agendas control the agencies. Instead of implementing congressional policies, they have become self-perpetuating, policy-making bodies in their own right. They make their own rules, enforce them at their own discretion, and choose the targets of judicial and regulatory action. Thus, they have a wide-open invitation to target and abuse perceived political enemies. Too often citizens are subjected to onerous regulations and find themselves at the mercy of arbitrary and imperial government action.

CHAPTER 33

Women in Rome

HISTORICAL STUDIES OF PAST societies rarely present a complete picture. Most are written from a top-down perspective, focusing on kings, consuls, wars, trials, and political conflicts. They focus on the actions of men but neglect the role of women, and it's impossible to have a full picture of a society without knowing the status and activities of women. This is the case with Rome, since our information mostly pertains to the upper classes and military campaigns. Nonetheless, with some extrapolation, sufficient information exists, from which to make reasonable inferences about the role and influence of Roman women and draw parallels to America.

One can reasonably infer that Roman women had a greater degree of freedom and power than women in other ancient societies. While Greece, Judea, and other nations separated women from men in almost all settings, Roman women sat in the stadiums, watching the games alongside men. They dined with men, and households didn't contain separate apartments as in Greece, where the women of the house remained concealed from the eyes of male nonrelatives. By the mid republic, it was possible for women to obtain divorces, and by the late republic, it was relatively easy. Some historians have contended that women of the late republic were less encumbered in both public and private matters than women were to be again until the twentieth century. Nonetheless, the legal status of Roman women was below that of men.

Roman laws provide a great deal of information about the family and the status of women. Justinian's *Institutes*, though composed five centuries after the republic, reflected the republic's patriarchal system, the rights of male citizens, and by inference the lesser status of female citizens.

> Our children, the issue of a valid Roman marriage, are in our power. (1) Marriage or matrimony is the union of male and female, involving shared life together. (2) The power which we have over our children is a right peculiar to Roman citizens, for there are no other men who have such control over their children as we have. (3) Therefore whoever is born of your son and his wife, that is to say, your grandson and granddaughter, are equally in your power, and your great-grandson and great-granddaughter, and so forth. But the child born of your daughter is not in your power, but in that of its own father.[271]

In the early republic, women were under the father's control. After the death of her father, a woman, unless married, could own and control her own property in the same manner as her brothers.

Upon marriage, she came under the power of her husband and became a member of the husband's paterfamilias just as if she had been adopted. However, it was always recognized that married women retained certain rights and a residual connection to their own paterfamilias. Women kept their name throughout their lives and didn't change it upon marrying.

In the early republic, marriage ceremonies were conducted in the old form of *cum manu*, or hanging over; however, the law allowed marriages *sine manu*, or marriage without being handed over, otherwise called "marriage by cohabitation."

In the latter type of marriage, a wife didn't become a member of her husband's paterfamilias but retained both her place in her father's paterfamilias and ownership of her property. A wife could retain her *sine manu* status by absenting herself from the home for three successive nights during the year. This customary law had been in effect since the Twelve Tables, table 6. "If

---

[271] Justinian, *Institutes*, 1.9 pr. 3; 1.11 pr. 10 L.

any woman is unwilling to be subjected in this manner to her husband's marital control, she shall absent herself for three successive nights in every year and by this means shall interrupt his prescriptive right of each year."

By the mid republic, *sine manu* marriages, cohabitation marriages, became prevalent. In either kind of marriage, dowries were customary, with the woman's family providing a dowry to the husband. In the *sine manu* marriage, the dowry did not pass into the absolute ownership of the husband; he controlled the dowry for only the duration of the marriage. Upon a divorce or the husband's death, the dowry was returned to the wife, less allowances for any children of the marriage. Return of the dowry could be especially important for the wife because it could be used again to secure a second marriage.

By the late republic, the prevailing view was that marriage was revocable and dependent on the continuing intentions of the parties, and women gained the right to divorce their husbands on almost any grounds. Divorces became common, and women often made second and third marriages of their own choosing.

The financial consequences of a divorce depended on the circumstances. Alan Watson summarized the rules.

> A husband could divorce his wife without any grounds whatever, and equally a wife could divorce her husband unless she was in his power. The heavy financial penalties for being the guilty party or for divorcing one's spouse without justification disappeared. Except when the parties had made their own arrangements, the wife's dowry had to be returned to her or her father if the marriage ended in divorce, but the husband was entitled to retain certain fractions of it, for instance, if there were children of the marriage, and he could retain other fractions if the wife had committed adultery or was unjustifiably

divorcing him. If the husband were at fault and not the
wife, he would lose his right to keep any of the dowry.[272]

Among the upper classes, marriages were often arranged to form alliances. While most girls of young ages would have complied with the
arrangements made for them, arranged marriages couldn't be permanently forced on them; they had the ultimate freedom of choice and the
final say regarding whether a political alliance could be made or would
last. Although a young, unwilling bride might be convinced or coerced to
accept the marriage, as she matured, she might assert herself.

Roman laws and customs provide a picture of the restraints placed
on women, but they don't capture the critical role women played in that
society. Paradoxically, while in many ways women held an inferior legal
status, in actual status, they were highly respected and honored, and they
exerted great influence in and outside their families. They were the teachers, arbiters, and judges of morality. Respect for the opinion and approval
of women strengthened Rome's morality and value systems. Tacitus described a woman's role in the family.

> It was the greatest honor for her to have charge of her
> household and to live for her children … Before her noth-
> ing could be said which was disgraceful; nothing could be
> done which was dishonorable. And not only the educa-
> tion and work of the children, but their games and hours
> of amusement were superintended by her with piety and
> modesty. In this way we have heard that Cornelia, the
> mother of the Gracchi, Aurelia, the mother of Caesar,
> and Atia, the mother of Augustus, took charge of their
> sons' education and brought them up to be great men in
> the state.[273]

---

[272] Alan Watson, *Roman Law and Comparative Law* (Athens, GA: University of Georgia
Press, 1991) 31.
[273] Tacitus, *Dialogues on Oratory*, 28.

Cornelia was the daughter of the great Scipio Africanus; she was married to a prominent and accomplished military commander, the elder Tiberius Sempronius Gracchus. They had twelve children, but only three survived. When Sempronius died, Ptolemy, the king of Egypt, wanted to make Cornelia his queen, but she declined, preferring to devote herself to rearing her children. Her daughter married the most respected *optimate* of his time, Publius Cornelius Scipio Aemelianus, the final conqueror of Carthage; her sons were the famous *populare* reformers Tiberius Sempronius Gracchus and Gaius Sempronius Gracchus, who tried to enact major land reforms. Both were killed, and Cornelia became renowned not only for her sons but also for the dignity with which she bore their deaths.

The steadfast worthiness of Rome's women was as important to the strength of Rome as the courage of the legions. Throughout their history, the Romans exhibited a strong respect for their women, and their women represented Roman morality. Traditional values were taught by legendary tales of the courage, chastity, and loyalty of women. The founding of the republic was attributed to the rape of Lucretia by the son of King Tarquinius. Lucretia's subsequent suicide incited the overthrow of the king. The preservation of the republic was attributed to Veturia, the mother of General Coriolanus. As Coriolanus approached the gates of Rome with his army, determined to destroy it, Veturia confronted him outside the gates. Her admonitions to him and her threat of suicide if he wouldn't turn back shamed him into retreating.

Less dramatic, more prosaic virtues were the mortar of Roman society. The story of Turiae provided an example for women to emulate. A eulogy from her husband was found inscribed on her tombstone. Known as the *Laudatio Turiae*, it presented a vivid and poignant portrayal of Roman marriage, values, and loyalties. Scholars have identified the couple as Quintus Lucretius Vespillo and his wife, Turiae. Vespillo's eulogy began by noting some of the difficulties Turiae had overcome during her early life, which included her successful effort to obtain justice for her murdered parents. He then turned to their marriage and her character.

Marriages as long as ours are rare, marriage that are
ended by death and not broken by divorce. For, we were
fortunate enough to see our marriage last without dis-
harmony for fully forty years. I wish that our long union
had come to its final end through something that had
befallen me instead of you; it would have been more just
if I as the older partner had had to yield to fate through
such an event.

Why should I mention your domestic virtues: your
loyalty, obedience, affability, reasonableness, industry
in working wool, religion without superstition, sobriety
of attire, modesty of appearance? Why dwell on your
love for your relatives, you devotion to your family? You
have shown the same attention to my mother as you did
to your own parents, and have taken care to secure an
equally peaceful life for her as you did for your own people, and you have innumerable other merits in common
with all married women who care for their good name.
It is your own very virtues that I am asserting, and very
few women have encountered comparable circumstances
to make them endure such sufferings and perform such
deeds. Providentially Fate has made such hard tests rare
for women.[274]

After giving other examples of her friendship, honesty, and generosity,
Vespillo told of her courage when he was proscribed and exiled during the
civil wars. By sending him supplies, she risked her life, for anyone who
provided supplies to a proscribed person was subject to death.

You provided abundantly for my needs during my flight
and gave me the means for a dignified manner of living,
when you took all the gold and jewelry from your own
body and sent it to me and over and over again enriched

---

[274] www.U.Arizona.edu/A.Futrell/surv/laud.

me in my absence with servants, money and provisions, showing great ingenuity in deceiving the guards posted by our adversaries.

You begged for my life when I was abroad—it was your courage that urged you to this step—and because of your entreaties I was shielded by the clemency of those against whom you marshaled your words. But whatever you said was always said with undaunted courage.

In the tumultuous period when the Senate authorized Pompey to restore order after Milo's men killed Clodius and the city was overrun by rioters, Pompey had Milo charged with the murder. Milo fled into exile before a verdict was rendered, and while Milo was in exile, Vespillo acquired his house. When the winds of the civil war changed, Milo returned to Rome, and Vespillo had to flee into exile, leaving his wife in possession of the household, which she courageously defended. "Meanwhile when a troop of men collected by Milo, whose house I had acquired through purchase when he was in exile, tried to profit by the opportunities provided by the civil war and break into our house to plunder, you beat them back successfully and were able to defend our home."

Eventually, Augustus rescinded Vespillo's exile. Vespillo attributed his rescue to the strenuous and dangerous efforts of Turiae and to her good counsel.

That I was brought back to my country by Caesar Augustus, for if you had not, by taking care for my safety, provided what he could save, he would have promised his support in vain. Thus I owe my life no less to your devotion than to Caesar.

Why should I now hold up to view our intimate and secret plans and private conversations: how I was saved by your good advice when I was roused by startling reports to meet sudden and imminent dangers; how you did not allow me imprudently to tempt providence by

an overbold step but prepared a safe hiding-place for me,
when I had given up my ambitious designs.

Vespillo went on to describe more personal details of their marriage, and he expressed his love and his grief. "Natural sorrow wrests away my power of self-control and I am overwhelmed by sorrow. I am tormented by two emotions: grief and fear—and I do not stand firm against either. When I go back in thought to my previous misfortunes and when I envisage what the future may have in store for me, fixing my eyes on your glory does not give me strength to bear my sorrow with patience. Rather I seem to be destined to long mourning."

This marriage was obviously between equals despite the customs and legalities of the patriarchal system.

Although women didn't have the right to vote, they weren't silent. In 195 BC, women demonstrated in the forum for the repeal of the Oppian Law, which had been passed during the Second Punic War and required women to deposit their valuable possessions in the treasury. The Oppian Law also forbade women to wear gold jewelry or expensive clothes in public. With victory won and peace restored, the women demanded the repeal of the law. However, the conservative faction, led by the consul Marcus Procius Cato the Elder argued that the law should remain in force to repress women and prevent their corruption by luxuries. To the contrary, the tribune Lucius Valerius argued for the repeal of the law.

What, may I ask, are the women doing that is new, having gathered and come forth publicly in a case which concerns them directly? Have they never appeared in public before? Allow me to unroll your own Origins before you. Listen to how often they have done so—always for the public good ... Indeed, as no one is amazed that they acted in situations affecting men and women alike, why should we wonder that they have taken action in a case which concerns themselves? What, after all, have they done? We have proud ears indeed, if, while masters do not scorn the appeals of slaves, we are angry when honorable women ask something of us ...

Who then does not know that this is a recent law, passed twenty years ago? Since our matrons lived for so long by the highest standards of behavior without any law, what risk is there that, once it is repealed, they will yield to luxury? For if the law were an old one, or if it had been passed to restrain feminine license, there might be reason to fear that repeal would incite them. The times themselves will show you why the law was passed. Hannibal was in Italy, victorious at Cannae. Already he held Tarentum, Arpi and Capua. He seemed on the verge of moving against Rome. Our allies had gone over to him. We had no reserve troops, no allies at sea to protect the fleet, no funds in the treasury. Slaves were being bought and armed, on condition that the price was to be paid their owners when the war was over. The contractors had declared that they would provide, on the same day of payment (after the war), the grain and other supplies the needs of war demanded. We were giving our slaves as rowers at our own expense, in proportion to our property rating. We were giving all our gold and silver for public use, as the senators had done first. Widows and children were donating their funds to the treasury. We were ordered to keep at home no more than a certain amount of wrought and stamped gold and silver. At a time like that were the matrons so taken up with luxury and fancy trappings that the Oppian law was needed ... To whom is it not clear that poverty and misfortune were the authors of that law of yours, since all private wealth had to be turned over to public use, and that it was to remain in effect only as long as the reason for its writing did? [275]

---

[275] Livy, *History of Rome*, 34.1.

When the speeches for and against Valerius's motion for repeal had been made, vetoes were imposed to block the motion, but a large crowd of women besieged the forum until the vetoes were rescinded and the Oppian Law was voted on and repealed.

Women protested taxation. When the Second Triumvirate of Augustus, Antony, and Lepidus failed to raise enough money through proscriptions, they broke with tradition and proposed to tax the property of fourteen-hundred of the wealthiest women. In 42 BC, a crowd of women pushed their way into the forum to protest. Their spokesperson was Hortensia. She was the daughter of Hortensius, Cicero's great legal and oratorical rival. She boldly addressed the triumvirs.

> You have already stolen from us our fathers and sons and husbands and brothers by your proscriptions, on the grounds that they had wronged you. But if you also steal from us our property, you will set us into a state unworthy of our family and manners and our female sex. If you claim that you have in any way been wronged by us, as you were by our husbands, proscribe us as you did them. But if we women have not voted any of you public enemies, if we did not demolish your houses or destroy your army or lead another army against you; if we have not kept you from public office or honor, why should we share the penalties if we have no part in the wrongdoing?

All agreed that Hortensia had her father's flair and talent; long before the revolutionary American colonists, she raised the issue of "no taxation without representation." She continued,

> Why should we pay taxes when we have no part in public office or honors or command or government in general, an evil you have fought over with such disastrous results? Because, you say, this is a time of war. And when have there not been wars? And when have women paid taxes?

By nature of their sex women are absolved from paying taxes among all mankind …

But if there should be a war against the Celts or Parthians, we will not be less eager for our country's welfare than our mothers. But we will never pay taxes for civil wars, and we will not cooperate with you against each other. We did not pay taxes to Caesar or to Pompey, nor did Marius ask us for contributions, nor Cinna nor Sulla, even though he was a tyrant over this country. And you say that you are re-establishing the Republic! [276]

After Hortensia's speech, the triumvirs ordered the lictors to drive the women from the tribunal, but the crowd wouldn't have it, and the proceedings were postponed until the next day. Upon further thought, the triumvirs decided not to tax the women; instead, they raised taxes on men who were worth more than 100,000 sesterces.

Another woman with flair was Sempronia, the mother of Decimus Junius Brutus. Sallust described her.

[W]ell blessed by fortune in her birth and physical beauty, as well as her husband and children; well-read in Greek and Latin literature, she played the lyre, danced more art- fully than any honest woman should, and had many other gifts which fostered a luxurious life. Yet there was never anything she prized as little as her honor and chastity; it was hard to say whether she was less free with her money or her virtue; her lusts were so fierce that she more often pursued men than was pursued by them … Even so, she was a remarkable woman; able to write poetry, crack a joke, and converse modestly, tenderly or wantonly; all in all she had great gifts and a good many charms.[277]

---

[276] Appian, *Civil Wars*, 4.32–4.
[277] Sallust, *Bell Cat.* 25.

Sempronia was hardly the norm; the women of Rome weren't all of one mind, body, or character. Some adhered to the old values of chasteness, devotion, and piety; and they would uphold them to the death; others adopted a more libertarian mode of conduct. Some writers of subsequent periods, Livy among them, contended that as the republic deteriorated, there was a coincident deterioration of traditional morality. Others contended that the decline in morality preceded and contributed to the republic's demise. Under the latter view, if Cato the Elder returned to Rome two centuries after he had argued to preserve the Oppian Law, he would have said, "I told you so."

The questionable conduct of some women incited poets, critics, and satirists to extrapolate that the same conduct prevailed among the many. They painted the whole class of elite women as immoral. In the second century AD, the poet Juvenal satirized the attachment of Roman women to luxuries and dissipation. Apparently, he was a misogynist who exaggerated the moral decay of his time. He wrote,

> Poverty made Latin women chaste in the old days, hard work and a short time to sleep and hands calloused and hardened with wool-working, and Hannibal close to the city, and their husbands standing guard at the Colline Gate—that kept their humble homes from being corrupted by vice. But now we are suffering from the evils of a long peace. Luxury, more ruthless than war, broods over Rome and takes revenge for the world she has conquered. No cause for guilt or deed of lust is missing, now that Roman poverty has vanished. Money, nurse of promiscuity, first brought in foreigners' ways, and effete riches weakened the sinews of succeeding generations. What does Venus care when she's drunk? She can't tell head from tail when she eats big oysters at midnight, and when her perfume foams with undiluted wine, when she drinks her conch-shell cup dry, and when in her dizziness

the roof turns round and the table rises up to meet two
sets of lights.[278]

No doubt the private conduct of women varied, but it would be a
mistake to give too much credibility to Juvenal's viewpoint or to cast
blame for the deterioration of society on promiscuous women. For every
supposedly profligate woman, there were far more who maintained the
traditional values and held the mores of society in place. One must be
skeptical of generalizations and exaggerated views of past indiscretions.
The statesman and philosopher Marcus Seneca kept matters in perspective
and recognized that complaints of moral decay have always been, and will
always be, with us. "[I]t was the complaint of our ancestors, as it is ours,
and will be that of posterity, that morality has changed, and wickedness
rules, and mankind goes from bad to worse, and everything sacred is falling into disrepute. This one thing is and will ever be the same—changing
its extent from time to time, like sea waves which the incoming tide drives
on and the ebb keeps back and constrains."[279]

Howsoever one views the conduct of individual Roman women, certainly women played major roles in the destiny of the republic. Roman
politics operated through networks of the great families, and the influence
of women on their families equated with a great influence on political alliances. Ronald Syme wrote, "Marriage with a well-connected heiress therefore became an act of policy and an alliance of powers, more important
than a magistracy, more binding than any compact of oath or interest. Not
that women were merely the instruments of masculine policy. Far from it:
the daughters of the great houses commanded political influence in their
own right, exercising a power beyond the reach of many a senator."[280]

Julius Caesar's destiny was set early by the marriage of his aunt Julia
to Marius, which established a connection between Caesar's patrician clan
and the plebeian Marius. Then, when Caesar married Cinna's daughter,
Cornelia, he further solidified his connection to the *populare* faction.

---

[278] Juvenal, *Satires*, VI.

[279] Marcus Seneca, *Ad Helv.*, 16, 3.

[280] Ronald Syme, *The Roman Revolution* (Oxford University Press, 1939) 12.

Evidently, Caesar's love for Cornelia was genuine because when Sulla demanded that he divorce her, Caesar refused at the risk of his life. They had a daughter, Julia, who later played an important part in Roman politics.

In 69 BC, Cornelia died in childbirth; and in 67 BC, Caesar married Pompeia, the daughter of Sulla, the deceased dictator. This shift in alliances may have been for political convenience, since the marriage helped his election to *pontifex maximus*, an office that provided him with a residence. The marriage came to an early ending in the midst of a tremendous scandal that had far-reaching political consequences. The scandal erupted when, according to a yearly custom, Caesar's wife, Pompeia, hosted an all-female religious ceremony of the vestal virgins at the residence. While the ceremony proceeded, the roguish Publius Clodius Pulcher snuck into the house dressed in women's clothes. It was alleged that his purpose was to consort with Pompeia. He was charged with sacrilege but was acquitted. Guilty or innocent, Caesar divorced Pompeia, proclaiming that, although there had been no consorting, "Caesar's wife must be above suspicion."

Whether Clodius was secretly acting on Caesar's behalf and the divorce was part of a scheme to further Caesar's political plans is unclear; surely it must have looked that way when Caesar married Calpurnia, the eighteen-year-old daughter of Lucius Calpurnius Piso, Pompey's associate. This followed the arrangement in which Pompey married Caesar's seventeen-year-old daughter, Julia (from his marriage to Cornelia), to seal their pact for the control of the growing empire. The arrangement proved even more successful than hoped; despite their great difference in age, Pompey and Julia were quite happy together. However, plans and hopes are one thing; death in childbirth again played an immense part in the fate of the republic. When Julia, like her mother, died in childbirth and her newborn son died shortly thereafter, the alliance of Pompey and Caesar, which had been functioning peaceably, began to unravel. Had Julia lived and the triumvirs' mutual grandson lived, the civil war that followed might never have occurred.

Many women influenced Caesar's fate. Servilia, although married to another man, was Caesar's mistress for twenty years. She was Cato's half-sister, a fact that created some interesting situations because Cato was Caesar's most virulent enemy. For instance, in 63 BC, during the debate over the execution of the Catiline conspirators, Cato claimed that a letter handed to Caesar was from the conspirators and demanded that it be read aloud. Caesar allowed it to be read aloud; it was actually a love note from Servilia.

Servilia had a son from a previous marriage, Marcus Junius Brutus, and she naturally lobbied Caesar on his behalf. Caesar indeed formed a strong affinity for the young man, and this affinity was instrumental in Caesar's clemency to him after the Battle of Pharsalia, even though Brutus had fought on the side of the defeated Pompey. As dictator, Caesar made Brutus a praetor in 44 BC, which placed him in a prominent position to approve the assassination of Caesar, his benefactor.

Women also influenced Cicero's fate. When Clodius was tried for the sacrilege of infiltrating the ceremony of the vestal virgins, he claimed the alibi of having been out of Rome on the day in question. Cicero knew differently because he had met with Clodius that day. He resisted testifying against Clodius, but his wife, Terentia, accused him of not wanting to testify because he'd been having an affair with Clodius's sister, Clodia. Browbeaten, Cicero testified, inciting the enmity of Clodius, who in revenge would force Cicero into exile.

It would be a mistake to contend that women played only indirect or lobbying roles in connection to national events. Fulvia Flaccus (circa 83–40 BC) controlled and greatly influenced the political conduct of her three husbands—Publius Clodius Pulcher, Gaius Scribonius Curio, and Marc Antony—and she also had a marked influence on the destiny of Caesar and the republic. She was of the Fulvii, a distinguished plebeian family that had backed the reforms of Gaius Gracchus. Fulvia supported the *populare* ideology and saw Clodius as a potential leader of that cause because of his popularity with the urban masses and his control of collegia and street gangs. She picked Clodius as her husband and encouraged his political career. She had two children with him, including their daughter, Claudia Pulchra.

Clodius, while campaigning for praetor and participating in a fierce rivalry with Milo, was killed on the Appian Way in a clash with Milo's men. It was Fulvia who had Clodius's body carried through the streets of Rome, inciting an angry mob to invade the Senate house and build a funeral pyre inside to cremate the corpse. The fire spread and destroyed the building.

After his death, Clodius's supporters transferred their loyalty to Fulvia, who transferred that support to her second husband, Curio. Upon their marriage, Curio switched his allegiance from the *optimates* to the *populares*. He aligned with Julius Caesar, became a tribune, and continued many of Clodius's policies. In the civil war of 49 BC, he was killed while fighting for Caesar's faction.

Fulvia still maintained the allegiance of Clodius's supporters, and with her wealth, she was a sought-after widow. In 47 BC, she married Marc Antony and had two sons with him. The marriage was politically beneficial to him, and he became Caesar's master of the horse and coconsul in 44 BC, the year of the assassination.

After Caesar's assassination, while Antony was away from Rome on campaign, Fulvia defended him against Cicero's political attacks. What part she played in the formation of the Second Triumvirate is uncertain, but to cement the alliance, she married her daughter, Claudia Pulchra, Antony's stepdaughter, to Augustus. According to Appian, Fulvia had input into the proscriptions that followed and was joyous at Cicero's murder—not only because of his attacks on Antony but also because he had been Clodius's worst enemy and had defended Milo, Clodius's murderer, in court.

In 42 BC, when Antony and Augustus left Rome to fight Brutus and Cassius, the other triumvir, Lepidus, stayed in Rome. Fulvia also stayed in Rome, and she controlled the political scene. According to Cassius Dio, "She, the mother-in-law of Octavian [Augustus] and wife of Antony, had no respect for Lepidus because of his slothfulness, and managed affairs herself, so that neither the Senate nor the people transacted any business contrary to her pleasure."[281] So, for a time, she was the de facto third member of the triumvirate.

While Augustus and Antony were in Greece, fighting Brutus and Cassius, Fulvia schemed with her husband's brother, Lucius Antonius, who was consul in 41 BC, to undercut Augustus and pave the way for Antony to be the uncontested ruler of Rome. Her plans went unfulfilled.

---

[281] Cassius Dio, 48.4.1.

After Philippi, Augustus returned to Italy while Antony stayed in the East, where he consorted with Cleopatra. Fulvia continued plotting. Exploiting the bitterness caused by Augustus's massive program of confiscation and redistribution of land in Italy, she instigated a movement to overthrow the triumvirate. Rumors spread that her real motivation was to start a war in Italy to draw Antony back and away from Cleopatra. When Augustus learned of her activities, he divorced Claudia, Fulvia's daughter and Antony's stepdaughter.

Fulvia openly proclaimed her opposition to Augustus and Lepidus. She raised six legions, under the command of Lucius Antonious, and drove Lepidus out of Rome. However, Augustus had ten legions, and he maneuvered Lucius Antonious to retreat into the city of Perusia, trapping him there. Augustus, with the aid of Marcus Agrippa, cut off all supplies to the city. After months of siege, in February 40 BC, Lucius surrendered. Augustus spared him and his troops, but Perusia was plundered and destroyed.

Meanwhile, Fulvia fled with three thousand cavalry to Greece and met Antony in Athens. It was a strained meeting, with the relationship of Antony and Cleopatra in the air. Antony severely criticized Fulvia for starting the Perusine War, and he left her without saying good-bye. Fulvia was distraught, reputedly stopped eating, and died shortly thereafter. Conveniently, everyone blamed her for the conflicts between Antony and Augustus, and the two triumvirs renewed their alliance, with the widower Antony marrying Augustus's sister, Octavia. It was assumed that Antony would break off his relationship with Cleopatra, and this would finally bring an end to the conflict.

Octavia was an upstanding woman, and she took in and reared the children of Fulvia and Antony. Her match to Antony seemed incongruous—she had lived a life of dignity while he had lived a life of profligacy. Nonetheless, she had a strong influence on him, and she often played the role of peacemaker between Antony and Augustus, helping to maintain calm in a situation that seemed to call for a military resolution. Of course, Antony soon dishonored Octavia when he continued his relationship with Cleopatra, becoming completely absorbed in her orbit. When he divorced Octavia, the civil war between Augustus and Antony followed.

Augustus tried to solidify another alliance by marrying Scribonia, an in-law of Sextus Pompeius, the son of Pompey. Scribonia was ten years older than Augustus. She became pregnant with another Julia, but Augustus wasn't happy in the marriage. In 39 BC, he met Livia Drusilla, a nineteen-year-old beauty. Her statues portray a serene, commanding woman with perfect features; large, striking eyes; and thick, wavy hair. She was already married to the much-older Tiberius Claudius Nero and had a three-year-old son, also named Tiberius Claudius Nero; she was pregnant with a second son. That aside, Augustus and Livia had an affair and decided to marry.

Although Augustus was only twenty-four years old, he ruled family matters with the same iron will with which he ruled all other matters. He waited for Scribonia to deliver their daughter, Julia, then immediately divorced her. Next, he persuaded Livia's husband, Claudius, to divorce her. That done, Augustus married Livia, and, adding salt to the wounds, made Claudius preside over the wedding.

A few months later, Livia delivered her second son, Drusus Claudius Nero. Under Roman custom, her two sons were sent to the father, Claudius, to be raised, while Augustus and Scribonia's daughter, Julia, stayed with Augustus and Livia. When Claudius died in 32 BC, Livia's two sons joined the Augustus household.

The marriage lasted fifty-one years until Augustus died. Livia bore him no children but was friend, guide, and ally to her husband. She established an independent identity in the fashion of a queen, was granted the inviolate status of a tribune, received large numbers of clients, commissioned public buildings, dedicated temples, sponsored charities, and helped her protégés advance to political office.

On the dark side, the rumor was that since Augustus had no sons, Livia pushed her own sons into power at the expense of other more capable young men. She arranged for her son Tiberius to be married to Augustus's daughter, Julia; and for her other son Drusus to be married to Augustus's niece. Both Tiberius and Drusus became generals and won victories across the Rhine in Germany. Drusus was more popular, but in 9 BC, on his way back from Germany, he was thrown from a horse and killed.

With Drusus gone, Tiberius was the undisputed candidate to succeed Augustus, and in AD 4, Augustus adopted him and named him as his heir. When Augustus died in AD 14, Tiberius became emperor. As the mother of the emperor, Livia continued her prominence as the first lady of Rome until her death in AD 29.

CHAPTER 34

Cultural Divide

IN *COMING APART*, CHARLES Murray argued that the second half of the American twentieth century saw "the formation of classes that are different in kind and in their degree of separation from anything that the nation has ever known. He argued that "the divergence into these separate classes, if it continues, will end what has made America America."[282]

Murray pointed out that many people among the most elite and influential of American society—the academic intelligentsia, elite-school graduates, news media and entertainment producers—no longer feel the imperative of traditional American values or believe in the supremacy of Western culture, but instead they subscribe to a postmodern relativism. They disparage patriotism or the belief in American exceptionalism. Leaders of the media and entertainment industries readily present anti-American themes in their productions, and the leaders of academia emphasize the negatives of American history while minimizing its achievements. This position is contrary to the advice of the founders. Thomas Jefferson advised that education should encourage a love of country and an appreciation for our form of government; all students should study and understand the benefits of American representative democracy

---

[282] Charles Murray, *Coming Apart*, 11.

and the need to preserve it.[283] Jefferson's thought mirrored Livy's succinct maxim "An empire remains powerful so long as its subjects rejoice in it."

To the contrary, many Americans today lack confidence in their nation. Some criticize American corporatism and power broking; others see hypocrisy in traditional religions and institutions; and many obsess over long-ago injustices. They view as enemies those who hold different opinions and attribute the worst intentions to their adversaries.

How did these circumstances come about? How did we come so far from the proud, self-confident nation, victorious in the First and Second World Wars, to a nation uncertain of itself, a nation steadily losing faith in its institutions and pride in its people?

For one explanation, juxtapose America's experience after winning the First and Second World Wars with Rome's experience after winning the wars against Carthage and Greece. In the post-Punic War period, Rome's continued eastward expansion brought enormous wealth to Rome, and as the soldiers and businessmen returned home, they came back with Greek ideas and practices. Tensions between traditional Roman values and the imported Greek values were acted out in the political battles between Cato the Elder and philhellenes, such as Scipio Africanus and Scipio Aemelianus. This social conflict endured, and a century later, Cato's grandson, Cato the Younger, also tried to suppress Greek influence and profligate practices. Whereas Cato the Elder could claim victories, though not an overall one, Cato the Younger lost his fight.

In much the same way that the Romans became fascinated with Greek ideas, Americans became fascinated with European culture. Like the Romans who transported Greek sculpture to their estates throughout Italy, wealthy Americans imported European art, architecture, and fashions. Like the Romans who sent their sons to Greek academies to be educated in rhetoric and philosophy, the American intelligentsia adopted European theories of moral relativism, Marxism, atheism, and existentialism—notions that would have been inimical to the founders, pioneers, and early Congregationalists.

Just as Greek tutors, sophists, and philosophers left their decimated

---

[283] Preamble to the 1779 bill for the More General Diffusion of Knowledge.

cities for opportunities in Rome, European intellectuals brought their war-torn ideas to America. But unlike the Greek sophists, whom Cato the Elder banished, the European intellectuals were welcomed in America. It was a time when America was flush from its victories of Nazi Germany and Imperial Japan, when it was enjoying unprecedented prosperity and prestige, and when it wasn't on its guard against inimical European threats to its way of life.

Marxist professors from the University of Frankfurt, such as Herbert Marcuse, Max Horkheimer, and Theodor Adorno, left Germany to teach at American Ivy League universities. They espoused critical theory, a modern form of Greek skepticism. The advocates of critical theory held that every foundational tenet of Western civilization should be questioned, challenged, and attacked; and the Frankfurt circle and other intellectuals set about undermining American assumptions and moral codes.

Along with critical theory, the existentialism of Jean Paul Sartre and Simone de Beauvoir spread from Europe to America. The existentialists proselytized that life was meaningless except for action on behalf of a cause, and causes abounded, ranging from antinuclear proliferation to social justice to sexual liberation. Later, the French philosopher Jacques Derrida proselytized deconstructionist theories at several American universities. Deconstructionism questioned the basic assumptions of Western philosophy and culture, and like the Greek Carneades, whom Cato banished for arguing that there was no such thing as truth, Derrida contended that "there are no truths; reality is negotiable." He promoted the politicization of universities and wanted a reconstruction of Western values, replacing them with Marxist principles. The acceptance and adoption of the "isms" and their derivative causes wasn't exclusive to the intelligentsia but spread through news and entertainment mediums to the general population.

To be sure, traditional American institutions and prominent conservatives tried to resist the onslaught of progressive, Marxist, and atheistic ideas. In response to libertine tendencies in Hollywood movies, the motion picture production codes were established. Thirty-seven states established state censorship boards, and the movie industry empowered Will H. Hays, a Presbyterian elder, to act as an arbiter. Like a Roman censor, Hays established a list of don'ts pertaining to profanity, nudity, sex, drugs, and other matters. In 1929, when Jesuit Catholics recommended a code, the movie industry voluntarily agreed to adopt it to avoid more government censorship. The code sought not only to ban certain troubling or provocative materials but also to affirmatively promote traditional values. Sexual relations outside of marriage couldn't be seen as permissible; all crimes had to be punished; authority figures, including clergy, had to be treated with respect. Thomas Doherty, a Brandeis University professor, described the code as "no mere list of Thou-Shalt-Nots but a homily that sought to yoke Catholic doctrine to Hollywood formula. The guilty are punished, the virtuous rewarded, the authority of the church and state is legitimate, and the bonds of matrimony are sacred. What resulted was 'a Jewish owned business selling Roman Catholic theology to Protestant America.'" [284]

As American morals and values continued to change, the enforcement of the code became problematic. In 1968, it was abandoned and replaced by a rating system, but the tide of change couldn't be held back by quasi-regulations. Anti-Americanism became increasingly common in novels, textbooks, movies, and even comic books. It may seem trivial, but it was telling that in the April 2011 issue of the *Superman* comic book, Superman renounced his US citizenship after eighty years of being an American superhero with the motto "Truth, justice, and the American way."[285]

As the "isms" and their derivatives gained sway and were adopted by large segments of the population, they replaced traditional values and mores, and many social and sexual taboos were abandoned. Coincidentally, marriage rates and church attendance declined while out-of-wedlock births, drug use, and crime increased.

While many welcomed the relaxation of social restrictions, others were affronted by what they saw as licentiousness, and the divide between those with opposing social views widened. Among conservatives, pessimism prevailed, and analogies to Rome proliferated. The noted historian Victor David Hanson wrote that Rome's deterioration "was a result not of imperial

---

[284] Henry Scott, *Shocking True Story* (New York: Pantheon, 2010) 14.
[285] Dixon and Rivoche, "How Liberalism Became Kryptonite for Superman," *Wall Street Journal*, June 14, 2014.

overstretch on the outside but something happening within that was not unlike what we ourselves are now witnessing. Earlier Romans knew what it was to be Roman, why it was at least better than the alternative, and why their culture had to be defended. Later in ignorance they forgot what they knew, in pride mocked who they were, and in consequence disappeared."[286]

The changing mores of American society were nowhere better described than by Daniel Patrick Moynihan, the Democratic senator from New York, in his article "Defining Deviancy Down." He argued that conduct that would have been excoriated in earlier times as immoral had become accepted as normal, and the acceptance of this conduct was contributing to a disintegration of civil society.

In the 1980s, the presidency of Ronald Reagan interrupted the perceived downward trajectory of American culture and spirit. His positive vision provided a jolt for America and also brought to the forefront the social issues dividing the nation. Religion in schools, affirmative action, and abortion became significant polarizing issues. Democrats and Republicans took opposite sides of the issues, and they often fought each other, not through rational argument but through character assassination.

In 1987, the conflicts came to a head when President Reagan nominated Robert Bork for the Supreme Court. Bork was a strict-constructionist jurist who declined to read implied rights into the Constitution. He was projected to vote against abortion rights, and liberal activists mounted a full-bore campaign to prevent his appointment. The liberal icon Senator Ted Kennedy spoke against Bork on the Senate floor. The tone of his remarks expressed the furious nature of the dispute. Kennedy said, "Robert Bork's America is a land in which women would be forced into back-alley abortions, blacks would sit at segregated lunch counters, rogue police could break down citizens' doors in midnight raids, schoolchildren could not be taught about evolution and artists could be censored at the whim of the government, and the doors of the federal courts would be shut on the fingers of millions of citizens.[287]

---

[286] Victor David Hanson, "I Love Iraq, Bomb Texas," *Commentary*, December 2002.
[287] Congressional Hearing, September 15, 1987, www.C-span.org./bork/nomination/hearing.

Bork's nomination was defeated in the Senate, and liberal partisans applauded Senator Kennedy's victory. They didn't denounce him for his exaggerated claims but instead adopted and repeated them. Party xenophobia was in full force. Kennedy became a hero to the left despite a scandal that in less-partisan times would likely have driven any politician from office. On July 18, 1969, after a social engagement, Senator Kennedy drove his car off a ferry into Chappaquiddick Bay, killing his female companion. According to the extensive reporting on the incident, instead of attempting to rescue her, Kennedy saved himself, left his companion to drown, and checked into a motel. He undoubtedly delayed reporting the incident to the police to gain time for the alcohol in his system to dissipate and to concoct a cover-up. Nevertheless, his political career continued. For his supporters, loyalty to a party leader trumped everything, and they reelected him to the Senate term after term until his death in 2009.

After the defeat of the Bork nomination, the confirmation process became increasingly combative. In 1991, when President George H. Bush nominated Clarence Thomas for the Supreme Court, a conservative African-American, the left attempted to "Bork" him. A woman who had worked with Thomas came forward to charge that he had sexually harassed her by making inappropriate remarks and implicit sexual jokes. Justice Thomas didn't remain passive as Bork had done but aggressively challenged his attackers. He testified at the Senate confirmation hearings. "This is not an opportunity to talk about difficult matters privately or in a closed environment. It is a circus. It's a national disgrace. And from my standpoint, as a black American, it is a high-tech lynching for uppity blacks who in any way deign to think for themselves, to do for themselves, to have different ideas, and it is a message that unless you kowtow to an old order, this is what will happen to you. You will be lynched, destroyed, caricatured by a committee of the U.S. Senate rather than hung from a tree."

Thomas survived his acrimonious nomination process, and the Senate confirmed him. However, the politicization of the nomination process spilled over to the court itself, damaged the prestige of the court, and undermined the perception of the court as an objective standard-bearer of the law. The court increasingly became the subject of accusations that it made decisions on the basis of partisanship.

Societies are held together by intangible forces, by moral systems. Without rational debate and compromise on difficult issues, partisanship evolves into class or group hatred that can shred and break the bindings that hold society together. In *The Righteous Mind*, Jonathan Haidt defined moral systems as "interlocking sets of values, virtues, norms, practices, identities, institutions, technologies, and evolved psychological mechanisms that work together to suppress or regulate self-interest and make cooperative societies possible."[288] As long as factions recognize and adhere to a society's moral system, disputes can be addressed through compromise. But when the moral system collapses and interlocking sets of values unlock, society divides into opposing forces, occupying the same crowded landscape with no means of avoiding collisions.

Disagreements about changing mores, philosophy, or religion can exacerbate the partisan acrimony more so than basic political or economic disagreements. People engaged in public affairs generally have much stronger feelings about abortion, affirmative action, same-sex marriage, or gun control than about marginal tax rates, economic theory, or labor-management relations. Modern political parties have aligned on opposite sides of a host of major social issues, polarizing the nation to a degree not seen since the conflict over slavery; and today Lincoln's admonition "A house divided against itself cannot stand" is again a realistic concern.

As always the case, political and social movements need adversaries, and when the issues are highly personal, adversaries become enemies. Recent statements and accusations made by today's partisans, on both the right and the left, have been extraordinarily contentious and demagogic. Some of these statements have come from high government officials. An example occurred in a remarkable radio interview on January 17, 2014, when Andrew Cuomo, the Democratic governor of New York, told WCNY's *The Capitol Pressroom* that, as for Republicans, "their problem is not me and the Democrats; their problem is themselves. Who are they? Are they these extreme conservatives who are right-to-life, pro-assault-weapon, anti-gay? Is that who they are? Because if that's who they are and

---

[288] Jonathan Haidt, *The Righteous Mind*, (New York, Pantheon Books, 2012) 170.

they're extreme conservatives, they have no place in the state of New York, because that's not who New Yorkers are."

Governor Cuomo pointed out that the right wing of the Republican Party had become increasingly extreme; however, he neglected to point out that the left wing of the Democratic Party had also become increasingly extreme. His comments highlighted the growing intolerance of each party for the other. Party affiliation had become a factor as divisive as religion, race, or ethnicity had been in earlier times. In social and personal relations, it became a predominant consideration. It's interesting that while interfaith and interracial marriages have increased, marriages of Democrats and Republicans have decreased. The owner of a prominent Internet matchmaking service stated, "People now say 'I don't even want to meet anybody who's from the other party, even if it's someone who's perfect in every other way."[289]

The political has become personal. Every action has a reaction, and those who have been labeled right wing extremists have been equally hostile to those with whom they disagree, pejoratively labeling them "left wing extremists." Debates about public policy have degenerated from practical and rational argument to political positioning based entirely on emotional attachments, a phenomenon prevalent during the disintegration of the Roman Republic. Cicero observed about Roman political debate, "Men decide far more problems by hate, love, lust, rage, sorrow, joy, hope, fear, illusion, or some other inward emotion, than by reality, authority, any legal standard, judicial precedent or statute."

Twenty-four-hours-a-day television and radio news and talk shows across the nation have become the platform for conservatives and liberals to lash out at their perceived adversaries with a constant drumbeat of criticism laced with outrageous and inflammatory characterizations. With only a few exceptions, most news outlets—whether television, radio, print, or the Internet—have adopted ideological platforms, and interested citizens patronize the outlets they agree with, rarely patronizing those with which they disagree. Party affiliation determines what news outlets

---

[289] Pew Research Center, "Political Polarization in the American Republic," June 12, 2014.

an individual follows, thus reinforcing an individual's position on social, moral, and political issues.

Besides the specific issues that divide Americans, a more profound division exists between those who affirm America's past, values, and vision as a positive force for the world and those with progressive values who believe American society is flawed and needs structural change. The former speak of American leadership in the world, individual merit, personal responsibility, and upward mobility; the latter, while hoping for a better future, speak of America's imperfections, social injustice, and the need to alleviate income inequality.

With such social and political conflicts continuing to escalate, national fragmentation is a possibility, and our unity and cohesion cannot be taken for granted. When political parties refuse to compromise and adherents of those parties are deeply divided over fundamental issues, a spark can unleash unpredictable events that can change the nature and character of our society. In recent decades, each succeeding presidency has seen the divide widen further, creating cracks in the nation's foundation as dangerous as those that surfaced in the last century of the Roman Republic.

CHAPTER 35

Domestic Violence

IN THE LAST CENTURY of the Roman Republic, an influx of displaced farmers, freed slaves, and immigrants from other parts of the empire swelled the urban population. In 60 BC, Rome had about one million residents. The affluent resided on the high ground, while the poor were crowded into severely congested tenements (*insula*) in conditions that generated tension and resentment. In that turbulent era, as opposing political factions jockeyed for power, the growing number of poor and unemployed loomed ominously over the city, and the increasing threat of mob violence affected elections and legislation. The bottom line was that the common citizens were always a threat to the political order. When the contract between the people and their representatives broke down, the people often rioted. In most instances, the rioting subsided in a few days, but sometimes it flared for months. Politics was always involved. At times, the rioting was orchestrated from the beginning for political purposes; other times partisan factions exploited it after the fact. Demagogues used mobs to enforce their demands, and civil debate was increasingly supplanted by violence.

Of all the demagogues who exploited mob violence, Clodius was the most treacherous. He tapped into the resentments of debtors and the poor, and he could instigate street violence whenever he wished. He intimidated opponents by mounting demonstrations at their homes and in the forum; on some occasions, he did so at the behest of Crassus or Caesar, while they maintained plausible deniability. In one instance, on election-day in 56 BC, Crassus was running for the consulship against the *optimate* Lucius Domitius Ahenobarbus, Cato's brother-in-law and a descendent of consuls. Ahenobarbus was favored to win one of the two positions; Pompey was heavily favored to win the other. At dawn, as Ahenobarbus walked toward the Campos Martius for the vote, surrounded by his entourage, a group of armed assailants attacked them. Ahenobarbus turned back. Consequently, Pompey and Crassus were elected unopposed. The assailants, who most likely were associated with Clodius, were never identified.

During the election campaign of 53 BC, tensions between political factions ran high; threats, disruptions, and street clashes were constant. Clodius was campaigning for praetor as a *populare*; Titus Annius Milo, an *optimate* senator, was campaigning for consul. Although they weren't running for the same office, they represented the opposing parties. The *optimates* chose Milo to run because he had assembled an armed security force and wouldn't be intimidated by Clodius's street gangs.

Supporters of both sides staged demonstrations, fought with one another, and terrorized the city. Because of the violence, elections had to be postponed, and without magistrates the city was left in a state of disorder, which lasted into the next year. Then, in January 52 BC, as chance or design would have it, Clodius and Milo were traveling in opposite directions on the Appian Way. As their entourages met and passed, they stared defiantly at one another. Milo's force included two famous professional gladiators, Eudamus and Birria, who pushed and shoved Clodius's slaves. When Clodius wheeled his horse to confront them, they attacked and stabbed him. Wounded, Clodius tried to escape into a nearby inn, but he was dragged out and killed, his body dumped on the side of the road.

The next day, two *populare* tribunes took Clodius's slashed body to the forum and displayed it on the rostrum. The people were infuriated, and riots erupted. Clodius's followers took his body inside the Senate house and built a funeral pyre with benches and manuscripts. The fire consumed the body and the Senate house with it, a vivid and symbolic event. The house from which Rome ruled the Mediterranean world was burned by its own people.

The American republic has experienced periods of disorder

comparable to those of the most turbulent Roman periods, and the same kinds of civil unrest and mob violence have affected American cities. To be sure, human nature and its most abhorrent aspects haven't changed, and under certain circumstances, mob violence bursts forth like a natural phenomenon. In *The Crowd*, a study published in 1895, Gustave Le Bon referenced the French Revolution and explained mob behavior.

> When the crowd changes into a mob, its individual members lose their identity and merge into a cruel, primitive body which has lost its civilized restraints and suddenly has no respect for those law enforcement agencies that resist it ... An isolated individual knows well enough that alone he cannot loot a shop or set a fire to a building, and should he be tempted to do so, he will easily and readily resist the temptation. As a part of a mob, however, he becomes conscious of the power he shares with others, and it is sufficient to suggest ideas of pillage, murder, or violence for him to yield immediately to temptation.

As in Rome, American political opportunists have used mob violence or the threat of it to achieve their ends. Crowded urban conditions in times of economic hardship often provide the tinder to fuel a fire. Beginning in the 1830s, waves of immigrants settled in New York City. The 1860 census counted 813,669 New York residents; half were foreign born, and a quarter of them were Irish. Affluent citizens lived in spacious housing and well-kept neighborhoods; the poor lived in overcrowded, unsafe, and unsanitary tenements. The Five Points section was the most populated area; it comprised the territory bounded by Broadway, the Bowery, Canal Street, and Park Row; and it contained theaters, rundown tenements, and 270 saloons. First-generation Irish Catholics, who had fled famine and oppression in Ireland, largely populated the area.

Charles Dickens described the area. "Let us go again, and plunge into the Five Points. This is the place; these narrow ways diverging to the right and left, reeking everywhere with dirt and filth ... Debauchery has made the very houses prematurely old. See how the rotten beams are tumbling down, and how the patched and broken windows seem to scowl dimly, like eyes that have been hurt in drunken frays."[290]

Notorious within this community were the gangs—the Plug Uglies, the Dead Rabbits, and the Bowery Boys—whose members were laborers, butchers, dock workers, gamblers, and full-time criminals. The Plug Uglies and the Dead Rabbits were mostly Irish, and they owed their allegiance to the Tammany Hall Democratic Party; the Bowery Boys were non-Irish, primarily Protestants, whose ancestors had immigrated in earlier periods. They supported the Know Nothing Party. These gangs had much in common with the Roman street gangs.

The Tammany Hall society was an American version of the Roman collegia, which demagogues such as Saturninus, Sulpicius, and Clodius had controlled. Tammany began as a fraternal society but turned into a political machine with its ward bosses running patronage throughout the city, deciding who got jobs and providing assistance to new immigrants in return for their votes. They provided meeting places and legal protection for gang members who worked for them during campaigns and on election day. Thus, the gangster underworld played an important part in city politics, and as the immigrant population grew, Tammany Democrats won most of the elections for local office.

A prerequisite for political activity is an opposition. For the Democrats, political opposition was provided by the landed gentry of the Whig Party and the Know Nothings. The Whigs and Know Nothings disapproved of the election of foreigners to public offices, and they demanded the repeal of Tammany Hall-sponsored naturalization laws that had provided the Democratic Party with a large base of immigrant voters.

As the Democrats and Whigs engaged in political stratagems, the Irish street gangs and the Know Nothing gangs regularly threatened one another and often fought in the streets. By 1855, thirty thousand men owed allegiance to one gang or another. To restore law and order, landowners and business leaders established a reform party to combat disorder and political corruption. The Reform Party didn't have city gangs at its disposal;

---

[290] Charles Dickens, *American Notes* (New York: Crowell) 108.

its main support came from farming and rural areas on the outskirts and beyond the city; and it could influence the legislature in the state capital at Albany.

In 1856, Fernando Wood, the Tammany Hall candidate, ran for re-election as mayor, despite having engaged in blatant corruption during his first term. The night before the election, Mayor Wood ordered most of the police force to stay off duty and away from the polling places, except to vote for the mayor. This left the election in the hands of the gangs, with the Dead Rabbits and Plug Uglies supporting the Democrats, and the Bowery Boys supporting the Know Nothings. After clashes throughout the day, the Dead Rabbits and Plug Uglies overwhelmed the Bowery Boys, and Wood was reelected.

During Wood's second term, gambling and prostitution houses continued to operate flagrantly, and police corruption was rampant. In response, the Reform Party passed bills in the state legislature to disband the city's municipal police, replacing it with the Metropolitan Police Department and commissioners appointed by the governor rather than by the mayor.

In 1857, the new commissioners called on Mayor Wood to disband his police force, but he refused and called on his officers to stand by him. Most did, but about eight hundred resigned and enlisted with the state-authorized metropolitan police. It was only a matter of time before the two forces collided, and on June 16, 1857, a hand-to-hand battle between the forces took place at city hall.

After the police battle, both police forces patrolled the city, but neither could maintain order, and just as the gangs of Clodius and Milo terrorized Rome's streets in 53 BC, so also the New York gangs ran wild throughout the summer months of 1857, fighting each other and terrorizing the citizens. A *New York Times* article of July 6, 1857, reported on a street battle. "Brick-bats, stones and clubs were flying thickly around, and from the windows in all directions, and men ran wildly about brandishing firearms. Wounded men lay on the sidewalks and were trampled upon. Now the Rabbits would make a combined rush and force their antagonists up Bayard Street to the Bowery. Then the fugitives, being reinforced, would turn on their pursuers and compel a retreat to Mulberry, Elizabeth and

Baxter Streets."[291] The fighting continued until two regiments of the state militia were called out to restore order.

The political stalemate over the police authority moved to the courts for adjudication. In the autumn, a state appellate court upheld the Reform Party legislation. The municipal police force was disbanded, and the metropolitan police took over. Normalcy returned for a time, but resentments and grievances simmered until the Civil War brought them to a boil.

In July 1863, draft riots brought a week of disorder, arson, and murder as extreme as, or worse than, the riots in Rome after the death of Clodius. Though many underlying causes existed, the riots began as a protest against the Civil War Conscription Act. To implement the act, President Lincoln issued a proclamation calling for the enlistment of three hundred thousand men. A draft lottery was to be held in New York City at the provost marshal's office on Lexington Avenue and Forty-Sixth Street. All married men between twenty and thirty-five years of age, and all unmarried men between twenty and forty-five were enrolled in the lottery. Those picked in the lottery had to join the army, find a substitute, or pay $300 for an exemption.

For the majority of the working classes and the poor in the city, it was repellant enough to go to war on behalf of slaves, a war with constantly rising death rates, and veterans returning armless or legless. Adding insult to injury was the ability of the wealthy to avoid service by paying $300, which provoked a sense of injustice among those who couldn't afford to pay. On the morning of July 13, 1863, the day the draft was to be held, a general strike was called, and the strikers marched past factories and construction sites, recruiting supporters as they did. A massive column of demonstrators formed, marched to the draft office, and attacked it. Some of the more determined stormed inside, destroyed the lottery wheel, and set the building on fire. From there, the demonstrators turned into a warlike mob, racing to destroy one site after another. The protest turned into a full-scale uprising, and for a few days, it appeared that the rioters would overwhelm the authorities. A writer in the *New York Times* described the roving mob.

---

[291] Herbert Asbury, *Gangs of New York* (New York: A.A. Knopf, 1928) 183.

It is for the most part made up of the vilest elements of the city. It has not even the poor merit of being what mobs usually are—the product of mere ignorance and passion. They talk, or rather they did talk at first, of the oppressiveness of the Conscription Law; but three-fourths of those who have been actively engaged in violence have been boys and young men under the age, and not at all subject to the Conscription. Were the Conscription Law to be abrogated tomorrow, the controlling inspiration of the mob would remain the same. It comes from a source quite independent of that law, or any other law—from a malignant hate toward those in better circumstances, from a craving for plunder, from a barbarous spite against a different race.

Parts of the mob sought African-Americans to attack; some rationalized that while they were being sent to war to fight on behalf of the slaves, no one seemed to care about the economic plight and conditions of the city's poor. Others acted out of racist hatred, and one of their most vile acts was setting fire to the Colored Orphan Asylum on Fifth Avenue.

In the first few days of the riot, the mobs overwhelmed the police. The metropolitan police force numbered 2,297 officers of all ranks. Heroically they battled the mobs but were outnumbered fifty to one. Five regiments from the Union army had to be diverted to the city, and the riot turned into the equivalent of a Civil War battle. Besides burning the draft office and the Colored Orphan Asylum, the mobs burned three police stations, the Second Avenue Armory, and hundreds of other buildings. The mob beat or lynched African-Americans and killed three police officers and fifty soldiers. Total casualties, mostly rioters, were estimated at two thousand dead, eight thousand wounded.

The carnage of the draft riots was certainly as terrible as the worst of the Roman urban riots. Also, the conduct of some political leaders was as irresponsible as that of the worst Roman tribunes. While the metropolitan police, the Union army, and volunteer citizens were fighting the mobs, Democratic Party members of the Board of Aldermen and the state legislature demanded the withdrawal of the police and soldiers from their districts, claiming that the suppression of the riot was too severe. A Democratic Party magistrate pronounced the draft law to be unconstitutional and urged the people to resist its enforcement. Democratic politicians came to the aid of jailed rioters and obtained their release. When all was said and done, only nineteen rioters were tried and convicted. They were sentenced to an average of five years in prison each.

In the twentieth century, economic concerns and racial animosities were the usual precursors to the urban riots that occurred in dozens of northern cities. One example occurred in the city of East Louis, Illinois, which in 1917 was a railroad, industrial, and cattle-processing center. It housed three major stockyards and meat-packing plants, aluminum and steel companies, and twenty-seven railroad lines. As the economy boomed, workers staged labor strikes for higher wages. The company owners opposed union organizers and brought in large numbers of African-Americans from the South to replace strikers and fill job vacancies. Rumors spread that thousands more were on the way to take all the jobs.

In the middle of this tinderbox, at a labor union rally on May 28, 1917, labor leaders shouted inflammatory speeches to large crowds of white workers, fanning the growing mob into the cruel, primitive mob described by Gustave Le Bon in *The Crowd*. About three thousand whites ran through downtown, beating any African-American they could find. On July 1, 1917, an African-American shot a white attacker, and more rioting broke out, lasting several days. By its end, eight whites and thirty-nine blacks were dead, and 312 buildings had been burned.

During the Second World War, job openings again drew southern blacks to northern cities and similar problems arose. In Detroit, Michigan, in June 1943, friction between whites and blacks ignited a riot, which resulted in thirty-four deaths.

After the war, the nature of urban riots changed. What had once been competition between groups for jobs evolved into outbursts by African-Americans living in poor urban ghettoes and enraged by their treatment as second-class citizens. In almost every instance, interactions with white police officers sparked the riots. The complaint was that the police behaved as an occupying force in the black ghetto and treated black citizens with less respect than they gave white citizens. Invariably, when a white police officer shot an unarmed black man, protests would erupt, often leading to riots.

The preaching of several radical activists fueled a growing sentiment in the black community against what was seen as white oppression; the most prominent at the time was Malcolm X. As a member of the Nation of Islam, he gained notoriety for his comment on the 1963 assassination of President Kennedy. Malcolm said it was a case of chickens coming home to roost and added, "Chickens coming home to roost never did make me sad; they always made me glad."[292]

In 1964, Malcolm X broke with the Nation of Islam and began a black nationalist movement, advocating for a separate black nation and black self-defense. On February 21, 1965, at the Audubon Ballroom in Manhattan, he was assassinated by members of the Nation of Islam. His death enhanced his stature and enhanced the sales of his supposed autobiography, *The Autobiography of Malcolm X* by Alex Haley. The book, although embellished with dubious suppositions, became a best seller, spreading Malcolm's ideas and inspiring potential revolutionaries, both black and white.

An annual summer riot cycle began in 1964, with major riots erupting in New York, Newark, Philadelphia, and Chicago. In 1965, a riot in the Watts section of Los Angeles resulted in thirty-four deaths and six hundred buildings burned or looted. In 1966, disorders or riots occurred in forty-six cities across the country. In 1967, the number increased to 33 serious and 123 minor riots. Newark and Detroit were hit the hardest. The situation in Detroit was so dire that Michigan Governor George Romney activated eight thousand National Guard troops and telegraphed President Lyndon Johnson to request, "The immediate deployment of federal troops into Michigan to assist state and local authorities in re-establishing law and order in Detroit ... There is reasonable doubt that we can suppress the existing looting, arson, and sniping without the assistance of federal troops. Time could be of the essence."

On July 24, President Johnson deployed six thousand fully-equipped

---

[292] "Malcolm X Scores U.S. and Kennedy," *New York Times*, December 2, 1963.

federal troops. The Detroit rioters now became insurgents, turning to sniper tactics. On July 26, troops and snipers engaged in gun battles; thirty-six people died that day. In one week, forty-three people died, seventy-two hundred were arrested, and three thousand buildings were looted or burned. That one week of rioting precipitated Detroit's decline from one million residents to less than four hundred thousand and bankruptcy in 2014.[293]

In the aftermath of the riots, President Johnson appointed the National Advisory Commission on Civil Disorders, chaired by Illinois Governor Otto Kerner. The commission's report famously offered a succinct warning. "Our nation is moving toward two societies, one black, one white—separate and unequal."

The report cast the blame for the rioting on racial discrimination against blacks in employment, education, and housing, which had prevented them from obtaining the benefits of economic progress. A national debate ensued, and it seemed for a time that progress was being made to address many of the problems identified in the commission report, and many hoped that riots wouldn't recur. However, on April 4, 1968, Martin Luther King Jr. was assassinated. He was a great civil right leader and an inspiration to most people. His murder, incited the most widespread, long-lasting, and damaging riots the nation had ever experienced. Cities burned, and the violence was of such magnitude that military units had to be called on to suppress it. One hundred thirty cities, including Washington, DC, suffered varying degrees of destruction. The final toll was forty-six people killed, seven thousand injured, and twenty thousand arrested. More than eighty thousand troops were called upon—thirty-six thousand US Army and forty-seven thousand National Guard.

This wasn't a minor disorder; applying a nation's military force to its own citizenry is the stuff of revolutions. When a government uses force, retaliatory force often follows. Radicals incited the crowds with fiery rhetoric, and while most of the rioters were merely looters or criminal opportunists, some were committed revolutionaries.

Dr. King had been a counterweight to those advocating violence,

---

[293] Willard Heaps, *Riots, U.S.A., 1765–1970* (New York: Seabury Press, 1970).

but in the wake of his death, radical groups that advocated "black power" and armed insurrection, such as the Black Panther Party and the Black Liberation Army, gained influence with a substantial segment of the black population. The most violent of the radicals carried out bombings and murders. They waged a war against the police, assassinating or assaulting dozens of police officers in 1971 and 1972. One well-known radical, George Jackson, disdained the nonviolence of Dr. King, writing from prison, "It may serve our purpose to claim nonviolence, but we must never delude ourselves into thinking that we can seize power from a position of weakness."[294]

Major rioting was confined mostly within the black communities and didn't spread beyond. Had radical whites, such as the Weathermen, joined the black radicals and coordinated their activities, the riots might have gained more strength and engulfed other areas. Some attempts were made to form a black-and-white radical coalition, but conflict between the groups scuttled a viable coalition. More importantly, law enforcement efforts, including arrests, indictments, and shootouts, decimated the radical groups, forcing many of the leaders to flee to communist Cuba and other countries. One among those who fled to Cuba was Joanne Chesimard of the Black Liberation Army. She had been convicted of murdering a New Jersey state trooper and in 1979 escaped from prison with the help of three of her associates, who entered the prison with guns and took guards hostage.

Law enforcement put most of the ultra-radical groups on the defensive; the 1980s saw a reduction in the number and intensity of riots. However, tensions hadn't diminished, and the antiwar and Marxist revolutionary causes were replaced by anti-police brutality movements. In 1992, full-scale riots erupted in the aftermath of the Rodney King incident, in which the state of California charged four California police officers with assaulting King. During the incident, police officers pursued King's vehicle for eight miles at speeds in excess of one hundred miles per hour. When King pulled over, the officers tried to arrest him, but he resisted. An officer

---

[294] *Soledad Brother: Prison Letters of George Jackson* (New York: Bantam Books, 1970) 165.

deployed a Taser electric stun gun, knocking King to the ground, but he was undeterred, rose from the ground, and charged toward an officer. Officers began beating King with batons until he allowed himself to be handcuffed. A bystander captured this action on video.

The videos of the beating were repeatedly shown on television stations across the nation, but the events leading up to the beating weren't shown. The reaction of most people to seeing several white police officers beating an African-American man with nightsticks was shock and abhorrence. Nationwide protests against police brutality took place in hundreds of cities. California charged the officers with assault, but when a Los Angeles County jury acquitted them, the worst rioting since 1968 followed. Over six days, the rioting caused the deaths of fifty-three people, two thousand injuries, and $1 billion in property damage. It took the California National Guard, the US Army Seventh Infantry Division, and the US Marines First Division to stop the destruction. All total, eleven thousand persons were arrested.

To quell the public outrage over the acquittals, the US Justice Department stepped in and, despite double jeopardy concerns, indicted the four officers in federal court for violating King's constitutional rights. Two of the four officers were convicted and sentenced to prison on the basis of the same conduct for which the state jury had acquitted them.

The Rodney King incident demonstrated the explosiveness of racial tensions. The possibility of a police incident, particularly a white-on-black incident, sparking disorders and riots in American cities is ever present, and radicals are ever ready to exploit such incidents.

A lesson can be drawn from the Roman Republic. In the first century BC, malicious demagogues and urban mobs threatened violence and exerted an enormous influence on trials, elections, and the political process. The inherent irrationality of the mobs was a major factor in the demise of the republic. In the United States, mobs can be just as irrational and destructive. If the nation enters a period of deep economic crisis or embarks on an unpopular war or a race war, these mobs could become more dangerous than anything the nation has ever seen. How mob action will affect the course of future events is unknown, but what is known is that mob action in Rome contributed to the end of that republic's rule of law. It should not be underestimated here.

CHAPTER 36

The Growing Divide

JUST AS IN ROME where unpopular wars, assassinations, riots, prosecutions, false accusations, and political vilifications widened the divide between *populares* and *optimates*, comparable events in the United States have pushed the left and right wings of the political parties to irreconcilable positions. In Rome, the murders of the Gracchi, Memmius, Saturninus, Drusus, and others were cataclysmic events that led to a series of civil wars, each of which heightened partisan animosity and made domestic political enemies more hated than foreign ones.

In the United States, the assassination of President John F. Kennedy on November 22, 1963, initiated a poisonous period that metastasized into the critical events of 1968. As discussed in a previous chapter, Kennedy's assassination paralleled the assassination of Marcus Livius Drusus, which precipitated the Roman Social War. Although Kennedy's assassination didn't ignite a declared, militarized war as occurred in Rome, it ignited a domestic conflict that encompassed riots, bombings, and assassinations of police officers so numerous and constant that it seemed like the nation was, in fact, experiencing an ongoing civil war.

Kennedy's successor, President Lyndon Johnson, tried to steer the nation on a positive path, enacting his Great Society program designed to alleviate poverty and inequality. However, he was unable to contain the spreading violence, and he compounded the nation's problems by escalating the Vietnam War, thus creating a toxic divide more threatening to national unity than anything since the Civil War. Johnson increased troop levels and ordered bombing raids to destroy the North Vietnamese army, but in what came to be seen as his biggest mistake, he didn't leave the military planning to the generals. He took over the planning of war operations, and his planning was infected by political considerations. His on-again, off-again bombing campaigns gave the enemy respite and time to regroup.

Although the outcome of military operations was uncertain, the Johnson administration consistently told the American public that the war was almost won. This misrepresentation became apparent in 1968 when the North Vietnamese launched the Tet Offensive, making it clear they were far from defeated. Although the US military won the battles in the field, Tet was a political and public relations disaster for Johnson. He didn't seek reelection.

Perhaps the most pointed and valid explanation for the president's Vietnam mismanagement was his obsession with partisan politics. As David Halberstam reported in *The Best and the Brightest,* Johnson "would talk to his closest political aides about the McCarthy days, of how Truman lost China and then the Congress and the White House, and how, by God, Johnson was not going to be the president who lost Vietnam and the Congress and the White House." Unfortunately for Johnson, he lost the White House; more unfortunate was the horrific slaughter of the war on all sides and the deaths of more than fifty thousand American soldiers. Many more were wounded physically and mentally. In 1968, the nation was just beginning to realize what a quagmire it had entered.

Adding to the nation's anger, was the assassination of Dr. Martin Luther King Jr. in April 1968. Then President Kennedy's brother, Senator Robert Kennedy, was assassinated while campaigning to replace President Johnson and end the war in Vietnam.

Antiwar demonstrations escalated, with hundreds of thousands participating across the nation. Communists, foreign and domestic, who hoped for an American defeat, supported the antiwar groups. The more radical of the antiwar groups advocated violence. Groups such as Students for Democratic Action (SDS) and the Weathermen instigated riots at the 1968 Democratic Convention in Chicago and the student occupation of

Columbia University in New York. Their tactics generated a strong public backlash against the demonstrators and left-wing organizations.

Richard Nixon rode the backlash into the presidency as a law-and-order candidate. He espoused the rights of the "silent majority" and castigated rioters, hippies, and bleeding-heart judges. He excoriated some antipoverty programs, thus fueling social division and partisan warfare. Although he reduced the military complement in Vietnam from five hundred thousand to seventy thousand, and tried to achieve "peace with honor," the extrication from that war wasn't fast enough, and the antiwar protests and social revolts continued unabated. To the consternation of leftist partisans, the protests only increased Nixon's general popularity, and he easily won reelection, carrying forty-nine states to one.

Nixon had several major accomplishments that furthered world peace and stability, including the opening of diplomatic relations with China and the signing of an arms treaty with the Soviet Union. However, the Watergate scandal overshadowed his accomplishments and reenergized the forces of partisan division. His resignation shifted the political momentum from the right to the left and led to the election of Jimmy Carter.

President Carter's term was also a time of acute partisanship. Distrust of government and major institutions became watchwords on the left; distrust of liberals and the press became watchwords on the right. Conservative political groups increased their activities and propaganda, and several new think tanks propagated conservative ideas. Right-wing activists attacked their adversaries in both polemical and personal terms.

On both sides, political disagreements turned into ideological hatred and intolerance. A leading Marxist theorist of the time, Herbert Marcuse, advocated the withdrawal of tolerance for right-wing groups or anyone who opposed the progressive collectivization of society. He proposed demonizing Republicans as people who wished the poor to starve, the sick and elderly to go uncared for, and children to be neglected. Conversely, Republicans argued that the welfare state, beyond a basic safety net, undermined the work ethic and the respect for earned success. In keeping with their political beliefs, Republicans criticized programs for the poor and often referred to government social programs and the clients of these programs in pejorative terms. Terms such as "poverty pimps" and "welfare queens" were commonly used, and many people imputed racism to the Republican complaints about social welfare programs. Which side of the debate citizens chose to support wasn't necessarily determined by economic status. Many high-income and wealthy Americans subscribed to leftist positions generally favored by low-income Americans, while many low-income and working-class Americans subscribed to conservative positions wealthy Americans generally favored.

In addition to acute partisanship, President Carter's term also saw economic stagnation, the Iran-hostage crisis, and social discontent. Those difficult circumstances laid the groundwork for the election of Ronald Reagan in 1980.

Within two years of President Reagan taking office, the national climate changed. The economy improved, the public's mood brightened, and international diplomacy turned in positive directions. Whether these dynamics were caused by Reagan's policies or by circumstances beyond any one person's influence is an open question. In any case, Reagan built on the momentum of the improving circumstances, and with his confident manner and extraordinary communication skills, he revived the nation's spirit. Time and again, he delivered inspiring speeches that expressed what had been the ineffable feelings of many Americans.

His televised "Time for Choosing" speech, which he had delivered years before on October 27, 1964, on behalf of presidential candidate Barry Goldwater, was the template for the hundreds of speeches he would deliver as president. In the 1964 speech, he proclaimed, "This is the issue of this election: whether we believe in our capacity for self-government or whether we abandon the American Revolution and confess that a little intellectual elite in a far distant capital can plan our lives for us better than we can plan them ourselves." He said, "And this idea that government is beholden to the people, that it has no other source of power except the sovereign people, is still the newest and most unique idea in all the long history of man's relation to man." He concluded, "You and I have a rendezvous with destiny. We'll preserve for our children this, the last best hope of man on earth, or we'll sentence them to take the last step into a thousand years of darkness." While his speeches were hopeful and positive in style, they were also critical and negative in their attacks on big government. In his speeches, he repeatedly pronounced, "Government is not the solution; government is the problem."

His speeches inspired an energized conservative movement, but his attacks on the government complex generated negative reactions from those who believed a centralized and engaged government benefited the nation. Although Reagan's overall message was positive, his presidency generated further political division and animosity. Left-wing partisans saw Reagan as a serious threat to their beliefs. Coincidentally, Democrats in Congress mounted an investigation into Reagan's administration, which would evolve into the Iran-Contra scandal. They alleged that to get around the Boland Amendment, which prohibited the use of treasury funds to support the Contras, an anti-communist rebel group in Nicaragua, members of the Reagan administration entered into a secret deal in which they sold arms to Iran to raise funds outside the budget and pass the funds to the Contras.

As the investigation closed in on the administration, the president admitted in a televised speech what had occurred and took responsibility. Many left-wing partisans called for his impeachment, but Democrats in Congress decided it wouldn't be to their benefit to bring impeachment proceedings against such a popular president.

Reagan supporters were appalled that their beloved president, whom they believed spoke for them, could be attacked from the left for trying to fight communism in Central America. Democrats justified their actions as necessary to preserve the rule of law. They claimed Reagan had violated the checks-and-balances system by circumventing the will of Congress. As is often the case, the investigation was a mask for the fight over broader ideological issues between progressives and conservatives, a fight that would escalate and threaten the unity of the nation.

As one partisan conflict subsided, another resurfaced. A growing antiwar, anti-imperialism sentiment came into conflict with traditional American pro-military sentiments. In 1991, when the Soviet Union collapsed, it appeared that the Cold War was over and with it the prerequisite for leaders to have military experience. In 1992, President Bill Clinton became the first alleged wartime draft dodger to hold the nation's highest office. In a nation with a long military tradition and a history of choosing presidents with military experience, Clinton's background was a departure from the customary résumé of American presidents. Although Clinton was generally a moderate, many citizens saw him as a representative of the antiwar radicals of the 1960s. To them, Clinton's election confirmed the perception that the radical and revolutionary movements, which had seemed dormant, had only changed their appearances. The revolutionaries had redirected their energies into conventional politics, academia, and journalism to lead the nation toward socialism and egalitarianism. They were increasingly successful, and many secured important positions of influence; Clinton was their most prominent success story until that time.

Those opposed to Clinton found an outlet for their animosity toward him in a scandal involving a White House intern. Republicans mounted an all-consuming and partisan investigation into the scandal, which many saw as payback for Watergate. The investigation resulted in the House of Representatives impeaching Clinton on charges of perjury and obstruction of justice, not in connection with the intern but for lying to a court in a lawsuit involving allegations of his unwanted sexual advances toward another woman. The Senate acquitted the president, but he was disbarred from practicing law for lying to the court. These events further exacerbated the divisions between Republicans and Democrats.

Despite the impeachment, the economy prospered. The nation benefited from the end of the Cold War, relatively peaceful years, and astounding technological advances with computers and the Internet. These favorable conditions allowed Clinton to reduce Reagan's military budget and concentrate on domestic issues. While Congress forced him to "end welfare as we know it," he built on President Johnson's Great Society programs and implemented what might be termed a soft-socialist agenda. His housing and banking policies were designed to uplift people from the lower economic strata into the middle class. Using the 1977 Community Reinvestment Act as authority, his administration implemented "democratization of credit" by lowering the requirements to obtain government-backed mortgages.

His adversaries alleged that President Clinton gained political power by promising benefits to the lower and middle classes but then exercised power by dispensing political favors to the moneyed classes in exchange for financial support. Clinton implemented socialist-leaning policies, but at the same time he implemented policies that directly benefitted the nation's largest banks. At the urging of banking lobbyists to ratify the illegal merger of Citibank and Travelers Insurance, he repealed the Glass-Steagall Act, a perfect example of what Louis Brandeis meant in his book *Other People's Money* about oligarchic combinations of politicians and financiers. This law had been passed in response to the 1929 stock market crash; it separated commercial from investment banking and prohibited banks from mixing depositor funds with proprietary investing operations, a practice blamed as a major cause of the crash.[295] Many critics argued that the repeal, in the combination with the reduced mortgage standards of the Community Reinvestment Act, led to the housing and financial crisis of 2008.

Clinton's presidency was also marred by other scandals. In violation of law, his campaign accepted donations from foreign nationals, several of whom had connections to China. Coincidentally, Clinton pushed for the admission of China into the World Trade Organization. More concerning was the transfer of missile technology to China in 1996 by the Loral Space & Communications Ltd. Company. The technology was transferred to correct problems in the guidance system of Chinese space satellite rocket launchers. The technology was also applicable to the guidance systems of intercontinental ballistic missiles. Such technology transfers had been banned for national security reasons, but Clinton waived the ban. The waiver occurred after Bernard Schwartz, the chairman of Loral, Space & Communications, gave $1.5 million to the Democratic Party in 1996.

While there might have been some putative explanation for the China technology waiver, little justification can be found for a pardon Clinton issued during his last days in office for Marc Rich, which had no explanation other than money. Marc Rich was an enormously wealthy financier, who had been indicted in 1983 on charges of tax evasion and violations of the oil embargo against Iran while that nation held fifty-three Americans as hostages. Rich became a fugitive from justice when he fled to Switzerland.

---

[295] Eric Dash, "A Stormy Decade for Citi since Travelers Merger," *New York Times*, April 3, 2008.

The US government tried to extradite him, but Switzerland refused. Meanwhile, his ex-wife, Denise Rich, donated more than $1 million to the president's party, the senatorial campaign of Hillary Clinton (the president's wife), and the president's library. Miraculously, on January 20, 2001, just hours before leaving office, Clinton pardoned Mr. Rich. He did so despite recommendations from the Justice Department prosecutors and the pardon committee that the pardon for this fugitive wasn't warranted. The *New York Times* called the pardon "a shocking abuse of presidential power."[296] As could be expected, it inflamed the hatred of anti-Clinton partisans and convinced them more than ever of the hypocrisy of those on the left who claimed to be working on behalf of the people but were really working for their own benefit.

Less well-known was Clinton's pardon of sixteen terrorists belonging to the Armed Forces of National Liberation (FALN). This pardon was also difficult to explain. The FALN was a Marxist organization intent on turning Puerto Rico into a Cuban-style communist state. Between 1974 and 1983, its members admittedly carried out more than 130 bombings, several armed robberies, six slayings, and hundreds of assaults as part of their campaign for Puerto Rico's independence from the United States. They pursued their campaign despite the fact that the people of Puerto Rico had consistently voted against independence—only 5 percent had ever voted for it.

Two of the FALN bombings were especially atrocious. On January 24, 1975, a bomb exploded at the historic Fraunces Tavern in New York City, where George Washington had delivered his farewell address to his officers in 1783, and where the Society of Cincinnati had held its annual reunions, a target obviously picked for its symbolic value. The bombing occurred during a busy lunch hour; four patrons were killed, and many others were seriously injured. Then on New Year's Eve, 1982, an FALN bomb exploded at New York City Police Department headquarters, severely injuring three police officers. One lost a leg, another was partially blinded, and the third permanently lost all sight and hearing.

In 1983, the terrorists were convicted of numerous crimes. The FALN

---

[296] Editorial, *NewYork Times*, January 21, 2001.

leader, Oscar Lopez-Rivera, was sentenced to fifty-five years in prison. Then in 1999, despite the deaths and catastrophic injuries the victims had to live with for the rest of their lives, President Clinton pardoned the terrorists because they had supposedly spent enough time in prison. Congress formally condemned the pardons (95 to 3 in the Senate and 311 to 41 in the House).

The pardons were conditioned on the terrorists renouncing future violence. Lopez-Rivera, the FALN leader, refused to do so and remained in prison.

The pardons were granted while Hillary Clinton was running for senator of New York. Some surmise that the Clintons believed the pardons would gain votes for her from among the New York Puerto Rican community. Without having more information about these political relationships, it's difficult to understand how pardoning these terrorists would have translated into Puerto Rican votes for Mrs. Clinton. In any case, it's not difficult to understand how these pardons further exacerbated the divide between citizens committed to law and order on one side and citizens sympathetic to revolutionary, leftist causes on the other.

In the succeeding administrations, as new circumstances and issues developed, the right and left ends of the political spectrum automatically chose opposing positions, and agreement on solutions to controversial problems was almost unthinkable. In each presidential cycle, partisanship and acrimony increased, with the losing side harboring bitterness and resentment against the other.

The partisan divide widened further during the 2000 presidential election between vice president Al Gore and Texas governor George W. Bush. Gore won the national popular vote, but Bush won the electoral college. Gore challenged the results in Florida, where the popular vote count was extremely close and where Bush held a slim lead. Whoever won Florida would win the national election. A recount commenced, and the outcome remained uncertain for weeks. Enmity between the political parties intensified, and when the Supreme Court stopped the Florida recount, Democrats believed the election had been stolen from them. Disappointment on one side and jubilation on the other fanned the flames of partisan animosities, and despite the fact that later recounts by independent agencies showed that Bush had won Florida, the Democratic Party's anger wasn't allayed.

In President Bush's first year in office, the terrorist attack on September 11, 2001, united the nation and abated partisan disputes for a short time. On September 14, 2001, Congress overwhelmingly authorized the use of force against the terrorists wherever they could be found. However, a year later, when President Bush proposed to invade Iraq and depose Saddam Hussein as part of the campaign against terrorism, national unity began to falter, and partisanship resurfaced as strong as ever. The Bush administration argued that the invasion was necessary because Iraq had weapons of mass destruction (WMDs), had sheltered and supported terrorists, and had fired missiles at US planes patrolling the United Nations-mandated no-fly zones. President Bush argued that America needed to fight the terrorists in the Middle East rather than in the United States. This was the same argument Publius Sulpicius Galba had made in 200 BC to the Roman Senate; he said that to defeat Phillip V, the Macedon king who threatened Rome, it was necessary to invade Greece rather than fight him on Italian soil.

Some of those opposed to the invasion claimed that the Bush administration was looking for a pretext to depose Saddam Hussein in retaliation for Hussein's alleged attempt to assassinate the elder George Bush during his presidency. By itself, if true, it would have satisfied the Roman "just cause" standard for initiating a war. Others claimed the real reason for the invasion was to seize Iraq's oil.

The authorization to invade Iraq passed in a divided Congress. The US military swiftly accomplished its mission and dismantled Saddam Hussein's government, but during the occupation of Iraq, native insurgents and outside terrorist groups mounted a fierce resistance. Thousands of American soldiers were killed or wounded, which caused senators and others who had voted for the war to change their stance and attack the president. Some called Bush a liar because WMDs weren't found, some called our troops murderers and Nazis, and others took every opportunity to disparage the president and his administration. This situation recalls Thucydides's remark after the failed Athenian invasion of Sicily in 415 BC. "They turned against the public speakers who had been in favor of the expedition, as though they themselves had not voted for it."

War is the ultimate crucible of a nation's cohesion and viability, and the level of patriotism in wartime reflects a nation's commitment to its own survival. However, unlike the sustained surge of patriotism after the attack on Pearl Harbor in 1941, the surge of patriotism after the 9/11 attacks rapidly weakened. As the shock faded, several among the intelligentsia suggested—some implicitly, some explicitly—that the blame for the attacks should be cast on America's foreign policy, its imperialism, and the capitalistic system that exploits the rest of the world.

Many on the right took the vilifications of President Bush and the military actions as traitorous, as giving aid and comfort to the enemy. They believed the statements sent a message to the Iraqi insurgents that Americans were fast tiring of the war; if the insurgents kept killing US soldiers, the American people would demand a military withdrawal. The insurgents were almost right, but President Bush sent a "surge" of additional troops, stabilizing the situation. Unfortunately, the damage to American unity was irreversible; supporters of the president and the troops felt that the outspoken critics of the war had blood on their hands for the thousands of American soldiers who, they thought, wouldn't have been killed or wounded but for the public statements that encouraged the enemy. On the other side, the critics of the war felt they were loyal and patriotic citizens properly exercising their right to dissent. They believed the invasion of Iraq had been a mistake and not worth sacrificing American lives and treasure. Most of the criticism of the war came from people who genuinely believed their concerns were justified, but pure partisan politics motivated a substantial amount of the criticism.

CHAPTER 37

The Road toward Augustan Despotism

THE AMERICAN FOUNDERS FOUGHT against the despotism of King George III, and they designed their new government to prevent the emergence of an autocracy. Led by Hamilton, Madison, and others, they formulated a mixed system of government as the best means of maintaining the principles of individual liberty, private property, and free enterprise. For Hamilton, more so than Madison, the primary purpose of mixed government was to counteract a populist takeover of government that would infringe on those principles. He clearly leaned toward hierarchy, and he was more critical of the partisanship coming from the popular quarters than from the oligarchy. He believed populism produced demagogues. In *Federalist*, no. 1, he wrote,

> [I]t will be equally forgotten that the vigor of government is essential to the security of liberty; that, in the contemplation of sound and well-informed judgment, their interest can never be separated; and that a dangerous ambition more often lurks behind the specious mask of zeal for the rights of the people than under the forbidden appearance of zeal for the firmness and efficiency of government. History will teach us that the former has been found a much more certain road to the introduction of despotism than the latter, and that of those men who have

overturned the liberties of republics, the greatest number
have begun their career by paying an obsequious court
to the people; commencing, demagogues, and ending
tyrants.

Roman history was the template for how unrestrained partisanship could lead to the subversion of republican principles. Until the last century of the republic, the Romans held their nation together by staying within the parameters of their constitutional system, but when they began breaking traditional rules and threatening the balance of power, they doomed the republic. *Populare* demagogues achieved power and political victories by breaking constitutional traditions and abrogating the checks-and-balances system. Tiberius Gracchus persuaded the tribal assembly to pass his land reform bill over the Senate's disapproval; in the process, he expelled a fellow tribune from the assembly for trying to exercise his lawful veto power. Saturninus coerced senators to swear to support his bills or face exile. Sulpicius overruled the Senate's authority by having the assembly assign Marius to the command against Jugurtha in North Africa and later to assign Marius to replace Sulla in command against Mithridates in the East. Sulla reclaimed his command, and the political discord reached new levels of intensity when the consul Cinna initiated a war against his coconsul, Octavius, which ended with the murder of Octavius.

For a short time, Sulla succeeded in restoring the checks-and-balances system, but upon his death, *populare* forces immediately began rescinding his measures. The powers of the tribunes were restored, and in the following years, the tribune Clodius used potential and actual violence to intimidate his adversaries. Then in 59 BC, Julius Caesar, like Tiberius Gracchus, bypassed the Senate to pass a land reform bill in the assembly. It was as though in the United States the House of Representatives could pass laws without a corollary law passed in the Senate. Again, like Tiberius Gracchus, all legality was abandoned when Caesar, by physical coercion, prevented his coconsul from exercising his lawful veto power.

Populare victories by illegal methods pushed the *optimates* to respond with equally corrupt and illegal measures. Oligarchic factions, led by reactionaries such as Scipio Nasica, Lucius Opimius, Catulus, Lucullus, and Cato, refused to compromise; and they frequently violated the constitution themselves. They abused the power of the senatus consultum ultimum and authorized the deaths of the Gracchi. In 100 BC, they executed without trial the tribune Saturninus and his followers; then again in 63 BC, led by Cicero and Cato, they condemned the Catiline conspirators to death without a trial or appeal.

In the final analysis, as the demagogues of the tribal assemblies succeeded in overruling the decrees of the Senate, the door was opened for ambitious politicians to grab extraordinary powers for themselves. When the assembly abrogated the Senate's authority to assign military commands and granted extended pro-consulships to the triumvirs, they destroyed the balance of their republican government.

Despite the resistance of the oligarchy, the *populares* continued to win victories. These weren't victories of the plebeians over the patricians; the plebeians had already won their equality by political action; they had assimilated into the higher economic and social orders, and they had produced great noble families of their own. To the contrary, the new *populares* didn't assimilate; they undermined the social order, vilified their adversaries, and breached the inviolability of the tribunes and consuls.

The *optimates* eventually tired of fighting, as demonstrated by their frequent losses in the assembly, and many retired as the *populare* victors transformed Rome from an imperfect republic into the autocracy of the Caesars. In America, populist leaders periodically inspired political and economic reforms, and like the Roman *populares*, they pitted the debtors and the poor against creditors and the wealthy. Yale professor Ludwig von Mises wrote, "Public opinion has always been biased against creditors. It identifies creditors with the idle rich and debtors with the industrious poor. It abhors the former as ruthless exploiters and pities the latter as innocent victims of oppressions. It considers government action designed to curtail the claims of creditors as measures extremely beneficial to the immense majority at the expense of a small minority of hardboiled usurers."[297]

---

[297] Ludwig von Mises, *Human Action: A Treatise on Economics* (New Haven, CT: Yale University Press, 1949) **537.**

Banks, conglomerates, and Wall Street have been easy targets for castigation. President Andrew Jackson, the great American populist, railed against the banking establishment and then extinguished the Bank of the United States despite its lawful establishment by Congress and despite a Supreme Court decision upholding its constitutionality. Later populists continued assailing creditors and capitalists—notably, William Jennings Bryan with his "Cross of Gold" speech, Theodore Roosevelt's breaking up the industrial monopolies, and Franklin D. Roosevelt's regulating banks and the economy. But the checks-and-balances system continued to function, and pragmatic compromises were reached that produced beneficial results.

In recent decades, however, ideologues have increasingly supplanted pragmatists, politicians have disregarded the parameters of the checks-and-balances system, and presidents have circumvented Congress to implement their agendas through executive orders and regulations. President Nixon used his budget and administrative powers to advance his own agenda, reallocating authorized funds from some programs or departments to others. He claimed to be enforcing the popular will and refused to spend money Congress had appropriated until a federal district court declared his actions unconstitutional, forcing him to comply with the law.[298] To avoid congressional restraints, President Reagan used arms sales outside the budget to fund anti-communist rebels in Central America. President Clinton tried to legalize what Nixon had tried to do when he persuaded Congress to give him line-item-veto authority, which would have allowed him to cancel appropriations for parts of statutes already enacted into law. The Supreme Court struck down the line-item veto, holding, "There is no provision in the Constitution that authorizes the president to enact, to amend, or to repeal statutes."[299] The Constitution authorized the president to veto only entire bills; he couldn't pick and choose the parts he liked.

President Obama joined the parade of presidents who have circumvented the constitutional authority of Congress. At first, he had no need to

---

[298] *Local 2677 et al. v. Phillips*, US District Court, District of Columbia, J. Jones (1973).
[299] *Clinton v. City of New York*, 524 U.S. 417 (1998).

go around Congress. With the Democratic Party in control of both houses of Congress, he secured a near trillion-dollar spending package, a major health insurance reform (the Affordable Care Act), and the Dodd-Frank Act, which regulated banks and virtually all consumer financial transactions. However, after the historic 2010 Republican landslide election, in which the Democrats lost their majority in the House of Representatives, the president shifted his focus from passing laws in Congress to issuing executive orders and directing federal agencies to promulgate rules and regulations to implement his policies, often in contravention of legislation. Although article 2, section 3, of the Constitution states that the president "shall take Care that the Laws be faithfully executed," Obama failed to execute several important laws as they were written. He enforced laws he favored, changed some by regulations, and ignored others that ran counter to his policies. By picking and choosing which parts of a law he would enforce, the president imposed an unofficial veto, something the courts had rebuffed Nixon and Clinton for doing.

In contravention of the separation-of-powers doctrine, he gave health insurance companies a windfall of $135 billion as part of the Obamacare cost-sharing subsidies, even though Congress had not appropriated the funds, a violation of article 1, section 9, of the Constitution. "No Money shall be drawn from the Treasury, but in Consequence of Appropriations made by Law."

Congress sued the president to stop the allocation of the funds, and in May 2016, a US district court in Washington, DC, ruled that the president had exceeded his authority by earmarking the money for the insurance companies. The judge stayed her ruling to allow the government to appeal; by the time the appellate courts adjudicate the matter, Obama would be out of office.

While the president surely had sound policy reasons for taking measures he thought necessary, highly respected legal experts complained that he had acted unconstitutionally when he usurped the functions of Congress or disregarded it as a coequal partner in government. The laws the president ignored had been publicly debated and passed by the majority. Nullifying the vote of the people, he subverted the democratic process.

Experts pointed out that by arbitrarily negating parts of legislation, the president undermined the basis for political parties to work out bipartisan solutions. As a consequence, when members of Congress found they couldn't trust that the laws would be enforced as passed, they declined to reach compromises with members of the opposing party. Giving up an item in negotiations to the opposing party in return for getting an important item was no longer a viable process because the president might enforce only one party's item but not the other party's item. After 2010, congressional action came to a virtual stalemate. Republicans in the House of Representatives declined to pass laws or take actions the president proposed. For laws passed by the Republican-controlled House, the Democrat-controlled Senate refused to bring them to the floor for debate, so little was accomplished. With Congress in stalemate, President Obama issued more executive orders, and administration agencies issued more regulations, actions that had the de facto effect of law. This was done neither subtly nor privately but openly and proudly. Obama launched a public relations campaign called "We Can't Wait," repeatedly saying, "We can't wait for an increasingly dysfunctional Congress to do its job. Where they won't act, I will."

Appointments to the National Labor Relations Board (NLRB) require the Senate's advice and consent. When the Senate declined to ratify Obama's appointments to the board, the president made "recess" appointments, claiming he could do so because the Senate wasn't in session during a three-day period. Although the Senate didn't consider itself in recess, the president decided it was and made the appointments. The NLRB, with its improperly appointed members, issued more than four hundred decisions that affected labor-management cases. Despite a federal court ruling that the board was illegally constituted, it continued issuing decisions with the president's backing until the 2014 Supreme Court decision in *NLRB v. Canning* unanimously ruled, nine to zero, that the appointments were unconstitutional.

In July 2015, President Obama reached an agreement with Iran in which the United States would rescind economic sanctions on that country, release impounded funds, and even pay interest of 1.5 billion dollars in cash, In exchange Iran would stop or limit its development of nuclear weapons. This agreement fit the definition of a treaty for which the Senate would normally have to confirm by a two-thirds majority. However, the Senate would not have confirmed such a treaty or such payments, so Obama circumvented the treaty requirements and implemented the agreement without Senate approval. This executive action was a major abrogation of constitutional checks-and-balances.

Although it might have seemed that President Obama's actions were just part of the give-and-take of politics, his actions brought to mind the Roman *populares* circumvention of the Senate and their step-by-step challenges to traditional constitutional procedures. The president, instead of seeking compromises on important issues as previous presidents had done in similar circumstances, bypassed Congress. In his 2014 State of the Union address, he told the nation, "America does not stand still—and neither will I. So wherever and whenever I can take steps without legislation to expand opportunities for more American families, that's what I'm going to do."

Not only conservatives but also some liberal/progressives criticized the president's actions. Shortly after the 2014 State of the Union speech, a well-respected constitutional law professor, Jonathan Turley of George Washington University, testified at a House Judiciary Committee hearing that there has been a "massive gravitational shift of authority to the executive branch" and that President Obama has become "the very danger that separation of powers was designed to avoid." Professor Turley pointed to "hundreds of thousands of regulations that are promulgated without direct congressional action and outside the system created by the framers." Turley's testimony was of great import because he supported the president's social policies, yet he had to protest the president's violations of the Constitution. Another renowned legal scholar, Professor Lawrence Tribe of Harvard Law School, published an article, criticizing the president's actions to implement a "Clean Power Plan" through Environmental Protection Agency (EPA) regulations. Professor Tribe wrote, "The brute fact is that the Obama administration failed to get climate legislation through Congress. Yet the EPA is acting as though it has the legislative authority anyway to re-engineer the nation's electric generating system and power grid. It does not."[300]

---

[300] Lawrence Tribe, "The Clean Power Plan Is Unconstitutional," *Wall Street Journal*, December 23, 2014.

In addition to the usurpation of legislative authority, the president brushed aside congressional attempts to oversee executive branch activities. In what came to be known as the fast-and-furious scandal, Congress investigated allegations that US agents had supplied guns to members of Mexican drug cartels. At a committee hearing, the attorney general, Eric Holder, allegedly provided misleading information, made misleading statements, and refused to produce subpoenaed documents. On June 20, 2012, Congress held Holder in contempt, but the president neither fired the attorney general nor appointed a special prosecutor to investigate the matter. In effect, the contempt charge was ignored and forgotten.

Of greater concern to the nation were revelations that members of the Obama administration had used the Internal Revenue Service (IRS) to systematically target and harass political opponents, reminiscent of Nixon's attempt to use the IRS and other agencies to punish his enemies. The question is always, How could they have been so foolish? The answer is always the same: power corrupts.

The president didn't have to give direct orders for his appointees to target his adversaries, but like Augustus, to let his wishes be known, only had to express his opinions, and his people would have implemented his wishes. The IRS scandal provided an example of how this dynamic can work. During the 2010 midterm elections, a grassroots movement of conservative groups, generically referred to as the Tea Party, began to organize. These groups advocated policies averse to those of President Obama and his expansive government agenda. To function efficiently, these groups applied to the IRS for tax-exempt status, which would aid their budgeting and fund-raising. On August 9, 2010, the president warned, "Right now all around this country there are groups with harmless-sounding names like Americans for Prosperity, who are running millions of dollars of ads ... And they don't have to say who exactly the Americans for Prosperity are. You don't know if it's a foreign-controlled corporation." On August 21, 2010, the president in his radio address to the nation referred to "attack ads run by shadowy groups with harmless-sounding names. We don't know who's behind these ads and we don't know who's paying for them ... You don't know if it's a foreign-controlled corporation ... The only people who don't want to disclose the truth are people with something to hide."

Through September and October, the president repeatedly made similar comments.[301] Coincidentally, the IRS and other government agencies began targeting these Tea Party groups by arbitrarily delaying, in some cases for years, their applications for tax exemptions. The IRS didn't similarly target groups supportive of the Democratic Party platform.

As a consequence of the IRS actions, many Tea Party groups were thwarted and significantly weakened for the 2012 election campaign; to some degree, the results of the election may have been affected.

Congress tried to perform its oversight function to investigate the IRS, but the administration's stonewalling thwarted them. Lois Lerner, a key IRS official, asserted the Fifth Amendment and refused to answer questions before Congress about the performance of her duties. Notwithstanding her failure to explain her job performance, the IRS didn't fire her but merely suspended her with full pay until her retirement. Congress held her in contempt for refusing to answer questions, but the Justice Department failed to prosecute her, thus nullifying the congressional action. It has been speculated that the Justice Department didn't indict her because President Obama publicly stated, before the investigation was complete, that "not a smidgen of corruption was involved."

This scandal illustrated the difficulties of holding members of the executive branch accountable and made it clear that citizens had little immediate recourse against an executive branch insulated from outside investigation. In this case, some recompense was attained after the Obama Administration left office. Several Tea Party groups sued the IRS for violating their rights, and in October 2017, a $1.5 million settlement was reached.[302]

Obama's loss of Congress to Republican control greatly diminished his ability to lawfully accomplish his remaining projects. Many people assumed that he would become a lame duck; they underestimated his perseverance. Undaunted, he doubled down on executive actions as a means to achieve his goal of transforming America. Early in 2014, the president said,

---

[301] Kimberly Strassel, "An IRS Political Timeline," *Wall Street Journal*, June 7, 2013.
[302] Emily Cochrane, "Justice Department Settles with Tea Party Groups after IRS Scrutiny," *New York Times*, October 26, 2017.

"We're not just going to be waiting for legislation in order to make sure that we're providing Americans the kind of help they need. I've got a pen and I've got a phone. And I can use the pen to sign executive orders and take executive actions and administrative actions that move the ball forward."[303]

After his losses in the midterm elections, the president bypassed Congress and issued an executive order, implementing major immigration reforms, including the grant of legal status and work permits to approximately five million illegal immigrants. Seemingly, this was a violation of article 1, section 8, of the Constitution, which states, "Congress shall have the power ... To establish an uniform Rule of Naturalization."

By issuing this executive order, the president enacted what Congress had considered but declined to enact. His apparent motivation was to gain for his party the loyalty of the growing Hispanic population by establishing a path to full citizenship, just as Caesar had done for the Gallic population of his Cisalpine Gaul province. The president may not have been thinking of Caesar, but by issuing the executive order, he challenged Congress to do anything about it. Congress did nothing; however, twenty-six states sued to stop the implementation of the order, sending the issue into the courts. In November 2015, the Fifth Circuit Court of Appeals upheld a district court injunction that blocked the administration from implementing Obama's executive order because the president had exceeded his constitutional authority. In June 2016, the US Supreme Court upheld the injunction.

The president justified his executive orders on the grounds that Republicans in Congress had blocked legislation he favored. He seemed to forget that Republicans are Americans, and for some issues congressional Republicans represent the views and wishes of more than half of all Americans. By issuing executive orders, the president had disenfranchised those Americans. On a particular issue, if more than half of the population, whether Republican or Democrat, reject a proposed law and a president autocratically imposes his views on them by dictate as a substitute for the rejected law, he violates the democratic principle of majority rule.

---

[303] Bill Archer, "The Obama Uncertainty Principle," *Investor's Business Daily*, January 28, 2016.

As the Obama term neared its end, a political crisis arose over his chosen successor, the Democratic Party presidential nominee, former secretary of state Hillary Clinton. During the congressional investigation into Clinton's conduct in relation to the terrorist attacks on the US consulate in Benghazi, Libya, it was discovered that she had used an unauthorized personal e-mail system to conduct official State Department business, transmitted classified and top-secret material over the system, and destroyed voluminous e-mail records in violation of the law.

Congress held additional hearings to investigate the unauthorized e-mail server system. During the hearings, Secretary Clinton testified that she hadn't sent or received classified information on her personal system. She also testified that she had turned over all work-related e-mails to the State Department.

The Justice Department and the FBI conducted a year-long investigation. The administration failed to appoint an independent special prosecutor to conduct the investigation despite the obvious conflict of interest of the administration's investigating a cabinet member and the person whom the president had endorsed as his successor.

The FBI investigated whether classified information had been improperly stored or transmitted on Clinton's personal system in violation of a federal statute, making it a felony to mishandle classified information either intentionally or in a grossly negligent way, or in violation of a second statute, making it a misdemeanor to knowingly remove classified information from appropriate systems or storage facilities.

FBI Director James Comey announced that he had taken personal charge of the investigation. At the time, Director Comey enjoyed an incredibly favorable press. He had an outstanding reputation as a straight shooter, as someone above partisan politics who had stood up to his bosses in the Bush administration. President Obama praised his "fierce independence and deep integrity." He seemed almost a modern Cato the Younger, ready to prosecute his political ally, Licinius Murena, for election bribery. However, as it turned out, Comey was no Cato.

Skepticism about the integrity of Comey's investigation was raised when it was revealed that the Justice Department had not empaneled a grand jury, had not issued subpoenas for documents and computers, and had given immunity to five of Clinton's staffers without obtaining grand jury testimony from them. Skepticism was heightened by the fact that Secretary Clinton's lawyers had used Bleachbit on her e-mails to prevent their recovery and had destroyed her mobile devices, actions that in legal forums are regularly used to establish a "guilty mind" and "intent."

On July 7, 2016, Director Comey, in an unusual press conference, announced the results of the investigation, which found that Secretary Clinton had, in fact, sent, received, or stored classified information on her personal system. From indirect sources the investigation recovered thousands of e-mails Clinton had tried to delete, including more than fifteen thousand work-related e-mails that hadn't been turned over to the State Department, as Clinton had claimed before Congress and before a federal judge in a civil lawsuit under the Freedom of Information Act. Nevertheless, Director Comey announced that he wasn't recommending a prosecution of Secretary Clinton, saying, "Although there is evidence of potential violations of the statutes regarding the handling of classified information, our judgment is that no reasonable prosecutor would bring such a case."

Many critics said there were plenty of reasonable Republican prosecutors who would have brought such a case. Comey's explanation for his recommendation not to prosecute sounded like something Thomas Jefferson once called "legal twistifications." Comey said it would have been difficult to prove that she intended to violate the classified information laws, but section 973 of the United States code regarding the protection of classified information does not require intent but only "gross negligence." Comey said Clinton had been "extremely careless," a phrase that sounds remarkably like the equivalent of gross negligence, yet Comey nonetheless defended his recommendation not to prosecute.

The failure to prosecute was a further erosion of the rule of law and added to the common perception that the rules for the politically connected are different from the rules for the average person—that some in the government are above the law. Tyranny occurs not only when an administration acts unfairly against citizens but also when it fails to hold accountable its own members who violate the law.

In Rome, it wasn't one man who undermined the rule of law and transformed the republic into a dictatorship but a series of men who seized power by demonstrating more ability and ruthlessness than their competitors. Men such as Marius, Sulla, Pompey, and Caesar paved the way for Augustus. They transformed the republic from a nation that worshipped and abided by the rule of law into a nation that succumbed to legal and political chaos, and thus they established the preconditions for the people to submit to the protection of a strongman.

Augustus was the culmination of the march to dictatorship. He won military battles, cemented strategic alliances, and destroyed enemies one after another. His political acumen was undeniable, and as his stature rose, he gained the support he needed to transform the nation. Although he pretended to be a freely chosen leader, he was a military dictator who had seized control by buying armies and threatening the Senate. When he gained control of the state's revenues, he dispensed them for his own purposes; when he gained control of the courts, he transformed a purportedly democratic-republican government into a despotic autocracy.

The extent and complexity of our society militates against one man or woman taking control and establishing a tyrannical despotism in one lifetime, but it is not inconceivable that a succession of men and women, building on the work of their predecessors—decade after decade—could effectively establish a totalitarian despotism.

President Obama's term in office was a dry run for a tyrannical executive branch that would dominate all aspects of American life. His presidency established a road map for transforming one form of government into another while keeping the same names. Had Obama been more successful, had he maintained the Augustan artful deception of appearing as the restorer of the republic while dismantling it, had he persuaded rather than confronted, and had he kept the Democratic majority in Congress, he might have been able to fully achieve his goal of "fundamentally transforming America." However, the Democrats suffered a resounding defeat in the 2014 midterm elections. They lost control of the Senate, nine Senate seats, additional seats in the House of Representatives, five governorships, and hundreds of other elective positions. These losses weakened Obama's ability to enact his agenda. While he maintained the support of his base constituency, he lost favor among the broader population—first, because of legislative paralysis; second, because of the administration scandals; and third, because of foreign policy mistakes. In the end, he was unable to transform America as he had hoped.

Another president at another time or a series of presidents over a period of time, with more competence and acumen, might easily pick up the big-government mantra and lead the nation down the path to complete executive branch control. The courts repeatedly restrained President Obama, but if a future president gains full control of the judiciary, as Augustus controlled the Roman jurists, our nation will be vulnerable to the autocratic will of the executive.

CHAPTER 38

Transforming America

SENATOR BARACK OBAMA COULD have been a Roman demagogue. As the Roman *populare* demagogues, in the name of the plebeian class, attacked the *optimates*, so also Obama, in the name of the poorer classes, attacked the rich. He ran a skillful and effective campaign for president primarily on a platform for egalitarian policies, health insurance reform, transparency in government, and bank regulation. He promised to transform America by protecting civil rights, resetting foreign relationships, and distributing wealth in a more equitable manner.

With his great speechmaking abilities, Obama tapped into the vestigial instinct to elevate leaders to Olympian stature. As Julius Caesar and Augustus enhanced their images by the means available to them—for example, coins, statues, festivals, rituals, and deification—Obama used the mediums of modern image making to raise his stature far above the run-of-the-mill politician. At his nomination party in Denver, Colorado, he spoke from a stage with giant faux-classical columns as his backdrop. Wherever he spoke, his eloquent speeches gained for him the allegiance and even adoration of millions.

He claimed to be a unifier, saying, "There is not a black America and a white America and Latino America and Asian America—there is the United States of America." However, once in office, he quickly resorted to partisan politics. To gain popular support, he escalated class warfare and expressed enmity for those who opposed him, regularly excoriating big business and the rich. He accused doctors of performing unnecessary surgery, insurance companies of abandoning customers, pharmaceutical companies of price gouging, bankers of reckless greed, and energy companies of polluting the environment. His demagoguery had its effect, and after solidifying his left-wing base of support, he began his plan to transform America, a goal not likely to proceed without an explosive clash with the right wing.

In the first year of his term, partisanship worsened with the passage of the Affordable Care Act (ACA), popularly known as Obamacare, a law the president considered his most important legislative achievement. The one-sided manner in which the act was passed alienated the Republicans and exacerbated the animosity between the parties. With inadequate time for senators to read or debate the bill, and due to last-minute parliamentary maneuvers in the Senate, the two-thousand-page bill passed by one vote on Christmas Eve with only Democratic votes. The sheer immensity of the bill demanded compromise. The law disregarded the prudent warning James Madison gave in *Federalist*, no. 62. "It will be of little avail to the people … if the laws be so voluminous that they cannot be read, or so incoherent that they cannot be understood." Opponents of the law and some who saw themselves as a target of the president's disparaging rhetoric responded with increasingly bitter and hateful language, sounding rather like the Roman *optimates*, who claimed the demagogues were inciting the "rabble" to seize autocratic power.

Adding fuel to the fires of class warfare, President Obama targeted and vilified "special interests" or wealthy individuals and corporations. He claimed that through large campaign contributions, they controlled the political process to the detriment of the general public. In his 2011 State of the Union address, with members of the Supreme Court seated directly in front of him, he criticized the court's decision in *Citizens United v. Federal Communications Commission*, which had held that the First Amendment allowed American corporations to spend unlimited funds for political advocacy.[304] Obama stated, "Last week, the Supreme Court reversed a century of law to open the floodgates for special interests—including

---

[304] *Citizens United v. Federal Communications Commission*, 558 U.S. 310 (2010).

foreign corporations—to spend without limit on our elections. Well, I don't think American elections should be bankrolled by America's most powerful interests, and worse, by foreign entities. They should be decided by the American people, and that's why I'm urging Democrats and Republicans to pass a bill that helps to right that wrong." To be accurate, the ruling didn't overturn the ban on foreign contributions to elections. In any case, putting aside the inaccuracies of the president's characterization, his words sent a strong signal to his political operatives in the executive branch to take whatever actions they could to counteract the influence of "America's most powerful interests." His words conformed to the tenets of the burgeoning progressive, anti-capitalist movement within the Democratic Party.

Throughout his presidency, Obama assailed core Republican Party principles, and Republican animosity toward him ran so strong that partisans vehemently criticized him, even in areas where his policies copied those of President Bush. As a candidate, Obama campaigned against the Iraq War and for the repeal of controversial provisions of the anti-terrorism Patriot Act; however, as president, he initially followed Bush's military plan in Iraq and even expanded the war in Afghanistan. He continued most of the anti-terrorist practices of the Bush administration, including increased surveillance of American citizens. In addition, he increased the prior administration's drone missile strikes, killing more than two thousand people in foreign countries.

On the receiving end of Republican Party criticism, President Obama responded with equal truculence. As the campaign for his second term in office approached, he returned to the class-warfare rhetoric of his first campaign. Speaking to an audience of Latinos, he urged them to vote against their "enemies." He referred to "fat-cat bankers," and in the last days of the campaign, he urged his supporters to vote for "revenge." He didn't specify on whom to take the revenge, but based on his rhetoric, one could fairly surmise that he meant large corporations, banks, Wall Street, and the wealthy. His hate-the-rich and hate-Republicans rhetoric wasn't very different from the demagoguery of the *populare* radicals against the patrician *optimates*.

In the election campaign of 2012, a Democratic advertisement portrayed the Republican vice presidential candidate Paul Ryan as pushing an elderly woman in a wheelchair over a cliff. As for Mitt Romney, the president's challenger, the Obama campaign spent millions of dollars to impugn his character and destroy his reputation, prompting the *Wall Street Journal* editorial to note, "President Obama spent his formative years in academia, so he's no doubt familiar with postmodernism, the literary theory that rejects objective reality and insists instead that everything is a matter of interpretation and relative 'truth.' At any rate he's running the first postmodern Presidential campaign, now organized almost exclusively around allegations about his opponent that bear no relation to the observable universe."[305]

President Obama blamed the real estate and financial crash of 2008 on the "failed Republican policies of the past." He blamed Republicans for the financial crisis when Democrats were as much to blame as anyone. He blamed bankers and Wall Street without acknowledging that they had acted in accordance with President Clinton's housing and lending policies and his repeal of the Glass-Steagall Act.

Obama's castigation of Wall Street and the banks fed a wave of class envy that helped him win reelection despite a relatively poor record in his first term. Although he had borrowed and spent nearly a trillion dollars on a stimulus package, the unemployment rate remained high throughout his term, the gross national product stayed weak, poverty levels worsened, debt increased to record levels, the nation's credit rating was downgraded, and the gap between black and white living standards grew wider. Nevertheless, like Pliny's racing fans rooting for their team's colors, Obama's fans kept rooting and voting for him.

In his second term, problematic issues arose with the implementation of the Affordable Care Act. Although the law had been passed three years earlier, the public began to learn that many citizens would lose their private insurance coverage and the ability to keep their doctors. It also became clear that the president and his party had misled the public about the contents of the bill when they promised numerous times, "If you like your insurance, you can keep it. If you like your doctor, you can keep him."

---

[305] Editorial, *Wall Street Journal*, June 10, 2012.

As the public learned that the Affordable Care Act had been sold under false pretenses, the president's approval ratings dropped significantly to a point lower than his predecessor's during the worst years of the Iraq War. Partisanship also reached new heights. A study by Alan Abramowitz, a leading scholar of polarization at Emory University, found that between 1978 and 2012, the percentage of voters with extreme antipathy to the opposing party tripled, and nearly two-thirds of voters expressed anger at the other party's presidential candidate.

The hope that the Obama presidency would unify the nation was unfulfilled. The standing divide between right and left shifted from a disagreement about the best means to improve the state of the nation to a disagreement about the very nature of American society and government. The right subscribed to a philosophy of limited government, less regulations, fewer entitlements, and a nationalistic outlook; meanwhile the left adopted a big-government progressivism that included a socialist agenda, sympathy for communist movements, and a "Lennonite" globalism in the mold of John Lennon, imagining a world without nations or religions.

Just as the Roman *populare* radical reform movement evolved from the Gracchan revolution to the autocracy of Caesarism, American populism evolved from a focus on land and financial reforms into a progressivist agenda for government control and domination of society. Its evolution can be traced from the Homestead Acts of the 1860s, the "Cross of Gold" speech of William Jennings Bryan in 1896, and the communistic movements of Huey Long and presidential candidate William Z. Foster in the 1930s to the far-left wing of today's Democratic Party, with its emphasis on racial, gender, and economic inequality.

During the Obama administration, the progressive and radical groups seized on police incidents, particularly on white-on-black police shootings, to energize their supporters. They used police incidents in Ferguson, Missouri; Staten Island, New York; Baltimore, Maryland; and Dallas, Texas, to spur anti-police demonstrations that turned into riots. These demonstrations included overheated and often-fallacious demagoguery that accused the police of endemic racial animus toward Afro-Americans, the kind of rhetoric that could reach angry and unstable people who were readily susceptible to calls for violence.

In the Dallas incident on July 1, 2016, many of the demonstrators wore military clothing, bulletproof vests, gas masks, and automatic rifles slung over their shoulders. As the demonstrators marched, a deranged man, using a high-powered rifle, suddenly began shooting at the police officers who were policing the demonstration. Five officers were killed, and seven others were wounded. Police killed the shooter, and the subsequent investigation disclosed that the shooter had been incited by anti-police rhetoric.

In the Ferguson and Baltimore incidents, the demonstrators protested the failure to indict the police officers involved in the death of black suspects, and the demonstrations turned into riots. In Baltimore, the district attorney, to placate the rioters, indicted several officers. At their trials, the officers were acquitted, inciting new demonstrations and riots.

In Rome, Clodius and Milo prosecuted each other for organized street violence. Threats and violence disrupted their trials. Clodius's two trials were dismissed for fear of mobs, and Milo's trial was disrupted by violence at the court and abandoned. Rome's vaunted respect for law and adherence to legal process was rendered null and void, and in America, mob actions surrounding trials have increasingly threatened to undermine the legal process.

Dr. Thomas Sowell, the noted historian, economist, and philosopher, described the problem of using indictments and trials to placate mobs.

> Do we want people punished based on other people's preconceptions, rather than on the facts of the individual case? Apparently there are ranting mobs who do, and many in the media who give them a platform for spouting off, in exchange for the mobs' providing them with footage that can attract an audience ...
>
> If grand juries are supposed to vote on the basis of what mobs want, instead of on the basis of evidence that they see—and which the mob doesn't even want to see— then we forfeit the rule of law and our freedom that depends on it.[306]

---

[306] Thomas Sowell, "Is the Rule of Law, So Hard-Won, Now Optional?" *Investor's Business Daily*, December 9, 2014.

A difference between these recent incidents and disturbances from prior years was the coalescing of black and white protesters. In some cities, more whites than blacks protested, indicating the formation of new coalitions and associations that could be stronger than those of earlier periods. Race, ethnicity, class, and religion have been important factors in the formation of mobs in the past, but today political partisanship is the most powerful factor, bringing together persons from all groups who share the same attachments.

Groups committed to fighting police brutality, racial and gender discrimination, economic inequality, capitalism, and other issues have combined to form large and powerful coalitions, and the Internet facilitates the coordination of group members who will take to the streets and engage in violence. This growing network of activists raises the possibility of mass protests undermining the rule of law and inciting what could become lynch mob justice through improper indictments.

In a nation with stark divisions, access to instant communications, and a populace susceptible to propaganda and emotional appeals, the threats of violence posed by radical revolutionaries shouldn't be underestimated, and support for these revolutionaries from some of our political leaders should be of concern. Clear inferences can be drawn that some of our highest political leaders harbor sympathies for revolutionary causes.

In the last days of President Obama's term in 2016, he granted unconditional clemency to Oscar Lopez-Rivera, the FALN terrorist whom President Clinton had tried to pardon in 1999. Obama decided to give the clemency despite the fact that Lopez-Rivera was the leader of a terrorist group that had murdered many people. Apparently, Obama agreed with those who had made Lopez-Rivera a hero in the same category as Che Guevara, the murderous Cuban revolutionary whom the left idolized. Apologists for Lopez-Rivera offered that one man's terrorist is another man's freedom fighter, but freedom fighters don't blow up innocent, unarmed people by sneaking bombs under their feet.

Upon the release of Lopez-Rivera from prison in 2017, he was to be honored at the New York City Puerto Rican Day Parade as a "National Freedom Hero" until protests from the police and other groups forced him to drop out. The pardon did not advance Obama's goal of transforming

America into a more equitable society, but it widened the social and political divide, and ratcheted up the level of partisan political hatred.

Obama's presidency did not transform American in accordance with his progressive visions, but it exacerbated the nation's polarization, which carried over into the next administration.

CHAPTER 39

Modern Proscriptions

ALEXIS DE TOCQUEVILLE PREDICTED that the growth of centralized government, even in America, would lead to a soft tyranny; and the
evidence is mounting that his prediction will prove to be an understatement. He didn't foresee the ingenious methods modern central governments would use to oppress their citizens.

He predicted a soft tyranny for America rather than the hard tyranny
of the dying Roman Republic. He was surely familiar with the draconian
measures Roman politicians imposed on their adversaries, especially
through proscriptions. Time and again, during the civil wars, Roman
citizens were proscribed with no justification other than simple affiliation with a defeated opposition party. Proscription meant death or exile.
Of course, most of the proscribed chose exile if they could, but they lost
their property and the right to bequeath an inheritance. Marius used de
facto proscriptions to murder his adversaries and steal their property, and
Sulla responded in kind, though he couched it in the legality of the official
de jure proscription with the prior approval of the assembly. Antony and
Augustus used proscriptions with a vengeance. After the civil war between
them, Augustus used proscriptions to crush those who had opposed him,
taking the land and property of entire towns that had supported Antony.
What property Augustus didn't take for himself, he distributed to his
associates and soldiers.

In America after the Revolutionary War, the government proscribed

English loyalists, confiscating their property and even executing some. When the United States was formed, the Constitution banned such proscriptions. It banned bills of attainder, thus preventing the legislature from identifying particular groups and declaring them guilty of an offense. It also banned corruption of blood, thus preventing the legislature from punishing the descendants of a convicted traitor or nullifying his or her rights of inheritance. However, these protections have eroded as our government hasn't always abided by the spirit of those laws. The internment of Japanese-Americans during the Second World War is a prime example.

In recent years, confiscations by our government, or what might be termed "soft proscriptions," have increased to an alarming extent, differing only in form, degree, and complexity from those of Rome. More indirect, impersonal, and corporate, the proscriptions usually play out within regulatory or legal contexts that lack the violent aspects of Rome's proscriptions; nonetheless, they have devastating effects. Targeted individuals aren't exiled, but their property is confiscated through administrative penalties, fines, lawsuits, and forfeitures. Under the Obama administration, confiscations increased to levels far greater than at any time in our history.

When President Obama took office, his goal was to redistribute wealth, which meant taking money and property from some to give to others, even if he had to disregard constitutional due process. He forecasted his position in an interview he gave in 2001 as an Illinois state senator to WEBZ radio. When asked about the Constitution and Supreme Court activism, he clearly found the document and the court's interpretation of it inadequate for his purposes. He stated,

> The Supreme Court never ventured into the issues of redistribution of wealth, and of more basic issues such as political and economic justice in society ... [The Supreme Court] didn't break free from the essential constraints that were placed by the Founding Fathers in the Constitution, at least as it's been interpreted, and the Warren Court interpreted in the same way, that generally the Constitution is a charter of negative liberties.

[It] says what the states can't do to you. [It] says what the
federal government can't do to you, but [it] doesn't say
what the federal government or state governments must
do on your behalf.

To facilitate what the government must do—in other words, redistribute wealth—the obvious measure was to raise taxes on the rich, but
Obama could raise taxes on the rich only to a limited degree, not enough
to finance his goals. Other means had to be used, and the president wasn't
reticent. He publicly announced, "We're gonna punish our enemies, and
we're gonna reward our friends"; and in a radio interview with Univision,
he urged Latino voters to do the same on his behalf.[307] If the "enemies"
were foreign adversaries, it would have been one thing, but the president's
enemies were American citizens with investments in banks, energy companies, and large and small corporations.

Large banks, practicably and symbolically, presented the most inviting
targets. Using the 2008 financial crisis as justification, the administration
filed hundreds of lawsuits and regulatory actions against the largest banks.
The basis for many of these actions arose from the Bush administration's
attempt to stabilize the financial markets by encouraging or coercing the
large banks—Bank of America, J. P. Morgan Chase, and Wells Fargo—to
buy several troubled institutions that were on the brink of insolvency.
The large banks complied by buying Countrywide Financial, Bear Sterns,
Merrill Lynch, Washington Mutual, and Wachovia Bank.

Allegations were made that the troubled institutions had engaged in
fraudulent practices in connection with mortgage lending and collateral-
ized debt obligations (CDOs); however, since the troubled institutions no
longer existed, the administration sued the large banks for actions of the
troubled banks that had been consummated before they were taken over.
Irrespective of the help that the large banks had given to end the crisis,
they became defendants from whom the government extracted billions
of dollars in penalties.

JPMorgan Chase was on the receiving end of a barrage of regulatory

---

[307] Daily Caller.com, October 25, 2010.

actions and lawsuits. Some say the bank was targeted because Jamie Dimon, chief executive officer of the bank, had publicly criticized the policies of President Obama and implied that he shouldn't be reelected. He also called the Dodd-Frank legislation "downright idiotic." The bank was targeted despite the fact that JPMorgan Chase was the strongest bank in America, hadn't needed a government bailout during the financial crisis, and in the midst of the crisis had stepped forward at the request of the government to buy two of the collapsing financial institutions—Bear Stearns and Washington Mutual. The government extracted tens of billions of dollars in fines and settlements. The *Wall Street Journal* editorial board summarized the situation this way: "Federal law enforcers are confiscating roughly half of a company's annual earnings for no other reason than because they can and because they want to appease their left-wing populist allies."[308] In addition, as further punishment of the bank's shareholders, the bank had to spend $28 billion on legal expenses trying to protect their interests.

Bank of America was also sued. It held out for years but eventually settled for $17 billion rather than risk a trial. Bank of America's sin was buying, at the request or demand of the government, the collapsing firms Countrywide Financial and Merrill Lynch.

Allegations were made that financial institutions that openly opposed the administration were sued, while others that had been supportive and had ties to the administration weren't; it was also alleged that even if they were sued, administration supporters were given favorable treatment and allowed to settle for less than nonsupporters.

Citibank settled for $7 billion for the tainted CDOs (collateral debt obligations) it had issued. To the uninitiated, it is difficult to understand why the Citibank settlement was so much less than the settlements of JPMorgan and Bank of America. Citibank issued more tainted CDOs in its own name than the other banks did; it had more risk on its balance sheets than any of the other banks, and it had to have the government bail it out three times. To understand the more favorable treatment of Citibank, the revolving door between Citibank officials and Democratic

---

[308] Editorial, *Wall Street Journal*, October 21, 2013.

administrations must be considered. Timothy Geithner, a protégé of Citibank's Robert Rubin, President Clinton's secretary of the treasury, became President Obama's first secretary of the treasury. When Geithner resigned, Jacob Lew, who had worked in the unit at Citibank that handled the "toxic" mortgage CDOs, succeeded him as Obama's second secretary of the treasury.

Another bank that appeared to receive relatively favorable treatment from the government was Goldman Sachs, the giant financial investment firm. Goldman Sachs was a major creditor of the AIG Insurance Company when that firm entered a government-sponsored bankruptcy. In an unusual outcome for a bankruptcy settlement, Goldman Sachs received 100 percent on the dollar, while other creditors received far less. Coincidentally, Goldman Sachs and its employees were the second largest group of donors to the 2008 Obama presidential campaign, and before and after the bankruptcy settlement, Lloyd Blankfein, the firm's chief executive officer, publicly supported administration policies.

Overall, by 2014, the Obama administration extracted over $127 billion from the large banks or, more accurately, from the shareholders of those banks. The money extracted came not only from the very wealthy but also from middle-class Americans who owned bank stocks through pension and retirement funds. Adding salt to the wounds, the money extracted from the bank shareholders was distributed not to the investors allegedly defrauded by the CDOs but to housing-activist groups associated with the Democratic Party and borrowers in democratic areas, whose default or failure to stay current on the loans had contributed to the crisis. A substantial part of the money was used to reduce the interest or principal owed by the defaulting borrowers—a neat way to redistribute wealth.[309]

Another means the government used to attack the banks was by filing or threatening to file lawsuits alleging racial discrimination in the banks' lending practices. None of the lawsuits were based on cases of actual, intentional discrimination; they were brought on a theory of statistical disparate impact. This theory ignored other credit factors that could have

---

[309] Editorial, *Investor's Business Daily*, August 28, 2014; Dan Epstein, "Masking Bank Shakedowns by DOJ as Public Services," *Investor's Business Daily*, July 8, 2015.

accounted for differences in loan rates between racial or ethnic groups. The banks denied the allegations and argued that any difference in loan rates was attributable to nondiscriminatory factors, such as poor credit ratings or employment histories. However, rather than fight the government, the banks settled and paid billions of dollars to avoid unfavorable publicity and costly litigation. None of the cases were litigated to completion, and no actual liability in any case was ever proved.

Whatever the merits of the disparate impact theory were, the confiscated funds were neither distributed to actual victims of discrimination nor deposited in the US Treasury; the funds were distributed to a national network of favored left-wing community organizations allied with the Democratic Party.

The Obama administration used substantial amounts of the money extracted from banks and other businesses to fund programs Congress wouldn't fund in the budget. Supposedly, Congress has the power of the purse, but the administration now had its own purse to fund programs run by activists groups; no doubt most of these groups will work on behalf of Democratic Party candidates. Kimberly Strassel of the *Wall Street Journal* wrote, "It works like this: The Justice Department prosecutes cases against supposed corporate bad actors. Those companies agree to settlements that include financial penalties. Then Justice mandates that at least some of that penalty money be paid in the form of 'donations' to nonprofits that supposedly aid consumers and bolster neighborhoods. The Justice Department maintains a list of government-approved nonprofit beneficiaries. And surprise, surprise: Many of them are liberal activist groups."[310]

It also appears that besides favoring political friends, the administration marked for prosecution those it saw as political adversaries.

Another financial institution the Obama administration targeted was the Standard and Poor's rating agency (S&P). Prior to the financial crisis of 2008, the three major rating agencies—S&P, Moody's, and Fitch—had been equally involved in the rating of the critical mortgage CDOs, and all three agencies had given high ratings to the securities. Then, in 2012,

---

[310] Kimberly Strassel, "Justice's Liberal Slush Fund," *Wall Street Journal*, December 4, 2015.

S&P downgraded the credibility of the US debt, while the two other rating agencies didn't. Reportedly, Obama administration officials, including Treasury Secretary Geithner, made veiled threats to S&P. Then, in 2013, the administration sued S&P for what it claimed were fraudulent or negligent CDO ratings. The government didn't sue the other two rating agencies, making the lawsuit look suspiciously like the use of government power to punish an entity that had embarrassed the administration.

The public rarely empathizes with financial institutions, and little concern was voiced about the fairness of the government actions. Under such conditions, financial executives and major investors were reticent to publicly complain about their treatment. Nonetheless, sometimes jokes or off-hand remarks expose what people are thinking to themselves in all seriousness. On September 20, 2013, Warren Buffett, the renowned billionaire investor, made a telling remark during an interview he gave on CNBC television. When asked about the government lawsuits against the banks, he expressed caution, saying, "If you think something the government is doing is unfair, it is unwise to express it on national television."

On October 22, 2013, in an interview on Bloomberg Television, Mr. Buffett was more specific. Discussing a $13 billion settlement that the federal government had extracted from Mr. Dimon and JPMorgan Chase, Buffett said, "If you're a financial institution and you're threatened with criminal prosecution, you have no ability to negotiate. You pay what's asked. You've got a gun to your head. Basically, you've got to be like a wolf that bares its throat. When it gets to the end, you cannot win."

Buffett has always been a realist, and the reality he saw was government despotism of the kind that can strangle American freedom. As governmental power has increased and intruded into all aspects of society, many businesses and individuals, out of fear of government disapproval and retaliation, have altered their conduct and have become reluctant to exercise their rights of free speech, a sure sign of tyranny.

While banks have been the most prominent targets of government regulatory actions, an increasing number of smaller businesses and individuals have been targets of government confiscatory practices. Federal asset-forfeiture laws designed to combat organized crime have been regularly used against otherwise-lawfully functioning businesses and individuals. These draconian forfeiture laws allow the federal government, before a trial or conviction, to seize a defendant's funds without a judicial hearing to establish that the funds were the proceeds of a crime. The defendants, without access to their funds, are often prevented from hiring competent attorneys, investigators, and experts. Consequently, in the overwhelming majority of such cases, the defendants are compelled to plead guilty to criminal charges or settle a civil lawsuit under terms set by the government.

With thousands of federal laws and regulations to choose from, the government can easily find some law with which to prosecute or sue any company or individual engaged in business. Furthermore, with broad discretionary powers, the government can charge some while not bothering others. An interesting case involved the Gibson Guitar Manufacturing Company. In 2009 and 2011, federal agents from the Environmental and Resources Division of the Justice Department raided Gibson's offices and factories in Nashville and Memphis, Tennessee. The agents seized computers, files, guitars, and rosewood and ebony fingerboards. Gibson's alleged crime had been to import the rosewood from India and the ebony from Madagascar in violation of the Lacey Act, which prohibits importing flora or fauna in violation of a foreign nation's laws.

The rosewood, ebony, and finished guitars seized were worth more than a million dollars, and the seizure of the raw materials crippled the company's production. The seizure by the government without first conducting a hearing was an egregious violation of due process because Gibson had documents from India and Madagascar showing that those governments didn't consider the exportation of the wood unlawful. Nevertheless, because Gibson couldn't resume manufacturing with the criminal prosecution hanging over its head, in 2012 it entered into a deferred prosecution agreement with the Justice Department.

In the agreement, the Justice Department explained that it deferred prosecution regarding the wood from India because "certain questions and inconsistencies now exist regarding the tariff classification of ebony and rosewood fingerboard blanks pursuant to the Indian government's Foreign Trade Policy. Accordingly, the Government will not undertake enforcement actions related to Gibson's future orders, purchases, or imports of ebony or rosewood fingerboard blanks from India." The government agreed that its seizure of the wood from India had been wrong; however, they wouldn't concede regarding the wood from Madagascar, and the settlement was based on that. Gibson agreed to pay a $300,000 fine and a $50,000 payment to the Fish and Wildlife Foundation.

Circumstantial evidence raised the suspicion that partisan politics had motivated the prosecution of Gibson. The catalog of Gibson's main competitor, C. F. Martin & Company, showed several guitars made of the same kind of wood seized from Gibson, but C. F. Martin was never raided or prosecuted. Coincidentally, the CEO of C. F. Martin & Company had contributed to Democrats, while the CEO of Gibson had contributed to Republicans.[311]

Smaller businesses have also been subjected to prehearing and pretrial property seizures and forfeitures. A law frequently used against small businesses is the Bank Secrecy Act, which requires banks and other financial institutions to report cash deposits greater than $10,000. The law was designed to counteract "structuring," in which criminals intentionally try to hide the proceeds of their crimes by keeping their deposits below $10,000. Although the law was designed to catch drug dealers and other racketeers, the government has used the law to go after run-of-the-mill business owners who have committed no crime. The government can impound the money in the bank accounts of these owners without filing a criminal complaint. The owners must then prove they are innocent to get the money back, and most cannot afford to fight the government, so they settle.

The Internal Revenue Service (IRS) is just one of several federal agencies that pursue these cases. The IRS doesn't track the number of cases it pursues, but the Institute for Justice, a public-interest law firm, found 639 seizures by the IRS in 2012. In only one of five of these cases were criminal charges filed. Most of the other cases settled with the targeted business forfeiting substantial amounts of money.[312]

---

[311] John Fund, *Obama's Enforcer* (New York: Broadside Books, 2014) 23-28.
[312] Shaila Dewan, "Law Lets I.R.S. Seize Accounts on Suspicion, No Crime Required," *New York Times*, October 25, 2014.

Individual property owners have also felt the might of the government. One egregious case went all the way to the Supreme Court. Mr. and Mrs. Sackett owned a two-thirds acre residential lot in Idaho. The lot lies just north of Priest Lake but is separated from the lake by several lots containing permanent structures. In 2007, to prepare for constructing a house, the Sacketts filled in part of their lot with dirt and rock. Some months later, the Sacketts received a compliance order from the Environmental Protection Agency (EPA), which ordered them to remove the dirt and rock, and restore the property under an EPA work plan. The EPA contended that the Sacketts had polluted wetlands in violation of the Clean Water Act; however, their contention was subject to legal debate. Federal jurisdiction under the Clean Water Act encompassed navigable waters. Priest Lake was a navigable body of water. The question was whether the Sackett lot, several building lots from the lake, was connected to the lake. The Supreme Court had addressed similar issues in previous cases, and the outcomes of those cases were neither clear nor consistent. Thus, with the ambiguities of judicial precedents on which to rely, the Sacketts challenged the order rather than immediately comply.

Under EPA regulations, however, a party who doesn't immediately comply with an order is fined $75,000 per day, and the EPA fined the Sacketts. They sued to stop the fines, claiming that the order was arbitrary and capricious. In response, the EPA argued that the Sacketts hadn't exhausted their administrative remedies. The district court agreed with the EPA and ruled that the Sacketts' lawsuit was premature. Meanwhile, the $75,000-per-day fines continued to accumulate. The Sacketts appealed to the Ninth Circuit Court of Appeals, which ruled against them, holding that the Clean Water Act precluded pre-enforcement judicial review of compliance orders and that such preclusion didn't violate due process of law.

The Sacketts then appealed to the US Supreme Court, which in 2012 unanimously reversed the Ninth Circuit, holding that the couple was entitled to due process and judicial review of the EPA action. This didn't mean they had won the case; it meant only that they were entitled to a judicial hearing to contest the EPA finding that their residential lot was connected to navigable waters. In a concurring opinion, Justice Samuel Alito wrote,

"The reach of the Clean Water Act is notoriously unclear. Any piece of land that is wet at least part of the year is in danger of being classified by EPA employees as wetlands covered by the act, and according to the federal government, if property owners begin to construct a home on a lot the agency thinks possesses the requisite wetness, the property owners are at the agency's mercy."[313]

The Sacketts were among the few who could bear the costs of a five-year legal battle with the federal government. Most others in their position couldn't have afforded to resist such government tyranny. The EPA issues approximately fifteen hundred compliance orders per year, and most of the recipients have no choice but to comply.

The Gibson guitar case, the Sackett case, and many other cases recall the sentiments that Thomas Paine expressed before the Revolution when he wrote, "We still find the greedy hand of government thrusting itself into every corner and crevice of industry, and grasping the soil of the multitude. Invention is continually exercised to furnish new pretenses for revenue and taxation. It watches prosperity as its prey, and permits none to escape without a tribute."[314]

Like the victims of the Roman proscriptions, whose names have been lost to history, thousands of American citizens and small businesses have been financially ruined by government "soft" proscriptions. Most are not heard from because they don't have the means to mount a protest.

---

[313] *Sacketts v. EPA*, 566 U.S. 120 (2012).

[314] Thomas Paine, *Rights of Man, Part the Second* (Norwalk, CT: Heritage Press, 1961).

CHAPTER 40

Military Leadership and Foreign Entanglements

GEORGE WASHINGTON WANTED THE nation to avoid foreign entanglements, but that hope quickly proved impossible. From the quasi-war
with France in 1798 onward, the US has been continually involved in conflicts with foreign nations. Under such circumstances, military experience
was considered a primary qualification for the presidency, and throughout the nineteenth century, the majority of presidents had been military
generals. However, in the twentieth century, this trend reversed, even as
the nation fought two world wars. The only general elected president in
the twentieth century was Dwight Eisenhower, the commander of the
allied armies in Europe during the Second World War. He might be the
last general ever to become president, which would be a clear indication
of the nation's changing attitudes and character.

Eisenhower's success as a military commander stemmed from his
study of military history, including Roman military history. In his childhood reading, his first hero was Hannibal. He wrote, "Every ground commander seeks the battle of annihilation; so far as conditions permit, he
tries to duplicate in modern war the classic example of Cannae."[315] In
January 1945, Eisenhower employed the double envelopment maneuver
Hannibal had used at Cannae for his plan to encircle and capture the
German army in the Ruhr Valley. His plan succeeded, and at the news con-

---

[315] Dwight Eisenhower, *Crusade in Europe* (New York: Doubleday, 1948) 325.

ference to announce the victory, General Walter Bedell Smith proclaimed, "Of all the campaigns I have known this one has followed most exactly the pattern of the commander who planned it. With but one small exception, it proceeded exactly as General Eisenhower originally worked it out."[316]

The Second World War generation might be the last to consider at least some military experience as a required qualification for the presidency. Presidents Lyndon Johnson, Richard Nixon, and Jimmy Carter served but didn't see major combat. Gerald Ford served as a lieutenant commander in the navy and saw action on the USS *Monterey*. John F. Kennedy and George H. W. Bush saw major combat. Kennedy commanded a torpedo patrol boat in Japanese-controlled waters in the Pacific. A Japanese destroyer rammed and sank his boat, and the eleven-man crew swam to a deserted island, where they hid until they were rescued six days later. Bush flew fifty-eight combat missions. On one mission, Japanese anti-aircraft fire shot down his plane, and it crashed in the ocean. A US submarine rescued him from the water.

After the Vietnam War, military leadership or service lost its primacy as a presidential qualification. Neither Bill Clinton nor Barack Obama or Donald Trump served even in peacetime. Senator Bob Dole, a wounded war veteran, lost the election to Clinton, and Senator John McCain, who had been a prisoner of war in Vietnam, lost the election to Obama.

This trend away from military primacy hasn't been confined to the presidency. The number of senators and congressmen who served in the military declined from 386 to 118, and many were elected based on their protests against the Vietnam War. The US Supreme Court, which always had at least one member with military experience, lost its last veteran when Justice John Paul Stevens retired in 2010. Presently, not one member of the court has served in the military.

President Nixon ended the military draft to avoid repeating the problems encountered with draftees during the Vietnam War and to counteract the antiwar movement, which was led primarily by affluent youths, who would be less inclined to protest once they were no longer subject

---

[316] Richard Ambrose, *Supreme Commander*, (New York: Penguin Random House, 2012) 612.

to the draft. Eliminating the draft was a step along the same problematic path Rome took when Marius revolutionized the army by recruiting landless citizens into the legions, which changed the character of the legions because many soldiers, rather than returning home after serving a year in a province, remained in the province to await the arrival of the next proconsul. They became a permanent cadre, almost a mercenary class. Consequently, fewer citizens had to serve in the legions, and this fact changed the character of the nation.

Today American volunteers who serve in the armed forces represent only a small percentage of the population, and the majority of citizens have lost direct contact with the military and the pride of military service. The wars in Iraq and Afghanistan have been fought for almost two decades by a cadre of approximately two million soldiers—less than 1 percent of the population and a fraction of the sixteen million who served during Second World War. Today's soldiers serve repeated tours of duty, while the rest of the population remains uninvolved.

Although moving to an all-volunteer army enhanced the quality and efficiency of the military, it exempted most of the population from military service, training, and discipline. Thus, the concept of reciprocal obligation that requires citizens to render military service in exchange for the rights and benefits of citizenship seem inapplicable to the general population, and many citizens have become ambivalent about the nation's military endeavors. The ramifications are difficult to calculate. It may be that the public will tolerate small wars fought by volunteers, but if the need arises to fight a large war, in which a greater number of citizens would have to participate, it's questionable whether the nation could muster the necessary effort.

The United States could be suddenly forced into an all-out war requiring the full participation of the nation. In the first days of the Second World War, General Eisenhower learned the perils of sending untrained and unprepared recruits into battle. He advised, "Thorough technical, psychological, and physical training is one protection and one weapon that every nation can give to its soldiers before committing them to battle, but since war always comes to a democracy as an unexpected emergency, this training must be largely accomplished in peace. Until world order is an accomplished fact and universal disarmament a logical result, it will always be a crime to excuse men from the types and kinds of training that will give them a decent chance for survival in battle."[317]

Since Vietnam and the end of the Draft, Eisenhower's advice has been largely ignored, and the nation has lived under the delusion that our nation would never suffer a major attack or be drawn into a war not of our choosing. However, in 1979, when the revolutionary guards of the Islamic Republic of Iran seized the American embassy in Tehran and held fifty-two diplomats and other personnel hostage for 444 days, an undeclared war began. Since the seizure of the embassy, Iran has supported terrorist attacks on the United States, either through its own agents or through proxy organizations. In Beirut, Lebanon, two devastating attacks occurred in 1983. On April 18, 1983, the US Embassy was bombed, killing sixty-three people, seventeen of them Americans. A jihadist organization took credit for the attack, claiming, "This is part of the Iranian revolution's campaign against imperialist targets throughout the world."[318]

On October 23, 1983, the US Marine barracks in Beirut was bombed by a suicide-truck bomber; 299 soldiers were killed, including 241 Americans; 225 of them were marines. The soldiers were part of a United Nations peacekeeping force. It was the single deadliest day for the US Marine Corps since Iowa Jima in the Second World War. Shortly thereafter, the United States and the UN withdrew their forces from Lebanon. The United States didn't respond forcefully enough to discourage additional attacks. Its response was limited to diplomatic protests and economic sanctions, which had limited effect. In 2004, the Iranian government erected a monument in Tehran to commemorate the 1983 bombing and the terrorist "martyrs."

Another conflict arose in 1991 when Saddam Hussein's Iraq army invaded Kuwait. President George Bush the elder assembled a US-led coalition of more than four hundred thousand troops that defeated the Iraq army in just six weeks, a textbook case of how overwhelming force

---

[317] Dwight Eisenhower, *The Crusade in Europe*, 158.

[318] Terry Anderson, "Bomb Kills 28 at U.S. Embassy," *Syracuse Herald Journal*, April 18, 1983.

should be employed to decisively win a war. The war strategy appeared to follow the advice of General MacArthur, speaking before a Joint Session of Congress in 1951. "Once war is forced upon us, there is no alternative than to apply every available means to bring it to a swift end. War's very object is victory—not prolonged indecision. In war, indeed, there can be no substitute for victory."

Surprisingly to many, after the initial victory, President George H. Bush limited the goal of the war to the ejection of the Iraqi army from Kuwait. Although ample justification existed for proceeding to Baghdad and toppling Hussein, the president chose to withdraw the troops and leave Hussein in power. Apparently, he did so because he saw Hussein as a bulwark against Iran.

After the war, the United States suffered more attacks by Middle Eastern terrorist organizations. On February 26, 1993, the North Tower of the World Trade Center in New York was bombed, killing six people. On June 6, 1996, Khobar Towers, a US Air Force housing facility in Saudi Arabia, was bombed, killing nineteen airmen. On August 7, 1998, US embassies in Kenya and Tanzania were simultaneously bombed, killing 224 people and injuring more than four thousand. On October 12, 2000, the USS *Cole*, a missile destroyer, docked in the harbor of Aden, Yemen, was bombed, killing seventeen sailors.

The United States investigated these attacks as criminal acts and arrested some of the responsible individuals, but again, the United States did not respond forcefully enough to discourage additional attacks; thus, the attacks escalated until the devastating attacks by the Al-Qaeda terrorists on September 11, 2001, in New York, Washington, and Pennsylvania. Appeasement in the Middle East has never worked. When Osama bin Laden declared war on the United States in 1996, he cited American weakness, taunting, "Where was this false courage of yours when the explosion in Beirut took place in 1983?" He also cited the American withdrawal after the 1993 Black Hawk Down incident in Mogadishu, Somalia. "You left the area carrying disappointment, humiliation, defeat and your dead with you."

The American equivocation in the Middle East leading up to the 9/11 attacks in many ways resembled the Roman equivocation in North Africa, leading up to the Jugurthine War. Lessons can be drawn from this history. Rome claimed the role of ruler and arbiter over foreign territories, making it the target of revolts and the enemy of other ambitious nations. In an equivalent way, the United States has exercised its military and economic might and has assumed the role of the dominant world power, making it the natural target of resentments and rebellions. When Rome equivocated instead of confronting head-on the challenges to its hegemony, the eventual costs in lives and resources escalated exponentially. Similarly, when the United States failed to decisively defeat those who attacked Americans, it encouraged additional attacks.

After the September 11, 2001 attacks, President George W. Bush retaliated by bombing Afghanistan where Al-Qaeda had been harbored and invading Iraq in 2003. Going further than his father, President George Bush the younger proceeded to Baghdad and toppled Hussein and his government. After the initial military victory, however, Bush limited the number of occupation forces and the rules of engagement because of domestic criticism of the war. This limiting strategy proved ineffective, and in 2007, Bush reversed course and ordered a troop surge to crush the insurgents. The surge restored stability and decimated the Al-Qaeda terrorist organization that had been operating in Iraq. By 2009, the United States had aggressively asserted its power and gained control of Iraq.

With the presidency of Barack Obama, however, US military policy shifted from offensive to defensive. The president endeavored to fulfill his campaign promise to withdraw US troops from Iraq. On December 14, 2011, at Fort Bragg, Georgia, the president announced the withdrawal of the last remaining troops, stating, "We are leaving behind a sovereign, stable, and self-reliant Iraq, with a representative government that was elected by its people."[319]

The president issued the order to withdraw from Iraq against the advice of his generals and senior cabinet members. Many critics thought it was a strategic error not to leave a residual force and a military base from which to maintain security, political influence, and intelligence

---

[319] Charles Krauthammer, "Iraq's Collapse Dates to 2011 Abandonment," *Investor's Business Daily*, May 22, 2015.

capabilities. As events unfolded, the vacuum left by the withdrawal weakened the new Iraqi government and allowed reconstituted insurgent groups to pose a serious threat to that nation and surrounding nations. The vacuum also left many of those who had put their lives on the line to aid the US Army vulnerable to retaliation by insurgents; the withdrawal was seen as a betrayal that undermined American credibility. Moreover, by relying too heavily on diplomatic negotiations with untrustworthy adversaries, the president allowed a host of more serious and dangerous problems and conflicts to develop.

In Libya, President Obama joined a military campaign to oust the Libyan dictator, Muammar Gaddafi. However, he didn't order a robust military commitment but limited the campaign to airstrikes in support of various rebel groups. The airstrikes helped the rebels bring Ghaddafi to justice, but the vacuum in Libya allowed extremist Islamic groups to gain control within strategic areas of the country. No American or allied occupation force was employed to maintain order or provide support for the institution of a new government.

In the ensuing chaotic state, on September 11, 2012, the anniversary of the 9/11 attacks, the American consulate in Benghazi, Libya, was attacked; and four Americans, including the ambassador, were killed. Subsequent to the attack on the consulate, the chaos spread, and in September 2014, the United States had to close its embassy in Tripoli and withdraw all personnel from that country.

Other errors in Egypt and Syria contributed to the loss of American influence and prestige. In Egypt, during the mass anti-government protests, called the "Arab Spring," the president made the decision to abandon President Hasni Mubarak, who had been an American ally for thirty years. In doing so, he created a vacuum that allowed the previously outlawed Muslim Brotherhood, an organization that had engaged in and supported terrorist activities, to take control of the Egyptian government. He then endorsed the Muslim Brotherhood's legitimacy and supplied it with weapons, including tanks and jet fighters, despite that organization's imposing a theocratic autocracy in contravention of the majority's wishes. Subsequently, in June 2013, thirty million Egyptians took to the streets in the largest peaceful demonstrations in history to protest the regime and support a military coup that ousted and banned the Muslim Brotherhood.

As for Syria, President Obama announced that Bashar Assad would be removed from power within a year. He encouraged rebel groups to overthrow him and provided them with training and equipment but not enough to defeat Assad's army. When evidence arose that the Syrian regime might use chemical weapons, the president publicly warned the regime that it would pass a "red line" if it used chemical weapons in its military operations against pro-democracy rebel groups. When Syria, in fact, used chemical weapons, it was assumed that the president would bomb the regime as punishment for doing so, but the president backed off and didn't order bombing or other retaliation. By not backing up his word, he again undermined American credibility, and thus he encouraged the Syrian regime to increase the indiscriminant bombing of its own people. Aleppo, the second largest city in Syria, and a stronghold of the rebels, was bombed and reduced to rubble. Hundreds of thousands were killed or forced to flee as refugees.

President Obama wasn't the only president reluctant to commit forces to the Middle East, but his stated policy of withdrawal or only limited involvement highlighted the reduction of American influence. His policies were tantamount to transferring American hegemony to other powers and forces.

His reluctance to remain forcefully engaged became most apparent with his failure to take timely action against the rise of the self-proclaimed Islamic State in Iraq and Syria (ISIS), the new insurgent terrorist group that rushed into the power vacuum. In 2013, this group announced its intention to establish an Islamic caliphate. It recruited a coalition of the most extreme radical Islamists, disaffected Sunni Muslims, and former military personal from the Saddam Hussein regime. Conducting a hellacious campaign, they conquered substantial territory in Iraq and Syria, forced Christians to convert to Islam or be killed, and murdered many Iraqis who had cooperated with Americans, including the judge who had sentenced Saddam Hussein to hang. ISIS murdered people by crucifying them, beheading them, or burying them alive; and forced more than a million people to flee their homes to avoid the slaughter. While this event was occurring, the United States didn't take decisive action against ISIS, giving the terrorists time to recruit as many as thirty thousand fighters. Then, in the spring and summer of 2014, having grown in strength, ISIS defeated the Iraqi army and took control of several cities, including Ramadi, Fallujah, and Mosul; the latter, the second largest city in Iraq, had a population of more than a million. In Mosul, ISIS stole millions of dollars from bank vaults and seized the military equipment left behind by the fleeing Iraqi army, including more than two thousand Humvee vehicles. The United States had supplied the equipment.

In the summer of 2014, ISIS threatened the Yasidi people, a religious minority, with genocide, forcing them to flee from their homes to mountains in Kurdistan. When ISIS began to overrun Kurdish forces at the Kurdistan border, threatening the American embassy in the capital city of Irbil, President Obama finally ordered air strikes to stop the terrorist advance.

When asked why he hadn't ordered air strikes or other action sooner, the president explained, "We did not just start taking a bunch of airstrikes all across Iraq as soon as ISIL [ISIS] came in because that would have taken the pressure off Iraq's Prime Minister Nori al-Maliki. ... and those Shiites would have thought: 'We don't have to go through the difficult process of figuring out what we've done wrong in the past. All we have to do is let the Americans bail us out again. And we can go about business as usual.'"[320] This statement raised the question of how many innocent people ISIS terrorists had crucified, beheaded, or buried alive while Obama applied political pressure on al-Maliki to resign. It also raised the question of just how ruthless a president can be—in this case, passively ruthless.

In August 2014, ISIS broadcast videos of the beheadings of two American journalists and a British aid worker. These men and others had been held captives for more than a year, and the United States had been unable to rescue them. The videos were shown on the Internet and televisions around the world. In response to public outrage over the beheadings, the president was forced to announce an expanded military campaign against ISIS, and the United States began bombing its strongholds in

---

[320] Thomas Friedman, "On the World," *New York Times,* August 8, 2014.

Syria. However, the genie was already out of the bottle as ISIS rampaged across the Mideast and North Africa, demonstrating its viciousness with escalating atrocities, including mass beheadings. Some critics argued that had President Obama acted sooner, using the full strength of the United States, he could have quickly defeated ISIS before its successes strengthened it. Had he maintained and asserted a strong American posture in the region, the chaos and slaughter may have been avoided; millions of people, families, and children may not have been expelled from their homes and forced to become refugees and suffer hardships and destitution.

The situation the United States faces in the Middle East and North Africa in many ways resembles not only the situation the Romans faced with Jugurtha but even more so the situation in 90 BC when Mithridates VI, the king of Pontus on the Black Sea, began testing Roman power by seizing regions in Roman provinces. Mithridates proclaimed that he intended to eject Rome from the East and reestablish an eastern empire, of which he would be the overlord. Rome, divided by internal conflicts, equivocated about taking action and sent envoys to negotiate. In 88 BC, sensing Rome's weakness, Mithridates ordered the execution of all Latin-speaking people in the territories he controlled in Asia Minor. Eighty thousand Roman citizens or allies were slaughtered.

In Rome, political infighting prevented an immediate counterattack; and in the meantime, Mithridates took advantage and seized control of Athens and other Greek cities. When Sulla was able to take his army to the East, he tracked Mithridates for three years and in 85 BC cornered and defeated him. However, despite the atrocious slaughter three years earlier, Sulla negotiated a lenient peace treaty because of the domestic conflicts still plaguing Rome. Mithridates had only to withdraw to the borders of his kingdom and cease his aggression. He didn't have to pay reparations for the destruction and deaths he had wrought.

Predictably, Mithridates didn't abide by the peace treaty, and he again seized territories and incited rebellion in Roman provinces. Finally, in 66 BC, the Roman Senate gave Pompey an extraordinary commission to eliminate the threat. In 63 BC, Pompey won several battles that led to diplomatic victories and control of the region. Mithridates committed suicide. Although Pompey accomplished his mission, this was another case in which Rome should have acted immediately after the first attack, before the 88 BC slaughter. Had it done so, it would have saved eighty thousand lives and decades of savage warfare.

In the wake of 9/11, the United States asserted its power in Afghanistan and Iraq, but it didn't effectively deal with its most formidable enemy in the Middle East—Iran. During the US occupation of Iraq after 2003, intelligence agencies uncovered evidence that Iran's military arm, the Quds force, had secretly armed and aided the insurgents in Iraq and supplied the roadside explosive devices that killed more than one thousand American soldiers. The United States never held Iran responsible for those deaths, and when President Obama took office, he offered to negotiate agreements with Iran.

As for the victims of the Beirut bombings in 1983 and the Khobar bombing in 1996, the US government told the victims to sue Iran. Some did, filing claims that senior officers of the Iranian government directly supported, approved, and assisted in carrying out the attacks. In 2005, a US district court found Iran liable for the Beirut embassy attack and awarded $320 million in damages to forty-seven American victims. Similar judgments have been found against Iran for the 1983 Beirut marine barracks bombing and the 1996 Khobar Towers bombing. Although victims in the three cases prevailed in court, they have been unable to enforce the judgments and haven't been paid.[321]

In response to Iran's clandestine war against the United States and Iran's violations of UN resolutions regarding the production of nuclear weapons, the United States imposed economic sanctions, freezing Iranian assets in international banks. By 2015, the sanctions were having an effect on the Iranian economy, and the Iranians agreed to negotiate. On July 14, 2015, an agreement was reached for Iran to curtail its nuclear activities in exchange for a lifting of the sanctions. More than $100 billion in frozen assets were released to Iran. No mention of Iran's terrorist activity was made. No provisions were made to pay the judgments to the victims of

---

[321] Anne Dammarell, "Iran Owes Millions to Victims of Its Terrorism," *Wall Street Journal*, June 18, 2015.

the Beirut and Khobar bombings. No agreement was reached to free four American citizens held prisoner in Iran.

While it may be hoped that this agreement will improve relations between the United States and Iran, reduce the terrorist activities, and further the interests of peace, that remains to be seen. Many experts predict that it's more likely that the agreement will prove to be an irresponsible appeasement to an ambitious terrorist state. If history repeats itself, this agreement and the continued appeasement of Iran will lead to less peace and more devastation in the same way Rome's appeasement of Jugurtha and Mithridates led to more death and devastation in the same regions of the world.

CHAPTER 41

Trump Arrives

THE ELECTION OF PRESIDENT Trump was like throwing gasoline on the already burning fires of partisanship. Leftist were incensed, and many vociferously insulted those who voted for him. The Trump voters were equally incensed at what they saw as unjustified attacks on themselves and their president.

The Trump election shifted the traditional paradigm of American politics. It demonstrated that a populist movement can come from the right as well as the left. Populist movements stem from resentments of the common people against the elites. Left-handed populists seek to disrupt the social order; they focus on the economic elites, whom they perceive as exploiters of the poor and working classes. Right-handed populists also seek to disrupt the social order but do so by rejecting the social elites, whom they perceive as undermining traditional, national values. Trump rode the right-handed populists to the presidency and has since become the focus of every conflict in America. Since his election, political vitriol has escalated, and comparisons to Roman civil strife have become even more frequent than before. Like the Roman *populare* protests at the homes of unpopular consuls, demonstrations against Trump erupted at his home at Trump Tower in New York City where protesters called for his removal by any means possible. Signs carried by protesters and postings on the Internet maliciously depicted him in the worst manner, often as a target of violence.

The Romans did not have the Internet, but they were known to display the severed heads of politicians stuck on the top of poles. In America, a well-known comedienne posted a photograph on the Internet of herself holding what appeared to be the bloody severed head of Donald Trump. She was only pretending, but the thought was the same.

During the 2017 summer season at the Delacorte Theater in Central Park, New York City, Shakespeare's play *Julius Caesar* was performed. The leading character was costumed in modern dress, unmistakably to resemble Donald Trump with his distinctively-styled reddish-blond hair, blue overcoat, white shirt, and long red tie. The play was an allegory for the Trump presidency. In the assassination scene, the Roman senators repeatedly stabbed Trump/Caesar until he fell, his white shirt soaked in red blood. The New York audience enthusiastically applauded. Although only make believe, this event was a strong indication of the nation's deep divide.

A real event occurred on July 14, 2017, in Alexandria, Virginia, when an extreme leftist, distraught over the election of President Trump, opened fire with a high-powered rifle at a group of Republic congressmen practicing for a baseball game. Four people were shot, including Congressman Steven Scalise, the majority Republican whip.

Another real event occurred on August 12, 2018, in Charlottesville, Virginia, when alleged Neo-Nazi, white nationalist groups demonstrated against the removal of a statue of Civil War Confederate General Robert E. Lee. Leftist counterdemonstrators equated the white nationalists with Trump and used the event as a means to protest Trump and his supporters.

The white nationalist groups were armed with bats and helmets, and were clearly ready to fight. The counterdemonstrators were likewise armed, and serious fighting ensued. One of the white nationalists intentionally drove his car into the crowd, killing a woman and injuring several other people. This battle, although involving only a miniscule percentage of the population, epitomized the national polarization.

The battle instigated a movement across the nation to remove statues and plaques commemorating Confederate leaders. Throughout history, removing or restoring statues and plaques of controversial figures has frequently been the spark that ignited political violence. In Rome, Marius ordered the destruction of a monument commemorating Sulla's capture of Jugurtha. When Sulla came to power, he ordered the removal of monuments to Marius. Caesar restored the Marius monuments, and by doing so, he sent a message that he was reigniting the conflict between the pro-Marian *populares* and the pro-Sullan *optimates*. Similarly, the recent American controversy over historic statues and monuments signals that the nation is on a dangerous course toward a major internal conflict.

President Trump aggressive actions, his extraordinary energy, his embrace of every controversy, and his media omnipresence have super-charged partisan animosities and eroded the chances for resolving conflicts through negotiation and compromise. Instead of rational debate, partisans ignore facts and attack their opponents with hyperbolic claims. Climate-change-believers attack non-believers as though they were Holocaust deniers. Advocates for reasonable gun control are accused of leading a totalitarian takeover. Those seeking tighter immigration and border controls are called bigots and racists.

When the Democrats lost the election to Trump, as a departing salvo, they set in motion a collusion-with-Russia narrative, apparently hoping to drive Trump from office or cripple his presidency. They used operatives to dig up and publicize dirt on him and his associates, and this led to the appointment of a special counsel charged with investigating and prosecuting members of the Trump campaign, if not Trump himself. Some critics contended that the dirt and the collusion allegations were fabrications designed by a cabal of Democratic Party conspirators.

In response, the Republicans instituted congressional investigations of alleged unlawful acts committed during the Obama administration and the Clinton campaign. They alleged that members of the Obama Justice Department engaged in politicized activities rather than impartial law enforcement and unlawfully spied on the Trump campaign.

Criminalizing politics is a dangerous game. The current political warfare is not dissimilar to the periods when the Romans regularly used prosecutions as political weapons. The back-and-forth Roman prosecutions exacerbated animosities and led to civils wars, which led to the dictatorships of Cinna, Sulla, Caesar, and Augustus.

The initial actions taken at the beginning of the Trump administration further infuriated his adversaries. He decimated programs and policies of the Obama administration, and he imposed a travel ban of people from several predominately Muslim countries. He used executive orders to reverse Obama's executive orders, such as the subsidy payments from the Treasury Department to health insurance companies, the amnesty for undocumented aliens brought into the country as minors, the ban on building the Keystone pipeline, and numerous environmental regulations. He also reversed international accords, such as the Paris Climate Change Agreement and President Obama's agreement with Iran about nuclear development. Thus, we now have government by dueling executive orders, with policies and practices increasingly set by the unilateral decisions of one man, rather than by congressional legislation.

President Trump likely will be able to appoint several Supreme Court justices and scores of federal circuit and district court judges. This will strengthen his position and allow him to exercise presidential powers in ways that would make the Obama presidency look constrained. As it now appears, Trump will be able to do far more than Obama to centralize power in the executive branch. Ironically, he may do so while claiming to disperse power to the states, just as Augustus claimed to be restoring the Republic while he transformed it into an autocracy.

In the same way that President Obama used the threat of executive orders to pressure Congress to pass legislation, President Trump has done the same. Going further, he has requested that Congress give him the power of the line-item veto, even though President Clinton's line-item veto was ruled unconstitutional by the Supreme Court.

He has also advocated doing away with the filibuster rule in the Senate for all legislation. During the Obama administration, the Democratic Party Senate majority leader, Harry Reid, did away with the filibuster for the confirmation of federal judges, and Trump apparently wants to go further, extending it to all legislation. Doing away with the filibuster would allow bills to proceed without the necessary sixty votes for closure of debate and would allow legislation to be enacted by a simple majority. This might seem practicable, but it would destroy any need for compromise, further alienating the opposing parties. Without the filibuster rule, the majority could force through legislation without any support from the minority party. This would give a president with control of Congress more unchecked political power than any president has ever had before.

Whether the most beneficial policies are those of the Clinton-Obama democrats or those of the Trump populist-republicans is not the point; too much centralized power in the executive branch is the point. If the current trajectory remains intact, future presidents will dominate all aspects of government and society.

To a degree, President Trump has been constrained by unrelenting political and personal attacks from the press, attacks apparently designed to delegitimize his presidency; however, a future president, with a favorable press or diminished press, might face no such constraints and might be able to exercise unchecked, unprecedented power. As has been said before, a page of history is worth a volume of logic, and a president with unconstrained and broad Augustan power could readily impose despotic measures in ways that abrogate the checks-and-balances system, individual rights, and the long-cherished ideals of American freedom and liberty.

CHAPTER 42

Conclusions

BOTH ROMAN AND AMERICAN republics reached unprecedented levels of prosperity and social development. Their successes changed the course of history. The Roman Republic survived and prospered for almost five centuries; the American republic still prospers. Both republics produced generations of highly productive, well-intentioned, resourceful people who contributed greatly to the success and prosperity of their societies.

Achievements that distinguished both republics from most other nations included the following:

1. Assimilating people of different races and ethnicity while maintaining the core values of their own cultures
2. Fostering upward mobility on the basis of merit and fitness
3. Respecting the rights of private property
4. Promoting the distribution of land through liberal inheritance laws rather than adhering to a stagnant system based on primogeniture
5. Protecting individual civil liberties and rights
6. Embracing the rule of law as a categorical imperative
7. Spreading the best aspects of their laws and culture to other nations

Both nations created enormous wealth, which provided the funds to finance military operations and massive infrastructure projects. Much of Rome's revenue came through conquest, but the greater proportion of revenues came from commerce and trade. Likewise, American military victories opened opportunities for entrepreneurs to reap economic benefits. The Roman equestrian class and the American Protestant middle class were each driven to succeed economically, and religious and moral obligation underpinned their conduct to a lesser or greater degree.

Each nation encountered problems, and they endured periods of extraordinary crisis, disorder, violence, economic depressions, and social upheavals. Problems arose from their hegemonic status and their roles as the world's policemen. We know Rome's expansion reached a point of diminishing returns, with the costs outweighing the benefits. It's an open question of whether the United States has reached its hegemonic limits and whether its extensive reach is more detrimental than beneficial. Undoubtedly, the larger its footprint, the more likely it will be subjected to difficult and unpredictable challenges.

As Rome expanded, it increasingly faced unanticipated challenges; for example, the Romans didn't expect their conquests in North Africa to have such damaging long-term consequences as they did. The Jugurthine War not only was costly in lives and treasure but also soiled politics and inflamed class warfare. In that war the incompetence and corruption of the Roman generals opened the oligarchy to attack, weakened Rome's self-confidence, and planted seeds of division. With the ruling class undermined, populist demagogues seized the opportunity to gain power for themselves, opening the door for men such as Marius and others to dismantle traditional rules, subvert the rule of law, and initiate the processes that eventually destroyed the republic.

In the United States, the Vietnam War was comparable to the Jugurthine War. The American war effort, while it achieved some of its goals, couldn't be deemed a success. Many viewed it as an utter failure—not only for the lives lost but also for the domestic turmoil and political acrimony it generated. The perceived failure in Vietnam weakened the faith in American leadership and the belief in American exceptionalism, and it provided opportunities for radical and revolutionary leaders to begin the process of fragmenting the culture and dividing the nation.

In addition to the parallels between the Vietnam and Jugurthine Wars, other comparisons relating to overextension can be drawn. The terrorist bombing of the US Marines barracks in Beirut, Lebanon, in 1983 and the attacks by Al-Qaeda on the United States on September 11, 2001, were as shocking as Mithridates's slaughter of Roman citizens in 88 BC and the Parthians' capture of Crassus's legions at Carrhae in 53 BC. The two Roman disasters portended the end of the republic's invincibility.

While the Romans, as always, recovered from their defeats by making adjustments and demanding more of their citizens, the adjustments changed the nature of their society and transformed their republic into an autocracy. Rome reclaimed its dominance, but it did so at a terrible price—the end of the democratic republic, the loss of individual liberties, and a corruption of the Roman character.

The United States has made considerable adjustments to deal with terrorist attacks and other ongoing threats, and it can surely find ways to overcome the difficulties it will encounter in the future, but it remains to be seen what further adjustments will be made in both foreign and domestic affairs.

In Rome, the transition from an independent-farm economy to a slave-labor society produced a nation overburdened with unemployed and disgruntled citizens. Gaius Gracchus tried to address those problems, but by instituting the dole, he unintentionally added fuel to the mix, creating an explosive situation. Free grain drew masses of poor into the city; and Saturninus, Sulpicius, Cinna, and Clodius each increased the dole, adding to the congestion in the slums and exacerbating tension in the streets and assemblies. On those occasions when drought, war, or piracy interrupted the grain supply, those dependent on the grain for survival became a menacing mob, susceptible to calls from demagogues to attack the rich. Demagogues exploited the power of the mobs to push for confiscation and redistribution of land. While some of the more prudent conservatives initiated or accepted reforms, other more reactionary conservatives refused to make concessions or adopt reasonable reforms, thus setting the stage for a series of escalating conflicts. The demagogues, of course, were playing with fire, and most of them came to bad ends. Nonetheless, the forces of demagoguery and mobocracy inevitably overwhelmed the more conservative elements of the state. The process took a hundred years, with the pendulum swinging between disorder and stability, until the disorder became so prevalent that the Romans took security over liberty and accepted autocratic rule.

During the Depression of the 1930s, President Roosevelt, as the leader of the American oligarchy, didn't make the same mistake as the Roman oligarchs who had refused to accept reforms and other measures. Roosevelt implemented reasonable economic and social measures to address the crisis; the watchword was *reform* rather than *revolution*. Later in the 1950s and '60s, when the civil rights movement demanded reforms, American leaders responded with substantial programs to address grievances relating to poverty, segregation, and discrimination. They did not copy the intransigence of the Romans who refused the demands of the Italians for citizenship rights and equality; thus, America avoided the kind of social war that occurred in Rome.

However, past performance doesn't necessarily predict future results. The United States will undoubtedly face new problems and challenges, and it must be of concern that the nation has become so polarized that partisanship often overrides the interests of the nation. The two major political parties have shifted toward their ideological poles, and the nation's political center has eroded. In this climate, political, social, and cultural disagreements inhibit the nation from reaching the solutions needed to resolve critical problems. To borrow from the Kerner Commission, our nation is moving toward two societies, one left, one right—separate and irreconcilable.

Deepening the polarization is the growing perception of income inequality. It's not that the poor are getting poorer; it's that globalization has exponentially increased profits for corporations and the wealthy. In the same way Roman commerce expanded across the Mediterranean world, American commerce has expanded across the entire world. Until globalization fully arrived, a successful American business would generate revenue from within a city or region—in some cases nationally or in a few, internationally. Now the reach of American business encompasses the entire world, and businesses strive for international trade. Where we had millionaires, we now have billionaires. Understandably, a perception has arisen that the working class is standing still while the richest are becoming astronomically wealthy. This is a recipe for class warfare and for attacks on the foundations of the American system.

John Adam warned, "Democracy never lasts long. It soon wastes, exhausts and murders itself. There was never a democracy that did not commit suicide." America has so far defied his warning, but signs of the fraying of the American fabric are seen everywhere. We should heed Roman history. When the Romans defeated their enemies and external threats were reduced, internal struggles intensified; partisans turned on fellow citizens; and ambitious politicians, looking for fame, power, and wealth, fanned the flames of hatred. Thus, the republic's downfall came from within.

The destruction of the Roman Republic has shown that without the rule of law or checks and balances, those with executive power will aggregate more power to themselves. In the late republic, politicians from both sides proscribed their opponents, refused to share power, disregarded the traditional rules of political engagement, and destroyed the people's faith in fair government. The *populare* demagogues and the *optimate* reactionaries may have been well intentioned, but by abrogating their constitution and the rule of law, they launched the ship of state downstream on a treacherous journey until it cascaded over the precipice. Picking up the broken pieces of the wreckage, Caesar and Augustus imposed their dictatorships. As the people gave up their freedom, their character changed. The nobles were no longer equals sharing the responsibility of leadership, but they became pawns of dictatorship. The commoners were no longer unified and patriotic citizens, dedicated to their commonwealth (res publica), but they were subjects of their rulers.

At the American Constitutional Convention in 1787, Benjamin Franklin warned that the republic "can only end in despotism, as other forms have done before it, when the people shall become so corrupted as to need despotic government, being incapable of any other."

How long our republic has lasted might have surprised Franklin. It has survived civil war, ideological divides, and long stretches of one-party rule, but it might not yet survive political parties that demonize their adversaries and treat them as though they were potential enemy combatants from foreign foes. It might not survive a ubiquitous press that foments partisan conflicts either out of commitment to an ideology or simply to increase ratings for fast profits.

Democratic-republican government made America's prosperity possible, and the character of its people made the possibility a reality, but the people must remain on guard. If they give up their balanced constitutional government in favor of an autocratic imperial presidency, their character will change. If they give up their founding principles, the spirit of freedom and independence that made them great will be lost. Leonardo da Vinci once said, "It is easier to resist at the beginning than at the end," but to do so, we must first recognize that a potentially destructive transformation is upon us. Following in the footsteps of the Roman Republic's demise is not inevitable, but the American people must resist the passions of extreme partisanship, ever-expanding bureaucracy, intensified government control, and the tendency of partisans to put all their faith in a single exalted leader. They must never lose sight of the need to preserve the rule of law, the primacy of the individual, and our marvelously designed system of constitutional government.

Index

A

Actium 439, 441, 445

Adams, John 5, 14, 45, 54, 55, 85,
89, 109, 112, 114, 154, 257,
261, 262, 268, 270, 271, 272,
334, 416

Adams, John Quincy 153, 154,
258, 314

Addison, Joseph 6

Adherbal 193, 194

Aedui 64, 67, 235, 236

Aemilianus, Publius Cornelius Scipio
142, 143

Aequians 24, 35, 53

Affordable Care Act 428, 529, 540,
542, 543

Afghanistan 460, 463, 466, 541, 561,
564, 569

Agrippa 125, 437, 439, 446, 487

Ahenobarbus, Domitius 125, 243, 502

Alesia 237, 377

Alien and Sedition Acts 112, 268, 270,
271, 334, 416

Ambiorix 37

Antiochus IV, King 143

Antonius, Lucius 486

Antony, Marc 244, 248, 249, 267, 432,
485, 486

Appian (Appianus) 124, 125, 126, 130,
144, 190, 202, 212, 215, 220,
240, 325, 372, 402, 434, 435,
465, 481, 485, 486, 502

Appian Way 124, 126, 130, 220, 240,
325, 372, 485, 502

Appius Claudius Crassus 72, 124,
334, 335

Arausio, Battle of 393

Ardennes 375

Argonne 363

Assad, Bashar 566

Atia 431, 474

Augustus Caesar (Octavian) xi, 59, 86,
267, 268, 431, 432, 486

B

Bacchanalia 188, 189

Barca, Hamilcar 129

Bastogne 375

Beirut 562

Bibulus, Marcus Calpurnius xi, 231,
248, 412

Biddle, Nicholas 317

Bills of Attainder 415, 416, 548

King, Martin Luther Jr. 357, 400, 510, 514

King Phillip's War 35

King, Rodney (riots) 511, 512

Know Nothings 504, 505

Knox, Henry 12, 39

Korean War 378, 424, 466

Kunkel, Wolfgang 47, 281, 454

Kuwait 562

L

Laenas, Gaius Popillius 143

Latifundia 91, 170, 171, 308, 387

Latin War 123

Laudatio Turiae 475

Lentulus, Publius Cornelius 104, 296

Lentulus, Publius Cornelius Spinther 296

Lepidus, Marcus Aemilius 219, 302, 433

Lex Appuleia 202

Lex Aquilia 278

Lex Calpurnia 284, 401, 410

Lex Calpurnia de Ambitu 410

Lex Cornelia de Iniuriis 285

Lex Cornelia de Sicariis et Veneficiis 217

Lex Gabinia 410

Lex Hortensia 49, 82

Lex Julia et Papia 447

Lex Maiestas 454

Lex Poetelia 82

Lex Pompeii de Provinciis 413

Lex Sempronia 403

Lex Tibia 434

Lex Tullia de Ambitu 410

Lex Varia 405

Libby, Lewis "Scooter" 427

Libya 464, 535, 565

Licinian-Sextian 79, 80, 123

Licinian-Sextian laws 79, 80

Licinius, Gaius 79

Lincoln, Abraham 15, 22, 73, 167, 303, 312, 330, 335, 336

Little Turtle 38, 40

Livia Drusilla 488

Livingstons 87

Livy 3, 4, 5, 9, 10, 11, 25, 26, 27, 29, 30, 51, 52, 61, 63, 67, 68, 69, 72, 73, 74, 76, 77, 78, 82, 132, 139, 141, 160, 184, 186, 188, 189, 334, 340, 479, 482, 492

Long, Huey 390, 543

Louisiana Purchase 145, 150, 153

Lucretia 475

Lucretius 191, 475

Lucullus, Lucius Licinius 222, 230, 233

Lyon, Matthew 269, 416

M

MacArthur, Douglas 167, 168, 376, 381, 389, 458

Macedon 48, 125, 133, 139, 140, 142, 144, 169, 170, 171, 189, 196, 276, 522

Madison, James 54, 86, 97, 113, 145, 163, 270, 540

Maecenas 437

Maiestas 202, 210, 268, 406, 454

Malcolm X 509

Manlius, Marcus Capitolinus 29, 77, 88

Marcellus, Gaius Claudius 243

Marcuse, Herbert 493, 515

Marius, Gaius 197, 201, 224, 302, 404

Marshall, John 58, 89, 98, 118, 315, 356, 418

Scipio, Gnaeus Cornelius 133

Scipio, Lucius Cornelius 187

Scipio, Publius Cornelius 129, 133, 134, 142, 143, 176, 187, 475

Scipio, Quintus Metellus 239, 241

Scribonia 488

Second Bank of the United States 146, 315

Second Punic War 51, 129, 140, 169, 184, 364, 462, 464, 478

Second World War x, 167, 364, 369, 377, 391, 394, 423, 459, 460, 466, 492, 508, 548, 559, 560, 561, 562

Seminoles 151, 152

Sempronius 51, 52, 173, 475

Senatus consultum Silanianum 448

Senatus consultum ultimatum 244, 302

Seneca, Marcus 483

Sertorius, Quintus 217, 219

Servilia 484, 485

Servius, Rufus 295

Servius, Tullius 26, 27

Seward, William 350

Shawnee 38, 40, 41

Shays 88

Silanus, D. Junius 276

Social War 203, 207, 208, 209, 211, 358, 395, 397, 400, 405, 424, 513, 580

Sowell, Thomas 544

Spanish-American War 359, 363

Spartacus 17

Stanton, Edwin 351

Starr, Kenneth 426

St. Clair, Arthur 38

Stevens, Ted 427, 429

Stevens, Thaddeus 354

Stoicism 191, 192

Story, Joseph 289

Sulla, Lucius Cornelius 102, 199, 241, 406

Sulla, Publius 411, 412

Sulpicius, Publius Rufus 205

Sumner, Charles 326, 354

T

Tacitus 2, 38, 285, 286, 442, 453, 474

Taft, Howard 388

Taney, Roger 317, 333

Tarentum 126, 132, 140, 186, 479

Tarquinius Superbus 3

Tea Party 532, 533

Tecumseh 40, 41, 237, 337

Temple of Concord 11

Temple of Jupiter 6, 170, 210, 301, 303

Tenth Legion 227, 367

Terentia 485

Teutoburg Forest 39, 465

Thames, Battle of the 41

Third Punic War 143, 171

Thirteenth Amendment 354

Thomas, Clarence 496

Tiberius Claudius Nero 454, 488

Tiber River 1, 9, 29, 170, 222

Ticinus River 129

Time for Choosing 516

Tocqueville, Alexis de 165, 166, 547

Torquatus, Titus Manilius 132

Transcontinental Railroad 351

Trasimene 129, 159, 294

Treaty of Fort Jackson 42, 311

Treaty of Ghent 148

Treaty of Greenville 40

Trebia River 129

Trenton, Battle of 150

Truman, Harry 391

Trump, Donald 560, 572

Turiae 475, 477

About the Author

Walter Signorelli is a practicing attorney and an adjunct professor of law and police science at John Jay College of Criminal Justice in New York City. He was previously a member of the New York City Police Department for thirty-one years, and today he is a criminal defense attorney and a police practices and procedures expert. Signorelli graduated cum laude from St. John's University School of Law before later graduating from the Columbia University Police Management Institute. He has written three books related to law and police science: The Crisis of Police Liability Lawsuits (2006), Criminal Law, Procedure, and Evidence (2011), and The Constable Has Blundered (2012), which received a recommended rating by the Choice Review for Academic Libraries.